Accountancy *for* non-accountants

Volume II

MANAGEMENT ACCOUNTING

Paul Norkett BA. MSc. FCCA. ACIS. AMBIM.

Longman

Longman Group Limited
Longman House
Burnt Mill, Harlow, Essex.

*Published in the United States of America
by Longman Inc. New York.*

First published 1982

British Library Cataloguing in Publication Data

Norkett, P.T.C.

Accountancy for non-accountants, management accounting. — (Longman business management series).

1. Managerial accounting
1. Title
658.1'51 HF5635

ISBN 0-582-41208-0

Contents

DIAGRAMS

to my wife Aktan

Preface

This book is almost double the size that was planned, which is rather ironic because one of the book's themes is planning and control. The reason I am admitting this planning error, is because it can be used as a simple illustration of some key issues relating to planning and control.

Firstly, *events rarely proceed according to plan.* When a deviation from a plan is likely to occur, or has occurred, then the basic choice is to alter the plan and/or impose tighter controls. What you decide to do will depend upon the objectives towards which your plan is directed. With this book my objectives were quite clear:-

(a) To provide a useful learning and reference text on management accounting for non-accountants.

(b) To take a broad interdisciplinary approach to the subject that will show that management accounting is not just an esoteric form of arithmetic.

(c) The book should be an integral part of a three volume reference work on accountancy for non-accountants.

These objectives upon which the initial plan was based justified the continual revision and enlargement of the text.

The fact that I am convinced the textual re-direction was correct, leads to the second key issue. *Changes in a plan will always be justified by someone.* My justification for including aspects of economics, personnel, law, marketing, mathematics, statistics, psychology, sociology, organisation and management theory, industrial relations and computing, was that all these subject areas have a contribution to make towards effective planning and control. As cost and revenue data from management accounting provides the core for planning and control, it is appropriate that this accounting core includes relevant information principles and techniques from other specialist subject areas.

Having reviewed some aspects of the planning of this book we can now consider the control system. This leads us to the third key issue. *Control cannot exist without a plan.* With this book, the continual revision of the plan did not weaken the system of control that was applied with Volume 1 and will be applied with Volume 3. A preliminary framework was constructed for each chapter from a wide collection of articles, books and personal notes. Each framework was discussed with subject specialists on the chapter's structure, relevance and coverage. All chapters passed through at least two draft stages before the final draft was proof read by two independent subject specialists. If I agreed with a reviewer's comments, the text was revised. There was then a final proof reading whilst compiling the index.

Even with all these controls, there are still probably some errors in the text and this leads us to the last key issue. Errors *will occur with all planning and control systems.* This final point is often used as a reason for not formalising the planning function. Managers can often quote numerous examples of carefully constructed detailed plans becoming completely irrelevant because of a change in events outside their control. They therefore conclude that planning is a waste of time. This cannot be true, because every planning exercise should be of educational benefit to all participants. If a plan fails it will be due to faulty planning and/or weak controls. Providing the participants *honestly* determine the reasons for a plan's failure, then subsequent planning and control should improve. If plans need to be based on the uncertain outcome of events, then risk calculations and contingency plans are necessary.

This book has been written primarily for managers who need to know about planning and control techniques and have to interpret information given by specialists such as accountants. The book is suitable for the following uses:-

(a) As a reference source for the non-accountant who needs a 'working knowledge' of management accounting and its terminology.
(b) As a course book for business and management courses.
(c) As an independent study programme for management accounting for non-accountants.
(d) As a reference source for accountancy students where the dictionary should be of particular use to students for whom English is a second language.

The approach to this book will depend upon your circumstances. *If you are following a programmed course of study then seek reading instructions from the tutor.* This is most important because in many chapters the amount of detail will probably far exceed the course requirements. For irnstance few courses would go into the detail that is given on basic costing in chapter 3 or all the decision techniques explained in chapters 6 and 7. However, it is very useful to have this detail available for reference purposes. If you are studying accountancy independently then please read the relevant section of the following notes:-

Independent study categories

(i) Owners/directors of small and medium sized businesses

Chapter 1 Interesting but not essential reading.
Chapter 2 You will probably have existing knowledge of this subject, but it is still worthwhile reading because the planning and control principles that are explained have practical relevance for the owner/director of a business.
Chapter 3 Do not try and read the entire chapter - there is too much detail. Use it mainly for reference purposes. Although section 6 could be useful general reading.
Chapter 4 You need to know a lot of the detail contained in this chapter especially the employment and dismissal procedures in section 2, remuneration policy in section 3:8 and labour planning in section 5. You may not agree with some of the views expressed in section 4 on organised labour.
Chapter 5 Read the introduction carefully, it will help you determine the relative importance of inventory management for your company. Only read the remainder of the chapter if you need to get involved in the detail.
Chapter 7 An important subject that can get quite complex. Basic essential reading would be sections: 2, 3, 7 and 8. Although it would be useful to have some knowledge about the risk calculations explained in section 7.
Chapter 8 Read this chapter several times, it contains a lot of useful information about Budgeting, planning and control. You may not agree with the views expressed in section 4.
Chapter 9 Only read sections 1 and 2, the other sections are for reference purposes.
Chapter 10 If you have, or will have, a micro/mini computer. then read sections 2 and 4.

(ii) Senior executives of large companies

Chapter 1 Useful reading
Chapter 2 You will probably already have a good understanding of the principles and details for planning and control and will find this chapter interesting.
Chapter 3 There is a lot of detail in this chapter explaining accounting terms that you should understand. Do not become too involved in the detail.
Chapter 4 A lot of the detail in this chapter will be dealt with by specialist departments in a large company. Therefore only read the sections where you require the detailed knowledge.

Chapter 5 Unless you have responsibility for inventory control this chapter would be for reference purposes only.
Chapter 6 Essential that you read and understand the entire chapter.
Chapter 7 As a senior executive you should understand investment appraisal techniques. Do not get too involved in the detailed calculations. But you need to understand the techniques that adjust cash flows for risk and the time value of money. Read all of this chapter.
Chapter 8 A most important chapter covering topics that need to be understood by senior executives. Pay particular attention to section 4.
Chapter 9 Read sections 1 and 2. If you receive standard costing reports then read the relevant sub-sections on how to interpret the variances.
Chapter 10 If your company is considering integrating existing information systems into an MIS read all of this chapter.

(iii) Engineers, scientists, systems analysts and other specialist functions.

Chapter 1 Interesting but not essential reading.
Chapter 2 Useful reading.
Chapter 3 Essential reading for systems analysts. Other specialist functions, do not attempt to work through the detail, just use the chapter for reference. purposes.
Chapter 4 Mainly reference, except for systems analysts designing manpower and/or remuneration systems.
Chapter 5 Mainly reference except for systems analysts designing inventory systems.
Chapter 6 Worthwhile reading all of this chapter. Minimum reading, sections 2 and 3.
Chapter 7 Mainly reference unless you have to prepare an investment proposal, then read sections 1, 2, 3, 4 and 7.
Chapter 8 An important topic. Read all the chapter but do not get too involved in the detail.
Chapter 9 It is unlikely that you will need all the detail in this chapter. Use only for specific reference purposes.
Chapter 10 If your company is using computers and is developing an MIS then minimum reading would be sections 2 and 4.

(iv) Service industry executives such as bankers, insurance brokers and investment analysts.

Chapter 1 Useful reading
Chapter 2 Should be relevant for your needs. Read all this chapter.
Chapter 3 Do not get involved in the detail, this is mainly for reference purposes. Useful for you to read sub-section 5:9 and section 6.
Chapter 4 An important reference chapter that you should find useful. You may not agree with the views expressed in section 4.
Chapter 5 Unlikely that you will ever need to read this chapter.
Chapter 6 The break even model does not generally apply to service industries therefore do not get too involved in section 2. Sections 3 and 4 could be useful.
Chapter 7 Unlikely that you will need all the detail given in this chapter. Although bankers and investment analysts should be aware of the principles explained in sections 8,9,10 and 11.
Chapter 8 Some of this chapter is probably relevant to your work situation. Therefore useful to read all of the chapter.
Chapter 9 Unlikely that you will ever need to read this chapter.
Chapter 10 If your company is using computers and is developing an MIS then minimum reading would be sections 2 and 4.

(v) Shop stewards (Author's note - I have taught accountancy to shop stewards on TUC courses and found with many delegares a 'strong need to know' about accountancy. To bargain effectively and responsibly the shop steward needs some knowledge about accountancy and I sincerely hope this book will satisfy some of their information needs).

Chapter 1 Useful reading.

Chapter 2 If you are participating in the decision making process then read all of this chapter. You will probably disagree with some of the views.

Chapter 3 Too much detail in this chapter. Only read sections when you need to understand some specific terms used by managers and accountants.

Chapter 4 For your purposes this is the most important chapter in the book. Read the entire chapter, even though you will probably disagree with some of the statements about organised labour.

Chapter 5 ignore this chapter unless it is useful for your job.

Chapter 6 It is not necessary for you to read this chapter unless you are participating in the decision making process.

Chapter 7 During negotiations you may receive details of investment proposals or decisions. This chapter explains the appraisal techniques that are often used by management for investment decisions. Do not get involved in the detail unless you are good with figures and have a lot of spare time. If you are participating in the decision making process then read sections 2, 3, 4 and 7.

Chapter 8 It is not necessary for you to read this chapter unless you are participating in corporate planning.

Chapter 9 It is unlikely that you will ever need to refer to the detail in this chapter.

Chapter 10 If your company is developing a management information system on a computer then one of the negotiating issues could be trade union access to the system. If this occurs you will need to read sections 2 and 4.

These guidance notes are based on my experience of interactive accountancy teaching to a wide range of interest groups. Since founding *Tekron College*, an independent management education college, I have been actively involved in teaching accountancy to non-accountants. Indeed this book is based on the course manual I wrote for short courses in management accountancy for non-accountants. Most of the course material has now been produced as independent study cassette packages.

Acknowledgements

Acknowledgements are due to a number of people who were prepared to proof read and give a professional opinion on several chapters in this book. Every chapter has been independently proof read by at least two qualified people and I trust this will have ensured the text does not have too many errors. In some instances the reviewers did not entirely agree with my views and raised some very valid points. I am sincerely grateful to the reviewers who actively contributed to the development of this book. In alphabetical order the reviewers were: John Blake, Herbert Hahn, Alan Gully, Chris Haliburton, Vic Marchesi, Peter Mathews, Ian Mearns, David Parker, Sylvio Prodano, Tony Roche, Tim Seville and Maurice Ward. Acknowledgements are also due to the Certification Officer for permission to reproduce statistics from his annual report. Contributions have also been made by delegates on accountancy courses I have run during the last few years, where a lot of this book originated from.

PAUL NORKETT

Management and Accountancy 1

Objective
To explain the structure of this book and attempt to show the close relationship that exists between management and accountancy.

Content *Page No.*

Management and Accountancy

Introduction

The business environment is passing through two fundamental changes that will inevitably reform traditional management practices. The first change is being caused by low cost electronic data processing. This has been appropriately described as an 'information revolution' and the term 'revolution' is certainly not an overstatement. The capability of modern electronic technology to store, analyse and transmit data over long distances is phenomenal. Moreover, this incredible data processing and communication power is obtainable even for the small business with a low financial profile. The low cost of micro computers and access terminals to large computer data bases can place a warehouse of information at the fingertips of any decision maker. The problem is that many decision makers do not know how to use this powerful management tool. This is certainly not a criticism of decision makers. The rate of technological change has been so fast that there will inevitably be a time lag before the full benefits of the information revolution are reaped. In the interim period there will be a lot of false promises made about software capability and many disappointments, until decision makers know precisely what they want and what they are paying for.

The other fundamental change is related to people and workplace relationships. Social values are a luxury only developed economies can afford and transition from luxury to necessity is just a matter of time. From necessity emerges political expediency and then economic reality. This general trend becomes evident from a study of UK workplace relationships. Fifty years ago the rights of capital were virtually unchallenged and management used labour simply as a factor of production that would maximise the 'return on capital'! The social consequences arising from decisions were virtually irrelevant because the over-riding criteria was to maximise profit on behalf of the owners. It was this 'stewardship criteria' that formed the foundation of accounting. This foundation has now been eroded to such an extent that directors and shareholders frequently refer to a 'fair return for capital'. Also directors are now talking about their tripartite responsibility to employees, shareholders and the public. Thus the rights of capital are being shared with the rights of labour and rights of consumers and local communities. This change in social values has been brought about by education, organised labour, the media and some outstanding politicians. During the last decade the political emphasis has shifted in favour of employees and this shift appears to be gathering momentum in Europe. The scope of collective bargaining has certainly broadened when compared with early negotiations that were limited to wage bargaining. This broadening process is moving towards participation in decision making at the strategic level and there is already an EEC directive on participation. In the UK the existing employment legislation will probably be supplemented with industrial democracy legislation (Refer to chapter 2 section 4:2:4) Accordingly, traditional authoritarian management practice is unlikely to be as successful as a participative approach that recognises the factor input of labour, as people with dignity and rights, that need to be taken into consideration in the decision-making process.

The information revolution will enable managers to make better decisions and the changes in workplace relationships will certainly test a manager's ability 'to get things done through people'. Where then does management accounting fit into this changing environment?

• The primary function of management accounting is to serve managers. Managers require information for planning and controlling business activity and a large proportion of this information is converted into costs and revenues. As accounting is the only profession that has the necessary expertise and experience for recording, analysing and reporting on cost and revenue data, it is clear that accountants have an important role to play in serving managers. However, if managers cannot understand accounting the service has no function. The cause for a non-accountant's lack of interest and misunderstanding of accounting is probably due to the inability of accountants to sell their service. The legally imposed aspects of accounting explained in Volume 1, Financial accounting for non-accountants, do not have to be sold. But before a decision maker is going to spend time and money on using a management accounting technique he/she has to be convinced that it is worthwhile. Clearly some compromise is needed, managers need to learn how to use accounting and accountants need to learn how to communicate to non-accountants. The emphasis in this book for non-accountants is how to use management accounting. Therefore we first need to distinguish between financial accounting, management accounting and finance. (These subject areas are covered in detail in Volumes 1, 2 and 3 in this series After distinguishing management accounting we then need to establish the frame work for this book.

Financial accounting developed from the stewardship function of keeping a record of account. Indeed the roots of financial accounting can be traced back to a seventeenth century treatise on double entry book keeping. This system of recording financial data has remained virtually unchanged over the centuries and still forms the basis of most advanced double entry book-keeping systems. However, with electronic processing alternative forms of self checking financial record systems are being developed and the functions of double entry book-keeping are being eroded. The traditional output of double entry book-keeping has been some form of income statement, (total revenue minus total cost) and a statement of net worth (a list of assets and liabilities). These aspects of financial accounting have become legal requirements under company and fiscal legislation. Thus the core of financial accounting is to keep a record of account of business activities and at regular intervals to report to the owners (stewardship reporting). The reports are mainly, a profit and loss account and balance sheet that are a true and fair view of the underlying records.

As business activity became more complex, professional managers were demanding more cost and revenue information from accountants. Initially the main demand was for cost data such as how much does it cost to produce product 'X' and how can the costs be reduced? This specialised information requirement created the birth of a new kind of accounting called cost accounting. As Taylor's scientific management (Refer to sub-section 2:1) gained credence, this contributed to the increased demand for more cost information. In the UK in 1919, a new accountancy body was formed called the Institute of Cost and Works Accountants (Now called the Institute of Cost and Management Accountants) and costing was gradually becoming an accepted part of accountancy. Gradually costing developed to encompass a far broader base and was appropriately re-named management accounting. The emphasis of management accounting was a total approach to planning and control of which costing was just one part. This total approach emcompassed *expected* costs and revenues as well as *actual* costs and revenues. Moreover, management accounting became more interdisciplinary utilising useful work done by mathematicians, economists, psychologists, sociologists and marketing, production and industrial relations specialists. It is this broad inter-disciplinary approach to management accounting that is taken in this book.

The parameters of finance are not so clear as management and financial accounting. There is, of course, an overlap between these three areas of accounting and this is especially noticeable with finance. Basically, finance is concerned with cash flow. In the long run this will include management accounting techniques such as investment appraisal and in the short run working capital management techniques that have been developed under the umbrella of financial accounting. Where finance becomes very specialised is in the broad choice of financing options between debt and equity. In Volume 3 finance (and taxation) are approached from the viewpoint of the small businessman. Topics such as how to calculate financial needs, and how and where to apply for finance are explained.

Having briefly distinguished between the three broad areas of accounting let us develop a framework for management accounting that will provide a structure for this book. The hub of management accounting is the recording, analysis, interpretation and reporting on cost and revenue data for planning and control. The cost and revenue data can be broadly divided into two main categories; *expected* costs and revenues used for planning and control and *past* costs and revenue that are mainly used for control. Because planning and control is the focal point of management accounting, it forms the structure for this book. This structure is illustrated in diagram 1. And, in chapter 2 the principles of planning and control are explained. An-

DIAGRAM 1

HOW THIS BOOK IS ORGANISED – PLANNING & CONTROL APPROACH

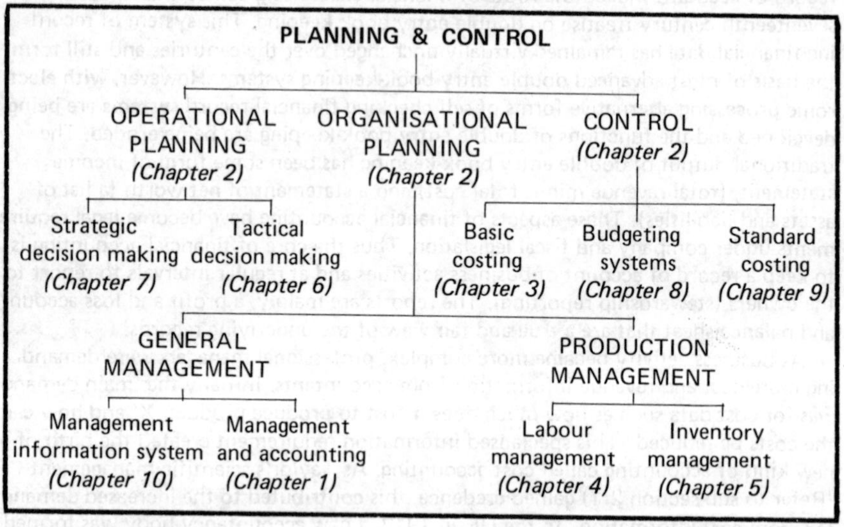

other way of viewing management accounting is the input/output approach illustrated in diagram 2. This shows the three inputs of materials, labour and capital passing through a conversion process into a saleable output. The overall planning and control of the enterprise is developed in chapters 2 and 10. The planning and control of each input is explained in chapters 4, 5 and 7. And specific planning and control aspects of the conversion process are explained in chapters 3, 6, 8, 9 and 10. The approach in some chapters is very broad encompassing areas not normally associated with management accounting. For example, sections in the labour management chapter cover aspects of industrial relations and personnel. The decision making chapters include selected areas from mathematics, statistics, economics, marketing. And in the budgeting systems chapter, a section summarises some useful work done by psychologists and sociologists. The final chapter attempts to bring together the entire subject of management accounting by taking a computer users viewpoint of a management information system. This very broad and detailed approach to management accounting is meant to reflect the changing nature of the subject that is due to:-

(a) The changes that are occurring in workplace relationships and the trend towards participation.
(b) The increasing professionalism of managers who are becoming more numerate
(c) The impact of low cost computer hardware and sophisticated software packages.

DIAGRAM 2 HOW THIS BOOK IS ORGANISED – INPUT/OUTPUT APROACH

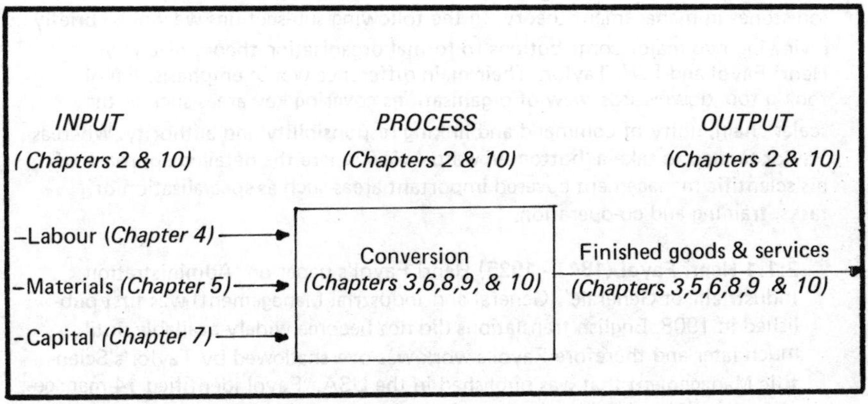

These trends indicate that management accounting must become more interdisciplinary if it is to serve management effectively. Managers are already being served by a wide range of specialists that have developed decision making techniques. Also, most businesses have at least one 'ancilliary department' that exists simply to serve managers. In this introductory chapter we will briefly review the development of some management theory and then summarise a wide range of management techniques. The glossary of techniques is cross referenced to the text.

2. Review of some management principles

The need for some form of overview of management principles in this introductory chapter is quite clear. But so much work has been done by very competent writers based on years of research and/or personal experience, it is exceedingly difficult to select an appropriate sample. Indeed, it is probably overbold to even attempt a simple review of the subject.

This review will begin with the principles of organisation provided by two well known writers from the classical school, Fayol and Taylor. These traditional views have been challenged by many writers and in the following sub-sections we will be reviewing the contributions made by some writers from the human relations school. Of course the principles summarised in these sub-sections represent only part of a vast store of literature on this subject, but a larger review is beyond the scope of this section. For readers who require a broader review there are numerous management books to choose from.

2:1 Classical The classical school of management theory has no precise boundaries. A number of writers are often referred to as being part of the classical school, such as Taylor, Fayol, Weber, Gilbreth, Gantt, Emerson and Mooney. The general characteristic that seems to link these writers' to the classical school is their formal approach to organisations. In some of these writers formal organisation models accounting has a clear role. For example, in Taylor's scientific management model there is a clear need for cost accounting to be linked to time and motion study. Indeed, Taylor's management principles probably played an important role in the development of early cost accounting techniques.

During the last thirty years the classical school has come under increasing attack from many 'modern' management writers. Although many of the critic isms may be valid, formal organisation theory still represents one of the foundation stones in management theory. In the following sub-sections we will be briefly reviewing two major contributions to formal organisation theory given by Henri Fayol and F.W. Taylor. Their main difference was in emphasis, Fayol took a 'top downwards' view of organisations covering key areas such as the scalar chain, unity of command and linking responsibility and authority. Whereas Taylor tended to take a 'bottom upwards' view where the detailed approach of his scientific management covered important areas such as specialisation of tasks, training and co-operation.

2:1:1 Henri Fayol (1841 - 1925) Henri Fayol's paper on 'Administration Industrielle et Generale' (General and Industrial Management) was first published in 1908. English translations did not become widely available until much later and therefore Fayol's work was overshadowed by Taylor's Scientific Management that was published in the USA. Fayol identified 14 management principles that have been copies, criticised and built upon by subsequent writers on management. Briefly the principles were:-

1. Division of work into specialised tasks. This results in the functional division of an organisation into departments, such as production, marketing, administration and finance.

2. Authority and responsibility need to be closely linked, i.e. responsibility should not be given without some form of authority that is linked to the reward/penalty system.

3. Discipline is a necessary part of an organisation 'Discipline is what leaders make it'. Fayol identified three elements:-

(a) Good superiors at all levels
(b) Clear and fair agreements
(c) Sanctions judiciously applied

4. Unity of command where an employee should receive orders from only one superior.

5. Unity of direction for a group of activities with only one objective, one plan and one head.

6. Subordination of individual interest to the general interest, where three elements were identified:-

(a) Superiors to provide firmness and good example
(b) Fair agreements
(c) Constant supervision

7. Remuneration of personnel should be fair, encourage effort and not lead to over payment. Various methods of payment were identified including profit sharing. Fayol said '...... profit sharing is a mode of payment capable of giving excellent results in certain cases, but is not a general rule. It does not seen to me possible, at least for the present. to count on this mode of payment for appeasing conflict between Capital and Labour. (Refer to chapter 4 sub-section 3:6)
8. Centralisation of planning and control is a question of proportion and a matter of finding the optimum degree for a particular organisation.
9. The scalar chain is the chain of superiors ranging from the ultimate authority to the lowest ranks. The principle is illustrated in diagram 3 that shows if E wanted to formally communicate with J it would be necessary to go up the A - F chain to A then down the A - K chain to J. Fayol recognised the need for the use of 'gang plank' communication (represented by a dotted line between E and J) but emphasised that it must be authorised by superiors.

DIAGRAM 3 SCALAR CHAIN

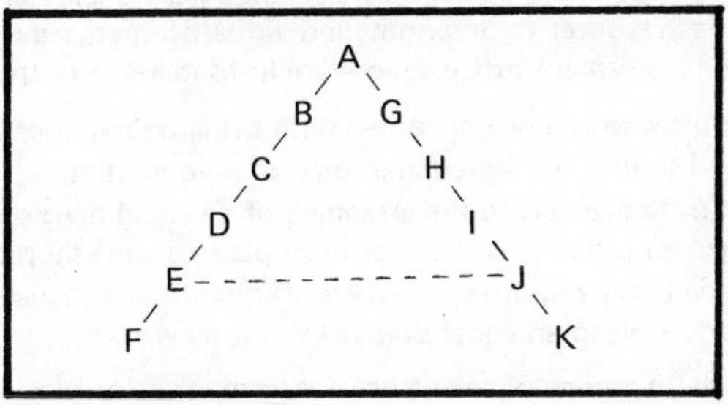

10. Order This is divided into material order where tangible assets are organised with an emphasis on neatness and cleanliness. And social order which is seen as 'A place for everyone and everyone in his place'. Formal organisation charts are an example of Fayol's social order.
11. Equity is distinguished from justice, because justice is just putting into execution established conventions. Equity requires kindness and the application of justice requires good sense, experience and good nature.
12. Stability of tenure relates to the time required for an employee to get used to the work and succeed in doing it well. If there is instability during this time period the work will never be done properly.
13. Initiative refers to the need for an organisation to encourage managers to think out plans and ensure their success. Initiative is a powerful stimulent and 'The manager must be able to sacrifice some personal vanity in order to grant this satisfaction to subordinates'.
14. Esprit de corps refers to the loyalty of personnel towards the organisation and Fayol identifies two important points:-

(a) 'Dividing enemy forces to weaken them is clever, but dividing one's own team is a grave sin against the business'
(b) The abuse of written communication where internal messages that should be verbal are written and distributed through the scalar chain.

From this brief review of Fayol's 14 principles it is evident that there are areas where accounting can play an important role. The authority and responsibility principle is embodied in many budgeting systems (Refer to chapter 8) and the remuneration principles are included in many wage payment systems (Refer to chapter 4 section 3).

2:1:2 F.W. Taylor (1856 - 1915) Taylor's main contribution to the classical school was in the 'Principles of Scientific Management' first published in 1911. The principles were divided into four different groups of duties that should be undertaken by managers:-

First group of duties would include gathering all the knowledge of workmen which had been acquired through skill and experience. Scientific management would then reduce this knowledge to laws, rules and formulae. These laws and rules would then be applied to everyday work with the co-operation of the workmen. As a result output would increase, profit would increase and higher wages could be paid.

Second group of duties is related to the scientific selection and the progressive development of workmen. Managers would study the character, nature and performance of each worker to determine individual strengths and weaknesses. This selection and assessment process would help to increase output.

Third group of duties would be concerned with bringing together the scientifically selected and trained workmen in a spirit of co-operation.

Fourth group of duties relates to the arranging of an equal division of work between workmen and the managers. For example in a workshop, the calculation of the workload may require say three workmen to one manager and this proportion would result in an equal share of the total work.

To illustrate these groups of scientific management principles Taylor used an example of workmen shovelling pig iron at the Bethlehem Steel Works. The research team gathered knowledge from two 'first class shovellers'. Details were systematically analysed to determine the optimum shape and size of a shovel and the way it should be used. Subsequently several different types of shovel were introduced for different types of work and workmen were persuaded to accept the new work practices. A wage payment system was introduced that related to results. The outcome of this experiment in scientific management was an increase in output, profit and workmens' wages. This scientific method of analysing work and workmen and paying by results gave rise to the following management practices that are still widely used:-

(a) Motion study of work practices to determine the best way of completing tasks.

(b) Time study of workmen to establish work performance standards.

(c) Payment by results schemes based on time and motion studies.

(d) Scientific selection and training of workmen.

(e) Functional management where supervisory functions became specialised and relate closely to work being done.

Taylor did convert many managers to 'scientific management' and this probably helped create a demand for cost accounting. Indeed, early cost accounting techniques were closely related to motion studies (Refer to chapter 3) and remuneration systems were linked to payment by results schemes. (Refer to chapter 4 sub-section 3:3).

2:2 Human relations Since the late 1920's the focus of research into industrial organisations has shifted from the classical formal organisation approach towards the social influences on work groups and the psychological influences on individuals. The reason for this shift was mainly because classical theory did not represent reality. For instance, many principles of formal organisation theory rest upon an assumption of rational human behaviour. General principles should help to predict the outcome of events from a given set of circumstances. But it became evident from experiments that predictable changes in output arising from changes in working conditions were unreliable. This was because powerful social and psychological factors were influencing events. These influences are often referred to as the informal organisation and the human relations school has tended to concentrate on this aspect of organisations. The main research methods adopted by the human relations school have been a range of observation techniques and interview techniques. The results of the research findings have been interpreted in many ways but in general the outcome has been to stress the importance of the individual and the work group in an organisation.

In the following sub-sections we will be briefly looking at some of the well known research findings and attempting to relate them to accounting. In subsequent chapters human relations theory has been directly related to accounting. For instance in chapter 8 section 4 the 'people effect' on budgetary systems refers to Maslow's motivational pyramid. However many aspects of accounting still closely relate to classical management theory.

2:2:1 Hawthorne studies (1927 - 1932) These studies undertaken by Elton Mayo and associates F. Rothlisberger and W. Dickson at the Hawthorne Works of the Western Electric Company, Chicago, are generally considered to represent the beginning of the human relations school of management theory. The early experiments were to determine the effects of varying lighting levels on productivity. With one of the control groups the lighting was reduced to a level where the operators could just about see their work, yet output increased. The cause of the increased output was identified as a human relations factor. The groups of workers had routine monotonous tasks. Thus when they received attention from management and the researchers it gave them a feeling of importance and greater satisfaction. As a result output increased.

The failure of the illumination experiments to clearly identify the cause of increased output provided the incentive for research into human relations. The experiments in a relay assembly test room lasted for a year where wages, rest pauses and other variables were altered. The final conclusion however, was that increased productivity was mainly due to improved human relations.

Further studies in a bank wiring observation room revealed a network of informal relationships that established social bonds and created common norms. These group norms were in effect a set of rules for conduct at work. One group norm had established a 'fair day's work' that was below management's productivity standards. The workers were afraid that increased productivity would result in the piece rate being cut. Therefore fast workers would slow down to conform with the informal rules. The informal control of output levels also tended to strengthen worker solidarity by reducing competition and increasing job security. Several positive factors were noted about cohesive work groups such as good timekeeping, reduced absenteeism and fairly high morale.

Since the pioneering work of the Hawthorne studies a large amount of research effort has been directed into studying human relations at work. The outcome of the research has been a change of managerial emphasis that recognises the existence and importance of the informal organisation. Where accounting fits into this aspect of management is in the design of control systems (Refer to chapters 8, 9 and 10) and remuneration systems (Refer to chapter 4).

2:2:2 Motivation - hygiene theory Frederick Harzberg's research in the 1950's and 60's provided the basis for his general theory on motivation at work. This is generally referred to as the motivation - hygiene theory. The theory first identifies factors at work that can lead to satisfaction and dissatisfaction. These factors are summarised in the following table:-

Satisfying (motivating) factors	Dissatisfying (hygiene) factors
Achievement	Company policy
Recognition	Administration
Responsibility	Supervision
Work satisfaction	Salary
Advancement	Inter-personal relationships
Possibility of personal growth	Job security
	Status

These two sets of factors represent different parallel sets of needs that are pursued by individuals. The hygiene seekers are mainly concerned with their environment, over-react to changes and are generally dissatisfied and apathetic to work. Motivation seekers are primarily concerned with the nature of their work and the opportunities it provides for achievement and personal benefit. They tend to react less to hygiene conditions and have balanced sincere belief systems.

Herzberg's earlier work was criticised because wide conclusions were being drawn from a limited study of accountants and engineers. However, the work has influenced management thinking because it is now fairly widely accepted that there is a duality of motivation. People do tend to respond differently to work content in one way and the working environment in another way. Thus interesting work still needs a satisfactory environment. Conversely a good environment still needs to be linked to the feeling that the work is interesting and worthwhile.

Accounting can play an important role in motivation through the design of wage payment systems and work control systems. Herzberg's writing have encouraged the development of job enrichment schemes and management accounting has a role to play in their development to ensure proposed schemes are cost justified.

2:2:3 Theory X and Theory Y A lot of planning and control is based upon the assumptions that managers make about human nature and behaviour. These assumptions can be based on a traditional view of the need for directing and controlling employees towards organisational goals. Or, the assumptions can be based on the view that individual employee needs can be directed towards organisational goals without strong external direction and control. The basic principle of Theory X and Theory Y is to identify two opposite sets of assumptions about human behaviour. Douglas McGregor's well known exposition of contrasting management philosophies under the headings of Theory X and Theory Y are summarised below:-

Theory X managers believe:-

(a) People have an inherent dislike of work and will avoid it whenever possible.

(b) To get people to work towards organisational objectives they must be coerced, controlled, directed and threatened with punishment.

(c) The average person prefers to be directed and does not want responsibility.

(d) The average person has little ambition.

(e) People have a high need of security.

Theory Y managers believe:-

(a) People do not inherently dislike work and that physical and mental effort in work is as natural as play or rest.

(b) External controls are not the only means of ensuring effort towards organisational goals. If a person is committed to objectives the self direction and self control will ensure sufficient effort.

(c) The personal committment to organisational objectives does not necessarily require specific monetary reward. Self satisfaction from achievement can provide sufficient motivation.

(d) Given proper conditions the average person accepts and seeks responsibility.

(e) Most people have a relatively high degree of imagination, ingenuity and creativity for solving organisational problems.

(f) Modern industrial life only partly utilises the intellectual potential of human beings.

These two sets of assumptions can be viewed as opposite ends of a horizontal scale.

Theory X Manager ———————————————— Theory Y Manager

The point on the scale that represents management attitudes in an organisation will reflect the nature of the organisation's control systems. McGregor provided many reasons why management should move more towards the Theory Y position.

Many accounting systems relate to a Theory X position and appear to have lagged behind in the management shift towards Theory Y. For instance, few budgetary control systems provide for full participation in target setting because of the risk of 'budgetary slack'. (Refer to chapter 8 sub-sections 4:2 and 4:3)

3. Review of management techniques

The purpose of most management techniques is to help managers with their planning and control function. There are also a miscellany of techniques developed by 'behavioural scientists' that concentrate on the management function of getting things done through people. The traditional role of management accounting techniques has tended to fit neatly into the former category. Indeed this book is packed with detail relating to the traditional cost based decision making and control techniques. But management accounting techniques have generally been widening their quantitative approach to planning and control. For example, budgeting systems are being designed to accommodate participative management styles. Although the accounting technique of budgeting has not undergone fundamental change, the arrangements for target setting have certainly changed (Refer to chapter 8 section 4). In wage payment systems, it is no longer just an arithmetic exercise, but a complex problem incorporating many variables that are generally considered to be outside the scope of accounting (Refer to chapter 4 section 3:8)

This review is intended to provide a quick reference source and contains brief descriptions of 94 management techniques. Most of these techniques are explained in greater detail in various sections of this book as indicated by references. It should be clear from this review, that there is a close relationship between accounting and management.

GLOSSARY OF MANAGEMENT TECHNIQUES

Absorption costing A cost control technique that charges all costs incurred in bringing a product to its current condition and location. The accumulated costs are often used for unit pricing decisions *(Refer to chapter 3 section 5:1)*

Algorithms A problem solving technique that reduces a task/problem to a logical sequence of operations *(Refer to chapter 2 section 2:3:6)*

Analytical estimating A production planning technique that breaks down a job into a sequence of operations for measuring estimated costs and/or times. Similar to work measurement that takes place when work is actually being done.

Auditing An independent appraisal of one or more aspects of business activity. There are many types of audit. The most well known being the statutory audit *(Refer to Volume 1 Financial accounting for non accountants chapter 1 section 8)*

Batch processing An administrative technique where documents are collected, recorded and filed in batches. *(Refer to chapter 10 section 2:1:1) also chapter 2 section 5:12).*

Bonus schemes A range of motivational techniques where additional wages are paid to encourage improved performance. *(Refer to chapter 4 section 3).*

Brainstorming A problem solving technique that encourages the participants to generate new ideas. *(refer to chapter 2 section 2:3:1).*

Breakeven analysis A technique that illustrates the relationship between cost, volume, price and profit. Widely used for price/output decision making. *(Refer to chapter 6 section 2).*

Budgeting A planning and control technique that requires a plan to be quantified in terms of volume, output and sales and costs and revenue. The detailed quantified plan is then used as a performance measure against which results are compared). *(Refer to chapter 8).*

Cash forecasting A number of techniques to determine the future cash requirements of a business. *(Refer to chapter 8 section 2:4:4 and Volume 3 Finance and taxation for the non-accountant).*

Collective bargaining A rule making process between the representatives of employers and employees to determine employment relationships and conditions of employment. *(Refer to chapter 4 section 4)*

Contract costing A costing technique that enables a manager to determine the profit or loss and cash flow arising from a single contract. *(Refer to chapter 3 section 5:11).*

Contribution analysis A costing technique used to determine the contribution (selling costs less variable costs), that a product or service makes towards paying the fixed costs of an enterprise *(Refer to chapter 6 section 2).*

Corporate planning A range of techniques used to establish the medium and long term plans of a business. The plans would be broadly divided into operations and organisation. *(Refer to chapter 2 sections 3 and 4)*

Cost-benefit analysis A technique that attempts to place values on the benefits arising from a decision. The notional value of the benefits are then compared with the expected costs to produce a favourable or unfavourable cost/benefit ratio. *(Refer to chapter 7 section 4:2).*

Cost effectiveness analysis A costing technique used to find the cheapest way of achieving a clearly defined objective. *(Refer to chapter 7 section 4:3)*

Costing A very wide range of techinques generally used for cost control and numerous kinds of decisions. *(Refer to chapter 3).*

Credit control A number of techniques that attempt to ensure customers pay within the agreed credit period. *(Refer to Volume 3 Finance and taxation for the non-accountant).*

Critical path analysis A planning and control technique which illustrates the sequence and relationship of a project's activities. *(Refer to chapter 6 section 3:6:1)*

Cybematics The application of automatic control systems to relieve management from routine decision making. *(Refer to chapter 2 section 5:1)*

Decision trees A technique that illustrates the choice between alternative courses of action for a series of decisions. *(Refer to chapter 6 section 3:5).*

Differential costing A decision making technique that excludes all costs that do not differ for each alternative course of action. *(Refer to chapter 6 section 3:1).*

Direct costing A cost control system that collects costs in cost centres and/or cost units. A direct cost is one that can be exclusively attributed to a cost centre or cost unit. *(Refer to chapter 3 section 3:4).*

Discounted cash flow An investment appraisal technique that makes adjustments to future cash flows to allow for the time value of money. *(Refer to chapter 7)*

Disinvestment appraisal An investment appraisal technique that includes project abandonment values in the calculations to determine the economic life of a project. *(Refer to chapter 7 section 8:5).*

Expected monetary volume A technique that makes allowance for risk in cash flow calculations. *(Refer to chapter 7 sections 9:1:1 and 9:2:3).*

Factoring An arrangement where a business hands over all, or part of its debtors to a collection agency in return for guaranteed payments less the factoring company's changes. *(Refer to Volume 3 Finance and taxation for the non-accountant).*

Feasibility study A method of appraisal to determine whether a project's objectives can be achieved within known financial and time constraints. *(Refer to chapter 7 section 4:1).*

First in first out A stock valuation technique based on the assumption that the first stock items received are the first issued. *(Refer to chapter 5 section 5:3:1).*

Formula pricing A technique that calculates price by adding a percentage margin to the cost. (Cost may be defined in a number of ways). Alternatively a percentage margin is deducted from the market price to determine a target cost. *(Refer to chapter 6 section 4:2).*

Gantt chart A horizontal bar chart that shows planned work against actual work.

Group bonus system A payment by results scheme where the output of a group is measured to determine the premium payment. Also arises as lieu payments for groups of workers that see their differentials being eroded because of a separate incentive payment scheme. *(Refer to chapter 4 section 3:3:3).*

Hedging A range of techniques applied to minimise risk, usually in commodities and currency dealings. *(Refer to Volume 3 Finance and taxation for the non-accountant).*

Human resource accounting This comprises of three proposed methods of measuring the human resources of business: the historic costs of recruitment, training, etc, the replacement costs, or the economic value defined as the present value of future net income streams. *(Refer to chapter 4 section 5:1:3).*

Incremental costing A decision making technique used to calculate the change in total costs and revenues arising from a change in the level of activity.*(Refer to chapter 6 section 3:2).*

Inflation accounting A technique that produces current cost figures from historic cost figures in an attempt to allow for the effects of inflation on accountancy reports. *(Refer to chapter 8 section 3:4 and Volume 1 Financial accounting for non-accountants chapter 10).*

Internal audit An independent appraisal activity within an organisation for the review of operations as a service to management. *(Refer to Volume 1 Financial accounting for non-accountants, chapter 1)*

Internal check A system of organising and sub-dividing work so that a single person does not have complete control over a set of activities. The main purpose is to reduce the risk of fraud. *(Refer to Volume 1 Financial accounting for non accountants chapter 1).*

Internal rate of return An investment appraisal technique that produces a percentage figure for a project that represents the discount rate where the net present value will be zero. *(Refer to chapter 7 sections 7:3 and 11:1).*

Inventory management A broader concept than stock control. Inventory management covers requisitioning, purchasing, receiving, inspecting, storage, issues to work in progress, receiving from work in progress, valuing stock, calculating economic order quantities, optimum stock levels, re-order levels, safety stocks and stores administration. *(Refer to chapter 5).*

Investment appraisal A wide range of techniques that relate to decisions concerning the medium and long term activities of a business. *(Refer to chapter 7).*

Job costing A costing technique for the 'one off' type of job where costs are totalled and a margin added to determine the price to be charged. *(Refer to chapter 3 section 5:10).*

Job evaluation A number of techniques that attempt to resolve the problem of 'differentials' in wage payment systems. The four main techniques are: point rating, factor comparison, grading and ranking. *(Refer to chapter 4 section 3:1:2).*

Joint costing A costing technique for production processes that automatically produce more than one product. *(Refer to chapter 3 section 5:7:1).*

Key factor analysis A technique that identifies and assesses the effect that limiting factors will have upon achieving an objective. *(Refer to chapter 6 section 2:8:4).*

Labour administration A large number of techniques and systems that relate to the recruitment, employment and dismissal of employees. *(Refer to chapter 4 section 2).*

Labour planning A range of techniques used to determine the future size, composition and nature of the labour force. Often called 'manpower planning' *(Refer to chapter 4 section 5).*

Labour remuneration A large number of methods for calculating wage payments. *(Refer to chapter 4 section 3).*

Labour turnover A set of techniques used to measure the movement of employees in and out of an organisation and to determine their reasons for leaving. *(Refer to chapter 4 section 5:1:2).*

Last in first out A stock valuation technique based on the assumption that the last items of stock received are the first issued. *(Refer to chapter 5 section 5:3:2).*

Learning curve A technique that attempts to establish a relationship between labour efficiency and the length of the production run. The principle of learning curves are also applied to individuals during practical training periods.

Life cycle costing An investment appraisal technique that divides a project's life cycle into seven costing stages: specification, design, make or buy, installation, start up, operating and terminal stage. *(Refer to chapter 7 section 2:3:3).*

Linear programming A mathematical technique constructed with a set of linear equations to determine an optimal position. Can be used for multiple limiting factor problems, product mix, machine scheduling, labour utilisation, warehousing and transportation problems. *(Refer to chapter 6 section 3:7).*

Management by exception A management principle based on the principle 'if things are going alright, leave them alone'. This means arranging business affairs so that only deviations from the plan are brought to a manager's attention. Standard costing is an application of MBE principles. *(Refer to chapter 9 section 2:1).*

Management by objectives A planning and control technique that concentrates on participative goal setting throughout an organisation. *(Refer to chapter 8 section 5:4).*

Marginal costing A costing technique that divides costs into fixed and variable as an aid for price/output decision making. *(Refer to chapter 3 sections 5:2 and 5:3 and chapter 6 section 2).*

Measured daywork An incentive payment method where a fixed amount is paid above the basic rate if an agreed level of performance is achieved. There are three main categories of MDW schemes: high day rate system, flat rate plus bonus system and premium pay plan system. *(Refer to chapter 4 section 3:5).*

Merit rating An incentive payment method that calculates additional payments to employees based on personal performance.*(Refer to chapter 4 section 3:1:3).*

Net present value An investment appraisal technique that multiplies a project's net cash flows by a discount factor to determine the discounted cash flows. The initial cost of the project is then deducted from the discounted cash flows to derive the net present value of the project. *(Refer to chapter 7 sections 7:1 and 11:1).*

Net terminal value An investment appraisal technique that uses compounding calculations to determine a future value of present cash flows, instead of a present value of future cash flows that is calculated by discounting techniques. *(Refer to chapter 7 section 7:4)*

Networks A range of techniques used for planning and control of projects. Network techniques include critical path analysis (CPA) and program evaluation and review techniques (PERT). *(Refer to chapter 6 section 3:6).*

Operations research The application of mathematical techniques to complex problems. Techniques include linear programming, simulation models, queuing theory and networks.

Opportunity costs A technique that attempts to assess the cost of lost opportunities arising from sub optimal decisions. *(Refer to chapter 6 section 3:3).*

Organisation and methods (O and M) A service for managers that provides advice on the structure of an organisation, its planning and control and its procedures and methods.

Output budgeting Used to describe a quantitive statement of future production. Also used to describe a programme budgeting system. *(Refer to chapter 8 section 2:4:2 and 5:2).*

Output costing A simple costing system where the total costs are divided by the related output. Can be used in single product enterprises such as mining or quarrying. *(Refer to chapter 3 section 5:8).*

Payback A project appraisal technique that answers the question 'How quickly do I get my money back?' For regular cash flows divide the net cash outlay by average annual net cash flows until they equal the initial cash outflow. *(Refer to chapter 7 section 3:3).*

Percentage yield An investment appraisal method that equates the discounted cash inflows and outflows of a project to derive a project percentage figure often called the 'internal rate of return' *(Refer to chapter 7 sections 7:3 and 11:1).*

Process costing A costing system that divides a continuous production process into cost centres. Each cost centre then charges its costs to production as it passes through the process. *(Refer to chapter 3 section 5:7).*

Product life cycle A technique that attempts to assess the life of a product (or service) into four phases: introductory, growth, maturity and decline. *(Refer to chapter 7 section 2:2:2).*

Product matrix A technique that illustrates in a matrix the relationship between corporate cash flows and market share. *(Refer to chapter 2 section 3:2:1).*

Profit planning A medium term planning technique that begins with a profit target. The profit target is then 'grossed up' to a total turnover figure using average net margins. A similar process can be undertaken using P/E ratios. *(Refer ro chapter 2 section 3:4).*

Profit sharing A form of incentive payment that is intended to improve the good will of employees towards the enterprise. *(Refer to chapter 4 section 3:6).*

Program evaluation and review technique (PERT) A technique similar to critical path analysis, but PEAT allows several time estimates to be included for a single activity on a probability basis. *(Refer to chapter 6 section 3:6:2).*

Programming, planning, budgeting system (PPBS) A planning and control tech nique that derives a programme from the organisation's objectives. The programme then provides a framework for a budgetary control system. *(Refer to chapter 8 section 5:2).*

Quality circles A technique where a small group of employees, between 3 and 12, who do similar work meet regularly to discuss problems, analyse the causes and propose solutions to management. These groups are often encouraged to implement the solution themselves.

Quality control A range of techniques that record and analyse inspection data to ensure that the quality of a product (or service) is maintained within specified limits and where possible improved.

Ratios analysis A range of techniques that establish relationships between two or more variables that enable the effects of scale to be removed and valid comparisons to be made. *(Refer to chpater 9 section 7 and Volume 1 Financial accounting for non accountants, chapter 12).*

Relevant costs A decision making technique that only considers costs that relate to the future and will be different for the decision alternatives. *(Refer to chapter 6 section 3:4).*

Responsibility accounting A budgeting system where budgets are directly related to a manager's span of responsibility. Each budget only contains costs/revenues that are within the control of an individual manager. *(Refer to chapter 8 section 5:3)*

Risk analysis A range of mathematical techniques that attempt to quantify and allow for risk in forecasts. The techniques are of limited value under conditions of uncertainty where there is no data available to help predict future events. *Refer to chapter 7 section 9).*

Sensitivity analysis A technique that is used to assess the sensitivity of a project to changes in specific variables. For instance, if a 10% rise in the costs of a specific in put could destroy a project's economic viability then sensitivity analysis techniques would be used in the decision making process. *(Refer to chapter 7 section 9:3).*

Simulation A range of mathematical techniques that enable the decision maker to predict the outcome of events within specified constraints. For instance, the effect on market share arising from a change in price. *(Refer to chapter 7 section 9:4)*

Standard costing A planning and control technique that establishes a set of pre-determined costs and revenues, against which actual costs and revenues are compared. *(Refer to chapter 9).*

Synectics A problem solving technique that requires the decision maker to distort, transpose or invert the familiar to make it strange. *(Refer to chapter 2 section 2:3:2)*

Systems analysis A technique where the decision maker breaks down a problem into manageable parts and then applies rigourous procedures for analysing each sub-problem and its solution. The technique is normally associated with computer personnel who have described themselves as systems analysts. *(Refer to chapter 2 section 2:3:5).*

Terotechnology A broad cost/engineering concept that is mainly concerned with the design of assets to reduce maintenance costs. *(Refer to chapter 7 section 2:3:2).*

Time span of discretion A kind of job evaluation scheme based upon the length of time a manager can continue without needing decisions from superiors. Also the length of time it is possible for an employee to produce sub-standard work without being noticed by the immediate supervisor. *(Refer to chapter 4 section 3:1:4).*

Uniform costing An agreement between business units to use the same costing principles and practice. *(Refer to chapter 3 section 5:5).*

Value analysis A technique that compares the cost of an item or service with the value obtained from it. Similar to cost/benefit analysis.

Variance accounting An accounting system that compares planned/expected costs and revenues with actual costs and revenues. The differences between the actual and expected costs/revenues are called variances. *(Refer to chapters 8 and 9).*

Variety reduction A range of techniques aimed at simplifying and standardising products and packaging to reduce costs.

Work study A range of techniques that measure, record and analyse work practices in relation to output. The techniques include: time study, method study, work meas-measurement, activity sampling, ergonomics and predetermined motion time systems (PMTS).

Zero budgeting A budgeting system that requires all existing activities to apply for resources during the budgetary planning phase in the same way as new proposals. All departments start from a zero base and have to justify their claims for resources as though they were new departments. *(Refer to chapter 8 section 5).*

Summary

Management accounting exists to provide a service for managers. It is therefore appropriate that this book should begin with a review of the management function to identify where accounting fits in. Although this may be the appropriate starting point, it is certainly no easy task to adequately describe the management function in just one chapter. There is a vast volume of literature on management, with contributions from some eminent writers. A lot of the literature is based on valid experience and research. Accordingly, any attempt to review this warehouse of knowledge will be incomplete.

The approach taken in this chapter has been first to highlight the main changes that are occurring in electronic data processing and industrial relations. The second section then took a brutally brief review of management theory by only covering the the work done by people such as: Fayol, Taylor and Mayo. There are of course many other valid contributions and management. However, the management principles developed by these writers provide a useful starting point. The third section is primarily a quick reference source for information about management techniques and provides many references to sections in this book that explain the techniques in greater detail, Naturally, most of the techniques reviewed in section 3 are management accounting techniques and provide an indication of the practical relationship that exists between accounting and management.

The management function covers a very broad area and managers can draw upon a wide range of techniques to help with specific tasks. In this introductory chapter we have been mainly concerned with the techniques developed by accountants for management. Most accounting techniques are generally developed to help with the planning and control of an enterprise. Indeed, most of the chapters in this book are related to planning and control. The principles of planning and control are explained in the next chapter.

Accountancy Quiz No.1.

1. What is the difference between financial accounting and management accounting? *(1.)*

2. Briefly explain the difference between the classical and human relations schools of management/organisation theory. *(2, 2:1, 2:2.)*

3. What did Fayol mean by 'unity of direction and unity of command'? *(2:1:1.)*

4. What is a scalar chain? *(2:1:1.)*

5. Explain the principles of scientific management. *(2:1:2.)*

6. Briefly describe the Hawthorne studies and explain their significance. *(2:2:1.)*

7. Why is it important for managers to be aware of the informal organisation in an enterprise? *(2:2:1.)*

8. Briefly explain the motivation - hygiene theory. *(2:2:2.)*

9. Describe the difference in attitudes between a Theory X manager and a Theory Y manager. *(2:2:3.)*

10. Briefly describe five management techniques developed by accountants. *(3.)*

2

Planning and Control

Objective

To provide a broad framework of the principles of planning and control as a foundation for the techniques that are explained in subsequent chapters.

Content *Page No.*

An outline of the principles of decision making.

An explanation of the principles, and some methods, for planning the operations of a business.

An explanation of the principles of planning the organisation of a business.

An explanation of the principles and problems of controlling a business.

Planning and Control

Introduction

In chapter 1 we reviewed some general management principles and techniques, and related them to accountancy. The rest of this book is primarily concerned with techniques for planning and controlling business activity. However, before we get involved in the detail of accounting decision making techniques it is first necessary to consider some of the principles of planning and control.

Have you ever considered why some businesses grow and others fail? Or, why some market leaders retain their leadership and others sink into oblivion? Although every business situation is different, business growth or decline will always be dependent on the quality of management's planning and control. Even in a short run situation with very favourable trading conditions planning and control is vitally necessary. Fast business growth creates many problems and good trading conditions rarely last for a long time. Just as the squirrel plans for winter so managers need to anticipate, and be prepared for change. Indeed the primary function of planning and control is survival. Bad planning and weak control can ruin a business.

Most of this book is devoted to the use of accounting and related techniques for planning and control. This was illustrated in diagram 1, chapter 1. This chapter is structured into four main parts; decision making, operational planning, organisation planning and control. The first part reviews some decision concepts and then some practical aspects of decision making such as generating and evaluating ideas and problem solving. Planning is divided into operations and organisations. Operational planning is broadly divided into strategic and tactical decisions. Some emphasis is placed on corporate life risk decisions, because decisions of this nature must be identified and then great care taken in the decision making process. Organisational planning is mainly concerned with getting the organisation structure right. Although these two aspects of planning are treated separately in this chapter the reader needs to be aware that the organisational and operational aspects of a business are totally interdependent. The last part, or control, reviews some control principles to provide a foundation for subsequent chapters on the control techniques of budgeting and standard costing.

2. Making decisions

We are all making decisions every day of our lives. Most of these personal decisions are relatively unimportant, but once in a while a decision is made that can affect one's future life style. Similarly, most business decisions are routine, repetitive, low risk and easily delegated. At the other end of the scale a single decision can place the entire business at risk.

Scale of decision importance

Routine decisions	________________________	*Corporate life risk decisions*

In this section on decision making we will be directing our attention towards the life risk end of the decision importance scale. The routine decision making is mainly a matter of organisational planning and operational controls.

Decisions are made individually and/or collectively under a variety of different circumstances. The first thing that needs to be established is the framework within which decisions are being made. Secondly, the class of decision and third the decision process. If a decision maker is unaware of the framework and class of decision he/she will probably be asking the wrong questions and deriving the wrong solution Defining the problem and asking the right questions requires a clear understanding of where the decision fits in the overall pattern of business activity. For instance, any person who has played a business game will be aware of the problem of matching production and sales. The effectiveness of planning output to meet demand quickly shows itself in stock levels. The decision to reduce high stock levels in a business game is usually simplified down to reducing production and/or increasing marketing. Diagram 4 illustrates this production/sales matching decision as a continuing planning and control process. The important point to grasp here is that any decision made in this continuing process is inter-related to many other decisions.

DIAGRAM 4 CONTINUOUS PLANNING & CONTROL PROCESS

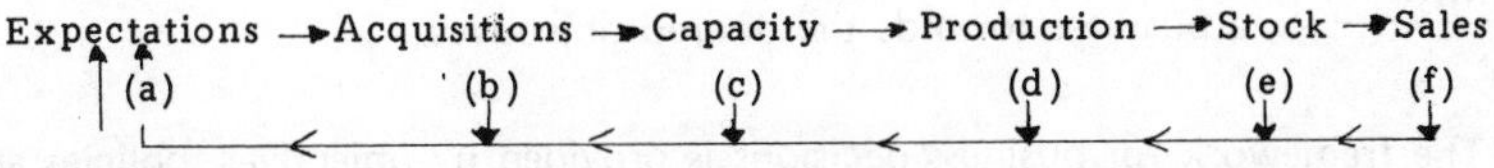

Where:-

(a) Expectations are the attitudes of management that result from endogenous and exogenous information flows.

(b) Acquisitions represent materials, labour and facilities that result from expectations.

(c) Capacity refers to the firm's capacity to affect the market. This is a wider concept than the practical description of productive capacity.

(d) Production of goods and/or services.

(e) Stock of finished goods available for sale (For a business that provides services and not goods, 'production' would be replaced in the diagram by 'services' and stock would not usually be significant.)

(f) Sales of goods and/or services.

In the following sub-sections on decision making we will be looking at the elements of a decision, the different classes of decision and methods for making decisions.

2:1 Decision framework There is a substantial amount of theory and a lot of techniques related to business decisions. Contributions to this body of management theory and practice have been made by economists, psychologists, mathematicians, statisticians, systems analysts and accountants. It is therefore appropriate that we first try to develop some kind of framework into which all these contributions can be given some perspective. Consider the following brief notes on the stages of decision making:-

Framework for business decisions

Objectives	These represent the desired outcome from decisions and subsequent action
Policies	These represent a broad framework for general courses of action providing direction for decisions towards stated objectives.
Plans	These are policy statements representing a series of decisions that need to be taken.

Decision process

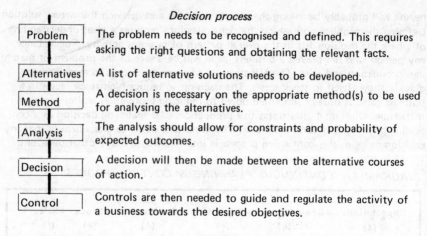

Problem	The problem needs to be recognised and defined. This requires asking the right questions and obtaining the relevant facts.
Alternatives	A list of alternative solutions needs to be developed.
Method	A decision is necessary on the appropriate method(s) to be used for analysing the alternatives.
Analysis	The analysis should allow for constraints and probability of expected outcomes.
Decision	A decision will then be made between the alternative courses of action.
Control	Controls are then needed to guide and regulate the activity of a business towards the desired objectives.

The framework for business decisions is provided by objectives, policies and plans. Decisions are then made by applying the generally accepted problem solving process of making a choice between feasible alternative solutions. The accountants' contribution in this process is usually restricted to providing data and analytical methods. This narrow approach to decision making has been frequently criticised and accountancy is now taking a wider multi-disciplinary approach in problem solving.

The classical decision model was based on assumptions such as:-

(a) Managers were rational decision makers and would make decisions in pursuit of their firm's objectives.
(b) Optimal decision making was possible.
(c) Outcomes were single valued, even when uncertainty was known to exist.
(d) That accurate performance measurement was possible.
(e) That labour was a fully controllable factor of production.
(f) Little interdependence existed between decisions.

Whilst the classical decision model does not represent reality, many decision making methods are based on this certainty framework within which no allowance is made for human behaviour. Although this book takes a wide approach to decision making, encompassing subjects not normally associated with accountancy, it is still primarily a practical text. Therefore it is inappropriate to discuss decision theory in detail.

2:2 Decision classes Both planning and control require decisions to be made. The decisions made in the planning stage relate to the long and medium term strategy of the firm and are generally referred to as strategic decisions. These strategic decisions can be broadly divided into operations and organisation. The decisions made in the control stage tend to be related to the short term tactics of the firm and are generally referred to as tactical decisions. This type of decision can also be divided into operations and organisation. These broad decision classes are illustrated in diagram 5. The general principles of strategic and tactical decisions are outlined in the following sub-sections and discussed in greater detail in section 3 - Planning the operations and section 4 - Planning the organisation.

DIAGRAM 5 MAJOR DECISION CLASSES

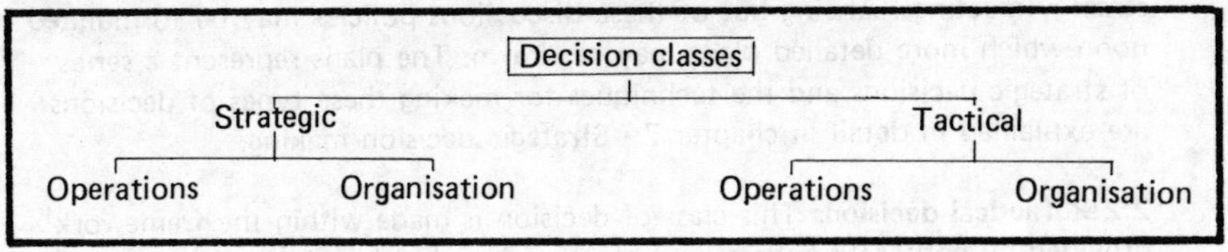

2:2:1 Strategic decisions Decision making often requires asking questions that may appear unnecessary. For instance, at the strategic level it is necessary to ask questions such as:-

What business are we in?
What business do we expect to be in, in say five or ten years time?
What business do we want to be in?
Why do we want to be in this business?
Are there any better alternatives?
What are our objectives?
What are the constraints on achieving these objectives?
What are our strengths and weaknesses?
Are our objectives relevant and realistic?
What plans do we have for achieving these objectives?

These soul searching type of questions are not an irrelevant academic exercise. Their purpose is to draw managers out of daily decision making routines and get them to think *long term*. Naturally, there is a danger that corporate strategy meetings will degenerate into irritating discussions on irrelevant issues. However with rapidly changing technology and markets, corporate strategy must be regularly and rigourously reviewed. Accordingly strategy meetings need to be very carefully planned with clear objectives, proposals for discussion and relevant information. There is a valid role in these meetings for management consultants and/or non-executive directors. Let us consider some of the questions that should be asked at a strategic meeting concerning business growth:-

Is the economy likely to be in a boom or recession during the next five years?
Is the state of the industry and its market suitable for a growth strategy?
What is the existing and projected size of the market?
What is the company's existing and projected market share?
What are the major competitors' existing and projected market shares?
Are there any technological developments that will significantly alter the nature of the market?
Should the company be in this market?
Should the company diversify?
Should the company expand through acquisition?
What are the expected outcomes of existing investment proposals?
What are the financial constraints on the growth strategy?
What are the organisational constraints on the growth strategy?
Are there any resource constraints such as materials, labour or equipment on the growth strategy?
Will the strategy create industrial relations unrest?

These types of questions provide the focus for a structured discussion at strategy meetings. Arising out of these discussions policies may be formulated upon which more detailed plans may be drawn. The plans represent a series of strategic decisions and the techniques for making these types of decisions are explained in detail in chapter 7 - Strategic decision making.

2:2:2 Tactical decisions This class of decision is made within the framework provided by corporate policies and plans. It is a decision that relates to the short term, tends to be repetitive and is generally delegated to all management levels below the board of directors. In small and medium sized enterprises directors would probably be involved in tactical as well as strategic level decision making. Indeed for some directors it can be very difficult to break away from tactical problems such as price, output or staffing and think in strategic terms.

A characteristic of tactical decisions is that they are mostly problems of costs, revenue or output. Questions such as:-

How much to produce of different types of product?
What price to charge?
How much stock to hold?
How much overtime to allow?
How to operate an incentive payment scheme?
What staff to employ?
How to cut costs?
How to improve efficiency?
Whether to accept or reject a special contract?
Whether to make or buy a product?

To cope with these kinds of problems the decision maker needs accurate, up to date and relevant information. Most of this information is quantitive and is the result of the analysis of data using some form of decision making technique. Tactical decision making techniques are explained, in detail, in chapter 6 - Tactical decision making.

2:3 Decision methods In this sub-section we are going to review some of the methods used to encourage creative thinking and help with problem solving. Decision making should be a creative process and not always a choice between the obvious alternatives. The creative decision maker will initially take a very wide view of the problem and actively seek alternative solutions. This creative process has been analysed by psychologists and the following five stages identified:-

1. Problem recognition
2. Gathering data related to the problem
3. Analysing the data
4. Recognising possible solutions
5. Testing and selecting a solution

Techniques for gathering and analysing data for decision making are explained throughout this book. Our concern here is with the methods that decision makers can use to generate ideas and systematic ways of evaluating these ideas. The methods used for generating ideas can be broadly divided into the following categories:-

(a) Analytical methods which use objective questioning on a specific problem. These tend to be used by systems analysts.

(b) *Free association methods* where anything goes. In the early stages these techniques encourage all ideas on a completely random basis with no attempt at evaluation.
(c) *Fixed relationship methods* that usually result in some form of logical listing such as a check list.

In the following sub-sections we will be reviewing methods for generating ideas such as: brainstorming, synectics, and role playing. We will then direct our attention to methods for evaluating solutions such as model building and some techniques used by systems analysts.

2:3:1 Brainstorming This is a well established technique that is used to help solve problems and generate new ideas. The group undertaking a brainstorming session is often referred to as a *buzz group*. The principle of brainstorming is to encourage ideas that would normally be suppressed by an individual, or if they were expressed, they would be squashed by the hasty judgement of others. A brainstorming session would comprise between 4 and 12 people from diverse backgrounds, knowledge and experience. Each person would be briefed on the principles and purposes of brainstorming. The room should provide a relaxed atmosphere with a board for writing on all the items as they are generated. There are several types of brainstorming techniques.The following guidelines relate to the Osborn's[1] brainstorming method.

Brainstorming guidelines
(i) Problem not revealed before the session
(ii) Problem clearly stated at the beginning of the session
(iii) Large number of ideas are wanted, regardless of quality.
(iv) Freewheeling is encouraged even if ideas are only remotely connected to the problem.
(v) Combinations of ideas and improvements are encouraged
(vi) No evaluation is allowed on any ideas

Once all the ideas have been listed a separate session is necessary for evaluation. The evaluation process should be clearly separated from the ideas generation process. Brainstorming is for generating ideas, it may not be suitable for evaluation.

2:3:2 Synectics[2] The principle of synectics is to make the familiar strange or the strange familiar. The use of this technique in problem solving is to help the decision maker break out of the analytical phase. In most decision situations the decision maker uses familiar solutions for problems. Even when the decision represents a strange situation, the decision maker may still attempt to force the strangeness into a familiar pattern, thus seeking a solution to the wrong problem. The use of sinectics requires the decision maker to distort, transpose or invert the familiar to make it strange. A similar process is undertaken using the principles of *lateral thinking.*

2:3:3 Role playing This is a popular teaching technique where students play personality roles and/or functional roles. The technique may also be used for

---

(1) Alex. F. Osborn - Applied Imagination. Charles Schribrier's Sons, New York (1953)
(2) W.J. Gordon - Synectics - Harper and Son (1961)

generating ideas. In a personality role play the decision maker can try to become say a trade union representative faced with the same problem. Or in functional role playing the decision maker may attempt to approach the problem as a salesman, a production worker or customer. The role playing may take place in a small group, or an individual decision maker can attempt role playing to obtain a wider view of the problem.

2:3:4 Model building The traditional use of models is to represent objects. For example a model ship made to scale, could be used in simulation tests for stability in rough seas. The same principle applies to abstract models, except they represent the relationships of variables. For example, a simple model explained in chapter 6, is the break even model. This is a mathematical/accounting model with two functions:-

Total revenue function	=	Price x Quantity
Total cost function	=	(Unit variable cost x Quantity) + fixed cost

To build a model the decision maker has to bring together all the parts of the problem into a framework that expresses their relationships. For instance, in the simple total revenue model above, revenue is a function of unit price and quantity sold. This relationship is the revenue model. Given this model, the decision maker can simulate what will happen if the unit price is increased or decreased, or the quantity sold is altered. Of course most models are ore complicated than this. But the same principles apply. Once the relationships have been established then simulation exercises may be undertaken to answer the What if....? type of questions. Decision models are without doubt the most powerful tool available to the decision maker. With the falling costs of hardware and packaged software, sophisticated decision making models are now within the reach of many decision makers.

There exist many kinds of models for a variety of different functions. There are however some broad categories that the decision maker should be aware of. The main categories are:-

(a) Static models in which it is assumed all the variables are in a steady state and any changes are at a constant rate throughout the decision period.
(b) Dynamic models where the influences of decisions in earlier and later periods are taken into consideration. This type of model is necessary for sequential decision problems such as inventory levels.
(c) Report models that simple generate reports of filed data in a prescribed format at specified time intervals. For example, budgeting statements or interim accounts.
(d) Deterministic models that assume single volume outcomes, (i.e. no risk calculations) For example interest calculations on a fixed interest investment
(e) Stochastic models (probabilistic models) allow for a range of possible out comes in relation to the range of performance possibilities.
(f) Optimising models use mathematical techniques such as linear programming or integer programming to derive an optimal solution.
(g) Heuristic models that search the data for a satisfactory solution. Each search produces an improved solution on the previous one. The program then ensures that the following trial solution will be an improvement on the previous solution.

Accountants have been building models for centuries. The earliest financial models were expressing relationships between business transactions according to sets of rules that categorised all costs and revenues. In this book we are concerned with accountancy models that help the decision maker. Although in most instances these models tend to be static, deterministic or report models. Indeed one of the criticisms that is levelled at accountancy models is they generally provide single value outcomes to complex problems. This is now changing due to low cost electronic data processing and software development.

2:3:5 Systems analysis This activity is usually associated with computers and computer personnel such as systems analysts and programmers. But systems analysis existed long before computers were invented. Systems analysis is a method where the decision maker breaks down a problem into a number of manageable parts and then adopts a rigorous procedure for analysing the problem and its possible solutions. As an illustration of the method, consider the following procedure that would be undertaken by a systems analyst for problem solving:-

Systems approach to problem solving

(i) Define objective and sub-objectives
(ii) State parameters and constraints on achieving objectives
(iii) List and evaluate different methods of achieving objectives within constraints
(iv) Select best method
(v) Develop model to simulate situation to test the method
(vi) Test the model
(vii) Evaluate results and adjust where necessary
(viii) Produce and run pilot study
(ix) Evaluate results of pilot run
(x) Make necessary adjustments and re-run until all problems resolved
(xi) Decision for full run
(xii) File loading
(xiii) Full run parallel with old system
(xiv) Review and monitor
(xv) Decision to stop parallel running and go 'live' with new system

In addition to rigorous procedures the systems analyst and programmer uses techniques such as decision trees, algorithms and flowcharts to help in the decision making process. Decision trees are explained in chapter 6 sub-section 3:5. The following sub-section explains the principles of algorithms and flowcharts.

2:3:6 Algorithms and flowcharts An algorithm is a structured series of procedural steps necessary for solving a specific problem. In most instances it is just a list of instructions. A flowchart is a diagramatic representation of an algorithm. For example, an algorithm for preparing an invoice could be as follows:

1. Check description and quantity on delivery note
2. Check unit price on prices list
3. Calculate invoice price
4. Type invoice out
5. Update sales ledger
6. Post invoice and file copy

A simple flowchart of this algorithm would have a start, a set of description frames and a stop, as shown in diagram 6.

DIAGRAM 6 *SIMPLE FLOWCHART*

This simple flowchart for an invoicing procedure makes no allowances for situations such as short deliveries, returns and discrepencies. When a system is being designed for electronic data processing then contingencies must be allowed for and the appropriate machine instructions given. Therefore a more complicated flowchart is used called a *'program flowchart'*.

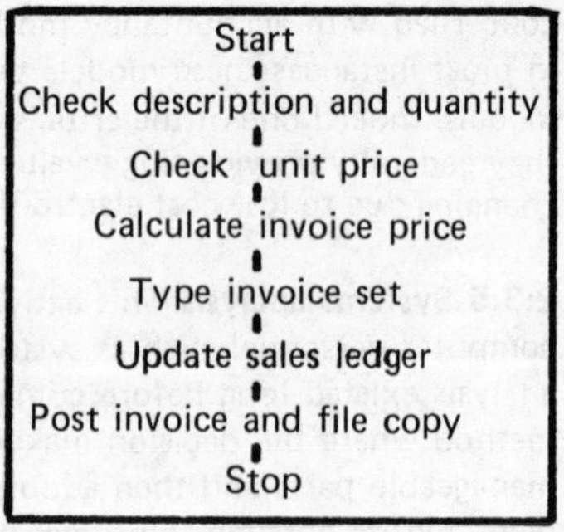

An extract from a program flowchart is illustrated in diagram 7 below.

DIAGRAM 7 *PROGRAM FLOWCHART*

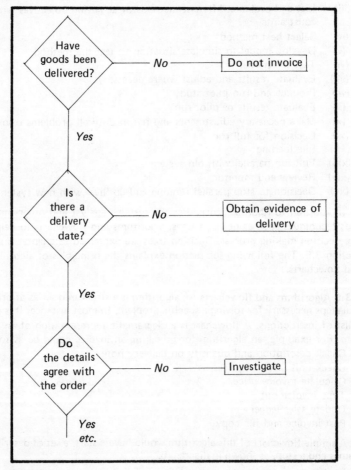

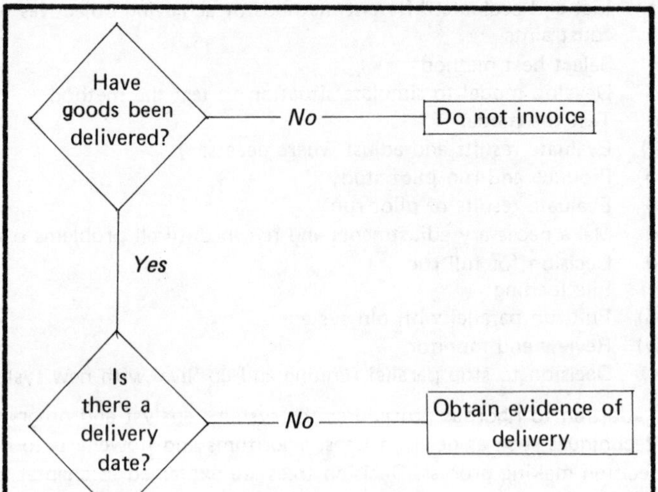

There are a number of rules for drawing flowcharts that have been created by programmers, system analysts and organisation and methods personnel. Departments tend to have their own set of house rules for flowcharts and they are often used as a form of esoteric communication. However, the individual decision maker can make his/her own rules to fit whatever problem is being examined, because the purpose of the flowchart is to help the decision maker. For example, consider the flowchart constructed by the author (diagram 8) for a small direct selling campaign. The diagram adheres to few flowcharting rules and is similar to a decision tree (Refer to chapter 6 sub-section 3:5) The point to note here is that you utilise techniques to serve a purpose and *results are more important than rules.*

DIAGRAM 8 *AD–HOC FLOWCHART*

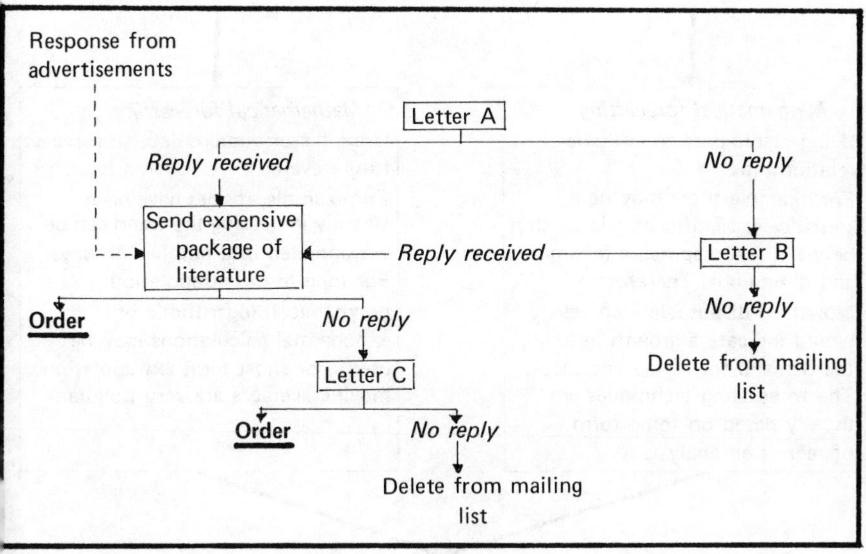

3. Planning the operations
This section is divided into three main parts forecasting, long range planning and profit planning and represents a broad approach to the procedure for the planning of the operations for a business. The first part on forecasting, takes a broad view of forecasting systems and does not explain any forecasting technique in detail. The second part on long range planning is divided into four sub-sections. The first sub-section explains how the product matrix can be used by decision makers for long range planning. The remaining three sub-sections explain the principles of diversification, synergy and corporate life risk that are important aspects of long range planning. The final part on profit planning examines the principles of this planning technique and how it is closely linked to budgetary process explained in detail in chapter 8.

3:1 Forecasting Business decisions are made in anticipation of future events. Thus in the early stages of planning the operations of a business it is necessary to make long, medium and short term predictions. These predictions of future events can

DIAGRAM 9 *FORECASTING SYSTEMS*

Macro-forecasting

This would include collecting data such as:-

Disposable incomes
Investment
Consumer's expenditure
Inflation
Exchange rates
Interest rates
Specific industries and the business cycle

Micro-forecasting

This would include collecting data such as:-

Sales of specific products and market shares
Costs trends
The future order book

Mathematical forecasting

Using macro-data to evaluate relationships.
For example there may be a statistically significant relationship between real disposable incomes and dining out. Therefore a growth in disposable incomes would indicate a growth in the demand for restaurant space. The forecasting techniques are usually based on some form of regression analysis

Mathematical forecasting

Using historic micro-data to forecast future events.
For example, if sales have been steadily increasing the trend can be extrapolated in a number of ways. For long term extrapolation polynamical, logarithmic or exponential calculations may be used. For short term extrapolation moving averages are very popular.

Co-ordinated forecasting

This is where the macro, micro, long snd short term forecasts are brought together. In most instances this is intuitive forecasting, where experienced executives examine the available information and make predictions. Mathematical forecasting has extended into this level with probabalistic models. But no matter how sophisticated the computer program, the decision makers should *feel* the forecast is right. The macro, micro and mathematical forecasting techniques are only aids in the forecasting process. *Increased complexity does not necessarily mean greater accuracy, reliability and relevance. Accordingly, at the co-ordinated forecasting level, decision makers should use mathematical forecasts and not be overpowered by them.*

be formalised into forecasts and from the forecasts plans can be devised. It is important to distinguish between forecasts and plans. Forecasts are estimates of future events that are likely to affect the business. Whereas plans represent decisions to pursue policies towards stated objectives. All business activity is dependent upon decision makers forming views about future events. The way these views are influenced and formed will range fron ad hoc random data gethering by a single decision maker to highly formalised forecasting systems where the output is examined by a strategic planning committee, i.e.

Range of forecasting systems

Subjective ad hoc data collection with little analysis	————————————————	Objective formalised data collection and analysis

As companies grow they tend to move along the scale towards formalised forcasting systems that suit the specific decision making team. Although forecasting systems tend to be different in detail, they will all have one or more of the following characteristics:-

Micro-forecasting, where past data such as sales and cost trends are used as pointers for the future.
Macro-forecasting, where the future state of the economy such as boom or recession and its effect on the industry and the firm is assessed.
Mathematical forecasting, where macro and/or micro data is analysed using established mathematical techniques.
Intuitive forecasting, where decision makers subjectively analyse macro and/or micro data.

These characteristics are illustrated in diagram 9.

A forecasting method that is being used in some companies in high technology industries is the *Delphi approach.* In this method a team of 'experts' from different disciplines is put through a kind of brainstorming session (Refer to sub-section 2:3:1). Each expert then draws up their own intuitive forecast. These forecasts are then sent to more experts who attach probability estimates for their likely occurrence. The data is then analysed using mathematical techniques producing a broad based forecast that takes into consideration expected technological change.

The forecasting techniques that have been outlined in this sub-section have ranged from simple extrapolation of past sales using moving averages and graphs, to advanced statistical mathematical techniques. Decision makers have to decide at what point on this scale their corporate forecasting system should be developed. Good planning has an element of luck, but in the long run it will be dependent on a good forecasting system.

3:2 Long range planning (LRP) The starting point for LRP is to be clear about the corporate objectives. It was explained earlier in section 2:1, how objectives were an essential part of the framework for all business decisions. Most business are assumed to have multiple goals such as: profit maximisation, increasing market share, high growth and increasing shareholders' wealth. In theory, businesses are also generally assumed to have rational decision makers capable of making optimal decisions. Reality however, shows that the behaviour of decision makers is not always rational, and activity is usually directed towards *'satisfactory'* levels and not *'optimal'* levels of business performance. The chairmen of public companies naturally have to state objectives using the 'maximising shareholders' wealth' rhetoric, but for planning, the real objectives need to be more carefully and clearly defined.

There will always be multiple objectives in areas such as: profitability,market share, technology, industrial relations, social and welfare, ownership and control A company therefore needs to adopt a procedure to structure the objectives in some form of framework. An outline procedure would include the following stages:-

Outline procedure for structuring corporate objectives

Stage 1 List all possible objectives using some kind of brainstorming technique.

Stage 2 Identify any potential conflict in objectives.

Stage 3. Rank objectives in terms of relative importance.

Stage 4. Create a framework for the objectives that shows their relative importance and clarifies potential conflict.

The next phase in the planning process is often referred to as a 'SWOT' analysis. This planning technique is used to identify the strengths, weaknesses, opportunities and threats for the company. The output of this technique is mainly a listing of detail under each of the four headings with possible courses of action related to each item.

Up to this point we have used fairly simple methods to answer two fundamental questions:-

1. Where are we going? (Structuring objectives)
2. Where are we now? (SWOT analysis)

To avoid the corporate strategy jargon let us draw an analogy of a sea journey. We have established where we are and where we are going . Now, we have to *'plan'* the route. There are several aspects to this route planning:-

1. The general direction such as south west (Long range planning)
2. The specific route taken on each chart. (Profit planning)
3. Decisions made along the route to allow for changes in the wind and tide (Tactical decisions)
4. Constantly checking the actual position with the planned position on the chart (Control)

This sailing analogy is quite valid, because a captain has to achieve an objective with limited resources and faces constraints, risks and uncertainty. The main difference is that the chief executive's objectives, constraints and risks are not so tangible. Therefore planning the operations of a business will not be so precise as planning the direction of a ship.

In general terms LRP can be broadly directed into three classes:-

Growth strategy through investment, diversification acquisition or other methods

Hold strategy where operational and/or organisational problems are resolved before any growth plans are initiated.

Decline strategy that may be adopted for a subsidiary company as part of a holding company's overall strategy.

Hold or decline strategies are often adopted during a recession and are some times referred to as *survival strategies.* But as growth is a fairly widespread business objective we will direct our attention to some aspects of growth strategies

3:2:1 Product matrix There are a number of applications of the product matrix. One popular application uses some sparkling jargon, such as *'stars, cash cows* and *dogs!'* The matrix is intended to illustrate the relationship between corporate cash flows and product market share. To use the matrix the decision maker needs to understand the jargon -

Stars are products (or services) that are capable of rapid growth. To support this growth and become market leaders they usually need huge amounts of cash. But once these *stars* are established they are cash generators and provide substantial revenue. Therefore *stars* need to be looked after very carefully.

Cash cows are products (or services) that have a large market share in a mature market. Because the market has matured and settled, the products do not need substantial amounts of cash to maintain growth. However, they still generate large amounts of cash. Thus, *cash cows* are used to fund the stars that will hopefully become *cash cows.*

Dogs are products with a low market share and low growth prospects. Although they may become profitable, they will never become *stars or cash cows.*

DIAGRAM 10 *PRODUCT MATRIX*

Market share / Market growth rate	High	Low
High	STARS	?
Low	CASH COWS	DOGS

Diagram 10 shows the jargon in a product matrix with a question mark in the right hand quandrant. The question mark represents products in high growth markets where the company has a low market share. Long range planning of the operations requires a market strategy to be devised for the general direction of business resources. The product matrix can help the decision maker devise this market strategy.

Let us now briefly consider the strategic options of a product in each of these quadrants, using the following corporate planning terminology.

(i) Build strategy refers to investment in a product (or service) aimed at increasing market share and cash flows. Build strategies can be very costly and require careful planning.

(ii) Hold strategy is to maintain the market position and constantly review the effects of tactical pricing and output decisions. A hold strategy would not allow substantial investment in a product.

(iii) Harvest strategy is to reap the maximum revenue from the product with the minimum costs. This usually requires some kind of premium pricing.

(iv) Divest strategy is a decision to get rid of the product in a way that the company will secure the maximum possible revenue.

Summary of strategy options using the product matrix

(a) Question marks The important point about products in the question mark quadrant is that they are in a high growth market. The first decision for these kind of products is whether the company should adopt a *leader or follower strategy.* A decision to adopt a leader strategy would place the product in the *stars* quadrant and would be a build strategy requiring heavy cash outflows in research, development and marketing. Alternatively the company could opt to follow the market leader and take a smaller share of an expanding market, possibly harvesting on a premium price. Or, choose a divest strategy where the product is sold or licenced to a company with a build strategy Resources from divesting could then be directed into *stars* or other *question marks.*

(b) Stars This is an expensive high yield, high risk quadrant and should not contain too many products. *Stars* require great management skill and often bold decisions are necessary. The criteria for most decisions is cash flow.*Stars* need to be converted to *cash cows* as the market growth rate slows down.Continued fast market growth for *stars* in high technology industries can exhaust a company's financial resources. When this happens a harvest or divest strategy may be necessary for some products. A hold strategy would rarely be suitable for products in the *stars* quadrant.

Cash cows This is a good quadrant in which to have some products. The usual strategy would be to hold or possibly harvest for as long as possible. As the *cash cows* will not last for a long while the cash should be used for financing the development of new products.

Dogs These products are in low growth markets and would rarely warrant a build strategy. In most instances the strategy would be to hold or harvest. If any product in this category was not expected to produce positive net cash flows then a divest strategy would be necessary.

3:2:2 Diversification In the previous sub-section we were concerned with product strategies. Developing product strategies will often result in some kind of diversification, therefore we need to briefly direct our attention on to this subject area.

There are many kinds of diversification and the terminology is not standardised. The important questions to ask are:-

(a) Is the company producing a new product that is within its existing technological and productive capacity?

(b) Is the company selling the new product (or service) in its exisitng market or is it entering entirely new markets?

Let us take a simple example to illustrate the importance of the nature of diversification. Office equipment manufacturers have been forced to accept a change in the nature of their market. A lot of office furniture should be designed to meet the needs of the 'electronic office'. Companies therefore have to diversify by changing their classical office furniture design to designs that will house computer terminals, word processors and visual display units. Different approaches to this problem could include:-

(i) Simple design alterations.No technology or production changes. Continue selling to existing market.

(ii) Design alterations to include production changes by using different materials and technology changes by installing hidden wiring circuits in desk frames. Continue selling to existing markets.

(iii) Different marketing approach by selling direct to hardware manufacturers office equipment designed to meet their specific requirements.

(iv) Purchasing hardware, then making and selling complete office systems.

(v) Manufacturing hardward, fitting in office furniture and marketing complete office systems.

These alternative approaches to a common problem illustrate different degrees of diversification. An extreme example would be an office furniture company with strong financial resources may decide that computer stationery is the place to be, and diversify into printing continuous stationery. The range of diversification alternatives can be illustrated as a scale: i.e.

Scale of corporate diversification

Single product in a Single market	————————————	Diverse product range in diverse markets

Any company at the single product/single market end of the scale is at risk and needs to diversify. Conversely, at the other end of the scale the conglomerate type of company may have planning and control problems because it is too diversified. Accordingly, decision makers need to recognise the necessity and risks associated with diversification when planning the long term operations of their company.

3:2:3 Synergy The principle of synergy is often summarised as the '2 + 2 =5' rule. It has even been traced back to Aristotle who observed 'The whole is greater than the sum of its parts'. At a more practical level, an understanding of synergy is important for long range planning. Let us first consider some broad categories where the 2+2 = 5 rule applies:-

Marketing Synergy where the marginal costs of marketing additional related products are very low. For instance, if two drinks manufacturers producing non-competitive products such as alcholic and non-alcholic drinks were merged they would no longer need two salesforces. There could also be possibilities for combined sales promotion. Thus in such a merger there would be market ing synergy opportunities.

Distribution synergy can offer tremendous cost savings. In the above example of the drinks manufacturers there could be economies of scale advantages through a regional or centralised warehousing and distribution policy that could not be possible for either manufacturer on their own.

Production synergy has two elements, investment and operating. Investment synergy would be possible by sharing existing capital equipment and new investment opportunities could be planned from a far broader base. Operating synergy could be obtained by joint purchasing for larger discounts and possible reductions in administrative costs. Combined research and development, maintenance and training could also be undertaken.

Financial synergy is often claimed as the justification for conglomerates. Yet the group balance sheets of conglomerates rarely have healthy cash balances. The rapid growth of conglomerates is generally due to acquisitions. For instance if a declining company acquired another declining company every year there would be an apparent sales growth rate. Even though acquisitions may be funded with 'chinese money' (share exchange arrangements), this kind of continued acquisition may not produce the claimed financial synergy. *(Refer to Volume 1 Financial accounting for non-accountants).*

Administrative/Management synergy may be as illusive as financial synergy.One of the problems associated with growth is control and the usual method of solving this problem is more administration and managers. Indeed, as individual managerial status in an organisation may be enhanced by employing more junior managers and administrators, synergetic gains in this area may be from 'adjusted figures' and not represent the real position.

Thus decision makers cannot ignore the importance of synergy when developing the corporate long range plan. However, synergy can be positive or negative. In areas such as production or marketing, the synergetic effect can be crudely calculated on a marginal cash flow basis and the possibility of positive synergy is quite good. But in administration, finance and management the assessment of potential synergy has a fairly high degree of uncertainty. Moreover, there could be a possibility of negative synergy.

One other aspect of synergy that needs to be considered is when a company wishes to enter a new market. There are entry barriers for all markets. The barrier may be: the scale of production such as in ship building or a steel foundry, technological such as semi-conductors, or consumer preference barriers that have been built up by existing companies in the market. The entry price into a market can be very high thus companies often enter markets by acquisition. The synergetic effect in this situation has two components; entry synergy and operating synergy. The positive entry synergy can be very high because the acquired company could have market reputation, labour skills, productive capacity and contacts.

We can conclude this sub-section by saying that decision makers need to understand the rpinciples of synergy and make relevant calculations when deriving their long range plans.

3:2:4 Corporate life risk (CLR) After the spectacular business failures such as Rolls Royce in the U.K. and Penn Central in the U.S.A. and the continuing business failures of less well known enterprises, it is clear that corporate life risk is a reality for every business. There is a substantial amount of literature on why companies fail. Mathematicians have produced a single value solution (Z – score) based on published accounts, accountants have produced a range of ratios and management consultants have produced check lists. The mathematical 'magic figure' is based on the assumption that published accounts represent the real situation. There is however, ample evidence that the practice of 'cosmetic reporting' (data selected, analysed and presented in a favourable way) is quite widespread. Investment analysts and accountants also adopt quantitive techniques, but they have a far broader base providing multiple values for assessing the risk of corporate failure. An even broader view is taken by management consultants. One such view we will be briefly examining, is the corporate failure process that is well presented by John Argenti[3]. After looking at the corporate failure process we will consider some types of corporate life risk decisions that may be made in long range planning. These CLR decisions can be grouped into the following classes:-

High conflict risks	High technology risks
High market risks	Cost trap risks

The objective of this sub-section is to alert the decision maker to the fact that CLR decisions exist and must be identified.

Argenti has observed three stages in the business failure process that are explained below and illustrated in diagram 11.

Phase 1 This is primarily a management defect stage that may be identified by managerial attitudes, organisation structure, systems of planning and control, and the company's responsiveness to change.

Phase 2 This phase is identified by mistakes that cause financial difficulties. Thus the defects identified in phase 1 have resulted in bad planning and control

Phase 3 The final phase where the symptoms begin to show in poor liquidity and performance. Most of the analytical corporate failure techniques attempt to identify the symptoms at the earliest possible date.

DIAGRAM 11 *BUSINESS FAILURE PROCESS*

Defects →	**Mistakes** →	**Symptoms**
Managerial attitudes and responsiveness to change	Bad planning and control	Performance indications and cash flows

Corporate failures can be broadly divided into three categories which we shall call: *non starters, high flyers* and *complacents.* These three categories are illustrated in diagrams 12, 13 and 14.

DIAGRAM 12 *BUSINESS FAILURE – 'NON STARTER'*

Non-starters are companies that never really get off the ground. The business does not generate enough cash flow to provide the funds for growth.

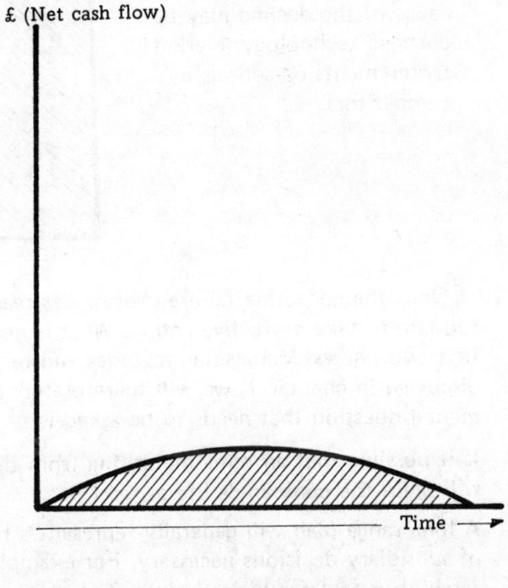

(3) J. Argenti - Corporate Collapse. McGraw Hill (1971). Also in 'Accountancy' October 1976 and August 1977.

DIAGRAM 13

BUSINESS FAILURE

'HIGH FLIER'

High fliers are companies with very fast sales growth. However the fast growth creates cash problems, organisation problems and eventually customer problems Once the business has lost credibility its decline is often faster than its growth.

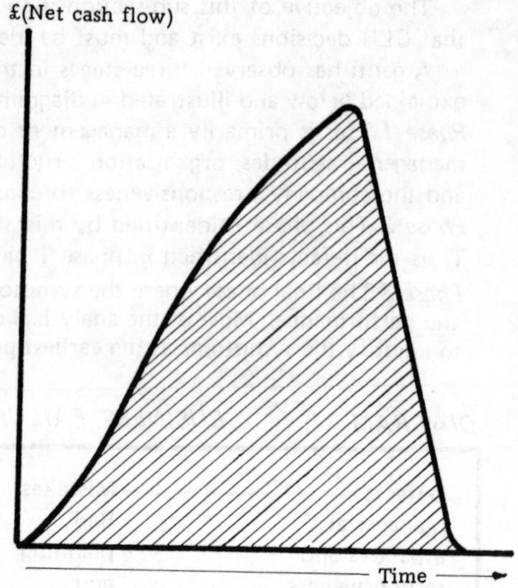

DIAGRAM 14

BUSINESS FAILURE

'COMPLACENT'

Complacents are companies that do not anticipate and react quickly to change. The cause of the decline may be changed technology, market requirements or actions by competitors.

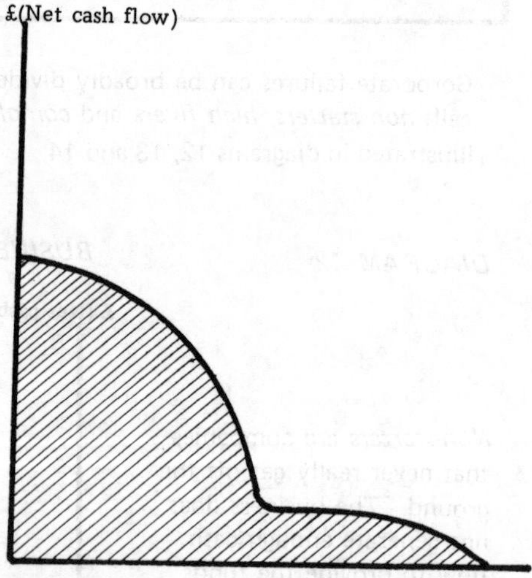

Once the corporate failure process has reached the third phase it may be too late to take corrective action. What is needed is preventative action in the first two phases. Managerial attitudes and responsiveness to change has been discussed in chapter 1, we will therefore concentrate on phase 2. The fundamental question that needs to be asked is:-

Is it possible that an outcome arising from this decision (or lack of decision) will place the company's life at risk?

A long range plan will generally represent a major decision that makes a series of subsidiary decisions necessary. For example, the major decision may be to establish a new production plant. The series of subsidiary decisions making up the detailed plan would include financial marketing, technical and administration tive areas. Just as a ship can be lost from a 'ha'panny of tar' so a long range plan could fail from a bad subsidiary decision. The failure of the plan could in turn cause the failure of the business. Thus there are two levels of corporate life risk. The major decision level that could ruin the business if it failed, and the subsidiary decision level that could cause a life risk plan to fail.

Identifying the life risk at the major decision level is mainly a financial appraisal and is very important for the *high flyers*. This type of company will probably have administration, management, production and distribution problems. Thus to launch into a substantial project, regardless of how profitable, may be a life risk decision. This is because the company has not had time to consolidate and prepare for a further growth phase. It would only take one or two mistakes at the subsidiary decision level for the plan to fail and the company to collapse like a pack of cards as illustrated in diagram 13. The areas where life risk may exist are:-

(a) High conflict areas that are likely to cause industrial relations unrest. For instance, assume a plan requires substantial and rapid changes in production methods. Any change that alters work practices can be a potential time-bomb The preparatory phase for any such change must sound out opposition through the consultative process, adapt where possible and have good training where necessary. A subsidiary decision at any level that ignores the 'people problems' associated with change may be creating a corporate life risk situation. There fore any potential CLR decisions must be identified before the task is delegated

(b) High market risks exist in markets where consumer preferences can change rapidly, or demand can fluctuate wildly. An investment in any such market should not be of a sufficient size to place the company at risk. For example. assume a company has an annual turnover of say £50,000 generating a net cash flow of £10,000. The company is considering a long range plan for entering an unstable but very profitable market, with an entry price of about £200,000. Clearly the company's existing cash flow cannot cope with this plan and substantial external finance will be needed. This would be a CLR decision There is nothing wrong with such bold decisions providing the decision maker is fully aware that the entire company is being placed at risk.

(c) High technology risks are a characteristic of decision making in industries such as micro-electronics and electronic data processing. The research and development race rewards winners and penalises the losers. The CLR decision here is related to the company's capacity to compete in specific races. If a decision is made to compete in a race requiring heavily externally funded negative cash flows, then this can place the company at risk.

(d) Cost trap risks arise when a plan is approved that can create heavy negative cash flows placing a tremendous financial burden on the company. This often happens with building contractors that make ambitious bids on large contracts that they may not be able to finance. Any delay with the contract work and related delay in stage payment results in a cash crisis. If a financial institution will not fund the company through the crisis, then that will probably be the end of the business, regardless of how profitable the contract may have been.

From this brief discussion we can conclude by noting that corporate failure can happen to any business. Accordingly, managers need to be concerned with preventative as well as corrective measures. The preventative measure is a good planning and control system which is capable of identifying CLR decisions and ensuring they are examined in great detail.

3:3 Profit planning This term has been widely applied by senior management to describe a variety of planning techniques. From published articles written by consultants, academics and businessmen, it appears that the term profit planning can be used to describe planning activities ranging from budgeting through to long range planning. For the purpose of this chapter we will place profit planning somewhere between the budgetary planning process and the long range planning process and refer to it as medium term planning technique.

The budgetary planning process explained in chapter 8 begins with a sales forecast from which a sales budget is constructed. The sales, production and finance budgets are then co-ordinated together with all the subsidiary budgets to produce a budgeted profit. Thus profit is a product of the budgetary planning process. With profit planning the process starts from 'the bottom line'. A target profit figure becomes the objective towards which the planning process is directed. For instance a company could start by setting a profit before tax target of say £100,000. With a 10 per cent average net margin this would require a turnover of about £1 million. A budgeted income statement could then be constructed with a £1 million turnover and a £100,000 before tax profit. As the detail was built up around the profit target it would soon become apparent if there was a gap between objectives and capability. The gap that generally arises is between the turnover requirements to achieve profit targets and sales forecasts as illustrated in diagram 15 below.

DIAGRAM 15 *PROFIT PLANNING SALES GAP*

Where:

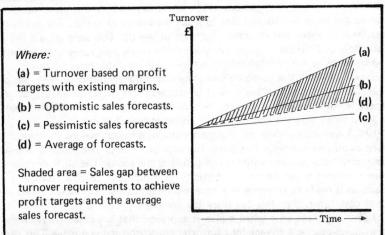

(a) = Turnover based on profit targets with existing margins.

(b) = Optomistic sales forecasts.

(c) = Pessimistic sales forecasts

(d) = Average of forecasts.

Shaded area = Sales gap between turnover requirements to achieve profit targets and the average sales forecast.

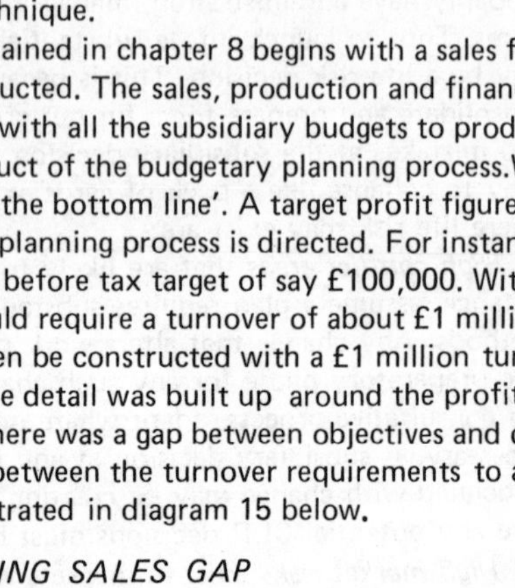

For the quoted company, the profit planning process will probably begin with the price earnings (P/E) ratio. This ratio is the number of years earnings that is represented by the market price. For instance, if a quoted company had one million ordinary shares and had made profits attributable to ordinary shareholders of say £3 million, then the earnings for each share would be £3.00. If the share price was £12.00 this would represent four years earnings. The calculation in its simplest form would be:

$$\frac{\text{Market share price}}{\text{Earnings per share}} \quad \text{i.e.} \quad \frac{12}{3} = \text{P/E of 4}$$

Shareholders are interested in future earnings and capital growth. Accordingly, the market price will tend to move on investor expectations of profit. A high P/E therefore represents high expectations creating a high share price. The high share price then provides opportunities for growth by acquisition, through 'share exchange' arrangements.

The planning departments of quoted comapnies need to seek answers to the following kinds of questions:-

(i) What is the relevant industrial average P/E and earnings likely to be during the planning period?

(ii) What profit will the company have to make to ensure its earnings per share is above the average?

These two questions are concerned with short term profit estimates. They provide an indication of required interim profit figures and published forecasts that will tend to raise investor expectations and thus the share price. The planning department would try to estimate the effect of its profit targets on the share price with a view to growth by acquisition. This type of calculation could show how an increase in published interim profits and forecasts would enable the company to use its high P/E to acquire other companies through share exchange arrangements. In turn the acquisitions would enable the company to show high growth in terms of turnover, and possibly profits, thus strengthening its position in the market.

Thus we have two aspects of profit planning. An inverted income calculation which starts with profit and works back to turnover and a speculative kind of arithmetic based on P/E ratios. Both serve a useful planning function.

4. Planning the organisation

In the previous section we examined some of the principles and methods of operational planning. For operational plans to be converted to action there needs to be a suitable organisation. Although organisational and operational planning are interdependent, business organisations are sometimes allowed to develop without clear statements of objectives and strategy. Whereas operational planning is normally subject to regular rigorous reviews of strategy and tactics. A popular approach to organisation planning appears to be allowing random growth for a number of years followed by a disruptive 'pruning' exercise where departments are rationalised, removed, combined or simply re-named.

Business organisations can be very complex and the organisation chart only reflect functional relationships. Equally important are the social relationships and both aspects need to be taken into consideration in strategic organisational planning meetings. A lot of useful research has been undertaken by sociologists on business organisations. Some of this work is reviewed in the first sub-section on formal and informal organisations. In the second sub-section we consider authority structures in organisations and their relationship to ownership. It is interesting to note that with very different forms of ownership, authority structures are often remarkably similar. After these two general sub-sections we then look at some practical problems of organisational planning such as the decentralisation/centralisation decision and examples of bad organisational planning.

4:1 Formal and informal organisations Organisations are a feature of modern society. They enable tens, hundreds and even thousands of individuals to be directed towards common goals. Organisations provide opportunities for improved standards of living and at the same time pose a great threat to individual liberty. It is therefore not surprising that this subject has attracted a substantial amount of research and debate. For our purposes we will define an organisation as a structure of interpersonal relationships governed by rules that denote function, authority and status For instance, a sailing club will have its Commodore, Treasurer, Secretary and various racing officials. These are functional positions with authority and status and their holders make decisions on behalf of the club members. The organisation enables people to work together towards the club's objectives. These would probably be to provide sailing and other social facilities for club members. The existence of an organisation provides stability, security, continuity and less risk of being destroyed by divergent interests. For example, if some members of the sailing club were interested in fishing or power boat racing, the organisation would probably prevent these interests being developed with the club facilities.

Clubs are a form of business unit with a democratic organisation structure and objectives that include the provision of benefit to members. However most forms of business organisation are not so democratic. They exist primarily for the benefit of owners. Employees are considered as a factor of production and are employed in the same way as materials and capital. Accordingly these types of organisations require an authority structure that directs and controls people. These types of organisation structures are generally based on the following principles:-

(i) *The Scalar chain.* A chain of command that is needed to direct and control people. The best examples of chains of command are military organisations.

(ii) *Delegation.* A necessary part of a command chain is the delegation of authority and responsibility. This creates a 'reporting back' function and in large organisations there is a lot of internal reporting based on this function.

(iii) *Specialisation.* The division of work by function that tends to create specialist departments in an organisation.

(iv) *Span of control.* The purported necessity to always control people in business organisations provides a function for managers. This control of people function is supposed to be limited to five or six subordinates, depending on the work situation. In practice this results in multi-layer mangement structures

(v) *Line and staff.* These titles refer to two types of formal relationships that often exist in an organisation structure. Line relationships refer to management subordinate roles in the scalar chain. Whereas staff relationships tend to represent advisory or specialist roles have not been clearly defined.

A formal business organisation will normally be based on the above principles and is represented diagramatically by an organisation chart. (Refer to diagram 16) These charts show scalar chains, specialist divisions and line and staff relationships However, in every formal organisation informal organisations will develop. The informal organisations tend to be work groups that have developed their own work practices, norms and social relationships. Often the informal organisations will determine the level of output and business efficiency. It is important for the informal structure to be identified and understood for the following reasons:-

(a) Research has shown that informal organisations resist change[4]. Therefore any proposals to change operational practice or the organisation need to be examined with an awareness of possible resistance.

(b) Informal groups often have an informal leader. It is important to know of the existence, roles and attitudes of informal group leaders because they can present a serious challenge to the formal leaders that represent the formal organisation structure.

(c) Informal groups have a communication network that can be very efficient. Management should be aware of what information is circulating through informal channels. The creditibility of formal channels of communication must not be weakened bv the informal networks.

---

4. L. Coch and J French Jnr. in Human Factors in Management. Harper and Brothers (1951).

(d) Informal group pressures are quite different from the reward/penalty pressures of the formal structure. The informal pressure is based on interpersonal relationships and can be far stronger than formal pressures. Managers need to understand that individuals can be placed in situations where the demands of the formal and informal organisation are in conflict.

DIAGRAM 16 FORMAL ORGANISATION CHART

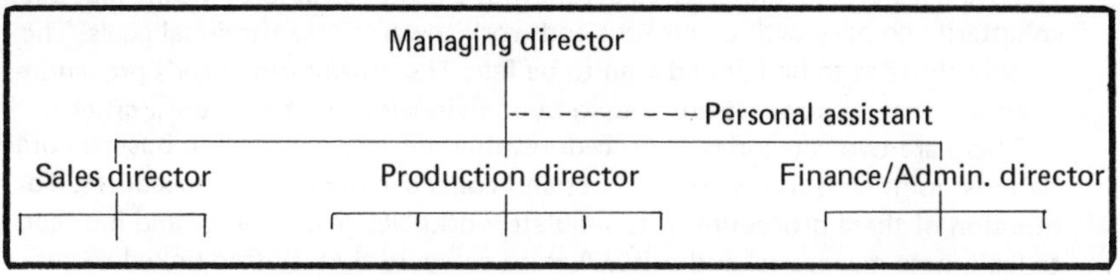

Clearly organisational planning is not simply a matter of re-drawing the formal organisation chart to meet changing circumstances. Change will probably face some kind of resistance and persuasion is generally more cost effective than coercion. Managers need to recognise that the informal structure will always exist and any threats to its existence will tend to strengthen a group's resolve. Recognition of the existence of informal organisations and the need to manage them has resulted in some managers adopting a more participative management style. Participation is discussed in the following sub-section on organisation structures.

4:2 Organisation structures We have defined an organisation as a structure of inter personal relationships. It therefore follows that if the structure is to be re-organise it will alter the balance of relationships. An important set of relationships in a business organisation is the authority structure. A breakdown in authority can leac to the destruction of the organisation. The term authority has a precise meaning to sociologists, who have made some interesting distinctions between authority, persuasion and power:-

Power is exercised through the threat of physical coercion, or by the manipulatior of conditions that forces people to act in a given direction.

Persuasion is where a person lets the opinions and arguments of another person influence his/her decisions and actions.

Authority is where a person is willing to suspend their own judgement in advance and voluntarily comply with commands. The voluntary acceptance of commands implies *legitimate authority*.

There are many types of legitimate authority. Weber[5] defined three pure types; legal, traditional and charismatic and then applied the principles of legitimate authority to his theory of bureaucracy. Our interest here is in planning a business organisation that will have a legitimate authority structure. We have identified the existence of informal organisations that can challenge the legitimacy of the formal organisation. This kind of challenge often forces managers to exercise power instead of authority. Some managers may try persuasion, but in the long run if the structure does not have legitimate authority, the organisation will not achieve its objectives. The use of power or persuasion will not produce long term solutions for

5. Max Weber in The Theory of Social and Economis Organisation, translated by A Henderson and T. Parsons. Free Press (1947).

organising and directing labour. There is ample evidence that when individuals have formal power in an organisation the privilege will be abused. The result of the abuse of power is that labour organises to produce a counter veiling power. Thus some business organisations operate on the principle of balancing power between vested interests and the existence of any legitimate authority rests on the restricted charisma of individuals.

It must surely be clear that organisational planning can be a very complex issue. To have a legitimate authority structure (not a power structure) means that people voluntarily comply with commands and work towards organisational goals. The organisation has to be fair and seen to be fair. The organisation needs procedures to ensure that its power is not abused by individuals or vested interest groups.

There are two categories of procedures that are very common in business organisations: joint consultative procedures and collective bargaining procedures. The function of these procedures is to regulate workplace relationships and indirectly, to legitimate managerial authority. A third category that is often linked to consultation and collective bargaining is participation. But genuine participation is fundamentally different. These aspects of business organisations are examined in the following sub-sections.

4:2:1 Joint consultation The distinguishing feature of joint consultation is that management retain the right of decision. The purpose of setting up joint consultative procedures is to encourage discussion on matters of joint concern. It is really a widening of communication channels in an organisation where management and employee representatives can express their views on selected topics. The traditional areas for joint consultation are; health and safety, welfare, education and training, codes of discipline, changes in production and related matters.

During the early 1950's the government made several attempts to pursuade business organisations to develop joint consultative procedures. Consultative procedures were encouraged in the public sector and are now highly developed. Managers in industry and commerce have made many attempts to develop consultative procedures, but many consultative issues were taken over by collective bargaining. For example, production efficiency, work practices and health and safety are generally regarded by trade unions as negotiating issues. Thus the areas for discussion in consultative meetings have diminished. Indeed many companies now operate through a single channel of communication by collective bargaining procedures. The failure of joint consultation has been attributed to the inability of employees to influence decisions that will affect their lives. Probably many so called consultative meetings were really briefing meetings where management just explained what decision had been taken.

4:2:2 Collective bargaining This is now a well established part of most business organisations and any organisational planning process will have to take collective bargaining procedures into consideration. Indeed, a mature collective bargaining system can provide an effective organisational control on the abuse of power by any individual in the organisation. It is therefore useful to look at the development of collective bargaining and its role in business organisation structures.

Collective bargaining is the product of an evolutionary process that gathered momentum during the economic industralisation of the U.K. in the nineteenth century. Rapidly changing technology and the principles of laissez-faire forced employees to bargain collectively to protect their interests. In the vanguard of collective bargaining were the skilled craftsmen who organised to restrict entry into their trade and bargained for their sectional interests. New factory trades such as textiles quickly followed suit and during the 1830's there were bitter recognition disputes. After the 1867 Royal Commission, which recommended that trade unions should not be considered illegal, there was a significant shift in government opinion in favour of the trade unions. A number of statutes in the 1870's established the legal position of a trade union's right to participate in collective bargaining. By 1900 the principle of voluntary collective bargaining was fairly well established, although most negotiations were still on a local or district level basis.

During the First World War the movement for national level negotiations developed and this mood was given impetus by the Whitley Committee recommendations for Joint Industrial Councils (JIC). Such was the enthusiasm for national level negotiations that between 1918 and 1921, 73 JIC's were formed and 33 IRC's (Industrial Reconstruction Committees for badly organised industries hopefully to become JIC's later) By 1939 a lot of JIC's had been abandoned but industry wide bargaining was still the central feature of Britain's system of wage determination. Since the Second World War the system of collective bargaining began to fragment and become very complex. At industry level there were the pre-Whitley Ad-hoc bodies and Wages Councils and a number of JIC's and IRC' Then there were the subsidiary levels of; district, company, plant and sub-plant In evidence to the Donovan Commission the Ministry of Labour listed some 500 pieces of negotiating machinery at national level for just manual workers. Clearly the negotiating machinery was becoming too complex and too remote from the people it was representing.

The unions support for industry wide agreements stemmed from the high unemployment inter-war period, where unemployment averaged between 10% and 15%. Bargaining at national level provided unions with more collective strength against the employers during a period when bargaining power at a local level was very weak. However after the war the employment position improved considerably and the unemployed percentage fell as low as 2%. Against this background of improved economic conditions local bargaining strength of the trade unions increased and the power of the shop steward also increased. This change in emphasis from industry to local bargaining is what the Donovan Commission referred to as the growth of the 'informal' system of industrial relations

Clearly collective bargaining does have a role to play in business organisation Naturally some managers attempt to vitiate the role because it reduces their area of discretion in decision making and places limits on their power. But from an organisation viewpoint, collective bargaining can help to legitimate authority because it institutionalises conflict between different interest groups. This is because collective bargaining is a rule making process that enables the parties to an agreement to understand each others position and the limits of their actions.

Earlier we defined an organisation as a structure of interpersonal relationships governed by rules. Collective bargaining can help to make these rules, by negotiating agreements which regulate terms of employment and procedures for the settlement of disputes. This constructive aspect of collective bargaining requires responsible behaviour, and a lot of hard work is needed to produce sets of rules that govern the conduct of parties in an organisation. There are two types of rules;

Procedural rules that refer to methods of settling disputes. These are often called *disputes of right* which relate to rights under exisitng agreements. An example of procedural rule setting would be a grievance procedure.

Substantive rules that refer to wages and working conditions. These are often called ***disputes of interest.***

Generally speaking procedural rules relate to collective bargaining behaviour and substantive rules relate to job regulation. In both instances the rules impose a constraint on managerial and labour behaviour. Really they are rules for co-existence that legitimise the differing 'interest groups' powers.

The British rule making process of collective bargaining is not a one off agreement for a specific period as in the U.S.A. It is concerned not only with the making of the rules, but also the administration of rules in the day to day conduct of the business. The main principles that may be extracted concerning collective bargaining are:-

(i) It is a rule making process jointly determined for regulating the relationships between parties who have differing objectives.

(ii) It is a process of power equalisation where the parties recognise each others position and right to negotiate.

In theory collective bargaining is a democratic process. But in practice, expediency is often considered to be a more appropriate criteria than democracy. From a social viewpoint, collective bargaining has the following disadvantages:-

(i) Tends to fortify the strong and neglect the weak

(ii) Bargaining power is never in equilibrium

(iii) The outcome of negotiations may not be socially or economically desirable from a national viewpoint

The collective bargaining aspect of business organisations has attracted a lot of criticism, because the press naturally highlights disputes of interest, when the parties to the dispute are just making tactical manoeuvers to improve their relative bargaining positions. For every one dispute of interest that results in a protracted power struggle, there are probably a thousand disputes that are settled by mature negotiation. Providing both parties are prepared to compromise, collective bargaining is an appropriate way of regulating employment relationships. Trade unions have a fine heritage of defending the rights and dignity of the working class and are capable of moderate and responsible behaviour. Unfortunately some trade union organisations are being used as vehicles for the advancement of political ideologies and this tends to distort their valid collective bargaining role in business organisations.

From an organisational planning viewpoint trade unions pose a particular problem because of the uncertainty of their conduct. If management could be certain of responsible behaviour on the part of trade unions, then the collective bargaining role could be widened into a form of participation in the planning process.

4:2:3 Participation This is a general term that is widely used to describe anything from disclosure of information to employees to complete equality in the decision making process. The most common abuse of the term is to describe a consultative process as participation. In practice, participation can be achieved in a number of ways at different levels in a business organisation. In this sub-section we will briefly look at four ways in which a business organisation may achieve some form of participation:-

Terms of employment
Management style
Ownership
Control

(i) Terms of employment Participation in this area is usually achieved through collective bargaining procedures explained in the previous sub-section. Trade unions and employers make joint decisions on matters affecting the terms and conditions of employment. Genuine participation in this area would result in a system of rights for employees. Any change in these rights would require full consultation at all stages before a decision is made and either party woul have the right to delay or veto the decision.

(ii) Management style Participation in the decision making process is sometimes formalised by committee styled organisation structures. Management by comm-mittee has been heavily criticised because it tends to dissipate responsibility and individual authority can be achieved by manipulation. At an informal level, a manager may adopt a participative management style. However most so called participative management styles are based on consultation. To share the decision making process with employees or their representatives would require a significant change in attitudes of both managers and employees.

(iii) Ownership There are three main ways that a business organisation can attempt to achieve participation through collective ownership:-

(a) Employee shareholdings taking advantage of tax concessions provided in the Finance Act 1978

(b) Co-operative societies permitted by the Industrial and Provident Societies Act 1965

(c) Common ownership using the provisions of the Industrial Common Ownership Act 1976

The employee shareholding principle is really a form of incentive scheme based on profit sharing. It was believed that this approach would encourage employees to appreciate management's points of view and thus improve efficiency. In practice however, individual employee shareholdings tend to be small and the return on dividends insignificant when compared with wages. Because of the small amount that employees are able to invest in shares it is unlikely that employee shareholders will ever be in a position to influence corporate strategy. Indeed the wider spread of share ownership increases the gap between ownership and control.

The Co-operative movement has become established mainly in the retail trade where customers are the members. They receive a fixed interest on the their investment and control is vested in an elected committee of management On voting issues the rule is one member one vote regardless of the size of individual investments.

Business organisations based on the principles of common ownership are probably the most democratic form of business unit where participation through joint ownership is a reality.

(iv) Control This is where most of the debate on participation has been focussed. The EEC in 1972 published a proposal (fifth directive) on employee participation aimed at the establishment of a two tier board system where employees would participate in the supervisory board. Some member states already have legislation on employee participation. In the U.K., a Committee of Enquiry on Industrial Democracy published its proposals in 1977 (The Bullock Report). A summary of this report is given in the next sub-section.

4:2:4 Industrial democracy The Bullock Report[6] provided a sound basis for discussion on industrial democracy legislation. The Committee could not reach

6. *Report of the Committee of Enquiry on Industrial Democracy. HMSO Cmnd 6706 (1977)*

agreement. Therefore, the report was divided into a set of majority proposals, mainly from trade union representatives and academics, and a set of minority proposals from representatives of industry and commerce.

The majority proposals centred on two main alternatives:

(a) A two tier system similar to West Germany, or

(b) A unitary board

The W. German two tier system that has been in existence for 23 years has a supervisory board on which employees are represented and a management board is responsible for the running of the company and has a reporting responsibility to the supervisory board. The Committee argued that the W.German system was not suitable for the U.K. because of company law difficulties requiring two separate company law systems and the need to maintain flexibility that the formalised W. German system did not allow. The French experience of a volun tary two tier structure was reported as not working particularly well and that the problems of a passive body or conflict development could occur in the U.K Several modifications of the W. German system were considered. The Danish system provided an example of an overlap between the two tier functions that overcame many of the objections but it did not resolve the problem of changing Company Law. Consequently the Committee opted for a modified unitary board on a 2x plus y basis, where the 2x is an equal number of shareholders and union members who jointly choose a smaller odd number called the y group. Full time union officials may be elected into the y group. (Refer to diagram 18) Employee representation would be introduced by a process starting with a request from one or more independent recognised trade unions, representing 20 per cent of the companies' employees, and a secret ballot of all employees. The arrangements for the selection of employee representatives would be made by a new style joint union committee - called a joint representation committee - representing all independent and recognised trade unions in the company.

The employee representatives would all be employees of the company, not full time trade union officials. They would not receive special directors' fees on top of their normal pay but they would have a right of access to secretarial and similar services plus time off from their normal work. The Committee agreed that all directors should have the same legal duties and liabilities. It will therefore, be necessary for trade unions to provide some indemnity for their member representatives.

Chapter ten outlined the proposed role of the trade unions. The main argument for using trade union machinery instead of works councils is the experience of many companies indicated that this type of formal negotiating was mainly consultative and lacked independence. The trade union mechanism was independent and had established and trusted channels of communication. Also to link representation into the trade union mechanism would be one way of ensuring that it did not conflict with the process of collective bargaining. The problem of the estimated 30% non unionised employees was covered by saying '...... our proposals in this chapter do not provide any special rights for employees who are not members of a trade union.' The proposed sequence of events in companies employing over 2000 employees would be:

(i) A request for board level representatives from one or more recognised trade unions.

(ii) A ballot of *all* employees to see if there is the required majority in favour of representation on the board.

(iii) Constitution of a Joint Representation Committee (JRC)

(iv) Agreement on the size of the reconstituted board.

(v) Selection of employee and shareholder representatives.
(vi) Co-option of additional directors (the y factor)
(vii) New Board assumes office

It may be useful to consider each of these stages separately:-

(i) The request must be from a 'recognised' trade union; where the term 'recognised refers to recognition procedure under the Employment Protection Act. The aim of the first stage is to encourage the parties to reach an agreed solution suited to:-

(a) The company circumstances
(b) Company size
(c) The number of trade unions
(d) The number of members on the board
(e) The selection of a y group

(ii) The ballot stage is likely to create some difficulties. The report suggests a single question:

'Do you want employee representation on the company board through the trade unions recognised by your employer?

The proposed ballot question does not provide the opportunity for non-union members to ask for representation outside the trade union mechanism. It appeared to be a choice of representation through the trade union or no representation. As the right to request a ballot would rest with the trade union the issue could be avoided providing none of the recognised unions made a request. The objective of the secret ballot was to ensure that board representation was desired by the majority of employees. Clearly if employees do not want representation, then to impose a statutory obligation of board representation is unlikely to be successful.

(iii) The constitution of a Joint Representation Committee (JRC) is without question a desirable objective. Any incentive to bring unions together within an organisation will in the long run, benefit employees and employers. For board representation to take place the unions will have to come together in some form of committee. There really could be some in fighting at this stage as the different unions bargain with each other for seats on the board. As Bullock cautiously stated:

'Even with the best will in the world, all the members of the JRC may not always be able to agree amongst themselves'.

(iv) The size of the reconstituted board will most probably be a more discreet power struggle than the earlier conflicts. To apply the 2x + y formula some existing directors will have to retire otherwise many boards would consist of too many directors. Bullock size suggestions are:

		X_1	X_2	Y
Number of employees -	2000 - 999	4	4	3
	10000 - 24999	5	5	3
	more than 25000	7	7	5

The Times 1,000 survey showed that only one third of companies with over 2,000 employees had more than ten directors. Possibly many non-executive directors will accept some form of loss-of office compensation and vacate their seats graciously. It would be a great loss if a director who gained a board seat by ability and hard work has to vacate for an employee representative. Many boards contain technical directors or senior executives from production and sales who make valuable contributions to the planning function It is difficult to see how a company will benefit by replacing these men with representatives of sectional interest groups.

(v) The selection of employee and shareholder representatives would probably be a time of power manoeuvers. For the shareholder representatives it will tend to be a 'who is going' problem, but the employee representative choice is quite different. The recommendations for selecting an employee representative are covered in the following extract:-

'We have already said above that we expect the method of selecting employee representatives to be built on trade union machinery. We expect this machinery generally to result in the selection of company employees, and more often than not of shop stewards. The members of the Joint Representation Committee will probably in most instances act as an electoral college and select employee representatives from among the community of shop stewards or equivalent representatives in the company.'

In firms where union representation is not in the majority, it is possible that internal disputes will arise between non-unionised employees seeking their own representative and the officially elected trade union representatives. Once the employee is elected he/she will hold office for a recommended three year period with the possibility of the period being renewed. As the employee director is a representative not a delegate the power of removal will only arise at the end of the three year period. With regard to remuneration, employee representatives would not be paid.

(vi) The co-option of additional directors is likely to be a discreet affair. As agreement is necessary between the two 'x' groups on the selection of the 'y' group. A trade off situation is bound to develop on the basis of 'you accept our nomination we will accept yours. The real problem arises in the odd number requirement; one nominee has to be acceptable to both parties. The power of the acceptable nominee could in some situations be considerable If conflict developed and the battle lines drawn the voters would be 50/50. Therefore, if the decision was to be based on a simple majority the 'y' nominninee would have the power of an arbitrator. Both of the 'x' groups will be fully aware of the piwer the 'y' group will have in times of conflict. Therefore the selection of 'y' candidates will have a natural objective of trying to ensure that the nominee is sympathetic to whatever side one represents. It would be naive to assume that during the transition phase there will be mutual trust and understanding. It would be a power struggle and the election of the 'y' group would be part of the fight.

(vii) According to the report the last stage is the new board taking office. Although it is the last stage of employee board representation, it is the first stage in the redistribution of industrial and commercial power.

The basic areas of conflict between the majority and minority proposals were on two main issues:-

(a) The level of representation: and

(b) The electoral base for representatives.

The level of representation recommended by the minority report was on the basis of a two tier structure where a supervisory board would be created above the Board of Directors. (Refer to diagram 19)

Diagram 17 shows the existing situation where the ultimate power rests in the shareholders Annual General Meeting. In practice shareholders power over the board of directors is rarely exercised but it is a power that influences the action of directors. Under the majority proposals in diagram 18 the shareholders lose their role as the ultimate power and are relegated to the role of creditor with information rights and control over their elected representatives. They do not

have control over the employee representatives or the independent members. Therefore they have effectively lost their right of ultimate power. With the minority proposals shown on diagram 19 the shareholders have lost their ultimate power position but as they have the elective power for board representation they are still in a good central position. Indeed the supervisory board may become divorced from the realities of control that is exercised by the board of directors. Thus under the minority proposals it would be possible for the existing power position to remain unchanged. If the one third employee representatives cannot draw support from the one third independent members, then they will be in a minority and subsequently a quasi consultative capacity.
The electoral base for representation from the majority recommendations was through the trade union machinery. The minority report argued it was not democratic and that all employees should be eligible to vote and that potential candidates should satisfy certain conditions of eligibility.
In addition to the electoral procedure the minority report proposed the creation in the organisation of a representation substructure that would support the supervisory board. Basically this would have been a number of works councils similar to the West German situation.

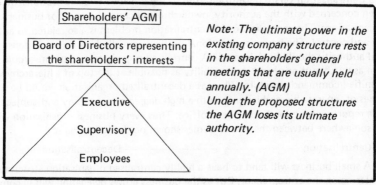

If industrial democracy legislation ever gets to the statute book it will cause business organisations to fundamentally rethink their organisational plans.

DIAGRAM 17 EXISTING CORPORATE CONTROL STRUCTURE

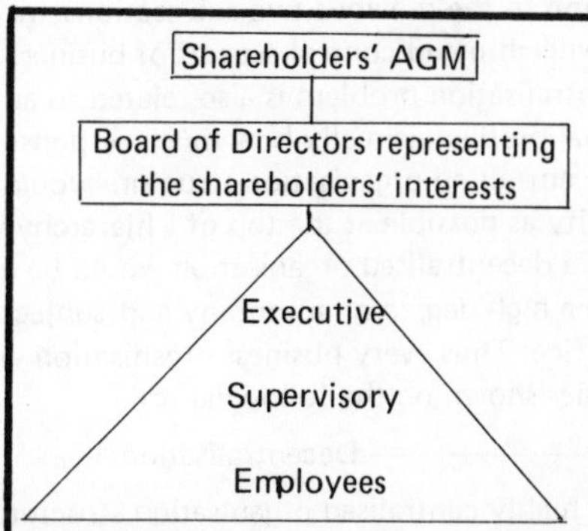

Note: The ultimate power in the existing company structure rests in the shareholders' general meetings that are usually held annually. (AGM)
Under the proposed structures the AGM loses its ultimate authority.

DIAGRAM 18
PROPOSED CORPORATE CONTROL STRUCTURE (MAJORITY)

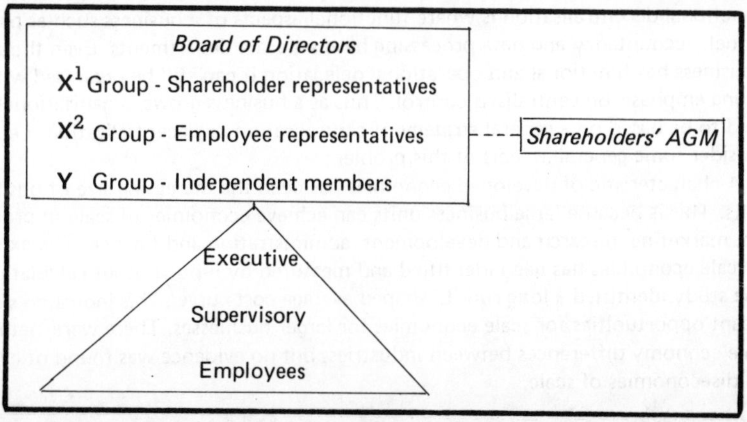

DIAGRAM 19

PROPOSED CORPORATE CONTROL STRUCTURE (MINORITY)

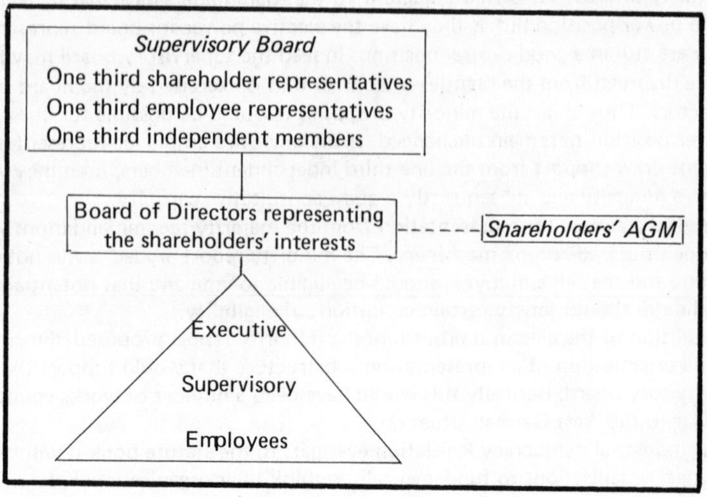

4:3 Centralisation versus decentralisation In the previous two sub-sections we have been concerned with the authority, ownership and control aspects of business organisations. The centralisation/decentralisation problem is also related to authority and control. The basic organisational problem is really how much responsibility and authority should be delegated? A centralised organisation structure would retain as much authority and responsibility as possible at the top of a hierarchy with a unified command structure. Whereas a decentralised organisation would be a series of separate hierarchies each with a high degree of autonomy and subject only to a reporting function for the head office. Thus every business organisation will be somewhere between the two extremes shown on the following scale:-

Centralisation ——————————————— Decentralisation

A small business will tend to have a highly centralised organisation structure centering on the entrepreneur. But as the business grows delegation will become necessary. This will result in two forms of decentralisation: operational and functional. Operational decentralisation is the delegation of command responsibilities. Functional decentralisation is where functional aspects of a business such as personnel, accountancy and data processing have separate departments. Even though a business has functional and operational delegation it can still be organised with a strong emphasis on centralised control. Thus as a business grows, organisational plans need to be based on a general strategy of centralisation or decentralisation. Let us consider some general aspects of this problem.

A characteristic of developed economies has been the increasing size of business units. This is because large business units can achieve economies of scale in production, marketing, research and development, administration and finance. The existence of scale economies has been identified and measured by input/output calculations. One study identified a long run 'L' shaped average cost curve[7]. This indicated significant opportunities for scale economies for larger businesses. There were naturally scale economy differences between industries, but no evidence was found of eventual diseconomies of scale.

As a business grows an important change occurs in the organisation, it is a disproportionate growth of administration. This growth is generally referred to as bureaucratisation. A satirical observation of administrative growth was stated in one of Parkinson's laws[8]. Suggesting that the less work there was in an organisation the greater would be the increase in administrative staff. There is a substantial amount of theory on the effect of bureaucratisation that is outside the scope of this book[9].

The centralisation of authority demands systems of control where power is concentrated at the top of the hierarchy. One outcome of this demand for control is an increased emphasis on the reliability and predictability of behaviour from subordinates. A consequence of this emphasis is that behaviour becomes rigid, impersonal and increases the difficulty in dealing with people external to the organisation The demand for control also increases the need for delegation and training in specialist functions. The outcome of this need is the mushroom growth of service departments that are continually competing for status and influence in the hierarchy

Some general disadvantages of centralisation appear to be:-

(a) Bureaucratisation, leading to a weakening of interpersonal relationships external to the business and a substantial rise in administrative costs.

(b) Slow response to change in trading conditions due to external lines of communication and delegation.

(c) Misdirected managerial motivation because a manager's future is often more dependent on 'internal activities' than on entrepreneurial activity.

To overcome these disadvantages some large companies have approached organisational planning with a view to the decentralisation of authority. This can be difficult if the nature of the business is say a large inter-dependent production process on a single site. But for some large businesses such as conglomerates, decentralised operationally autonomous group companies is the most appropriate form of organisation structure.

Thus long run organisational planning has to be directed towards centralisation or decentralisation objectives that are believed to be suitable for future growth of the business.

4:4 Practical organisation structure problems Most of the discussion so far on planning the organisation has been directed at broad principles. It is therefore appropriate to conclude this section with some practical illustrations of bad organisation planning. Each of the following examples are presented in the form of simplified diagrams and brief notes.

---

7. Pratten and Dean in The Economics of Large Scale Production in British Industry. Cambridge University Press (1965)

8. C. Parkinson in Parkinson's Law and Other Studies in Administration. Houghton - Miffin (1957)

9. Readers interested in the characteristics and problems of bureaucracy are referred to the following authors:-

M. Weber in The Theory of Social and Economic Organisation. Free Press (1947)

A. Gouldner in Patterns of Industrial Bureaucracy. Free Press (1954)

R. Merton in Social Theory and Social Structure. Free Press (1957)

J. March and H. Simon in The Dysfunctions of Bureaucracy. Wiley (1958)

DIAGRAM 20 ORGANISATION WITH TOO MANY MANAGEMENT LEVELS

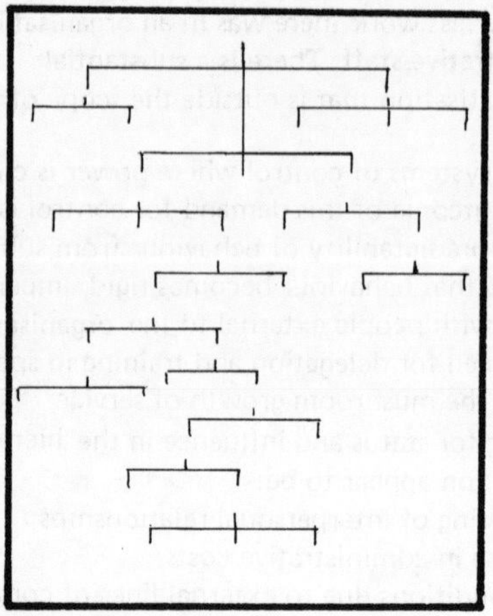

The problems with this kind of structure are extended lines of communication decision making and control. This can create operational delays, inflexibility and high adminstrative costs.

DIAGRAM 21

ORGANISATION WHERE SPAN OF CONTROL IS TOO LARGE

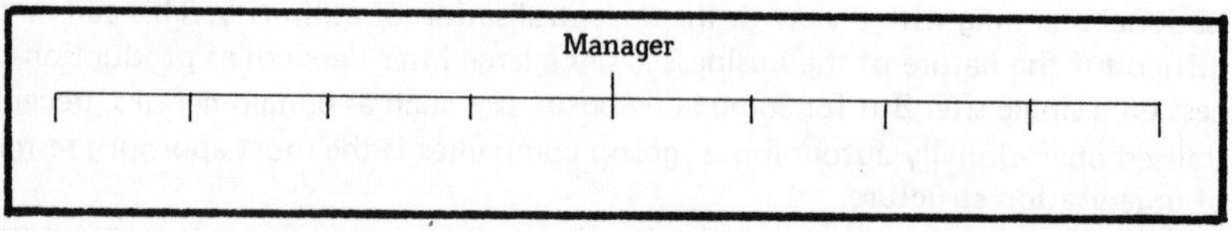

The manager represented in this diagram cannot manage all the subordinates effectively. This could create control problems such as subordinates assuming authority that has not been formalised. Decisions could be delayed because the manager does not have time, or bad decisions could be made through excessive work pressure. Care is needed when correcting this kind of situation because there is a risk that the kind of problems illustrated in diagram 20 may arise.

DIAGRAM 22

ORGANISATION WHERE LINE STAFF RELATIONSHIPS ARE OUT OF BALANCE

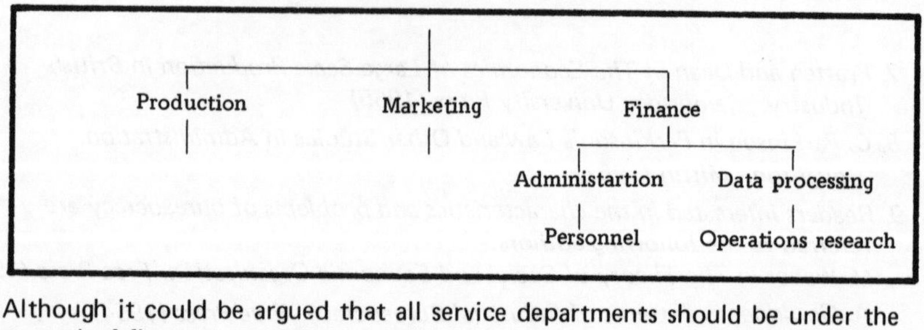

Although it could be argued that all service departments should be under the control of finance, a number of difficulties can arise from establishing line relationships for staff functions. Staff positions are usually held by people with specialist skills that should be available to all the organisation. In the above organisation structure the finance director would effectively be in control of the organisation.

DIAGRAM 23

ORGANISATION WHERE THERE IS POTENTIAL CONFLICT IN AUTHORITY

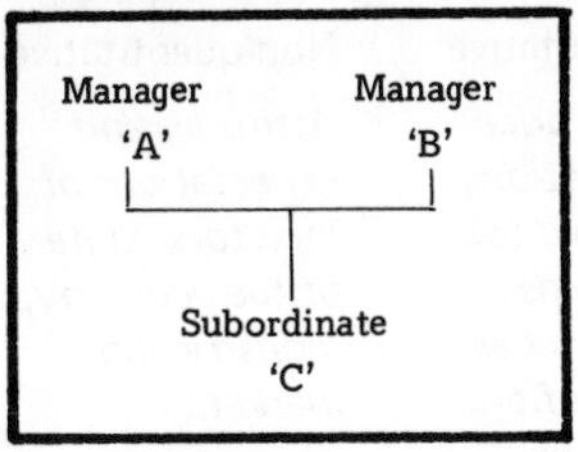

This kind of organisation structure creates problems for all three parties. For instance: what if managers A & B give contradictory orders to subordinate C? Or, should C report to A what work has been done for B?

DIAGRAM 24

ORGANISATION WHERE THERE IS A POSSIBLE DUPLICATION OF RESPONSIBILITIES

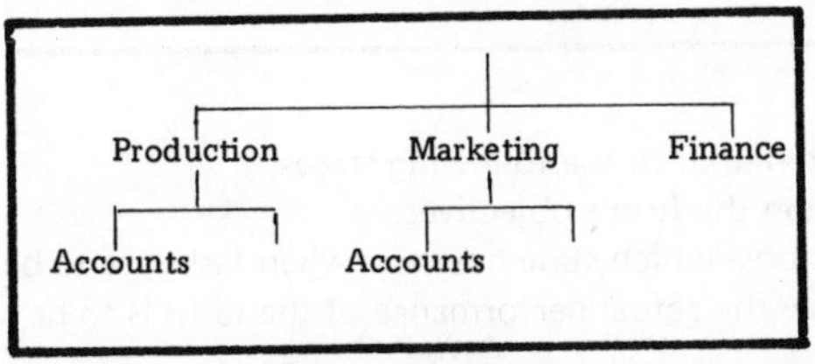

In this example different departments are maintaining their own little accounting sections. For this kind of situation to exist without conflict there has to be a very clear work structuring and co-operation between the central and subsidiary accounting sections. Even with good co-operation there is still a possibility of work duplication and conflict in results.

5. Control

The control of a business depends upon plans and an organisational structure that is capable of converting these plans into action. Planning can exist without control, but control cannot exist without planning. In the previous sub-sections we have looked at decision making, , the planning process and organisational structures. We are now in a position to look at the principles of control.

In an accounting book, the emphasis will naturally be on accounting controls such as standard costing and budgeting systems. These accounting control systems are explained in detail in chapters 8 and 9. But accountancy controls are only a part of the picture and it is first necessary to see where they fit in the control framework. An attempt to illustrate the control framework is given in diagram 25. This shows the primary division of controls into internal and external. These broad divisions are then sub-divided into quantitative and qualitative controls with some examples of each kind Most of the control systems produced by accountants fit into the internal quantitative category and are therefore only partial control systems. There are financial models, such as the P/E calculations discussed in sub-section 3:4, that provide some form of internal control measurement based on external factors. But they are not so well established as budgeting systems.

DIAGRAM 25 THE CONTROL FRAMEWORK

CONTROLS

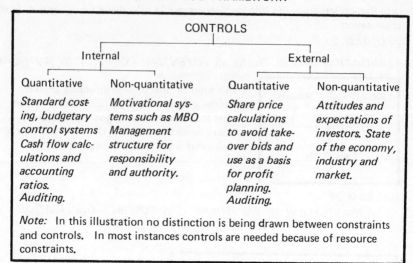

Internal		External	
Quantitative	Non-quantitative	Quantitative	Non-quantitative
Standard costing, budgetary control systems Cash flow calculations and accounting ratios. Auditing.	*Motivational systems such as MBO Management structure for responsibility and authority.*	*Share price calculations to avoid takeover bids and use as a basis for profit planning. Auditing.*	*Attitudes and expectations of investors. State of the economy, industry and market.*

Note: In this illustration no distinction is being drawn between constraints and controls. In most instances controls are needed because of resource constraints.

The control process can be broken up into the following stages:-

(i) Quantified plans based upon the firm's objectives.

(ii) A set of procedures (decisions) which state how and when tasks are to be done, who is to do them and how the actual performance of the tasks is to be measured.

(iii) Controls which compare actual performance with planned performance and alter the procedures (sets of decisions) where necessary to ensure goals are achieved

This viewpoint of a control process is generally referred to as a single loop feedback control system, because the control loop is just process, feedback and control, i.e.

DIAGRAM 26 SIMPLE CONTROL LOOP

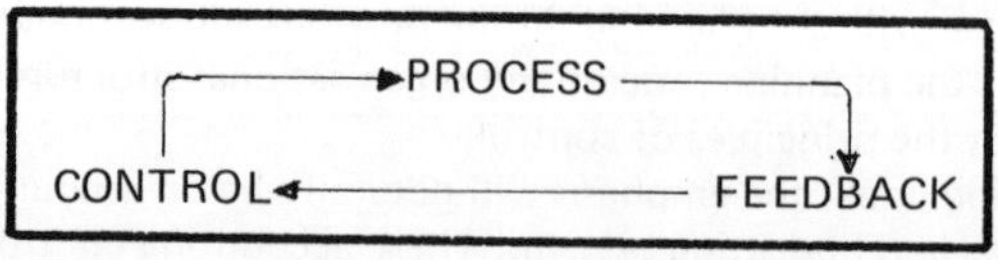

The single loop control system can be drawn in a number of ways. Diagram 27 for example shows the control process receiving information from a number of sources

DIAGRAM 27 ALTERNATIVE CONTROL LOOP

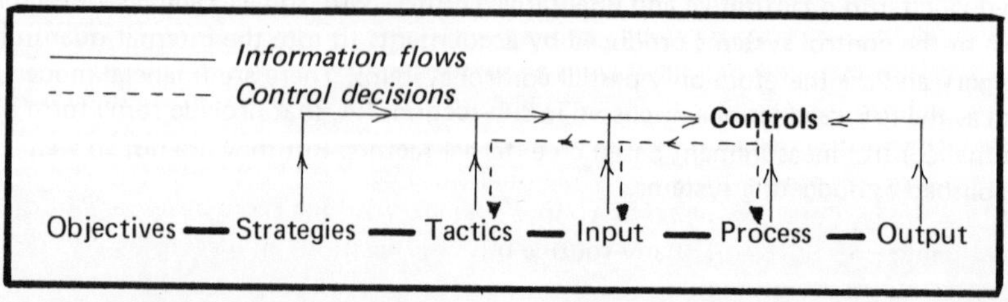

and making control decisions that will affect the production process. Diagrams can also be drawn to include external controls. However, all these diagrams adopt a mechanistic approach and do not make sufficient allowance for human behaviour. A large amount of useful work has been done by psychologists and sociologists on the behavioural implications of control systems. Some of this work is reviewed in chapter 8 section 4.

What we will be considering in this chapter are levels of control and types of control. The levels of control are divided into three categories:-

(i) Lower management that have routine decision making tasks which keep the company running.

(ii) Middle management that are involved in making tactical changes such as price/output decisions to achieve corporate goals.

(iii) Higher management that are concerned with making strategic changes.

The types of control can be broadly divided into cash flow, expenditure controls, production controls and people controls. All of these controls have a measure of accountability where someone in the organisation has a duty to account for the resources which are under their control.

5:1 Levels of control Control means different things to different people. All managers in an organisation have control over some business resource and are themselves subject to controls. At the lower management levels the resource control would include ensuring the correct materials are ordered and delivered and that employees arrive and leave at the right times. At middle level management tactical decisions are made that may alter production levels and production mix. Whilst at the higher levels, strategic changes are decided upon such as the introduction of new technology or the building of a new factory. Clearly management at each of these different levels have different control information requirements and different control responsibilities. In the following sub-section we will be briefly looking at each of these management control levels.

5:1:1 Keeping the business running At the lower levels of management the prime purpose of control is to keep the business running according to plan. A lot of this routine decision making is now capable of being done by electronis data processing. For example, most inventory management decisions explained in chapter 5 can be made by a computer. This aspect of control can be illustrated in the *cybemetic* model. *Cybemetics* is about a body of theory relating to the communications and control mechanisms of living beings and machines. A living being has a set of control mechanisms that maintain a constant state such as body temperature. These are referred to as *homeostatic controls* and *cybemetics* seeks to apply these principles to machines.

As a simple illustration of a cybemetic control cycle consider heating and retaining water at say 90°c. The plan would be to raise the water temperature to 90° and hold it at that temperature. There would be a *decision* to switch on The *control* would be some way of measuring heat. Part of the control process would be a *feedback* where actual results were compared with the plan. There would then be further *decisions* to switch the heat off and on to maintain the planned temperature of 90°c. This control cycle is illustrated in diagram 28 The control of maintaining the temperature at 90°c could be mechanised by us using a thermostat that switched the heat on and off automatically. This is refered to as part of a *homeostatic control system.* With the rapid development of computer programs, many routine business decisions are becoming part of a homeostatic control process.

DIAGRAM 28 HOMEOSTATIC CONTROL SYSTEM

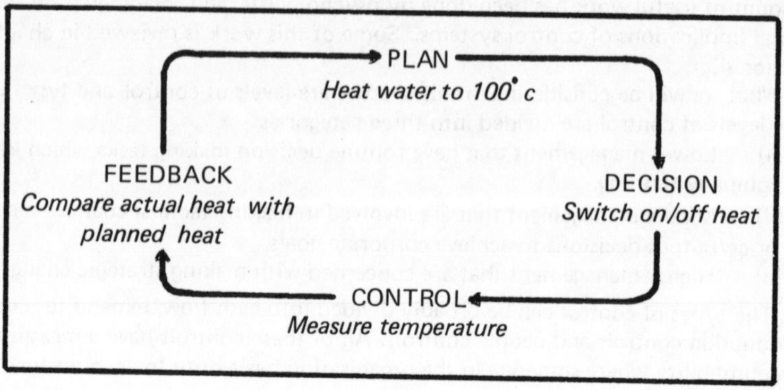

5:1:2 Controlling tactical changes From a control viewpoint, tactical change can be usefully divided into high and low conflict changes. Some tactical decisions such as changes in price or simple product design alterations may not pose a control problem and can be delegated to the routine control level. However a tactical decision that can involve a change in work practices can be a potentially high conflict change. In this situation a separate monitoring/control system has to be devised until the conflict has passed and routine controls can cope with the new production arrangements. As routine controls are only designed to cope with routine decisions it should be clear that any tactical changes will require separate controls until the changed situation can be built into the established control system.

5:1:3 Controlling strategic changes There are two control stages relating to strategic decisions: control of a project's development until it comes on stream and the development of new routine controls when the project is running. Once a strategic decision has been made, such as to set up a new production process, a whole series of sequential decisions are needed to implement the plan. A popular control technique for this development phase is the Program, Evaluation and Review Technique (PERT) that is explained in chapter 6 sub-section 3:6:2 This control process is mainly concerned with getting the project on stream in line with the corporate plan. Before the project comes on stream, organisational planning is needed to ensure that there will be a system of routine controls ready to control the production process. Thus at the senior levels of management, the concern with control is that the systems are designed properly and working well Whereas at the lower levels of management the control emphasis is on getting the job done according to plan.

5:2 Types of control To keep a business on course towards desired objectives, managers need to exercise a number of controls. In the following sub-sections we will be considering three levels of control and four types of control. The levels of control range from routine controls that are needed to keep the business running, to the special controls necessary for tactical and strategic changes. The types of control are divided into the main categories of expenditure, cash, production and people controls. All these controls are explained in greater detail in subsequent chapters. The point to note about this overview of controls, is their interdependence with one another. Also that the co-ordination of control systems should take place in the planning phase, especially organisational planning (Refer to chapter 8, sub-section 2:3).

5:2:1 Expenditure controls The most widely used forms of expenditure control are budgeting and standard costing. Because of their importance for business planning and control, over sixty pages in this book have been allocated to these two types of control systems. In this sub-section we will just look at some of their general principles as a form of introduction to the detailed subject coverage given in chapters 8 and 9.

There is no doubt whatsoever that an important management function is strict expenditure control. If departmental spending was allowed to operate without any controls, then probably the business would be bankrupt within a year. It is so easy for people in organisations to justify expenditure and it takes strong management to resist the pressure. Often managers do not face their expenditure control responsibility. They just pass the problem on to the accountant. When the accountant has the strength to question and resist expenditure demands the conflict can arise between managers and accountants. Budgeting can avoid this shift of responsibility and subsequent conflict, providing managers are involved in the budgetary planning phase. Once cash expenditure limits for the planning period have been agreed by a manager, then expenditure responsibility is delegated to where it should be. There are two general points to note about delegating expenditure responsibility:-

(i) Managers should participate in the setting of expenditure targets that relate to their area of authority and responsibility.

(ii) The agreed expenditure categories should be within the control of a manager. (This is explained in chapter 8 sub-section 5:3 - Responsibility Accounting) Ideally the expenditure would be stated in cash terms by excluding provisions such as depreciation.

Once managers have agreed planned expenditure controls, the remainder of the budgetary process is mainly comparing actual expenditure with planned expenditure to ensure cash limits are not exceeded.

Standard costing works on a similar basis by comparing actual costs with expected costs. The control principle of standard costing is based on management by exception (MBE). A manager who is responsible for a wide range of expenditure, such as a purchasing manager, needs some form of expenditure control system. A standard costing system would provide a manager with a list of expected costs, called standard costs, for the control period. As actual costs are incurred they would be sutomatically compared with their related standard costs producing favourable or adverse differences, called variances. Under MBE principles a manager only looks at exceptions, i.e. where actual events differ significantly from planned events. Thus a list of variances are a list of exceptions that may need management attention. Although standard costing is a well established expenditure control technique there are two aspects of a standard costing system that need careful attention:-

(i) The system is dependent upon 'correct' standards. If the standards are not properly set and regularly revised then the variances will be meaningless.

(ii) Standard costing can become quite complicated, especially the analysis of variances, and if managers do not understand the output of the control system then the entire costly exercise is wasted.

Any method of expenditure control needs a good cost collection and analysis system. The costing system can use a wide variety of techniques and these are all explained in chapter 3 - Basic costing.

Standard costing and budgetary control are not mutually exclusive cost control systems. Indeed, they are often linked together. The difference in the systems, tends to be in the level of detail. Standard costing is a unit concept for cost control of specific costs. Whereas budgeting, is a total concept that is used for planning, co-ordinating and controlling the activities of a business.

5:2:2 Cash flow controls The control of cash flows is usually the sole responsibility of the accountant. It is a particularly difficult control problem for a fast growing company. Controls are required on the *amount and timing* of cash flows. When a business is growing very quickly, the levels of stocks, work in progress and debtors have to be tightly controlled. For instance, assume a production cycle took eight weeks, the average stock turnover was six weeks and the average credit period was six weeks. This means that when cash is converted in the production phase, it would take at least five months for it to be converted back to cash again. If during the production period there was any kind of delay due to shortage of materials, machine breakdowns or industrial disputes it would lengthen the time cash was tied up in working capital. The technique the accountant uses for working capital control calculations is called cash budgeting and is explained in chapter 8 sub-section 2:4:4. (Also refer to *Volume 3 - Finance and Taxation for the non-accountant)*

There are two types of cash control: short term controls relating to working capital and longer term controls that are mainly concerned with capital expenditure. The controls for capital expenditure are explained in chapter 7. The cash controls are partly based upon expenditure controls explained in the previous sub-section. For the accountant to plan and control the cash flow, expenditure needs to be controlled by managers within pre-set limits. Indeed, the co-ordination of revenue and expenditure controls usually occurs in cash control calculations.

5:2:3 Production controls There are a very wide range of necessary production controls. In diagram the controls are broadly grouped into input, process and output controls. At the input stage controls are needed for material purchases to ensure the correct quantity and quality of materials are purchased at the right time at the best price. (Refer to chapter 5 section 3). Controls are also

DIAGRAM 29 PRODUCTION CONTROLS

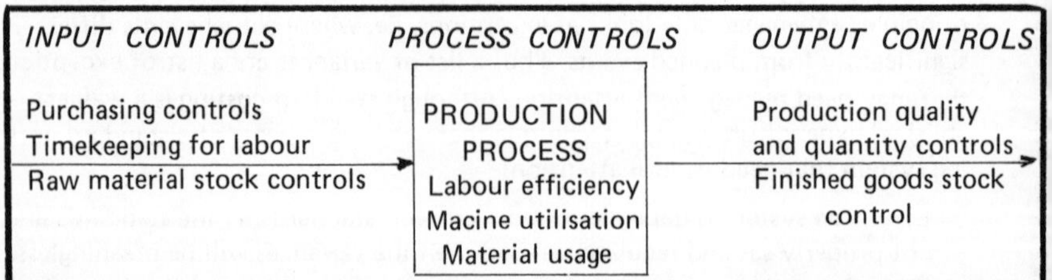

needed in raw material stores to minimise losses from theft or deterioration and avoid excessive stock holdings. The other major input is direct labour where the main input control is timekeeping.

The process controls are primarily concerned with the efficient utilisation of materials, labour and machines. The controls are usually based on some form of input/output relationship such as one direct labour hour or machine hour should produce say ten units of output. Probably, over 90 per cent of a production manager's time is spent on control. Therefore higher level management should be constantly reviewing production control systems to see if homeostatic controls can be introduced (Refer to sub-section 5:1:1)

5:2:4 People controls Controlling people at work is difficult, expensive and can have unpredictable results. Earlier it was explained that informal group pressures can exercise far greater control on individuals than the established 'carrot and stick' pressures adopted by a formal organisation structure. Therefore some fundamental questions that need to be asked about any formal control system would be:-

(i) Is this a control over the behaviour of people at work?
(ii) Is there likely to be any resistance to this control? If so, why?
(iii) What are the costs and benefits of this control?
(iv) What would the costs be if the formal control did not exist?
(v) Is the control really necessary?

A large proportion of management time is spent on trying to control people in workplace situations where they are probably quite capable of controlling themselves. With proper training and suitable motivation many supervisory functions would become unnecessary. In these first two chapters we have continually referred to participative management styles and the changing nature of workplace relationships. Clearly, with an educated and skilled labour force, 19th century 'stick management' is an entirely inappropriate form of people control Throughout this book we will be referring to the people problem in business organisations. Chapter 4 is about labour management and sub-sections of chapters 8, 9 and 10 refer to practical people problems with accountancy control systems.

6. Summary

The purpose of this chapter has been to provide a framework for the accounting techniques and related topics explained in this book. The traditional management accounting approach to planning and control placed great emphasis on budgeting and standard costing. These techniques only represent part of the picture. Accordingly, a lot of recent accounting theory has been drawing upon other subject disciplines such as; sociology, psychology, industrial relations economics, mathematics, statistics, organisation and management theory. Because an interdisciplinary approach has been applied throughout this book, it was necessary in this foundation chapter to draw a very broad framework for planning and control.

The subject area has been divided into four broad areas that are inter-related and interdependent; decision making, planning the operations, planning the organisation and control.

In the first part of the chapter we examined some principles and methods for decision making. The decision process was explained, with its application to tactical and strategic decisions. Some important decision methods were reviewed, such as brainstorming and flow charting.

Business planning was divided into two parts: planning the operations and planning the organisation. These are totally interdependent activities but it is useful to separate them for the purposes of analysis and discussion. With operational planning a distinction was drawn between long range planning and profit planning. Also, the neglected subject of corporate life risk was developed. It was emphasised that life risk decisions should be identified at the planning stage. Organisational planning examined the people problems related to business organisations. The topics covered the importance of the informal organisation and the organisation structure needed for regulating employment relationships. Because of the importance of some topics, such as collective bargaining and industrial democracy, explanations were fairly detailed. Some practical problems were also examined such as the centralisation/decentralisation issue and organisation structures.

The last part of the chapter reviewed the principles of business control. There were two approaches to this problem: levels of control and types of control. The levels of control were divided into: routine controls for keeping the business running and specific controls that may be needed for tactical and strategic change. The types of control related to the broad categories of expenditure, cash, production and people controls.

It is hoped that this broad approach to planning and control will provide a suitable foundation for the principles and techniques that are explained in subsequent chapters.

Accountancy Quiz No.2.

1. Describe the decision process and its relationship to objectives, policies and plans *(2:1)*

2. Define and give examples of tactical and strategic decisions*(2:2:1, 2:2:2)*

3. Explain how each of the following methods can help a decision maker:-

Brainstorming *(2:3:1)*
Synectics *(2:3:2)*
Role playing *(2:3:3)*
Model building *(2:3:4)*
Systems analysis *(2:3:5)*
Algorithms and flow charts *(2:3:6)*

4. Describe a procedure for long range planning. *(3:2)*

5. What is a product matrix and how can it be used for corporate planning *(3:2:1)*

6. Explain the principles of profit planning *(3:4)*

7. What is meant by 'informal organisation' and why should it be taken into consideration during organisational planning? *(4:1)*

8. Explain what you understand by the following terms in relation to organisational planning:-

Joint consultation *(4:2:1)*
Collective bargaining *(4:2:2)*
Participation *(4:2:3)*
Industrial democracy *(4:2:4)*

9. What factors do you consider should be taken into consideration when deciding on the centralisation/decentralisation policy of a company? *(4:3)*

10. Do you consider homeostatic control is possible for tactical and/or strategic change? *(5:, 5:1, 5:1:1, 5:1:2, 5:1:3)*

3 Basic Costing

Objective
To provide the non-accountant with an overview of costing principles and techniques.

Content

Basic Costing

1 Introduction

The origins of accounting can be traced back many centuries, when books of account were kept by stewards for landowners. With the development of joint stock companies and the divorce between ownership and control the nature of book-keeping changed into a wider dimension generally called financial accounting. Just as the history of financial accounting can be traced back through centuries of book-keeping management accounting can be traced back to basic costing. Costing is a relatively new branch of accounting because it began during the industrial revolution when the practice of management was changing. In chapter 1, Taylor's principles of scientific management were summarised. The effect that Taylor had on management practices during the early 1900's should not be underestimated. Basic costing, developed out of the changed attitude of managers who wanted to be more scientific and required information for planning decision making and control. As businesses became larger and more complex, managers demanded more information. The traditional financial accounts that produced an annual income statement and balance sheet were of little use. Cost information was needed on products for pricing and output decisions. Controls were needed for material and labour used in production, and departmental controls were needed to ensure that departments did not overspend. The practice of costing therefore developed spontaneously in many businesses to meet an urgent information need. In 1919 the Institute of Cost and Works Accountants was formed in the UK. This institute (now called Institute of Cost & Management Accountants) subsequently made a significant contribution to the development of costing and management accountancy.

In this chapter we will be looking at basic costing. The subject area is very detailed has a lot of specialised terms and sometimes gets quite complicated. Section 2 explains some costing principles and section 3 describes the different types of costing classifications. There are a number of ways that cost data is classified to satisfy specific purposes. For example, if managers require cost data for departmental control, then costs are classified according to organisational function. If cost data was required for decision making, then costs may be classified according to whether they vary in relation to production. It is important to distinguish between cost classifications and the costing bases or methods that are explained in section 5. This is a long section and the reader is advised not to attempt to understand all the costing bases and methods. However, it is useful to know the difference between marginal and absorption costing and be aware of the range of costing methods that exist. Section 4 explains how costs are recorded with an emphasis on computerised records and section 5 summarises the different costing bases and methods. Then section 6 brings together many of these topics with an explanation of the principles of a costing system.

This chapter covers a very wide and detailed subject. Therefore the non-accountant needs to be quite selective in his/her reading. To provide the reader with an overview, the really detailed sections, numbers 3 and 5 are logically structured and explained with diagrams, then you will understand the structure of costing and be in a better position to select the sections that are appropriate for your needs.

2. Costing principles

The appropriate starting point is to define what is meant by cost. We know that profit is the difference between revenues and costs and that the different categories of profit are derived by using different categories of cost. Therefore the term cost cannot stand alone, it has to be described. Examples would be material cost, labour cost, average cost or total cost. There are hundreds of cost descriptions representing a wide range of cost data and different cost concepts. At the practical level there are many cost descriptions that state what money has been used for. These kind of costs usually have two components, quantity and price. For example:

Quantity x Price	=	*Cost*
10 items of Y	*@*	*£1.00 each = £10*
3 hours of labour	*@*	*£3.00 per hour = £9*

This division of costs into quantity and price is used in costing systems such as standard costing. Another broad division of costs is into product and period costs, where product costs are related to output and period costs related to the time period in which they were incurred, irrespective of the level of output. Section 2:2 explains an application of product costs and section 2:3 an application of period costs.

For an economist, cost has a different meaning. The cost of using something in an enterprise is the benefit foregone, or opportunity lost, by not using it in its best alternative use. The measurement of the economist's opportunity cost presents many practical problems. Allowance is to be made for imputed factors such as the use of the business owner's time or personal resources. Allowance is also made for an expected yield to compensate for the risks involved. For the manager, the economist's cost concepts are useful but their practical measurement difficulties prevent their application. Accordingly, costing has developed as a range of practical techniques designed for specific purposes. Most of the basic costing techniques are explained in this chapter. Although they are different in nature and purpose, some general characteristics exist in most costing systems. These common characteristics such as cost elements, cost units, cost centres and averaging are explained in the following sub sections.

2:1 Cost elements. The primary division of costs is based on the reasons why expenditure was incurred. These reasons are divided into three expenditure categories of materials, labour and expense, where expense represents any expenditure that is not for materials and labour. Thus any expenditure can be referred to by its primary reference of materials, labour or expense. These three categories are called cost elements. Anything that is done with these cost elements is a cost classification, cost base or cost method. The costing classifications, bases and methods are explained in sections 3 and 5. The distinction between cost elements and cost classifications is illustrated in diagram 30. The three cost elements are the

DIAGRAM 30 COST ELEMENTS & CLASSIFICATIONS

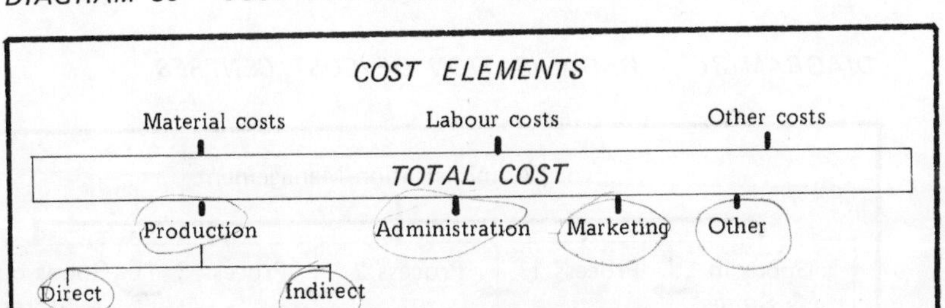

starting point for any costing system and need to be clearly separated and identified.

2:2 Cost unit For costing to exist there must be something to be costed. It may be a product or a service. Products such as books, pencils, cars etc. can become a cost unit in a costing system. This means the costs are collected and analysed relating to the cost unit. For some cost units the analysis can be very complicated and occasionally provide meaningless results. However there is one principle that must be understood and that is the relationship of output to unit cost. When mak ing products some costs do not vary with output, such as the rent of the factory o the managers salary, whilst other costs such as materials and some labour will vary with output. These are called fixed and variable costs and are explained fully in sections 3:3, 5:1, 5:2, 5:3 and chapter 9. At this stage we will just use a simple example to illustrate the relationship of unit cost to the level of output.

Fixed Cost	*Variable cost per Unit*	*Output*	*Total Cost*	*Total Unit Cost*
10,000	10	100	11,000	110
10,000	10	1,000	20,000	20
10,000	10	10,000	110,000	11

The important point to grasp at this stage is that unit costs vary with output therefore one cannot talk about a total unit cost unless it is related to a given leve of output. Unit costs become more difficult to measure with services. Transport may be measured in passenger miles or with haulage in ton miles. Whatever the business it is possible to derive some kind of cost unit but the usefulness of the measure is something only the manager can decide.

2:3 Cost centre For cost control purposes costing systems are often based on th organisation structure of the enterprise. Often this results in costs being collected by a department. A department that is costed would be called a cost centre. Cost centres can relate to people, items of equipment as well as departments. Any part of an organisation or a person can be designated as a cost centre. The main featu of cost centres is that they can only be charged with costs that relate to their loca tion and sphere of operations. When an organisation is divided into cost centres the cost collection and analysis system can be used to derive unit costs. Diagram 31 shows a simplified organisation of a factory that is divided into six cost centres. The factory has a three stage manufacturing process with centralised administration for management, distribution and sales. A cost unit may be derived from this costing system as follows:-

DIAGRAM 31 ORGANISATION OF COST CENTRES

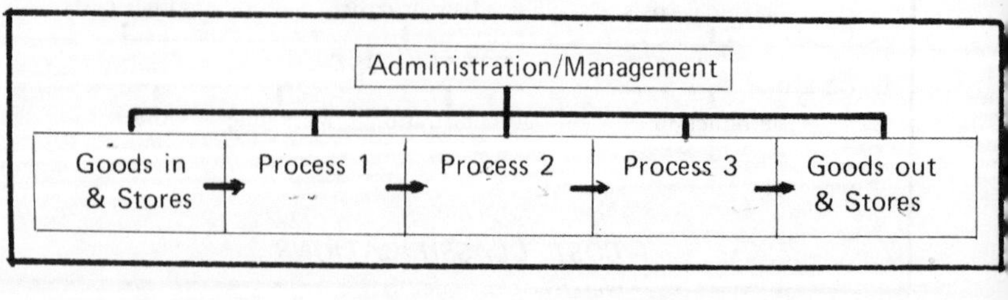

	£	£
Direct materials	5.00	
Direct labour working in processes 1,2 and 3	5.00	
Unit variable cost		10,00
Fixed costs:-		
Process 1 1 hr @ £1.00 per hr	1.00	
Process 2 1 hr @ £2.00 per hr	2.00	
Process 3 2 hrs @ £1.00 per hr	2.00	
General overhead from stores,administration and management	2.00	7.00
Total unit cost		£17.00

In this example as the cost unit passes through each process it is charged on a time basis with the costs of each cost centre. There are a number of complications that arise from this kind of costing that are explained in later sections. At this stage you need to be aware what cost centres are and how they can be used for cost control and unit costing.

2:4 Averaging. A total cost figure will usually contain some 'average cost data'. The averaging process may occur when accumulating and/or dividing costs. Let us consider each cost element to see where averaging may occur.

(a) *Materials* in stock have often been purchased in different quanties and at different prices. A common method of stock valuation is to calculate a simple or weighted average cost for specific stock items. There is sometimes a slight variation in the quantity of material used in a continuous production process. This variation will probably be averaged out in the cost calculations. (Refer to chapter 5)

(b) *Labour* rates can vary due to the amount of overtime or bonus payments. An average rate is usually calculated. Labour efficiency will vary between individual employees but efficiency calculations are often averaged between a number of employees. (Refer to chapter 4)

(c) *Expense* items such as rent and rates are normally divided between cost centres on a kind of averaging basis.

From the above summary you will appreciate that cost data is not necessarily as precise as the figures imply. Averaging will be part of any costing system and the user should be aware whether the averaging process is likely to significantly distort the results.

3 Costing classifications

This area of costing can be very confusing therefore it is important to place costing classifications into some perspective before explaining what the main classifications are. Costs are classified for a specific purpose. For example you may want to know how much it costs to run a particular department. Therefore you would classify the costs according to organisational functions such as production department costs, re-

DIAGRAM 32 *COST CLASSIFICATIONS*

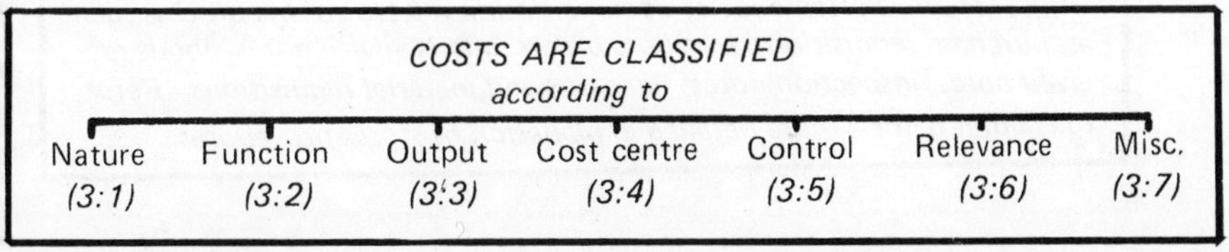

search department costs or administration department costs. You may also decide to classify the same cost data for pricing and output decisions. Common classifications for this function are: fixed and variable, direct and indirect, or relevant and irrelevan The important point to grasp about cost classification is that it represents the sorting of cost data into specific categories for specific functions. The main classifications are shown in diagram 32 and explained in the following sub-sections.

3:1 Nature. When costs are classified by their nature they are grouped according to common characteristics. There are three main groupings: materials, labour and overheads.

3:1:1 Materials. Costing of materials is not as simple as it may seem. There are problems of description, quality, discounts, returns, stock losses, productio wastage, price movements and issue prices to work in progress. It can be a most important part of a costing system, therefore great care is necessary at the systems design stage to ensure *all* the correct costs are recorded from the appropriate documents. The material costs are normally taken from the financial accounting system when suppliers' invoices are received. Specific jobs, units, processes or departments are then charged with the relevant costs when materials are issued from stores. Some businesses have remarkably complex costing systems to fulfill this fairly simple costing function. With the increased use of electronic data processing, costing large varieties and volumes of materials should not be an excessive administrative burden. The basis of most material costing systems is shown in diagram 33 below.

DIAGRAM 33 COSTING OF MATERIALS

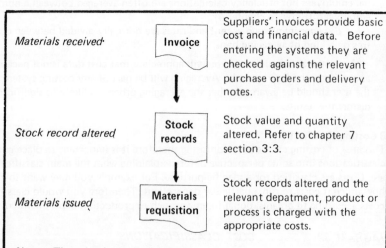

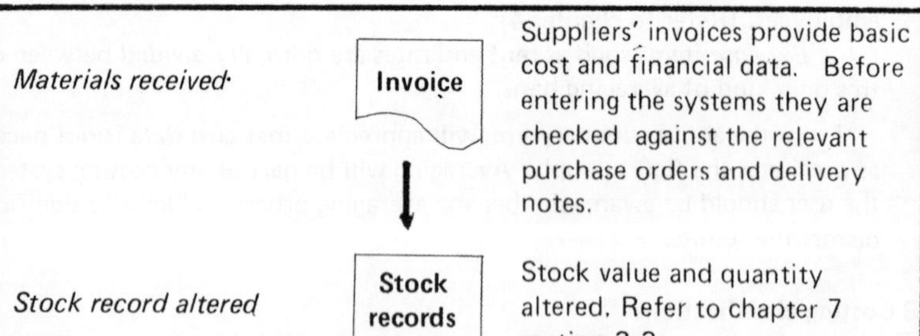

Materials received

Suppliers' invoices provide basic cost and financial data. Before entering the systems they are checked against the relevant purchase orders and delivery notes.
Stock record altered
Stock records
Stock value and quantity altered. Refer to chapter 7 section 3:3.
Materials issued
Materials requisition
Stock records altered and the relevant depatment, product or process is charged with the appropriate costs.

Note. There is often a lot of documentation related to this process such as; purchase requisitions, purchase prders, goods advice notes, goods received notes, inspection notes, bin cards and material requisitions. Refer to chapter 5 for a more detailed explanation of stores procedures

3:1:2 Labour. The cost data for labour can be extracted from the payroll when there is a simple costing system and only a few methods of remuneration. However, when remuneration and costing systems are complex, a different data source is necessary. For example during 'The Times' labour dispute it was reported that there were over 160 different types of wage payment systems in just one Fleet Street print room. Incentive payment schemes need tight cost control and therefore a good cost collection and analysis system is necessary. A basic labour costing system is shown in diagram 34 below.

DIAGRAM 34 COSTING OF LABOUR

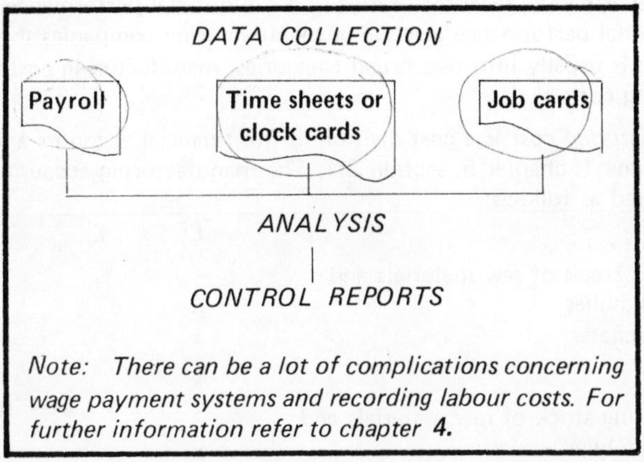

DATA COLLECTION
Payroll
Time sheets or clock cards
Job cards
ANALYSIS
CONTROL REPORTS
Note: There can be a lot of complications concerning wage payment systems and recording labour costs. For further information refer to chapter 4.

At this stage we are only considering labour as a cost element within cost classifications. However, labour cannot usually be treated as a factor of production like materials and capital. Therefore, if you wish to take a broader view of labour costing refer to chapter 4.

3:1:3 Overheads. An overhead cost is any cost that cannot be charged direct to a cost unit. For example the depreciation of a machine, the rent and rates or the managing director's salary. The common feature of these cost elements is that they are not affected by changes in the volume of production. For businesses in the service industries a large proportion of their costs are classified as overheads. The term overhead is usually synonymous with fixed costs but not necessarily with indirect costs. Refer to sub sections 3:3 and 3:4. There are two basic ways of dealing with overheads in a costing system: they can be *allocated* or *apportioned*. These terms have specific meanings. If an overhead cost is to be allocated all of it is charged to a cost centre or cost unit. For example, if a production department that was a cost centre had say, four machines, the depreciation on these machines would be *allocated* directly to the cost centre. Whereas if a unit of production was passing through each machine in a production process a proportion of the overhead costs of depreciation would be *apportioned* to the cost unit. The problems associated with overhead absorption are explained in sections 5:1 and 5:3

3:2 Function. This form of classification is most common with budgetary control systems where each department has a cost budget. Aspects of functional cost classification that require caution are the possibility of double costing, problems of equitable apportionment of overheads and the inclusion of all relevant costs. Departmental functions have to be very clearly defined for costs to be classified on this basis. For example most departments have some kind of administration. It would therefore be difficult to isolate an accurate total administration cost. Also there can be a high degree of interdependence between some departments. Thus dome departments that are carrying other departments' costs may look very expensive because the way the costs are collected and analysed. Consequently the costing system may provide a false view of departmental cost efficiency. To introduce a rigid departmental costing system may damage interdepartmental co-operation. Indeed producing optimal 'paper performance' at each departmental level may result in a sub-optimal performance at aggregate operational performance levels. For manufacturing companies the functional division is usually into two broad categories; manufacturing costs and non-manufacturing costs.

Manufacturing cost is a cost division in the financial accounts and was explained in Volume 1, chapter 5, section 3:1. The manufacturing account is normally structured as follows:

	£	£
Opening stock of raw materials and sub assemblies	x	
add Purchaser	x	
	x	
less closing stock of raw materials and sub assemblies	x	
Cost of materials used in production		x
add manufacturing wages		x
Prime costs		x
add factory overheads		x
Opening work in progress	x	
less closing work in progress	x	x
Manufacturing costs of goods transferred to finished goods stock		£ x

The popular terms here are 'prime costs' which are the costs of direct material and direct labour; and 'conversion cost' which represents the total cost of converting raw material into the product transferred to finished goods stock.

Non-manufacturing costs are all the other costs incurred by the firm and are sometimes referred to as 'general overheads'. These costs tend to be related to time whereas the manufacturing costs are related to output. For example non-manufacturing costs of say general administration would be estimated per month regardless of output. On the other hand, some manufacturing costs such as materials, would be strictly related to the level of output.

This point is explained in more detail in the following sub section on fixed and variable costs.

3:3 Fixed and variable costs. When output is tangible and measurable a popular cost classification is into fixed and variable costs. There are also intermediate classification stages of semi-fixed and semi-variable costs.

Fixed costs do not vary in relation to the level of output within a specified range. For example a production manager's salary would not usually change if production increased or decreased. Fixed costs tend to be time based; such as rent, rates or insurance.

Variable costs vary directly in relation to production. For instance, if the product was wooden tables there would tend to be a direct relationship between the number of tables produced and the total cost of wood.

It can be argued that in the short run almost all costs are fixed and in the long run almost all costs are variable. However cost collection and analysis relates to discrete time periods, therefore the variability of costs should be related to the appropriate accounting time period. Inevitably, many cost elements cannot be neatly classified into fixed and variable and they fall into the semi-fixed or semi-variable region. That is, they vary, but not directly in relation to out put. Electricity for example has a fixed charge based on time and a variable charge based on consumption. Or, the use of rags and lubricating oil would tend to increase as production increased but it could not be easily measured. For some decision making techniques, such as pricing and output problems, it is necessary to separate *all* costs into fixed and variable. This can be a lengthy process but there is a 'short cut' method.

3:3:1 Quick method of dividing costs into fixed and variable. This method may be used where the costing system produces total costs but does not classify all costs into fixed and variable categories. It is a fairly crude technique and the results should only be used as a rough guide. For the purposes of illustration a graphical technique will be used that is suitable for simple price/output decisions when the costing system does not divide costs into fixed and variable.

Assume the costing system has produced the following total cost figures for different levels of output over a number of accounting periods.

Output level (units)	*Total cost £*
5,000	17,500
7,000	20,500
10,000	25,000

This data is plotted on a graph with output on the horizontal axis and total cost on the vertical axis. A line is then drawn between the points and continued back to the vertical axis. Where the line intersects the vertical axis will be the fixed costs (estimated). In diagram 35 the above data is entered on a total cost graph and the line intersects the vertical axis at £10,000. Having established from the graph that the fixed cost is £10,000 the variable cost per unit can be calculated as follows:-

Stage 1 Total cost - fixed cost = variable cost. Therefore at an output level of 10,000 units the variable costs are £25,000 – £10,000 = £15,000.

Stage 2 Variable cost per unit $= \dfrac{\text{Variable cost}}{\text{Unit output}} = \dfrac{\text{£}15{,}000}{10{,}000} = \underline{\underline{\text{£}1.50 \text{ per unit}}}$

Thus the total cost function can now be expressed as 10,000 + 1.5q where q represents the level of output. For each level of output the equation can

be multiplied out as follows:- 5,000 units = 10,000 + (1.5 x 5,000) = £17,50
7,000 units = 10,000 + (1.5 x 7,000) = £20,50
10, 000 units = 10,000 + (1.5 x10,000)= £25,00

DIAGRAM 35 *TOTAL COST GRAPH*

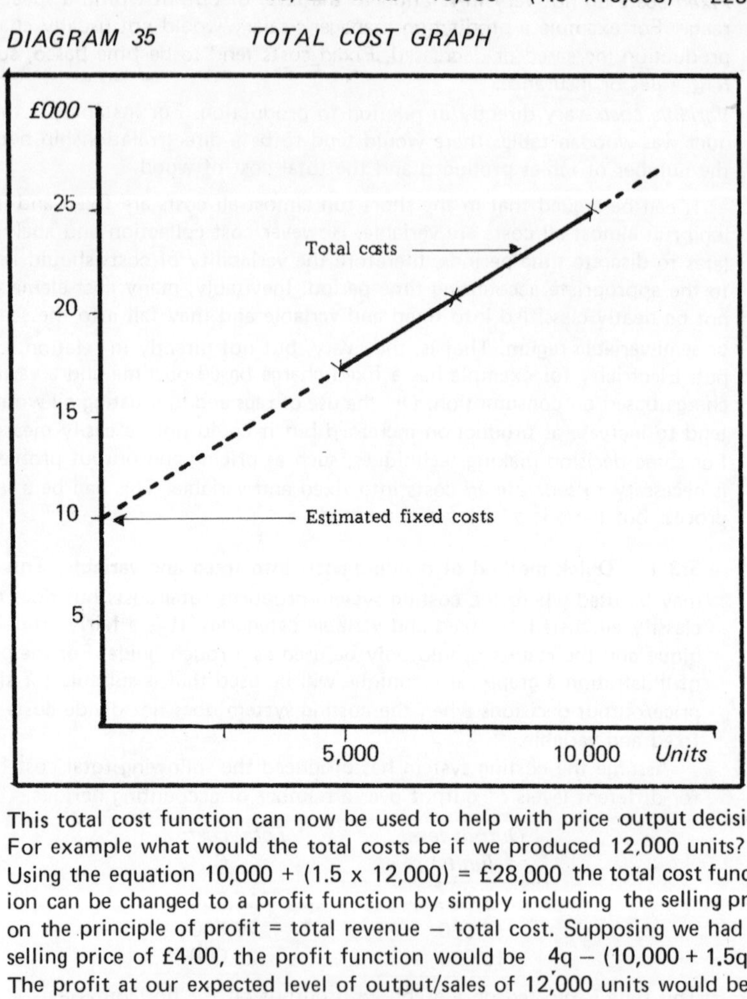

This total cost function can now be used to help with price output decisions. For example what would the total costs be if we produced 12,000 units? Using the equation 10,000 + (1.5 x 12,000) = £28,000 the total cost function can be changed to a profit function by simply including the selling price on the principle of profit = total revenue – total cost. Supposing we had a selling price of £4.00, the profit function would be 4q – (10,000 + 1.5q) The profit at our expected level of output/sales of 12,000 units would be:-

(12,000 x 4) – 10,000 + (1.5 x 12,000) = £20,000

A pricing decision such as what would the profit be if we reduced the selling price to £3.00 to sell 14,000 units could be calculated as follows:-

(14,000 x 3) – 10,000 + (1.5 x 14,000) = £11,000

From this example you will appreciate that the division of costs into fixed and variable is very useful for decision making. However, there are many limitations to this technique (often called break even analysis) and it is important that you read chapter 6 to appreciate the applications and limitations of using costs that are divided into fixed and variable. One further point concerning this example: when the total cost points are plotted on graph paper, they will rarely form a straight line as in this example. You will need to draw a line of best using some kind of regression analysis.

3:4 Direct and indirect costs. The terms direct and indirect are in common usage, even though the costing system being used may not use a direct costing basis for cost classification. As a working definition one can say that a cost is direct if it can be identified as belonging exclusively to a cost centre or cost unit. Conversely, a cost is indirect if it cannot be exclusively attributed to whatever is being costed. For example if a machine shop (the cost centre) was producing steel screws then the steel, the machine shop wages, the depreciation of the machines would all be direct costs of that cost centre. If this machine shop was part of a factory then other costs relating to general administration, general management and sales would be indirect costs for that cost centre.

A common error is to assume that direct costs and variable costs are the same. Direct costs are those directly related to a cost centre or cost unit therefore they may be either fixed or variable. In the machine shop example, the fixed cost of depreciation was a direct cost to the cost centre. Popular usage of the term direct where direct and variable costs are synonymous include:

Direct materials—A variable cost where material costs are directly related to output.

Direct labour—A variable cost where labour costs are directly related to output.

Direct expense—General expense items that are directly related to output.

The main point to remember about the terms direct and indirect is that they relate to whatever is being costed. If the cost centre is a department then the department managers costs are direct but if the costing is related to cost units his costs will be indirect.

3:5 Controllable and non-controllable costs. The term controllable refers to the extent that an *individual is able to influence cost behaviour.* This kind of cost classification is generally referred to as responsibility accounting and explained in chapter 8. At this stage we will just be concerned with the principles of classifying costs into these two broad categories. The first point to note is that costs are related to individuals who have departmental responsibility and should be capable of controlling selected cost elements. For example, at the foreman level cost responsibilities may be limited to say; efficient use of direct material and direct labour. Whereas at the executive level the ability to influence cost is spread over a wider area and a longer time span. This leads to the second point, for costs to be classified by responsibility, the business must have a clearly defined prganisation structure with identifiable scalar chains and good delegation of responsibility and authority. It entirely defeats the purpose of responsibility accounting to hold managers responsible for costs over which they have no control. The classifications can be defined as follows:-

Controllable costs are those cost elements that a manager is capable of influencing within specified time periods.
Non-controllable costs are those cost elements that are outside the control of a manager over a specified time period.

You will have noticed that those definitions referred to time periods. This is because cost control is directly related to time. For instance overtime payments have a short time control period, whereas rent and rates have a longer time period. In the long run *all* costs are controllable, therefore at the board of director level all costs are considered controllable.

3:6 Relevant and irrelevant costs This kind of costing classification will probably be made on the 'back of an envelope' instead of in a computer data base. Indeed it would be virtually impossible to instal a valid formalised relevant costing system. *The division of costs is based upon their relevance to a specific decision problem involving alternative choice.* Therefore the costs relevant for one decision maybe irrelevant for another decision. The task facing the manager is to select from a list of costs those that are *considered relevant for a specific decision.* Relevant costs have two main characteristics :-

(a) They relate to the future. In most instances historic costs are irrelevant for decision making. For example if you paid £10,000 for a machine this figure is irrelevant for decision making once it has been paid. The relevant figures are its *future income earning potential* and its *future net realisable value.* Past costs are usually only useful as indicators for the future.

(b) They are different between alternatives. Decision making is about choice between alternatives. *If the cost for each alternative is the same, then it is irrelevant for the decision* and should be excluded. This aspect of costing is sometimes referred to as 'incremental' or 'differential' costing where calculations are made to derive the cost difference between alternatives. However, these costing techniques do not necessarily use relevant costs.

3:7 Miscellaneous cost classifications. There exists a very wide range of costing classifications that have been developed to meet specific needs in an industry or special businesses. For example in publishing, the terms 'first copy costs' and 'run on costs' refer to cost classifications useful to the industry. In engineering terms such as 'set up costs' and 'oncosts' refer to cost classifications that are important to a production manager. This wide range of specialised terms, are in most instances, a slight variation on the fixed and variable cost classification explained in section 3:3. The best thing you can do when faced with a specialised cost classification is to ask what cost elements go into it? Then you will probably find it is just a variation of a fixed and variable cost classification or direct and indirect cost classification. Some of these specialised classifications apply the economist's principle of marginal costing that is explained in section 5:2

4. Cost recording

Cost recording is an ideal application for electronic data processing. From the previous sections on costing classifications you will be aware that cost data can be classified into a wide range of categories for a variety of purposes. In the next section on costing techniques the wide range of applications for costing are briefly explained. It will then be clear that the costing system and its applications upon which planning decision making and control rest, is dependent on a good cost recording system. The entire process is therefore weakened if the cost collection and recording system is inadequate. The following points need attention:-

(i) All cost data is collected. A lot of the costing data will be extracted from the financial accounts, but detail such as unit quantities purchased, in stock and issued to work in progress will be obtained from other sources. The important part of this operation is to ensure all the data is collected.

(ii) Cost data is collected accurately. Many costing systems are now computerised This means that cost data is entered on computer input documents. Production statistics, stores issues etc. are all part of the input process. However, the design of input documents often makes little concession for the user. They are sometimes difficult to understand, not suitable for the job and employees are not given adequate instruction on how to use them. Consequently the systems analyst's saying

of 'garbage in garbage out' is applicable. With bad input documentation that results in incomplete or inaccurate data entering the system the cost reports may be misleading management.

(iii) Cost data is not double recorded It is very easy for the same data to be entered twice unless there is a good system of input control. There is also a possibility of duplication due to a system design fault where one type of cost is entered in two categories because the same figures are derived from two separate sources.

If the cost data collection and recording system is inadequate the entire costing process is weakened. We will now briefly look at some important aspects of cost recording.

4:1 Memorandum or double entry. The simplest form of cost recording is based on a memorandum system where specific costs are recorded on separate records that have nothing to do with double entry book-keeping. They are recorded for a specific purpose. In many businesses stock records (in value terms) are on a memorandum basis and excluded from the double entry system. Whilst memorandum records are usually easier to maintain (and understand) than double entry, their disadvantage is the limitations on checking their accuracy and reliability. Moreover, there is a danger that a memorandum cost record maintained for a specific purpose could be misleading if used for another purpose.

One of the principles of double entry book-keeping is that every transaction has two components, a receipt and a payment. Let us not get involved in the debits and credits but simple be aware that for every transaction two equal entries, one debit, one credit, appears in separate accounts Thus when all the accounts are totalled, the total debits equal the total credits. From this partly self checking recording system we can then analyse the data into a variety of cost classifications for use in a wide range of applications. Double entry book-keeping has stood the test of time in financial accounting and there appears to be no reason why it should not serve cost accounting in the same way.

4:1:1 Integrated accounts. A fully integrated system would hold cost accounts and financial accounts together by double entry where no distinction was made between the two types of accounts. The advantage of a fully integrated accounting system is that the accounting function has less tendency to become separated into the two common divisions of financial and management accountancy. This practical division of accountancy was relevant for large organisations, but now with the low cost recording and analytical power of computers a fully integrated system is mainly a programming problem.

If full integration is not acceptable to a company then there are some half way stages between this and totally separate systems. A common form of integral accounting is with the use of control accounts. (Accounts that aggregate the totals of other accounts) The management accountant and financial accountant have their own recording systems and at the end of each accounting period attempts are made to reconcile their figures through central control accounts.

The long development of cost recording systems has been based on manual record keeping, requiring many cost clerks and several management accountants. With low cost electronic data processing most of these costing systems are being replaced and it is therefore appropriate to briefly introduce the concept of a computerised common data base.

4:1:2 Common Data Base. The accepted method of controlling and directing business activity towards a common goal is the functional division of an enterprise into departments such as marketing, production, personnel, administration and accounting. One of the outcomes of this divisionalisation is a proliferation of filing cabinets, multiple copy documents, photocopying machines and internal memorandums. Each department receives and sends a number of internal documents that attempt to ensure each separate filing system is kept up to date. Management consultants have continually recommended reduction of internal paperwork and some companies have attempted centralised filing systems to reduce duplication. The trend is towards the common data base.

The common data base is a file of records which is not designed to meet a specific application but is used as a data source for a variety of recording, analysis and reporting functions. The early centralised filing systems were a form of common data base but multiple access to hard copy files created many problems. For example the file would have to be requested, collected and returned which is inconvenient, especially if the file was being used by someone else. Inevitably, departments would take copies of files and gradually develop their own filing systems thus defeating the purpose of the common data base. With a computerised common data base all the disadvantages of centralised filing are eliminated. An interactive terminal will provide a department with instant access to the data base.

As the computerised common data base is likely to become a feature of many business administration systems let us consider how this will affect cost recording. An appropriate starting point is to identify the main sources of cost data and then consider how the cost recording function will differ if a common data base is used. A costing system will draw its data from production records, labour records, stock records, purchasing records and the financial accounts. The system will then accumulate the data in double entry cost accounts or memorandum records. A common data base does not need separate cost accumulation records. The purpose of costing records is to enable cost analysis and reports to be undertaken that will help management. As cost analysis is an ideal application for electronic data processing it follows that a large amount of costing can be programmed, drawing upon the common data base as a data source, instead of cost accumulation records. However, the data base may be structured on double entry costing principles, where data is stored in coded accounts. The following sub sections explain how accounts may be coded and some of the principles of cost data collection. (Also refer to chapter 10 sub-section 2:2:2)

4:2 Coding of accounts. A good system of codification has the following charactistics:-

(a) Capable of being understood by an employee who may have to provide input or operate the system. A complex system where employees have to search long lists of codes to compute input documents will inevitably cause input errors.

(b) Comprehensive, so that all cost elements and related data can be entered in the system.

(c) Have spare capacity to allow for increases in cost elements and for new broad categories to be introduced.

(d) Able to deal with exceptional items, so that all data still enters into the system.

(e) Capable of being easily adapted for electronic data processing.

The choice for coding can be grouped into three main categories: alphabetic, numeric and alpha-numeric. A simple alpha system will generally adapt a mnemonic form, i.e. S = Sales, SM = Sales Management, SR = Sales Representatives etc. The main limitation of an alpha system is expansion because the same letters should not represent different accounts. Once the mnemonic principle is broken, the main advantage of the alpha system is lost. Most large accountancy coding systems are numeric. An outline of numeric coding for financial and cost accounts is shown below:-

Financial accounts	*0 - 999*	
e.g.	0 - 100	fixed assets
	101 - 200	liabilities
	201 - 300	sales ledger
	301 - 400	purchase ledger
	etc.	

Cost accounts	*1,000 - 1,999*		
e.g.	1,000 - 1,100		Raw materials category A
	1,101 - 1,200		Raw materials category B
	1,201 - 1,300		Direct labour
	1,301 - 1,400		Service costs
		e.g. 1301	Service engineers basic wages
		1302	Service engineers overtime
		1303	Service materials
		1304	Service tools
			etc.

With this kind of numeric codification different departments only need to know the cost codes that concern them for input documents. The author knows of two large companies that provided employees with a complete coding and no clear instructions, then expected error free input.

4:3 Data collection. Data entering a costing system will usually be in one of the following categories:

Specific costs (or revenues) from invoices.

Specific quantities and units of measure from a variety of sources.

Total costs or quantities from one or more record systems.

Average costs or quantities from one or more record systems.

In this sub section our concern is with how this data is collected, in later sections we look at how it is analysed, presented and used.

Methods of data collection will vary according to the nature of the organisation. A manufacturing company which has a measurable output will collect quantities as well as costs, whereas a service company that does not have a tangible output will tend to concentrate on department costs instead of unit costs. The most appropriate way of covering this wide area is to divide it into the three well known cost classifications explained earlier; materials, labour and expense.

4:3:1 Materials The term materials covers, raw materials, bought in sub-assemblies and sub assemblies produced by the company and returned into stock. The movement of materials and the data collection points are shown in diagram 36 below.

DIAGRAM 36 MATERIALS – DATA' COLLECTION POINTS

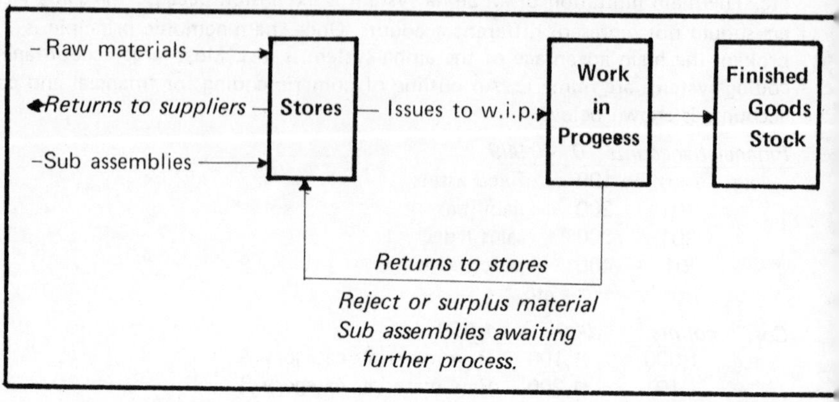

This diagram shows the movement of materials and sub-assemblies into the stores and then issued to work in progress. (w.i.p.) From work in progress most materials become finished goods but some will require further processing and be returned to stores. Other returns to stores will be reject or surplus materials. Whenever materials are moved documentation is needed to update the stock records. The data collection points are summarised in the following notes:-

(a) *Materials and sub assemblies received from and returned to suppliers* will be recorded on the following documents; purchase order, suppliers' invoice and delivery note, goods received note, inspection note, goods returned note, stock records and the financial accounts. Selecting the appropriate documents for input into the costing system is an individual matter for each organisation. However care is needed to ensure that the selected documents provide a complete and reliable record. The problem areas at this stage are units of measure and returns to suppliers.

(b) *Issues to work in progress* are normally recorded on materials requisition, job cards and stock records. This data collection stage is to provide information for costing; jobs, processes, units and/or cost centres. There are two problems here: the human factor in getting the right cost codes and all the costs entered on input documents and valuation of issues to work in progress The human problem can be overcome by good input document design and adequate training, but the valuation problem can become very complex. Stock valuation methods are explained in chapter 5.

(c) *Returns to stock* of surplus or reject material is recorded on internal goods returned notes, reject/scrap notes, job cards and stock records. The return of completed sub-assemblies for use in a subsequent production process would be recorded on job cards and stock records. Returns usually create administrative problems, but the records need to be adjusted unless the amounts involved are insignificant. Where amounts are small then a single account may be used to accumulate this data and thr total extracted at the end of each accounting period.

(d) *Transfers from work in progress to finished goods stock.* The main input source for this stage would be job cards and finished goods stock records. The valuation methods for goods passed in to finished goods stock are explained in chapter 5.

4:3:2 Labour The major data source for labour costs is the payroll. However, most payrolls are structured for financial accounting into: gross pay, P.A.Y.E., National Insurance, Graduated Pensions, other deductions and net wages. For a costing system we need to identify labour costs by product, pro cess, unit, job and/or cost centre. Thus the financial and costing systems have separate functions concerning labour records. The financial system has to meet the cash obligations to employees and meet the company's legal obligations for collecting P.A.Y.E., National Insurance and pensions' payments. The costing system has to meet management's information requirements for planning, decision making and control. Where the systems tend to come together is when the company has incentive payment schemes. The calculations from the costing system are then entered in the payroll as part of the gross wages. Accordingly, labour costing systems tend to develop separately from the payroll. Labour time and other output data is collected from; clock cards, job cards, time sheets, piecework tickets and then this data is multiplied by the relevant wage rates extracted from the payroll. This system separation will probably continue in many companies because the popular software packages for payroll have remarkably little capacity for cost analysis.

We are therefore left with a costing system that extracts time and output data from production documents, and wage rate data from the payroll. When collecting this data the following points need to be considered:-

(a) *Nature of employment.* Our concern here is if the employee's labour can be directly traced to a cost unit or cost centre. Thus a broad division is made that separates employees into direct and indirect labour (Refer to section 3:4).

(b) *Labour time.* There are three categories of direct labour time that need to be recorded :-

(i) Time on premises
(ii) Time on specific job
(iii) Non productive time, i.e. (i) – (ii)

(c) *Wage rate* For direct labour the wage rate paid by the employer will comprise, basic wages, incentive payments and employer's contributions. The analytical part of the costing system should divide this total sum by the productive hours to get a wage rate. Because this can be quite complicated, direct labour rates are often costed on the basic hourly rate which will generally understate the cost to the employer.

4:3:3 Expense An expense item is any cost that is not included in the mat erials and labour categories. (See diagram 30) Almost all this data will be extracted from the financial accounts. The division of expenses into direct and indirect would be through account codes on the input documents and subsequent analysis. The financial accounts usually provide a sufficiently wide range of expense analysis that can be transferred directly to the cost accounts For example, expense elements such as rent, rates and electricity can be easily extracted from the financial accounts and then apportioned or allocated to cost centres through the costing system.

DIAGRAM 37 THE STRUCTURE OF COSTING BASES & METHODS

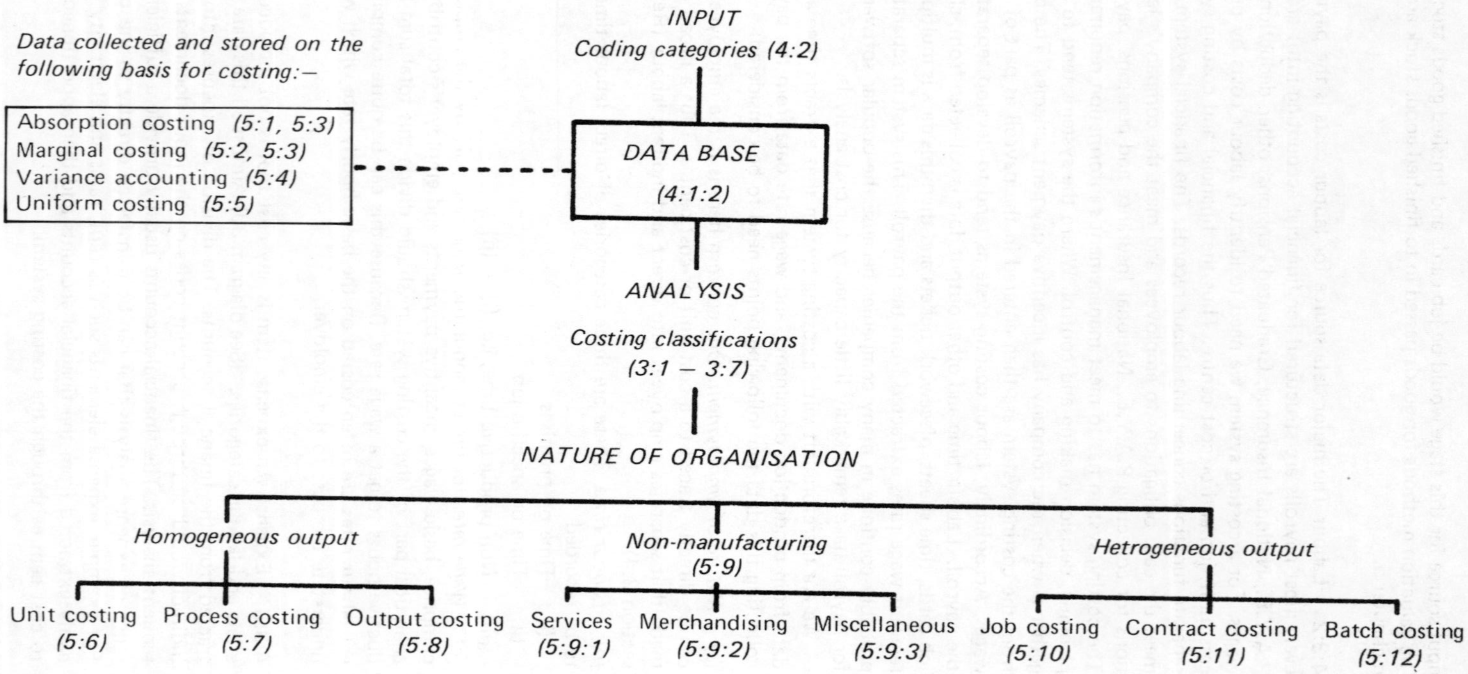
INPUT
Coding categories (4:2)
Data collected and stored on the following basis for costing:–
Absorption costing (5:1, 5:3)
Marginal costing (5:2, 5:3)
Variance accounting (5:4)
Uniform costing (5:5)
DATA BASE
(4:1:2)
ANALYSIS
Costing classifications
(3:1 – 3:7)
NATURE OF ORGANISATION
Homogeneous output
Non-manufacturing
(5:9)
Hetrogeneous output
Unit costing
(5:6)
Process costing
(5:7)
Output costing
(5:8)
Services
(5:9:1)
Merchandising
(5:9:2)
Miscellaneous
(5:9:3)
Job costing
(5:10)
Contract costing
(5:11)
Batch costing
(5:12)

5. Costing bases and methods.

The following sub sections explain four costing bases and twelve costing methods The structure of costing illustrated in diagram 37 is cross referenced to the following sub sections. Much of the detail is intended for reference purposes and the reader is advised not to attempt to understand every costing method. However, the four costing bases: absorption costing, marginal costing, uniform costing and variance accounting need to be understood. It is especially important to be aware of the distinction between marginal and absorption costing because all costing systems are based on either marginal or absorption principles. The principles of uniform costing are quite simple and variance accounting is used by many business enterprises. Accordingly it is suggested that you read sub sections 5:1 to 5:5 to obtain a general understanding of costing bases and then just read the costing methods that are relevant to your working environment.

5:1 **Absorption costing.** This is sometimes referred to as total cost accounting and is based on the principle that all costs incurred by a business should be charged to production. In practice absorption costing systems do not usually charge selling costs and financial expenses to products or processes. Therefore, strictly speaking total cost accounting or total absorption accounting are different from absorption accounting..Absorption cost accounting may be defined as a costing technique that charges all costs, except selling and financial costs, to operations, products or processes. The principle of absorption costing is illustrated in diagram 38 below.

DIAGRAM 38 PRINCIPLES OF ABSORPTION COSTING

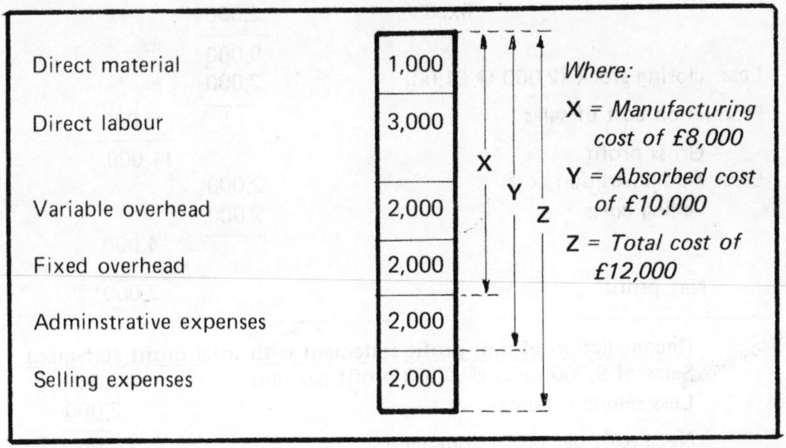

If 10,000 units were produced then the cost per unit would be £10,000 divided by 10,000 units and the stock value would be £1.00 per unit. To bring the 10,000 units to their current condition and location it cost £10,000 and using absorption costing principles the stock value becomes £10,000. Assuming the unit selling price is £2.00 the unit profit statement would be as follows:-

Unit Profit Statement

	£	£	£
Selling price			2.00
Less:			
Direct Materials	0.10		
Direct Labour	0.30		
Variable Overhead	0.20		
Prime cost		0.60	
Add fixed costs:-			
Production		0.20	
Administration		0.20	
Total cost			1.00
Profit per unit			£1.00

The unit profit excludes selling amd finance costs, but the figures can be reconciled with a type of financial accounting profit statement. Assume an opening stock of 1,000 units and a closing stock of 2,000 units then the profit state ment would be:-

Profit Statement

	£	£
Sales (9,000 units @ £2.00)		18,000
Less: production cost of sales:-		
Opening stock (1,000 @ £1.00)	1,000	
Add: Direct material	1,000	
Direct Labour	3,000	
Production overheads: variable	2,000	
fixed	2,000	
	9,000	
Less: closing stock (2,000 @ £1.00)	2,000	
Production cost of sales		7,000
Gross profit		11,000
Less: Administration costs	2,000	
Selling costs	2,000	
		4,000
Net profit		7,000

Reconciliation of unit profit statement with total profit statement

Sales of 9,000 units @ £1.00 profit per unit	9,000
Less selling expenses	2,000
Net Profit per profit statement	£7,000

An important point to note is how absorbed overhead costs will affect stock valuation and consequently the profit and loss account and balance sheet. The statement of standard accounting practice on stock valuation (SSAP 9) recommends that cost should be calculated as being the 'expenditure that has been incurred in the normal course of business in bringing the product or service to its present location and condition' (*Refer to Volume 1 Financial Accounting for the non-accountant*). Therefore the principle of absorbing overheads into unit costs is well established. However, overhead absorption creates a number of problems that are explained in the following sub sections.

5:1:1 Equitable allotment. The problem here is how to spread the overhead costs fairly between cost centres, products or processes. The following table lists possible bases for overhead allotment.

TYPE OF OVERHEAD	*BASIS FOR ALLOTMENT*
Depreciation and maintenance:	
Buildings	Cubic capacity, floor area
Plant & Machinery	Machine manning time
Supervision	Number of employees
Heating and lighting	Cubic capacity or floor area
Canteen and welfare facilities	Number of employees
Transport	Ton/miles, passenger miles
Administration	Output, number of employees
Rent, rates	Cubic capacity, floor area

Because of the administrative difficulties and cost of operating a wide range of 'fair' methods for the allotment of overheads, it is common practice to include most overhead costs in a general overhead category and then allot on a common base. Some popular common bases for absorbing overheads are summarised below:-

Percentage of direct labour		£
Detail:	General overhead costs to be alloted	100,000
	Costs of direct labour for equivalent period	400,000

$$\text{Absorption rate} = \frac{\text{Overhead cost}}{\text{Level of activity}}\ \%\ \text{i.e.}\ \frac{100{,}000}{400{,}000} \times 100 = 25\%$$

The overhead absorption rate of 25% on direct labour means that if a job had direct labour costs of say £1,000 then the charge for overheads would be £250. A similar calculation could be made using direct labour hours instead of direct labour costs. The disadvantages of using this method are:

(i) No allowance is made for jobs that use expensive equipment and should therefore absorb a larger proportion of overheads.

(ii) The different efficient of individual employees will result in larger job cost variations, because of the overhead absorption rate.

Percentage of direct material		£
Detail:	General overhead costs to be alloted	100,000
	Costs of direct materials for equivalent period	200,000

$$\text{Absorption rate} = \frac{\text{Overhead cost}}{\text{Level of activity}}\ \%\text{i i.e.}\ \frac{100{,}000}{200{,}000} \times 100 = 50\%$$

The overhead absorption rate of 50% on direct material means that if a job had direct material costs of say £800 then the charge for overheads would be £400. The disadvantages of this method are:

(i) Overheads tend to be time based costs such as rent, rates and depreciation, whereas direct material is usage based.

(ii) A job using few direct materials may utilise a lot of capital equipment and would not be charged its fair share of overheads

(iii) The price of some materials may fluctuate and cause erratic job costs to be made.

Rate per unit of output		£
Detail:	General overhead costs to be alloted	100,000
	Number of units produced for equivalent period	20,000

$$\text{Absorption rate} = \frac{\text{Overhead cost}}{\text{Level of activity}} \text{ i.e. } \frac{£1000,000}{20,000} = £5 \text{ per unit}$$

The overhead absorption rate of £5.00 per unit would therefore be added to the cost of every unit produced. The disadvantage of this method is that it is only suitable for businesses with a homogeneous unit output.

There are many methods of overhead absorption and businesses tend to develop methods that are best suited to their specific circumstances. Providing a method is applied consistently, then temporal total cost comparisons may be made. However, when making spatial total cost comparisons, such as between two different companies, it is important to be clear about their methods of overhead apportionment. For example, if we take the figures used to illustrate the above three general methods of overhead absorption the following detail can be compiled:-

	£000	£000
Direct materials	200	
Direct labour	400	
Variable cost		600
Fixed cost		100
Total cost		700

Assume the above cost detail has been extracted from two identical companies 'A' and 'B' Company 'A' absorbs its overheads in direct labour and Company 'B' on direct materials. If both companies made a product that contained £500 of direct material and £100 of direct labour, their total costs would be as follows:-

	Company 'A'		*Company 'B'*	
	£	£	£	£
Direct materials	500		500	
Direct labour	100		100	
Variable cost		600		600
Company 'A' overhead (100 x .25)		25		
Company 'B' overhead (500 x.5)				250
Total cost		£625		£850

You will now appreciate that the basis of overhead apportionment can distort total cost figures. This point is especially important if total cost figures are being compared as a measure of efficiency. In a company one department may be absorbing an unfair overhead cost burden and closure or rationalisation decisions may be made based on misleading total cost detail. Therefore, whenever you are using cost detail that includes overheads make sure you know what the overhead costs represent and how they have been absorbed.

5:1:2 Pre-determined absorption rates. One of the advantages of absorption costing is that a profit can be calculated for specific jobs or units of output. However, to calculate the total cost and hence the profit, for a specific job, the overhead absorption rate has to be calculated in advance. The formula is basically the same, except budgeted activity and overhead costs are substituted in place of the actual figures, i.e.

$$\frac{\text{Budgeted overhead costs}}{\text{Budgeted level of activity}}\%$$

Rarely will budgeted activity and costs be the same as the actual results. Thus, pre-determined overhead rates will create over or under absorption of overhead costs. The following example illustrates the problem of over/under absorption that is created by pre-determined overhead absorption rates.

Unit Cost Statement

	£	£
Selling price		2.00
Less: Direct materials	0.20	
Direct labour	0.50	
Variable Overheads	0.10	
	0.80	
Fixed overheads apportioned on a fair basis at an output of 1,000 units (i.e. Actual overheads £700)	0.70	
Total Unit cost		1.50
Unit Profit		£0.50

Comparative Profit Statement ***(abbreviated)***

Unit Output/Sales	*(500)*	*(1,000)*	*(1,500)*
	£	£	£
Sales	1,000	2,000	3,000
Less: Prime cost	400	800	1,200
	600	1,200	1,800
Less: Overheads @ £0.70 per unit	350	700	1,050
Total Profit	£250	£500	£750

It is necessary to ask - are these profit figures correct? Remember that the fixed overheads should remain fixed regardless of the level of output at £700 Therefore, the actual profits would be:-

Over/under Absorption Statement

Unit Output/Sales	*(500)*	*(1,000)*	*(1,500)*
Actu	£	£	£
Actual loss/profit	(100)	500	1,100
Absorption costing loss/profit	250	500	750
Over/under absorption	(350)	—	350

1,000 units As this was the expected level upon which the absorption rate was calculated the costing calculations are correct.

500 units The absorption rate should have been £1.4 per unit (i.e.700:/500) therefore, as output is lower than expected the overheads have been under absorbed.

1,500 units At an output of 1,500 units, the absorption rate should have been £0.46 (i.e. 700/1,500) consequently the overheads have been over absorbed.

The only time the overhead absorption will be correct is when the expected output equals the actual output.

5:1:3 Circular apportionments. This problem arises when several departments undertake work for one another. Take the following situation:

Department	*Own overheads to be apportioned*	*Apportioned to Department*	
	£		£
A	4,000	B	2,000
		C	2,000
B	4,000	A	2,000
		C	2,000
C	4,000	A	2,000
		B	2,000

Supposing A apportioned first then B would have £6,000 to apportion.When C came to apportion, it would have £9,000 (i.e. 4,000 + 2,000 + 3,000) to apportion. The circular apportionment would then return to A and so the circle would continue as shown in diagram 39 below.

DIAGRAM 39 *CIRCULAR APPORTIONMENTS*

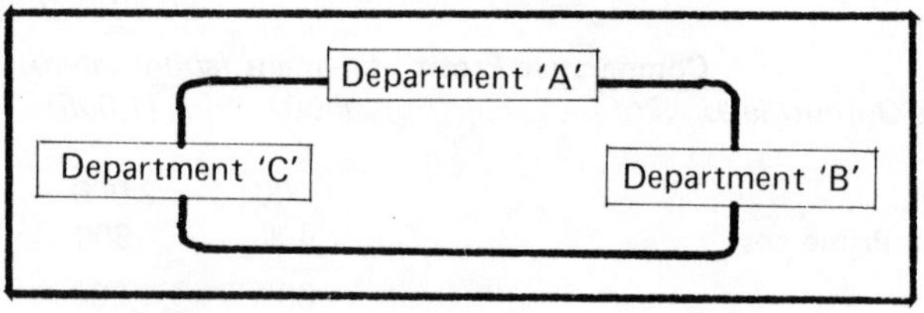

There are three main methods of breaking the vicious circle:-

(a) Algebraic method - takes the total service costs of each department and expresses them as algebraic equations. Mathematical procedures are then used to determine the amount to be apportioned.
With the increasing use of computers for costing systems, this method may gain popularity because the calculations could be programmed fairly easily.
(b) Trial and error - this method continues to allot the costs between departments until the amounts involved become insignificant.
(c) Clearing in a specified order - each department is cleared of overheads in a set order. The departments that do the most work for other departments are cleared first and no return charges are made.

For non-mechanised costing systems, method (c) is generally used, mainly because it is the easiest to calculate.

5:1:4 Summary. Absorption costing is a technique that attempts to determin mine total costs in relation to output. Many costs, however, are not output based; these include: rent, rates, depreciation, administration, supervision, storage and maintenance. The basis of the technique is to calculate an overhead absorption rate that can be applied to output for the above types of cost. This section has explained:-

(a) The principles of absorbing overhead rates.
(b) Methods of calculating overhead rates.
(c) The problems of overhead absorption, paying special attention to:
  (i) A fair methods of apportionment
  (ii) Pre-determined overhead rates where actual output differs from expected output
(d) The problem of apportioning several service department overheads.
(e) Different ways of presenting absorption costing statements.

Because of the difficulty of accurately estimating overhead costs in relation to output, the abosrption costing technique has been strongly criticised by many accountants. The argument is basically whether or not one accepts a cost averaging process. Averaging will inevitably result in some degree of inaccuracy. How wrong the results of the costing process are, will depend on the following:-
  (i) Efficiency of cost collection
  (ii) Efficiency of data processing
  (iii) Fairness of overhead absorption bases
  (iv) Accuracy of budgets for pre-determined absorption rates.

Assuming an ideal for the above factors, then the error arising from the averaging process should be 'acceptable'. However, if there are incorrect overhead absorption rates applied to output, then it can affect management decisions and corporate profits. An efficient department could be recorded as inefficient by the use of unfair overhead absorption rates to such an extent that management may consider taking corrective action where it is not needed. Conversely an inefficient department may be recorded as efficient by incorrect overhead absorption rates.

Corporate profits are affected by stock valuation. The absorption costing technique will include overheads in stock values. If the overhead absorption rate is wrong, the stock valuation will be wrong and consequently the profit figure will be wrong. Of course there are many other areas where profit calculation can be distorted but stock valuation has a direct effect. Consider the following figures:-

Closing Stock Valuation	*Direct Cost*	*Overhead Absorbed*	*Total Cost*	*Net Profit/Loss*
	£	£	£	£
	10,000	6,000	16,000	1,000
+ 20% error absorption rate	10,000	7,200	17,200	2,200
– 20% error absorption rate	10,000	4,800	14,800	(200)

Given a ± 20% error in the abosrption rate, the net income ranges between a profit of £2,200 and a loss of £200.

When considering the inventory valuation problem a decision has to be made regarding what costs are inventoriable? The eligibility of a cost for overhead absorption may be considered as any cost that directly or indirectly contributes to the product. Most companies would include indirect manufacturing costs as eligible but differences of opinion arise as the costs become more indirect. As a broad guideline, the following cost groups are ranked according to their inventoriable eligibility.

Direct costs
- Direct Material
- Direct Labour
- Direct Expenses

Indirect costs - Manufacturing expenses
- General administration expenses
- Financial expenses
- Selling expenses.

It becomes increasingly difficult to justify cost eligibility for stock valuation as the costs move away from manufacturing. Selling expenses are clearly ineligible because they are not even indirectly related to the making of the product. Where the line of cost eligibility for stock valuation is drawn will vary between companies according to circumstances and the opinions of accountants.

5:2 Marginal costing. In the previous sub-section we saw that unit costs were affected by the level of output. Generally speaking, the greater the output the lower the unit cost. The reason for this was that fixed costs were divided up between the number of units. Indeed one of the problems with absorption costing was how to charge the overheads fairly and accurately to production. With marginal costing this problem is avoided by not charging fixed costs to unit output. In marginal costing all costs are classified as either fixed or variable as explained in section 3:3. Then only the variable costs are charged to output. This means that profit per unit cannot be calculated because the total cost per unit will not be known. However, instead of the unit profit calculated under absorption costing, a marginal costing system will produce a *contribution* per unit. The term *contribution*, has a very specific meaning and is calculated by deducting the unit variable cost from the selling price. The contribution each unit makes towards paying the fixed costs is often used as a key figure for price/output type decisions. Two main features of a marginal costing system are:-

(i) the segregration of all costs into fixed and variable elements; and
(ii) the exclusion of all fixed costs from unit cost calculations.

When a marginal costing system is installed, a series of decisions have to be made regarding the variability of every cost element in relation to output. Every cost element that is regarded as fixed is then excluded from a unit cost calculation. Therefore, the valuation of stock and work in progress will only include costs that are considered to vary directly in relation to output. As stock value is a determinant of externally reported net income, there are some important issues relating to the use of marginal costing techniques as a basis for calculating stock values. The principles, practice and problems of stock valuation are explained in chapter 5. At this stage we will just say that marginal costing is not generally recommended for stock valuation purposes. Before looking at marginal costing statements it is worthwhile comparing the differing viewpoints of economists and accountants concerning marginal costs.

5:2:1 The accountants and economists views of marginal costs. The accountant's practical approach is to divide all cost elements into categories of fixed and variable. Where variable costs vary directly in relation to output and fixed costs remain fixed in relation to output. The variable cost of output is also called the marginal cost - hence the term marginal costing. The term marginal costing is synonymous with variable costing. However, there is disagreement over the term direct costing. Some say that direct costing is the same as marginal costing. Strictly speaking this is incorrect. Direct costing is based on the principle of collecting costs that are directly related to a cost centre or cost unit. Whereas marginal costing.principles are based on the variability of a cost in relation to output. For most situations, direct costs are also variable but there could be instances where a direct cost does not vary with output. For example, if one machine is used exclusively for one type of output, all the costs of that machine are directly related to output, but some of the costs, such as depreciation, may be time based and not output based. Therefore, the direct cost is not a variable cost and cannot be called a marginal cost. Consequently, the use of the term 'direct' requires understanding and a little caution. Under marginal costing the term should be mainly limited to direct material and direct labour. When referring to overheads, the terms variable or fixed should be used.

The economist's view of a marginal cost is the change in the total cost of production if output is varied by one unit. Thus the economist's marginal cost would normally be the variable cost per unit. But as production increases there will be an output level where additional fixed costs will be incurred At this output level, the marginal cost of the additional unit would be the unit variable cost plus the additional fixed costs. Consider the following table where fixed costs are £1,000 until production exceeds 1,000 units. then additional fixed costs are incurred of £100. The variable costs remain constant at £10 per unit.

(a) Unit Output	*(b) Fixed Cost*	*(c) Variable Cost per unit (Accountants Marginal Cost)*	*(d) Total Cost b + (cxa)*	*(e) Average Cost d/a*	*(f) Economists Marginal Cost per unit*
Units	£	£	£	£	£
1	1,000	10	1,010	1,010	1,010
100	1,000	10	2,000	20	10
1000	1,000	10	11,000	11	10
1001	1,100	10	11,110	11.1	110
1500	1,100	10	16,100	10.7	10

At an output level of one, the accountant will say the fixed cost is £1,000 and the variable or marginal cost is £10. The economist will say the marginal cost is £1,010 because if the unit was not produced, then £1,010 would be saved. Similarly at an output of 1,000 units if an extra unit is produced, it will cost £100 in fixed costs and £10 in variable cost, giving an economists marginal cost of £110. The accountant's equivalent to the economist's marginal cost is called *incremental costing*. However, incremental cost calculations *do not always relate to one* extra unit. The calculations may be made for a batch, a special order or a specific quantity.

There are some fine distinctions in costing terminology related to marginal costing, therefore it is appropriate to summarise the meaning of some of these terms:-

(a) *Differential costing* often uses marginal costs but is concerned with the cost and income *differences* between alternative courses of action.

(b) *Direct costing* also uses marginal costs but is *concerned with costs that directly* relate to a cost centre or cost unit.

(c) Incremental costing is the same as the economist's marginal cost as explained earlier.
(d) Marginal costing is concerned with the variable costs of production and the marginal cost is sometimes referred to as the cost that can be avoided if the extra unit was not produced. This is basically the same as the incremental cost.
(e) Variable costing refers to costs that tend to vary directly in relation to output.

The most widely used term is marginal costing, even though it may be referring to direct, variable or incremental costing.

5:2:2 Marginal costing statements. The two main types of marginal costing statement are unit statements and total statements. Consider the following data:-

Sales of 1,000 units @ £10 each had related costs of:
1,000 hours of direct labour @ £3.00 per hour
1,000 kilos of direct material @ £2.00 per kilo
Variable expense of £1,000
Production fixed costs of 1,000
Administration costs £500 and selling costs of £500.

The marginal cost statements would be:-

Unit Marginal Cost Statement

		£	£
Selling price			10
Less variable costs:	Direct labour	3	
	Direct Material	2	
	Variable overheads	1	
			6
	Contribution per unit		£ 4

Marginal Cost Statement

		£	£
Sales Revenue			10,000
Less Variable Costs:	Direct Labour (1000x3)	3,000	
	Direct Material (1000 x 2)	2,000	
	Variable Overheads (1000x1)	1,000	6,000
Contribution to fixed costs			4,000
Less: Fixed Costs:	Production	1,000	
	Administration	500	
	Sales	500	
			2,000
Net Profit			£2,000

The key figure in the unit cost statement is the contribution that each unit makes towards paying the fixed costs. It is important that you understand the term contribution because it is an important figure for price and output decision making.

Three uses of marginal costing statements are:
(a) To show the effect of changes in output,
(b) To enable comparisons to be made between cost centres, and

(c) To enable comparisons to be made between products.

Simplified examples of these types of marginal costing statements are shown below:

(a) CHANGES IN OUTPUT

Unit output	*200*	*500*	*1,000*	*1,500*
	£	*£*	*£*	*£*
Sales	2,000	5,000	10,000	15,000
less marginal costs	1,200	3,000	6,000	9,000
Contribution	800	2,000	4,000	6,000
less fixed costs	2,000	2,000	2,000	2,000
Profit (loss)	(1,200)	b/e*	2,000	4,000

* b/e = Break even where total cost = total revenue. Refer to chapter 6.

(b) COST CENTRE COMPARISONS

Department store	*Cost Centre 'A' (clothing)*	*Cost Centre 'B' (furniture)*	*Total*
	£	*£*	*£*
Sales	100,000	400,000	500,000
less marginal costs	66,000	300,000	366,000
Contribution	34,000	100,000	134,000
less fixed costs			100,000
Profit			34,000

(c) PRODUCT COMPARISONS

	Product X	*Product Y*	*Product Z*	*Total*
	£	*£*	*£*	*£*
Sales	10,000	14,000	26,000	50,000
less marginal costs	7,000	13,000	20,000	40,000
Contribution	3,000	1,000	6,000	10,000
less fixed costs				5,000
Profit				5,000

You will have noticed that statements (b) and (c) did not derive cost centre or unit profits. They could be calculated using absorption costing but then the problem of fair and accurate overhead allotment would arise. Marginal costing statements place the emphasis on contribution instead of profit.

5:2:3 Advantages and disadvantages of marginal costing. This system of costing is widely accepted as an aid for decision making in matters such as:

(a) Comparing the relative profitability of products or processes, and

(b) Determining profitability at different levels of output.

Indeed many of the decision making techniques explained in chapter 6, 'Tactical decisions', are applications of marginal costing. It is therefore useful to list the advantages and disadvantages of this important costing system.

Advantages

(a) The simple treatment of fixed costs avoids the complications of overhead absorption explained in section 5:1.

(b) Attention is focused on costs that are more controllable in the short run (Refer to section 3:5).

(c) A 'profit volume' relationship is established that helps with pricing and output decisions.
(d) The 'profit volume' relationship is easily understood when presented graphically in the break even chart (Refer to chapter 6.)
(e) A break even level of output/sales (i.e. where total cost = total revenue) can be calculated that is well known and used by managers.
(f) Pricing decisions using marginal costs tend to follow the principles of relevant costs (Refer to section 3:6) But note the importance of full overhead recovery in the long run.

Disadvantages

(a) Pricing based on marginal costs may mislead managers into prices that will not recover all the overheads in the long run. This is especially important for capital intensive businesses that have high fixed costs and low variable unit costs.
(b) The division of all costs into fixed and variable is, in some instances, arbitary. There will always be a number of cost elements that are semi variable or semi fixed. Moreover, the variability of costs is time based. In the long run almost all costs are variable and in the short run almost all costs are fixed.
(c) Simple marginal costing calculations for sales mixture problems can be misleading unless key factor analysis and linear programming methods are applied (Refer to chapter 6).
(d) Marginal costing is not well suited to one off type jobbing businesses where cost plus pricing is needed because the market value of each individual product would not be known. The cost plus calculation must make an allowance for overheads.
(e) Stock valuation using marginal costing is not recommended for financial accounts. The accounting standard SSAP 9 *(Refer to Volume 1 Financial accounting for non-accountants)* prefers all costs to be included that bring a product to its present condition and location.

5:3 Comparison of marginal and absorption costing. If you have worked through sections 5:1 and 5:2 then you are aware that the main difference between these two costing bases is in their treatment of overheads. Because most costing systems are based on either marginal or absorption principles it is important that we compare them. Although, a costing system can classify data for both marginal and absorption costing, especially if it is computerised. (Refer to section 4:1:2) Let us first work through a simplified example. Assume a business has a homogeneous output and has budgeted for 10,000 units to be produced and sold during the year. The cost data is illustrated in diagram 40.

The overhead absorption rate for this product could be calculated in a number of ways(Refer to section 5:1:1), but we will use a simple method:-

$$\frac{\text{Budgeted overheads}}{\text{Budgeted unit output}} = \frac{£(12{,}000 + 12{,}000)}{10{,}000 \text{ units}} = \underline{\underline{£2.40 \text{ per unit}}}$$

The overhead costs in this calculation have not included the marketing costs of £6,000. This is because these costs are not incurred until the products are sold and therefore cannot be included in the stock values.

DIAGRAM 40 COMPARISON OF MARGINAL & ABSORPTION COSTING

BUDGETED OUTPUT, REVENUE & COSTS FOR 1,000 UNITS

	Total	*Absorption*	*Marginal*
	£	£	£
Direct materials	6,000	0.60	0.60
Direct labour	20,000	2.00	2.00
Direct expenses	4,000	0.40	0.40
Production overhead	12,000	1.20	
Administration overhead	12,000	1.20	
Marketing overhead	6,000		
Profit	20,000		

Using this basic detail the unit cost statements would be:

Marginal Costing			**Absorption Costing**		
	£	£		£	£
Selling price		8	Selling price		8
less variable costs:			less total costs:		
Direct materials	0.60		Direct materials	0.60	
Direct labour	2.00		Direct labour	2.00	
Direct expense	0.40		Direct expense	0.40	
			Overheads	2.40	
Unit stock value		3	*Unit stock value*		5.4
Unit contribution		5	*Unit profit*		2.6

Let us assume that six months later the managing director realises that the sales budget was too optomistic. The company has only sold 2,000 units in six months and sales are not expected to improve during the remainder of the year. In this situation where the actual output/sales is different from the budgeted output/sales, the two costing systems will produce different results. This is shown in the table overleaf that compares marginal and absorption costing.

Statements of estimated profit/loss for the 6 months ending...

Marginal Costing	£	Absorption Costing	£
Sales	16,000	Sales	16,000
less variable costs(2000x3)	6,000	less total costs (2000 x 5.4)	10,800
Contribution	12,000		5,200
less fixed costs *	15,000	less marketing costs*	3,000
Loss	(3,000)	Profit	2,200

(* Assuming all fixed costs are incurred equally throughout the year)

The reason why absorption costing is giving misleading results is because absorption cost calculations are only correct when actual output is the same as the output used for pre-determined overhead absorption rates. In this instance overheads have been under absorbed. This example has assumed sales and production were equal and no stock variations occurred. In reality finished goods stock is the buffer between output and sales. When there is a large difference between production and sales that significantly affects closing stocks then this can make a large difference in the profit calculation. Consider the following example where two identical companies have produced 40,000 units but only sold 10,000 units, thus increasing their closing stocks by 30,000 units. The point to note about the calculations is the effect on the profit and loss account.

Detail

Comparative Unit Cost Statements

Company 'A' *(Marginal costing system)*	£	*Company 'B'* *(Absorption costing system)*	£
Direct material	3	Direct material	3
Direct labour	2	Direct labour	2
Direct expense	1	Direct expense	1
		Overheads	10
Unit stock value	6	*Unit stock value*	16

Assume this is the first year of trading with a nil opening stock and closing stock of 30,000 units. The fixed costs for the year were £250,000 for production, £150,000 for administration and £50,000 for marketing. For company 'B' the administration and production overheads have been absorbed into the unit costs (i.e. £400,000÷40,000 = £10 per unit). The summarised income statements would be as follows:-

Comparative Income Statements

	Company 'A' £000	£000	*Company 'B'* £000	£000
Sales (10,000 x £22)		220		220
less cost of sales:				
Opening stock	—		—	
add costs of manufacture:				
Direct costs (40,000 x 6)	240		240	
Production overhead	250		250	
	490		490	
less closing stock	180		480	

Continued......

		310		10
Gross profit (loss)		(90)		210
less: Administration	150		150	
Marketing	50		50	
		200		200
Net profit (loss)		(290)		10

This simplified example illustrates how two identical companies can have different profit/losses because of the difference in stock valuation methods arising from marginal and absorption costing. The main differences between these two well established costing methods are summarised in the table below.

Marginal costing	Absorption costing
Overheads Fixed costs are considered irrelevant for short run decisions because they are fixed regardless of the level of output within the 'relevant range'	*Overheads* Fixed costs are brought into all calculations on the assumption that they must be recovered
Production/sales differences High production and low sales results in a lower profit for marginal costing than in absorption costing due to lower closing stock valuation. Thus marginal costing tends to be more sales orientated.	*Production/sales differences* Low production and high sales results in a lower profit using absorption costing than in marginal costing due to higher closing stock valuation. Thus absorption costing tends to be more production orientated.
Stock valuation Marginal costing excludes overheads for stock valuation and therefore does not represent the full cost of producing finished goods. This can be misleading with capital intensive businesses	*Stock valuation* Absorption costing includes overheads, except marketing, so that the stock value represents all the costs of getting stock to its current condition and location.
Unit costs Only variable costs are charged to cost units on the principle that fixed costs are time based and should not be charged to output .	*Unit costs* All costs, except selling costs are charged to cost units on the principle that all costs relating to the product should be included in the unit cost.
Costing system Marginal costing is easier to use and understand by managers.	*Costing system* Over and under absorption of over heads are difficult to operate and sometimes difficult for managers to understand.
Price/output decisions Contribution represents a profit/ volume relationship that helps with price and unput calculations. However overhead recovery in the price cannot be ignored in the long run.	*Price/output decisions* Pre-determined overheads prevent a reliable profit/volume relationship being established. However, if the output can be fairly accurately assessed then the overhead absorption rate becomes more useful.

Any costing system that will attempt to cost output can either exclude or include overheads. To exclude overheads based on marginal costing principles clearly aids decision making for pricing output and relative 'profitability' of departments, branches or products because the overhead complication is ignored The problems of marginal costing are that many costs have to be arbitrarily classified as fixed or variable and that their behaviour is not linear in relation to output as break even analysis suggests. (Refer to chapter 9) If overheads are to be included based on the principles of absorption costing then there are problems of accuracy and relevance when alloting overheads to products, processes or departments. Clearly production cannot be undertaken without incurring fixed costs and these fixed costs must be recovered in the long run. Therefore both systems have advantages and disadvantages and it is important that managers using cost information are aware of how it is derived and the limitations of their company's costing system.

5:4 Variance accounting. With variance accounting, data is produced on the planned activities of a business in the form of budgets, standard costs, standard selling prices and standard profit margins based on expected results. This data is then compared with actual results which produces variances. These variances represent the difference between actual results and expected results. The detailed techniques of budgeting control and standard costing are explained in chapters 8 and 9. In this sub - section we will just consider the *principles* of variance accounting to distinguish it from other costing bases and methods.

The distinguishing feature of variance accounting is the use of expected results. This means that variance accounting is an *addition* to other costing bases or methods. For example you can have a costing base of standard marginal or standard absorption. These bases could be applied to methods such as unit costing or process costing. In other words the costing of say a process, could be on an absorption costing basis and then have standard costing added to it by the addition of expected results. The two main techniques of variance accounting are briefly explained in the following sub sections.

5:4:1 Budgeting. A budget is a quantitive plan relating to a future period of time of a policy to be pursued during that period towards stated objectives. This is an important technique for planning and control because in the first instance it requires managers to quantify their plans. Once the plans are quantified then the expected results are used as a performance yardstick against which actual results are compared. The variances (differences between budget and actual figures) then act as a control device to let management know if business activity is proceeding according to plan. Budgetary control is widely used and does not require a sophisticated costing system Budgetary control principles, techniques and applications are explained in chapter 8.

5:4:2 Standard costing. A standard cost is a pre-determined cost that is calculated based on a prescribed set of working conditions that include: technical specifications, material usage and price, labour efficiency and rate and overhead costs in relation to levels of output. You will therefore appreciate that standard costing is very detailed and requires a good cost collection and analysis system so that actual costs can be compared with the standard costs. The comparison of all the detailed standard and actual costs results in long lists of different types of variances that are analysed in a way that highlights areas of high cost and inefficiency. This is called variance analysis and can be a very useful management tool, Standard costing and variance analysis are explained in chapter 9.

5:4:3 Difference between standard costing and budgetary control. The main difference is that standard costing is a unit concept whereby all cost elements are given predetermined costs. Whereas budgeting is a total concept that is used for quantifying plans, co-ordinating business activity and overall control. Both techniques compare expected data with actual data. The two techniques are often linked together in a standard costing budgetary control system. Indeed, some parts of standard costing use budget figures therefore standard costing is almost always linked to budgetary control. But, budgetary control does not need a standard costing system.

5:5 Uniform costing. This is not a separate costing technique but represents a situation where a number of businesses agree to use the same costing principles and practices. It is not pragmatic for companies to have identical costing systems because each costing system should be designed to meet the specific needs of the business it serves. As most businesses are different, it follows that the costing systems will be different. However, it can be useful for a holding company, if its subsidiary companies can agree on common costing principles and practices. The following sub sections briefly look at some of the areas requiring uniform treatment and the advantages and disadvantages of attempting to establish uniform costing.

5:5:1 Areas requiring uniform treatment. Some important matters that need to be considered are detailed below:-
(a) *Classification of accounts* A common system of accounts coding first requires clear definitions of account classifications.(The principles and practice of accounts coding were explained in section 4:2) For example one subsidiary company may include in its labour costs; employers contributions, national insurance and graduated pensions, whilst another subsidiary may treat these as financial items. Clearly, if this situation existed uniform codification would atill not enable labour costs to be compared on a valid basis. When electronic data processing is used for costing in subsidiary companies then uniform codification will certainly help the parent company for centralised planning and control
(b) Treatment of overheads This subject has been covered in sections 5:1, 5:2 and 5:3. After reading these sections you will be aware that it is difficult for a company to establish a fair method of overhead allotment and calculate absorption rates that do not produce misleading results. Accordingly, it is even more difficult for a number of companies to develop a uniform-method for the treatment of overheads, The outcome could very easily be arbitrary methods that distort costing statements. Therefore great caution is needed if overheads are to be treated in a rigid uniform costing framework. The best that could be achieved would probably be an agreement on allotment and absorption principles.
(c) Stock valuation The different techniques fór stock valuation are explained in chapter 5. Even if companies had the same costing base of say, absorption costing, there is still a fairly wide choice of stock valuation methods available. Under most circumstances a comparable and compatible method

of stock valuation could be agreed between subsidiary companies.

(d) Accounting periods It is absurd for subsidiary companies to have different accounting periods. Once the primary period has been agreed for the financial accounts the interim periods of:-

52 separate calendar weeks
13 separate accounting periods of 4 weeks,
12 separate calendar months,
4 separate accounting periods of 13 weeks and/or
2 separate accounting periods of 26 weeks

should be agreed.

(e) Specific costs Because there are alternative methods of treatment for items such as depreciation or research and development a set of uniform costing principles could be agreed for each specific cost where variations in cost treatment are likely to occur.

(f) Cost centres Each company will probably have a slightly different organisation structure therefore it would be difficult to achieve uniformity with cost centres. However, wherever organisational similarities exist then there is no reason why some kind of agreement cannot be reached on uniform cost centre definitions for specific areas.

(g) Cost reports Companies develop their own internal reporting styles based on management needs and the opinions of accountants. In some instances the latter is the sole reason for the existence and style of a particular report. Discussions between accountants in subsidiary companies with a view to establishing a uniform style of cost reporting would probably improve the general level of reporting in the group.

5:5:2 Advantages and disadvantages of uniform costing. The main advantages of uniform costing are as follows:-

(a) *Comparability.* When subsidiary companies are sufficiently similar in the nature of their operations for comparisons to be made, then uniform costing enables valid cost comparisons to be undertaken. Without some degree of uniform costing the parent company needs to be very careful when making subsidiary company comparisons.

(b) *Staff mobility.* Administrative uniformity within subsidiary companies enables staff to work in any company at fairly short notice without needing additional training. The group is therefore in a better position to quickly help with temporary staff problems in a subsidiary company.

(c) *Data processing.* The high costs of software may be shared between subsidiaries if uniform costing is adopted.

(d) *Cost savings.* Standardised form design for input documentation etc. can be printed in larger print runs thus reducing unit print costs. There may also be savings with centralised training facilities for staff in subsidiary companies that are using a uniform costing system.

(e) *Centralised costing.* If the parent company wishes to centralise all planning and control then uniform costing enables cost data to be collected from subsidiaries, analysed and then comparative cost reports sent to each subsidiary.

The main disadvantages of uniform costing are:-

(a) *Rigidity.* Sometimes a uniform costing system imposed on a company prevents the flexibility that is necessary for good local planning, decision making and control. Costing systems should be designed to meet the information

needs of managers. A uniform system may not meet all their needs.

(b) *Costs.* The set up costs can be very high especially: software conversion, form design changes, training and data file adjustments.

(c) *Risk.* If uniform costing is not properly discussed, designed, agreed and implemented there is some risk of data corruption and an arbitrary uniform costing system replacing efficient individual systems.

5:6 Unit costing This method of costing can be applied where specific units of output are measurable and identical. The technique is quite simple being the application of the following formula:-

$$\frac{\text{Cost (a)}}{\text{Number of units (b)}}$$

(a) *Cost* may be defined as the total cost under absorption costing principles or the variable costs as used with marginal costing. In most circumstances it will be the total cost based on actual output for an accounting period.

(b) *Number of units* will be directly related to the costs for the level of output during a specified accounting period.

5:6:1 Defining the cost unit. Great care is needed when defining cost units. For example, if a factory produced refridgerators the cost units may be defined as the standard model or de luxe model at each different cubic capacity. There may be ten or more cost units even though every one is a refridgerator. Where the unit of output is small in terms of cost such as bricks or nuts and bolts the cost unit may be in hundreds or by the gross (144). Cost units can become esoteric. For example, a 'baker's dozen' may be defined as a cost unit of 13 loaves and a printer may refer to a ream of paper being 516 sheets which is 20 quires or 480 sheets plus an allowance for waste. The important point is that everyone should know what the cost unit represents.

5:7 Process costing. In the previous section we looked at a costing method for homegeneous specific units of output. There are however a number of industries that have a continuous flow of a homogeneous product from manufacturing processes such as oil, paint, ink, food, chemicals. plastics and paper. Companies in these types of industries often use process costing. The characteristics of process costing are illustrated in diagram 41 below.

DIAGRAM 41 PRINCIPLES OF PROCESS COSTING

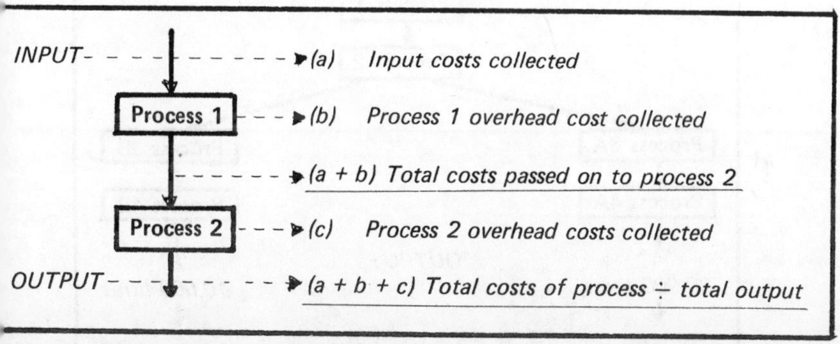

Basically, process costing divides production into its separate processes and treats each process as a cost centre. Each cost centre is charged with its share of overheads and the costs collected in the cost centre are charged to production as it passes through the process. As an illustration we will introduce some cost data into the two stage process shown in diagram 41. We will assume that there is no loss or wastage in either process and 10,000 kilos of 'X' are produced.

Simplified Process Cost Statement

		£	£
Raw materials			15,000
Process 1	Direct labour	10,000	
	Direct materials	1,000	
	Direct expense	1,000	
	Overhead for time period	13,000	
			25,000
Process 2	Direct labour	20,000	
	Direct materials	2,000	
	Direct expense	1,000	
	Overheads for time period	7,000	
			30,000
Total cost for 10,000 kilos of 'X'			70,000

Therefore cost per kilo = £7.00

This example has avoided all the practical complications that can occur in process costing , such as work in progress, material mixtures, process yields and overhead absorption. But there are two aspects of process costing that need to be explained; joint costing and by product costing.

5:7:1 Joint costing. This arises when a process automatically produces more than one product. For example the processing of crude oil will usually result in several products being jointly produced. The costing principles are basically the same as process costing but there is the complication of valuing the process output at the separation stage. Consider the following simplified example that is illustrated in diagram 42 where a production process results in two separate chemicals being produced from an input of a single raw material.

DIAGRAM 42 PRINCIPLES OF JOINT COSTING

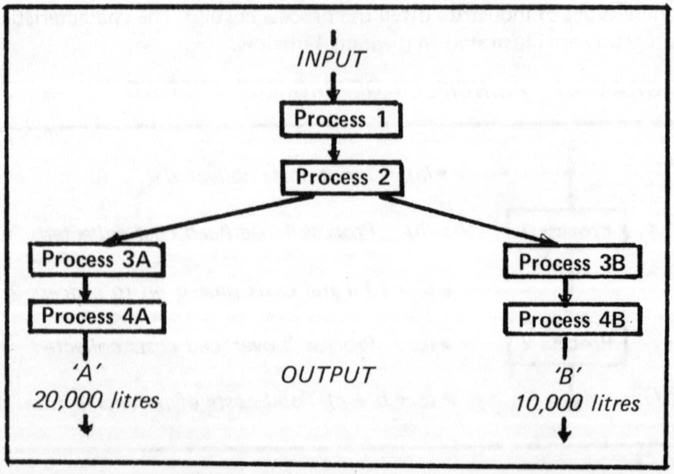

Simplified Joint Costing Statement

	£	£
Raw materials		20,000
Costs from process 1	30,000	
Costs from process 2	50,000	80,000
Total costs up to separation point		100,000

Separation	Process 'A' (60%)	Process 'B' (40%)
	£	£
Input from process 2	60,000	40,000
Costs from process 3	10,000	20,000
Costs from process 4	10,000	10,000
Total costs for 20,000 litres of 'A' and 10,000 litres of 'B'	£80,000	£70,000
Therefore cost per litre =	*£4.00*	*£7.00*

Clearly a useful costing of chemical 'A' or 'B' is dependent on a valid basis of cost apportionment at the separation point. The bases for apportioning costs at the separation stage may be made on:-

(a) *Selling price relationship* where the most expensive product is charged with more costs. In the above example we can assume that chemical 'A' can sell for £12 per litre and chemical 'B' £8 per litre. Thus the apportionment would be:

Chemical A $\frac{12}{20}\% = 60\%$ Chemical B $\frac{8}{20}\% = 40\%$

(b) *Physical relationships* where the apportionment is made on weight or volume. In the example we could assume that at the separation point 30,000 litres were required by process 'A' and 20,000 litres by process 'B'. Thus the apportionment would be:-

Chemical A $\frac{30}{50}\% = 60\%$ Chemical B $\frac{20}{50}\% = 40\%$

(c) *Market value* at the point where the process is divided can be a fair method of apportionment. In this example if the 50,000 litres were worth say £2.00 per litre then process 'A' that used 30,000 litres would be charged £60,000 an process 'B' using 20,000 litres would be charged £40,000.

5:7:2 By-product costing. During a production process there is sometimes an additional output of relatively low value which is treated as waste, scrap or as a by-product. If this by-product of the main process is sold, then the revenue can be added to the revenue from the main process. Sometimes it is worthwhile for a company to pass the by-product through a separate process. When this is done, the by-product process costs can be deducted from the by-product revenue and the net figure added to the revenue from the main process. There are several other methods of treating by-product costs and revenues but generally speaking they are either treated separately or added in to the main process.

5:8 Output costing. When an enterprise produces only one kind of product (with a few grades) such as a brewery, a mine, quarry or a cement manufacturer, then this simple method of costing may be used. The basic principle is to total all the costs and divide by the related output. The system may get a little more complicated if the different grades of the product are to be treated on joint costing principles. But in general, output costing is not a complex technique.

5:9 Costing of non-manufacturing organisations. There exists a very wide range of business activity that cannot be classified as manufacturing. For our purposes we will divide the non-manufacturing sector into three areas: services, merchandising, and miscellaneous. Whatever the nature of the enterprise it is always possible to undertake some form of costing. The costing method will still have the three main stages of: data collection, analysis and reporting and will be based on either absorption or marginal principles. There could also be some form of variance accounting in a budgetary control system and the enterprise may have to conform to centralised uniform costing requirements. You will therefore appreciate that costing of non- manufacturing operations will still follow basic costing principles. The methods will differ according to the needs of the organisation, but the costing bases remain the same. *The major costing problem for non-manufacturing businesses is to define a cost unit that represents what is being sold.*

The principles explained in the previous sub-section on manufacturing homogeneous output can also be applied to non-manufacturing homogeneous output in areas such as the extractive industries, transport and some services. This is sometimes referred to as operation costing. In the following sub-sections we will consider these principles and some of the problems of designing a costing system that meets the specific requirements of non-manufacturing businesses.

5:9:1 Services The cost unit for most services is usually based on labour hours because it is skilled labour that is being sold and not a product. The best examples of services costing are probably in accountancy practices. The client is invoiced according to the time spent by each grade of labour multiplied by their relevant charging rate. For instance a company requiring auditing, accounting and taxation services may have accumulated the following costs:—

	£
Junior articled clerks 160 hours @ £3.00	480.00
Senior articled clerk 40 hours @ £5.00	200.00
Audit senior 4 hours @ £12.00	48.00
Taxation specialist 6 hours @ £20.00	120.00
Partner 2 hours @ £30.00	60.00
Charged to client account	£908.00

The client's account would also be charged with any costs that can be specifically identified to the work. For example: if the audit team needed to travel and stay in a local hotel these costs would be directly chargeable to the client's account.

To operate this kind of costing system requires attention to detail for cost and time allocation. Every member of staff has a charging rate and is required to complete a daily time sheet so that costs can be apportioned and/or allocated. Where costs and time cannot be charged direct to a client's account they need to be charged to a department or cost centre. The accumulated costs in these cost centres then need to be recovered through apportionment to clients' accounts.

Deriving an appropriate charging rate for each grade of labour is, in principle, quite straight forward, but in practice may be very difficult. Consider the following simplified example.

EXAMPLE

A management consultancy has the following labour capacity structure:—

Labour grade	*Total hours per annum*	*Gross Salary*
Partner A	1,728	£21,000
Partner B	1,728	£14,000
Assistant A	1,862	£7,000
Assistant B	1,862	£7,000

The partners have estimated that their total costs not directly chargeable to client accounts for the next year will be £50,000. This figure includes costs such as rent, rates, power, telephone, administration and the secretary's salary. Their before tax profit target for the next year is £30,000.

To recover the fixed costs, salaries and achieve the profit target, they have made the following calculations for their charging rates:—

	£
Total costs	50,000
Salaries	49,000
Profit required	30,000
Total amount to be recovered in charging rate	£129,000

Grade of labour	*Labour rate ratio*	x *hours available*	= *total hours*
Partner A	3:1	1,728	5,184
Partner B	2:1	1,728	3,456
Assistant A	1:1	1,862	1,862
Assistant B	1:1	1,862	1,862
			12,364

Basic rate $\frac{£129{,}000}{12{,}364} = £10.4335$

Charging rate per hour

Partner A	(10,4335 x 3)	£31.30
Partner B	(10.4335 x 2)	£20.87
Assistant A	(10.4335 x 1)	£10.43
Assistant B	(10.4335 x 1)	£10.43

The example has avoided all the complications that would usually be associated with this type of calculation, such as accurately estimating future costs, and hours to be worked. However, charging rates are calculated by many service companies and the basis of the calculations will tend to be the same as illustrated in this example. In addition to the calculation complications, the charging rate system can create organisational difficulties and personnel problems. A high charging rate may be considered as an indication of importance to the organisation instead of value to the client. Moreover, individuals may resent a large difference between their charging rates and salary rates. Accordingly, great care is necessary when designing such a costing system, because arithmetic accuracy is not the only criterion.

5:9:2 Merchandising This term is being used to describe any non-manufacturing business that is buying and selling products. It is a very large area of commercial activity that includes: retailing, wholesaling, importing, exporting and agency work. The primary concern of any merchandising operation is margin control. This is not a simple matter of just the difference between buying and selling prices. The following factors need to be considered:—

(a) The range of product margins from 'special offer' products to luxury slow moving items.
(b) The volume sales of specific products.
(c) The competition
(d) Market trends
(e) Cost trends
(f) Product mix including complementary and competing products.
(g) Discount policy for quantity, cash, advance orders and regular orders.
(h) Delivery costs of specific products
(i) Storage costs of specific products
(j) Selling costs of specific products.

The gross margin arising from the sale of each product provides a contribution towards paying the storage, administration, selling and other costs of running the business. Thus costing for merchandising operations can be broadly divided into two categories: *margin control and cost control.* The function of margin control is to maximise the total contribution from buying and selling through pricing and marketing strategies. Whereas, the function of cost control is to minimise the costs of efficiently running the business through some form of budgetary control system and efficiency ratio measurements. (Refer to Volume 1 *Financial accounting for non-accountants* for efficiency ratios).

5:9:3 Miscellaneous There are many non-manufacturing businesses that do not fit into the merchandising and services categories. For example: agriculture, transport and the extractive industries. For these type of businesses it is not usually difficult to identify and measure the cost unit. With agriculture it may be the yield per acre, for transport it may be passenger/miles or ton/miles and for the extractive industries some form of weight/yield. Unlike the services' companies, the cost unit is often tangible and measureable. Thus with this kind of non-manufacturing business costing systems can be designed in the same way as manufacturing costing systems. Consider the following example.

Example

A small transport business with two ten ton delivery vehicles has estimated its costs for the next year to be:

	£
Indirect wages and administration	20,000
Other costs	10,000
Total fixed costs	£30,000

The variable costs of fuel, tyres, servicing etc. have been estimated as £1.00 per mile.

Based on past experience and the future order book, mileage is expected to be 50,000 per vehicle, and for half of this mileage the vehicles are expected to be empty. The director has a target profit figure of £20,000 for the year and calculates the charging rate as follows:—

Calculation of ton/mile costs	£
Total fixed costs	30,000
Total variable costs (25,000 x 2 x £1.00)	50,000
Required profit	20,000
Total revenue required	£100,000

Charging based on estimated 25,000 miles carrying 10 tons require a ton/mile charging rate of £0.40 (i.e. £100,000 250,000 ton/miles).

Let us now apply this charging rate to a delivery run for a customer that starts with a full load for 150 miles off-loads 6 tons and on loads 2 tons. Then another 80 miles and off-loads 4 tons. A further 90 miles to off-load the last two tons and then an empty run of 70 miles back to the depot. The Calculations would be as follows:–

Delivery	*distance*	x	*weight*	=	*ton/miles*
First	150		10		1,500
Second	80		6		480
Third	90		2		180
Return	70		0		0
Total					2,160

The delivery run would therefore be costed as 2,160 x 0.40 = £864.00

5:10 Job costing When a business produces a product to meet a customer's special requirements (i.e. a one off job), then some form of job costing is necessary to ensure the price is above the total job costs. Engineering and printing businesses are often asked to produce 'one off jobs' in addition to their regular production runs. Therefore a separate costing system is needed. Job costing is simply the totalling of all the costs related to a specific job. Most job costing systems are based on one document called the *'job card'*. The job card provides a record of material usage, labour time, machine time and time spent by different departments. This key document is identified by a job number that is used as an authority on stores issue documents, labour time sheets and departmental overhead apportionment records. The principles of a job costing system are illustrated in the following example:–

Example

A printer has been asked to produce 10,000 A.5 16-page booklets, centre fold, wire stitched, from supplied art work. The completed job card is shown below:–

JOB CARD	**Order No.**089712....... **Job No.**381..........
Customer	XYZ Booklet Publisher, Station Road, London.
Job Description	10,000 A.5 16-page booklets, centre fold, wire stitched, single colour, A/W supplied
MATERIAL USAGE	8 negatives and plates 40,000 sheets A.4 80 gsm bond 20,000 staples
LABOUR TIME	Machine setter 1 hour Machine minder 10 hours Collating/folding/stapling machine operater 6 hours
MACHINE TIME	Platemaking ½hour Printing 10 hours Finishing 6 hours
SERVICE DEPARTMENTS' TIME	Administration 2 hours Packaging 1 hour

The completed job card was then passed to the accounts department for cos
ing. The job cost schedule is shown below:—

JOB COST SCHEDULE **Order No.** 089712 **Job No.** 381

Customer XYZ Booklet Publisher, Station Road, London.

Job description 10,000 A.5 16-page booklets, centre fold, wire stitched, single colour, A/W supplied.

Material costs	£	£
8 negatives and plates	24.00	
40,000 sheets A.4 80 gsm	200.00	
20,000 staples	10.00	
Miscellaneous materials, ink, etc.	20.00	
		254.00
Labour costs		
Machine setter 1 hour @ £8.00 per hour	8.00	
Machine minder 10 hours @ £4.00 per hour	40.00	
Finishing machine operator 6 hours @ £4.00 per hour	24.00	
		72.00
Overheads		
Darkroom 0.5 hours @ £10.00 per hour	5.00	
Printroom 10 hours @ £6.00 per hour	60.00	
Finishing department 6 hours @ £5.00 per hour	30.00	
Administration 2 hours @ £12.00 per hour	24.00	
Packaging 1 hour @ £5.00 per hour	5.00	
		124.00
Total job cost		£450.00

The example has shown how labour, material and overhead costs are charge to a specific job based on the data provided in the job card. Most job costing systems will be based on absorption costing, therefore some system of pre-dete mined overhead absorption rates need to be calculated. (Refer to section 5:1:2

5:11 Contract costing This type of costing is similar to job costing because it i used for 'one off' type jobs. The distinction is that contract costing is generall used for jobs that take a long while to complete. For example the constructior industry tends to use contract costing for civil engineering work such as buildin roads, bridges or industrial estates. One of the features of a contract costing system is that most labour and material costs are easily identified as belonging to a contract. Indeed when materials are ordered they are specifically identifie by the contract number and direct labour is often engaged or sub-contracted fc specific contracts. Even plant and machinery is sometimes separately leased fo each contract. The most common contract costing method is to open up separ ate contract accounts for each contract. All costs are debited to their related contract account in some form of columnar analysis. Thus the cost accumulation and analysis aspects of contract costing pose few problems. Each contract account is a form of trading account that accumulates all the costs and revenue relating to a contract providing a contract profit or loss figure. There are however a few problems:—

(a) Calculating and agreeing stage payments.
(b) Assessing the profit on incomplete contracts at the end of a financial accounting period.
(c) Retention monies.

These contract costing complications are explained in the following notes.

5:11:1 Stage payments It is customary with long time period contracts for the negotiations to agree a number of stage payments to be made at certain stages of the work. With construction contracts each stage payment is usually based on an *'architect's certificate'*. These certificates normally detail work that has been completed satisfactorily and authorise the company to invoice a stage payment based on a proportion of the contract price. From a cash flow viewpoint *(Refer to Volume 3 Finance for the non-accountant)* these stage payments are extremely important.

5:11:2 Profit on incomplete contracts The accounting standard on the valuation of stocks and work in progress, SSAP 9 *(Refer to Volume 1 Financial accounting for non-accountants)* allows a profit to be taken on incomplete long term contracts.

"The amount to be reflected in the year's profit and loss account will be the appropriate proportion of this total profit by reference to the work done to date, less any profit already taken up in prior years. The estimated outcome of a contract which extends over several accounting years will nearly always vary in the light of changes in circumstances and for this reason the result of the year will not necessarily represent the proportion of the total profit on the contract which is appropriate to the amount of work carried out in the period: it may also reflect the effect of changes in circumstances during the year which affect the total profit estimated to accrue on completion". *(SSAP 9)*

The accountant has some discretion on the amount of profit to be taken up each year from incomplete long term contracts. However, the accounting convention of conservatism is usually applied to the apparent profit on incomplete long term contracts by applying some form of reducing formula such as:—

$$\tfrac{3}{4} \text{ of apparent profit } \times \frac{\text{Cash received}}{\text{Value of work certified}}$$

EXAMPLE

The following figures summarise the position of contract 123 at the end of the financial year:—

	£
Value of contract	200,000
Value of work certified during the accounting period	60,000
Cost of work done during the accounting period	30,000
Apparent profit for the accounting period	30,000
Cash received (£60,000 – £10,000 retention money)	50,000

Calculation of contract profit to be taken to the Profit and Loss Account

$$30{,}000 \times 0.75 \left(\frac{50{,}000}{60{,}000}\right) = \underline{\underline{£18{,}750}}$$

5:11:3 Retention money It is quite common for construction contracts to have a retention money clause. The purpose of this clause is to indemnify the customer for the rectification of faulty work. For example, if six months after a building had been completed and paid for, some structural faults occurred due to the contractor's negligence, then payment for correcting the defects would be deducted from the retention money. Thus there are three important points to note about a retention clause:–

(a) The amount of retention money.
(b) The time period it will be retained.
(c) The reasons for non-payment when the time period has elapsed.

With large contracts it is not difficult for a customer to find many points of detail that require rectification and then deducting the costs from the retention money. Accordingly, it is prudent to exclude retention money from contract profit calculations until it is actually paid.

5:12 Batch costing The term 'batch' is used to describe a quantity of identical cost units such as a specific size of nuts, bolts or screws. The batch may be produced for stock to be issued for a variety of production processes, or produced to meet a customer's requirements. A batch is costed in the same way job costing by accumulating all the related costs. The total batch cost is then divided by the number of units in the batch to derive a unit cost.

Example

An engineering company has just completed an order from a boat builder for 10,000 stainless steel 0.25" x 2" Unified thread bolts and 10,000 0.25" Unified thread nuts. The cost sheet is summarised below:–

BATCH 191 10,000 Stainless Steel 0.25" x 2" Unified thread bolts		
		£
Direct materials		400
Direct labour		200
Overheads		100
	Total cost	£700

BATCH 192 10,000 Stainless Steel 0.25" Unified thread nuts		
		£
Direct materials		100
Direct labour		200
Overheads		100
	Total cost	£400

The total costs to produce the 10,000 nuts and bolts are analysed below:–

	Total cost	*Unit cost*
	£	£
Bolts	700	0.07
Nuts	400	0.04
Nuts and bolts	£1,100	£0.11

6 Costing systems

All businesses at some time will have to undertake some form of costing. For the very small business the costing procedures are likely to be ad hoc. But as the business grows there will be a stage when the costing procedures will become formalised. But when a costing system has been developed to meet the specific needs of a particular business it may still have to be revised to meet the changing needs of decision makers. It is therefore appropriate that we look at costing from a systems viewpoint. Every costing system can normally be divided into four stages: data collection, recording, analysis and presentation. These four stages are treated separately in the following sub sections.

6:1 Data collection The main sources of cost data are from:—

Suppliers' invoices
Payroll and time sheets
Production records
Stores records

From these few sources the volume of cost data can be very large and complex. The design of the costing system should therefore ensure that all cost data is collected accurately. From an organisation viewpoint the costing department will require co-operation from other departments in the business for its data collection. If the costing department creates burdensome data collection procedures for other departments then probably not all the data will be collected. This is especially true for stores issues when a costing department requires excessive paperwork to be completed.

6:2 Data recording The principles and practice of recording cost data were explained earlier in this chapter in section 4. The main points were:—

(i) The book-keeping system There are two important decisions here: memorandum or double entry records and the level of integration with the financial accounts.

(ii) The coding system for recording data. Most coding systems are numeric.

(iii) The use of electronic data processing With the falling costs of hardware and improvements in software packages few new costing systems will be developed for manual data processing. Accordingly, the data collection (input documents) and recording (coding of data) need to be designed for EDP applications.

(iv) The integration of cost data with other business information in a common data base. (Refer to sub section 4:1:2);

6:3 Analysis of data Cost data can be broadly analysed in a wide variety of ways that have been explained in sections 3:1 to 3:7 and 5:1 to 5:12 in this chapter. For analysis purposes the coding system has to identify:—

(i) The cost element (Refer to sub section 2:1)
(ii) The nature of the cost (Refer to sub section 3:1)
(iii) The control function of the cost (Refer to sub section 3:2, 3:5, 5:4)
(iv) The decision making function of the cost. (Refer to sub sections 3:3, 3:4, 3:6, 5:1, 5:2, 5:3, 5:6 to 5:12).

Clearly, for cost data to be analysed for a variety of planning, decision making and control functions the coding system must enable the same cost data to be sorted in a number of different ways. Although this is mainly a problem for systems analysts, managers need to have a clear idea *why* they require cost information, so that the analysts are given clear systems' objectives.

6:4 Presentation of cost information An efficient, accurate and reliable costing system is of no use to a manager if he/she cannot understand the output and misinterprets or ignores the information. To ensure costing information is understood and used by managers three matters need to be considered:–

(i) The costing system should be 'user friendly'
(ii) Management training
(iii) Management acceptance.

These three aspects of presenting costing information are discussed in the following sub sections.

6:4:1 'User friendly' costing systems Some costing systems are remarkably hostile to their end users, making no concessions for lack of accounting knowledge and overwhelming the recipient with data. If some systems analysts and accountsnts are not firmly controlled they will probably present cost information that suits their needs and expect the end user to adjust. 'Friendly systems' adjust to the user, whereas 'hostile systems' expect the user to ad just to the system. However, 'hostile systems' are not necessarily the result of single minded accountants and systems analysts. Often managers have few clear ideas what they want from a costing system and are not prepared to genuinely participate in the system's design. Under these circumstances it is difficult for accountants and analysts to produce a valid costing system. Let us consider two general characteristics of a user friendly costing system.

(i) The system needs to be capable of answering questions immediately such as: How much has product X cost, contract Y cost, batch 921 cost, etc? In addition to providing historic cost data the system should also be capable of giving cost estimates such as: How much to produce 10,000 items of Z and what would the break even point be if they were sold at £Y each, etc?

(ii) The costing system should also be able to produce regular cost reports for control purposes comparing actual expenditure with planned expenditure. The reports would have a simplified summary page with detailed back up pages.

These general characteristics meet the two management information requirements for planning/decision making and control. The interactive part of the system is mainly for planning/decision making and the regular output from the costing system, for control. A hostile costing system will tend to produce a regular 'data dump' and expect the user to sort the data for planning and control purposes.

6:4:2 Management training To use costing information effectively for planning and control a manager needs to acquire some knowledge on costing tech niques and their applications. In addition to a general knowledge of costing and management accounting the manager also needs to fully understand the specific information flows that exist in his/her organisation. Thus there are two aspects of management education concerning costing systems: general knowledge about costing and management accounting, and specific knowledge about a company's management information flows. A manager cannot be expected to use cost information correctly if he/she does not have this knowledge. Accordingly, management training is an integral part in the design of a costing system.

6:4:3 Management acceptance If managers do not accept the validity, accur acy and/or usefulness of a costing system then there is little justification for the system to exist. A costing system exists to serve management, if management do not accept the system then there is no valid reason for its existence. The responsibility for the validity of a costing system ultimately rests with top management. For example, it is not uncommon in some companies for budgetary control to become a useless annual ritual where planned figures for the coming year are agreed then lost and/or forgotten until 12 months later. (Refer to chapter 8) Whereas in other companies budgets are key documents that all managers are aware of. This difference in attitude to wards cost data is created by top management. If the directors believe in costing systems then they will ensure that the systems provide the information service that their managers need. If senior management accept the validity of costing systems and attempt to understand and use them, then the systems' acceptance will pass down the scalar chains.

7 Summary

This chapter has covered a large and very detailed area of accountancy that contains a lot of important terminology. For instance, every manager should be aware of the difference between say; fixed and variable costs or marginal and absorption costing. An understanding of many of these basic costing terms is necessary before any further study is undertaken on management accounting techniques and their applications. Thus this chapter has explained in some detail, most of the basic cost ing terminology that the non-accountant is likely to encounter at work. In addition to explaining costing detail, an attempt has been made to place each costing technique in a general framework. For example the distinctions between cost elements, cost classifications, costing bases and costing systems have been illustrated in diagrams. Diagram 30 shows how the different cost elements make up the total cost. Then diagram 32 illustrates the different ways costs are classified and provides section references for each cost classification. Diagram 37 is probably the most important, because it shows a broad structure of costing with section references for most of the chapter. This diagram is intended to provide an overview of costing for the non-accountant and enable the interrelationship of costing classifications, bases and methods to be understood. Once this general framework of basic costing is known then the many different costing terms will be far easier to understand.

Accountancy Quiz No.3.

1. Explain the following terms:–

Cost element *(2:1)*
Cost centre *(2:2)*
Cost unit *(2:3)*

2. Define the following cost classifications:–

Fixed and variable costs *(3:3)*
Direct and indirect costs *(3:4)*
Controllable and non controllable costs *(3:5)*
Relevant and irrelevant costs *(3:6)*

3. What is absorption costing? *(5:1, 5:1:1, 5:1:2, 5:1:3, 5:1:4)*

4. Explain the difference between the accountant's and economist's views of marginal costs. *(5:2, 5:2:1, 5:2:2, 5:2:3)*

5. Compare the advantages and disadvantages of marginal and absorption costing. *(5:3)*

6. What is variance accounting? *(5:4, 5:4:1, 5:4:2, 5:4:3)*

7. Explain when, where and why uniform costing should be used. *(5:5, 5:5:1, 5:5:2)*

8. Explain three different types of costing system that may be used for a manufacturing company producing homogeneous output. *(5:6, 5:7, 5:8)*

9. What would be the main factors determining the design of a costing system for a non-manufacturing organisation? *(5:9, 5:9:1, 5:9:2, 5:9:3)*

10. Describe three different types of costing system that may be used for a company producing hetrogeneous output. *(5:10, 5:11, 5:11:1, 5:11:2, 5:11:3, 5:12)*.

4 Labour Management

Objective
To provide an overview of labour management that shows where accountancy inter-relates with other subjects such as personnel management and industrial relations.

Content

Labour Management

1. Introduction

The title and size of this chapter provide a clear indication of a broad approach to the subject. Therefore the reader is advised not to attempt working through the entire chapter in one sitting. There is an enourmous amount of detail that has been included for reference purposes. The accounting content is confined mainly to sections on wage payment systems, human asset accounting and disclosure of information for collective bargaining. (Disclosure of information direct to employees is covered in *Volume 1 - Financial accounting for non accountants*) Because of the importance of this subject, which probably should have been a completely separate book, it seemed inadequate to examine just the accounting part of labour management. The chapter is therefore divided into four major sections:-

Labour administration, labour remuneration, organised labour and labour planning

The last two major sections cover some controversial areas and the reader may not entirely agree with the author's approach to the subject. However, they are subjects that must be discussed objectively regardless of the strong views on this topic that may be held by the reader. Organised labour can and does play an active role in labour management. Accordingly, the matter needs to be taken into consideration in the development of a labour management policy.

With regard to the final section on labour planning, it is self evident that capital tends to replace labour. Therefore the capital/labour equation is part of the labour planning function and needs to be incorporated into a labour management policy.

Before getting into the detail, let us first take a brief macro view of UK employment trends. Diagram 43 below, shows the widening gap between the working population and the employed labour force. It is outside the scope of this book to

DIAGRAM 43 UK EMPLOYMENT TRENDS 1970 - 1980

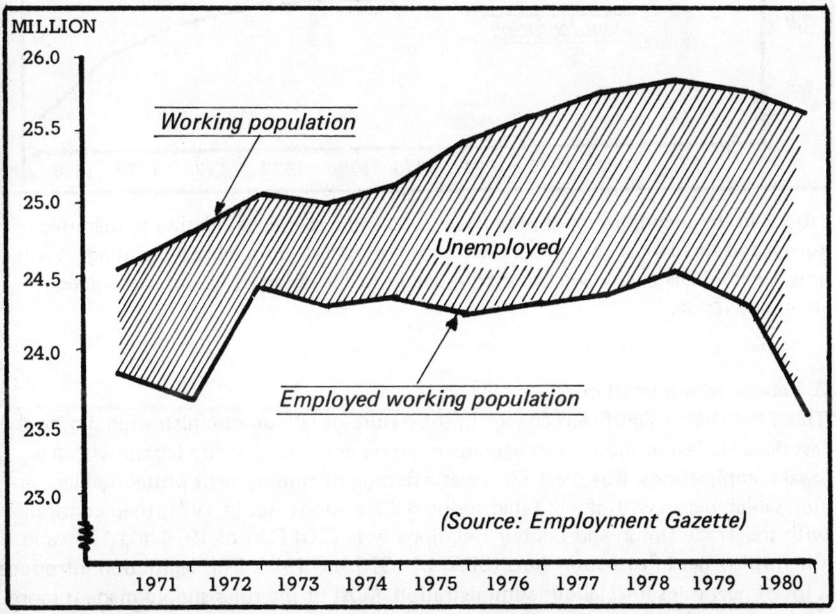

enter into a discussion on the social, economic and political consequences of this situation. Our concern here is with labour management in an enterprise. However, a large and sustained pool of unemployed labour will certainly influence corporate labour policies with regard to: labour planning, remuneration levels and the role of organised labour.

Another macro aspect that is worth considering, is the structural change in UK employment that has occurred over the last decade. Diagram 44 shows how there has been a substantial shift in employment away from manufacturing. This shift can be attributed to factors such as capital replacing labour and the strength of foreign competition. Whatever the reason, the trends indicate that a large proportion of

DIAGRAM 44 UK EMPLOYMENT IN MANUFACTURING 1970 - 1980

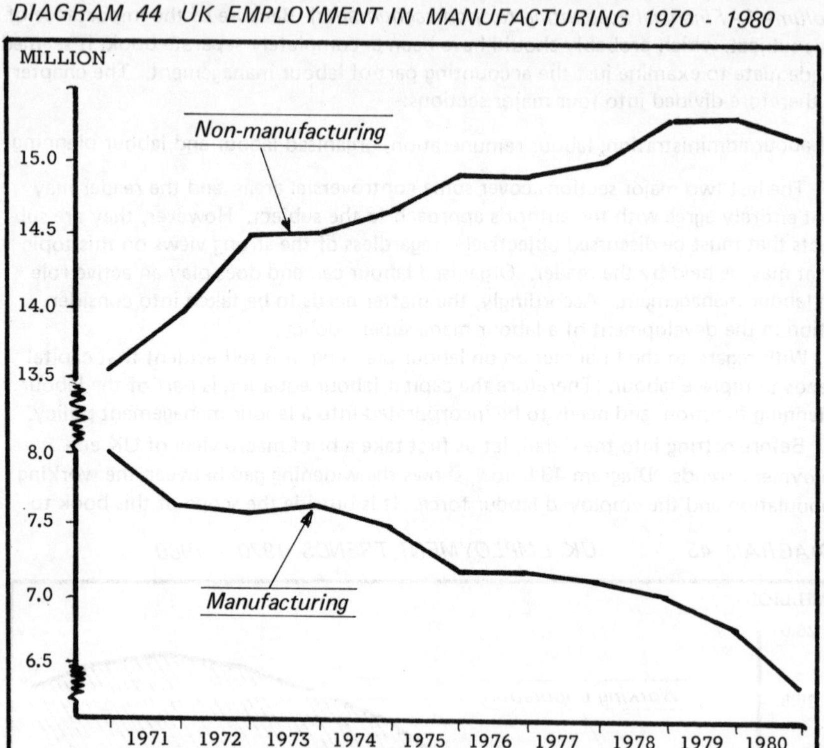

labour in the unemployment pool have skills and experience relating to manufacturing and this factor should be taken into consideration in labour planning. With this general background we can now move in to the detail of labour management in an enterprise.

2. Labour administration

There has been a significant change in the nature of labour administration during the last decade. Ten or more years ago an employer could hire or fire labour with few legal complications. But the 1970's was a decade of employment protection legislation which began with the ill fated Industrial Relations Act in 1971, then continued with the Trade Union and Labour Relations Acts (TULRA) of 1974 and 1976 and the Employment Protection Acts (EPA) of 1975 and 1978. This legislation introduced a lot of new rules into labour administration. Most of the rules simply made it more difficult and expensive to dismiss an employee. Because of these new rules, employers had to revise their recruitment, employment and dismissal procedures. To remove an employee can be an expensive process, therefore a lot more care is now necessary at the recruitment stage to ensure that there is a genuine job vacancy and that the right person is selected for the job.

In the first part of this section we will be briefly reviewing some of the procedures for personnel selection and related legal requirements. Once job applicants have become employees, then there are a number of employment procedures that need to be established and these are explained in the second part of this section. For instance, it is now fairly common for employees to be engaged on a trial basis called a probationary period. Also a company has to care for the health and safety of all employees and where necessary provide training and education. Employees now have many legal rights, and these should be allowed for in labour adminstrative procedures. The sub sections on dismissal explain a three stage warning procedure and provide examples of fair and unfair dismissals. Another sub-section distinguishes between dismissal and redundancy and explains some of the redundancy rules.

Labour administration is clearly a complex and specialised function requiring a manager to have a sound knowledge of labour law, industrial tribunals and some industrial relations experience. In most companies, this specialised function is undertaken by a personnel department industrial relations or labour relations department. The following brief review of the subject has been provided as a guide for the non-specialist and also to show where labour administration fits into the labour management framework.

2:1 Recruitment procedures The hiring of an employee is a remarkably complex matter when compared with the acquisition of other factors of production. Firstly there is no standard specification where you can be certain what you are buying. Secondly, employees can create control difficulties and thirdly, an employer faces a wide range of moral, social and legal responsibilities. Accordingly, the hiring of employees requires a set of recruitment procedures that satisfy legal requirements and provide a selection process that ensures the right person is recruited for the job In the following sub-sections we will briefly examine the principles of personnel selection and some of the legal requirements relating to recruitment.

2:1:1 Personnel selection The starting point of the selection process is usually a job description. The job analysis should describe the work activities, responsibilities, authority and if any special skills, knowledge and/or experience is needed. Using the job description the person(s) responsible for selection would then draw up a profile of the ideal candidate. The advertisement could then be drafted for internal and external advertising. There may be a company policy that all job vacancies are advertised within the company for a specified period before outside recruitment is attempted. A full selection procedure would have the following stages:-

Stage 1 A study of the application forms to identify applicants with suitable qualifications and experience.

Stage 2 Appropriate psychological tests of aptitude, character, personality and/or intelligence.

Stage 3 Technical testing that is related to the necessary skills required for the job.

Stage 4 Group observation session where candidates are encouraged to ask questions about the company.

These four stages are filtering devices to ensure a good short list of candidates can be drawn up for the final interview stage. Many companies may go direct from stage 1 to the short list, but the interview is usually the last stage in the selection process.

The interview

There have been a number of studies of interviews to determine the validity and reliability in the selection process. It was observed that many interviews were too short and unsystematic and thus provided unreliable results. To help with structuring an interview The National Institute of Industrial Psychology produced a seven point plan :-

1. Physical make-up	Are there any defects of health which might prevent good job performance?
2. Attainments	Are his/her education, training and previous experience satisfactory for the job in question? How well has he/she done in previous jobs?
3. General Intelligence	How much general intelligence does he/she display?
4. Special aptitudes	Has he/she any outstanding aptitude suited for the job, such as numeraccy, literacy or mechanical aptitude?
5. Interests	To what extent are his/her interests social, interlectual, practical, physical or artistic?
6. Disposition	How well does he/she get on with other people? Does he/she influence others? Is he/she self reliant?
7. Circumstances	What are his/her domestic circumstances? Are they compatible with success in the job in question?

Once the selection procedure is complete, the successful candidate will be offered a contract of employment. The next sub-section explains some of the legal aspects of recruitment.

2:1:2 Legal requirements Labour law can be broadly divided into laws for the protection of individual employees and laws that regulate collective labour relationships. Some important labour law statutes are listed below:-

Truck Acts 1831, 1887, 1896 and 1959
Disabled Persons Employment Acts 1944 and 1953
* Contracts of Employment Acts 1963 and 1972
Industrial Training Act 1964
* Redundancy Payments Act 1965
Race Relations Act 1968
Health and Safety at Work Act 1974
* Trade Union and Labour Relations Acts 1974 and 1976
Social Security Pensions Act 1975
Sex Discrimination Act 1975
* Employment Protection Act 1975

(These Acts were consolidated into the Employment Protection (Consolidation) Act 1980)*

Clearly a detailed coverage of labour law is beyond the scope of this book. However it is useful to extract a few important points of law such as:-

(a) During the labour selection process it is unlawful to discriminate on the grounds of race, sex or marriage. Thus some caution is needed with the wording of job descriptions, advertisements and advising unsuccessful job applicants.

(b) Employers are legally obliged to maintain a register of disabled people in the

their employ. Employers are also required to offer employment positions to disabled people equivalent to at least 3 per cent of their total labour force. A disabled person should not be dismissed if it would bring the number of disabled people employed below 3 per cent.
(c) The contract of employment exists when the employee proves his/her acceptance of an employer's terms and conditions of employment by starting work.
(d) Both employer and employee are legally bound by the agreed terms and conditions of employment. Within thirteen weeks of the employee starting work the employer must provide the employee with a written statement about the terms of employment and additional details on grievance procedures. The statement must contain the following particulars:-

(i) The scale or rate of remuneration, or the period of calculating remuneration (including, for example, any terms on piece-rates, or overtime pay)
(ii) The intervals at which remuneration is paid, that is weekly or monthly or some other period
(iii) Any terms and conditions relating to hours of work (including normal working hours)
(iv) Any terms and conditions relating to: entitlement to holidays, including public holidays, and holiday pay (sufficient to enable the employee's entitlement, including any entitlement to accrued holiday pay on the termination of employment, to be precisely calculated)
(v) Incapacity for work due to sickness or injury, including any provisions for sick pay, and
(vi) Pensions and pension schemes (except where employees are covered by special statutory pension schemes and their employers are already obliged by those statutes to provide pensions information about them)
(vii) The length of notice of termination which the employee is obliged to give and entitled to receive, or if the contract is for a fixed term, the date when the contract expires
(viii) The title of the job which the employee is employed to do.

The written statement must also contain an additional note on discipline and grievances. This additional note must include:-

(ix) specify any disciplinary rules (other than those relating to health and safety at work) which apply to the employee, or must refer to a document, reasonably accessible to the employee, which specifies the rules
(x) specify by description or name, the person to whom the employee can apply and the manner in which an application should be made if dissatisfied with any disciplinary decision relating to him or her, or for the purpose of seeking redress of any grievance relating to his or her employer.
(xi) expalin what further steps, if any, follow from an application, or refer to a document which explains them and is reasonably accessible to the employee.
(xii) state whether a contracting-out certificate under the Social Security Act 1975 is in force for the employment in respect of which the written statement is being issued.

(e) Employees are legally entitled to an itemised pay statement that must include the following detail:-

(i) The gross amount of the wages or salary;
(ii) The amounts of any fixed deductions and the purposes for which they are made;

(iii) The amounts of any variable deductions and the purposes for which they are made;

(iv) The net amount of wages or salary payable;

(v) The amount and method of each part-payment when different parts of the net amount are paid in different ways, for example the separate figures of a cash payment and a balance credited to a bank account.

(f) Employers are legally prevented from making deductions from wages unless they have been agreed and there is a contract signed by the employee. (Truck Acts) Deductions that can be lawfully agreed include:

(i) Rent of a house let by the employer to the workman
(ii) Medical services
(iii) Food
(iv) Tools

This brief survey of some legal aspects of employment illustrates the importance of establishing corporate policies and procedures for the recruitment of labour. The legal aspects of dismissal and redundancy will be reviewed in subsequent sub-sections.

2:2 Employment procedures In addition to the recruitment procedures there are a number of important aspects of employment that require procedures. For instance when a new employee attends work on the first day it can be quite a bewildering and sometimes distressing experience. To overcome this problem many large companies have established induction procedures that introduce new employees to the company. Procedures may also be needed for monitoring the work of new employees to see if they are suited to the job. Indeed legislation has indirectly encouraged employers to formalise this observation period into a probationary period. Procedures are required for training, health and safety, grievances, welfare, sickness, holidays and wage payments. Meeting all these social, moral and legal obligations of employment and controlling employees requires a lot of management time. To ensure management time is used effectively and not wasted on continued disputes on minor issues, employment procedures are needed. The procedures regulate employment relationships and may be determined in one of the following ways:-

(a) Unilaterally by management
(b) Unilaterally by management after joint consultation
(c) Bilaterally through collective bargaining or participation (Refer to chapter 2 sub-sections 4:2:2, 4:2:3 and 4:2:4)

In the following sub-sections we will be briefly reviewing four important areas where procedures are needed.

2:2:1 Probationary period Many companies engage employees on a trial basis that is usually specified in the letter of appointment as a probationary period. The length of time will probably depend upon agreement with the relevant trade unions but would rarely exceed six months. When an employee has been in continuous employment with the same employer for less than 52 weeks, then the dismissal provisions of the Employment Protection (Consolidation) Act does not apply. Thus during this time, there are fewer legal complications attached to dismissal should an employee's performance be inadequate. Dismissal procedure are explained in sub section 2:4.

The procedure for probationary periods would include:-

(a) Regular assessment of employee performance.
(b) Regular discussions with the employee about his/her performance.
(c) Advice and training given when performance is below standard.

(d) Providing written statements to an employee whose performance is likely to result in early dismissal, with copies to the relevant trade union.

(e) Providing written statements to employees on their successful completion of the probationary period or a statement stating the reasons for extending their probationary period.

Probationary period procedures will probably meet with resistance from trade unions and would therefore be a matter for negotiation and compromise.

2:2:2 Training and education This is one of the few subject areas in industry and commerce where all sectional interest groups have been making the same 'noises'. Although there appears to be consensus on the need for more training and education employers are cautious because training can be costly and the benefits are not easily measured. The government tried in its Industrial Training Act 1964 to persuade industry to spend more money on training. Basically, the idea was for Industrial Training Boards to charge a levy on employers and then give back some of the money in the form of grants to encourage training. The practical consequences of this legislation was the re-direction of a large proportion of training levies to fund form filling bureaucracies. Statutory enforced form filling at the company level was, for some companies, an exercise in manipulating training times, staff numbers and course content to maximise training grants. There is evidence that some industrial training boards have been successful in increasing training in their respective industries. But there must surely be a more cost efficient way of getting companies to spend more money on training?

Clearly every company needs to have a training policy statement. The policy statement could require all departments to submit an analysis of their training needs for the coming year as part of the budgetary planning process. (Refer to chapter 8 section 2) From these statements a complete assessment of the company's training needs could be made and plans drawn up to ensure that training was co-ordinated, met the company's requirements and gave good value for money. The last point concerning value for money is especially relevant for training. For most training programmes, a substantial part of the cost is staff time. Thus if an employee was to participate in an educational course rather than specific job training, the corporate policy statement may require this to be done in the employee's own time. The following notes briefly review some categories of training and education:-

Induction training The main purpose of this type of training is to introduce a new employee to a company. A company may opt for a simple booklet, a video film, a general talk by the personnel officer or an introductory session with the relevant line manager.

Job training This is to provide the employee with the skills required to do an existing job or a job that he/she may be transferred to a later date. Normally this is an internal training function.

Job education In many jobs it may be useful for an employee to widen or deepen his/her specific subject knowledge with regard to changes in: legislation, work practices, technology or new techniques. This kind of updating knowledge is generally acquired from external courses.

Management education The education of managers is a continuing process and a training policy statement may require minimum amounts of formal management education to be undertaken by every manager every year. The education of managers can be broadly divided into three levels:-

Level 1 The acquisition of specialised knowledge such as management practice and techniques, accountancy, law, industrial relations, marketing and industrial psychology/sociology. This would require a formal junior management training programme where trainee managers would undertake a large proportion of the study in their own time. This could be done by correspondence course or evening classes in a local further or higher education establishment.

Level 2 Experienced middle level managers rarely get the opportunity to think and discuss the broader aspects of management because they become too involved in the day to day running of their departments. The purpose of level 2 education would be to force managers to think in strategic terms by using established management education techniques such as: case studies, role playing and business games. Level 2 courses would also provide updating on the latest changes that may affect a manager's area of responsibility.

Level 3 Higher level management education is primarily aimed at the broader issues of strategic decision making. Generally this kind of education is provided by conference organisers that use leading speakers and experts on specific subjects Conferences also provide the opportunity for delegates to discuss general business problems with senior managers from other companies.

In the foregoing summary, training and education has been broadly structured into job training/education and management education. The former tends to be very specific and a one off updating exercise. Whereas management education should be a continuing process

2:2:3 Health and safety Employers have for a long while, been under a common law duty of care for the health and safety of their employees. Various statutes have been passed, such as the Factories Acts, that have codified some of the employers' responsibilities in this area. But the most important statute has been the Health and Safety at Work Act 1974. This Act brought together much of the existing health and safety legislation and codified some of the common law One important point that should be noted is that the Act transferred offences from the civil law into the criminal law. This means that an officer of a company who does not make sufficient provisions for the health and safety of the company's employees has committed a criminal offence and may be charged accordingly.

The Act provided for the setting up of a Health and Safety Commission which in turn engaged a Health and Safety Executive which in turn took control and unified the various inspectorate bodies and administrations. The statutory health and safety inspectors have formidable powers that include:-

i) A right of access at any reasonable time
ii) A right to take photographs, measurements, or any recordings considered necessary
iii) A right to demand answers to relevant questions and for individuals to sign a declaration that the answer is true.
iv) A right to demand assistance and facilities necessary for his/her investigations.
v) A right to be accompanied by a police constable if he/she has reasonable cause to believe that there will be obstruction in the execution of his/her duty.
vi) A right to sieze, render harmless or destroy any article or substance which he/she believes could be a cause of imminent danger to employees.

If the inspector was not satisfied with the health and safety precautions taken by a company he/she may serve an *improvement notice* or a *prohibition notice* The former requires an employer to remedy defects within a specified time period and the latter can require a production process to cease until the danger is removed. From this brief summary of the legislation it should be clear that *every* organisation must have a health and safety policy and procedures. The policy statement and procedures could include the following points:-

i) To provide a safe system of work, informateon, instruction and training

ii) Setting up safety committees with representatives from different departments.

iii) Regular inspection by safety represeentatives

iv) A participative approach towards decisions concerning health and safety.

(Refer to chapter 2 sub-section 4:2:3)

v) Providing training for safety representatives on matters such as first aid and fire prevention

vi) Identifying the major health hazards and taking relevant precautions such as warning signs and machine guards

vii) Recording all accidents, identifying the causes and taking suitable precautions to prevent their recurrence.

The health and safety of employees is an important issue that was traditionally discussed in joint consultative meetings. However, in many companies it has become a negotiating issue in collective bargaining. This is not necessarily a bad development except when health and safety issues are used as a trade off factor in wage negotiations. Employers cannot remove their statutory obligations by agreements with individual employees or their representatives.

2:2:4 Grievances Employees have the following legal rights concerning grievances

i) A right to receive a written statement that explains the company's grievance procedures.

ii) A right to seek redress for grievances relating to their employment

As employees have these legal rights, it is necessary for employers to establish a formal grievance procedure. In small businesses where there is close personal contact between the employer and employees a formal system may not be needed. When a company has recognised trade unions then the disputes procedure will almost always be a negotiating issue. The aims of a grievance procedure should be:-

i) To settle a grievance fairly and as near as possible to the point of origin

ii) To be simple and rapid in operation

iii) To be in writing

An example of a three stage procedure would be:-

Stage 1 Complaint would be dealt with by the immediate supervisor possibly accompanied by a trade union representative. The complaint should be discussed at this level within two or three days of it arising.

Stage 2 If the employee is dissatisfied with the stage 1 outcome,then he/she would have a right to be heard by the head of the department within seven working days. If required, the trade union representative could be present at the meeting

Stage 3 If agreement is not reached at stage 2 level, then the matter may be referred to the trade union branch secretary, who will meet with a company representative to resolve the problem within one month of the original complaint.

The purpose of any complaints or disputes procedure is to institutionalise conflicting interests. Accordingly, managers need to treat grievances with respect and due consideration. If managers abuse a grievance procedure then conflict may emerge. There are no real winners in industrial conflict situations, only differences in the extent of loss.

2:3 Payroll procedures In section 3 we will be looking at many different methods of calculating an employee's remuneration. From an administrative viewpoint we can divide these wage payment systems into time based and incentive based. The calculation of wages for incentive based systems can be quite complex but it is only one part of a payroll procedure. In this sub-section we will divide the payroll procedure into the following stages:

i) Collect relevant data
ii) Calculate wages and salaries
iii) Collect cash from bank
iv) Sort cash and cheques
v) Deliver pay to employee

1. Collect relevant data

a) Each employees details such as: full name, address, department, national insurance number and tax code.

b) Each employees employment contract details such as: wage rate, basis of calculation, incentive schemes, holiday entitlement and agreed deductions such as trade union and social club subscriptions.

c) Weekly time sheets, where appropriate, giving basic time, overtime and shift working time.

d) Performance data where incentive payment scheme is operating giving individual or group output figures.

2. Calculate wages and salaries

From all this detail the payroll section has to calculate each employee's gross wage national insurance contribution, graduated pension payment, PAYE tax payment and other deductions to derive a net wage. Clearly this part of labour administration is vitally important. Wages and salaries must be calculated correctly in accordance with the agreed terms and conditions of employment, and paid regularly. Procedures need to be established to reduce the opportunity for fraud. For instance any alteration of pay rates must be authorised in writing. There should be frequent spot checks on the payroll register to ensure:

a) No dummy employees that enable a person to draw more than one wage

b) Dates of employees joining and leaving the company agree with personnel records.

c) Wage rates agree with personnel records.

d) Incentive payments agree with production records.

3. Collect cash from bank

The handling of cash requires a lot of security procedures, therefore many companies are attempting to persuade employees to accept payment by cheque. Where the wages are to be paid by cash, the cash request should be precisely the same amount as the total cash figure on the payroll. The delivery of cash will normally be by a security firm on the day wages are paid. It is prudent to hold large amounts of cash for the minimum possible time on the premises.

4. Sort cash and cheques

The sorting of cash needs to be in a physically secure place with strict entrance regulations. The person(s) sorting the cash and cheques into the envelopes with the pay slips should not be the same person that calculates the wages. Indeed the wage calculation and physical sorting/payment of wages should be completely separate functions. The wages envelopes should include an itemised individual payslip that has a duplicate entry on the payroll register. The cash sorting process will have the following stages:-

a) Insert cash into each envelope in accordance with the net pay on each payslip

b) Supervisor to make random checks on pay envelopes for correct contents

c) If there is a shortage or an excess of cash at the end of the sorting process then a mistake has occurred and all the envelopes have to be checked until the error is located.

d) When all checks have been made and totals agree the envelopes may be sealed and sorted for delivery.

5. Deliver pay to employees

Physical security measures are still necessary at this stage of the payroll procedure. Some companies allow a supervisor to openly carry a tray of pay envelopes around a factory floor for personal delivery. There could be several thousand pounds in the tray and this places the supervisor in potential physical danger. The administrative aspect of wage delivery is simply to get a signature for every separate cash payment Any kind of cash payment such as petty cash or wages must always be recorded and signed for.

This brief survey of payroll procedures illustrates the importance of this function. Wages must be calculated accurately and delivered on time. Whenever cash is involved precautions are needed for physical security and fraud.

2:4 Dismissal procedures. The principle of unfair dismissal was introduced into UK legislation in the ill fated Industrial Relations Act 1971. Many of this Act's provisions were incorporated into subsequent Trade Union and Labour Relations Acts and Employment Protection Acts. Prior to this legislation, an employer did not have to give reasons for dismissal and provided proper notice was given and wages paid, an employee had no legal redress for dismissal. Thus, after years of loyal service an employee could have been unfairly dismissed without any reason being given. *Now, most employees have a legal right not to be unfairly dismissed.* There are some exceptions, such as employees who have been in continuous employment with the same employer for less than 1 year. This qualifying period is 2 years for small firms employing less than 20 full time people during the claimant's service. Pensioners (women over 60 and men over 65) and part time employees working less than 16 hours a week or 8 hours after 5 years continuous service also have no statutory protection for unfair dismissal.

In principle, this kind of legislation should help to prevent the abuse of organisational privelege and power that is given to managers. In practice it is a legal minefield which managers have to cautiously work through if they wish to *fairly* dismiss an employee, A dismissal will usually be considered 'fair' when it can be proved by the employer that he acted fairly and reasonably in dismissing an employee on the grounds of his/her misconduct or incapability. However the burden of proof rests on the employer and an industrial tribunal may ask questions such as:-

i) Did the situation merit dismissal?
ii) Did management have all the facts?
iii) Were there mitigating circumstances?
iv) Was the manner of dismissal correct? i.e. Did management follow the correct procedures?

With this kind of questioning, managers need to have clear procedural guidelines to maintain their authority and their right to fairly dismiss an employee. In the following sub-sections we will be looking at some of the details relating to warnings, dismissals and redundancy.

2:4:1 Warnings The manner of dismissal is very important. An industrial tribunal will want to be satisfied that the company's procedures were adequate and fair. Also, that the employee understood what was expected of him/her. Accordingly, many companies establish a disciplinary procedure based on a sequence of warnings. Often these disciplinary procedures are established through negotiation with the relevant trade unions who normally require a trade union represetative to be involved at each warning stage. A three stage warning procedure could be as follows:-

Informal warning This would be an oral warning in the form of advice, assistance and/or reprimand for an employee whose behaviour and/or performance is below standard. A sutiable period of time should be allowed for an improvement to take place. Details of the oral warning should be recorded and a copy sent to the relevant trade union representative.

Formal warning If after the stated time period the employee's performance and or behaviour has not improved, then a formal interview would be arranged to which the trade union representative would be invited. The warning given in the interview would be given in writing to the employee and a copy sent to the trade union representative.

Final warning If after a suitable time period and informal and formal warnings, there is still no improvement in the employee's performance and/or behaviour, then a final warning may be given. This would take place in an interview to which the trade union representative would be invited. The final warning would make it clear that unless the employee improved, he/she will be dismissed.

At all these interviews the employee needs to be given an opportunity to state his/her point of view. The purpose of disciplinary procedures is to promote fairness and order in the treatment of individuals and in the conduct of industrial relations. They should not be viewed simply as a preliminary process for dismissal.

2:4:2 Dismissals A dismissal represents a failure by management to select the right person for the job or to provide the right kind of motivation if the selection process was valid. A high or rising labour turnover figure is generally regarded as an indicator of bad management. There are of course many occasions where an employee cannot, or will not, adjust to the requirements of an organisation and dismissal becomes necessary. Where this type of situation arises and a manager decides an employee must be dismissed then generally speaking there are two options:-

Option 1 - Dismiss and damn the consequences.
Option 2 - Learn the dismissal rules and play the game.

Let us first consider *Option 1* to see what could happen. The employer may get away with it, because the employee just leaves without causing any trouble. This is possible because the shock of dismissal can affect people in different ways. However, the chances are, that the employee will seek advice and subsequently submit a written statement to an industrial tribunal claiming unfair dismissal. There is a three month time period for the effective date of termination within which the complaint should be submitted. But the industrial tribunals have the discretion to receive complaints after the three months if there are mitigating circumstances.

The first stage in the process would be when a conciliation officer from the Advisory Conciliation and Arbitration Service (ACAS) calls. He/she will attempt to 'plaster over the cracks'. If the manager and/or employee will not compromise then the next stage would be a tribunal hearing, where the manager has to prove the dismissal was 'fair'. Assuming the tribunal found that the dismissal was 'unfair' then the remedies offered would be reinstatement or re-engagement, or a compensation payment. The tribunal would ask the employee if he/she wanted an order for reinstatement or re-engagement and would decide on this remedy after carefully considering if that course of action was practicable. If the tribun-

decided on a compensation order then there would be a basic award calculated under the principles of the Redundancy Payments Act 1965 with a minimum entitlement to two weeks pay. In addition to the basic award the tribunal will usually make a compensatory award. This would be based on the assessment of loss which the employee has incurred as a result of the dismissal to a maximum of £5,200. With remedies like this, managers would be well advised to learn the rules of the game.

If a manager decides on *Option 2* then there are a lot of rules to learn. Before reviewing a few of these rules it is useful to identify situations where dismissal is automatically unfair.

Examples of unfair dismissals

i) Dismissed solely on the grounds of race, religion or sex, or because he or she is a disabled person.
ii) Dismissed solely because she is pregnant.
iii) Dismissed for exercising his or her rights in connection with Trade Union activity or membership.
iv) Dismissed because of sickness, where sickness is not specified in the company rules as grounds for dismissal.
v) Dismissed for taking part in industrial action where selection is for an inadmissible reason or for selected non re-engagement after a dispute.
vi) Made redundant where the reason is inadmissible or in contravention of an accepted or customary practice.
vii) Terminated arising out of a 'constructive' dismissal. That is a situation where an employee resigns because of unreasonable or unfair conduct on the part of the employer.

Thus if a manager wanted to dismiss a pregnant disabled jewish negro taking part in trade union activities then it would be difficult to claim fair dismissal.

There are circumstances when an employee may complain that he/she has been treated unfairly and that the treatment constitutes *constructive dismissal.* The burden of proof for this situation rests on the employee. But if it is proved then a tribunal may treat the case as unfair dismissal. If a manager's reply is yes to any of the following questions then constructive dismissal may have occurred:-

i) Has the employee's pay or conditions been reduced without his agreement?
ii) Has any attempt been made to force the employee to resign?
iii) Has the employee been publicly treated with marked discourtesy?
iv) Has the employee's status been lowered without his agreement?
v) Have steps been taken to replace the employee without informing him?
vi) Has a higher performance been demanded from the employee then from others with similar jobs?
vii) Has the employee been treated in a discriminatory manner?
viii) Has the employee been denied his rights?
ix) Has the employee's authority been consistently undermined?
x) Has the employee been required to do work other than his own against his wishes?

Examples of possible fair dismissals.

i) Lack of capability to do the job
   Ensure not due to sickness
   Ensure adequate warnings have been given
   Ensure training and/or councelling has been given where appropriate

ii) Misconduct and breaking company rules
Ensure all the facts have been collected and can be proved
Ensure sufficient evidence to satisfy a tribunal
Ensure no mitigating circumstances such as personal stress or lack of experience
Ensure employee given the opportunity to be heard and warnings given where appropriate.

iii) Lack of qualification to do the job
Ensure formal qualification is necessary to do the job
Ensure lack of qualification is contrary to company policy
Ensure employee has been given the opportunity to obtain the necessary formal qualification.

iv) Senior employee's behaviour incompatible with position
Ensure employee has been warned
Ensure there have been genuine attempts to help employee
Ensure no mitigating circumstances such as personal stress
Ensure dismissal is a reasonable and fair course of action.

The foregoing notes relating to fair and unfair dismissals provide some indication of how comples dismissal can be and the need for a company to establish clear procedures for grievance, discipline and dismissal.

2:4:3 Redundancy Dismissals due to redundancy would normally be acceptable to a tribunal if the following conditions were satisfied:-

i) The need for the employee's work has ceased or been substantially diminished.
ii) The employee(s) to be made redundant have been selected under a recognised procedure such as last in first out.
iii) A genuine attempt has been made to find alternative employment that is acceptable to the employee
iv) The treatment of the employee(s) has been as fair as possible

If an employee is legitimately redundant, he/she is entitled to a redundancy payment. Naturally the trade union will try to extract a redundancy payment above the statutory levels, which only represent minimum payments. There is evidence that employers often pay over double the statutory levels, especially for employees with only a few years service. Not all employees are entitled to redundancy payemnts. The legal provisions do not cover

i) Anyone who is not an employee, for example an independent contractor or free-lance agent
ii) Employees who ordinarily work outside Great Britain under the terms of their contracts of employment, but most employees working on offshore oil and gas installations in British sectors of the Continental Shelf are covered.
iii) Members of the police service and armed forces
iv) Merchant seamen
v) Registered dock workers engaged on dock work
vi) Masters and crew engaged in share fishing who are paid solely by share in the profits or gross earnings of a fishing vessel
vii) Crown servants
viii) Employees who have not completed two years continuous employment Service under the age of 18 does not count
viii) Employees covered by collective agreements on redundancies who have been excluded from the provisions by an Order made by the Secretary of State for Employment

x) Employees who have not completed two years continuous employment. Service under the age of 18 does not count.

Calculating redundancy payments

If an employee is legally entitled to a redundancy payment the amount can be calculated by referring to the age of the person and length of service (to a maximum of 20 years). Three examples are given below:-

Examples of redundancy payment calculations

a) Age of person between 41 and 65 (60 for a woman). The entitlement is 1½ weeks pay for each year. e.g. 63 year old man with 35 years service currently earning £100 per week. Redundancy payment entitlement would be £3,000 (20 x 1.5 x 100).

b) Age of person between 22 and 40. The entitlement is 1 weeks pay for each year. e.g. 39 year old man with 15 years service currently earning £175 per week. Pay over £110 per week is excluded in the calculations therefore the redundancy entitlement would be £1,650 (15 x1 x 110)

c) Age of person between 18 and 21. The entitlement is ½ weeks pay for each year. e.g. 21 year old woman with five years service currently earning £140 per week. Service before the age of 18 is not allowable therefore the redundancy entitlement would be £165 (3 x 0.5 x 110)

The employer will get back 41% of the redundancy payment from the government's Redundancy Fund. Thus, the actual cost of the above redundancy examples would be:-

	Employer pays £	*Government pays* £	*Employees receive* £
a)	1,770.00	1,230.00	3.000.00
b)	973.50	676.50	1,650.00
c)	97.35	67.65	165.00
Total	2,840.85	1,974.15	4,815.00

The foregoing examples of redundancy payment calculations were for illustration and are therefore a simplified version of the kind of calculations that are needed when planning redundancies. In reality, the calculations would have to take into consideration *all* the detailed legal rules and any related arrangement with the trade unions. Total cost calculations would have to take into consideration:-

i) Notification periods necessary for employees.

The Secretary of State needs to be notified if more than 10 workers are to be made redundant.

ii) Time off allowances for redundant employees to search for alternative employment

iii) Collective agreements on redundancies that may result in long serving employees volunteering for large redundancy payments instead of the shortest serving employees being selected by management

iv) The possible costs and cash flow consequences of industrial action

Clearly redundancy decisions require careful planning within an established procedural framework.

2:5 Company rule book This section on labour administration has reviewed the procedures necessary for recruitment, employment and dismissal. Managerial discretion in these areas is almost always limited by labour law, collective agreements and social responsibility. Any manager that resents these restrictions on their actions, ought to think honestly for a few moments, whether he/she would abuse their privelege of organisational power if they had complete freedom of action. There is substantial evidence throughout the world that shows when labour is not organised and prepared to fight for themselves and their families, people in organisations will abuse their privelege of power. Fortunately, many managers are sufficiently mature and confident to accept a reduction in their managerial discretion when making decisions that concern employees. The attitudes of managers in an organisation is generally reflected in the Company Rule Book.

Many company rule books have been drafted unilaterally and must be accepted as a condition of employment by the employee if he/she wants the job. Once accepted the rule book becomes part of the contract of employment and the rules may be used by an employer as a reason for dismissal. Although this would not prevent the employee from claiming unfair dismissal. Some companies have adopte a broader and more enlightened approach to their rule books. They tend to be called employee handbooks and provide information about the company, and employee rights and responsibilities. Instead of being prepared unilaterally, the book would be compiled through joint consultation, collective bargaining or even participation. Such a book could be the working document for managers and employe that establishes workplace relationships of authority and responsibility. It could explain all the procedures relating to: recruitment, training, health and safety, welfare, holidays, sickness, salaries, overtime, incentive schemes, discipline, dismissals redundancies and trade union activities. Indeed most aspects of labour administration could be incorporated in an employee handbook.

If an organisation wishes to give a fair deal to its employees it has to be seen to be fair. Employees should see that they have rights as well as duties and responsibilities. The company rule book (or 'Employee Handbook') can play an important role in labour administration and industrial relations.

3. Labour remuneration

All employees are linked to their employing unit by some form of remuneration system. This remuneration linkage is the prime mover of most organisations (The exceptions are mainly voluntary worker groups) Put simply, if the wages do not get paid then the organisation will cease to function. The importance of money as a motivating force is the main reason why so many incentive payment schemes have been devised. In the following sub-sections we will be looking at over thirty different incentive payment schemes and ten kinds of employee benefits. Although this is a comprehensive coverage, the emphasis is on schemes that differ in principle. Under just one principle, say a piece rate system, there can be thousands of schemes that differ in detail. The important point about each remuneration scheme is that it has been devised to meet specific circumstances. The problem here, is that all incentive payment schemes are subject to natural decay and become unsuitable when circumstances change. But to try and change a scheme once it has been introduced can be a time consuming, frustrating and costly exercise. Accordingly, many companies avoid complex incentive payment schemes and just have a flat rate time based remuneratation system.

If a financial incentive scheme is to be introduced into a remuneration system then a key concept that must be considered is the effort/reward relationship. This relationship is illustrated in diagram 45 [1] which shows how some incentive schemes such as profit sharing, have a remote relationship between reward and the effort of an individual. Whilst other schemes, such as piece rates or sales commission have a close

---

(1) *Based on a diagram by T. Lupton & D. Gowler - Selecting a wage payment system. Engineering Employers' Federation (1969)*

reward/effort relationship. A financial incentive payment scheme aimed at increasing output should have a close reward/effort relationship, but this may not be possible because of production circumstances. For example, extra effort from an individual employee in a large continuous production process cannot be easily measured in output terms, therefore a group incentive scheme may be considered more appropriate.

DIAGRAM 45 *EFFORT/REWARD RELATIONSHIP*

Reward / Effort	Frequent payments (weekly, monthly)	Infrequent payments (6 monthly,annually)
Reward related to individual effort	*Piece work*	*Measured daywork*
Reward related to group effort	*Group bonus*	*Profit sharing*

Or, an incentive scheme may be designed to improve the goodwill and co-operation of employees on a plant wide or company basis. It is inevitable that this tyoe of scheme will also reward the inefficient, but providing the overall effect is improved co-operation, then the incentive payment system may be considered successful. However, a scheme that is successful in one factory may cause chaos in another factory. Therefore we need to consider what factors will exert some influence on incentive payment schemes.

i) Demand and supply for labour

When a particular skill is in short supply in a local area, then employers may need to devise some form of incentive scheme that helps them retain existing and attract new, skilled workers. Conversely, when there is a plentiful supply of a particular labour skill and high unemployment, then an incentive payment scheme may not be necessary

ii) Differentials and relativities

A distinction is sometimes drawn between differentials and relativities arising from a Relativities Board that was established during one of the price and income restraint periods. The distinction is that relativities exist outside the bargaining unit and differentials within the bargaining unit. There are of course many classes of relativities and differentials that include differences due to: industry, region, male or female, white collar or blue collar, and skilled or unskilled. The differences that tend to have the greatest effect on incentive payment schemes are within the plant. A common problem arises between direct and indirect labour where direct labour may be earning high wages through a payment by results scheme. The differentials then have to be restored by some form of lieu bonus for indirect workers.

iii) Technology

The acquisition of technically advanced equipment is normally cost justified because of improved efficiency. The improved efficiency may enable employees working under old incentive payment schemes to earn disproportionately large bonus payments. Thus incentive payment schemes may have to be re-negotiated before new technology is purchased.

iv) Collective bargaining

This is one of the most important factors that will determine the success or failure of an incentive payment scheme. A company with a mature collective bargaining system and established disputes procedures will be able to 'adjust' the incentive payment schemes to meet changing circumstances. Indeed, one of the constructive aspects of collective bargaining is the development of procedures that enable the part ies to live together under an agreement. Moreover, a negotiated incentive payment scheme will probaqly be more successful than a unilaterally imposed remuneration system.

v) Structure of the labour force

Two similar companies may have quite different labour force structures in terms of age, education, sex, skills, unionisation, full time/part time, wage payment system and organisation. These aspects of the labour force need to be taken into considera- tion when designing an incentive payment system.

vi) Ability to pay

If a large proportion of a company's total costs arise from labour remuneration, then great care is necessary when introducing an incentive payment scheme to ensure that the company will have the ability to pay the additional costs. When the proport- ion of labour costs to total cost is small, then there is unlikely to be an ability to pay problem, even during periods of depressed demand for the company's products or services.

The central problem of labour remuneration is to equate payment with effort and skill thus providing an incentive for higher output and enabling the business to achieve a satisfactory return on capital employed. As no two employing units are identical there cannot be a panacea for this problem. Each remuneration system has to be designed to fit specific circumstances that include the six factors outlined abov

In the following sub-sections we will be reviewing the principles of many differen types of incentive payment schemes. But before looking at the detail it is important that remuneration systems are placed into some kind of framework. Diagram 46 shows labour remuneration divided into these broad categories: time based, direct incentive and indirect incentive systems. The indirect incentive category is sub- divided into cost reduction and general incentive systems. Under each of these head- ings a list of schemes are given with their relevant sub-sections. It is hoped that this overview will enable the reader to see where a particular scheme fits into the frame- work before looking at the detail to determine if it is suitable for a specific set of local circumstances.

3:1 Time based payment Time rates are the most common form of wage pay- ment base. A time based payment is calculated by multiplying the number of hour 'worked' by the appropriate rate. Hours 'worked' generally means hours on the premises and is basically a management control problem. Traditionally, blue collar workers have had individual time record cards punched on some mechanical or electrical clock. White collar workers were subject to less formal controls and not required to 'clock in'. Indeed this timekeeping difference was often given an organ- isational status distinction where certain white collar workers were referred to as salaried staff. This kind of artificial status structuring still exists in some companie The really important variable in the time based payment method is determining the appropriate rate.

Wage rates are normally determined through collective bargaining (Refer to chapter 2 sub-section 4:2:2) This aspect of wage determination is discussed in som detail in section 4 of this chapter. In this sub-section we are concerned with time based remuneration methods. These can be based on premium payments such as overtime, shirt premiums or dirty money. Also there are time payment methods based on merit rating and job evaluation. The main difference between these two systems is that the former attempts to grade people and the latter to grade jobs. These time based payment systems are briefly reviewed in the following sub sectio

DIAGRAM 46 *STRUCTURE OF LABOUR REMUNERATION SYSTEMS*

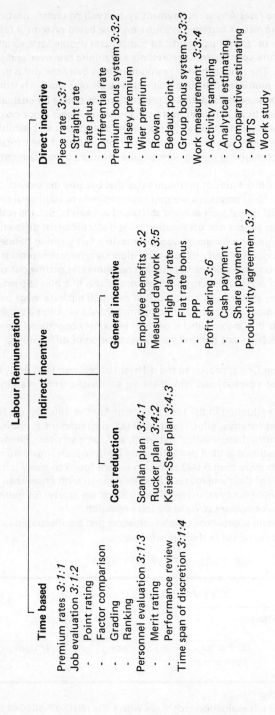

Labour Remuneration

Time based

Premium rates *3:1:1*
Job evaluation *3:1:2*
- Point rating
- Factor comparison
- Grading
- Ranking

Personnel evaluation *3:1:3*
- Merit rating
- Performance review

Time span of discretion *3:1:4*

Indirect incentive

Cost reduction

Scanlan plan *3:4:1*
Rucker plan *3:4:2*
Keiser-Steel plan *3:4:3*

General incentive

Employee benefits *3:2*
Measured daywork *3:5*
- High day rate
- Flat rate bonus
- PPP

Profit sharing *3:6*
- Cash payment
- Share payment

Productivity agreement *3:7*

Direct incentive

Piece rate *3:3:1*
- Straight rate
- Rate plus
- Differential rate

Premium bonus system *3:3:2*
- Halsey premium
- Wier premium
- Rowan
- Bedaux point
- Group bonus system *3:3:3*

Work measurement *3:3:4*
- Activity sampling
- Analytical estimating
- Comparative estimating
- PMTS
- Work study

3:1:1 Premium time rates Any wage payment system will be under constant pressure from employees. A common pressure on time based systems is for 'special allowances' or 'special payments' to compensate people for a variety of different reasons. Any such payment represents a premium rate over and above the basic time rate. The most common premium rates is overtime and is generally calculated as a multiple of the basic rate such as 1½ or 2 times. Overtime should offer managers some flexibility in production scheduling by enabling peak demand periods to be met with overtime, instead of higher stock holdings and/or under utilised labour. However, once overtime becomes an established practice, employees begin to rely on the premium rate as part of their total wages This can lead to slow working during normal time to ensure a management request for overtime.

There are many other kinds of premium rates that become the subject of continued disputes. Shift premiums are quite common where additional rates are paid for 'unsocial hours' such as night shifts and weekends. But the real danger in premium rates are the one off decisions that distort internal differentials and create precedents for subsequent wage claims. In a fast growing business where organised labour can easily disrupt a continuous production process,managers have to be strong and vigilant to prevent premium rates getting out of control. An example of wage rates getting out of control was in a Fleet Street print room where a survey showed one company had over 500 separate wage payment arrangements. It is most important that companies should establish a wages policy that prevents the uncontrolled growth of separately negotiated premium payments and the subsequent demand for the restoration of differentials.

3:1:2 Job evaluation One approach to the differential problem is to analyse and assess every job (not a person) and rank them for a balanced remuneration system.

A survey of job evaluation in the U.K. was carried out in 1967 by the National Board for Prices and Incomes, which sampled 8,000 organisations in mining, manufacturing, construction, utilities, transport, and some services. The findings were that job evaluation was used predominantly by large-scale organisations. Establishments with more than 5,000 employees were found to apply job evaluation to nearly 40% of their employees. In establishments with fewer than 500 the coverage was only 6% of employees. Some 25% of the nearly 6½ million employees in the sample, were covered by job evaluation.

There are four main approaches to job evaluation that are illustrated in diagram 47 below and explained in the following notes.

DIAGRAM 47 JOB EVALUATION METHODS

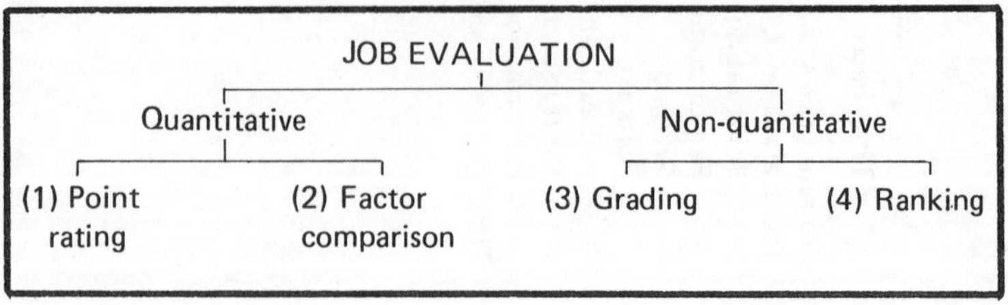

i) Points rating

This is a popular job evaluation technique where the relative 'value' of a job is determined by adding together the quantitative assessments for selected factors. The stages in a points rating scheme would be:-

Stage 1 Obtain agreement with the relevant trade unions for the scheme
Stage 2 Identify key factors for a job such as skill, effort, responsibilty and working conditions
Stage 3 Attach weights to each key factor
Stage 4 Assess selected jobs in terms of key factors, multiply by appropriate weights and total to give the points rating for each job.
Stage 5 Correlate points ratings for existing pay levels using acceptable regression analysis technique to determine pay/points relationship
Stage 6 Attempt to structure existing pay arrangements with 'minor adjustments' into a points rating structure and seek agreement with the trade unions.

ii) Factor comparison

This quantitative method is not so popular as the points rating method because it has been found that employees find the scheme difficult to understand. A factor comparison scheme would have the following stages:-
Stage 1 A representative committee is appointed to prepare a detailed job evaluation proposal
Stage 2 A committee selects four or five key factors for job evaluation
Stage 3 The committee then select a number of key jobs that represent the whole range of jobs to be evaluated. This would normally be more than the jobs selected if a points rating method were used.
Stage 4 Each job is then ranked against each key factor to produce a separate hierarchy of jobs for each factor
Stage 5 A second set of hierarchies is then constructed based on the money paid for each job which is divided between the key factors
Stage 6 The two scales for each factor are then compared and amounts assigned for job levels for each factor. These amounts are totalled across the factors giving a ranking of jobs and rates.
Stage 7 Seeking agreement with the trade unions

iii) Grading

The government survey in 1967 identified this as the second most popular job evaluation technique in the U.K. (The first was points rating) The National Coal Board for example has been operating a job grading scheme since 1955 covering over two hundred thousand employees. A job grading scheme will have the following stages:-
Stage 1 Separating the organisation into different hierarchies such as manual, clerical and management where promotion paths can be identified
Stage 2 Defining the hierarchy of grades for each division based on significant differences in a few key factors such as skill and responsibility
Stage 3 Reading all the job descriptions and allocating them to relevant grades
Stage 4 Determining salary ranges for different grades and seeking agreement with the trade unions.

iv) Ranking

This technique is similar to grading. The main difference is that ranking is done by using job descriptions, whereas with grading the hierarchy is determined first without reference to job descriptions. Job ranking would have the following stages:-
Stage 1 Dividing all jobs into occupational groupings
Stage 2 Ranking all jobs within occupational groupings according to their contribution to the organisation

Stage 3 Comparison of occupational ranking and allocating grades to each rank

Stage 4 Allocating rates of pay to each grade and seeking agreement with the trade unions

It is evident that job evaluation is a complex exercise that needs careful planning. The four basic methods that have been explained can be adapted to suit the particular needs of an organisation. If a job evaluation scheme is successful, it can provide a sound framework for employee remuneration decisions and help to avoid the problems of pay anomolies and disputes over internal differentials.

3:1:3 Personnel evaluation In the previous sub-section we were concerned with the problem of grading jobs as a framework for a wages structure. In the job evaluation process it is the job not the individual that is being assessed. As some employees will be better at a job than others, then some form of differential payment can be devised that will provide additional rewards to some employees based on merit. These merit awards are a form of incentive payment but they do not readily fit into any of the incentive remuneration schemes explained in subsequent sub-sections.

There are many ways of assessing the performance of individual employees. We will consider two popular methods; merit rating and performance review.

i) *Merit rating*

Merit rating enables the differences in personal abilities and qualities of employees doing the same job to be assessed. The assessment would be undertaken once or twice a year by a supervisor and departmental manager. Points would be awarded against a list of factors and the total points would produce a merit rating. An illustration of a merit rating form in diagram 48 shows the principle quite clearly. The advantages of merit rating are that it provides an incentive for the good employee to maintain high standards and it highlights individuals who require training and/or discipline.

DIAGRAM 48 PRINCIPLES OF MERIT RATING

MERIT RATING FORM

Name .... Department ....

Date of assessment .... Assessors ....

Performance factor	*Assessment*
Quality of work (Max. 50 points)	
Quantity of work (Max. 50 points)	
Loyalty and integrity (Max. 50 points)	
Co-operation and helpfulness (Max. 40 points)	
Use of initiative (Max. 40 points)	
Timekeeping (Max. 30 points)	
Total points	

Rating		*Merit Award*
A 220 to 260 points	=	£2.00 per week
B 180 to 219 points	=	£1.00 per week
C 140 to 179 points	=	£0.50 per week
D Below 140 points	=	No award

ii) Performance review

The purpose of a performance review is to objectively assess an individual employees performance against pre-determined tasks and objectives. It would normally be undertaken once a year in advance of the salary review. The employee would be advised of his/her targets and know that he/she will be assessed on their performance. During the interview the employee should be allowed to comment on his/her own performance. The manager(s) will assess the employees performance and set targets for the following year.The assessment should include a statement on the employees strengths and weaknesses. The review file on each employee enables managers to make objective assessments for salary increases, promotions, additional training or discipline.

3:1:4 Time span of discretion. This is a kind of job evaluation scheme that was developed at the Glacier Metal Company in London. The principle of their remuneration system is that all jobs have a *prescribed* and a *discretionary* element. The prescribed parts of the job are the rules and instructions such as operating a machine. The discretionary element of the job is the part where the employee has to use his/her own discretion and make decisions. For example, a skilled machine operator working from drawings may have to decide how to produce a product. The time span theory is concerned with the amount of discretion there is related to a job. The greater the discretion the greater the responsibility and possibly greater anxiety.

The process of measuring the time span of discretion is based upon how long it is possible for an employee to carry out sub-standard work without being noticed by an immediate supervisor. Thus each job in a production process is analysed to determine its discretionary content and the pay is varied accordingly.

This kind of remuneration system virtually eliminates pay bargaining because pay claims tend to be based on comparability, cost of living, productivity and the employer's ability to pay. Of these four, pay bargaining elements, only comparability is relevant for time span systems. And even then the comparability studies are based on job evaluation and analysis which tends to limit the scope of comparability based pay bargaining. Accordingly, trade union negotiators do not tend to be very enthusiastic about proposals for time span wage systems.

3:2 Employee benefits The last decade has witnesses a shift in remuneration emphasis towards increasing employee benefits. The reasons for this shift have been due to taxation, government incomes policies and a greater awareness of the incentive effect of benefits. Employment benefits used to be only for senior executives and became an established part of their total remuneration package. Many senior executives would expect a pension plan, company car and private patients insurance policy to be a normal part of their conditions for employment. But benefits have now spread to a far wider range of employees. In this sub-section we will briefly review different types of employee benefits.

1) Company car This kind of benefit often has a high status value and can create complications on choice due to the different status distinctions in the hierarchy. Moreover, not all employees necessarily want a company car. They may prefer to use their own car and receive a mileage allowance.

ii) Food Employees may be subsidised by the employer with luncheon voucher or company dining rooms where the cost of a meal is very low. Status in the hierarchy also enters into this type of employee benefit by multiple ranking of dining rooms for different levels of employees.

iii) Holidays Most companies offer above the statutory minimum holiday entitlement to executives. Increases in holiday entitlements are also sometimes awarded to all employees in relation to the number of years they have worked for the company.

iv) Health insurance This is an important benefit for companies in countries that do not have a free health service. In the UK health insurance may be in the form of a private patients plan for the employee and his/her family.

v) Sickness benefits Companies have become increasingly generous in this area. A common arrangement is for time off with full pay to be increased in relation to the number of years the employee has worked for the company.

vi) Pension plans A substantial amount of companies have opted out of the government pension scheme and have made pension arrangements with insurance companies or run their own pension fund. This benefit is available in different amounts to almost every employee.

vii) Death and injury benefits It is quite common for companies to take out some form of life insurance for their employees that will provide funds for the widow if an employee dies or specific amounts for the loss of a limb and similar injuries.

viii) Education Companies quite frequently pay the education fees and expenses fo employees that are attending vocational courses. Financial assistance can also be made available for the private education of an employee's children.

ix) Company's products/services Some companies provide their products or services to employees at a substantial discount. For instance airlines often have generous flight arrangements for their employees. Comapnies that produce consumer durables or packaged food sometimes have a 'company shop' where employees car purchase specific products at very low prices.

x) Housing assistance This can be provided in several ways. Assistance with house purchase, allowances for moving and subsidised accommodation.

A survey undertaken by the British Institute of Management in 1970 concluded that benefits were unlikely to play an important part in increasing productivity and improving performance. Once a benefit has been established it just becomes part of an employees total reward and another cost of employment. Like most other forms of incentive payments, employee benefits need to be tailored to meet the specific needs of a business and can be part of an employee remuneration strategy.

3:3 Payment by results incentives (PBR) Every payment by results scheme is based on output. The output may be measured in physical units of weight, quantity volume etc, in value terms or in terms of standard hours (Refer to chapter 9 section 5 for an explanation of standard hours of production) One of the earliest PBR schemes was developed by F. Taylor in his book Scientific Management (1881). It was a simple piecework scheme that is probably still being applied today in some companies. There are now many kinds of PBR schemes because each incentive based remuneration system needs to be designed to meet the specific needs of an organisation. However some general characteristics of PBR schemes can be identified:-

i) Proportional schemes where wages increase directly in relation to output

ii) Progressive schemes where wages increase proportionately more than output

iii) Regressive schemes where wages increase proportionately less than output

iv) Variable schemes where wages increase or decrease according to variations in output

v) Individual schemes where any of the previous schemes are based on individual effort and the individual is rewarded accordingly

vi) Group schemes where schemes (i) to (iv) may be applied to group effort and the work group rewarded accordingly.

The choice of scheme really depends upon workplace circumstances. For example, outworkers (people who work at home) that, say, assemble a product from supplied components, are ideally suited for a proportional piece rate. They simply get paid an amount per unit assembled. If however the workplace is part of a continuous production process for hetregeneous output, then any PBR scheme will be far more complicated. The incentive scheme would probably require some form of job evaluation to ensure that pay differentials were not distorted. In workplace situations where output cannot be measured with any degree of accuracy or relevance, such as an office, a PBR scheme is inappropriate. The advantages and disadvantages of a PBR scheme are listed below.

Payment by Results Schemes	
Advantages	*Disadvantages*
Provides incentives for higher output	May create problems due to pay differentials and individual job rates
Higher output reduces average cost per unit	Tight quality controls needed
Less supervision is required	Increased administration costs
	Reduces labour mobility because some jobs may have higher earning potential

Great caution is necessary before introducing a PBR scheme. Even though output may be measureable and employees request some form of output incentive there are a number of problems with PBR schemes. The National Board for Prices and Incomes (NBPI) made a substantial investigation into PBR systems(2). They found a wide range of PBR schemes, some were under close control and others where management had lost control. A key issue in most schemes was the 'conversion factor' that was multiplied by the standard time to produce acceptable earnings. Indeed PBR schemes were identified as one of the main causes of divergence between wage rates agreed at national level and industry level and local earnings. The NBPI reported that 'natural decay' will occur in most PBR systems. The development and natural decay of PBR systems has been identified as occurring in four phases:-(3)

Phase 1 Introduction of a scheme relating wages to output based on scientific work study.

Phase 2 Unilateral regulation of the scheme by management begins to create earnings anomalies due to: changes in production methods, the learning curve effect, allowances for waiting time and changes in standard times and conversion factors.

Phase 3 Joint regulation of the PBR scheme develops as shop stewards start bargaining on conversion factors, standard times, minimum earnings and waiting time allowances.

Phase 4 Fractional bargaining develops where individual bargains are struck for specific jobs. This is distinguished from collective bargaining which should be based on established procedures. Fractional bargaining is the signal of a complete breakdown in the system because rates are fixed by haggling instead of by objective measurement. The consequences of too many individual bargains being struck

(2) *Payment by Results Systems. NBPI Report No. 65 and Supplement. HMSO Cmnd.3627 (1968).*

(3) *W. Brown. Piecework Bargaining. Heineman (1973)*

are; discontent over differentials, leap frogging effect of each bargain and the ratchet effect of total wages drifting upwards. Once the effort/earnings linkage is broken, the PBR scheme has failed.

In the following sub-sections we will review some of the main types of PBR schemes. However, it must be emphasised that any kind of incentive payment system has to be tailor made for an organisation. Accordingly, the established methods only provide a basis upon which to develop a PBR scheme within a company.

3:3:1 Piece rates A piece rate system is where an employee is paid a fixed amount per unit of output regardless of the time taken. Piece rate systems can be divided into three categories:-

i) Straight piece rate
ii) Piece rate plus guaranteed day rate
iii) Differential piece rate

i) Straight piece rate This is often used for part time employees and outworkers engaged in repetitive work producing a measurable output. The formula is:

Total wages = Number of units produced x piece rate per unit

ii) Piece rate plus guaranteed day rate With full time employees there is normally a guaranteed pay based on the number of hours 'worked'. The management options were basically to adopt a position somewhere along the following scale that will provide the maximum incentive.

Piece Rate Scale

Low guaranteed pay with high piece rate	————————	High guaranteed pay with low piece rate

iii) Differential piece rate This is quite a popular system and is generally an application of the guaranteed day rate principle explained above. There are several methods that are attributed to their designers, i.e. Taylor plan, Merrick plan and Gantt task and bonus plan. Their main difference is in the number of steps between the piece rates. Taylor used a high and low rate, Merrick used three different rates and the Gantt plan has three rates where the lowest is the guaranteed minimum pay level.

The choice of piece rates and output levels is really a matter for individual organisations to decide. Whatever decision is made, a lot of calculations are needed to ensure the results of the system will not distort the company's existing pay structure.

3:3:2 Premium bonus systems. The difference between premium bonus systems is in the way the saving of time is shared between the employees and the employer. Premium bonus systems are output based, but tend to be more complicated than piece work systems. The characteristics of a premium bonus system are:-

(a) Incentive payments increase with output, but not in direct proportion to changes in output.

(b) There is a guaranteed day rate.

(c) The cost savings from increased output are shared between the employer and employees according to an agreed formula.

There are many kinds of premium bonus systems, but the differences are primarily in the way the cost savings are calculated and divided between the employer and employees. We will briefly examine the following methods:-

i) Halsey premium system
ii) Weir premium system
iii) Rowan system
iv) Bedaux point premium system

i) Halsey premium system. A standard time is agreed for a job. If the worker finishes the job in the standard time or takes longer, then he/she will still receive the guaranteed day rate. But if the job is completed in less than the standard time, the time saved is shared between employer and employee at an agreed ratio which is usually 50:50. For example: assume an employee has a guaranteed day rate of £2.00 per hour and has a time allowance of say, 10 hours for a job. If the employee finishes the job in 8 hours then he/she will receive 9 hours pay for 8 hours work, i.e.

Time rate x (Time taken + (Time saved x 0.5)) = Gross pay
£2.00 x (8 + (2 x £0.5)) = £18.00

ii) Weir Premium system. Weir introduced the Halsey system in the U.K. and it is therefore sometimes called the Halsey-Weir system. This system is a little more complicated and best illustrated with an example.

A work study assessment of a job provided the following figures:-

	Hours
Observed time	6
less lost time due to production delay	0.5
	5.5
Estimated efficiency of worker 80%	x0.8
100% efficiency rating	= 4.4
Add allowance for fatigue, personal needs and production delays.	1.0
Basic time	5.4
Add incentive allowance of 66.6%	3.6
Standard time @ 66.7% efficiency	9.0

The bonus is calculated on the standard time of 9 hours. An employee who completes the work in the basic time of 5.4 hours receives a 33.3% increase in wages and a worker who achieves the 100% efficiency rating will receive a 50% bonus.

iii) Rowan system. This is similar to the Halsey premium system. But under a Rowan system the bonus hours are calculated in a different way. Using the example given in the explanation of the Halsey system we have:-

$$\text{Time rate x} \quad \text{Time taken} + \frac{(\text{Time taken x Time saved})}{\text{Time allowed}} = \text{Gross pay}$$

$$2.00 \times \left[8 + \frac{(8 \times 2)}{10} \right] = £19.2$$

In this example a higher bonus was paid under the Rowan system. But as efficiency increases Halsey rates become higher. This is illustrated in diagram 49 and its accompanying calculations.

(iv) Bedaux point premium system. This system derives standard times from work study. The time unit is a minute and is called a 'Bedaux Point' or 'B'.

The original Bedaux system paid a bonus of 75% on time saved multiplied by one-sixtieth of the hourly rate. The other 25% was paid to Supervision and other indirect labour in agreed proportions. The principle is illustrated in the following example that uses the same data given in earlier examples:-

Time allowance	(10 hours)	called	600 B's
Time taken	(8 hours)	called	480 B's
Bedaux points saved			120

$$\text{Bonus} = 120 \times \frac{£2.00}{60} \times \frac{75}{100} = 3.00$$

Plus basic rate (8 x 2)	=	16.00
Gross wages		19.00

Comparison of systems

All the premium systems are based on time savings where the benefits are divided between the employer and employees at agreed ratios. They all require standard times to be set for specific jobs. The setting of standard times requires an analysis of past output to assess approximate times and work study to determine more precise times. When the standard times and rates have been determi ined, calculations are needed to measure the effect of the proposals on wage costs and differentials. Diagram 49 and its accompanying calculations illustrate the effect of different incentive payment schemes at different levels of efficiency. The straight piece rate is illustrated as the most expensive, (depending on rate) and the time rate the cheapest (depending on efficiency)

DIAGRAM 49 COMPARISON OF INCENTIVE PAYMENT SCHEMES

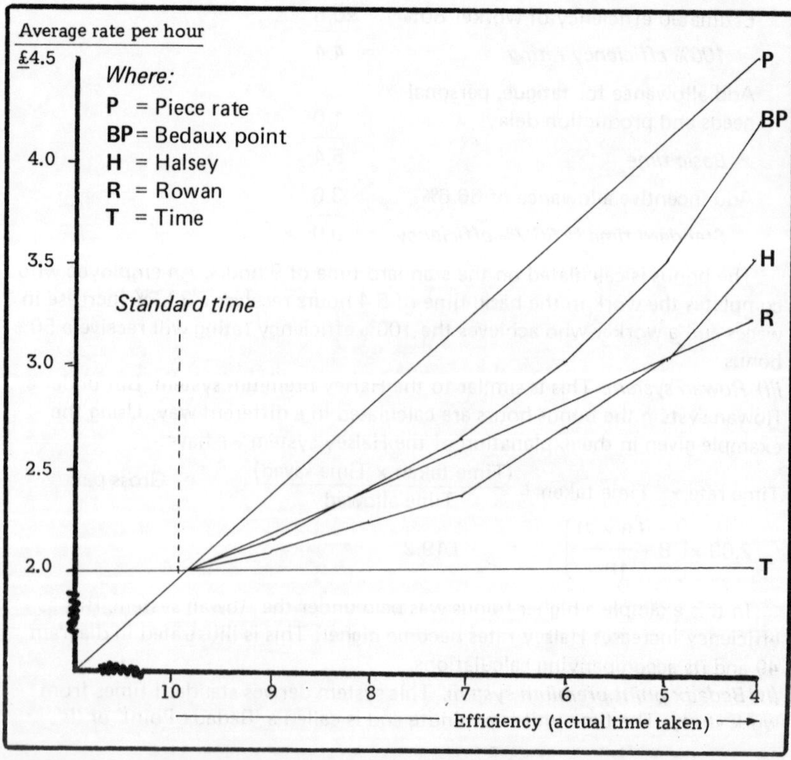

Calculations for diagram 49
The calculations are based on the data used in earlier examples, i.e. A time allowance of 10 hours and a basic rate of £2.00 per hour.

Time taken	Total pay Halsey	Rowan	B.Point	Average per hour Halsey	Rowan	B. Point
10	20.00	20.00	20.00	2.00	2.00	2.00
9	19.00	19.80	19.50	2.11	2.20	2.17
8	18.00	19.20	19.00	2.25	2.40	2.40
7	17.00	18.20	18.50	2.42	2.60	2.64
6	16.00	16.80	18.00	2.67	2.80	3.00
5	15.00	15.00	17.50	3.00	3.00	3.50
4	14.00	12.80	17.00	3.50	3.20	4.25

3:3:3 Group bonus systems. Throughout this section on labour remuneration systems it has been frequestly stated that each system has to be tailored to meet the specific needs of the organisation. An organisation may wish to introduce some form of PBR system but the production circumstances may make it difficult to measure an individual's output accurately and fairly. Under these kinds of circumstances a group PBR system may be used. The following table shows some production characteristics for individual and group PBR schemes:-

Individual PBR	Group PBR
Individual output can be measured	Individual output cannot be measured but group output can.
Changes in output dependent mainly on effort of individual	Changes in output dependent upon a group and not an individual.
Management wish to encourage individual effort	Management wish to encourage group effort and team spirit

A number of studies have been made about individual and group bonus schemes [4]. The group schemes had group sizes ranging from 5 to 50.For example a group PBR system used in a foundry could have over 50 employees. The *Priestman group bonus system* that is used in some foundries fixes a level of output for a specified time period. If the actual output exceeds the standard then a formula is applied to calculate the group bonus.

The problem of fairly dividing the group bonus amongst the employees can create difficulties if there are different grades of workers. A common group payment scheme is called the *lieu bonus* that can be viewed as an indirect cost of a PBR scheme. The need for a *lieu bonus* arises because skilled (and sometimes not so skilled) indirect workers become upset when they see other employees with whom they work, earning a bonus. For example, a skilled maintenance fitter or a foreman may find that an efficient semi-skilled machine operative is earning more than they are. This erosion of differentials is 'smoothed' with a *lieu bonus* and the 'ratchet has moved another click! (Refer to earlier notes on the 'ratchet effect'.)

3:3:4 Work measurement All PBR schemes are aimed at recording extra effort by an employee or group of employees. In many schemes the extra effort is

(4) R. Mariot Incentive Payment Systems, a Review of Research & Opinion Staples Press (1968)
Also see the NBPI Report No. 65, Payment by Results Systems

measured in output terms. However, work measurement in terms of physical output is not always the appropriate measure, therefore a wide number of work measurement schemes are in existence to suit specific work circumstances. Sometimes work measurement schemes are closely related to job and personnel evaluation schemes. (Refer to sub-section 3:1:2 and 3:1:3) The following notes provide a summary of work measurement techniques:-

Activity sampling. This technique is sometimes referred to as *work sampling* or *work measurement.* A series of observations of work activity are made at random intervals over a period of time and measurements of time and output are taken, Statistical techniques are then used to produce standard work times. These standard work times can then be used for planning, pricing and incentive payment schemes.

Analytical estimating. A technique where a job is broken down into identifiable components. Each component is then given a time estimate based on existing knowledge, experience and work study data if available. The job component times and costs are then aggregated to produce a standard upon which planning pricing and incentive payment schemes may be based.

Comparative estimating. Applications of this technique appear under a variety of titles that include: *Dominant job evaluation, integral job evaluation, job factor comparison, job grading, job ranking, points rating* (Refer to sub-section 3:1:2) and *time span analysis.* (Refer to sub-section 3:1:4). Basically all these work measurement techniques compare the work content of one job with similar work contents of other jobs. Jobs are then given broad time bands generally referred to as *'slotting'*. These job time bands can then be used in planning, pricing and incentive payment schemes.

Predetermined motion time system (PMTS). This is a synthetic time measurement system where a job is broken into a series of human motions for which a time is allocated. The time measurements make allowance for the nature of the motion and the conditions under which it is made. Alternative titles for this technique are: *methods time measurements (MTM)* and *work factory study.* This work measurement method can be used for manpower planning and production scheduling for new production processes where there is no relevant historical data upon which to base the measurement.

Work study. This technique is also referred to under the following titles: *time and motion study, time study, method study and work measurement.* This is based on the traditional 'stop watch game', where a job is broken down into a number of measurable components and then an employee's work is accurately measured with a stop watch. The times are then aggregated and adjustments made for 'normal working conditions'. The times can then be used for planning pricing and incentive payment schemes.

3:4 Cost reduction incentives The PBR systems explained in the previous subsections were based mainly on labour time savings in relation to some kind of output measure. Cost reduction incentive systems operate on a broader base that always includes labour time savings. Cost reductions are achieved through improved productivity, less material wastage and better co-operation between em-employees and management. A proportion of the cost savings then paid to employees based on an agreed formula calculation. A cost reduction incentive system is normally negotiated for an entire plant or cpmpany and is therefore referred to as a *company wide or plant wide incentive scheme.* The most well known company wide schemes are the: Rucker, Scanlan and Kaiser-Steel plans. Less well known cost reduction schemes have been operated with smaller groups. For instance, the *budgeted expenditure bonus scheme* is generally based on departmental cost savings. Under this scheme a bonus payment formula is applied to the cost savings when actual expenditure is less than budgeted expenditure. However this type of scheme would tend to create difficulties at the budgetary planning phase. (Refer to chapter 8).

The advantages and disadvantages of cost reduction schemes are summarised in the following table:

Cost Reduction Schemes

Advantages	*Disadvantages*
An incentive to increase overall efficiency including higher output and less material wastage.	The link between individual reward and effort is very weak
The plant wide scheme encourages co-operation and teamwork	Bonus payment can be affected by factors outside the workers' control such as material price increases.
Encourages employees to become more cost conscious	Time lag between effort and reward may may be too long

The following sub-sections briefly review the Scanlan, Rucker and Kaiser-Steel cost reduction plans.

3:4:1 Scanlan plan. This incentive payment system was developed by an American steelworker, Joseph Scanlan. The bonus payment (usually monthly) is based on a simple relationship of:-

$$\frac{\text{Total manpower costs}}{\text{Total sales value}}$$

The agreed labour cost/sales ratio will normally be derived by some averaging process from a number of years' figures. If productivity improves, the difference would be divided between the employer and employees on an agreed ratio of say 50/50. Consider the following simplified example:-

Example

A company operating a plant wide Scanlan Plan with a labour cost/sales ratio of 60% had the following trading results:-

Total manpower costs	£550,000
Total sales value	£1,000,000

As the standard manpower costs for this level of sales was £600,000 (i.e. £1,000,000 x 0.6) the cost saving was £50,000. The agreement was a 50/50 division and therefore a bonus of £25,000 was paid to the employees.

With the rapid changes in technology that can substantially increase output per manhour, some provision is needed to revise the labour cost/sales ratio. A revision of the ratio may be difficult to negotiate and an additional cost factor for the introduction of new technology may be a high bonus payment under a Scanlan Plan incentive scheme.

One of the objectives of the Scanlan plan was to encourage teamwork. Therefore,the plan includes a number of consultative committees aimed at improving work practices, production scheduling and reducing wastage.

An application of the Scanlan Plan was installed at The Pressed Steel Company at Linwood in 1963. It is sometimes referred to as the *'Linwood Plan'* but it was based on the Scanlan principle of a labour cost/sales ratio.

3:4:2 Rucker plan This incentive payment plan was developed by an American, Allan Rucker. It is similar to the Scanlan Plan except that the labour cost ratio is based on added volume instead of sales, i.e.

$$\frac{\text{Total manpower cost}}{\text{Value added by manufacture}}$$

The labour cost/added value ratio will be derived by an analysis of wages and related added values for a number of years. In the original Ruker Plan the added value was called the 'production value' and was based on the belief that in every industry there exists a proportional relationship between annual 'production value' per worker and annual pay per worker.

When there was an improvement in the ratio an agreed percentage of the actual cost saving would belong to the employees. Three quarters of this amount would be paid to employees on a monthly basis in proportion with their basic wages. The remainder would be held in a reserve fund to set against any adverse ratio results and the balance would be distributed at the end of the accounting period.

The Rucker plan does not have a strong consultative emphasis like the Scanlan plan. However, under the Rucker plan there is a 'Share of Production Committee' comprising eight to twelve members representing management and trade unions. The function of the committee is to promote and help implement cost reduction ideas.

3:4:3 Kaiser-Steel plan This plan was developed in America by a tripartite committee representing management, employees and the public. The committee was set up after the 1959 steel strike and their proposals were implemented by the United States Kaiser Steel Corporation.

The company wide incentive plan replaced individual and crew incentive payment schemes. The basic payments were made on a monthly basis based on a four year plan. The calculation of the bonus payments were related to the *planned* savings in the materials and labour costs of producing finished steel. The planned savings were calculated in terms of the costs of producing steel in 1961 but this was adjusted to take account of price variations. The plan also provided some employment safeguards such as:-

(a) A company employment pool as a protection against redundancy from changes arising from technology, and:

(b) Guaranteed future wage payment levels to keep at least level with other steel companies. However, in principle this plan was not significantly different from the Scanlan plan.

3:5 Measured daywork (MDW) This is an incentive payment method where a fixed amount is paid above the basic rate if an agreed level of performance is achieved. All MDW schemes are based on an agreed incentive performance level. If the employee, or group of employees, maintain performance at the agreed level then the bonus will be paid. MDW schemes do not porvide such a direct incentive as PBR schemes and tend to have the wage stability of some time based remuneration systems. Surveys have extablished that companies have adopted MDW schemes under the following circumstances:-

(a) When moving away from PBR schemes MDW schemes are often negotiated.
(b) To improve the earnings of time based workers and restore differentials MDW schemes are sometimes used.
(c) Changing of shift working arrangements are often negotiated on an MDW basis.
(d) Changes in work practices due to the introduction of new technology are sometimes negotiated on an MDW basis.

Like any other incentive payment method, MDW scemes will be tailored to fit the needs of the organisation and there will propably be an element of compromise arising from negotiations. MDW schemes tend to be simpler than PBR schemes and can be divided into three broad categories:-

High day rate system
Flat rate plus bonus system
Premiun pay plan (PPP) system

The high day rate system has a time based payment per hour, shift or week linked to a requirement to work to a specified level of performance. Although the wage payment aspect is quite simple the negotiated rules for running the scheme can be complicated. For example, it would be management's responsibility to ensure that there were no production delays such as material shortages or bad production scheduling. Assuming management kept to their side of the bargain,then the arrangements would allow sanctions to be applied against individual employees who failed to meet their agreed performance targets.

The flat rate plus bonus system has been criticised because it tends to be based on a penalty for failing to meet the performance standard, instead of being an incentive. In practice it would often be quite difficult to withold a bonus if there were strong trade unions involved in the arrangements, The subsequent negotiations would probably be based on both sides blaming each other for the poor performance.

The premium pay plan (also called graded or graduated MDW) provides an employee with the opportunity to increase earnings by improving personal performance. The PPP system has graded levels of pay for different fixed levels of performance. One of the early PPP systems had five job classifications from A to E and seven levels of performance from 1 to 7. The highest paid job would therefore be E7 and the lowest A1. An employee wishing to increase his/her wage could try to move up the job alphabet say from A6 to B2. Or, improve their performance and move up the performance scale say from C3 to C5. This system is similar to the job evaluation and merit rating schemes explained earlier. (Refer to sub-sections 3:1:2 and 3:1;3).

The advantages and disadvantages of measured daywork are summarised in the following table:-

Measured Daywork	
Advantages	*Disadvantages*
Lower administration costs than PBR methods	Productivity may be less than under PBR method
Provides stability of earnings	Stronger supervision may be necessary
Reduces opposition to mobility which often occurs with PBR methods	Disciplinary action may be needed for individuals not meeting performance targets
Avoids the 'ratchet effect' that can occur with PBR schemes	A lot of work necessary to agree job descriptions, pay levels and differentials.

The introduction of an MDW system is often the first step towards pay structuring. This can be a very difficult step to make if differentials have been eroded by PBR schemes and then 'smoothed' with lieu payments. However, an MDW system could provide the foundations for a structured pay policy.

3:6 Profit sharing The principles and practice of profit sharing have been established for a long time. In 1889 there was an International Congress on Profit Sharing in Paris. Since then,successive UK governments have continually debated and sometimes even legislated for different aspects of profit sharing and co-partnership schemes. The latest examples of UK legislation in this area are the tax incentives for employee shares in recent finance Acts. One of the reasons for these repetitive surges of interest in this subject is a desire to improve co-operation between employees and employers. However there is no valid evidence to support the assertion that profit sharing schemes improve workplace relationships. They certainly have a role to play in a general industrial relations strategy. But a profit sharing scheme on its own, is not the panacea that it is sometimes claimed to be.

If we sweep away the trite rhetoric that clusters around this topic and just look at the facts, we can broadly divide profit sharing schemes into the following categories:-

(a) Immediate cash payment where the company agrees to paying a proportion of profits directly to employees in cash immediately after income calculation dates.
(b) Deferred cash payment where a proportion of profits are regularly credited to employee accounts and then paid at agreed times such as retirement or after a number of years service.
(c) Immediate share payment where an employee's proportion of profits is given in the form of shares immediately after income calculation dates.
(d) Deferred share payment where employees' proportion of profits is invested in the company and shares are not distributed to employees until they die, retire or leave the firm after a specified number of years service.

Profit sharing schemes do not fit into the direct incentive category. Their function is simply to improve employees' goodwill towards the company. Therefore any scheme has to be part of an industrial relations strategy to improve co-operation between employees and employers. If a profit sharing scheme is to be introduced then the following key questions require answers:-

(i) What profit figure is to be used?

There are many kinds of profit (Refer to *Volume 1, Financial accounting for non-accountants)* It may not be difficult to define a profit figure such as: before tax, after interest, after extraordinary items and after minority interests for a 52 week accounting period. But there may be difficulty in explaining the basis and fairness of the calculation to a suspicious workforce. Moreover, if the profit figure used for the calculation does not readily reconcile with the published profit figure in the shareholders' accounts, then the entire costly excerise to secure employees' goodwill may be wasted.

(ii) What happens if there is a loss?

Employees normally claim that a loss is due to management inefficiency and employees should not be expected to suffer because of poor management. It would be quite difficult to get employees to contribute to a company loss. Thus the main options when a trading loss occurs, is to pay nothing or make a token payment as a sign of goodwill.

(iii) How much is to be paid out?

The popular choice here is to make a percentage payment equivalent to the individual yield. This has a superficial appeal, but is an invalid comparison because the bases of the calculations are entirely different. The amount payable can be just a simple percentage that has been agreed through negotiations.

(iv) How is the payment to be divided between the employees?

The alternative ways of distributing the total payment would include:-

A simple percentage of basic pay
A percentage of basic pay with increments related to length of service
A percentage of basic pay with increments based on performance assessment
Simple division equally amongst employees regardless of earnings and length of service.

According to a British Institute of Management (BIM) survey in 1962 the most popular method was some kind of formula relating to basic pay and length of service

(v) How should the payment be made?

This is mainly a choice between shares or cash. Generally, employees prefer to receive cash and employers prefer to pay out in shares. The legislature has tried to persuade employees to want shares, by providing tax incentives. From an employer's point of view there are a number of benefits from share issues such as:-

Does not affect corporate cash flow
Encouraging employees to be 'part' owners of the business
A wider spread of share ownership amongst small investors.

Employers therefore usually encourage share payments and provide lists of 'advantages' for employees who take shares in the company.

(vi) When should the payment be made?

The choice is basically between immediate or deferred payment. In the BIM survey most of the schemes paid out quarterly, half-yearly or annually. None of the 21 companies operated a deferred payment scheme for employees Deferred payment schemes are however a feature of some executive remuneration packages.

The advantages and disadvantages of profit sharing schemes are summarised in the following table:–

PROFIT SHARING

Advantages	*Disadvantages*
Improves employee goodwill towards the company	The reward is too remote from the effort by employees
Does not disturb the pay structure or encourage the 'rachet effect'	Can be difficulties when determining how and when payment should be made

Profit sharing schemes are unlikely to provide instant results in terms of increased output and improved efficiency. It is therefore difficult to objectively assess the results after introducing a scheme. Naturally, figures can be produced by any company proving the success of a scheme, but the link between cause and effect is so weak that figures are simply for support and not illumination. Indeed, some claims of success in profit sharing may have been made to justify a managerial decision instead of being an objective appraisal based on valid criteria.

3:7 Productivity agreements A productivity agreement is where employees agree to make a change or changes in working practices and manning levels that will improve efficiency. In return, the employer agrees to higher levels of pay and/or benefits. There are three main types of productivity agreement:-

1. *Partial agreements* that are restricted to just one or two groups of employees within an organisation. Partial agreements can distort differentials.

2. *Comprehensive agreements* that cover most of the employees in a plant or company.
3. *Framework agreements* that are negotiated at a national level to provide a framework for individual prouuctivity agreements within an industry.

The need for productivity agreements became apparent during the late 1950s when British companies were identified as having low labour productivity based on international comparisons. The reasons for poor labour productivity were generally ascribed to restrictive practices, excessive overtime and ineffective management. Many managers were in a particularly difficult position in their dealings with organised labour, because of fragmented plant level bargaining where several trade unions were often competing for membership in the same plant. Thus to remove restrictive work practices and reduce overtime was a formidable task. Then during the early 1960s a productivity agreement was successfully negotiated at the Esso Fawley Refinery near Southampton. It was a well documented and widely reported agreement that aroused great interest in productivity agreements.

The government during the 1960s supported productivity agreements by allowing them to be used as a means of increasing wages above the statutory incomes policy levels. The National Board of Prices and Incomes (NBPI) reported at that time that many productivity agreements were being reached. Although some of these agreements were probably just devices to circumvent incomes policy restraints. However, the 1960's were certainly a very active time with regard to productivity agreements.

The advantages and disadvantages of productivity agreements are summarised in the following table.

Productivity Agreements *Advantages and Disadvantages*	
Management Reduction of excessive overtime Greater flexibility in the use of labour (less demarcation) Reduction of manning levels Improved efficiency Acceptance of change	*Management* Grievances arise from employees excluded from an agreement, such as middle management. Rewards inefficient as well as efficient employees
Employees Higher earnings and shorter working week Greater stability of earnings Improved job satisfaction	*Employees* Reduction in some individuals' earnings who are used to working a lot of overtime. Threat of redundancy Possibility of unsocial working hours due to shift work agreements

The additional payment that an employer makes in a productivity deal is usually a negotiated increase in basic wage rates. It is often argued that this payment is simply buying off restrictive practices and that these practices will subsequently re-emerge and have to be brought off again. However, if an employer is expecting a surge in demand and the company's present working practices will prevent output targets being met; then it would probably be cheaper in the long run to make some kind of productivity deal before attempting to increase output.

3:8 Remuneration policy The previous sub-sections on labour remuneration have covered a wide range of incentive payment schemes. As some of these remuneration schemes may be tactical to meet the requirements of small pressure groups it is important that they fit into some kind of policy framework. If a remuneration framework does not exist then wages and salaries can easily become distorted in terms of differentials and make up of total rewards. The principles explained in chapter 2, Sub-section 2:1 can be applied for decisions concerning wages and salaries. Consider the following illustration:-

Framework for wages and salary decisions

Objectives	To attract, maintain and motivate labour. To provide a fair reward for effort
Policies	To move towards a 'clean' wage and salary system through negotiated settlements
Plans	The development of responsible collective bargaining The continual revision of incentive payment schemes and their removal where possible The development of internal career structures and the shift of wage earners into salaried staff

The policy in this illustration is to get out of incentive payment schemes. From this policy statement,a set of outline plans have been developed. The point to note about this grossly simplified illustration is that the objective, policies, plans approach helps to create a framework for wages and salary decisions. The detail concerning matters such as how total reward is made up, how differentials can be maintained and how the remuneration system can be used as an incentive device, can then be fitted into the broad policy guidelines.

In the following sub-sections on remuneration policy we will first distinguish between wage and salary systems, then examine some policy aspects of these two broad remuneration categories. The following sub-section explains why all wage and salary systems need to be constantly monitored and the final sub-section reviews the need for communicating to employees about the remuneration system.

3:8:1 Wage and salary systems The distinction between wages and salaries can be established by identifying some of the characteristics of wage earning and salary earning employees as shown in the following table:-

Characteristics of Wages and Salaries

Wage earners	*Salary earners*
Basic rate-hourly	Basic rate - annually
Payment frequency - weekly	Payment frequency - monthly
Payment method - cash	Payment method - cheque
Fixed working hours	Flexible working hours
Paid for overtime	Overtime not usually paid
Incentive payment usually part of total wage	Total salary does not usually include an incentive payment
Wage rates and bonus payments usually subject to collective bargaining	Salary levels usually based on individual performance and individual negotiations
Motivated primarily by wage and job security	Career and status motivation very important
Few fringe benefits	Many fringe benefits

Over the last two decades the wage/salary distinction has been becoming increasingly blurred. A noticeable change has been the erosion of job security and status of the white collar worker. This has been accompanied by increasing unionisation of clerical workers. Conversely, for many blue collar workers there has been a shift towards salary type structures with improved fringe benefits and career opportunities, flexitime working and payments by cheque. From a remuneration policy viewpoint,some managers may attempt a strategy of moving employees towards a salary based system. Once an employee is in a salary structure with career opportunities, status and job security,the scope for collective bargaining will not necessarily diminish. For example in the civil service or education,most employees are in salary structures. But the trade unions representing the employees still bargain effectively on behalf of their members.

With the changing nature of workplace relationships and advances in technology the shift of remuneration characteristics from wage systems towards salary systems will probably continue. However, from a remuneration policy viewpoint it is still useful to distinguish between wages and salaries. In the following two sub-sections we will first consider some aspects of a wages policy and then a salaries policy.

3:8:2 Wages policy Most of the incentive payment schemes that have been explained in Section 3 can be incorporated into a wages policy. However, a wages policy does not necessarily have to include output or cost reduction incentives. Indeed an objective of a wages policy could be to move towards a 'clean wage' system where there are no incentive payments whatsoever. But even a time based 'clean wage' system would still have to establish some form of differential wage structure.. The usual criteria for differentials such as levels of skill, experience, responsibility, age and service with the company would still apply. Also a 'clean wage' system would still have to recognise the demand and supply conditions in the company's relevant labour markets to be able to attract and retain certain kinds of labour.

As many parts of a wages policy are negotiated issues, managerial discretion in this area will probably be limited by collective bargaining, custom and practice and established procedures. Thus a policy shift away from incentive based systems may be very difficult to implement. The 'ratchet effect' of many incentive payment schemes, explained earlier, can lead to 'leapfrogging' parity disputes that become particularly difficult to structure in multi union negotiations. Under these circumstances a wages policy framework is essential. Otherwise, a single seemingly innocuous settlement could have costly ramifications.

We can summarise this complex issue by noting that a wages policy should provide a framework within which wage negotiations are structured. This structuring will help to reduce parity disputes by agreeing differentials. It will also help to provide some balance between the components that make up an employee's total reward. For example the components that make up total reward can easily get out of balance due to excessive overtime and/or high bonus payments becoming greater than the basic wage. As all incentive payment schemes are subject to natural decay, their revision needs to be undertaken within a wages policy framework.

3:8:3 Salaries policy A salaries policy needs to adopt a broader total reward concept than a wages policy. The total reward of a wage earner has traditionally contained few legitimate perks. Although this has changed a little, the prime motivator is still the wage packet and therefore this is the central issue in a wages policy. With a salaries policy, the £x,000 per annum for an employee is only one aspect of the total reward. The key factors for determining this £x,000 level are: the demand and supply of the skills, qualifications and experience needed for the job and the calibre of the employee. Thus a structured salary system based on 'clean salary' principles (i.e. no overtime or incentive payments) can be established on market rates and a personnel evaluation system. Managerial discretion may be greater with salaried staff if they are not members of any organised labour movement such as a staff association and/or trade union. Thus a salary policy could be imposed unilaterially and any individual would tend to be in a fairly weak bargaining position.

Taking a broad total reward approach to a salary policy provides senior management with a wide range of motivational devices. A powerful and relatively inexpensive motivational device is status. This can be achieved in absurd ways such as a bigger desk diary, the design of a chair (top status chairs have arms, swivel, tilt and look expensive), a larger desk, a carpet and other office trimmings. The more expensive status symbols are access to ranked staff restaurants, company cars and secretaries. A remarkable amount of time can be wasted by intelligent high level management in discussions concerning organisational status objects. Although many of these status objects have little objective function, they can be an effective motivational substitute for an increase in salary. Decision makers are not always rational and objective.

Sub-section 3:2 explained many kinds of real employee benefits such as: pensions, holiday entitlements, health insurance, education and housing assistance. All benefits form part of a total reward package and would be included in a salary policy. However, as one of the prime objections of any salary policy must be to increase staff motivation and improve goodwill, each aspect of an employee's total reward has to be cost justified. For some staff, a simple and cheap status object may be a more powerful motivational device than say a costly improvement of a staff pension plan.

Clearly a salaries policy is not just a matter of structuring salary levels. It is inter-related with organisational planning, (Refer to chapter 2, section 4) and encompasses the total range of rewards and motivational devices that are applicable to salaried staff.

3:8:4 Monitoring wage and salary systems All wage and salary systems need to be continually monitored and appropriate adjustments made to meet changing circumstances. Examples of changed circumstances include: production changes due to new plant and machinery or production scheduling, labour market changes in the supply and demand of people with special skills, changes in differentials brought about by incentive payment schemes or agreements through collective bargaining, changes in the law, markets and technology. Monitoring is also needed because total wages and salaries tend to drift upward. 'Wage drift' can occur because of badly negotiated and organised incentive payment schemes, special payments such as dirty money, shift premiums, etc getting out of control and excessive overtime. 'Salary drift' can occur because of organisational agreements where salary increments are based on length of service and employment grade. With these arrangements, organisations can become 'top heavy' where most of the members of staff are at the top end of the salary structure. This 'top heavy' type of organisation is particularly noticeable in some educational establishments where staff grading provides a safe career path for academics. Because of changing circumstances and the tendency for wages and salaries to drift upwards monitoring and subsequent corrective action is essential.

Monitoring is mainly a quantitative analytical function comprising the following stages:-

Stage 1 Data collection. The main sources of data are personnel records, production schedules, incentive payment agreements and payroll analysis.

Stage 2 Data analysis. The organisation and analysis of wage and salary data will depend upon the circumstances of each employing unit. For instance, if an organisation has a clearly defined set of job grades (Refer to sub-section 3:1:2) then some form of analysis could be undertaken as shown in diagram 50 which

DIAGRAM 50 JOB GRADING – ANALYSIS

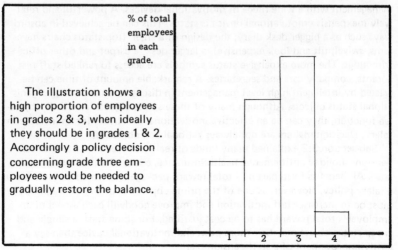

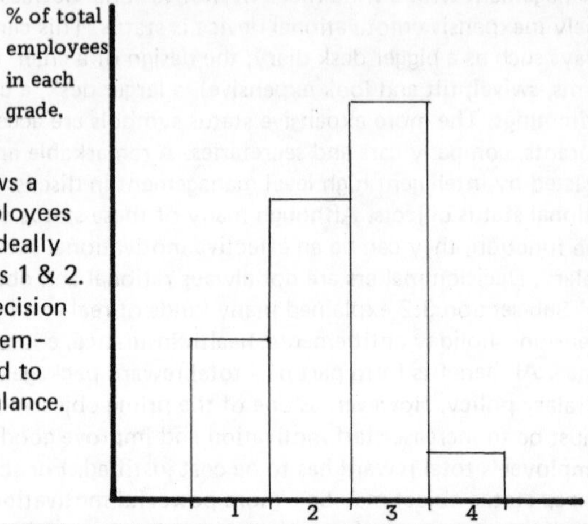

The illustration shows a high proportion of employees in grades 2 & 3, when ideally they should be in grades 1 & 2. Accordingly a policy decision concerning grade three employees woudl be needed to gradually restore the balance.

shows a 'top heavy' organisation. An analysis based on the distribution of wage levels shown in diagram 50 can provide an indication of the area of wage drift There are of course may analytical techniques that can be applied to the basic data. The choice of technique will depend upon the circumstances and the preferences of the decision maker.

Stage 3 Interpretation. The interpretation stage is concerned with identifying defects in the wage and salary systems and finding out why they have arisen. For example the standard setting process for an incentive payment scheme may have become slack and large bonus payments are being easily earned. Or there may be some mal practices concerned with the record keeping side of bonus payments. It is not uncommon for time sheets or job sheets to 'adjusted' by employees. A good data collection and analysis system will enable interpretation to be relevant and accurate.

Stage 4 Corrective action. Defects in a remuneration system are rarely,easily corrected. Malpractices can generally be stopped unilaterally by management, but any payment scheme that requires alteration will probably be subject to the rigors of collective bargaining. However, the difficulties normally associated with changing remuneration methods do not justify a slack monitoring system. Monitoring is an essential part of a remuneration policy.

3:8:5 Communicating wage and salary systems to employees. Employees have legal rights under the Contract of Employment Act 1963 and 1972 to receive details of the composition of their total wage and deductions. These rights represent the minimum information employees should receive about their *own* wages. Our concern in this sub-section is with communicating to employees details about their wage and/or salary *system.*

All incentive payment systems are intended to act as motivators for increased output, improved efficiency, cost reduction and improved goodwill. It is therefore important that an agreed incentive payment system is *sold* to employees. Indeed, communicating this important information should be viewed as an internal marketing exercise. Because unless employees understand,believe and support the system, then its motivational effect may be quite small.

Organisations that have clearly defined salary structures and staff grading can publish salary system details that show how an employee can progress through the grades. Each grade will have a salary band and employees will therefore know the approximate salary levels of all the members of staff. This 'open salary system' operates in the civil service, education and in some large companies. However, many companies have a 'closed salary system' where salary levels are strictly confidential. A 'closed salary system' with unorganised labour provides senior management with a considerable amount of discretion and flexibility. This type of secret system enables all kinds of anomalies to exist and honest communication would probably create a lot of staff discontent. Accordingly, communication within a 'closed salary system' will tend to be superficial.

When labour is organised and recognised by a company for collective bargaining, then the wage and salary system becomes more open and managerial discretion is limited. Under these circumstances, honest communication about wages and salaries becomes necessary. The communication can take the following forms:-

(a) Personal letter to each employee included in the pay packet
(b) General communication through a circular, notice boards and/or a house journal
(c) Verbally through briefing groups given by Supervisors, personnel officers and/or shop stewards.

It is remarkable that after months of intensive work and hard bargaining that usually precedes an incentive payment scheme, so little attention is given to communicating the system to employees. A logical conclusion to a negotiatiated settlement would be for the parties to agree a joint statement that explains:-

(i) How the new system works
(ii) How it affects existing arrangements
(iii) Why it was introduced
(iv) Who should be contacted for further details

This open approach should give employees trust and confidence in changes that affect them personally.

4. Role of organised labour

An important point raised in chapter 2 was that the corporate strategy comprises of two inter-related plans; the operational plan and an organisational plan that will support the operations. Both aspects of corporate strategy will include some aspect of labour planning. And before any labour plans can be devised the company needs to identify the role that organised labour will play in the planning process. The position may already be established by custom and practice and will be somewhere on the scale shown overleaf.

Existing collective labour relationships

100% membership of independent body representing organised labour	———————————	No independent body representing organised labour

Senior executives will have a fair idea where their company fits on this scale. Some companies with closed shop arrangements will be on the extreme left of the scale and many small businesses will be on the extreme right. It is important to establish the existing position with regard to *independent* organised labour because independent labour representation limits managerial discretion. If a company is well to the left of the scale, their organised labour already plays a role in labour management and any related policy decisions will tend to reflect this position. Thus after identifying the current position, the policy decision making group needs to consider their own attitudes towards organised labour. Their attitudes will be somewhere along the following scale:-

Attitude of senior management towards organised labour

Encourage formation and responsible participation in decision making	———————————	Prevent formation and restrict development

Some companies appear to have adopted a policy of encouraging the formation of organised labour. Consider the following extract and tables from the Certification Officer's 1979 Annual Report concerning staff associations:(6)

'The evidence in Chapter 2 shows that more than half the 88 associations were actually created or inspired by management, or received active encouragement from them in the early stages of their existence; this encouragement went beyond what would be expected of an employer simply prepared to respect the wishes of his staff, and is in marked contrast to traditional management attitudes to the the development of white collar unionism in many industries' (Refer to sub-section 4:1:2)

The Certification Officer's 1979 Annual Report contained a number of tables showing how some managements had actively encouraged the formation of organised labour. Extracts from this Report are given on the next page. The first table shows the main factors that caused the formation of 88 labour representative bodies. The largest number were initially set up as social/welfare bodies or consultative bodies. Probably, some of these representative bodies would not have been actively encouraged by management if they had considered that their function may lead to press ures for negotiating rights to replace their intended consultative role.

---

6. *Supplement to annual report of the Certification Officer, 1979. Certification Office for Trade Unions and Employers' Associations.*

Cause of formation				
Main factor	*Formed before 1970*	*Formed 1970 - 1974*	*Formed 1975 or after*	*Total*
As a social/welfare organisation.	4	-	-	4
Employees wish for collective representation where no representative system previously existed	9	10	4	23
Employees' wish to replace a pre-existing consultative body by one with negotiating functions	1	6	3	10
Employees wish for an alternative to a TUC union	1	2	5	8
Employees' reaction to a specific event(eg.threat of redundancy, unsatisfactory pay settlement, nationalisation)	2	5	5	12
As a management dominated consultative body or a management inspired association	7	10	3	20
Merger of associations	2	3	-	5
Not known	5	1	-	6
Total	31	37	20	88

Employers' attitudes to formation						
Date formed	*Inspired*	*En-couraged*	*Accepted*	*Hostility*	*Not known*	*Total*
Before 1970	7	5	10	1	8	31
1970-1974	10	17	7	1	2	37
1975 or after	3	6	7	4	-	20
Total	20	28	24	6	10	88

In the above table there are suprisingly few hostile employers' attitudes to the formation of representative bodies. Therefore companies that have had favourable experiences with responsible organised labour may have attitudes to the left of the scale.

Other companies that have experienced difficult and frustrating times with irresponsible organised labour representatives, will probably be to the right of the scale. Thus there will be a wide difference in managerial attitude towards the role of organised labour. At this point it will be useful to consider some ideologies that help to identify reference frames[7].

Unitary frame of reference views the firm as analogous to a team with one common purpose, one authority structure and one focus of loyalty.
Pluralist frame of reference views the firm being composed of sectional groups with divergent interests.
Radical frame of reference that views managerial perogative as a result of social conditioning and that there is no legitimate basis for managerial authority. Under this reference frame there are no common interests and the firm is just one of the many battlefields in the class war.

If employees, their representatives and management all had a unitary frame of reference, then the role of organised labour could be constructive and participative. However, trade unions are often forced into a negative role of opposing decisions after they have been made, instead of a positive role of making a contribution to the decision making process. This negative role generally causes mistrust on both sides and makes the transition from an opposition movement to a participative movement very difficult. For this transition to take place, concessions need to be made by managers and the employee representatives. If any of the parties involved hold a radical reference frame, then genuine concessions are not possible.

Probably the most generally held viewpoint is the pluralist frame of reference based on the assumption that employers and employees have some common interests such as the survival of the firm and some divergent interests such as work practices and levels of remuneration. Our concern here is to consider the role that organised labour can play to help reconcile these divergent interests. We have established that the role will differ according to circumstances and attitudes.

Every place of work can be viewed as a system of power relationships. One viewpoint[8] that is illustrated in diagram 51, sees the workplace system being based on three power groups referred to as actors workers, employers and the government. These power groups can interact at various levels such as national, industry and plant. For the system to survive, some consensus is needed between the power groups. And the system is held together by a common ideology that defines the role and place of each actor. Any differences between workplace systems would result from environmental influences that can be broadly divided into: economic, technological, political and social. The output of the system will be rules that govern the conduct of the 'actors'.

In the following sub-sections we will be briefly considering the different forms of worker organisations, the importance of procedures, and the provision of information for collective bargaining.

4:1 Forms of organised labour Organised labour can be broadly divided into three categories; consultative, negotiating and participative. (Refer to chapter 2 sub-sections 4:2:1, 4:2;2, 4:2:3 and 4:2:4) There are few examples of labour representatives fully participating in the decision making process where they have a

7. *A. Fox. Industrial sociology and industrial relations. Royal Commission Research Paper No. 3. H.M.S.O. (1966)*

8. *J. Dunlop. Industrial Relations System. Holt-Dryden (1958)*

DIAGRAM 51 WORKPLACE POWER RELATIONSHIPS

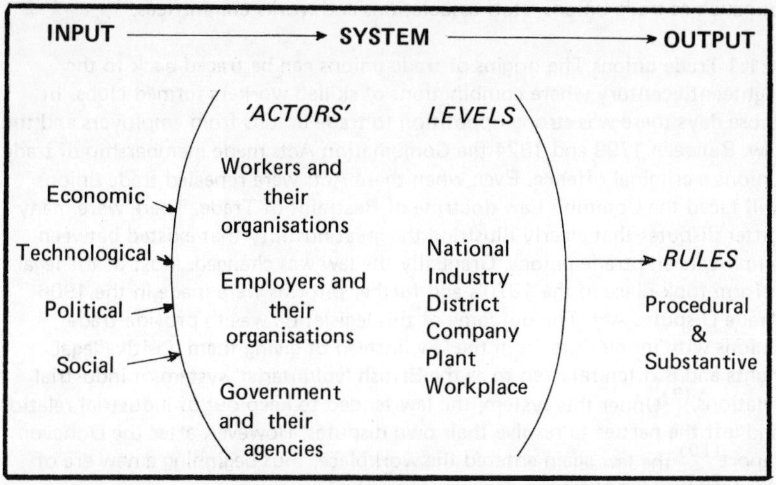

right of veto. Sometimes so called participation is a public relations exercise where employee representatives play a consultative and 'rubber stamping' role. Consultation is an important and useful organised labour function, but it should not be confused with participation. Full participation in the decision making process is the ultimate form of organised labour and exists in co-ownership business organisations. Any other form of organisation that distinguishes between capital and labour will tend to create employer and employee power groupings in which powerful organisations gain advantage from maintaining divergent interests. For instance, a trade union's strength is based on the need for labour to have an independent organisation represent their vested interests. This is because decisions made by an employer concerning manpower requirements, working practices and remuneration can have a dramatic and traumatic effect on an employee's life style Indeed , all the decision making principles and techniques explained in this book, make no recognition whatsoever of the personal interests of employees. Most business decisions are based on economic criteria such as the best utilisation of resources. Labour is a resource, and utilising it for maximum efficiency will inevitably create areas of personal tension and conflict. There are, of course, numerous trite platitudes uttered by managers about concern for employees, but generally the only time employee interests are really taken in the decision equation is when they are organised and have the *power* to influence events.

If we refer back to diagram 51 it illustrates that there are external and internal influences capable of destroying the system. Indeed, this is the objective of individuals operating within a radical frame of reference. What holds the system together are the rules that govern the role and place of individuals within the organisatiom. Most of the formal rules are generally determined unilaterally by management (Refer to sub-section 2:5). However, work groups will develop their own set of informal rules (Refer to chapter 2 sub-section 4:1). It is this rule making process where organised labour can and often does make a valuable cóntribution to labour management. Ideally, the outcome of the rule making process would be a system of organisational rights where employee representatives were consulted *before* decisions were made and then had strong *rights in decisions* that could directly affect an employee's life style. However, as such a system of formal rules would reduce the power of management and the influence of trade unions, it would probably be resisted.

In the following sub-sections we will briefly review some forms of organised labour such as trade unions, staff associations and works committees.

4:1:1 Trade unions The origins of trade unions can be traced back to the eighteenth century where combinations of skilled workers formed clubs. In those days there was strong opposition to trade unions from employers and the law. Between 1799 and 1824 the Combination Acts made membership of trade unions a criminal offence. Even when these Acts were repealed, trade unions still faced the Common Law doctrine of Restraint of Trade. There were many bitter disputes that clearly illustrate the great hostility that existed between employers and trade unions. Gradually the law was changed. Most of the legal reform took place in the 1870's and further reforms were made in the 1906 Trade Disputes Act. The outcome of this legislation was to provide trade unions with immunities from the law, instead of giving them positive legal rights and is often referred to as the British 'voluntarist' system of industrial relations.[9] Under this system, the law tended to keep out of industrial relations and left the parties to resolve their own disputes. However, after the Donavon report[10] the law again entered the workplace, thus beginning a new era of third party intervention.

The early attempts at intervention 'In Place of Strife' and the Industrial Relations Act were defeated by political pressure from the trade unions. During this period (1969 to 1974) the Commission of Industrial Relations (CIR) was set up to improve industrial relations generally and collective bargaining in particular. Their emphasis was long term reform and they produced some excellent research papers. However, this organisation was disbanded by the Trade Union and Labour Relations Act 1974 (TULRA). Subsequently, a new body was formed, under the Employment Protection Act 1975, called the Advisory Conciliation and Arbitration Service (ACAS). The service is purported to be independent of ministerial authority and is run by a Council consisting of three CBI nominees, three TUC nominees and three independent members. ACAS functions cover:-

(a) *Resolving disputes* by conciliation, arbitration, advice and enquiry.

(b) *Developing collective bargaining* such as helping with recognition applications

(c) *Improving industrial relations generally* which is similar to the earlier CIR function.

The need for more third party intervention into industrial relations was considered necessary, because at national level, trade unions had lost control of their membership. Thus negotiations and agreements at national or industry level often had no bearing on what was happening at the factory level. This meant that high level agreements to help control wage drift and reduce strike activity had little effect. Accordingly, a shift of emphasis was needed and plant/company wide agreements have now become the centrepiece of industrial relations. Although the leaders of large trade unions speak on behalf of their membership, the real power of the trade unions is on the shop floor.

---

9. A good coverage of the development of trade unions is given by Henry Pelling in a History of British Trade Unions. Penquin (1963)

10. Report of the Royal Commission on Trade Unions. HMSO (1968)

Shop floor power is partly evidenced by the growth in the numbers of shop stewards. One estimate places the growth from 90,000 in 1961 to 300,000 in 1978[11]. In 1961, trade union membership was 9,883,000 and this had risen to 13,053,596 by 1978. This represents an average increase of 61% from 9 per 1,000 in 1961 to 23 per 1,000 in 1978. A partial analysis of trade union membership is provided in the table on the following page.

At plant/company level, shop stewards play a key role in labour management. But before collective bargaining can take place, each side must recognise each other for negotiating purposes. Formalisation of recognition procedures was recommended by Donavon[10] and appeared in 'In place of Strife', the Industrial Relations Act, TULRA and the Employment Protection Act. Recognition claims by trade unions do not usually create the well publicised disruption that arose from the APEX claim at Grunwick Laboratories Limited in London. Formal recognition applications are submitted to ACAS who apply the independence criteria defined in section 30(1) of TULRA 1974 as:-

'a trade union which -

(a) Is not under the domination or control of an employer or group of employers or of one or more employers associations;

and

(b) Is not liable to interference by an employer or any such group or associateon (arising out of the provision of financial or material support or by any other means whatsoever) tending towards such control'

Once all the investigations have been completed a decision is made by the Certification Officer. Cumulative totals of certification application details from 1 February 1976 to 31 December 1979 were:-

Certificates issued	306
Applications refused	48
Applications withdrawn or lapsed	6
Applications under consideration at 31 December 1979	16
Total number of applications received(including references by ACAS	376

The list of trade unions at 31st December 1979 comprised 477 organisations of which about 200 were affiliated directly or indirectly to the TUC. For trade unions, listing with the Certification Office is a simple process and an essential preliminary to applying for a certificate of independence. *Listing* entitles a trade union to tax relief for expenditure on provident benefits and *certification* provides the trade union with legal rights.

In addition to the formal aspect of a certificate of independence, a trade union has to establish its right to be recognised. *Recognition* may be full or partial. *Partial recognition* is where a trade union may only represent members on an individual basis, whereas *full recognition* allows representation for collective labour and individuals. When deciding on recognition it is necessary to determine the size and nature of the bargaining unit. For example should say toolmakers representing 5% of the total labour force have separate collective bargaining rights? Trade unions tend to seek separate negotiating rights at the workplace, leading to the fragmentation of the bargaining unit. Whilst management generally prefer company wide negotiations and a reduction of

11. A. Fox. Socialism and shop floor power - the British predicament. Fabian research series 338 (1978)

ANALYSIS OF TRADE UNION MEMBERSHIP (1979)

	Number of Members	INCOME		
		From Members	From Investments	Total Income
Unions each with 100,000 members or more:		£000s	£000s	£000s
Transport and General Workers Union	2,072,818	20,308	2,635	22,987
Amalgamated Union of Engineering Workers	—	—	—	—
Constructional Section	35,235	622	79	720
Engineering Section	1.199,465	13,683	1,070	14,821
Foundry Section	58,728	646	96	742
Technical Administrative and Supervisory Section	200,954	2,705	103	2,817
National Union of General and Municipal Workers	964,836	12,947	1,193	14,264
National and Local Government Officers Association	729,405	9,831	382	11,421
National Union of Public Employees	712,392	7,880	855	8,736
Association of Scientific Technical and Managerial Staffs	471,000	6,143	28	6,220
Union of Shop Distributive and Allied Workers	462,178	4,671	451	5,298
Electrical Electronic Telecommunication and Plumbing Union	438,269	5,444	331	5,921
National Union of Mineworkers	371,470	7,126	1,523	8,905
Union of Construction Allied Trades and Technicians	325,245	3,519	116	3,662
National Union of Teachers	293,378	2,693	399	3,157
Civil and Public Services Association	224,780	4,136	278	4,486
Confederation of Health Service Employees	215,246	2,579	65	2,657
Society of Graphical and Allied Trades 1975	201,665	3,013	38	3,538
Union of Post Office Workers	197,157	4,109	177	4,333
National Union of Railwaymen	171,411	3,519	998	4,523
Association of Professional Executive Clerical and Computer Staff (APEX)	152,543	2,054	148	2,371
National Association of Schoolmasters/Union of Women Teachers	140,701	1,436	84	1,613
Royal College of Nursing	134,389	1,168	—	1,168
Amalgamated Society of Boilermakers Shipwrights Blacksmiths and Structural Workers	131,099	1,602	276	1,878
Banking Insurance and Finance Union	126,343	1,190	22	1,217
Post Office Engineering Union	121,404	2,591	25	2,636
National Union of Tailors and Garment Workers	116,095	1,015	312	1,327
Iron and Steel Trades Confederation	113,432	1,472	834	2,316
National Graphical Association	109,904	2,214	767	3,502
Society of Civil and Public Servants	106,903	2,400	78	2,561
Total of above unions with 100,000 members or more	10,598,445	132,716	13,363	149,797
Total of 366 other listed unions with less than 100,000 members	2,448,063	35,598	4,069	45,081
Total of listed unions	13,046,508	168,314	17,432	194,878
Trades Union Congress	—	2,394	123	2,525
Total of 29 other unlisted unions which have submitted returns	7,088	285	13	311
TOTAL of all unions for 1978	**13,053,596**	**170,993**	**17,568**	**197,714**
TOTAL of all unions for 1977	*12,718,911*	*151,637*	*16,935*	*176,931*

(Source: Annual Report of the Certification Officer)

multiunionism at plant level, once a trade union is recognised, a written recognition and procedure agreement will be drafted (Refer to sub-section 4:2)

In this review of trade unions we have briefly considered their historical development, legal position, listing, certification, recognition and the shift of power to the shop floor. Although the coverage has been brief, it is evident that trade unions can play an active role in labour management.

4:1:2 Staff associations The term 'staff association' does not have a generally agreed definition. However, the following definition given by the Certification Office identifies the main characteristics:

'Organisations usually of white collar workers, not affiliated to the TUC, whose membership is confined to the employees of a single employer (or associated employers) in sections other than central and local government and the nationalised industries'

The principal characteristics identified in this definition are:-

(a) Membership is confined to employees of a single employer (or associated employers)
(b) Employees are almost always in non-manual/white collar occupations
(c) The association does not regard itself as a trade union and may even be hostile to trade unions.

Many staff associations regard themselves as negotiating bodies and have applied for certificates of independence. Indeed, a study made by the Certification Office of certification applications between 1 February 1976 and 31 December 1978 comprised 88 organisations that came within the above definition. The table on the following page shows staff associations are strongest in banking and insurance. In fact, staff associations have established a majority membership in 3 of the 5 English clearing banks and their total membership of about 90,000 has been brought together in the Clearing Bank Union. This is comparable with the main TUC affiliated union in this area - the Banking, Insurance and Finance Union (Refer to details on page 166). In the insurance sector, the position of staff associations has been eroded by mergers with TUC affiliates. According to one survey[12] staff associations play a secondary role to the Association of Scientific, Techanical and Managerial Staffs (Refer to table on page 166) which has collective bargaining rights in more than half of the top 30 insurance companies.

The staff associations supplement to the Certification Officer's annual report 1979 shows that there was a high casualty rate amongst the 88 staff associations. By the end of 1979, 9 had merged with TUC affiliated unions and 6 were disolved. An indication of the shift of staff associations towards TUC affiliated unions is given in the following list of staff associations that were absorbed into ASTMS during 1974 and 1975:-

Staff associations absorbed by ASTMS during 1974 & 1975

Pearl Agents	1974
Midland Bank Staff Association	1974
Clydesdale Bank Technical & Services Staff Association	1974
Forward Trust Staff Association	1974
Midland Bank Technical & Services Staff Association	1975
Engineer Surveyor Association	1975
Kodak Senior Staff Association	1975
ICI Staff Association	1975
Norwich Union Group Staff Association	1975
United Friendly House Staff Association	1975

12. *Union recognition in the largest insurance companies, Industrial Relations Review and Report No. 204. July 1979*

THE DISTRIBUTION OF STAFF ASSOCIATIONS BY SECTOR AND SIZE (1979)

Sector	Less than 100	100–249	250–499	500–999	1,000–2,499	2,500–4,999	5,000–9,999	10,000+	Number of staff associa-tions	Number of members
Banking		4	1			1		3	9	96,284
Insurance	2	1	2	1	1	3	4		14	39,073
Building Societies		2	1	5	2	1			11	12,271
Aerospace	1	2	2	3	1				9	4,750
Food/Drink/Tobacco	4		5		3				12	6,569
Engineering and Allied Industries	4	5							9	1,135
Other Manufacturing Industries	1	2	1	1		2			7	8,572
Construction/Retail/Services	1	4	2	2		1	1		11	16,653
Public Sector		2	2		2				6	4,428
TOTAL	13	22	16	12	9	8	5	3	88	189,735

(Source: Annual Report of the Certification Officer)

The point to note here is that if the attitude of senior management towards organised labour is to encourage the formation of consultative bodies with quasi negotiating rights, staff associations may appear to be a reasonable form of labour representation. However, pressure arising from the changing social attitudes of white collar workers and the membership drives by trade unions may make staff associations a half way house between consultative representation and fully developed trade union representation. Accordingly, any decision analysis concerning the introduction and/or support of staff association has to include the possibility of it opening the door for a variety of trade union activities.

4:1:3 Works committees This term is generally used to describe a consultative body that is part of a formal organisation structure. Its members are elected representatives of the entire workforce and they regularly meet with management to discuss areas of common interest. Joint consultation has been an accepted labour management technique for over 50 years. Indeed during the 1914-18 war the Whitley Committee recommended in its proposals for the post war development of industrial relations the establishment of joint industrial councils (JIC) for major industries. The JIC's sought co-operation at national level but recognised that support was needed at all levels and therefore proposed that district joint councils and works committees should also be set up. The works committees were not supposed to discuss matters such as wage rates and hours of work, these were to be settled at district or national level. At the works committee level, discussions were meant to be on matters of joint concern where management retained the right of decision.

The recession during the inter war period weakened the interest in works committees, but the principles of joint consultation were still applied in some large companies such as Cadbury and ICI. During the 1939-45 war, joint consultation was revived in the form of Joint Production Committees (JPC).After the war may industries had two systems of worker representation: collective bargaining through shop stewards elected by trade union members and joint consultation through representatives elected from the entire workforce. However, the JPC's were rapidly disappearing and the strength of collective bargaining was increasing. The traditional distinctions between areas for consultation and negotiation were no longer generally accepted and trade unions successfully fought for a single channel of labour representation through shop stewards. In some organisations, managerial acquiescence became capitulation when the closed shop was accepted. Some companies still maintain two channels of labour representation,where negotiation is concerned with remuneration and job security and consultation with health and safety, welfare, training and education, changes in production and codes of discipline, But when the consultative process is used as a rubber stamp by management, then it is not surprising that shop stewards are able to widen their sphere of influence on behalf of the trade union movement. For example, productivity agreements (Refer to sub-section 3:7) were traditionally an area for works committees, or other types of consultative bodies. But when management abuse their privelege of organisational power and simply walk over legitimate consultative concern, then productivity deals would probably become an official negotiating issue. Most productivity deals are now negotiated settlements, whereas in the 1950's many agreements were reached through the consultative process.

The point that is being made in this sub-section is that management get the labour representation system they deserve. If they are arrogant, dogmatic, insincere and/or have little genuine concern for their employees, then consultative labour representation will not be able to survive against the pressures of independent organised labour. This is unfortunate, because joint consultation with sincere, caring management and responsible employee representatives could help to provide an industrial relations system that would move towards unity ideals.

4:2 Procedures. Industrial relations procedures have the following characteristics:-

(i) A set of rules that may be written or unwritten
(ii) The rules govern employment relationships
(iii) The rules govern the conduct of the parties
(iv) The rules may exist at a number of levels such as: sub plant, plant, company, district, industry, national and be interelated and interdependent
(v) The rules may relate to one or more employers and one or more trade unions in one or more situations

From diagram 51 in section 4, it can be seen that rules are the output of an industrial relations system and that they provide a framework within which power relationships can exist. Procedures serve many functions that include:-

(i) A source of precedents for the orderly conduct of employer-employee relationships similar to the role of precedent in the development of law
(ii) A reference point for employers, managers and employees on the equitable solution to labour problems
(iii) An aid to administration and management because decisions relating to specific situations have been agreed by the parties and therefore courses of action can be planned
(iv) An important part of a company's system of communications (Refer to sub-section 2:5)
(v) Defines the relative boundaries of trade union and managerial power
(vi) A means of achieving co-operation between employers and employees

Having reviewed the characteristics and functions of industrial relations procedures we can now consider some practical applications. What procedures are trying to do, is establish some kind of machinery for reconciling the differences between various interest groups. This machinery can be broadly divided into two parts:-

(a) Machinery to make collective agreements such as determining the nature of collective labour representation. This has been explained in sub-sections 4:1:1, 4:1:2 and 4:1:3.
(b) Machinery to live under the agreements once they have been made, because agreements serve little function if they are ignored. This kind of machinery would include procedures for the interpretation of agreements, disciplinary and grievance procedures.

At national level, most trade unions have agreements with employers' associations relating to their members in all industry. For example, in the paper, print and publishing sector there are some 30 separate formal industry wide procedure agreements. Whilst at the domestic level (sub plant, plant, company) procedures tend to be more informed and many are unwritten. It was at the domestic level that Donavon[10] recommended changes that included:-

(a) Changes in the form of agreements to make them more formal and precise
(b) A change in the relative importance of agreements where domestic level agreements become more important

(c) A widening of the scope and contents of agreements
(d) A broadening of the bargaining unit

If these recommendations for a widening, broadening and greater formality for procedures at domestic level are accepted, it would clearly be a very important part of labour management. Therefore we need to look a little more closely at the types of procedure.

Let us first consider an aspect of the machinery to make collective agreements. When a trade union is recognised for collective bargaining (Refer to sub-section 4:1:1) a written recognition and procedure agreement would include the following points:-

(i) The scope of collective bargaining and its relationship to other forms of labour representation.
(ii) The election and terms of appointment of trade union representatives.
(iii) The arrangements for joint negotiations where more than one trade union has full recognition.
(iv) The facilities available for elected representatives such as time off for trade union duties.
(v) The circumstances under which management can change established work practices.
(vi) The procedures aimed at preventing industrial action such as grievance and disputes procedures.
(vii) The circumstances under which management or trade unions can revise or rescind existing agreements.

It is clear from the above outline that there is a lot of hard work, discussion and negotiation needed to produce such a procedure agreement. But once full recognition is accepted,there must be a set of rules to govern the conduct of the parties Similarly, once the parties have reached agreement, then there needs to be some machinery to help them live under the agreement. A common form of procedure in this category is the grievance/dispute procedure. The purpose of the procedure is to allow individuals or groups to have a formal channel for grievances relating to employment conditions. The grievance becomes a dispute when the trade union supports a case and cannot reach a satisfactory agreement with an employer. The stages in a grievance procedure would generally be as follows:-

Stage 1 Individual or group take problem to supervisor. If no satisfaction:
Stage 2 Shop steward informed and both parties speak to supervisor. If no satisfaction within a specified number of days:
Stage 3 Shop steward takes problem to line manager. If no satisfaction within a specified number of days:
Stage 4 Senior shop steward takes problem to industrial relations manager/ personnel officer. If no satisfaction within a specified number of days:
Stage 5 Problem discussed at plant works conference with shop stewards and management. If no satisfaction and the company is federated in an industry agreement then:
Stage 6 Problem discussed at regional conference level between full time trade union officials and representatives of employers' associations.

The defects in this grievance procedure are the length of time for the problem to pass through the process and the remoteness of the full time officials from local problems. Accordingly many grievance procedures aim to settle the problem quickly at its source.

From this outline of industrial relations procedures it should be clear that they can play an important role in labour management. Attempts have been made to create ideal industrial relations procedures and there are some useful guides available such as:-

The Code of Industrial Relations Practice. HMSO (1971)
Disputes Procedures C.B.I. (1971)
Model Procedure Agreements. The Industrial Society (1972)

Although these kinds of guides are useful for check listing they cannot be applied direct to any situation. Not only do procedures need to be tailored to meet the specific needs of organisations,they also need to be monitored and revised to meet changing circumstances.

4:3 Provision of information for collective bargaining The outcome of collective bargaining will usually have some effect on a company's costs and output and some effect on employees' working conditions and remuneration. Therefore, before entering into negotiations, both parties will collect information that:-

(a) Will help to determine their bargaining objectives in terms of a high settlement, a probable settlement and lowest acceptable settlement: and
(b) Will help in the negotiations as levers in the bargaining process. An example of this kind of information would be 'ability to pay' discussions where accounting data can be manipulated to suit the argument.

Traditionally, management have normally had an information advantage in negotiations, which meant trade union negotiators were forced to negotiate from strength and dogma. Trade union bargaining power can be expressed as an equation, i.e.

$$\frac{\text{The costs and inconvenience the company would suffer if they were to disagree with the trade union proposal}}{\text{The costs and inconvenience the company would suffer if they were to agree with the trade union proposal}}$$

If this equation could be quantified and the resultant figure was above 1, then the stronger the trade union bargaining position would be, and vice versa. The same equation can be used to determine management bargaining power by substituting trade union for company and company for trade union in the numerator and denominator.

Disclosure for collective bargaining has traditionally been at managements' discretion and the extent of disclosure to trade unions would depend on factors such as; management/trade union relationships, management attitudes, custom and practice and specific bargaining circumstances. Trade union information rights would have developed from local negotiation procedures and practice. There was certainly no legal obligation to meet demands for information. Moves to change the status quo developed during the 1960's. A Working Party Report by the Labour Party on Industrial Democracy and the Donavon Report on Industrial Relations both recommended some form of disclosure legislation. Both major political parties then enacted disclosure legislation. The Conservative Party with their ill fated Industrial Relations Act and the Labour Party with the Employment Protection Act and Industry Act. The disclosure provisions in the Industry Act are part of the Act's claim of extending the state's involvement with companies that make a 'significant contribution' to manufacturing in the UK economy. Consequently the aims are quite different to the Employment Protection Act that is directly concerned with workplace relationships

In the following sub-sections we will be examining the legal disclosure requirements, the information requirements of trade unions and management, and information agreements.

4:3:1 Legal requirements A legal requirement to disclose information to trade unions for collective bargaining and direct to employees, first appeared in the Industrial Relations Act 1971 (Sections 56 and 57). Quite a lot of the repealed Industrial Relations Act re-appeared in the Employment Protection Act 1975. Interestingly, the disclosure provisions to trade unions was re-introduced but direct disclosure to employees was not. There is no legal requirement to report direct to employees, but under Sections 17 to 21 of the Employment Protection Act an employer has a general duty to disclose information to a representative of a recognised independent trade union. The Act provides two criteria for the kind of information to be disclosed:

(a) The trade union representative would be, to a material extent, impeded in carrying on with him such collective bargaining, and
(b) would be in accordance with good industrial relations practice.

(Guidance on good industrial relations practice was given in the ACAS code. Details of the code are given in the table on the following pages)

When complying with this duty to disclose an employer shall not be required to:-

(a) produce or allow to be inspected any document, copy or extracts from a document, other than a document prepared for the purpose of providing information for the unions
(b) compile or assemble information where the amount of work or cost involved would be out of reasonable proportion to the value of the information in conducting collective bargaining.

The Act also lists the following circumstances when an employer does not have to disclose information

(a) would be against the interests of national security
(b) would contravene a prohibition imposed by or under an enactment
(c) was given to an employer in confidence, or was obtained by the employer in consequence of the confidence reposed in him by another person
(d) related to an individual unless he has consented to its disclosure
(e) would cause substantial injury to the undertaking (or national interest in respect of Crown Employment) for reasons other than its effect on collective bargaining
(f) was obtained for the purpose of any legal proceedings

If a trade union believer that an employer has not complied with these disclosure provisions then sections 19 to 21 provide a complaints procedure. This procedure is presented in flow chart form, in diagram 52.

The legal pressures for increasing disclosure of information appear to be strengthening. The main sources of pressure are from the EEC industrial democracy and company law proposals and the accounting bodies. Therefore any policy decisions concerning the provision of information need to allow for the possibility of subsequent legislation increasing not reducing the disclosure requirements.

COMPARISON OF DISCLOSURE RECOMMENDATIONS

T.U.C. REPORT (1970)	*C.B.I. REPORT (1975)*	*ACAS CODE No. 2. (1977)*
Manpower Number of employees by job descriptions; rates of turn-over, short-time, sbsenteeism, sickness and accidents; details of existing provisions for security, sickness, accidents, recruitment, training, re-deployment, promotion and redundancy.	**Manpower** Average numbers employed; numbers employed by sex, grade, occupation, departments etc.; labour turnover, redundancies and dismissals; absenteeism; redeployment, training and retraining days lost through disputes. Industrial relations: grievance procedures; safety rules, policies and programmes; health and welfare matters; disciplinary and dismissal procedures; trade unions; recruitment and promotion policies and methods; induction programmes; working rules, social matters.	**Manpower** Number employed analysed according to trade, department, location, age and sex; labour turnover; absenteeism; overtime and short-term; manning standards; planned changes in work methods, materials equipment or organisation, available manpower plans, investment plans.
Performance Unit costs, output per man activities; home and export return on capital employed, value added, etc.	**Performance** Export performance: details of main national and international competitors; competitive possibilities; orders, production and marketing situations; production schedules; work levels and standard performance levels; labour costs per unit of output; savings arising from increased productivity. Comparative departmental production fi[illegible]	**Performance** Productivity and efficiency data; savings from increased productivity and output; return on capital invested; sales and state of order book.

Incomes; directors remuneration; wages and salaries; make-up of pay - negotiated rates, PBR (payment hy results), overtime and bonuses.	Rates of pay; notice periods; hours of work; holidays; sick pay; pension schemes; results negotiations affecting pay and conditions; principles and structures of payment systems; job evaluation systems; holiday schedule arrangements; profit sharing, stock option and savings schemes; life assurance schemes; average earnings.	Principals and structure of payment systems, job evaluation systems and grading criteria; earnings and hours analysed according to work-group, grade, plant, sex, out-workers and homeworkers, department or division, giving, where appropriate, distributions and make-up of pay showing any additions to basic rate or salary; total pay bill; details of fringe benefits and non-wage labour costs.
Conditions of Service Details of new enterprises and locations; prospective close-downs; mergers and takeovers. Trading and sales plans; investment plans, including R&D (research and development). Manpower plans; plans for recruitment, selection and training; promotion, regrading and redeployment; short-term and redundancy provisions.	**General** Mergers and takeovers; investment and expansion; closures; changes in location; research and development; product changes.	**Conditions of Service** Policies on recruitment, redeployment, redundancy, training, equal opportunity, and promotion; appraisal systems; health, welfare and safety matters.
Financial Sales turnover by main activities: home and export sales; non-trading income including income from investments and overseas earnings, pricing policy. Costs: distribution and sales costs; production costs; administrative and overhead costs; costs of materials and machinery; labour costs including social security payments; costs of management and supervision. Profits: before and after tax taking government allowances, grants and subsidies into account; distributions and retentions. Worth of company: details of growth and up-to-date value of fixed assets and stocks; growth and realisable value of trade investments.	**Financial** Turnover; profits; dividends; losses; liabilities; total fixed assets; details of directors' remuneration and emoluments; details of chairman's renumeration and emoluments; total wages and salary bill; total labour costs as a percentage of operating costs; administration costs as a percentage of total costs; costs of materials.	**Financial** Cost structures; gross and net profits; sources of earnings; assets; liabilities; allocation of profits; details of government financial assistance; transfer prices loans to partent companies and interest charged.

DIAGRAM 52 COMPLAINTS PROCEDURE FLOWCHART

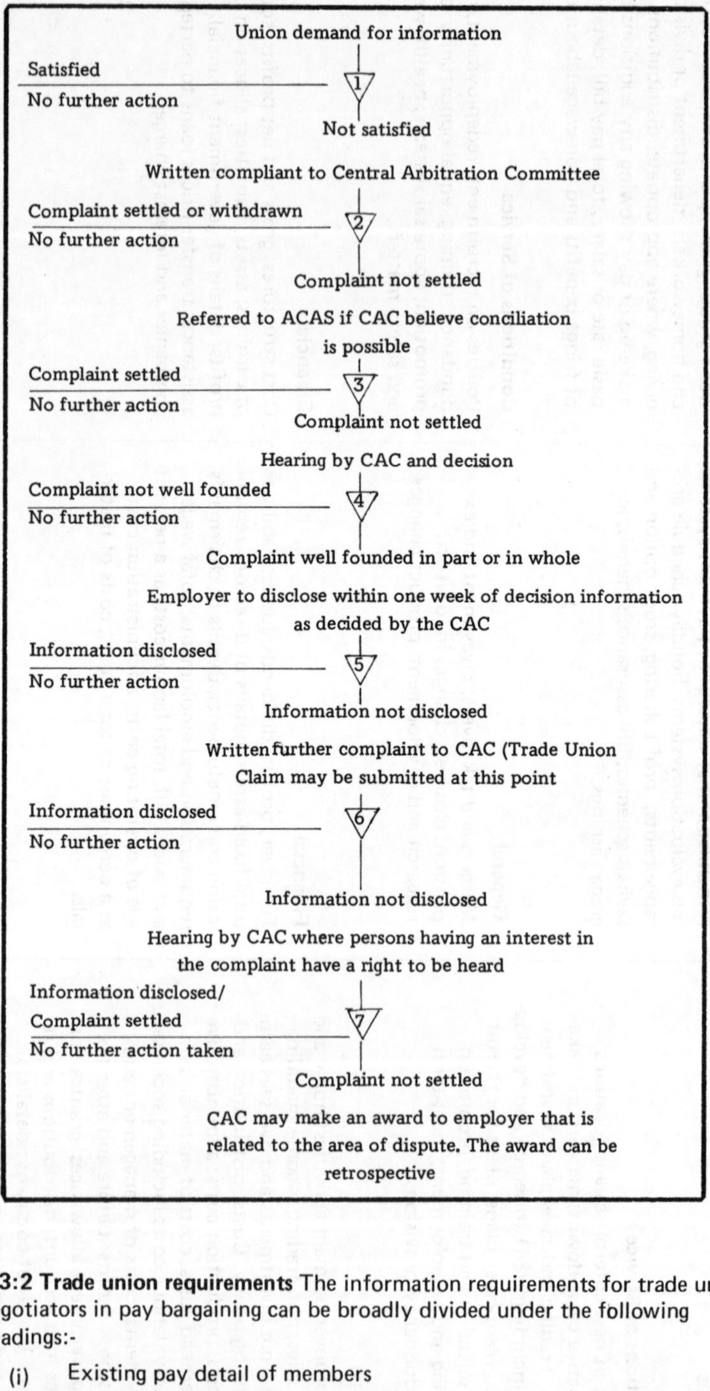

4:3:2 Trade union requirements The information requirements for trade union negotiators in pay bargaining can be broadly divided under the following headings:-

(i) Existing pay detail of members
(ii) External wage rates for comparison

(iii) Cost of living detail such as the Retail Price Index
(iv) The company's investment intentions
(v) The company's ability to pay
(vi) Miscellaneous financial detail

Information under the first three headings will tend to influence the level of wage claims. Whilst ability to pay detail (mainly level of profit) will be used to support a claim if profits are large. Low profits or loses may be viewed as limiting bargaining power and therefore rejected. To improve their bargaining position trade union negotiators may also seek miscellaneous information such as:- increases in directors' remuneration and dividend payments, increases in productivity or any relevant cost reductions. The important point to note about these categories of information is that they are required as bargaining levers.

There is however another use for information that responsible trade union representatives and honest management can attempt. If both sides genuinely wish to participate in the decision making process then the provision of information has a different perspective. Investment, costs and revenue detail are needed for trade unions to participate in decision making. However some trade union representatives would not necessarily want information for this purpose because:-

(a) It limits their pay bargaining
(b) They may have to accept management practices and values, thus becoming an extension of management
(c) They will not fully understand the information
(d) They may not be given all the relevant information
(e) Management may bypass the negotiators and report direct to employees in an attempt to weaken the trade union position

There is probably some justification for trade union concern about information provided by management and this has been expressed in a number of publications produced for trade unions[13].

4:3:3; Management requirements Prior to collective bargaining, a management negotiator may need the following information:-

(i) Existing pay details such as:
Internal detail relating to basic rates, overtime, productivity deals, bonus, piecework and other payments. External wage rates that may be compared with company rates. Also current levels of other external comparable wage settlements.
(ii) Details concerning: controls on prices and incomes, productivity deals, pension rights, redundancy rights, minimum wage levels, trade union rights and past collective agreements both substantive and procedural
(iii) Cost of living details, how pay has/has not kept pace with inflation. Forecasts of cost of living tax cuts/increases and other relevant factors.

---

(13) Examples of publications for trade unionists that express views about disclosure are:-

B. Brown	*Opening the Books A Workers Control pamphlet*	*(1968)*
R. Moore	*Company Information for Negotiators. Apex*	*(1974)*
C. Hird	*Your Employer's Profits*	*(1975)*

(iv) Ability to pay. Cost calculations of different wage claims and ability to meet demands with existing pricing structure.

(v) Corporate strategy, including investments, marketing and personnel plans.

The level of information requirements will be determined by circumstances and the attitudes of the negotiators. Research in the USA (14), revealed that some management bargainers had less accounting information than the union bargainers. The union bargainers were using published accounts and other published data.

4:3:4 Information agreements The ACAS Code of Practice on Disclosure of Information to Trade Unions for Collective Bargaining Purposes concludes with the following recommendation:-

'Employers and trade unions should endeavour to arrive at a joint understanding on how the provisions on the disclosure of information can be implemented most effectively. They should consider what information is likely to be required, what is available, and what could reasonably be made available. Consideration should also be given to the form in which the information will be presented, when it should be presented and to whom. In particular, the parties should endeavour to reach an understanding on what information could most appropriately be provided on a regular basis.

Procedures for resolving possible disputes concerning any issues associated with the disclosure of information should be agreed. Where possible such procedures should normally be related to any existing arrangements within the undertaking or industry and the complaint, conciliation and arbitration procedure described in the Act'

From the employer's viewpoint an information agreement would be part of an overall disclosure policy as explained in Volume 1, Financial Accounting for Non-Accountants. If a disclosure policy is being developed then a method of handling the detail could be as follows:

(a) List all information currently being provided as available to trade unions.

(b) List trade union expected information requirements

(c) Construct a disclosure matrix to handle the above information as shown in diagram 53 below.

DIAGRAM 53 *DISCLOSURE MATRIX*

Information detail	Currently provided/available			Expected requirements arising from negotiations
	Published Accounts	Employee Accounts	Other Sources	

(14) *J. Palmer. The use of Accounting Information in Labor Negotiations. National Association of Accountants (1977)*

The trade union negotiators may initially request the list of information recommended in the ACAS Code or recommended by the TUC (Refer to the table on pages174/5) to form the basis an information agreement. These lists are probably too long and detailed for most companies and a negotiated low content information agreement may be reached by management making concessions in other areas such as an incentive payment scheme or work practices. The use of the matrix illustrated in diagram 53, will enable management to determine what detail to include in their offer of information. There are however four ideal characteristics of an information agreement :-

(a) Reliability - The trade union should trust the information as being accurate and honest

(b) Comparability - The information provided should not conflict with other sources of information

(c) Regularity - Ideally the information flows should be on a regular basis

(d) Standardisation Regular information flows should try to adopt a standard acceptable form or presentation.

As management are under no legal obligation to prove the information given is accurate, reliable and comprehensive, there will be a certain amount of goodwill in an information agreement. Moreover, regular data can be given where the trade union representative has little chance of understanding it and could therefore be placed at a disadvantage in negotiations. Thus an information agreement is more than a matter of intention than of detail. If management genuinely want to communicate then this is more important than the listing of detail in an information agreement.

5. Labour planning

This topic is usually presented under the umbrella title of manpower planning which embraces diverse activities analysed at various levels. It represents an area of great interest to governments that attempt some form of centralised planning. At the national level there are demographic studies of 'manpower' resources related to changing patterns of employment and education and training needs. Arising out of these studies are some very sophisticated econometric models that establish economic and demographic relationships. The term 'manpower has become established in the civil service where this description has appeared in the early Ministry of Labour's 'Manpower Research Unit' and todays 'Manpower Services Commission' (MSC). The avoidance of the word 'labour' at national level is understandable, but our interests here are not with macro-economic studies for forecasting the aggregate demand and supply for labour. We are interested in labour management in a company of which labour planning is just one vital component. The objectives of labour planning at company level are:-

(i) To convert corporate objectives and policies into estimates of labour requirements

(ii) To identify existing and potential labour strengths and weaknesses that can affect corporate policy

(iii) To produce labour policies and plans that meet the corporate objectives

(iv) To integrate labour policies into the corporate planning process.

To meet these four objectives labour planning has the following stages:-

(a) A strengths and weaknesses analysis of existing labour

(b) A forecast of labour requirements

(c) A labour plan based on (a) and (b)

These three stages are discussed in the following sub-sections:-

5:1 Existing labour analysis The purpose of this kind of analysis is to provide an overview of the labour force. Accordingly, personal data about individuals is only useful if it can be aggregated. Thus we are not concerned with personnel assessment results unless they can be used to provide general efficiency indicators. Indeed, in a labour force analysis, personnel evaluation of individuals must be avoided, because it is quite a different function and will tend to divert attention away from important aggregate data. The types of analysis we will be reviewing in the following sub-sections relate to: the composition of the workforce, labour turnover and human resource accounting

5:1:1 Composition analysis To determine the composition of the workforce, labour has to be divided into a number of categories such as: male or female, part time or full time, age groups, direct or indirect, manual, clerical or managerial, levels of management and levels of skill such as: unskilled, apprentice, semi-skilled and skilled. For whatever categories are chosed, an analytical coding system needs to be designed. The appropriate code given to each employee would then enable all kinds of analyses to be undertaken with a fairly simple program on a micro computer (Refer to chapter 10 sub section 4:2:3). A temporal analysis of the data can then be presented in a graphical form as illustrated in diagram 54. This diagram shows the effects on the composition

DIAGRAM 54 LABOUR COMPOSITION ANALYSIS

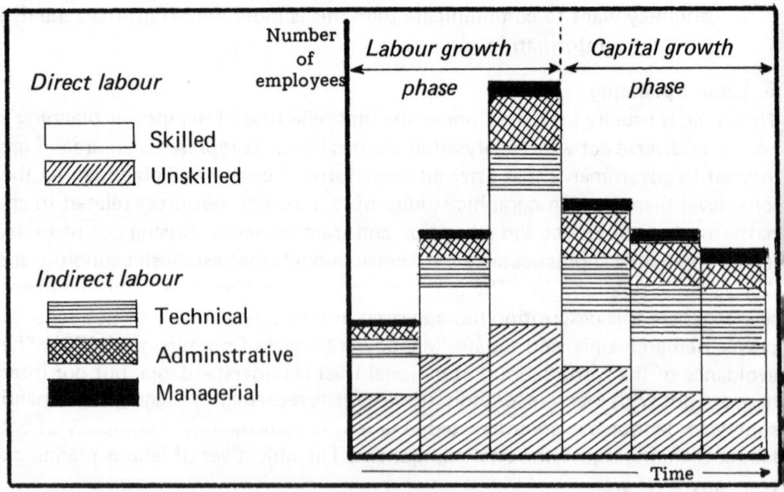

of labour as a company passes through two distinct phases. The first phase represents a rapid growth of the company where output/sales growth was achieved by large increases in direct labour and administrative staff. The second phase represents a labour rationalisation period where labour was being replaced by capital. Initially the direct labour was reduced and technical support increased as work practices became more automated. In the last period capital began replacing labour in the office and administrative labour decrease Thus the shift in the composition of the labour force over the growth period was from direct to indirect where the greatest losses were the workers whose skills could be replaced by a machine. This kind of structural analysis is most important for labour planning.

5:1:2 Labour turnover It is important for an organisation to know how many employees are leaving and why. The unplanned loss of skilled and experienced employees can be very expensive because of the costs of recruitment and training that is needed to replace them. Accordingly, personnel officers generally undertake quite a lot of labour wastage calculations. With regard to labour planning, a wider approach is needed that includes labour wastage and labour survival calculations. Let us first consider labour shortage.

The easiest calculation is to divide the number of leavers during a specific time period by the average number employed over the same period and express the result as a percentage. This calculation may be made for a department category of employees and/or company.

$$\frac{\text{Number of employees leaving during a specific period}}{\text{Average number employed over the same period}} \times 100$$

For example, if a department employed an average 100 people, and during one month 10 employees left then the labour turnover would be 10%. If the annual rate was also averaging 10% then for labour planning we could work on an assumption of a 10% 'natural wastage' rate. From a control viewpoint some form of labour turnover report would be needed as shown in diagram 55 overleaf. Labour turnover calculations are particularly important for skilled workers whose skills are in short supply. Some companies produce a skilled worker index to show if the company's pool of skilled labour is in danger of drying out. This index can be derived by applying the following formula:-

$$\frac{\text{Current number of skilled workers with over 1 year's service}}{\text{Number of skilled workers one year ago}}$$

The movement of skilled workers can be shown graphically to illustrate the trend.

The other main method of assessing the extent of labour wastage is to calculate employees survival rates based upon their lengths of service. The principle of the analysis is shown in the following table:-

Labour Survival Rates

No. of years service	*No. of employees*	*No. of leavers during the period ending...........*	*No. of Survivors*	*Survival rate*
Less than 1	1,500	300	1,200	80%
1 and less than 3	4,000	400	3,600	90%
3 and less than 5	6,000	500	5,500	92%
5 and less than 10	5,000	300	4,700	94%
10 and less than 15	3,000	100	2,900	96%
above 15	2,500	200	2,300	92%
Totals	22,000	1,800	21,200	96%

In this illustration the average labour turnover is 8%. However, for labour planning a continued natural wastage of 8% could not be assumed because most of the wastage occurs in the first year of service. Thus if the plan was to reduce labour through natural wastage, after the first year the wastage rate would be well below 8% because the remaining employees have high survival rates. Accordinaly, natural wastage calculations need to include an analysis of employees ages and lengths of service with the labour turnover figures.

DIAGRAM 55 *LABOUR TURNOVER REPORT*

Labour Turnover Report

Department .... Period ending..........

Detail	*This month*	*Last month*	*Year to date*	
			This year	*Last year*
Number leaving				
Average labour force				
Labour turnover				
Reasons for leaving				
Involuntary				
Poor performance				
Misconduct				
Illness/accident				
Retirement				
Redundancy				
Totals (%)				
Voluntary				
Pay				
Prospects				
Working conditions				
Transport				
Housing				
Other				
Totals (%)				

5:1:3 Human resource accounting (HRA) A good labour force is probably the best asset a business can have, but it is never shown on a balance sheet. The reason for this is that an accounting balance sheet is concerned with showing the ownership of assets. Capital is then derived by deducting the long term debt (For a precise definition of capital employed, refer to Volume 1 Financial Accounting for non-accountants). As *humans cannot be owned* and therefore sold, conventional accounting does not include human capital. Economists however, generally make no distinction between human and non-human, capital, because capital represents a source of income, the value of which is determined by its discounted future net income streams. Indeed, some theories see all non-human capital as representing the exploitation of labour and therefore belonging to the workers. Our concern here is not with the economics and politics of the ownership and distribution of wealth. We are operating at a practical level of getting an efficient utilisation of resources for wealth creation, where labour is a major resource.

Pressures from economists, sociologists and management theorists have caused some accountants to reconsider their traditional position of only measuring non-human resources. The movement seems to have started during the 1960's in America. Some original researchers set up an experiment [15] where

(15) Dr. R. Likert and Professor W. Pyle of University of Mitchigan research at the R.C. Barry Corporation, Columbus, Ohio. Also see R. Likert - The human organisation: its management and value. McGraw-Hill (1967)

they calculated the asset value of 150 salaried staff. The cost profile was based on the historical cost of recruitment, training and development. The cost profile was subsequently revised on replacement cost principles. At about the same time, some other researchers[16] were developing an economic value measurement of human resources based on discounted future earnings. From this brief background we can now move on to consider how HRA can help with labour management.

From the outset it is necessary to accept that a lot of the data is subjective. Accordingly, if the data is to have any meaning it has to be based on valid criteria and consistently applied so as to provide a set of useful yardsticks. Moreover, the purpose of this data analysis is to help with the decision making process and should not be used solely to support or contest decisions that have already been made. Unfortunately, a lot of 'subjective accounting' is used for support and not illumination. Converting labour into asset values enables this intangible resource to be built into decision calculations relating to recruitment dismissals output and investment. A list of the possible uses of HRA has been compiled[17], and included the following points:-

(i) Measuring the return on capital employed where organisational assets, include the value of human assets.
(ii) Integrating human asset values in the financial accounts for external reporting purposes.
(iii) Valuing businesses, where the human asset value is a relevant factor in mergers and takeover decisions.
(iv) Examining the disposition of resources, by allocating relative human asset values to different job grades. The location of organisational investment in human resources would be highlighted.
(v) Evaluation of personnel expenditure in relation to human resource value.
(vi) Preparing organisation charts to plan the disposition of human assets.
(vii) Industrial relations, where human asset values could provide a rational basis for discussing remuneration systems.

Just as value measurement enables diverse non-human assets to have a common unit of measure, so does HRA enable human assets to be included in the calculations. The value measurement of non-human assets may be precise, but it is only vaguely right (Refer to Volume 1 Financial accounting fo, non-accountants Chapter 3 section 4). The same principle applies to human asset measurement. The arithmetic will provide a precise result but the important point is the criteria upon which the arithmetic is based. The following notes briefly review some of the criteria for measuring human resources:-

Historic costs

This is a traditional costing approach to resource valuation and therefore represents a cost and not a value. The accounting system could record all costs relating to the recruitment, hiring and training of each employee. Many of the costs would have to be apportioned 'lumps' of overheads such as the personnel department. The resultant figures would be precise, like most historic costs,but their usefulness is questionable.

---

(16) B. Lev and A. Schwartz. On the use of the economic concept of human capital in financial statements. Accounting Review. (January 1971)

(17) W. Giles and D. Robinson. Human asset accounting. Institute of Personnel Management and Institute of Cost and Management Accountants (1972)

Replacement costs

This is based on the principle of how much it would cost to replace an employee, and tends to use more subjective data than the historic cost method. With many employees the cost of replacement would not be known until it was tried. That is, assuming the employee would be replaced. However, an experienced personnel officer could probably make some fairly accurate guestimates. The resultant figures would be more useful than historic cost but they would need to be constantly revised.

Economic value

The economic value of an asset is generally defined as the present value of its future net income streams. It is assumed that each asset makes some contribution to future profits and therefore the present value of its future contribution is seen as the economic value. This is just another example of an economic theory having no practical application. Even if the capitalisation of future income streams from an individual employee could be assessed, there are still problems such as the time horizon and the choice of discount factor (Refer to chapter 7 sub-section 2:2:1 and section 6)

Human resource accounting (also called human asset accounting) appears to have gained fairly widespread acceptance by academics. This is fortunate because there is still a lot of work needed to devise an objective method of measuring human resources. Once a measurement system has been tested, used and accepted by decision makers, then HRA will certainly be of great value for labour management.

5:2 Forecasting labour requirements The principles of forecasting explained in chapter 2 sub-section 3:1 apply to labour forecasts. Short, medium and long term forecasting will normally be based on forecasted sales and related production plans. In the short term forecasts, labour calculations will be part of the budget co-ordination process explained in chapter 8 sub-section 2:3. Therefore when the sales forecast is above normal productive capacity then detailed estimates of additional labour are required. If the sales forecast is below existing output levels and the company does not want to stockpile, then detailed labour rationalisation calculations are needed. For direct labour working on a measurable output basis, production plans can be converted into labour hours and labour requirements can be fairly accurately calculated. However, most work situations have so many variables that have to be taken into consideration, direct labour hour requirements cannot be precisely calculated. Short term adjustments to the labour force on a hire and fire basis could be costly and difficult to implement. Thus in the short run, production will rarely have precisely the right amount of labour in the grades required. To overcome this short term labour constraint, a series of buffers need to be built into the system, such as:-

(a) Labour work flexibility, including a willingness to change work practices and removal of demarcation. Also increased training of workers so they can do several jobs.

(b) The use of overtime during periods of peak demand.

(c) The use of part-time labour.

(d) Two-way sub-contracting arrangements.

(e) Widening the product base to smooth demand fluctuations (Refer to chapter 2 sub-section 3:2:2)

(f) Flexibility in finished goods stock levels (Refer to chapter 5)

Probably few companies will ever achieve true labour flexibility and will therefore use stocks and overtime as the main production/sales buffer.

A lot of labour planning is related to hiring and firing so that labour is cost/effective to meet corporate objectives. We have established that 19th century hire/fire labour management is not applicable to contemporary conditions. However in the medium and long run, 'adjustments' to the labour force are possible and this is a vital part of labour planning. In the following sub-sections we will look at two aspects of medium/long run labour planning: the corporate plan and the impact of technology.

5:2:1 The corporate plan A corporate plan would normally be for three, five or even ten years depending on the size of the company and nature of the industry Within the corporate plan timescale, there will be marketing, production, finance, and investment intentions. Any or all of these intentions can affect the labour plan. For example, if it was known that the market for a particular product or service was declining and/or competition was getting tougher, then the plan may include intentions of entering a new market. This would affect production and labour during the transition phase. The labour plan would therefore have to increase the flexible factors on the old product line such as overtime and stock piling and make labour wastage calculations and re-training preparations. Part of the labour plan would be to ensure no new employees were recruited for the declining process. There are however circumstances when a smooth transition from one type of production process to another type is not possible.

Earlier in section 4 we considered the role of organised labour and noted that it can be constructive or destructive. Some managers face tough organised labour where any planned change in work practices would be strongly resisted. Under these circumstances where compromise is not possible, labour planning may have to adopt an aggressive posture which could more appropriately be described as *strike planning.* To state the issue bluntly - if there is going to be a 'battle', a wise General will attempt to choose the time and place, know the enemy and have a strategy. Even if management was not seeking a 'battle', it would still be pragmatic to have some form of contingency strile plan.

In a commercial environment of changing markets, tough competition, political uncertainty and astonishing developments in technology, the corporate plan will be subject to continued revision. From a labour planning viewpoint, a revision may result in the need to prepare for an 'adjustment' in the size and/or composition of the labour force. Ideally, such 'adjustments' should be undertaken gradually. Indeed, it could be argued that rapid large scale labour reorganisations and redundancies are an indication of weak planning and control where employees suffer because of inefficient senior management. But such an argument needs to recognise the role of organised labour. If the representatives of organised labour are incapable or unwilling to accept responsibility for helping to alter the composition of the workforce to meet changing circumstances, then change cannot be a gradual process through agreed procedures.

5:2:2 Impact of technology There is a likelihood that any discussion on this topic will inevitably move into the social ramifications of technological advance. Ever since Ned Lud destroyed two stocking frames in 1779, employees have been concerned about how machines will affect their jobs and their lives. This concern has found various forms of expression: from the 'Luddite' bands of English artisans that caused riots for destroying machinery between 1811 and 1816, to modern day restrictive work practices that attempt to prevent the introduction of technologically advanced equipment. This concern that spans more than 300 years of 'progress' is based on the fact that *capital replaces labour.*

The history of applied technological innovation in the nineteenth and twentieth century has been mainly to extend man's physical capabilities. For instance, machinery has enabled tremendously high output to be achieved and large loads to be lifted and transported with just a fraction of the labour that would be required if the machinery was not available. Although this type of machinery tended to replace labour, its main characteristic was that it was dumb and needed human beings to bring it to life. Thus, one kind of labour skill was generally being replaced by another skill. The increased output provided higher standards of living which in turn created more demand. The overall effect was often structural changes in a company's labour force, rather than a reduction in total labour. From a labour planning viewpoint, the problem was mainly training and re-training. However, recent developments in technology will have a significant impact on labour planning because the new machines are intelligent!. Many tasks and processes can now be completely replaced by machines and the planning decision can be whether to use man or machine. It is not only the shop floor worker that is threatened with automation, the electronic office will reduce the requirement for clerical workers. With this general background on the impact of technology let us consider how this is likely to affect labour planning.

In the previous sub-section we considered how labour planning was based on the corporate plan. During growth periods a decision has to be made whether to increase capital or labour or a mixture of both, to meet higher output expectations. This can be a difficult decision and the kind of calculations that would be needed include:-

(i) Risk of excess capacity calculations (Refer to chapter 6 sub-section 2:7 and chapter 7 sub-section 9:2)

(ii) The cost difference between the alternative courses of action (Refer to chapter 6 sub-section 3:1 and chapter 7 sub-sections 2:3, 7:1 and 8:1)

Clearly, the capital/labour mix decision has to be included in the corporate plan for labour requirements to be forecasted. The 'mix' is especially important if the plan is to replace labour with capital, because it is often more difficult and costly to remove labour, then to recruit labour. The capital/labour mix changeover phase would probably be a disruptive time. There is ample evidence to show that organised labour usually fights the introduction of technology that replaces craft skills and causes members to lose their jobs. Accordingly part of labour planning is to identify which capital purchasing decisions are likely to cause an industrial dispute. The effects of the dispute can then be costed on a worst/best outcome basis and included in the decision making process. If the decision is made to acquire labour replacing technology, then labour planning would reflect the company's managerial style, i.e.

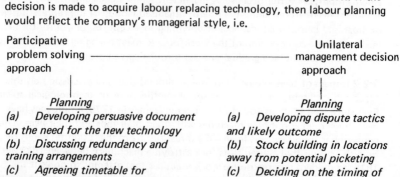

Participative problem solving approach	Unilateral management decision approach
<u>*Planning*</u>	<u>*Planning*</u>
(a) Developing persuasive document on the need for the new technology	*(a) Developing dispute tactics and likely outcome*
(b) Discussing redundancy and training arrangements	*(b) Stock building in locations away from potential picketing*
(c) Agreeing timetable for introduction of new technology	*(c) Deciding on the timing of the dispute*

Whatever the management style, the transition period when new technology is being introduced will generally be a difficult time. It therefore follows that labour planning is especially important for this kind of decision.

5:3 Producing a labour plan A labour plan is a statement of how future labour requirements are to be met. The underlying detail upon which the statement is based includes an analysis of existing labour and forecasted labour requirements. (Refer to sub-sections 5:1 and 5:2), an assessment of structural changes such as a shift from direct labour to indirect labour, training and education needs, cost efficiency calculations, key employee succession arrangements and a monitoring system to provide a feedback/control loop (Refer to chapter 2, section 5). A large proportion of this underlying detail is programable and explained in chapter 10. In the following sub-sections we are going to consider four aspects of the labour plan: improving labour efficiency, training and education, succession planning and the importance of a monitoring system.

5:3;1 Improving labour efficiency Our first task in this sub-section is to establish what we mean by labour efficiency. Profit is not a valid measure because this is determined by sales value, volume and accounting conventions relating to costs. The amount of work done is not necessarily the best measure, because work often increases just to fill the time available. There are also a wide variety of invalid output measures used to support the viewpoints of vested interests, rather than seek the truth. Living in this jungle of statistical deceit, are managers that seek genuine measures of labour efficiency. Measures that make allowance for the nature of the work, the type of equipment, the level of training, the continuity of production, the supply of materials and all the other variables that can effect the labour input/output relationship.

To improve labour efficiency using existing capital equipment, the following stages need to be considered:-

Stage 1 Identify meaningful measures of labour efficiency. The measures chosen will depend mainly upon the nature of the work and expected level of co-operation from the labour force.

Stage 2 Establish recording systems to monitor different aspects of labour efficiency such as: causes of non productive time, levels of illness and absenteeism and various labour cost/output ratios.

Stage 3 Identify causes of inefficiency from analysis of labour efficiency data

Stage 4 Examine alternative ways of rectifying the causes of inefficiency

Stage 5 Select best methods and implement

These five stages are stated in fairly general terms because there are so many different efficiency measures and reasons for inefficiency. However it is worthwhile briefly considering a few kinds of labour efficiency measurements such as:-

(i) Causes of non-productive time
(ii) Productivity comparisons
(iii) Absenteeism
(iv) Cost efficiency

(i) Causes of non-productive time There will occasionally be times when direct labour is not actually producing goods during working hours. The reasons may be waiting for work, breakdown of a machine or waiting for instructions. It is therefore important for management to know how much non-productive time occurs and why. A common recording system is the 'time sheet' where employees enter a job number and other details for the

costing department. Part of this time sheet can contain a non-productive analysis section that would enable aggregate figures to be quickly calculated. An example of the kind of analysis is given below.

DIAGRAM 56 ANALYSING NON PRODUCTIVE TIME

CAUSES OF NON-PRODUCTIVE TIME								
	Cause	*Minutes lost*						*Totals*
1.	Awaiting work							
2.	Awaiting machine							
3.	Awaiting materials							
4.	Awaiteng equipment							
5.	Awaiting instructions							
6.	Waiting for other trades							
7.	Breakdown of machine							
8.	Union business							
9.	Labour dispute							
10.	Other							

(ii) *Productivity comparisons* The measurement of productivity is usually undertaken as part of a productivity incentive agreement (Refer to sub-section 3:7). Many of these comparisons are cost based such as value added type ratios and are discussed later under the heading of cost ratios. The comparison of productivity over discrete time periods and/or between comparable work shifts or departments can be done from existing records. But care is needed to ensure that valid comparisons are being made. For example if the productivity of different shifts was being compared then adjustments would probably have to be made for the number of workers and number of hours to bring them to a comparable base.

(iii) *Absenteeism* A number of studies have shown that far more days are lost through absenteeism than through strikes. For instance a 1972 Government survey estimated that for every 1,000 working days lost due to strikes. 13,000 working days were lost through absenteeism.Moreover a high rate of absenteeism provides an indication of low staff morale. It is therefore important that absenteeism records are maintained and frequently analysed at individual, departmental and company levels. A weekly attendance record could have the following kind of coding:-

1. Absence without permission
2. Absence with permission
3. Education and training
4. Leave in lieu of overtime
5. Holiday
6. Sickness and accident
7. Jury service
8. Official trade union activities
9. Unofficial trade union activities
10. Industrial action

If employees' codings are included in the weekly return then a wide range of absenteeism analysis is possible such as: work group, age group, sex, length of service, shifts, and timing, say near public holidays. The important point about this kind of measurement, that is programable, is that management need to have details about absenteeism before the appropriate corrective action can be taken.

(iv) *Cost efficiency* This aspect of labour efficiency measurement is directly concerned with cost whereas the previous measures discussed were indirectly cost related. A major labour cost that can get out of control is

payment for overtime. Accordingly overtime must be tightly controlled. There can be exceptions to this general rule such as when companies operate a low basic rate with 'guaranteed' overtime as an undeclared wages policy. (Refer to sub-section 3:1:1) Or, if custom and practice and strong organised labour make it difficult to reduce overtime working. Whatever the reasons for overtime, there is no valid reason why it should not be measured and analysed in cost/efficiency terms. The analysis should show *where and why* overtime is being worked. For instance a single department may have a high overtime rate becuase there are not enough employees and/or machines to cope with demand. Or a maintenance department may have to work overtime because of the nature of their work (i.e. maintaining machines after the operatives have finished work). Once management are aware how much overtime is being worked, where it is being worked and why, then they are in a better position to make decisions to improve the cost efficiency of overtime working.

In terms of cost efficiency a wide variety of ratios can be produced such as:-

Overtime costs/total labour costs at department and company level

Direct labour/indirect labour costs

Recruitment costs/total labour costs

Training costs/total labour costs

Absenteeism costs/total labour costs

These kinds of ratios taken over time can provide a trend of labour cost efficiency that will enable management to make decisions to improve efficiency.

This brief survey about improving labour efficiency has concentrated on improvement with existing work practices, equipment and levels of training. Improving efficiency through the introduction of new technology was considered in sub-section 5:2:2. Education and training is discussed in the next sub-section.

5:3:2 Education and training An important part of any labour plan is to determine the future education and training needs of existing and future employees. For instance a high labour turnover could indicate a continuing need for in-house training.Or a planned change in capital equipment and working practices may require a separate education and training programme. Thus the starting point is to establish future education and training needs with regard to number of employees, the time to acquire necessary knowledge and skills and training resources needed. Moreover, the training should take place without disrupting production.

At an individual level personnel records should be maintained that show the strengths and weaknesses of employees so that appropriate training/education needs can be determined. Once future needs have been established, proposed training programmes would be developed to satisfy them. But each proposal has to be critically examined to ensure it is cost/effective. Indeed the appraisal of training must be a continuing process where every person who has attended a course is required to complete a questionnaire. Line supervisors could also complete questionnaires on their opinion of the relevance and usefulness of courses their subordinates have attended. Thus for education and training the following steps should be part of the labour plan :-

(a) Identify future education and training requirements
(b) Prepare detailed training programme proposals
(c) Critically evaluate all proposals on cost/effective criteria
(d) Evaluate every training course after it has run
(e) If the evaluation identifies specific course weaknesses alter training programme
(f) Continually review the overall programme to ensure it fits into the labour plan.

5:3:3 Succession plans With any organisation there are a number of key positions that require people with specific skills, knowledge and exoerience. But from the outset it is important to distinguish between the importance of an organisational function and the importance of an individual. To state the issue bluntly - cemeteries are filled with people who considered themselves indispensable. Whilst key individuals can determine the strength of an organisation, dependence upon individuals constitutes an inherent organisational weakness. Accordingly succession planning can be viewed as having three purposes:-

(i) To reduce organisational overdependence upon an individual's skills, experience and knowledge
(ii) To provide incentives that will retain and motivate key personnel within the organisation
(iii) To provide a career structure and internal promotion policy that ensures several successors are able to take up key positions at short notice.

Most discussions on succession planning are directed at the third objective but we will briefly consider all three objectives.

(1) Reducing organisation overdependence

Many small businesses are totally dependent upon the entrepreneur that created them. But as an enterprise grows and authority and responsibility is delegated to a wider group of executives, the organisation becomes less dependent for its survival on a single individual. Even so, there are still opportunities for individuals in large organisations to secure their positions and increase their spheres of influence by informal groupings that control the free flow of information. Organisational dependence upon an individual's abilities is acceptable, but procedures need to be developed that prevent individuals abusing their privilege of organisational power to strengthen their own positions. Such procedures could include: the free flow of information, decentralisation of decision making, and where practical, moving executives to different positions within the organisation. The objective of this type of procedure is to prevent individuals creating circumstances which make the organisation dependent upon them. For example, a systems analyst who does not docoment a systems design makes it very difficult, often impossible for the program to be modified by another analyst.

(ii) Retaining and motivating key personnel

Once key functions have been identified and the individuals performing the functions are assessed, then the following kinds of question need to be asked:-

(a) Is the individual worth retaining?
(b) If no, can he/she be easily replaced?
(c) If yes, can he/she be retained and motivated?

Our concern here is with employees who fit into the latter category. Subsection 3:2 outlined a number of perks such as a company car, private medical care etc. but for the real high flyer special remuneration packages have to be devised. These packages are often referred to as compensation and have given rise to a new breed of consultants referred to as 'executive compensation consultants'. Compensation would be divided into:-

(i) Salary and corporate performance related bonus

(ii) A wide range of 'perks'

(iii) Longer term incentives which are usually linked to some form of equity rights.

For example share options enable executives to purchase shares at a given price after a specified period. These options can be sold or taken up. Or, an executive may be given shares, a fixed sum or options that are related in some way to corporate performance.

It is the long term incentives that are normally the lock in devices aimed at retaining the individual. Unfortunately, when individuals achieve board of director status they may consider themselves key personnel requiring compensation packages. Thus the award of very expensive compensation may be made by an organisation to individuals who are not necessarily key personnel. Indeed some compensation contracts may be for the protection of an individual and not for the benefit of the organisation.

(iii) Career structure and promotion policy for successors

Key personnel are not necessarily on the board of directors even though many compensation packages are 'arranged' for that level in an organisation. Throughout the managerial and technical hierarchy there will be key individuals that may be approaching retiring age. Therefore an important part of this aspect of succession planning is an age distribution analysis. This kind of analysis will reveal succession weaknesses. For example it may show that a large proportion of senior staff are all about the same age and will therefore be due for retirement at about the same time. If many of their potential successors are also in the same age group then there will be a break in managerial continuity. To avoid such a break, a succession policy would be needed that developed, monitored and promoted individuals within the right age/experience groups. Where suitable internal candidates were not available, then a recruitment policy would attempt to fill the gap. To identify these gaps a bar chart could be constructed as illustrated in diagram 57. This shows a five tier management structure with an internal succession gap for the third tier.

DIAGRAM 57 MANAGEMENT SUCCESSION ANALYSIS

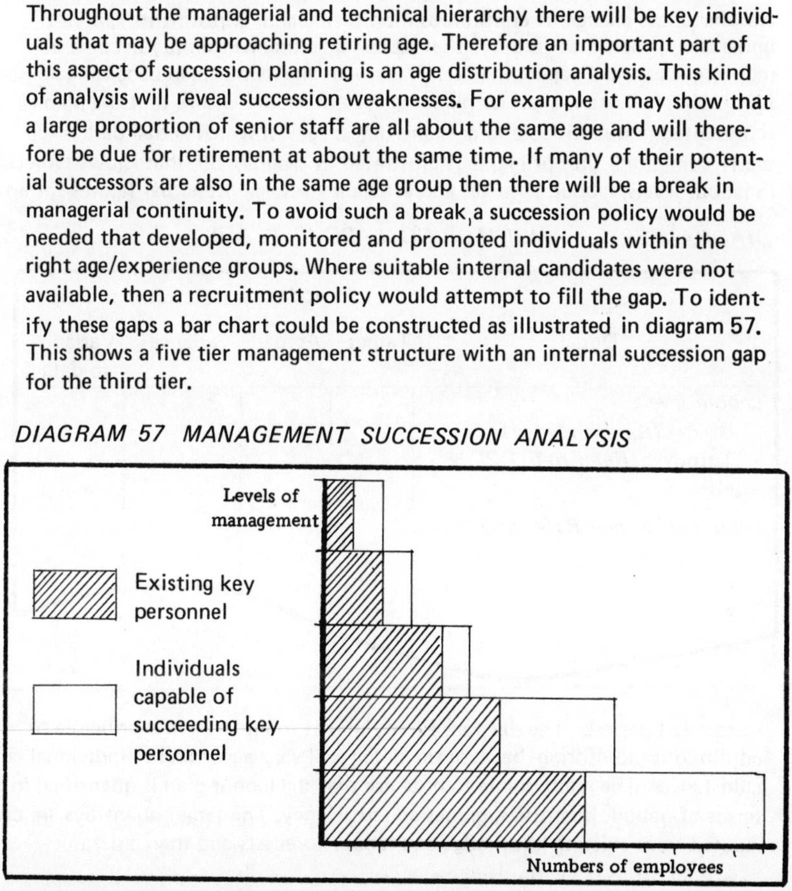

5:3:4 Labour planning system The labour plan represents a series of decisions that are based on the corporate plan and forecasted labour requirements. But like any other plan, a feedback loop is required to ensure that actual events are proceeding according to planned events. This is illustrated in diagram 58 below.

DIAGRAM 58 PRINCIPLES OF LABOUR PLANNING

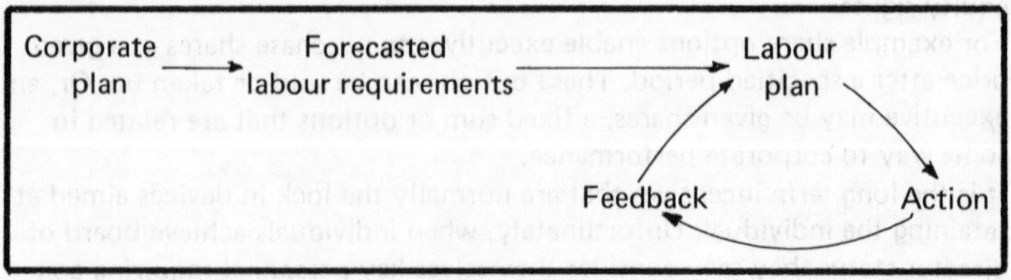

This feedback loop means that labour details that have been explained in previous sub-sections need to be monitored and related to the labour plan. Accordingly, a major part of any labour planning system are the arrangements for monitoring labour efficiency, labour turnover, labour composition, successions for key positions and training. An important feature of the monitoring system will be the *continuous flow of information*. Labour planning should be a continuous function of constant monitoring, decisions and revision of the plan if circumstances change. If continuous monitoring and 'adjustments' are not undertaken, then there is a risk that labour planning will simply become a meaningless annual paper exercise. To prevent the labour plan becoming a filing cabinet fixture, a labour planning system should ensure that the plan is represented in quantifiable targets and dates, against which actual data is regularly compared. This principle is illustrated in diagram 59, that shows targets in labour levels, labour turnover and efficiency set against actual figures for an

DIAGRAM 59 MONITORING LABOUR PLANS

	Period ending			
Detail	Target	Actual	Variance	Variance to date
Labour levels				
Grades *(Refer to 5:1:1)*				
Turnover *(Refer to 5:1:2)*				
etc				
Labour efficiency (Refer to 5:3:1)				
—				
—				
etc				

assessment period. The diagram is only meant to illustrate the principle of continuous monitoring, because the detail will vary according to individual circumstances. The main points to note are that the labour plan is quantified in terms of: labour quantities, grades and efficiency. The target quantities are calculated from existing knowledge and labour forecasts and then a data collection/analysis system provides regular actual data for feedback and control purposes. The provision of relevant data could come from a management information system as described in chapter 10.

6. Summary

This is the largest chapter in the book, yet in the first draft it was amongst the smallest. In the early stages of writing this chapter a fairly strict accounting approach was taken. But it quickly became evident that this was inadequate and a wider viewpoint was necessary. As a result of this wider view, the accounting content now occupies less than half the chapter.

The appropriate starting point for a study of labour management was taken as being labour administration. Thus the first major section concentrated on recruitment, employment and dismissal procedures. There is a tremendous amount of law relating to employment and dismissal, that tends to change according to political rather than commercial criteria. Thus the review of the law stated in this sub-section needs to be supplemented by specialist recent publications. However, the purpose of this sub-section was to alert managers to the labour law minefield that surrounds most employees. The general message of section 2 was to get recruitment, employment and dismissal procedures 'right' and keep them under constant review.

Section 3 on labour remuneration is probably one of the broadest and most detailed coverages of labour remuneration systems that has ever been documented in one chapter. The section was summarised in diagram 46, that provided a broad framework labour remuneration systems and a set of reference points for the sub-sections. Clearly, before any decision is made on a type of remuneration system, the decision makers need to be aware of all the options available. It is hoped that section 3 illustrates the inter-relationship between different remuneration systems and provides sufficient detail about each method so that the best system can be devised to suit a firm's specific circumstances.

A chapter on labour management would be incomplete if the role of organised labour was not recognised. Every effort was made in section 4 to be objective about this subject. A rather ambitious attempt was made to overview some theory from industrial sociology and industrial relations so as to provide some kind of framework. Following this introductory framework the three main forms of organised labour were explained with a special emphasis on trade unions and the procedures that govern employment relationships. Indeed the emphasis of these sub-sections was that good collective agreements are an essential part of good labour management. The remainder of section 4 was about an accounting topic - the provision of information for collective bargaining. These sub-sections concluded with an amphasis on the importance of establishing an information agreement.

Section 5 on labour planning was primarily concerned with the decision to replace labour with capital. This section was divided into three main sub-sections; analysing existing labour, forecasting future labour requirements, and producing a labour plan. The principles of human resource accounting were explained in this section for reference purposes but they are not recommended for practical application.

The subject of labour management can be a sensitive area and it is possible that some statements in this chapter may offend a particular reader. However, the subject must be kept open for debate and it is hoped that this chapter will contribute to more informed and less predjudiced discussions.

Accountancy Quiz No.4.

1. Describe a personnel selection procedure *(2:1:1)*

2. How would you dismiss an employee? *(2:4, 2:4:1, 2:4:2, 2:4:3)*

3. What do you understand by the term effort/reward relationship? *(3)*

4. Describe four kinds of job evaluation scheme *(3:1:2)*

5. Explain the general characteristics of payment by results schemes and state their advantages and disadvantages *(3:3)*

6. Describe and distinguish between three different types of premium bonus systems *(3:3:2)*

7. How would you derive a remuneration policy? *(3:8, 3:8:1, 3:8;2, 3:8:3, 3:8 3:8:5)*

8. What factors would you take into consideration before establishing an information agreement? *(4, 4:1, 4:2, 4:3, 4:3:1, 4:3:2, 4:3:3, 4:3:4)*

9. What is human resource accounting? *(5:1:3)*

10. What factors would you take into consideration when deciding whether to replace labour with capital? *(5, 5:1, 5:1:1, 5:1:2, 5:2, 5:3, 5:3:1)*

5 Inventory Management

Objective
To provide for the non-accountant a detailed description of stores administration, stock valuation and stock control techniques.

Content *Page No.*

Inventory Management

1 Introduction

Inventory management covers all aspects of stocks and work in progress including: requisitioning, purchasing, receiving, inspecting, storage, issues to work in progress, receiving from work in progress, valuing stock, calculating economic order quantities, optimum stock levels, re-order levels, safety stock and stores administration. It is a specialised management function that is sometimes sadly neglected by companies because it does not seem to be important. Yet, it is absolutely vital for some production processes that the right materials of the correct quality and quantity are available at the right time. Also, it is important that not too much cash becomes tied up in stocks, especially if the business is growing fast and working capital is being heavily financed on a bank overdraft.

There are two extreme approaches to inventory management. At one extreme stores are treated with contempt, being given the worst parts of the factory, little capital investment and no staff training. The other extreme is substantial investment in advanced storage techniques, computerised stock control systems and highly trained staff. Every enterprise will have an inventory management policy somewhere between these two extremes. The inventory management policy of each business will depend upon its trading circumstances. Therefore the appropriate starting point is for management to assess the relative importance of inventory management for their company. A simple assessment would require:—

(a) To determine the proportion of inventory to total assets.

(b) To assess the impact of inventory on cash flow.

(c) To calculate the proportion of total revenue expenditure spent on bought in materials and components.

Firstly let us consider how much of the business assets are tied up in inventories. This can be done by taking the company's last five balance sheets and making the following calculation for each year:—

$$\frac{\text{Average stocks and work in progress}}{\text{Average total assets}} \times 100$$

The crude average figures are calculated by adding the opening and closing balances and dividing by two. If this calculation produced a figure as large as 35%, which is the UK average for book publishers, then clearly inventory management is very important. But if the figure was below say 5%, then on a cost/benefit basis the company would normally not direct a lot of resources into inventory management.

Secondly we can look at the impact that inventory has on the company's cash flow. To do this the working capital cycle should be calculated for five years. The principles and calculations of the working capital cycle are fully explained in *Volume 1 Financial accounting for non-accountants* but the concept is illustrated here in diagram 60. The five year analysis may show the working capital cycle to be out of balance due to bad inventory management. Consider the figures in the following table that illustrates how working capital can become tied up in large inventories.

EXAMPLE OF WORKING CAPITAL CYCLE – 5 YEAR ANALYSIS

Year	*Average Inventory*		*Average Debtors*		*Average Creditors*		*Average Cash Working Cap Cycle*	
	£000's	*Days*	*£000's*	*Days*	*£000's*	*Days*	*£000's*	*Days*
1	150	50	100	60	80	30	10	80
2	250	60	120	65	100	35	(5)	90
3	400	65	180	55	160	40	(20)	80
4	600	70	240	55	200	35	(90)	90
5	900	80	300	60	250	30	(150)	110

DIAGRAM 60 WORKING CAPITAL CYCLE

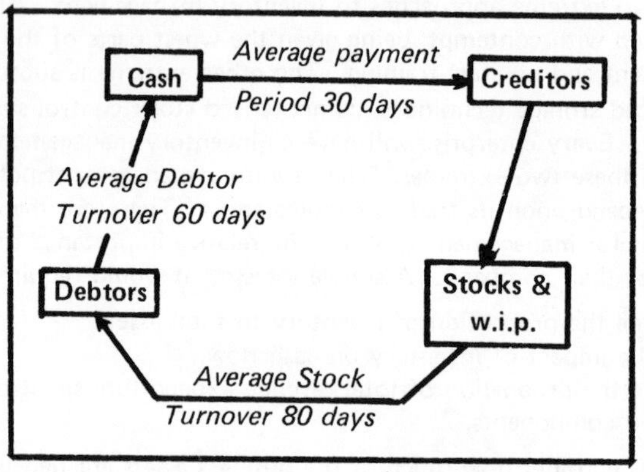

In this hypothetical example of a fast growing business, inventory has not been properly managed. Stock turnover has slowed down from 50 to 80 days and stock holdings have increased six times. The result of weak inventory management has been a severe strain on the company cash flow. Under these circumstances if corrective action was not taken quickly the inventory management policy, or lack of policy, could cause the company to go into liquidation.

Lastly we can look at the proportion of total revenue expenditure spent on bought in materials, in a kind of value added analysis. This assessment highlights the relative importance of the purchasing officer and his/her staff. If expenditure on bought in materials and components was above, say 20% of total revenue expenditure, then clearly purchasing is an important function for the business and merits closer attention from management. After making these three simple calculations management should be in a better position to assess the relative importance of inventory planning and control for the company.

In this chapter we first look at stock classifications because stock can be held in a number of different stores. We then examine the wider aspects of stores administration including: purchasing, receiving, recording, issuing, stock taking and the effect of computers on stock control. Section 4 is concerned with the practical aspects of storage such as identifying, locating and protecting stock and the problems of stores' queues. The section on stock valuation shows how there can be more than 60 possible stock values for just one stock item in the finished goods stores and explains seven ways of pricing issues to work in progress. Then section 6 reviews the two main problems for inventory planning and control; how much to order, and when to order?

This is a substantial chapter on inventory management containing a lot of detail The non-accountant is advised not to get too involved in all the methods of stock valuation and the detail of stores administration unless he/she is directly concerned with inventory administration, planning and control.

2 Classification of stock

A large manufacturing company will have a wide variety of stock in a number of different stores. Diagram 61 illustrates an enterprise with many different stores.

DIAGRAM 61 STOCK CLASSIFICATIONS' STORAGE & MOVEMENT

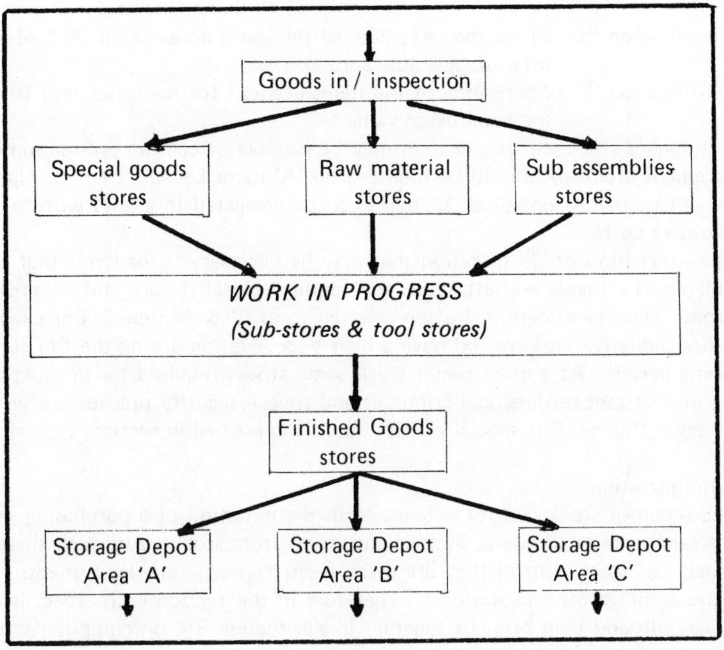

The main classifications to note from the diagram are: raw material stores, sub assembly stores, work in progress stores and finished goods stores. For merchandising companies there is usually only one main classification called finished goods. But for manufacturing companies, raw materials, work in progress and finished goods need to be treated separately in a stock control system. Thus our major stock classification categories are into:

(a) *Pre-process stocks* such as raw materials and bought in sub assemblies.

(b) *Intermediate stocks* that are often treated as work in progress. This classification represents items that have been partly processed but are not ready for sale.

(c) *Finished goods* are items that are ready for sale.

The second level of stock classification for a manufacturing company can be by usage value. The classification technique is based on an application of Pareto's

Law that is more commonly known as the 80/20 rule. The technique requires the average usage value of each item to be calculated and ranked in order, i.e.

Item reference number	*Unit value*	x *Usage*	= *Usage value*
	£		£
10897	100–00	100	10,000
10321	98–00	80	7,840
—etc......to	—	—	—
839121	0.001	100	0.10
		Total	£

Each item is then taken as a percentage of the total and broad classifications are drawn such as:—

Classification 'A' Where 10% of the items account for 60% of the total usage value,

Classification 'B' Where the next 30% of the items account for 30% of the total usage value, and

Classification 'C' Where 60% of the items account for the remaining 10% of the total usage value.

Although a stock-out of any item may be capable of causing production delays, management attention should be focussed on 'A' items because of their high usage value. Whereas the control of 'C' items can be delegated to a level with lower administrative costs.

One other kind of classification that may be necessary is for items that can be considered as valuable and attractive and require special storage and administrative controls. This classification is often referred to as 'V & A' items. For example in an office, adhesive tape would have a high V & A rating during the Christmas shopping period. At a more senior level, some stocks required for production processes may attract professional criminals and special security precautions would be necessary. This kind of special classification is explained in section 4 on storage.

3 Administration

The scope of stock control extends from the initiation of a purchasing procedure through receipt of goods, storage and issues from stock. Although these are all aspects of stock control they are often treated as separate departments with separate administrative procedures. Therefore in this section each aspect is explained separately and then brought together in sub section 3:4 on computerisation.

3:1 Purchasing The purchasing process must be controlled so that only authorised people in an organisation can order goods or services on behalf of the business. This basic control is absolutely essential. It would be absurd to allow anyone in a company to simply place orders as they thought necessary. Indeed stock control starts with purchasing procedures. Companies normally structure their administration so that one person and/or a department is responsible for placing *all* orders. This department will place orders on behalf of other people in the organisation based on internal documents called purchase requisitions. An administrative procedure for purchasing is illustrated in diagram 62. There can be a number of variations of the procedure shown in this diagram but several departments must know what has been ordered. Therefore the five part purchase order would be a minimum distribution.

From the ratio calculations explained in the introduction, management will

DIAGRAM 62 PURCHASING ADMINISTRATIVE PROCEDURE

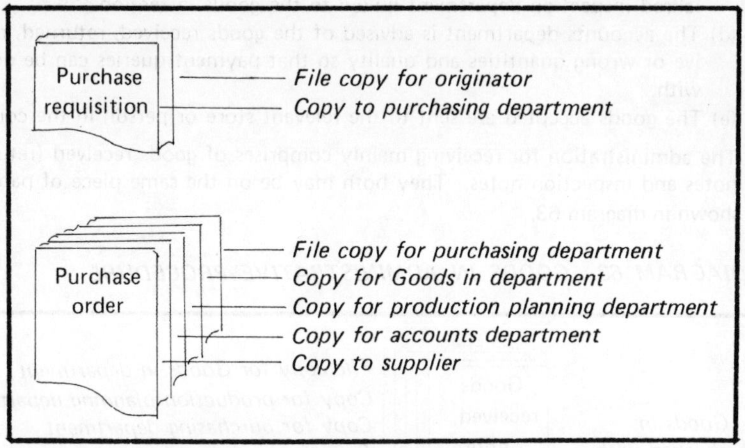

be able to assess the relative importance of their purchasing department. If for example the value added ratio expressed as:—

$$\frac{\text{(Sales} - \text{Bought in goods and services)}}{\text{Sales}} \ \%$$

was over 50% then purchasing would be one of the most important of all the business functions. Indeed purchasing is a skilled profession with its own professional body (Refer to Appendix 3). The purchasing officer would be responsible for:—

(a) An efficient purchasing administration system.
(b) Maintaining lists of reliable suppliers.
(c) Negotiating the best possible trading terms.
(d) Liason with other departments:—
 (i) With production manager for production scheduling.
 (ii) With accountants for budgets, cash flow calculations and bought ledger control.
 (iii) With goods in and inspection departments.
 (iv) With stores managers.
 (v) With managers authorised to sign purchase requisitions.
(e) Ensuring that production material requirements are met at the right time with the right quantity and quality at the best possible price.
(f) Monitoring price trends and advising management of items that are likely to have substantial price increases so that budgets can be adjusted and purchasing/storage policies altered accordingly.

A purchasing officer can increase corporate profitability and should be an integral part of the management team.

3:2 Receiving The function of the 'goods in' section is to provide a single point for the receipt of goods that:—

(a) Ensures goods received have been ordered.
(b) The quantity and description is the same as the purchase order.

(c) The quality is acceptable. For high technology goods there is often a specialised inspection department linked to the goods in section.
(d) The accounts department is advised of the goods received, returned, defective or wrong quantities and quality so that payment queries can be dealt with.
(e) The goods accepted are sent to the relevant store or person in the company.

The administration for receiving mainly comprises of goods received (returned) notes and inspection notes. They both may be on the same piece of paper as shown in diagram 63.

DIAGRAM 63 GOODS IN ADMINISTRATIVE PROCEDURE

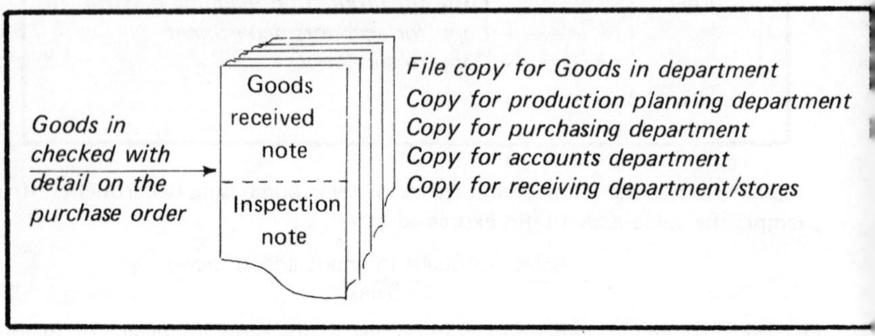

The accounting system would ensure that suppliers are not paid until ordered goods of the correct quantity and quality have been received. Therefore goods received notes would be the authorisation for invoice clearance in the bought ledger.

3:3 Storage and issues In this sub section we are concerned with the administration of stores. The physical aspects of storage are discussed in section 4, and the problems of pricing issues from stores and valuing stock are explained in section 5. For the moment we will concentrate on stores paperwork. There are two basic documents used by almost every storekeeper: the bin card and the material requisition.

(a) Bin card (Also called a 'Stock record card'). The storeman will keep one of these cards for every type of item in stock and on order. The basic detail on a bin card would be:–

(i) Material description and reference number.
(ii) Location in the stores usually called a 'bin number'.
(iii) The maximum and minimum stock level and re-order level.
(iv) Receipts, issues and stock level in quantity, value or both.
(v) Goods ordered not yet received.
(vi) Goods reserved for specific contracts or jobs but not yet issued.

Many storage administration systems are based only on bin cards.

(b) Material requisition This piece of paper represents the authority for a storekeeper to issue materials. When there are a lot of materials to issue for a contract or particular production run then the production planning department produce a list of material issues to be made that is often called a 'Bill of Materials'. The requisition or bill will contain the following basic detail:-

(i) Material descriptions and reference numbers.
(ii) Quantities.
(iii) Use, such as contract or job number.
(iv) Authorisation, such as foreman's signature.
(v) Costing records section. (Not usually completed by the storeman).

There are other documents that serve specific functions such as goods returned notes and stores transfer notes but the main documents are the bin cards and material requisitions.

3:3:1 Stock taking The bin card described in the previous section calculated a stock balance after every transaction. Thus the stock of any item can be determined by looking at the balance on the relevant bin card. This form of *perpetual inventory* system enables management to ascertain stock levels at any time, However differences can arise between the physical stock and the stock records due to:—

(a) Clerical errors such as addition, subtraction or entries on the wrong bin card.
(b) Mistakes when issuing due to counting, cutting or divisions of bulk goods
(c) Stock losses due to theft, deterioration or evaporation.
(d) Unrecorded issues and/or returns.

Because there tends to be a difference between the physical stock and stock records most businesses have some form of stocktaking. The stock taking may be an annual exercise linked to the statutory audit or continuous stock taking. The practice of continuous stocktaking usually involves independent staff making surprise checks covering a small number of stock items at frequent intervals. The organisation of continuous stock taking should ensure that all items of stock are checked at least once a year. The purpose of continuous stock taking is to ensure that the perpetual inventory system is working properly so that management can refer to stock records with the confidence that they represent the physical stock.

The advantages of continuous stock taking over annual stock taking are:—

(a) Stock discrepancies are revealed more quickly, thus reducing the risk of an unexpected stock out.
(b) Acts as a control on storekeepers and a measure of their efficiency.
(c) Production is not inconvenienced by a large annual stock taking exercise.
(d) Greater attention to detail is possible because there is more time for depth checking the stock records to find the *reasons* for discrepancies.

3:4 Computerisation In the previous sub sections the basic administration for purchasing, goods receiving, storing and issuing has been explained. If the entire procedure from ordering to issuing is computerised then a new approach has to be taken for stock administration. An input document would be required for each of the four stages of the procedure.

(a) Ordering A re-designed purchase order would be suitable.
(b) Goods received One or more input documents would be necessary to allow for inspection, rejects, returns and deliveries of the wrong quantity and/or quality.
(c) Goods stored An input document would be needed to identify location.

(d) Goods issued A re-designed requisition note would be suitable.

The main changes would be a large reduction in hard copy records filed in each department. Computer print out and/or terminals could provide the necessary departmental information. The need for numerous copies of forms to be sent to different sections would no longer exist providing there was adequate and relevant file access for user departments. But the real advantages of computerisation would be derived from improved stock control.

4 Storage

It is often said that the first priority with stock control is to lock the stores door. However this is only a precaution against theft. There are many other aspects of storage that require attention. In this section we will consider the problems of identifying stock, protection of stock, the costs of storage, the choice between central or sub stores and the problem of stores' queues.

4:1 Identifying stock Descriptions are sometimes inadequate for accurately identifying items of stock. For example an electrical stores may hold several hundred types of switches. Many of the switches may be identical in appearance but have different specifications. With storage problems like this companies usually identify all items of stock with reference numbers. The internal stock referencing system is then used by all relevant departments when ordering items from stock. Storage space is also organised around the stock referencing system where possible, so the storekeeper can quickly locate items of stock by their reference number. As items are received into store they will be marked with their appropriate stores reference numbers. For computerised stock records a stock referencing system is essential.

4:2 Protecting stock The kind of protection necessary will depend upon the nature of stock risk, the main categories being:—

(a) Deterioration can occur with many kinds of stock if they are not stored under proper conditions. For example if a printer stored paper outside his building and allowed it to get wet, then it would be of no use for printing.

(b) Fire precautions are taken with most types of stores but special precautions are necessary for certain chemicals or explosives.

(c) Special protection is sometimes needed for specific items of stock. Specialised packaging often provides the necessary protection. For example, electrical equipment must be free from dust and moisture or some metals protected from corrosion.

(d) Theft can be divided into two broad categories: petty and substantial. Petty theft from an office would include items such as stationery and pens or pencils. This level of theft is usually tolerated. However, organised substantial theft is possible where items of stock are valuable and easily disposed of. Stocks that are considered to be valuable and attractive (V & A stock) need special storage facilities and separate administrative arrangements, such as frequent inventory checks and audits.

(e) Damage can occur through careless handling and storage of delicate and sensitive items. For example sensitive measuring instruments should not be stored in or near a stock bin where heavy goods were often thrown. Stocks that can be easily damaged need to be stored separately and identified 'to be handled with care'.

4:3 Storage costs There are a number of costs incurred when storing materials, sub-assemblies and finished goods, these include:—

(a) Space costs such as rent and rates.
(b) Running costs such as heating, lighting and any special requirements.
(c) Security costs for alarm systems, security patrols and any special requirements.
(d) Labour costs of storekeepers and assistants.
(e) Administration costs such as stationery and telephone.
(f) Insurance costs for stock and the building.
(g) Equipment costs such as bins, racks and special equipment.
(h) Finance costs due to the cash that is tied up in stock.

It is important to note that larger stock holdings will cause many of these costs to rise. When stocks are held in stores for a long time the risk of obsolescence and deterioration increases and these costs can be quite large.

4:4 Centralised/decentralised stores In principle centralised storage should require lower stock levels, less administration, less space and have higher skilled labour than a number of departmental stores. Accordingly companies usually aim to centralise their stores whenever possible. However, the physical layout of a factory make sub-stores necessary, because a lot of labour time would be wasted walking long distances to and from the central stores. The correct number of sub-stores and main stores will depend on the nature and physical layout of the enterprise.

4:5 Stores queues Every time a queue forms outside a stores it represents lost production. This simple fact can be overlooked by accountants, systems analysts and administraters when they create complicated documentation for stores issues. For example, an engineer requiring say 30 different types of stock items may have to complete 30 separate forms each requiring reference number, items descriptions, job numbers, department reference and issue details. After the forms have been completed the items are located by the storekeeper who also has to alter bin cards and possibly other documents. Whilst this process is taking place a queue may form. Assuming that stores issuing administration and storage organisation has been streamlined to minimise wasted time in queues, then observations can be made that enable the cost of queues to be assessed. The observations should provide quantitative answers for the following questions:—

(a) What is the range of times between arrivals per day?
(b) What are the median and mean times between arrivals per day?
(c) What are the median and mean number of arrivals per hour?
(d) What is the range of individual waiting times per day?
(e) What are the median and mean waiting times per day?
(f) What is the average queue length per day?
(g) What percentage of the storekeeper's time was spent on serving?
(h) From the above data can any regular queuing times and days be identified?

If this data is compiled from representative observation period then a clearer picture will emerge showing if the enterprise has a stores queuing problem. An elementary costing of the problem would be simply to multiply the estimated lost man hours in stores queues by a productivity weighted average wage rate.

Analysis of the queuing data may make the solution quite clear. For example if most of the queues developed in the mornings then a part-time stores assistant may be the answer. However if the data shows irregular queues with a low percentage of the storekeeper's time spent on serving, then one of the many mathematical models may be of use. The important point is that managers should quantify their company's queuing problem by representative observations. After the observations have been analysed then management is in a far better position to assess the costs and benefits of alternative courses of action.

5 Stock valuation

There are two main reasons for valuing stock:—

(i) To be used in the periodic calculation of profit or loss; and,
(ii) To be used for costing jobs, contracts, products or processes.

Before explaining the different stock valuation methods it is first necessary to place stock valuation in some kind of perspective. It is important to distinguish between the different classifications of stock. For example raw material stores and finished goods stores may be treated in different ways for stock valuation pur poses. There are at least three alternative ways of costing materials going into stores. Once materials are in the stores, there is then sometimes a division into current stock and base stock with different valuations. When materials are issued to work in progress there are at least seven methods of pricing the issues. Then when the work in progress is completed and finished items enter the finished goods stores there are at least three methods of valuing finished goods stock. The interdependence between these stock valuation methods means that there can be more than 60 possible stock values for just one item in a finished goods store.

The structure of this section on stock valuation is illustrated in diagram 64 in sub section 5:1 we look at the problems of costing materials going into stores, then in sub section 5:2 briefly look at valuation of materials in the stores. Sub section 5:3 explains seven main ways of pricing stores issues and the final sub sec ion examines finished goods stock valuation methods.

DIAGRAM 64 CATEGORIES OF STOCK VALUATION

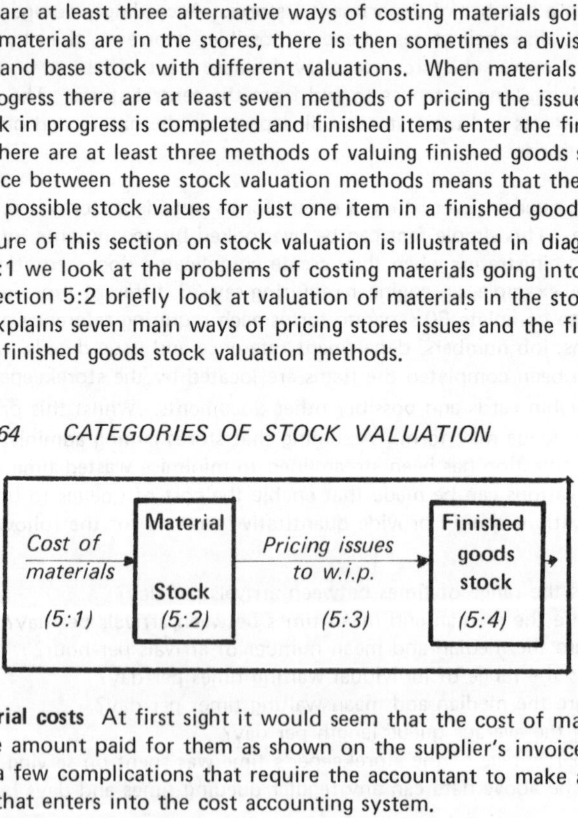

5:1 Material costs At first sight it would seem that the cost of materials is simply the amount paid for them as shown on the supplier's invoice. However there are a few complications that require the accountant to make a choice of the price that enters into the cost accounting system.

(a) *Value added tax* is easily dealt with by extracting it from the invoice in the financial accounts. The only time value added tax becomes a cost is when the final user pays for the item. At all other points the tax is only a colle ion stage and is passed on to the next user. *(Refer to Volume 1 Financial accounting for the non-accountant).* Thus VAT is excluded from stock values.

(b) *Transport or postage costs* that are charged to the customer should be included as a cost of materials.

(c) *Packaging costs* that are charged to customers should also be included as a cost of materials but if there is a refund on returned packages it would be netted off when (or if) claimed.

(d) *Discounts received* fall into three categories: trade discounts, quantity discounts and cash discounts. Trade discounts are clearly to be netted off the cost of materials. But some financial accounting departments consider quantity and/or cash discounts as financial items and exclude them from costing records.

The accounting standard SSAP 9 defines the cost of purchase as comprising of the purchase price, including import duties, transport and handling costs and any other directly attributable costs, less trade discounts, rebates and subsidies.

5:2 Material stores When materials are in the stores, there are a number of ways the stock can be valued. The stock could be valued on the issue pricing principle adopted by the company, such as LIFO or FIFO. (These are explained in the next sub section). Another popular method, especially with computerised stock control systems, is some form of averaging where unit quantities are multiplied by an average price.

The price actually paid for the materials in stock is unlikely to be used for stock valuation because it would require stocks to be identified by price. For instance if there were three separate deliveries of say material 'X' over a period of six months and the unit material costs at different dates were £1.00, £1.10 and £1.15 it would be difficult to ascertain what price related to specific items in stock if there were many issues of material 'X' during that period.

There is one instance where stock is physically separated and can be identified as having a specific price instead of an historic, current or average price. When a company decides that there must be a minimum stock level of specific items that are only issued in emergencies it is referred to as the *base stock method.* With this method, stock items are physically separated as emergency stocks and are valued at their specific historic cost. These stocks would not be included in the averaging process for overall stock valuation.

5:3 Pricing issues. If material costs were stable there would not be a stock valuation/issue pricing problem. However as input prices are rarely constant the basic problem is whether to issue stocks to work in progress at their historic cost, their current cost, their replacement cost or average cost. Once this choice is made then the appropriate valuation method can be selected. The following sub sections explain the different methods for valuing stock issues to work in progress. Where calculations are made to illustrate a stock valuation method, the following basic data will be used:-

Month	*Unit Purchases*	*Unit Cost*	*£*	*Unit Sales*	*Unit Stock*
March	100	£1.20	120	-	200
May	-	-	-	50	150
July	100	1.50	150	-	250
September	-	-	-	100	150
November	100	1.70	170	-	250
December	-	-	-	100	150

(a) Opening stock 100 units @ £1.00 each purchased during January.
(b) Replacement cost estimated to be £1.80 per unit.
(c) Standard cost per unit is £1.65.

5:3:1 First in first out (FIFO). Issues are priced on the assumption that the first stock received is issued first. For example if 100 items of stock were received at £1.00 each the next hundred at £.1.10 and another hundred at £1.20 each, the first issues would be at £1.00 until 100 items had been issued. Then the 101st item to the 200th item would be issued at £1.10 each and the last hundred at £1.20 each.

Calculation of stock value applying FIFO principles to the stock data in sub-section 5:3.

	£
100 items @ £1.70	170
50 items @ £1.50	75
FIFO stock value	£245

Advantages
(a) Logical assumption that the items in stock longest are used first.
(b) A fair method of pricing that uses actual prices for stores issues.
(c) The materials stock valued on this basis is a fair representation of the historic cost of stock.

Disadvantages.
(a) Too much detail for manual stock valuation systems.
(b) Similar jobs can be charged with different issue prices thus distorting comparative cost analysis.
(c) During periods of rapidly rising prices issue prices will be far below the replacement cost, especially with slow moving stocks.

5:3:2 Last in First out (LIFO) Issues are priced at the cost of the last material taken into stock. This is the reverse of FIFO explained in sub-section 5:3:1

Calculation of stock value applying LIFO principles to the stock data in sub-section 5:3.

	£
100 items @ £1.00	100
50 items @ £1.20	60
LIFO stock value	£160

Advantages
(a) Issue price will generally be near to the replacement cost.
(b) A fair method of pricing that uses actual prices for stores issues.

Disadvantages
(a) Too much detail for manual stock valuation systems.
(b) Similar jobs can be charged with different issue prices thus distorting comparative cost analysis.
(c) When stock levels get very low issue prices will probably be far below the 'items' replacement cost.

5:3:3 Simple average. There are two kinds of simple average calculations. One would be based on the stock available at the time of issue and the other on the stock available over an accounting period.

Calculation of stock value applying simple averaging principles to the stock data in sub section 5:3

(i) *Stock available simple average*

$$\frac{(1.7 + 1.5)}{2} \times 150 = \underline{\underline{£240}}$$

(ii) *Periodic simple average (i year period)*

$$\frac{(1.00 + 1.2 + 1.5 + 1.7)}{4} \times 150 = \underline{\underline{£202.50}}$$

Advantages

(a) Easy to apply and understand

Disadvantages

(a) Average can be distorted by small order surcharges or large quantity discounts.

(b) Stock value and issue prices rarely represent the actual price paid for the materials.

5:3:4 Weighted averages. The weighted average makes allowance for quantities purchased. There are two main kinds of weighted average based on either the stock available at the time of issue or stock over an accounting period.

Calculation of stock value applying weighted averaging principles to the stock data in sub section 5:3.

(i) *Stock available weighted average*

$$\frac{(100 \times 1.7) + (50 \times 1.5)}{150} \times 150 = \underline{\underline{£245}}$$

(ii)

$$\frac{(100 \times 1.0) + (100 \times 1.2) + (100 \times 1.5) + (100 \times 1.7)}{400} \times 150 = \underline{\underline{£202.5}}$$

Advantages

(a) The weighted average stock value is fairly representative and may be used in the financial accounts.

(b) The average is not distorted by fluctuations in order quantities.

(c) For computerised stock control the system is comparatively easy to programme.

Disadvantages

(a) Stock values and issue prices rarely represent the actual price paid for the materials

5:3:5 Replacement cost. The inflation accounting recommendations explained in *Volume 1 Financial accounting for the non-accountants* state that stocks are to be valued at their 'value to the business at the time the stock was consumed'. In most instances this would be the net current replacement cost. Where this could not be easily ascertained, an averaging calculation could be made using an appropriate specific index. The replacement cost method for materials uses the current replacement cost to price issues.

Calculation of stock value applying Replacement Cost principles to the stock data in sub section 5:3

Stock value = 150 items at a replacement cost of £1.80 per unit = $\underline{\underline{£270.00}}$

Advantages

(a) Conforms with inflation accounting recommendations for stock valuation.

(b) Issues to work in progress are costed at current prices.

Disadvantages

(a) Difficult to accurately estimate replacement costs.

(b) Substantial administrative problems unless stock records are computerised and specific indices are used for replacement cost estimates.

5:3:6 Standard cost. This method will follow the principles explained in chapter 3 sub-section 5:4 and chapter 9. Basically a standard (expected) price is given for every category of stock and the difference between the actual and standard price will be written off to a material variance price account.

Calculation of stock value applying Standard Cost principles to the stock data in sub-section 5:3.

Stock value = 150 items at a standard cost of £1.65 per unit = £247.50

Advantages

(a) Easy to use because there are not so many price adjustments.

(b) The standard costing principle of comparing actual and expected prices provide a check on the efficiency of the purchasing department.

Disadvantages

(a) If standards are not regularly revised issue prices and stock values will not reflect current economic values.

(b) A lot of administrative effort is necessary to set up a standard costing system.

5:3:7 Comparison of methods. The previous sub-sections have briefly explained most of the methods for pricing issues to work in progress. The method chosen for pricing issues will affect the cost of finished goods stock and the valuation of materials stock remaining in stores. The pricing/valuation methods can be grouped into the following five categories:-

1. *Valuation at original prices* where issues are made on a first in first out basis FIFO.
2. *Valuation at current prices* where issues are made on a last in first out basis LIFO
3. *Valuation at replacement prices* where issues are priced at their current replacement cost.
4. *Valuation at average prices* where issues are priced at either a simple or weighted average of original prices.
5. *Valuation at fixed prices* where issues are priced at the standard cost, or if base stock is issued at a fixed original cost.

The example that was used to illustrate these different methods provided the following stock valuations:-

Sub-section	*Stock valuation method*	*Stock valuation of 150 items*
		£
5:3:1	First in first out (FIFO)	245.00
5:3:2	Last in first out (LIFO)	160.00
5:3:3	Simple average (i) Stock available	240.00
	(ii) Periodic	202.50

5:3:4	Weighted average (i) Stock available	245.00
	(ii) Periodic	202.50
5:3:5	Replacement cost	270.00
5:3:6	Standard cost	247.50

Naturally the difference in stock values between the methods will depend on the basic data. The real problem is which method to choose? The early debates centred on a choice between LIFO and FIFO. In many ways these were similar to the debates on inflation accounting. The argument for LIFO was that current revenues should be matched with current costs and not historic costs. Thus during periods of rapidly rising prices LIFO should be used. The inflation accounting recommendations took the process one step further into pricing at current replacement cost instead of the latest purchase price as in the LIFO system. With computerised stock control systems the packaged software rarely provide a choice of stock valuation method. The weighted average method appears to have the greatest appeal for systems analysts and programmers. This limitation of choice is unfortunate. A replacement costing method using specific indices would be more appropriate because double digit inflation is now becoming a regular economic feature of the UK economy.

5:4 Finished goods stores. It has been explained that there are at least three bases for calculating costs of materials entering stores and at least seven ways of pricing stores issues to work in progress. This means that there are at least 21 alternative cost estimates for the material content of items entering finished goods stock from a manufacturing process. Once items are in finished goods stock we are then faced with more valuation alternatives. The recommendations in financial accounting for stock valuation are the 'lower of cost and net realiseable value'. This statement requires us to define cost. After reading chapter 3 you will appreciate that there are many kinds of cost. To assess the cost of finished goods stock we first have to decide whether to include or exclude overheads (Refer to chapter 3 section 5:3) Having made that decision it is then necessary to decide between historic costs, replacement costs, standard costs or average costs. The following sub-sections examine different aspects of these decision alternatives.

5:4:1 Lower of cost or net realisable value. The valuation of stock in the financial accounts is based on the principle that the cost and net realisable value of every item in stock is assessed and the lower figure is then entered in the stock valuation calculations. *(Refer to Volume 1 Financial accounting for non-accounts - SSAP 9).* Where this procedure is impracticable groups or categories of similar kinds of stock can be assessed together. The net realisable value is defined in the accounting standard as the actual or estimated net selling price less all further costs to completion and the costs of disposal. The cost is defined as being that expenditure which has been incurred during the normal course of business to bring the product or service to its current location and condition. This cost is divided into two categories: the cost of purchase and the cost of conversion. The cost of purchase was defined earlier in this chapter in sub-section 5:1. The cost of conversion comprises of:

(a) Costs which are specifically attributable to production such as direct labour, direct expense and sub contracted work.

(b) Production overheads based on a normal level of activity.

(c) Other overhead costs necessary to bring the product or service to its current location and condition.

The financial accounting requirements for stock valuation provide some guidance on the appropriate cost basis that is discussed in the following sub-sections.

5:4:2 Marginal or absorption costing. It was explained in chapter 3 sub-section 5:2 that many businesses have marginal costing systems because it provides useful data for price/output decision making. When a company adopts marginal costing, overheads are excluded from unit costing. Accordingly closing stock values are lower under marginal costing than under absorption costing (Refer to chapter 3 sub-section 5:3). The recommended financial accounting practice is to include overheads as costs of conversion for closing stock valuation. The use of marginal costing for closing stock valuation was challenged by the Inland Revenue.
Duple Motor Bodies Ltd. v Ostime (1961). In this tax case the company had been using a marginal costing system for many years. The Inland Revenue claimed that for tax purposes a proportion of indirect expenditure should be included for Stock Valuation purposes. It was held that providing the method of valuation was consistent from year to year, the long term effect on the accounts was the same whatever method was used. Therefore, there was no need for the company to alter their marginal costing system, consistency was considered more important than method.

5:4:3 Actual or standard costs. Items entering the finished goods store will tend to have varying costs over the accounting period. If actual costs are to be used for stock valuation then the principle of FIFO, LIFO and averaging apply. For example if the finished goods stock was say 200 units of 'X' at the beginning of the period and 300 units of 'X' at the end of the period a decision has to be made on what principles the 300 units are to be valued. Probably the same principle that is used by the company for valuing issues to work in progress will be used to value their finished goods stock. If the company is using a standard costing system then stocks may be valued at their standard cost on a marginal or absorption basis.

5:4:4 Historic or replacement cost. One aspect of the inflation accounting debate was stock valuation. It was argued that historic costs did not represent the economic value of stocks and therefore, the stock valuation criteria should be the lower of current replacement cost and net realisable value. if this argument is accepted it simplifies the decision on stock valuation because most of the valuation alternatives are based on past costs. Moreover, replacement cost principles imply absorption costing. Thus in the long run replacement cost stock valuation will probably become the most widely used system.

6. Stock planning and control.
The appropriate starting point for this section is to explain why stocks are necessary

(a) To ensure production has the correct quantity of materials at the right time.
(b) To enable integrated production processes that operate at different speeds to hold partly finished goods at various stages of the production process.
(c) To provide a buffer of finished goods between the production and sales to allow for demand fluctuations.

The necessity for stocks is clear. What is not so clear is the *level* of stocks. For every stock category there will be an optimum stock level that equates the costs of carrying stock with the risks and costs of not carrying enough stock. In practice the optimum point is not easily calculated because the costs and risks of not ca stock could not be accurately assessed for every stock category. Howe planning and control there are a lot of calculations that can be done. T are made to help answer two basic questions.

How much to order?
When to order?

The technique for calculating the economic order quantity (EOQ) range from fairly simple equations that seek an optimum point between the costs of carrying stock and the costs of ordering, to sophisticated models that attempt to calculate the optimum point as illustrated in diagram 69. To answer the question when to order, there are established techniques for calculating the lead time. Diagram 65 shows the structure of the sub sections that deal with these basic issues for stock planning and control.

DIAGRAM 65 STRUCTURE OF STOCK CONTROL

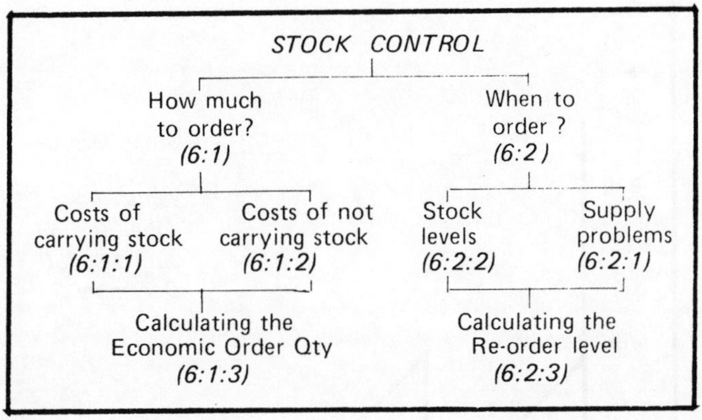

6:1 How much to order? Let us begin this section with the simplest situation of known regular demand. Assume a business sells a regular 10 items of 'X' a week and there are no supply complications. This situation is presented graphically in diagram 66 overleaf. The diagram shows a single order a year for 520 units giving an average stock of 260 units. The diagram also shows two orders a year.
This process could be continued down to weekly or even daily orders where average stocks are kept to an absolute minimum. The principle of low stock levels and frequent deliveries is applied in areas of retailing such as supermarkets and in assembly plants such as mass car production. Indeed a good purchasing officer will attempt to get supplies to bear the costs of stockholding and ensure frequent reliable deliveries. Whilst a good salesman should attempt to get the customer to take delivery quantities and dates that suit the supplier. Before looking at the more complicated stock level problems and calculations it is useful to consider the cost of carrying stock and not carrying enough stock.

DIAGRAM 66 STOCK LEVELS & AVERAGE STOCKS

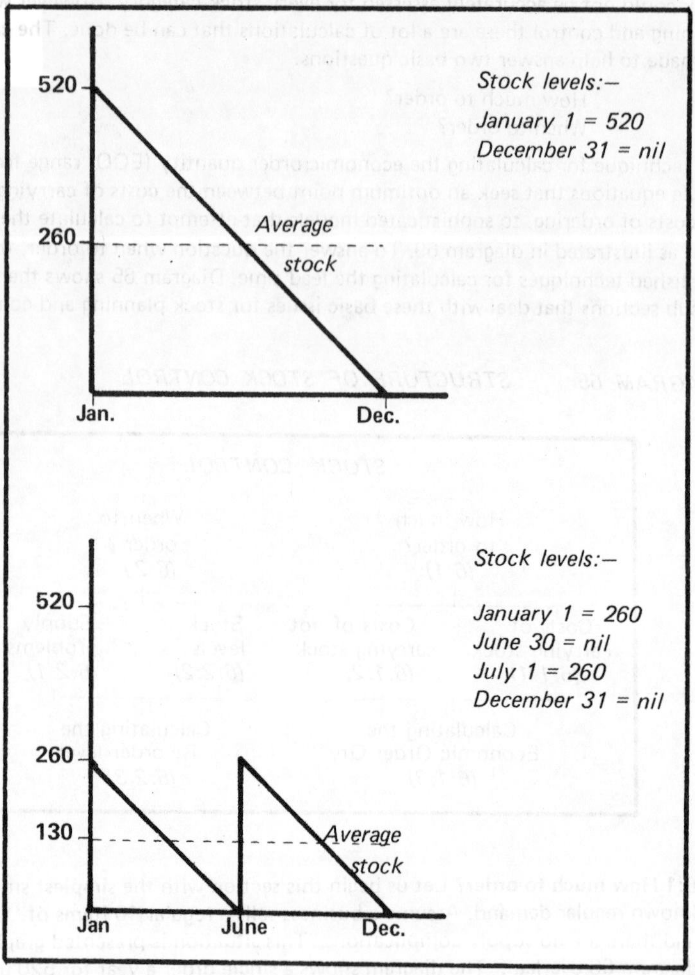

6:1:1 Costs of carrying stock. The costs of carrying stock can be broadly divided into physical storage, administration and financial. There is also the opportunity cost of carrying stock, but there are practical measurement difficulties with this cost category. (Refer to chapter 3 sub-section 3:7)

(a) *Storage costs* include: rent, rates, light, heat, direct wages, depreciation, spoilage, evaporation, deterioration and security.

(b) *Administration costs* include: administrative materials and wages, proportion of management time and telephone.

(c) *Financial costs* include: interest on capital tied up in stocks and insurance

(d) *Opportunity costs* represent the net benefits from opportunities if the resources tied up in stocks had been used on the next best economic alternative course of action.

Most of the storage and administrative costs tend to be fixed or semi fixed within a certain storage range. In the short run elaborate management techniques are not needed to determine when more storage space is needed. A purchasing officer should be aware of the size of the items that are being ordered and if they will fit in the available storage space. Also, most administrative costs will not vary significantly if slightly larger stocks are carried. However, for strategic planning, (Refer to chapters 2 and 7) the storage and related administrative costs need to be estimated. Where additional storage space and additional staff are required, this should be identified and the marginal cost of carrying additional stock calculated. The financial costs of carrying stock tend to be variable especially the interest on capital tied up in the inventory. Thus the cost of carrying stock can be viewed as fixed/semi fixed costs moving up in steps as stock increases and variable costs that increase with stock value. The likely cost behaviour of carrying stock is shown in diagram 67 which shows the stepped fixed costs added to the variable costs increasing as average stock levels increase. Now let us consider the costs of not carrying enough stock.

DIAGRAM 67 COSTS OF HOLDING STOCKS

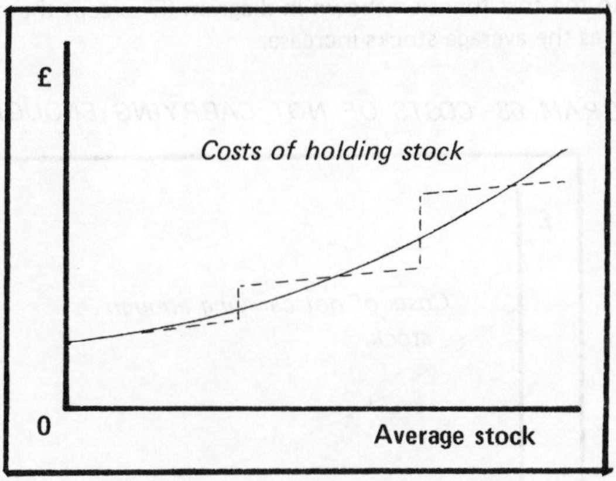

6:1:2 Cost of not carrying enough stock. The most damaging costs can be production inconvenience and lost sales/customer goodwill. It is not easy to quantify these costs therefore some stock control techniques do not include them in the calculations. If they are excluded, then management should treat the stock level recommendations with some caution. The other cost categories for not carrying enough stock are administrative and financial. The four main cost categories are summarised below:

(a) *Production inconvenience* can arise from a low average stock level policy. Low stocks can cause uneconomic production runs, excessive 'downtime' (time when machines are not actually producing due to setting up, cleaning, repairing etc.) and increase the risk of a stockout. If a stock-out does occur then the costs can be very large. For example consider a car assembly line with a stock-out of wheels or tyres. The entire assembly line would come to a halt. With inter-related and inter-dependent production/assembly processes the damage of a stock-out can be significant.

(b) *Lost sales* through stock-outs are well known in the retail trade. A customer simply goes to the next shop and makes the purchase there. A similar principle applies to manufacturers who need to convince their regular custom-

ers of reliability and continuity of supply. Many orders are lost through delivery dates, that are sometime more important than price. A loss of a customer often represents a loss of goodwill and the long term effect of a stock-out is difficult to assess.

(c) *Administrative costs* are easier to assess. Procurement costs such as purchase orders and related adminstrative time tend to vary in relation to the number of orders placed. But a lot of the adminstrative costs would tend to be stepped fixed. Above a certain level of orders, another purchase clerk would be needed together with desk, telephone and office space. Even if the purchasing process is computerised there will still tend to be a stepped fixed cost function for administrative costs.

(d) *Financial costs* such as: lost quantity discounts, additional carriage costs and increases in specific replacement costs cannot be easily calculated.

The costs of not carrying enough stock can be divided into those that are not easily quantifiable because they are related to the risk of a stock-out and those that can be quantified as the number of orders increases. The likely cost behaviour of not carrying enough stock is shown in diagram 68 which is similar to the cost function shown in diagram 67 except that the costs decrease as the average stocks increase.

DIAGRAM 68 COSTS OF NOT CARRYING ENOUGH STOCK

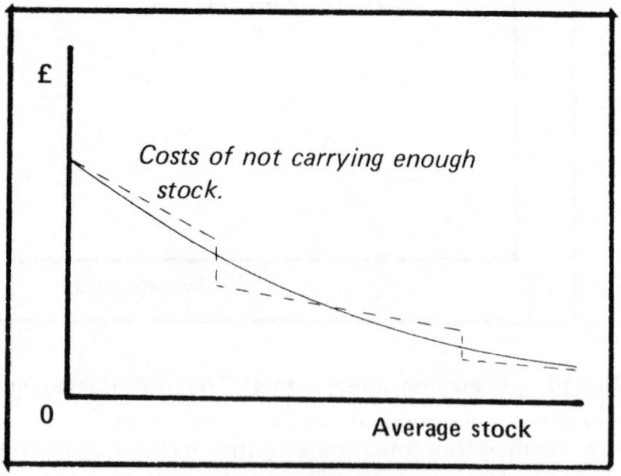

6:1:3 Calculating the Economic Order Quantity (EOQ) If we draw the two cost functions representing the costs of carrying stocks and costs of not carrying enough stocks on one diagram, the point where they intersect would represent the optimum average stock level. This is shown in diagram 69 that represents the data used in the following numerical example.

Example Assume a business is selling a regular10 items of 'X' a week with no supply complications. The company management accountant has made the following cost estimates:—

Cost of carrying one unit of stock a year	£
Storage and administration costs	0.50
Finance costs	0.20
	£0.70
Cost of placing a single order	£4.00

Using this data a tabulation can be compiled that will show the optimum average stock level, i.e.

Order size *O* *Units*	Average stock *O/2* *Units*	Number of orders *D/O* *Quantity*	Annual cost of ordering *P(D/O)* *£*	Annual cost of carrying *C(O/2)* *£*	Total annual cost *TC* *£*
520	260	1	4.00	182.00	186.00
260	130	2	8.00	91.00	99.00
104	62	5	20.00	43.40	63.40
52	26	10	40.00	18.20	58.20
26	13	20	80.00	9.10	89.10
20	10	26	104.00	7.00	111.00
10	5	52	208.00	3.50	211.50

The symbols used in the table represent:—

O = Order size in units
D = Annual demand in units which is 520
P = Cost of placing a single order which is £4.00
C = Cost of carrying one unit of stock for one year which is £0.70
TC = Total cost of holding stock and placing orders at specific order quantities

DIAGRAM 69 *ECONOMIC ORDER QUANTITY*

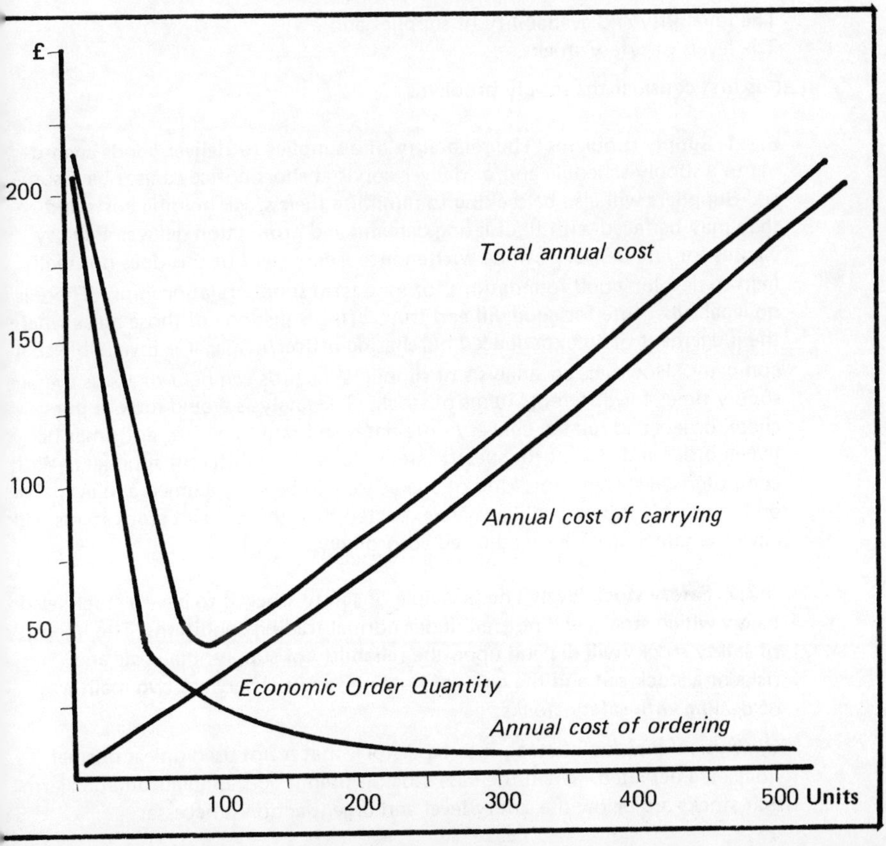

From the table if can be seen that the economic order quantity (EOQ) is somewhere near 52 units. The precise figure can be calculated using the following formula:—

$$EOQ = \sqrt{\frac{2DP}{C}}$$

$$= \sqrt{\frac{2 \times 520 \times 4.00}{0.70}}$$

$$= \underline{\underline{77 \text{ units}}}$$

Proof:—

TC for 76 units = 4(520/76) + 0.7(76/2) = £53.97
TC for 77 units = 4(520/77) + 0.7(77/2) = £53.96 *(EOQ)*
TC for 78 units = 4(520/78) + 0.7(78/2) = £53.97

The above example was a stock model for cases of known demand. However, in most instances demand is not known and a probabilistic model is required. The arithmetic is not too complicated, but if there are a lot of probability distributions then it is easier to use one of the stock control software packages. (Refer to chapter 6 sub section 2:7:1)

6:2 When to order? Once the economic order quantity has been determined the next problem is to decide, when to place the order? This will depend on two factors:

The reliability and availability of supplies and,
The levels of safety stocks.

Let us first consider the supply problems.

6:2:1 Supply problems The reliability of a supplier to deliver goods according to a supply schedule and/or deliver goods at short notice cannot be assumed. Suppliers will also be seeking to minimise their stock holding costs and they may be faced with fluctuating demand and production delays. Penalty clauses for late delivery can be written into a contract but this does not really help to develop good foundations for long term supply relationships. There is no legal substitute for goodwill and trust. This is just one of those areas where the judgement of an experienced purchasing officer/manager is invaluable to a company. However, an analysis of suppliers' records can help to assess average supply times for different items of stock. The analysis would look at purchase orders and related delivery note dates and rank the different times between order and receipt for specific stock items from different suppliers. With computerised systems this kind of analysis could be programmed and available on request. If supply problems are expected then the relevant stock items will have the safety stock level adjusted accordingly.

6:2:2 Safety stock levels The principle of safety stock is to have a stock level below which stocks will not fall under normal trading conditions. The quantity of safety stocks will depend upon the reliability of supply, the costs and risks of a stock-out and the costs of holding stocks. There are two main ways of dealing with safety stocks:

(a) Physical division of stock into base stock that is not used unless normal stocks are depleted. When the base stock is used it acts as an automatic alarm that stocks are below the safety level and urgent action is necessary.

(b) Administrative minimum stock levels that are reviewed with each new order in relation to production requirements to ensure the minimum level is not reached. The safety stock in the administrative system is not physically separated.

The physical division of stock is often called the *two bin method* because in some instances the safety stocks are stored in separate stock bins. The administrative approach to minimum stock levels is called the *constand order cycle system* or *cyclical review system.* Whatever method is used the problem of deciding the quantity for safety stock still remains. To calculate safety stock levels the following factors have to be considered:—

(i) The uncertainty of supply.
(ii) The variability of demand.
(iii) Acceptable level of risk for a stockout.

These factors are not easily quantifiable. However if they could be quantified with an acceptable level of accuracy then there are a number of mathematical techniques that can be used.

6:2:3 Calculating the re-order level A stock control system should have maximum and minimum stock levels and economic order quantities for every class of stock item. Between these maximum and minimum stock levels there also needs to be a stated stock level where goods will be re-ordered. The re-order level will depend upon the expected time interval between ordering and receiving the goods. This time interval is called the *'lead time'.*

Examples of calculating re-order levels
Using the data from the earlier example of known constant demand:—

Economic Order Quantity = 77 units
Average usage = 10 units a week
Estimated lead time = 3 weeks.

There are three types of calculation we can make:

(a) Re-order level with no safety stock and risk margin

Re-order point = Usage x lead time
= 10 x 3 = 30 units

(b) Re-order level with safety stock of 20 units

Re-order point = (Usage x lead time) + safety stock
= (10 x 3) + 20 = 50 units

(c) Re-order level with safety stock of 20 units and 10% risk margin

Re-order point = 1 + risk margin (Usage x lead time) + safety stock
= 1.1(10 x 3) + 20 = 53 units

The calculation of the re-order point is basically the expected usage multiplied by the lead time. If the items are vital for production then a risk percentage can be added as shown in example (c). When safety or base stocks are included in the total stocks levels then they need to be added to the re-order quantity as shown in examples (b) and (c). The re-order point and lead time is illustrated in diagram 70. The diagram shows four stock levels: maximum, minimum, average and re-order level. These four stock levels should be calculated for all items of stock.

DIAGRAM 70 CALCULATING STOCK LEVELS

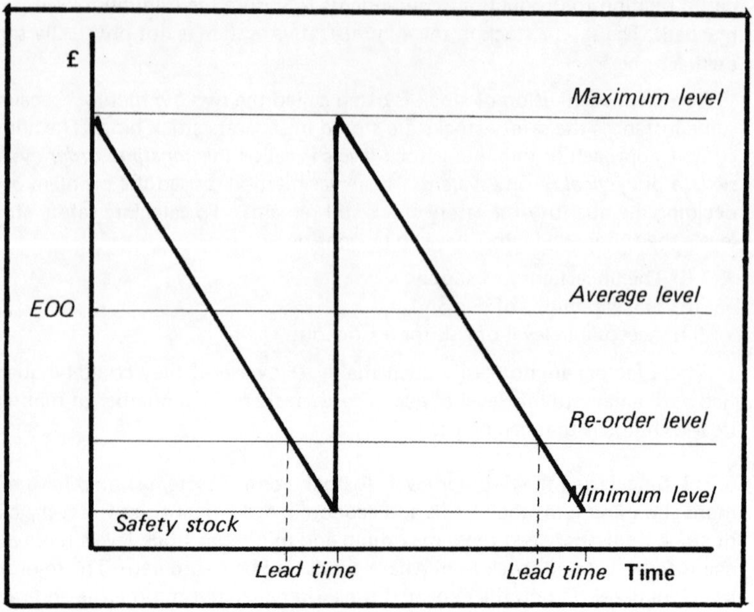

7 Summary

This chapter has provided a detailed reference base on stock valuation methods and stores administration. It has also explained the basic techniques for calculating economic order quantities, minimum, maximum, average and re-order stock levels. Although this is essential basic knowledge for anyone involved in inventory management it is worthwhile mentioning some other factors that will influence inventory decisions.

(a) Trade cycles are an accepted economic fact. There are boom periods and recessions. A characteristic of a recession is *de-stocking.* When a company adopts a de-stocking policy it will overide existing inventory management practice. Conversely, when the recession has bottomed out and there is an expectation of high demand then the minimum stock policy will be reversed.

(b) Cash flow problems within a company will affect management's attitude to stock levels.

(c) Specific inflation movements need to be taken into consideration concerning re-order quantities and dates. For example during the very rapid oil price increases in the mid 1970's it was inevitable that oil based products would also increase in price. Therefore, alert purchasing officers would have ordered early and helped to make stock profits for their company.

(d) Supply restrictions can occur due to changes in demand, political actions, industrial disputes or other factors. A good purchasing officer should be sensitive to any possibility of supply restrictions and order accordingly.

There are many other factors that can influence inventory decisions. The main point to grasp is that inventory management and its associated techniques should provide sufficient flexibility in the stores systems to allow for contingencies. Accordingly a selection of the techniques explained in this chapter would only provide a basis for an inventory management system.

Accountancy Quiz No.5.

1. Explain fully the term 'inventory management'. *(1, 2).*

2. Outline an administrative procedure for purchasing and explain the responsibilities of a purchasing officer. *(3:1).*

3. How would you assess the need for increasing or reducing the number of sub-stores? *(4, 4:1, 4:2, 4:3, 4:4, 4:5).*

4. What is the difference between FIFO and LIFO? *(5:3:1, 5:3:2, 5:3:7).*

5. Briefly explain the following stock valuation methods:–

Simple average *(5:3:3)*
Periodic simple average *(5:3:3)*
Weighted average *(5:3:4)*
Periodic weighted average *(5:3:4)*
Replacement cost *(5:3:5)*
Standard cost *(5:3:6)*

6. Explain what is meant by: 'the lower of cost and net realiseable value' and outline the problems of defining cost. *(5:4, 5:4:1, 5:4:2, 5:4:3, 5:4:4).*

7. What factors need to be taken into consideration when estimating re-order quantities and levels? *(6:1, 6:1:1, 6:1:2, 7).*

8. What is an economic order quantity and how is it calculated? *(6:1:3, 7).*

9. What factors need to be considered when deciding re-order stock levels? *(6:2, 6:2:1, 7).*

10. How would you calculate a stock re-order level? *(6:2:3, 7).*

6 Tactical decision making

Objective

To help the non-accountant understand and use tactical decision making techniques.

Content

Page No.

A detailed explanation of the break even model including principles, applications and limitations.

An outline of some popular tactical decision making techniques.

Tactical decision making

1 Introduction

The principles of planning , decision making and control were explained in chapter 2. In this chapter we are concerned with the *techniques* that can be used by managers to help with short/medium term related decisions. The techniques for medium/long run decisions are explained in chapter 7.

Tactical decision making is an interdisciplinary subject with useful contributions from accountancy, computing, economics, management, mathematics, marketing and operations research. The common component in the decision techniques of all these subject specialisations is the use of cost and revenue data. Most of the techniques attempt to quantify decision alternatives in terms of costs and revenues. Whilst an interdisciplinary approach is necessary for decision making, many subject specialists demonstrate a remarkable lack of basic accounting knowledge when analysing costs and revenues. It is therefore appropriate that management accounting should provide the core of knowledge in this subject area and become more interdisciplinary in its approach. Before using cost data the decision maker should understand the principles of cost collection, recording and analysis. (Refer to chapter 3) With a good basic costing knowledge the appropriate decision making technique can be selected and applied.

This chapter is divided into three broad areas. The first part provides a lot of detail on the break even model because of its wide acceptance in industry and commerce. The second part summarises eight decision techniques that can be applied in specific circumstances. Five of these techniques are suitable for computer users where packaged software is available. The last part of the chapter looks at the problems of pricing.

2 The break even model

Break even is one of the best known decision making techniques. The term break even point is in constant usage by managers as an accepted description of a no profit or loss position. The subject is regularly taught on most management courses and probably on all accountancy tuition programmes. It is therefore important that non accountants understand the principles, applications and limitations of the break even model.

The first part of this section explains break even principles and the different types of break even graph. This is followed by eight sub-sections explaining different applications of break even principles. Then the last part explains the limitations of the break even model. The reader is advised not to become too involved in all the applications that are explained in this section, but to concentrate on the principles and limitations of the break even model.

2:1 Basic principles You will find this subject area referred to under a variety of headings that include: Cost/Volume/Profit Analysis, Profit/Volume Analysis, Price/output Analysis, Cost/Output behaviour and other impressive titles. Basically they are all covering the same principle that profit is a function of costs, output and price. If you change cost, price or output, then you will alter the profit. Thus all the calculations and graphs are simply to determine the effect on profit if cost, price or output is altered. Let us first look at costs.

Under marginal costing and break even analysis, the assumption is that all costs can be neatly divided into compartments labelled fixed and variable. (This point is developed later under limitations of break-even). This is a most important division because of the cost relationship to output. For instance, suppose a person is employed to make straw table mats and was paid £0.10 per mat and the material costs per mat were £0.05. Clearly as output increases, so the total variable costs increase - 1 mat £0.15, 100 mats £15.00.

Other costs of the business could not be directly related to output and were therefore defined as fixed: say £100. The total cost function would be:

Total costs =	100 + 0.15q	Where q =	the quantity	
i.e.	Nil produced	100 + (0.15 x 0)	=	£100.00
	10 produced	100 + (0.15 x 10)	=	£101.50
	100 produced	100 + (0.15 x 100)	=	£115.00
	1000 produced	100 + (0.15 x 1000)	=	£250.00

The above cost detail is presented graphically in diagram 71.

DIAGRAM 71 TOTAL COST FUNCTION

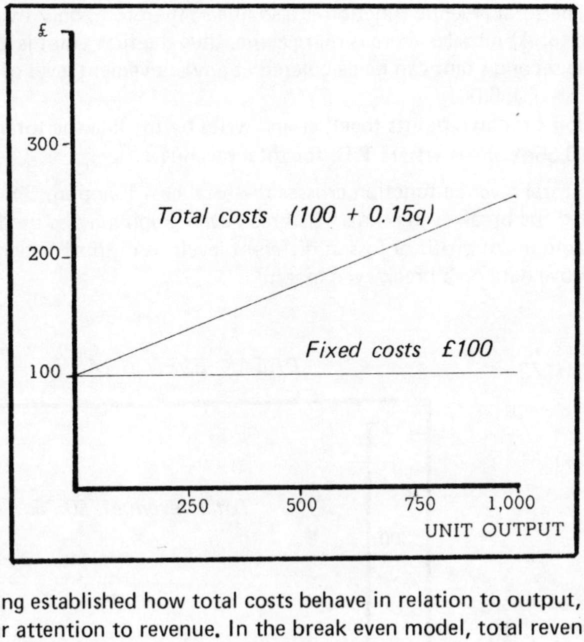

Having established how total costs behave in relation to output, we can now turn our attention to revenue. In the break even model, total revenue is simply the unit selling price multiplied by the quantity sold. Assume table mats sell for £0.35 each. If nil units are sold there is nil revenue, 10 table mats £3.50, 100 table mats £35.00 etc. It is therefore clear that the total revenue function will be a straight line starting at the origin as shown in diagram 72. At low levels of output total revenue will be below total cost representing a loss. Conversely at high levels of output where total revenue exceeds total costs a profit will be made. The level of output where total revenue equals total cost is called the break even point. If you work carefully through the next sub section on how to construct a break even graph the break even principle will become clear.

2:2 How to construct a Break Even Graph. The following example is based on the table mat detail in the previous sub section.

(i) First decide the scale of the axes. Conventionally the 'y' axis is value and the 'x' axis output, activity or sales. Determine the maximum value and output to be drawn and divide the axes accordingly.

(ii) At nil output the only costs to be incurred are the fixed costs; therefore plot that point i.e. Output nil, total cost £100,000.

(iii) As the cost function is linear (a straight line) only two points are needed. The first point was the fixed costs, the second point can be at any convenient calculation, i.e. Output 1,000 units, total costs £250.00 i.e. 100 + (1,000 x 0.15)

(iv) Join the points together and write by the line the total cost function (100 + 0.15q) or the letters T C for total cost.

(v) The cost output relationship is therefore the variable cost per unit x the volume of output plus the fixed cost. Moving on to the Revenue function: as the table mats were being sold for £0.35 each, the total revenue would be the number of units sold multiplied by the price per unit. Revenue function = £0.35q

i.e.	Nil sold	0 x .35 = Nil	100 sold	100 x .35 =	£35
	10 sold	10 x .35 = £3.50	1000 sold	1000 x .35 =	£350

(vi) The total revenue function is also linear; therefore, only two points need to be plotted. At nil sales there is nil revenue, thus the first point is at the origin (zero). The second point can be calculated at any convenient level of sales, i.e. 1,000 units = £350.00.

(vii) Joint the two points together and write by the line the total revenue function (0.35q) or the letters T.R. for total revenue.

Where the total revenue function crosses the total cost function, T.R. = T.C. and this is called the break even point. The break even graph may be used to deter mine the amount of profit or loss at different levels of output. Diagram 72 illustrates the above data on a break even graph.

DIAGRAM 72 *BREAK EVEN GRAPH*

Where:
(a) = area of loss (T.C. – T.R)
(b) = break even point (T.R = T.C)
(c) = area of profit (T.R – T.C)

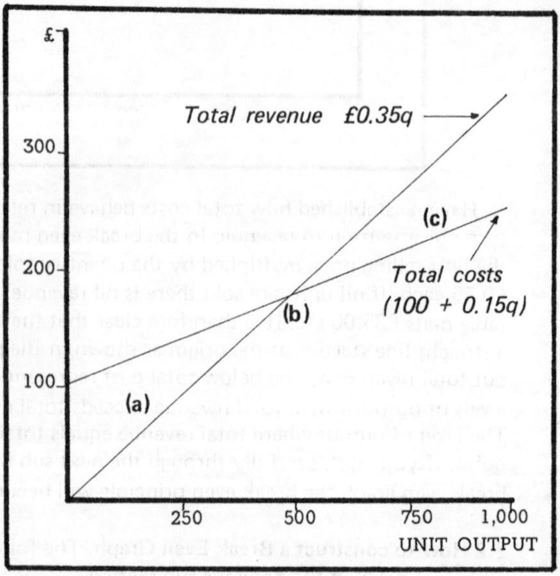

2:3 How to read a break even graph. The level of profit is calculated by deducting total cost from total revenue. From diagram 72 it can be seen that if 1,000 table mats were made and sold, the total revenue would be £350 and the total cost £250; therefore, the profit is £100. Alternatively the distance between the total revenue and total cost lines at a specific level of output can be measured and multiplied by the vertical scale. The diagram's vertical scale is calibrated in £50 points and at an output/sales of 1,000 units there are two points between the total revenue and total cost line resulting in a profit of £100. Using the diagram, try the following:-

(a) What is the profit or loss at output levels of 250, 350 and 750 units?
(b) What levels of unit output are necessary to make the following: a loss of £40 and a profit of £75?
(c) What levels of sales are necessary to make a profit of £60 and £80?
(d) What is the profit or loss at sales levels of £350 and £35?
(e) At what level of sales and unit output will the business make neither a profit nor loss?

Answer: *(a)* *Loss £50, Loss £30, Profit £50*
(b) *300 units, 875 units*
(c) *£280, £315*
(d) *Profit £100, Loss £80*
(e) *Break even = £175 or 500 units*

2:4 Different Types of Break Even Graph. There are many uses for break even graphs and consequently different ways of presenting the relationship between cost, volume, price and profit. The important thing is not just to learn the way the graphs are drawn but to understand what they represent. The following diagrams all represent the table mat data given in previous sub sections.

DIAGRAM 73 *CONTRIBUTION GRAPH*

Where:
(a) = area of loss (T.C – T.R)
(b) = break even point (T.R = T.C)
(c) = area of contribution (T.R – V.C)
(d) = area of profit (T.R – T.C)

Note; This is a normal B/E chart with a variable cost line to show the area of contribution.

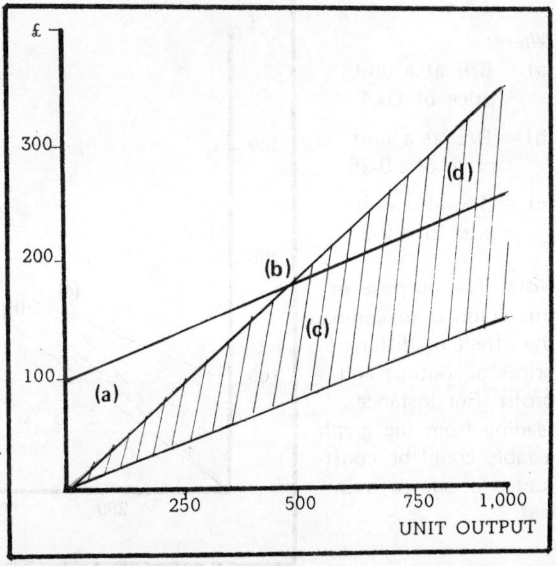

DIAGRAM 74 *PROFIT VOLUME GRAPH*

Where:
(a) = area of loss (T.C – T.R)
(b) = break even point (T.R = T.C)
(c) = area of profit (T.R – T.C)

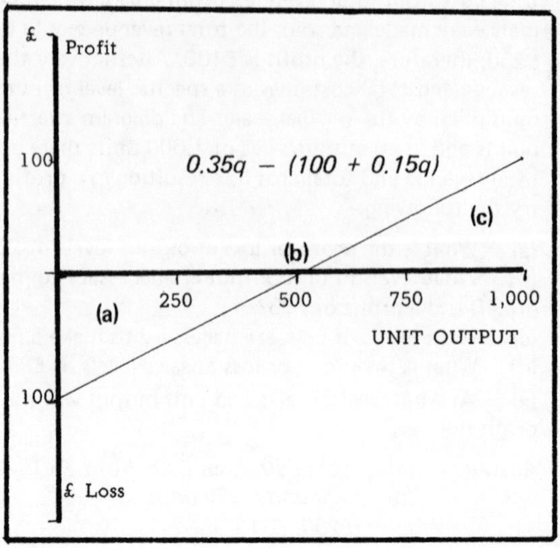

The total cost and total revenue functions are represented on the profit volume graph by the profit function. The line on the graph represents total revenue minus total costs and enables profit or loss to be read direct from the graph at any level of output. For example if you want to know what the level of profit is at say 750 units two readings would be needed from the break even graph of £262.5 and £212.5 giving a profit of £50. On the profit volume graph the figure of £50 can be taken with one reading

DIAGRAM 75 MULTIPLE REVENUE FUNCTIONS ON BREAK EVEN GRAPH

Where:
(a) = B/E at a unit price of £0.4
(b) = B/E at a unit price of £0.35
(c) = B/E at a unit price of £0.3

Note: The purpose of this graph is to compare the effect of different prices on output and profit. For instance, reading from the graph a table could be constructed as shown overleaf.

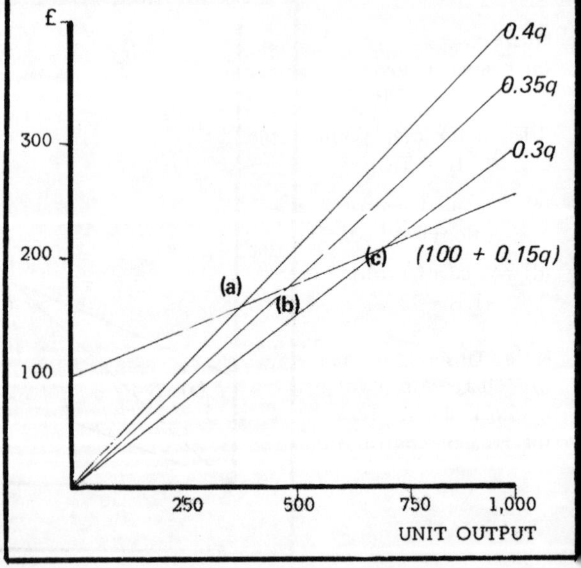

Price	Sales to Break Even		Profit/Loss at Sales/Output of 625 units
£	£	Units	£
0.40	160(a)	400	56.25
0.35	175(b)	500	25
0.30	200(c)	667	(6.25)

2:5 Margin of Safety and Operating Leverage. The margin of safety is the difference between the break even point and the budgeted level of output and is related to capital intensity. As a firm increases its capital a higher level of output/sales is necessary to recover its fixed costs. Consider the following example of a labour intensive firm and a capital intensive firm both selling the same product at the same price in the same market. The profit functions are:-

Company 'C'	Capital intensive	20q – (5,000 + 5q)
Company 'L'	Labour intensive	20q – (665 + 15q)

As 'C' has a higher contribution per unit than 'L' (i.e. C = 20 – 5 and L = 20 – 15) Cis said to have greater *operating leverage.* This means that as sales increase for both firms 'C's contribution will increase faster than 'L's. Conversely if sales fall 'C's contribution will fall faster. Therefore, 'C' requires a greater percentage margin of safety than 'L'. Diagrams 76 and 77 illustrate this point.

DIAGRAM 76 *OPERATING LEVERAGE – CAPITAL INTENSIVE*

Where:

(a) = B/E of 333 units or £6,660

(b) = margin of safety

(c) = budgeted output of 533 units or £10,660

Margin of safety:

Budgeted output	533
less B/E output	333
Margin of safety	200

$$\text{MoS \%} = \frac{200}{533}\ \% = 37\%$$

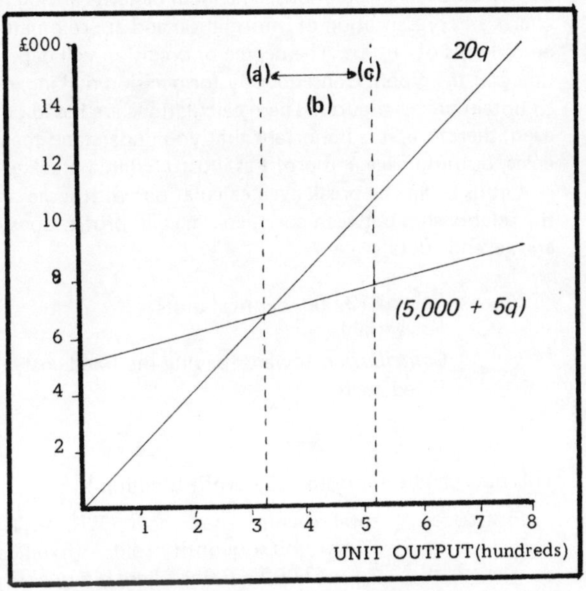

Although the margin of safety, in unit terms, is the same for both companies, if sales fall Company C is at greater risk than Company L because it has a higher operating leverage. Consequently C should have a higher margin of safety (The concept of financial leverage is explained in *Volume 1, Financial accounting for the non-accountant).*

DIAGRAM 77 *OPERATING LEVERAGE — LABOUR INTENSIVE*

Where:

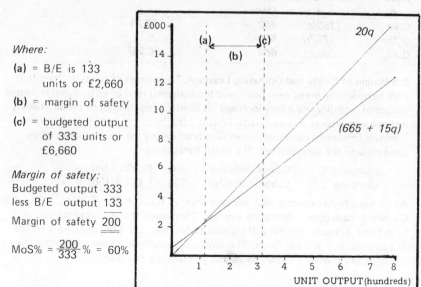

(a) = B/E is 133 units or £2,660

(b) = margin of safety

(c) = budgeted output of 333 units or £6,660

Margin of safety:

Budgeted output	333
less B/E output	133
Margin of safety	200

MoS% = $\frac{200}{333}$ % = 60%

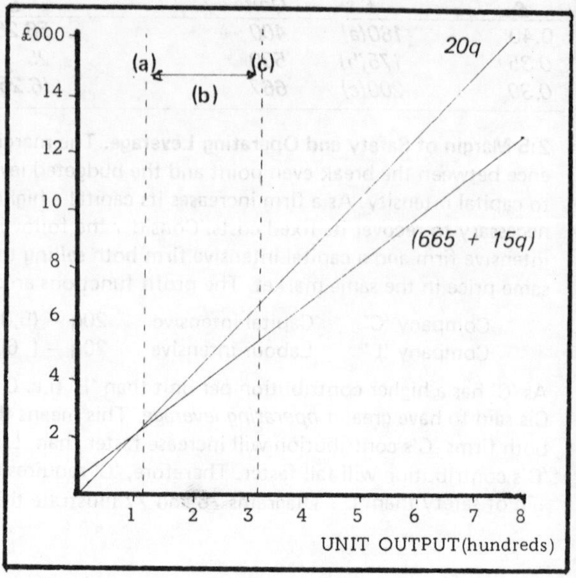

2:6 Break Even Calculations. The main benefits arising from the use of break even charts are; presentation of information and approximate profit/loss figures at different levels of output. The degree of precision will depend upon the scale and accuracy of the graph. Consequently for decision making, calculations are necessary to obtain precise figures. These calculations are based on the principles of break even; therefore, it is important that you understand the relationships between costs, output, price and profit as illustrated in a break even graph.

Let us begin the break even calculations with some simple figures to establish the relationship between costs, volume and profit. Consider the following cost and revenue data:-

	£
Sale of 10,000 identical units	10,000
less variable costs	6,000
Contribution towards paying the fixed costs	4,000
Fixed costs	2,000
Profit	2,000

This data can be expressed as a profit function :-

Profit = total revenue — total cost (T.R. — T.C.)
= £1 per unit x quqntity sold — (fixed cost + variable cost)
= 1q — (2,000 + 0.6q) *where q = quantity.*

Using this profit function we will now make three basic calculations:-

Calculating the contribution. The contribution is one of the most important figures in break even analysis. It is calculated by deducting the variable costs from sales. i.e.

Contribution per unit = 1 — 0.6 = £0.4

Calculating the profit/volume ratio (P/V). The P/V ratio represents the relationship between sales and contribution. Assuming the cost and revenue functions are linear, the P/V ratio will always be constant. This is shown in the following table:-

Units	Sales £	Variable costs £	Contribution/Sales	P/V ratio*
1	1.00	0.60	0.4/1.0	$^2/_5$
10	10.00	6.00	4/10	$^2/_5$
25	25.00	15.00	10/25	$^2/_5$

* The P/V ratio may be expressed as a fraction, decimal or percentage. i.e. $^2/5$, 0.4 or 40%.

Once the P/V ratio is known, the contribution can be quickly calculated from any given level of sales. For example with the $^2/5$ P/V ratio a £1,000 of sales would produce £400 contribution. (£1,000 x $^2/5$).

Calculating the break even point. At break even the total contribution must be exactly equal to the fixed costs because there is no profit or loss at break even. Thus to find the break even point, divide the fixed costs by the contribution per unit.

$$\text{B/E} = \frac{\text{Fixed Costs}}{\text{Contribution per unit}} \quad \frac{2{,}000}{(1.0\text{–}0.6)} = 5{,}000 \text{ units}$$

or in value terms 5,000 x the unit selling price of £1.00 = £5,000.
Alternatively to find the sales value of break even, the formula can be restated as:

$$\text{B/E} = \text{Fixed Costs} \times \frac{\text{Sales}}{\text{Contribution}} \quad 2{,}000 \times \frac{1.0}{0.4} = 5{,}000 \text{ units}$$

This method is useful when the unit detail is not available.

e.g. Sales £10,000, Variable Costs 6,000, Fixed Costs 2,000

$$\text{B/E} = 2{,}000 \times \frac{10{,}000}{(10{,}000 - 6{,}000)} = 5{,}000 \text{ units}$$

As sales over contribution is the reciprocal of the P.V.ratio, the above formula can be restated as :-

$$\text{F/C} \times \frac{1}{\text{P.V. ratio}} = 2{,}000 \times \frac{1}{0.4} = 5{,}000 \text{ units}$$

Summary of Break Even Formulae

Profit = Total revenue – total cost

Contribution = Sales – variable cost

Break even = *(in units)* $\dfrac{\text{Fixed costs}}{\text{Contribution per unit}}$

(in value) Fixed costs x $\dfrac{\text{Sales}}{\text{Contribution}}$

or Fixed costs x $\dfrac{1}{\text{P/V ratio}}$

P/V ratio = $\dfrac{\text{Contribution}}{\text{Sales}}$

2:7 Risk and the break even model Managers are well aware of the uncertainty and relative instability of the environment in which they make decisions. Material costs are rising, direct labour is sometimes volatile, rents, rate interest charges, energy costs are all rising rapidly, exchange rate movements are often unpredictable and markets are not reliable. In the real business world there appears to be little use for a break even model that assumes certainty, with linear cost and revenue behaviour. However, managers are used to coping with uncertainty and should therefore be capable of managing the break even model by making some allowance for risk.

In the following sub sections we are going to present risk profiles as probability distributions. It is therefore necessary to briefly explain the principle of probability before making general observations about risk and the break even model. If the reader is aware of probability and the binomial distribution the first sub section can be missed because it deals with the subject at an introductory level. The remaining sub sections are about identifying the downside risk and then, how to minimise risk.

2:7:1 Probability Mathematicians have developed many techniques for estimating probability. The techniques are attempting to measure the likelihood of particular events taking place. The mathematical probability of events taking place are measured from: 0 = the event will certainly not occur and 1 = the event is absolutely certain. To illustrate a probability technique we will work through a practical example and construct a probability distribution. By unbiased spinning of an unbiased coin, the probability of *Heads* is 0.5 and *Tails* is 0.5. On the second flip the probability of *Heads occurring twice* is 0.5 x 0.5 = 0.25. If we continue this process a probability table can be constructed:–

First spin of coin	H = 0.5
	T = 0.5
Second spin of coin	HH = 0.5 x 0.5 = 0.25
	TT = 0.5 x 0.5 = 0.25
	HT = 0.5 x 0.5 = 0.25
	TH = 0.5 x 0.5 = 0.25
Third spin of coin	HHH = 0.5 x 0.5 x 0.5 = 0.125
	etc.

Clearly this method of calculating probability is impractical when spinning a coin say 50 times. It is therefore easier to use the mathematical expression called the *Binomial Theorem.* At first sight the formula looks quite complicated. We will not be concerned with the proof or any elaborate calculations because the binomial is well established and widely available as software, even for programable calculators. The following calculations are just a continuation of the coin illustration to produce a binomial frequency distribution from spinning a coin ten times.

The important point to grasp about this binomial, is its usefulness for estimating probability. Do not become too involved in the calculations because with modern calculators it is just a 'press button operation'.

Probability of		Calculation	Probability
10H	H^n	$(0;5)^{10}$	= 0.000976
9H & 1T	$nH^{(n-1)}T$	$10(0.5)^9 x0.5$	= 0.009766
8H & 2T	$\frac{n(n-1)}{2x1}$ x	$\frac{10(10-1)}{2x1}$ x	
	$H^{(n-2)}T^2$	$(0.5)^8 (0.5)^2$	= 0.043945
7H & 3T	$\frac{n(n-1)(n-2)}{3x2x1}$ x	$\frac{10(10-1)(10-2)}{3x2x1}$ x	
	$H^{(n-3)}T^3$	$(0.5)^7 (0.5)^3$	= 0.117187
6H & 4T	$\frac{n(n-1)(n-2)(n-3)}{4x3x2x1}$ x $H^{(n-4)}T^4$		= 0.205078
5H & 5T	$\frac{n(n-1)(n-2)(n-3)(n-4)}{5x4x3x2x1}$ x $H^{(n-5)}T^5$		= 0.246094
6T & 4H	$\frac{n(n-1)(n-2)(n-3)}{4x3x2x1}$ x $T^{(n-4)}H^4$		= 0.205078
7T & 3H	$\frac{n(n-1)(n-2)}{3x2x1}$ x $T^{(n-3)}H^3$		= 0.117187
8T & 2H	$\frac{n(n-1)}{2x1}$ x $T^{(n-2)}H^2$		= 0.043945
9T & 1H	$nT^{(n-1)}H$		= 0.009766
10T	T^n		= 0.000976

The probabilities can be drawn as a histogram. This is shown in diagram 78 with a line drawn through the columns that represents the binomial distribution. If there were many more unbiased spins of the coin then the curve would become smooth and bell shaped. It is this bell shaped distribution curve that we will be initially using to illustrate the application of probability to the break even model. In this chapter we are concerned with the application of probability to the behaviour of costs and revenues for tactical decision making. The break even diagrams in the following sub sections will contain probability distributions to indicate the level of risk in price/output decisions. The probability is also used in the following chapter on strategic decision making, to illustrate the level of risk in investment appraisal.

DIAGRAM 78 BINOMIAL DISTRIBUTION

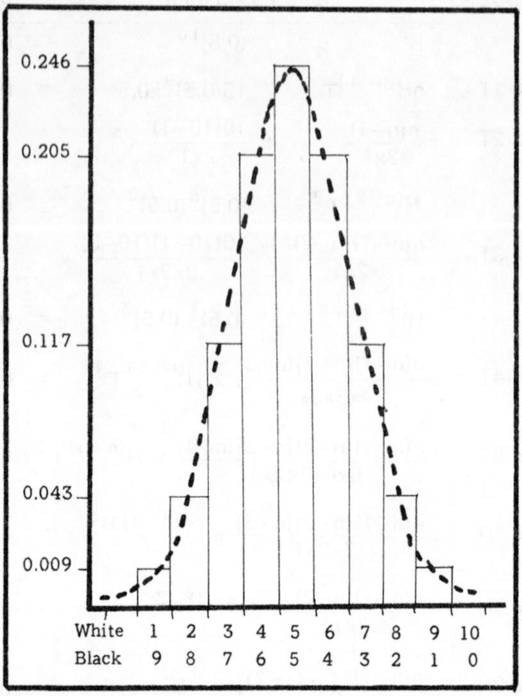

2:7:2 Identifying the downside risk The term 'downside risk' generally refers to the side of the business activity probability distribution that will result in the business trading at a loss. The term refers to a risk profile and not a specific value. Accordingly, statements such as "This project has a downside risk of £X" require clarification because the speaker/writer is probably referring to something quite different. The break even model is well suited for identifying risk profiles because it shows the relationship of costs, volume, price and profit. In sub section 2:5 the principle of operating leverage was explained as the relationship of the cost structure to the revenue function. Businesses with high leverage will have large fixed costs in their cost structures and require high levels of output to reach break even. Consider diagram 79 which shows two companies producing identical products and serving the same market. The level of activity is determined by the state of the market and the activity probability distribution is shown below the break even charts. Company 'A' with the high leverage has a higher downside risk than company 'B' even though the probability distribution is the same for both companies. This illustrates how relevant the break even model is for identifying risk.

Let us now turn our attention to the distribution curve. The curve represents the probability distribution of a range of outcomes for any critical limiting factor such as sales. It is improbable that the outcomes will be normally distributed as shown in the binomial distribution example. They will tend to be skewed to the left or right as shown in diagram 80 The important point to note is how much of the curve is to the left of the break even point. If a significant amount of the distribution is in the loss making area of activity and the slope of the curve into the loss area is steep, then the downside risk is high and management should consider ways to minimise this risk.

DIAGRAM 79 OPERATIONAL GEARING & RISK

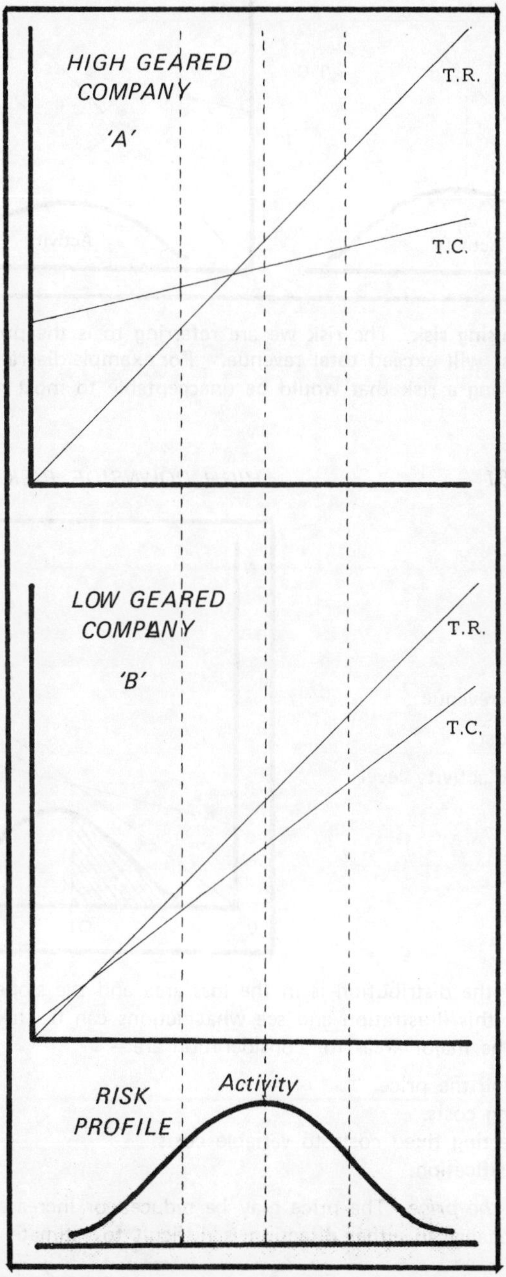

DIAGRAM 80 SKEWED DISTRIBUTION AND THE BREAK EVEN

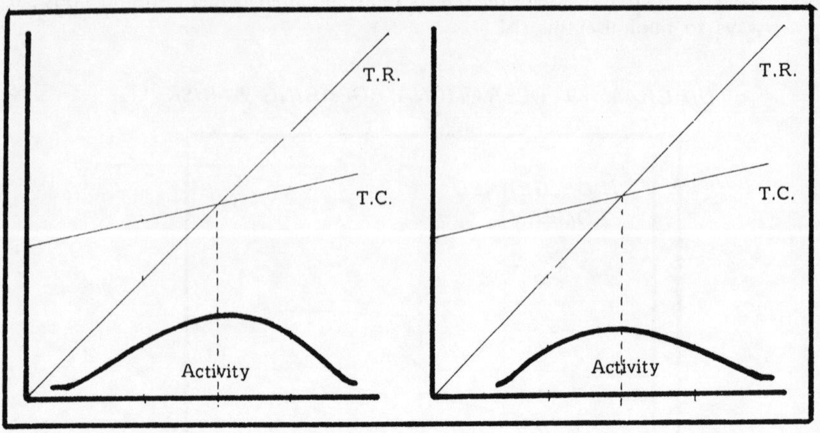

2:7:3 Minimising risk The risk we are referring to is the probability that total cost will exceed total revenue. For example diagram 81 shows a business taking a risk that would be unacceptable to most managers.

DIAGRAM 81 *HIGH DOWNSIDE RISK ACTIVITY*

Where:

(a) = total revenue

(b) total costs

OQ1 = risk activity level

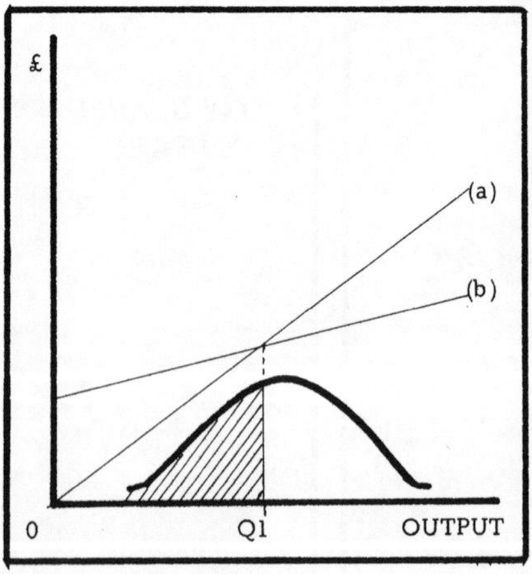

Almost half the distribution is in the loss area and the slope is very steep. Let us take this illustration and see what actions can be taken to minimise the risk. The major areas for consideration are:–

(i) Altering the price.
(ii) Cutting costs.
(iii) Converting fixed costs to variable costs.
(iv) Diversification.

(i) Altering the price The price may be reduced or increased. The effect of a price change in either direction is difficult to estimate with any

degree of accuracy. It will depend upon the price, elasticity of demand, competition and the state of the market. Diagrams 32A and 32B illustrate the possible outcomes of a price increase and a price reduction. Diagram A shows the downside risk being increased by a price reduction on the assumption that a higher volume of sales will be made. Conversely, diagram B shows a lower downside risk because of the price increase.

DIAGRAM 82   PRICE CHANGES & RISK PROFILES

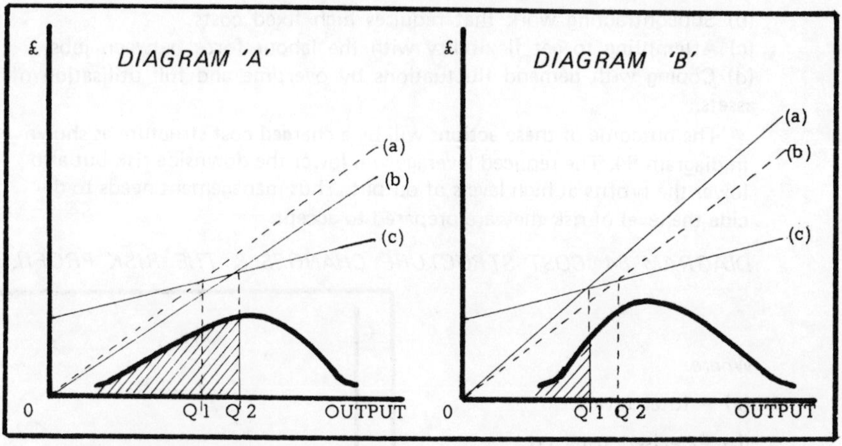

PRICE DECREASE	*PRICE INCREASE*
(a) = original total revenue	**(a)** = revised total revenue
(b) = revised total revenue	**(b)** = original total revenue
(c) = original total costs	**(c)** = original total costs
OQ1 = original risk activity level	**OQ1** = revised risk activity level
OQ2 = revised risk activity level	**OQ2** = original risk activity level

(ii) Cutting costs The effect of cost cuts will alter the total cost line but not the probability distribution. The shape of the distribution may be altered if say marketing costs were cut or the product quality was changed. Assuming administration and production costs were cut with no significant loss of efficiency or product change then the downside risk will be reduced as shown in diagram 83.

DIAGRAM 83
COST CHANGES & THE RISK PROFILE

Where:
(a) = total revenue
(b) = original total costs
(c) = revised total costs
OQ1 = new risk activity level.
OQ2 = old risk activity level.

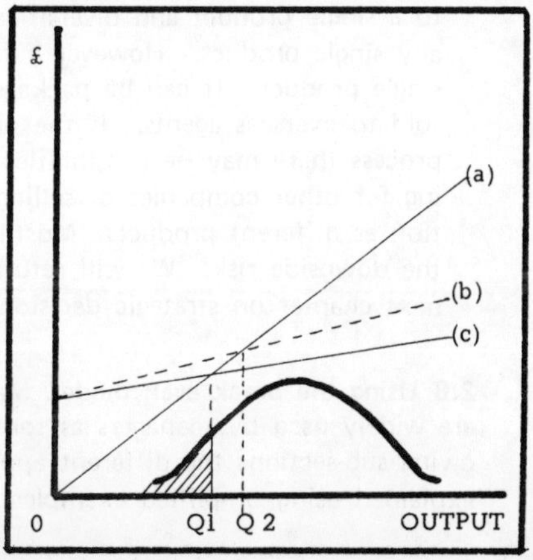

(iii) Converting fixed costs to variable costs This approach to the problem would be an attempt to match risk with the cost structure. Risk and reward tend to have an inverse relationship. High reward projects tend to have high risks. If the risks are reduced by say, sharing the venture, then the rewards are also reduced. The following methods may be used to convert fixed costs to variable costs:—

(a) Accepting use instead of ownership/use of assets by leasing or renting plant, equipment and premises.

(b) Subcontracting work that requires high fixed costs.

(c) Attempting to get flexibility with the labour force between jobs.

(d) Coping with demand fluctuations by overtime and full utilisation of assets.

The outcome of these actions will be a charged cost structure as shown in diagram 84. The reduced leverage will lower the downside risk but also lower the profits at high levels of output. Thus management needs to decide the level of risk they are prepared to accept.

DIAGRAM 84 COST STRUCTURE CHANGES & THE RISK PROFILE

Where:

(a) = total revenue

(b) = revised total costs

(c) = original total costs

OQ1 = new risk activity level

OQ2 = old risk activity level

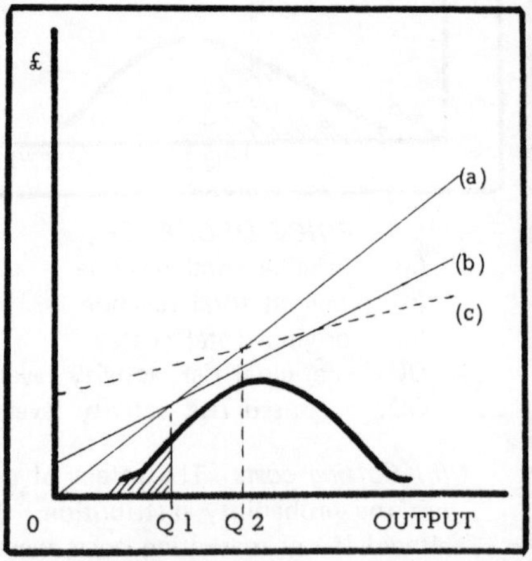

(iv) Diversification The break even model relates to a single product. The model cannot be used for multiple products that have different variable costs, selling prices and contributions. Accordingly, the risk relates to a single product and diversification will not alter the risk of a loss on any single product. However a form of diversification is possible with a single product. It can be packaged under a different brand name, and/or sold to overseas agents. If the product is subject to a lengthy production process there may be possibilities of joint products, by products, producing for other companies or selling the product at various stages of production as different products. Most kinds of diversification will tend to reduce the downside risk. We will return to the problem of risk again in the next chapter on strategic decision making.

2:8 Using the break even model. Marginal costing and the break even model are widely used by managers as tools for tactical decision making. In the fol owing sub-sections the different applications of break even analysis will be explained using simplified examples. All the examples are based on the assum ption that the limitations of the break even model explained in sub-section 2:9 do not apply. It is therefore necessary for the reader to understand that the results of break even calculations only provide guidelines for decision makers. The results are not as precise as the figures imply.

2:8:1 Changes in output. In chapter 3, sub-section 5:3 the effect on profit of changes in output was explained. Within the relevant range, the greater the output, the greater the profit. The actual effect on profit from output changes can be calculated quite quickly using the break even model.

Example.

A manufacturer has the following cost detail regarding a specific product:-

	£
Output/Sales 12,000 units @ £2.00 each	24,000
less variable costs of production	12,000
Contribution towards paying the fixed costs	12,000
less fixed costs	8,000
Profit	4,000

The accountant is asked to provide the expected profit/loss figures for the following output/sales levels on the assumption that all costs and revenues remain constant: £16,000, £23,000 and £29,000.

For this simple example the answer can be obtained without deriving the profit function. But as the profit function will be used in later more complicated examples, we will adopt a standard calculation technique.

Profit function	= 2q – (8,000 + 1q)		
P/V ratio	= 0.5		
Sales of £16,000=	(16,000 x 0.5)–8,000	= £nil	(B/E)
Sales of £23,000=	(23,000 x 0.5)–8,000	= £3,500	profit
Sales of £29,000=	(29,000 x 0.5)–8,000	= £6,500	profit

2:8:2 Changes in costs. In the break even model there are only two cost classifications; fixed costs and variable costs. A change in the fixed costs will alter the break even point and a change in the variable costs will alter the break even point, the contribution and the P/V ratio. Fixed costs such as supervision, time based depreciation, rent and rates are only fixed within a relevant range of output. At specific levels of output another supervisor may be needed or more machines and factory space. The result of these cost increases will be a stepped fixed cost as shown in diagram 85 As output passes OQ_1 additional supervision may be necessary for say: shift working. This would cause a fixed cost increase to OP_1 at output OQ_2 additional machinery is required and fixed costs increase to OP_2. Therefore, fixed costs are only fixed within a range of normal output.

Example:

A production manager has been provided with the following cost detail:-

	£
Output/Sales 5,000 units @ £5.00 each	25,000
less variable costs	20,000
Contribution towards paying the fixed costs	5,000
less fixed costs	2,000
Profit	3,000

DIAGRAM 85 STEPPED FIXED COSTS

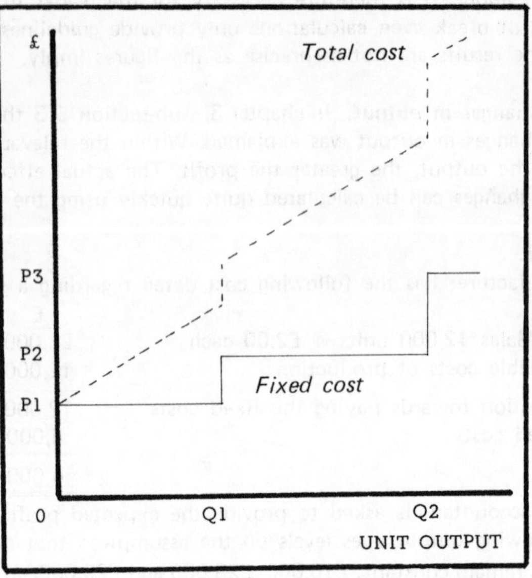

Some new plant is being purchased that will increase the fixed costs by £8,000 and reduce the variable costs by 25%. The plant is being purchasec to meet an expected annual demand of 10,000 units to be sold at the same price of £5.00. The manager would like to know: what is the difference in profit between the old plant and new plant at output levels of 5,000, 10,000 and 12,000 units and how will the break even be affected?

DETAIL	*OLD PLANT*	*NEW PLANT*
Profit functions	*5q–(2,000+4q)*	*5q–(10,000+3q)*
5,000 units	(5,000x1)–2,000 = 3,000	(5,000x2)–10,000 = B/E
10,000 units	(10,000x1)–2,000 = 8,000	(10,000x2)–10,000 = 10,00
12,000 units	(12,000x1)–2,000 = 10,000	(12,000x2)–10,000 = 14,00
B/E units	2,000 ÷ 1 = 2,000 units	10,000 ÷ 2 = 5,000 units
B/E value	2,000 x £5 = £10,000	5,000 x £5 = £25,000

2:8:3 Changes in price. A change in the selling price will alter the contrib- ution, P/V ratio and break even point. In many instances, an increase in price will tend to cause a reduction in sales, and a decrease in price an increase in sales. Naturally, market forces will determine the effect that price changes have on sales, but for the purposes of illustration we will assume the economist's downward sloping demand curve to be appropriate. The break even model is very useful for calculating the expected effects of price changes. For example, say a 10% decrease in price is expected to create a 5% increase in sales. The problem is: will this increase or decrease profit? For these calculations we are not concerned with market penetration, market share, reaction to competitors' actions or change in demand.

We have to assume all other factors remain constant when making these profit calculations.

Example:

A marketing manager has produced for a board meeting the following demand estimates and wants the company to reduce the selling price of its standard product which is currently selling at £3.00

Selling price £	*Estimated demand* *Units*	*Sales* £
2.00	5,000	10,000
3.00	3,000	9,000
1.80	9,000	16,200

Assuming the total cost function is (3,000 + 1q) and is not expected to change the different selling prices would provide the following profits:-

2q – (3,000 + 1q) for 5,000 units = (5,000 x 1) – 3,000 = £2,000
3q – (3,000 + 1q) for 3,000 units = (3,000 x 2) – 3,000 ==£3,000
1.8q–(3,000 + 1q) for 9,000 units = (9,000 x 0.8)–3,000 = £4,200

Based on this information the highest profit figure is achieved by reducing the price to £1.80. However, supposing the production manager has estimated that the increase in production will cause fixed costs to rise by 20% because of the new plant and equipment that would be needed. Also variable costs to increase by 10% because of increased overtime and incentive payments. Given these cost extimates would it be wise to reduce the selling price and increase output?

Firstly it is necessary to restate the profit function, then make the profit calculation.

Changes in fixed costs = 3,000 x 1.2 = £3,600
Changes in variable cost per unit = 1 x 1.1 = £1.10
Therefore the revised profit function is:1.8q – (3,600 + 1.1q)
Profit 9,000 units is: (9,000 x .7) – 3,600 = £2,700

Using the break even model with no adjustments for risk and making no allowances for otherfactors it would appear that a higher profit would be earned if the price remained at £3.00 because the marginal revenue from a change in price is less than the marginal cost.

2:8:4 Limiting factors. Every enterprise faces factors that restrict its growth. The factors may be sales, production, capacity, supply of materials, skilled labour or finance. These are called 'limiting factors' or 'key factors' For example, assume a business could not meet the demand for its two main products 'X' and 'Y' because of a material supply shortage. If both 'X' and 'Y' produced the same contribution per unit but 'Y' used twice as much material, then the business would concentrate its production on product **'X'**, because this would *maximise the contribution of the limiting factor.* If we use simple figures for 'X' and 'Y' this will help to illustrate the key factor maximisation principle.

	Product 'X'		Product 'Y'	
	£	£	£	£
Selling price		10		20
Direct labour	1		6	
Direct materials @ £1.0 per kilo	5		10	
		6		16
Contribution per unit		4		4

		Product 'X'	Product 'Y'
Contribution / Use of limiting factor	@	£4 / 5 kilos	£4 / 10 kilos
Contribution per limiting factor	=	*£0.80 per kilo*	*£0.40 per kilo*

If there was only 10,000 kilos of material available then to produce all product 'X' would provide a contribution of £8,000 and all product 'Y' a contribution of £4,000. This illustrates the importance of considering contribution per limiting factor for decision making.

Key factor method:

a) Identify limiting factor
b) Select the appropriate unit of measure for limiting factors, e.g. weight, volume length etc.
c) Calculate contribution per unit of output.
d) Divide unit contribution by limiting factor to obtain contribution per limiting factor for each type of output.
e) Select output that maximises contribution per limiting factor.

Example:

The following details relate to the production budgets of a multi product manufacturing company:-

Products	'A'	'B'	'C'	'D'
Selling price	25	20	15	10
Direct materials	5	6	10	5
Direct labour	15	10	2	3
Contribution per unit	5	4	3	2
Limiting Factors				
Raw material usage in kilos	5	6	10	5
Direct labour hours	15	10	2	3
Machine hours	20	30	4	6

We will now rank the product output priority under the following circumstances:

(i) No production limiting factor
(ii) Raw material limiting factor
(iii) Direct labour limiting factor
(iv) Machine capacity limiting factor

(i) *No limiting factor.* Maximum profit will be at maximum contribution from producing in the following priority:-

Product	'A'	'B'	'C'	'D'
Contribution per unit	£5	£4	£3	£2
Ranking	1	2	3	4

(ii) *Raw Material Limiting Factor.* Maximum profit will be where contribution per unit of raw material is maximised.

Product	*'A'*	*'B'*	*'C'*	*'D'*
Contributions	5/5	4/6	3/10	2/5
Contribution per limiting factor	£1.00	£0.66	£0.30	£0.40
Ranking	1	2	4	3

(iii) *Direct labour limiting factor.*

Product	*'A'*	*'B'*	*'C'*	*'D'*
Contributions	5/15	4/10	3/2	2/3
Contribution per limiting factor	£0.33	£0.40	£1.5	£0.66[1]
Ranking	4	3	1	2

(iv) *Machine hours limiting factor*

Product	*'A'*	*'B'*	*'C'*	*'D'*
Contributions	5/20	4/30	3/4	2/6
Ranking	3	4	1	2

Summary of ranking	*'A'*	*'B'*	*'C'*	*'D'*
No production limiting factor	1	2	3	4
Raw material limiting factor	1	2	4	3
Direct labour limiting factor	4	3	1	2
Machine hours limiting factor	3	4	1	2

This example illustrates how limiting factor calculations can alter production priorities. There are four different production priorities depending upon which limiting factor calculation was used. *The application of the contribution per limiting factor technique is only valid where there is a known single limiting factor.* In practice it is unlikely that a single limiting factor will prevent production optimisation. Moreover, as the production schedule is altered to maximise one limiting factor this may in turn change other factors which then become limiting factors. One cannot assume all factors will remain constant whilst just one factor is flexed. Consequently there has been some criticism of the limiting factor technique. A technique for production choice decision that overcomes some of the objections to contribution per limiting factor calculations is linear programming. The linear programming technique is explained later in this chapter.

2:8:5 Make or buy a product. Manufacturers are often faced with the decision to make a product or buy it from another manufacturer. A simple analysis of the problem would suggest that if the variable costs of producing the product were less than the cost of buying it the product should be made. There are however other factors that need to be taken into consideration.

(a) Is the plant working at full capacity?

(b) If there is spare productive capacity for making the product what alternative user could the resources be used for?

(c) What would the contribution be from the next best alternative use of these resources?
(d) Are there any limiting factors in producing the items that can be bought from another manufacturer?
(e) Would there be any stepped fixed costs if the product is made instead of purchased?
(f) Is the outside supplier reliable?

If we assume the supplier is reliable and there is a low risk of production disruption due to irregular supplies we can then make some cost calculations based on the break even model.

Example:

A large manufacturing company has been approached by a small manufacturer with an offer to provide a sub-assembly on a regular basis. The large manufacturer currently produces the sub-assembly for the following cost:-

	£
Direct labour	10.00
Direct materials	8.00
Direct expense	2.00
Variable cost per unit	20.00
Proportion of overheads	10.00
Total cost per unit	30.00

The machine used for making the sub-assembly is very expensive and could be used for making a new product with a unit contribution of £4.00 The machine takes two hours to make the sub-assembly and would take 1 hour to make the new product. The manager of the large company would like to know what is the maximum price he should consider paying for the sub-assembly.

The first point to establish is that the unit overhead absorption rate is irrelevant for this decision (Refer to sections on relevant costing) Currently it is costing £20 to produce the sub-assembly and using two hours of machine time, that is a limiting factor. The next best alternative use for the machine is to produce the new product with a contribution per limiting factor of £4.00 per hour. Accordingly the lost contribution is £8.00 for every sub-assembly that is made. When this is added to the variable cost of making the sub-assembly of £20 it provides the maximum price that the manufacturer should pay for the sub-assembly. Based on these calculations if the small company offers to sell the sub-assemblies for less than £28 each it is in the manufacturer's interests to buy and use the spare productive capacity for the new product.

2:8:6 Accept/reject a special contract. Producers are often approached by large retail organisations for special supply contracts. Because of the tremendous marketing power of the large retail chains they can make producers very attractive offers, but there is usually some tough bargaining on price and delivery schedules. It is therefore necessary for the supplier to calculate in advance the lowest price that can be accepted for a special supply contract. The key figure for the supplier is the unit contribution. Clearly the price cannot be below the variable cost, unless there are special circumstances, such as cash flow problems and the need to dispose of excessive stocks. Before applying the break even model to this kind of problem there are other factors to consider.

(a) Will the special supply arrangement affect the market for the product?

(b) Will the special arrangement become known to other regular customers who will want similar terms?

(c) Is there spare capacity to meet the contract?

(d) If there is no spare capacity what will the stepped fixed costs be for increasing output?

(e) Will variable costs change because of increased overtime or different product specifications required by the customer?

(f) Are there any better alternative uses for the extra productive capacity?

Example:

A company producing an 'instant fancy food' is approached by a supermarket chain to supply 2,000 packets a week under the supermarket brand label. The company is currently working at full capacity of 200,000 packets a year with a profit function of 0.65q – (20,000 + 0.45q). To increase output so that the special order could be met would mean additional fixed costs of £5,000 p.a. and an estimated increase in unit variable costs of 5% for overtime and bonus payments. The sales director will soon be negotiating with the supermarket's purchasing officer and needs to know the lowest acceptable price before discussing the contract.

Normally the lowest price would be slightly above the variable costs of £0.45 per packet. However, as the costs will alter if the contract is accepted, some calculations are necessary. Assuming the contract is for one year then it would be prudent to spread the additional fixed costs over the additional output for this period.

$$\frac{£5{,}000}{(52 \times 2{,}000)} = £0.04808 \text{ per packet}$$

It would also be necessary to adjust the unit variable cost by the estimated increase of 5%, i.e. £0.45 x 1.05 = £0.4725. Thus the minimum acceptable price would have to be above £0.52058 per packet. (o.04808+ 0.4725). One point to note here is that once the fixed costs have been incurred for the extra production, they become irrelevant to the decision and the minimum acceptable price would then fall to the variable cost per unit level.

2:8:7 Dropping a product line. The break even model is of limited use for this kind of disinvestment decision. The appropriate decision technique would be differential costing based on marginal costing principles. (Refer to chapter 3 sub sections 5:2 and 5:12). The cost difference between keeping and dropping a product line would be calculated on a marginal cost basis. Before making the calculations there are several factors that need to be considered:

(a) What are the reasons for closing the product line?

(b) If it is low profitability, can the selling price be increased and/or costs be reduced to improve the profit position?

(c) If it is a fall in demand, is it likely to be permanent or temporary?

(d) If a temporary fall in demand, is the decision to be a permanent or temporary shut down?

(e) What are the next best alternative uses for the spare productive capacity?

(f) What will the costs be for converting to the next best alternative use compared with full disinvestment?

(g) Are there any interdependent products, processes or markets for the product line?

There are clearly many other factors that could influence the decision. However once all the relevant factors have been taken into consideration it will be necessary to make some calculations to assess the different alternatives. Consider the following example:

Example:

A manufacturer produces four products with the following cost and revenue details:-

Detail	*'A' £000*	*'B' £000*	*'C' £000*	*'D' £000*	*Total £000*
Sales	100	180	120	200	600
less variable costs	60	150	110	130	450
Contribution	40	30	10	70	150
1) Identifiable fixed costs	10	10	20	10	50
2) Product profit (loss)	30	20	(10)	60	100
3) Other fixed costs					50
			Profit		50

Notes:

1) Identifiable fixed costs relate to those costs that can be specifically identified as belonging exclusively to the product.

2) Product profit makes no allowance for all the fixed costs and is a form of gross profit.

3) Other fixed costs represent all fixed costs not included in note 1.

For product 'C' there are no significant interdependent factors, the demand has been constantly falling and there are no opportunities for cost savings whilst the production line is running. The directors consider there are two alternatives:-

(a) *Disinvestment* by selling the plant and machinery and making redundancy payments to employees. The plant and machinery has a book value of £50,000 and net realiseable value of £5,000. The redundancy payments will cost £30,000.

(b) *New product development* by converting product line 'C' to new product 'X'. Costs of conversion and new machinery £100,000. Product life expected to be 5 years with sale value of machinery £50,000. Contribution from new product is expected to be £20,000 per annum. No redundancies would be necessary from product 'C' production line.

From this brief basic detail we can make some fairly crude calculations to illustrate the technique. To keep the illustration simple an allowance will be made for inflation and several other factors that should be included in the cost calculations. There are three alternatives; to keep the product line going, to disinvest or to replace product 'C' with product 'X'. As the new product is expected to last five years the differential calculation would be for this time period. We will assume that cost and revenue changes would affect each alternative in the same way and therefore hold all factors constant for the five years.

Alternative 1 Retain product 'C'
Profit over five years period would be 5 x £50,000 = £250,000
Alternative 2 Disinvestment

Profit over five years period (30 + 20 + 60 – 50) x 5	=	300,000
less net disinvestment costs 30,000 – 5,000	=	25,000
		275,000

Note: The book value of £50,000 is irrelevant for this decision)
Alternative 3 New product development

Profit over five years period for products A, B and D	=	300,000
Add: receipts from sale of product 'C' plant		5,000
contribution for five years from product 'X'		100,000
		405,000
deduct: net cost of product 'X' machinery		50. 000
		355,000

Comparing the three alternatives over the five year period the new product development clearly appears to be the best course of action. The main point to note from this simple example is the flexibility of the differential costing approach, that allows many factors to be approximately costed and included in the calculations. To simply apply the break even model with this type of decision would mean that any product not providing a contribution towards the fixed costs should be dropped. The decision process is far more complicated and the break even model approach is not as suitable as differential costing.

2:8:8 Sale or further processing. At most stages of a production process a manufacturer has the alternative to sell or continue processing. This decision is illustrated in diagram 86 that shows the basic alternatives. The cal-

DIAGRAM 86 SALE OR FURTHER PROCESSING

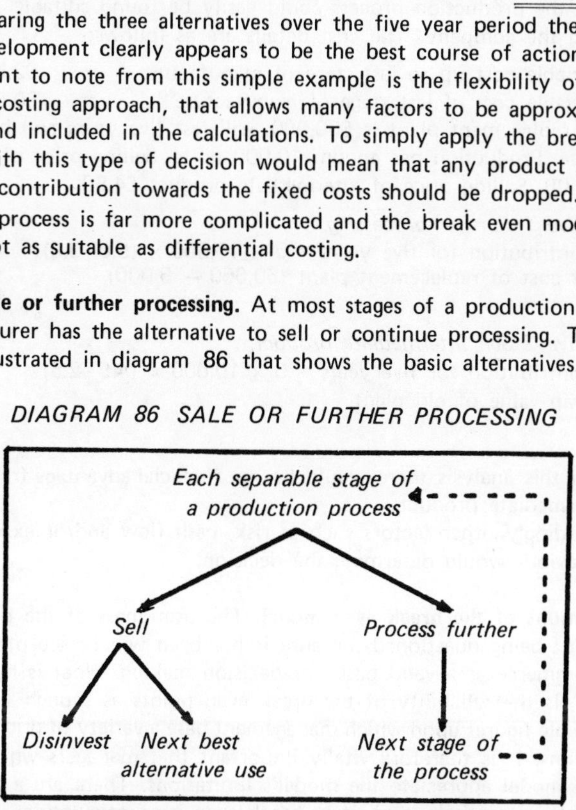

culations for this type of decision are similar to the previous example where the different alternatives were costed and compared. Before making any calculations other factors that can influence the decision should be considered.

(a) What is the market for the intermediate product?
(b) How does this market compare with the market for the final product?
(c) Would the decision to sell the intermediate product make the company dependent upon another manufacturer or just a few buyers?
(d) If the decision to sell the intermediate product was taken would it be very difficult and expensive to begin to manufacture the final product again?
(e) What is the next best alternative use for the spare capacity if the intermediate product is sold?
(f) Is there a half way stage where the intermediate product can be sold and additional production be processed for sale as finished goods?

Example:
A manufacturer is faced with the decision whether to replace some old plant at the end of the company's production process or disinvest and sell the intermediate product to another manufacturer. The old equipment has a £5,000 scrap value and the factory space could be used for badly needed inside storage of materials and partly finished goods. There would be no redundancy payments because the few employees working on the last stage of the production process could easily be found suitable jobs elsewhere in the company. The cost details are as follows:-

Unit variable cost up to last stage of manufacture	=	£2.50
Unit variable cost of last stage of manufacture	=	£0.50

Cost of replacement plant is £50,000, will last five years and has no terminal value. Production per annum 10,000 units. Selling price of final product £6.00. Selling price of intermediate product £4.50.

	£
Alternative 1 Further processing.	
Total contribution for five years = 5 x 10,000 x (6.0–3.0)	150,000
less: net cost of replacement plant (50,000 – 5,000)	45,000
	105,000
Alternative 2 Sell intermediate product.	
Total contribution for five years = 5 x 10,000 x (4.5–2.5)	100,000
add: scrap value of old plant	5,000
	105,000

From this analysis there would be no financial advantage from selling the intermediate product.

Accordingly other factors such as risk, cash flow and/or expected market behaviour would determine the decision.

2:9 Limitations of the break even model. The usefulness of the break even model is not being questioned, because it has been widely accepted in industry and commerce as a valid basis for decision making. What is being questioned here, is the reliability of the break even points as though they were precise reliable figures upon which management base a variety of price/output type decisions. It is therefore vitally important that managers who use the break even model appreciate the model's limitations. There are a number of fundamental assumptions implicit in break even type calculations that place limitations on the reliability of the results. The following sub sections are intended to alert the non-accountant not to be mislead by the precision that break even calculations imply. The break even model is only a decision making tool. Like all tools it is only as good as the user. If a manager understands the limitations of break even analysis then he/she will be more proficient in using this useful management tool.

2:9:1 Cost classifications. The break even model assumes that all costs can be neatly divided into fixed and variable. The criteria for the division is variability of cost behaviour in relation to output over a period of time. The period of time is not defined. In the long run most costs are variable and in the short run most costs are fixed. For example, if direct labour is calculated to produce say 2 units of production per hour then this would be the basis of a variable cost calculation. But in the short run, labour costs cannot be directly related to output in the same way as direct material costs. There is a short term fixed cost element in direct labour. The real problem however is the wide range of costs such as electricity, telephone, administration and miscellaneous materials that are semi variable or semi fixed in nature. Under the break even model all semi fixed or semi variable costs have to be classified as either fixed or variable. In brief, the classification is too arbitrary.

2:9:2 Non-linear functions and the 'relevant range'. The break even linearity assumption is based on the principle that unit costs and revenue vary directly in relation to output. For example, a linear revenue function would mean that the first unit would be sold for the same price as the millionth unit. This conflicts with the economist's downward sloping demand curve, where the greater the output the lower the market price. Consequently, revenue linearity in an imperfect market would only be within a range of output. As output increased, unit price would fall as shown in diagram 87.

DIAGRAM 87 CURVILINEAR REVENUE FUNCTION

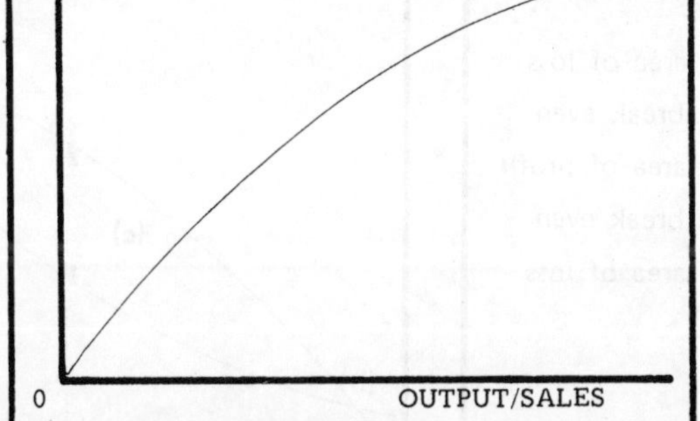

With regard to variable costs, it is unlikely that they will behave in a linear relationship to output. Direct Materials for instance, as demand increases

ases, the price will increase, but set against this will be the higher quantity discounts and the increased bargaining power of a big buyer. Direct labour costs will tend to increase at higher levels of output due to overtime and other wage bargaining agreements that are not output bases. Therefore, as output increases, unit variable costs will fall, level off and then rise. This is illustrated in diagram 88 as a smoothed total cost curve

DIAGRAM 88 CURVILINEAR TOTAL COST FUNCTION

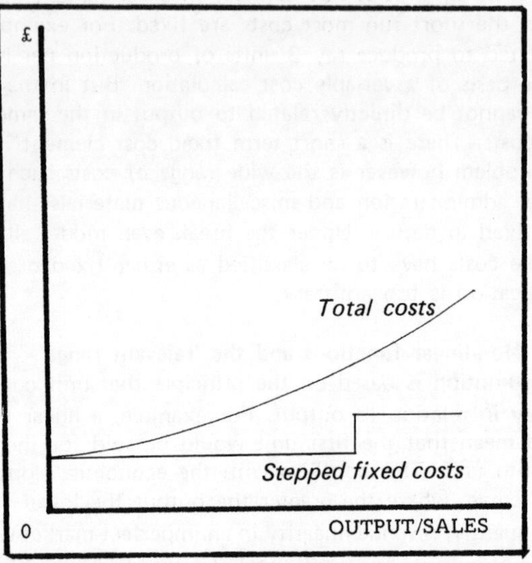

When the assumptions of non-linearity and stepped fixed costs are included in the break even diagram, the result is two break even points. This is often referred to as the economist's break even, where the effects of non-linearity and stepped fixed costs are shown as smoothed total revenue and total cost functions. This is shown in diagram 89 below.

DIAGRAM 89
ECONOMIST'S BREAK EVEN GRAPH

Where:

(a) = area of loss
(b) = break even
(c) = area of profit
(d) = break even
(e) = area of loss

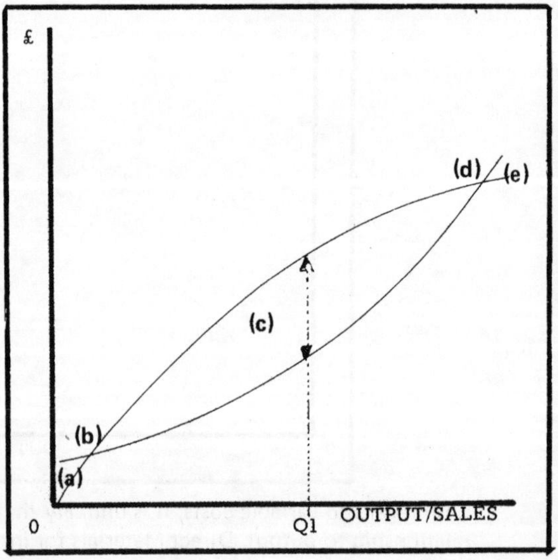

The economist's model is fundamentally the same but is based on different assumptions.. The economist's broad conceptual approach is usually applied to market behaviour. Whereas, the accountant's approach based on linearity assumptions will generally only be valid within a relevant range as shown in diagram 90.

DIAGRAM 90 RELEVANT RANGE OF BREAK EVEN MODEL

Where:

(a) = accountant's total revenue function.

(b) = economist's total revenue function

(c) = accountant's total cost function.

(d) = economist's total cost function.

OQ1 = economist's optimum output.

OQ2 = accountant's optimum output is equal to maximum capacity.

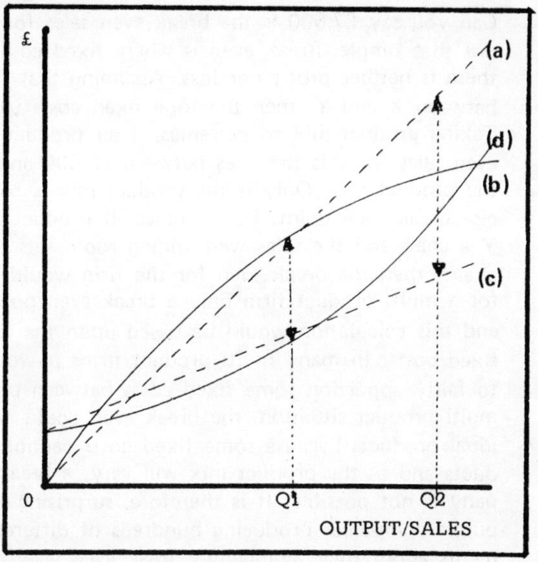

The two approaches are combined in diagram 90. The accountant's approach would recommend producing to an output level of say, 0Q2 which would provide a lower profit than other economist's output recommendation of OQ1. In principle the economist's cost and revenue functions are correct, but in practice they could not be ascertained within an acceptable degree of reliability.

Although the accountant's linearity assumption is conceptually invalid throughout the entire range of output within a *relevant range,* it could be acceptable as a reasonable approximation. Thus it may be concluded that the accountant's linearity assumption is necessary on practical grounds and is acceptable within a relevant range of output. The relevant range will vary according to circumstances. The factors affecting the relevant range will be:

(a) Stepped fixed costs
(b) Changes in variable cost per unit at certain levels of output
(c) Changes in th e unit selling price at certain levels of sales

Broadly speaking, the relevant range will tend to be from a point of low level output where unit costs and fixed costs are unlikely to change up to normal capacity. Outside this range, cost behaviour is unlikely to be linear

2:9:3 Output homogeneity If a company produces more than one type of product (i.e. heterogeneous output) then there cannot be a single break even point for the company unless the product mix is constant throughout the relevant range. Consider the following example of a firm producing two products.

Product	Profit functions	B/E Point Units	£
X	20q – (1,000 + 12q)	125	2,500
Y	10q – (1,000 + 8q)	500	5,000
	Total Sales		£7,500

Can you say £7,500 is the break even sales for the firm? The answer is not that simple. Break even is where fixed cost equals contribution and there is neither profit nor loss. Assuming that fixed costs can be separated between X and Y, then the total fixed costs to be recovered are £2,000. Taking product mix to extremes, if all product X or Y were sold, then break even sales for this firm lies between £5,000 and £10,000, depending upon the product mix. Only if the product mix is constant can we state a precise break even point. For instance, if product X was a table and product Y a chair and the sales were dining room sets of one table and four chairs, then the break even for the firm would be £7,500. Consequently, for a multi product firm only a break even point per product is possible and this calculation would be based upon the assumption of separable fixed costs. In many multi product firms it would be very difficult indeed to fairly apportion some fixed costs between products. Given a complex multi product situation, the break even could not be calculated for individual products because some fixed costs cannot be identified fairly to products and as the product mix will vary, a break even sales level for a company is not possible. It is therefore, surprising when directors of some public companies producing hundreds of different products make statements about their 'company's break even level of sales'.

2:9:4 Output equals sales. A basic assumption of the break even model is that all the production is sold during the period that is being analysed. For businesses with a seasonal output and sales this assumption cannot be made. Consider the following simple example:-

Example:

A single product firm with a profit function of: 10q – (1,000 + 6q) and an output of 50 units per month will break even at the end of the fifth month.

i.e. $$\text{B/E} \; \frac{1,000}{(10-6)} = 250 \text{ units}$$

$$\text{At 50 units per month} \; \frac{250}{50} = 5 \text{ months}$$

Management has to anticipate demand, and production levels reflect demand and expectations. In the example where the break even is 250 units, the demand may be seasonal where 250 units could be sold in one month. Therefore, five months production would be necessary to prepare for the one month's sales. For example, the relationship between output and sales for fireworks or christmas crackers would only be the same in the long run. The short run situation would be output greater than sales or vice versa.

In most production situations stocks act as a buffer between sales and output. Only in the long run, or occasionally by chance, will output equal sales. Therefore, it is important to bear in mind that the results if a break even analysis are based upon the assumption that all the output will be sold within the time period under consideration.

2:9:5 Multiple limiting factors. In sub section 2:8:4 the importance of calculating the contribution per limiting factor was explained. With multi-product firms a simple contribution approach cannot be used because of the different product's use of limiting factors. Accordingly the calculation of contribution per limiting factor is used. However, this technique is only valid if there is just one limiting factor. If there are multiple limiting factors then the break even model should be abandoned and a linear programming model used. The linear programming model is explained later in this chapter.

2:9:6 A static model. The break even model tends to be static making little allowance for changes in the following factors:-

(i)	Productive efficiency	(vii)	Wage rates
(ii)	Management efficiency	(ix)	Material costs
(iii)	Production capacity	(ix)	Competitors actions
(iv)	Technology changes	(x)	Consumer preferences
(v)	Methods of production	(xi)	Selling prices
(vi)	Product design	(xii)	Risk

Clearly these factors cannot be ignored for price/output decisions, but with the increasing use of computers it is possible for the break even model to be made more dynamic by introducing these factors into a program. This would enable the user of the program to alter the different factors and see the effect on profitability.

3. Ad hoc decision making techniques.

There are many techniques that have been developed to aid with specific decision making problems. Managers often develop their own decision criteria and their own decision techniques to meet the special circumstances of their particular business. Most of these 'one off' techniques will be applications of established management accounting. In the first four sub sections of this part of the chapter we will briefly review the principles of : differential costing, incremental costing, opportunity costing and relevant costing. These costing techniques often use subjective basic data and therefore only provide general guidelines for the decision maker. However, in the subsequent five sub sections we will look at some of the valuable contributions that mathematicians have made to this subject area The four techniques selected are briefly explained without too much attention to their mathematical content, because the application of these techniques would tend to be through the use of packaged software. All the user has to do is to provide the input and understand the output.

3:1 Differential costing. This decision technique has been applied to the specific problems explained in sections 2:8:7 and 2:8:8. The principle of differential costing is to total the relevant costs and revenues that are expected to arise for each alternative course of action. The costs that do not differ between alternatives are excluded from this decision.

Example:

A company director is trying to decide whether to continue using a local delivery van service or purchase a company van and employ a full time driver. The comparative cost details are as follows:-

Delivery service costs £1.00 per item within a radius of 10 miles, £2.00 per item within a radius of 25 miles. (The company's products are all standard size and weight) Purchase of delivery van £4,000, expected to last 5 years with a terminal value of £500. Average running costs of tax, insurance, repairs and fuel £2,000 per annum. Total cost of driver's wages including employer's contributions will be £5,000 per annum. Assume a 10% cumulative increase in costs every year. Deliveries are expected to be 2,000 items within a 10 mile radius and 2,000 items within a 20 mile radius in the first year. This is expected to increase by a cumulative 25% per annum and could be managed by a single driver and one van.

Alternative 1 Retain delivery service.

		£
Year 1	(2,000 x £1.00) + (2,000 x £2.00)	5,000
Year 2	5,000 x 1.25	6,250
Year 3	6,250 x 1.25	7,812
Year 4	7,812 x 1.25	9,766
Year 5	9,766 x 1.25	12,207
	Total	£41,035

Alternative 2 Purchase van and employ driver.
Total costs for five years (In cash flow terms)

		£
Year 1	Purchase of van	4,000
	Running costs (5,000 + 2,000)	7,000
Year 2	Running costs (7,000 x 1.1)	7,700
Year 3	Running costs (7,700 x 1.1)	8,470
Year 4	Running costs (8,470 x 1.1)	9,317
Year 5	Running costs (9,317 x 1.1)	10,249
	less: terminal value of van	(500)
	Total	£46,236

The difference between the two alternatives is £5,201 (46,236 – 41,035) in favour of retaining the delivery service. This particular problem should include the use of a technique that allows for the time value of money as well as using the differential costing approach. The time value of money technique is explained in the next chapter.

3:2 Incremental costing. This technique is ued to calculate the change in costs and revenues arising from a change in the level of activity. It is based on the economist's principle of marginal cost i.e the cost of one extra unit. This can be distinguished from the differential cost which is the calculation of the difference in costs and revenues from a change in policy. Incremental costs are calculated because the cost of an extra unit, or batch of units, may not simply be the variable cost difference. If the addition of the extra unit requires a stepped fixed cost then the incremental cost can be very high. It is therefore a useful basis for calculations relating to changes in output. Consider the following simplified example.

Example:

A manufacturer is operating at a 100% capacity of 4,000 units a year with a unit profit function of 20q – (20,000 + 10q). There is a six month delivery date for the products and any additional output will require:-

(a) Additional factory space of 5,000 sq. ft. @ £2 per square foot.
(b) A new machine costing £10,000, lasting 5 years with a nil scrap value.
(c) Another supervisor with gross salary plus employer's contributions of £6,000 per annum.

(d) All the variable costs will remain constant and the estimated set up time is three months.
An order has been received from a new customer wanting 10 units a month for one year. Deliveries to begin within three months from date of order.

The managing director is uncertain if acceptance of the order will increase the total profit of the company. The following calculations have been presented to the board of directors.

	£	£
Incremental revenue per annum (£20 x 10 x 12)		2,400
less: Incremental costs per annum:		
Supervisor's salary	6,000	
Depreciation of new machine (£10,000@20%)	2,000	
Additional factory space (5,000 x £2)	10,000	
Variable costs of production (£10x10x12)	1,200	
		19,200
Net incremental cost of order		16,800

The incremental cost calculations show that if the order is accepted and production expanded, total profit will be reduced by £16,800. However these calculations are based on an assumption that there will be no additional demand and that the new equipment will be operating below capacity. However a simple incremental break even calculation will provide the board of directors with an indication of the level of output necessary to recover the incremental costs. i.e.

$$\frac{\text{Incremental fixed costs}}{\text{Contribution per unit}} = \frac{18{,}000}{(20 - 10)} = 1{,}800 \text{ units}$$

If the board of directors believe that demand during the year will enable then to produce and sell a minimum additional output of 1,800 units then productive capacity should be increased and the order accepted.

3:3 Opportunity costs. This is an economic concept that is useful for decision makers. The opportunity cost represents the benefit foregone, or opportunity lost, by not using a resource in its best alternative use. In principle, a firm will measure opportunity costs by assigning a monetary value to all the factors of production it has used based on the amount it has sacrificed to have the use of the factor. In practice, there are many measurement difficulties. Even with a simple transaction such as say the purchase of raw materials, there are complications. For example if material was purchased for £10 per kilo then probably the amount sacrificed could be considered as the hist oric cost. But if prices have risen very quickly and the material could be sold without being processed for say £12, then this cost would be used. (This aspect of opportunity costs is developed in the next sub section on relevant costs).

The principle of opportunity cost also requires the inclusion of inputed costs such as the use of the business owner's personal assets and an allowance for risk. The risk allowance is supposed to be based on an amount sufficient to compensate for the risks involved. These opportunity costing principles can be applied in decision making techniques. One accountancy technique that applies opportunity cost principles is called relevant costing and is explained in the next sub section.

3:4 Relevant costs This decision making technique requires the manager to take an attitude towards costs that is quite different from traditional accounting. For example, if a manager has just spent £50,000 on a specialised machine it is quite difficult to accept that this historic cost is irrelevant. For decision making the relevant value would be the net realiseable value of the machine or its future income earning potential. There are occasions when traditional accounting principles and practices cause managers to make bad decisions. An example of this was when a production manager in a small manufacturing company had a new lathe installed. Unit output was costed on an absorption costing basis and the finance director had a prudent 'quick write off' policy for fixed assets. The outcome of these accounting practices was that the depreciation charge absorbed into the product costs was so high that the new machine was not used. In the words of the production manager 'I can produce them much cheaper on the old machines'. If the management of this company had adopted a relevant costing attitude towards decision making then depreciation policies would never have been allowed to influence production decisions.

Let us first consider the characteristics of relevant costs and then a few simple examples to illustrate the application of relevant costs for decision making.

3:4:1 Characteristics of relevant costs A decision is basically a choice between alternative courses of action that has to be made at a specific point in time. The point in time is often postponed and as a result the nature of the decision may change. At any point in time there will be costs that are relevant to the decision, but the costs and their relevance may change over time. Even though the costs may change the characteristics of relevant costs will remain the same. These characteristics are summarised below:–

(i) Future costs Decisions are made about the future not the past, therefore all expected future costs that are relevant to the decision should be included in the relevant cost analysis.
(ii) Past costs Once a cost has been incurred it becomes irrelevant for any decision. Managers often find this difficult to accept. The only relevance for past costs is the income earning capacity or net disinvestment yield represented by the asset not its historic cost.
(iii) Common costs As decisions are based on a choice between alternatives it follows that common costs for each alternative are irrelevant. Thus the relevant costs are those that will differ among alternative courses of action.

Given these characteristics we can now apply the principles of relevant costing to a few simple examples.

3:4:2 Applications of relevant costing The principles of relevant costing have already been used in some of the examples in this chapter. The following examples are intended to illustrate the importance of using relevant costs for decision making.

Example 1. Asset replacement decision.

A company purchased a computer for £100,000 and has been using it for five years with a depreciation rate of 10% per annum. A larger capacity machine is needed. This can be purchased for £25,000 due to the changes in technology. Because the existing computer is out of date it has no scrap value. The directors do not want to lose £50,000 and have therefore decided not to buy the computer.

If relevant costing principles were applied to this asset replacement decision the historic cost and book value of the existing computer would be ignored. The relevant costs would be the estimated future use value of the existing computer deducted from the estimated future use value of the new computer. If the difference is greater than £25,000 (after allowing for the time value of money) then the new computer should be purchased

Example 2. Use of materials decision.

A business had in stock 10,000 kilos of raw material 'A' that was purchased for £1.00 per kilo. The material was to be used on a production line that used 10 kilos per unit of output with a unit contribution of £12.00. The replacement cost of the raw material is now £2.00 per kilo and it can easily be sold from stock for £1.80 per kilo. Alternatively the material can be used on a new production line of a new product requiring one kilo per unit and providing a unit contribution of £1.50. Both production lines can use a substitute material 'B' that cost £1.00 per kilo for the 10,000 kilos in stock. This material has a replacement cost of £1.20 and a net realiseable value from stock of £0.80. The decision facing the production manager is what to do with material 'A'?

Using relevant costing principles we can ignore all the historic costs and just concentrate on the alternative courses of action:—

(a) Use material 'A' or 'B'? Even though both materials cost the same the replacement cost and net realiseable value of material 'A' is far higher. Therefore material 'B' should be used in production.

(b) Use or sell material 'A'? The contribution per kilo of material 'A' for the two production lines are:

Old production line $\dfrac{£12.00}{10 \text{ kilos}} = £1.20$ per kilo

New production line $\dfrac{£1.50}{1 \text{ kilo}} = £1.50$ per kilo

If the product is sold from stock its value is £1.80 per kilo. The alternatives can now be costed as follows:—

Use on old production line	1.20 x 10,000 = £12,000
Use on new production line	1.50 x 10,000 = £15,000
Sell from stock	1.80 x 10,000 = £18,000

Therefore the best alternative use for material 'A' is to sell and use material 'B' in both production lines.

Example 3 A pricing decision

A manufacturing company prices its output on a cost plus basis where unit cost includes an overhead absorption rate. The factory is working below capacity and has been offered a one off contract for a special job that will utilise the plant's spare capacity. An accountant has produced the following cost detail for the managing director who is negotiating on the contract price:—

Materials	*Historic Cost*	*Replace-ment Cost*	*Net realise-able Value*
	£	£	£
20,000 kilos of 'X'	20,000	30,000	26,000
10,000 kilos of 'Y'	5,000	2,000	1,000
1,000 kilos of 'Z'	10,000	11,000	10,000
Total	35,000	43,000	37,000

Direct labour 4,500 hours @ £2.00 per hour

Indirect labour of supervision and administration requiring no overtime or additional staff £10,000

General overheads such as proportion of rent, rates, depreciation, etc. £20,000

The managing director will naturally try to get the best price but he needs to know the lowest acceptable price. One manager makes the following calculation:–

	£
Materials	35,000
Direct labour (4,500 x £2.00)	9,000
Indirect labour	10,000
Overheads	20,000
Total cost	74,000
Minimum acceptable profit margin 10%	7,400
Contract price	81,400

These figures are rejected at the board meeting because of the spare capacity in the plant. It was decided that the overhead and indirect labour costs would be the same if the contract was accepted or not and were therefore irrelevant. Also the historic cost of the materials was considered irrelevant because they would have to be replaced for normal production to continue, therefore the replacement cost of materials was the relevant cost for the decision. Based on these assumptions the following relevant cost statement was produced:–

	£
Replacement cost of materials	43,000
Direct labour	9,000
Contract price should not be below	52,000

The final price for this contract will depend upon the skill of the negotiators and market conditions. The relevant cost calculations only provide the managing director with a secret base figure. Indeed it could be a negotiating tactic to use alternative accounting statements including overhead cost recovery.

3:5 Decision trees This popular technique can be used for tactical or strategic decision making. It is a visual aid that shows a logical structure for a decision process. Every decision is between alternative courses of action. Each course of action will have a path of events that require separate decisions. The decision tree technique is to produce a diagram of these different paths where a square represents a decision stage and circles represent expected events. Decision trees are normally laid out from left to right as shown in diagram 91 (A feature of decision trees is that they do not have any closed loops. Examples of closed loop type decision diagrams are explained in the next sub section on networks.) Once the decision maker has laid out the decision problem in this format, the expected outcome from the different decision paths can be quantified with their respective probabilities.

Example:

A company has developed a new product and is considering the following marketing alternatives

DIAGRAM 91 *SIMPLE DECISION TREE*

1A Sell direct
1B Sell through the trade
2A1 Advertise nationally
2A2 Advertise locally
2B1 Sell only through wholesalers
2B2 Sell direct to retailers

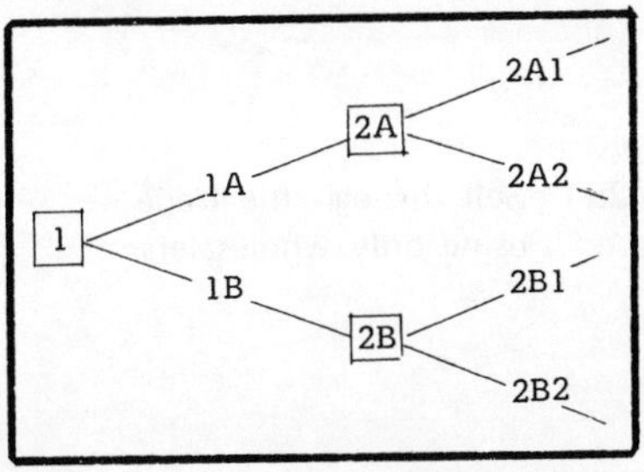

The total revenue and total costs have been calculated for each alternative with their probabilities. For example it is estimated that direct unit sales have an 80% probability of reaching 20,000 a year and a 20% probability of reaching 15,000 a year. Whereas the trade unit sales expectations are a 60% chance of 10,000 a year and 40% chance of 8,000 a year. All this detail can be entered on a tree diagram as follows:—

DIAGRAM 92 DECISION TREE WITH PROBABILITIES

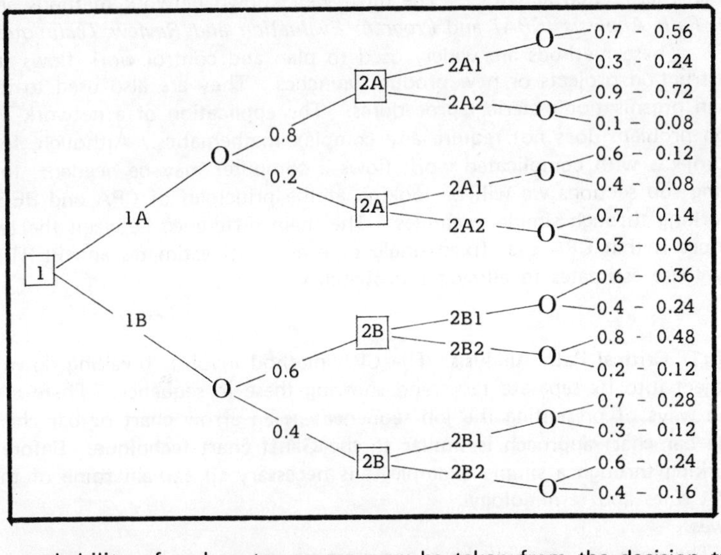

The probability of each outcome can now be taken from the decision tree and multiplied by the related expected profit.

Alternative		Probability	Expected Profit (£)	Expected Monetary Value (£)
2A1	Sell direct and advertise nationally	0.56	20,000	11,200
		0.24	24,000	5,760
		0.12	17,000	2,040
		0.08	19,000	1,520
		1.00	Total	20,520
2A2	Sell direct and advertise locally	0.72	21,000	15,120
		0.08	17,000	1,360
		0.14	18,000	2,520
		0.06	12,000	720
		1.00	Total	19,720
2B1	Sell through the trade using only wholesalers	0.36	25,000	9,000
		0.24	20,000	4,800
		0.28	15,000	4,200
		0.12	12,000	1,440
		1.00	Total	19,440
2B2	Sell through the trade direct to retailers	0.48	23,000	11,040
		0.12	19,000	2,280
		0.24	18,000	4,320
		0.16	10,000	1,600
		1.00	Total	19,240

The outcome of the analysis shows that the highest profits are expected to be earned by direct selling and advertising nationally.

3:6 Networks A network is a diagramatic illustration of complex problems involving inter-related activities. The most well known network methods are *Critical Path Analysis (CPA)* and *Program Evaluation and Review Technique (PERT).* These methods are widely used to plan and control work flows such as construction projects or new product launches. They are also used to improve an organisation's clerical procedures. The application of a network to a decision problem does not require any complex mathematics. Although, for large projects with complicated work flows a computer may be needed. In the following sub sections we will be looking at the principles of CPA and PERT and working through simple examples. The main difference between the two techniques is that CPA uses fixed single time and cost estimates and PERT can modify these estimates to allow for probability.

3:6:1 Critical Path Analysis The CPA method involves breaking down a project into its separate tasks and showing these in sequence. There are two ways of presenting the job sequence: as an arrow chart or bar chart. The bar chart approach is similar to the Gantt chart technique. Before working through a simple example it is necessary to explain some of the CPA rules and terminology.

Rules:

(i) The network can only have one starting and one finishing event.

(ii) Every activity represents a period of time and must be numbered and represented by an arrow.

(iii) The beginning or completion of each activity represents an event and must be represented by a numbered node.

Thus every CPA network will have numbered arrows and circles representing times and events. For example consider a simple invoice typing procedure:–

Events	*Activities*
1. Start	*1.* Insert multiple copy invoice set in typewriter. 10 seconds.
2. Invoice in typewriter	*2.* Type invoice in accordance with written instructions. 3 minutes.
3. Invoice typed.	*3.* Remove invoice set from typewriter. 3 seconds.
4. Invoice removed from typewriter	*4.* Top copy to be removed and inserted in window envelope. 1 minute.
5. Invoice inserted in envelope	*5.* Duplicate invoice filed. 1 minute.
6. Duplicate filed and procedure ended.	–

DIAGRAM 93 *SIMPLE NETWORK*

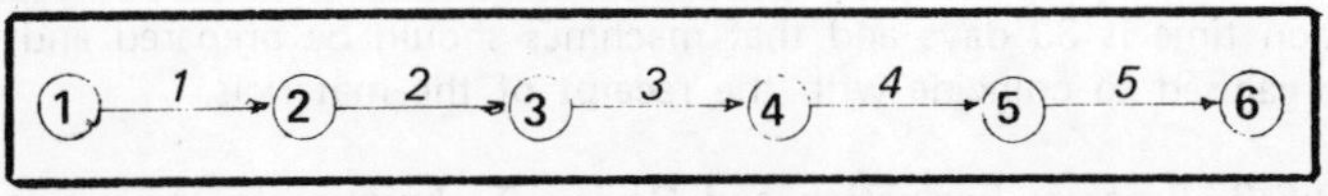

In this example the procedure was quite simple and the CPA technique was of little use but it does illustrate the application of the basic rules. Before moving on to a more complicated example we need to learn some of the terminology used with CPA.

Terminology:

(i) Critical path is the most important set of activities forming a continuous path through the network. These activities must have project priority.

(ii) Slack path represents any continuous path through the project which has a lower completion time than the critical path.

(iii) Float is the amount of spare time in an activity before the delay will affect other activities.

(iv) Dummy is the term used for an activity line showing dependence of activities and is represented by a dotted line.

With this basic knowledge we can now work through a simple CPA example.

Example

A company has just received a special order with a delivery date that must not be broken. The production planning department has produced the following work schedule and CPA diagram.

WORK SCHEDULE CONTRACT NO. 99

Event number	*Activity*	*Estimated activity time (days)*
1	Start	–
2	Plans prepared	1

3	Plans agreed with purchasing department	1
4	Plans agreed with production department	1
5	Materials ordered and received	10
6	Machines prepared	4
7	Production organised	1
8	Production completed	20
9	Goods despatched	1

DIAGRAM 94 CRITICAL PATH ANALYSIS

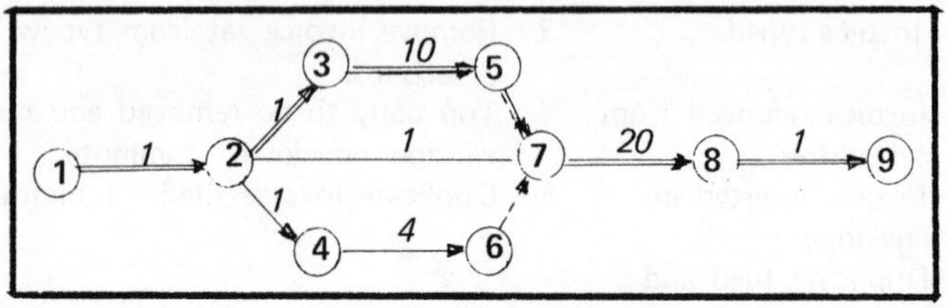

The critical path is 1, 2, 3, 5, 7, 8, 9 with a completion time of 33 days The slack paths are 2, 4, 6, 7 and 2, 7 with 6 days and 10 days float respectively. From this simplified CPA we can see that the earliest compl tion time is 33 days and that machines should be prepared and productio organised to coincide with the receipt of the materials.

3:6:2 Program Evaluation and Review Technique In the previous sub section a single time estimate was used for each activity. When estimatin times, it is often unwise to adopt such a deterministic approach. An alte native is to use the PERT probablistic model where different times can be assigned to each activity, i.e.

'o' = optimistic time, being the shortest possible time for the activity, often called the 'crash time'.
'p' = pessimistic time, being the worst anticipated time.
'l' = likely time, as would be shown in a CPA network.

The PERT/time model then combines these three time estimates by applying a beta probability distribution. Some PERT models include costs using the same probability calculation techniques and seek to identify the most cost efficient plan. The entire process can get so complicated that few managers are capable of using the technique. For our purposes we will look at a simple illustration of a PERT cost model.

Example

A marketing director has responsibility for co-ordinating all the functions of a new product launch such as production, distribution, advertising public relations and administration with an objective of maximising market impact and sales. The following PERT diagram and table is a summary of a detailed PERT example. The schedule has been divided into 12 specific event that are inter-related by 14 activities. Each activity is ascibed a normal time and cost and a crash time and cost. The cost differences between the normal times and crash times are then calculated as shown in the example.

	Normal		Crash		Cost difference per day	
Activity	*Time (days)*	*Cost (£)*	*Time (days)*	*Cost (£)*	*Increased (£)*	*Reduced (£)*
1	1	100	1	100	–	–
2	3	300	2	400	–	100
3	3	150	1	250	–	100
4	12	500	8	800	100	–
5	9	300	3	500	–	200
6	2	50	2	50	–	–
7	1	800	1	800	–	–
8	10	200	9	300	700	–
9	5	800	3	1,000		500
10	11	400	9	500	50	–
11	3	600	3	600	–	–
12	20	400	12	500	–	250
13	4	200	2	500	100	–
14	1	100	1	100	–	–

Example of cost difference calculation:–

$$\text{Activity 12} = \frac{(400 \times 20) - (500 \times 12)}{(20 - 12)} = £250 \text{ per day}$$

DIAGRAM 95 PROGRAM EVALUATION & REVIEW TECHNIQUE

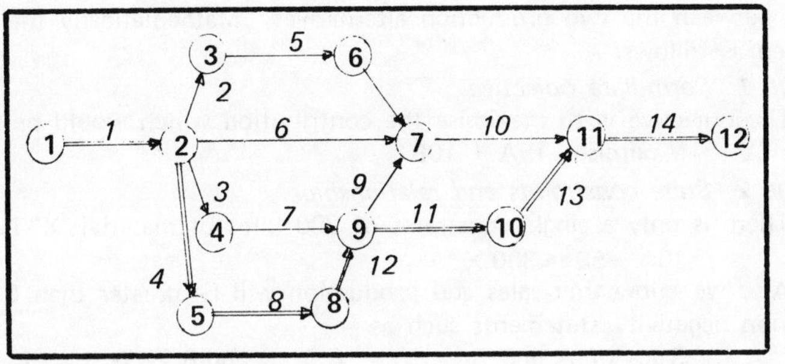

The critical path is 1, 4, 8, 12, 11, 13, 14 which has a normal completion time of 51 days and a crash time of 36 days. However it can be seen from the table that if activities 4, 8 and 13 are completed in reduced time the costs will increase due to overtime payments and other cost increases. The big cost and time saving on the critical path can be identified as activity 12 and is where management effort should be focussed. After each event of the product launch has occurred, it will be necessary to review the times and costs of subsequent planned activities to see if the critical path has altered. For instance, after event 9 the critical path may change to 9,10 & 14 instead of 11, 13 & 14. It is important to appreciate that PERT is a planning *and control* technique. Therefore the critical path needs to be under constant review throughout all the activities.

3:7 Linear programming Earlier in this chapter the principle of limiting factors (also called key factors) was explained. A technique called contribution per limiting factor was then applied to a single limiting factor problem. However, most output related problems have several limiting factors and for these types of decision the linear programming technique can be used. Linear programming can also be applied to many other kinds of business decisions such as product mix, raw material mix, machine scheduling, production scheduling, labour utilisation, warehousing and transportation. When ever there are limited resources and the relationships are estimated to be linear, then the application of this management tool will help the decision making process.

The first part of this chapter explained linear cost and revenue functions in the break even model. Similarly, the linear programming model is constructed with a set of linear equations, except in this model, we are trying to determine the optimal output after allowing for scarce resources. Consider the following problem with only one scarce resource.

Example with single limiting factor

A company produces two products; 'A' and 'B' for which the following detail is available:—

	'A'	'B'
Contribution per unit	£15	£10
Material 'X' usage per unit	10 kilo	5 kilo

The scarce resource for this company is material 'X' because only 300 kilos are available. Thus the production alternatives are to produce 30 units of 'A', 60 units of B or a mixture of 'A' and 'B'. The problem is illustrated in diagram 96, which shows the constraint of 300 kilos of 'X' as a straight line between the two production alternatives. Mathematically the problem is stated as follows:—

Stage 1 Formulate objective

The objective is to maximise the contribution which would be:

Maximise $15A + 10B$

Stage 2 State constraints and relationships

There is only a single constraint of 300 kilos of material 'X' i.e.

$10A + 5B \leqslant 300\ X$

Also we know that sales and production will be greater than 0 there will be non negativity statements such as:—

Sales of A and B $A \geqslant 0$ and $B \geqslant 0$

Production of A and B $A \geqslant 0$ and $B \geqslant 0$

Stage 3 Identify feasible alternatives

The feasible region is shown in diagram 96 below the constraint line. The purpose of identifying feasible solutions is so that calculations are not wasted on alternatives outside the feasible region.

Stage 4 Calculate optimum solution

The optimum solution is the product mix where total contribution will be maximised. With this simplified example we can make the calculations. But with complex problems mathematical techniques such as the Simplex method would be used.

Product Mix 'A'	'B'	*Calculation*	*Contribution* £
30	0	(30 x 15) + (0 x 10)	450
15	15	(15 x 15) + (15 x 10)	375
0	60	(0 x 15) + (60 x 10)	600

DIAGRAM 96

LINEAR PROGRAMMING MODEL WITH SINGLE CONSTRAINT

Product	*Material usage*
A	30 kilos
B	60 kilos

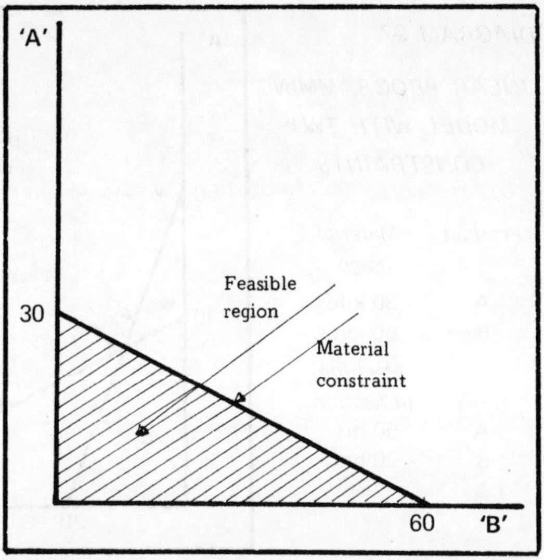

The optimum output for this problem would be 60 units of 'B'. Because the problem was a single limiting factor using simplified data the solution could easily be calculated without using linear programming. However, problems are rarely this simple. Let us now apply the technique to a problem that has two scarce resources.

Example with two limiting factors

The company in the previous example has just had a machine breakdown that is going to limit production to 1,000 machine hours. The detail is as follows:—

	'A'	'B'
Contribution per unit	£15	£10
Material 'X' usage per unit	10 kilos	5 kilos
Machine hour usage per unit	20 hours	50 hours

In this problem the optimal solution is not so clear because of the two limiting factors. We will therefore adopt the four stage approach used in the previous example.

Stage 1 Formulate objective

Maximise 15A + 10B

Stage 2 State constraints and relationships

Material 'X'	$10A + 5B \leqslant 300$
Machine hours	$20A + 50B \leqslant 1{,}000$
Sales of 'A' and 'B'	$A \geqslant O \quad B \geqslant O$
Production of 'A' and 'B'	$A \geqslant O \quad B \geqslant O$

Stage 3 Identify feasible alternatives

Refer to feasible region in diagram 97

Stage 4 Calculate optimum solution

Product mix 'A'	'B'	Calculation	Contribution £
30	0	(30 x 15) + (0 x 10)	450
25	10	(25 x 15) + (10 x 10)	475
0	20	(0 x 15) + (20 x 10)	200

DIAGRAM 97

LINEAR PROGRAMMING MODEL WITH TWO CONSTRAINTS

Product	*Material usage*
A	30 kilos
B	60 kilos
	Machine utilisation
A	50 hrs
B	20 hrs

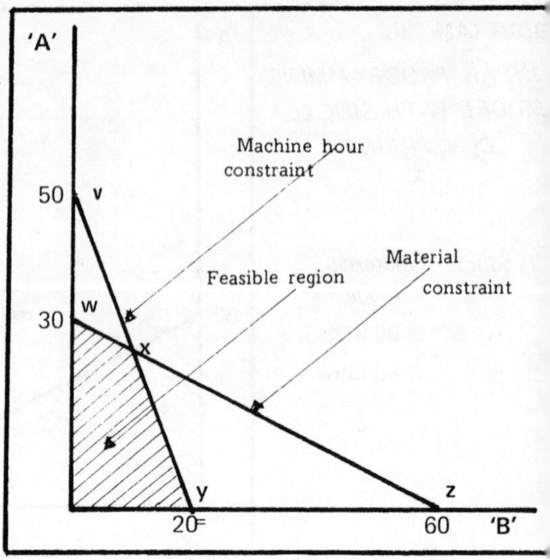

The optimum output mix for this problem would be 25 units of 'A' and 10 units of 'B' and was calculated by taking the optimum position from dia gram 97. The points to note on the diagram are:—

line vy = Machine hour constraint
line wz = Raw material constraint
point x = Optimum output mix

The diagram illustrates the principle of linear programming but in practice the optimum position would usually be calculated by mathematical techniques. For complex problems a computer would be needed and linear pro gramming software packages are readily available.

4 Pricing

In this section we are mainly concerned with pricing methods. There are two ways of approaching the problem of pricing a product or service:

(a) A market price approach where the criteria for pricing are based on marke conditions: or,

(b) A formula approach where pricing criteria are based on costs plus a percen age for profit.

Before looking at different methods of pricing let us see if we can place th fairly complex subject in some perspective. We can look at the problem from three viewpoints; accounting, economics or marketing. As accounting and mar eting tend to be practical applications of economic theory, the appropriate sta ing point would be a simplified economic model. An elementary economic theory on market price is the relationship between demand and supply. The general economic laws are as follows:—

(i) The lower the price of a commodity the greater the quantity demanded. This produces a downward sloping demand curve as shown in diagram 98

(ii) The higher the price of a commodity the greater the quantity supplied. This produces an upward sloping supply curve as shown in diagram 98.

(iii) When demand is greater than supply, prices will rise and when supply ex ceeds demand prices will fall.

(iv) At the point where demand equals supply the market will be in equilibrium where the price calls forth the quantity required by the market, as shown in diagram 98

DIAGRAM 98

ECONOMIC PRINCIPLES OF DEMAND & SUPPLY

D = Downward sloping demand curve

S = Upward sloping supply curve

E = Equilibrium where D & S are in balance

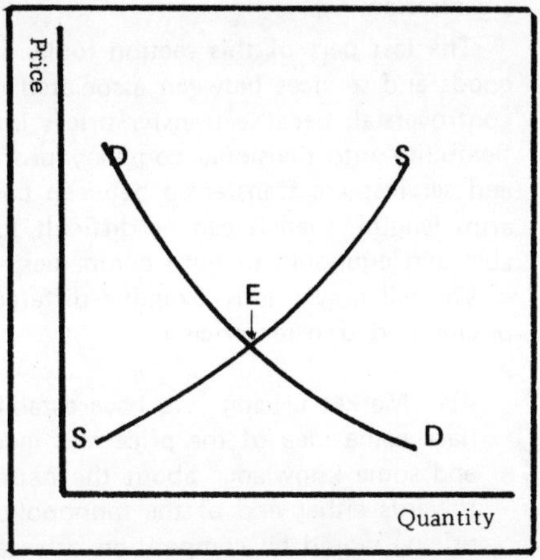

In reality, few markets ever achieve equilibrium pricing, but the basic laws of demand and supply seem to emerge in all types of market in the long run. However, there are so many interacting variables that can significantly affect demand and supply it is difficult to measure their effect for pricing decisions. Marketing departments certainly attempt to assess demand for a product or service and its responsiveness to price. But some products or services will also be responsive to income levels. These are generally referred to as price and income elasticities. For example, eating out may be fairly price elastic, (i.e. a change in price would cause a significant change in demand) and at the same time be fairly income elastic (i.e. a change in levels of income would cause a significant change in demand). Most managers that have to make pricing decisions, are intuitively aware of their products' price and income elasticities but they do not use these terms or attempt to construct a demand curve.

Having briefly considered the importance of demand and supply for pricing now let us think about the nature of the markets. Assuming the decision maker has a fair idea what the price and income elasticities are for a product or service he then has to consider the market. The nature of the market within which a firm operates will have a significant influence on pricing decisions. In a competitive market with many sellers offering identical products then the economic principles of demand and supply will determine price. In a monopolistic market where price can be controlled by the seller without the fear of actions by competitors then price can be determined from cost, volume profit calculations. Most markets however, fall between these two extremes of perfect competition and monopoly. Generally, companies have limited degrees of freedom for their pricing strategy.

In the following sub sections we will be looking at methods of pricing that are market and/or formula based. The market based methods are mostly marketing applications of economics and the formula based methods normally follow accounting principles. Although the methods are treated separately it is important that the reader is aware of their interdependence. Market pricing, in most circumstances, should be the dominant technique. But after a market price has been assessed the product or service must be costed to see if it represents the optimum use of the firm's resources. There are short run pricing strategies suc as product launches and market penetration that may not be acceptable to accountants. But in the long run, the generally accepted principle of total reven exceeding total cost cannot be ignored by even the strongest marketing organisation.

The last part of this section looks at the problem of transfer pricing for goods and services between associated companies. This subject has become controversial, because transfer prices introduce a certain amount of undesirable flexibility into divisional company profit calculations. When specialised produc and services are transferred between companies on transactions that are not 'at arms length', then it can be difficult to establish a transfer price that is accep able and equitable to both companies.

We will now briefly examine different aspects of market pricing, formula pricing and transfer pricing.

4:1 Market pricing We have established that the decision maker will usual have some idea of the price and income elasticities for the product or servic and some knowledge about the nature of the market. If the market tends towards either end of the monopoly/perfect competition scale then market pricing would be competition orientated. When a market is very competitiv for a homogeneous product such as the commodities market, then there is going rate for prices. At the other end of the scale towards oligopoly (a fe sellers) and monopdy (a single seller) a small firm will tend to be a price taker and not a price leader. Pricing will normally be related to the price leaders. However, around the middle of the perfect competition/monopoly market scale, decision makers have a lot more pricing discretion and can customer orientate their pricing, by creating brand images and developing brand loyalty. In this area of market pricing a marketing department will b attempting to alter the shape of their product's demand curve. Before cons dering some of the marketing aspects of pricing it is necessary to briefly me tion some circumstances when markets will not dominate pricing decisions. In free market economies, when governments attempt to control inflation with prices and incomes policies they distort the market. In centrally plann ed economies there usually exists a two tier pricing system; the official pric and the market price. The latter generally being referred to as the 'black market'. Lastly, legal or illegal price fixing arrangements will distort the market. Any market distortion should be known by the decision maker anc prices adjusted accordingly.

4:1:1 Parity pricing Homogeneous products with highly elastic demand curves will be priced at the going rate in the market. To price above the going rate without establishing a separate product identity will result in a substantial drop in sales. Conversely to reduce price with the objective of increasing volume sales will result in a price war, because competitors are forced to react to the pricing decision. Given these market conditions, parity pricing is the accepted pricing method

4:1:2 Price follower In some markets certain firms are capable of pulling prices upwards. For example, assume two companies dominate a market with say an aggregate market share of 70% and the remaining 30% was held by 15 other companies. The 15 companies would normally operate a kind of parity pricing that could be above, below, or the same as the market leaders. When the market leaders increased their price the followers would tend to change their prices to maintain parity. Price leadership can change. If a financially strong firm decided to pull prices down at a time when there was overcapacity in the industry then companies would probably have to follow the new price leader.

4:1:3 Promotion pricing The most common form of promotion pricing is the 'sale'. The promotion price normally represents a special price for a limited period of time that is used as a major sales tactic. An application of promotional pricing is when a company announces their price increases several months in advance so that salesman can use the existing price to help close a sale. This tactic is frequently used at trade fairs and exhibitions when a promotional price called a 'special exhibition offer' allows a discount on the existing price with an additional 'salesman's whisper' that the price will soon be increased. Retailers often use promotion pricing on specific goods to get customers into their store on the assumption that they will buy other items at the same time. This is a standard pricing tactic for supermarkets and department stores. Second hand car dealers sometimes employ an unscrupulous form of promotion pricing, often called bait pricing. The objective is to arouse demand with an advertisement for say a popular car at a low price. When potential buyers visit the showroom the car just happens to have been sold and the customer's attention is then directed towards alternative cars.

4:1:4 Psychological pricing There is a general assumption that price is directly related to quality. A low price product is often considered inferior, especially when people are giving gifts. Psychological pricing is based on this irrational aspect of consumer behaviour. A substantial amount of market research is directed towards this area where very large gross margins can be maintained. Most products that are priced on this basis have large packaging and promotion costs in relation to their manufacturing costs. Thus, the net margins do not necessarily equate with the high risk attached to this kind of pricing policy. A popular area of psychological pricing is referred to as odd pricing, where goods are priced at say £19.95 instead of £20.00. The consumer is naturally aware of the small difference, but research studies have shown that odd pricing does influence buying decisions. Conversely, even pricing may imply better quality and affect the purchase. Thus the £20.00 product may be purchased because the price indicates better quality.

4:1:5 New product pricing There is a large amount of marketing theory on this subject. The two extreme alternative pricing policies are described as market skimming and market penetration.
(a) Market skimming is when a firm that has introduced a new product charges a high price to 'cream off' the top part of the market. Gradually the price will be reduced as the scent of high profits attracts other firms into the market. To adopt a market skimming pricing policy the decision maker needs to be sure that demand is price inelastic. If there is a high market entry price or likely to be a long delay before competitors will enter the market then market skimming can be very profitable. Moreover, when competitors alter the market conditions it will not be difficult to lower the price.
(b) Penetration pricing is usually adopted by a firm introducing a new prod-

uct to a mass market where there is expected to be a high price elasticity of demand. It is intended to deter competitors from entering the market and is often referred to as 'keep out' pricing. This type of pricing policy would tend to be linked to high output and high operational gearing.

4:1:6 Multi-product pricing Many manufacturers make a range of products that are complementary or competitive with one another. For example an item may be produced as a standard or a de luxe model. Often the price of one model will affect the sales of the other. Although the basic product may not be significantly different the 'packaging' and pricing policy will clearly distinguish the products for separate markets. With products that will require replacement parts during use, a pricing policy is necessary for the product and the parts. The demand curve for the parts will usually be inelastic, therefore high gross margins are possible. Some manufacturers lock their customers into high priced service agreements because the pricing and distribution policy for parts make it difficult for anyone else to service their products. Attempts are made to measure cross elasticities (the effect on the sales of one product by a percentage change in another) for inter-related products but there are many practical measurement difficulties. Indeed optimal pricing for a multi-product manufacturer can become very complicated.

4:2 Formula pricing All formula pricing methods are cost related. The formula represents a cost calculation plus a percentage for profit or conversely a price less a specified margin to determine target cost figures. The break even model explained earlier in this chapter is often used for formula pricing.

Advocates of cost based pricing often maintain that it is 'fairer' than charging what the market will bear. Whereas, supporters of market pricing point out that prices serve a resource allocation function and in the long run, free markets will tend towards equilibrium. (Refer to diagram 98). One point that should be noted about cost plus pricing methods is that the higher a company's costs the greater their profit. Thus under strict cost plus pricing rules the cost efficient company would be less profitable than a cost inefficient company. This is why cost plus priced contracts for specialised goods and services have to be very carefully negotiated by a buyer. When products are priced on a cost based formula complications arise because of the alternative cost bases and methods that can be used. The alternatives include: absorption costing, marginal costing, replacement costs, historic costs and relevant costs. In the following sub-sections we will consider some of the formula pricing methods.

4:2:1 Variable cost pricing A product's price should always be above its variable cost so that there is some contribution towards overhead costs. Thus a cost plus formula based on variable costs would normally represent the minimum price in the short run. Variable cost plus pricing can be used when companies adopt a price discrimination policy. For example, a company with spare capacity may price its products for export markets on a variable cost formula whilst in the home market the price is calculated on a full cost basis. The calculation is quite simple and is illustrated in the following example.

Example

A marketing director is planning the sales tactics that will be used at an exhibition of the company's products and wants to allow the salesmen to have a special exhibition price to reduce stock levels of a slow moving product. The product's cost details are as follows:—

	£
Direct materials	15.00
Direct labour	30.00
Direct expense	5.00
Manufacturing overheads	20.00
General overheads	30.00
Total unit cost	100.00
Existing profit margin 20%	20.00
Selling price	£120.00

The accountant suggests that a promotional price based on a variable cost plus 20% formula should not be below £60.00, i.e. (15+30+5)x1.2.

4:2:2 Full cost pricing From the explanation of absorption costing in chapter 5 sub sections 5:1 and 5:3 you will be aware that the main problem with this pricing method is the overhead absorption rate. The importance of recovering all the costs in the long run is clear. Therefore long run pricing should allow for overheads. However, the unit overhead cost varies in relation to output. Consider the following example:

Example of output changes effect on full cost pricing

A company operating a full cost plus 10% pricing method is calculating its product price for the next accounting period. The budget figures were:—

	£
Variable costs	50,000
Fixed costs	150,000
Total costs	200,000
Expected unit output	100,000

Price calculation $\frac{£200,000}{100,000} \times 1.1 = £2.20$

During the year, however, it becomes clear that the sales forecasts were too optimistic and the revised sales estimates are for 50,000 units. This means the company will make a loss of £65,000, i.e. 50,000 x 2.2 — (150,000 + 25,000).

The profit/volume type problem was explained in the break even model sections of this chapter. In addition to the volume problem for overhead absorption rates, the reader should also be aware of the possible wide range of discretion that exists for calculating the 'full cost'. For instance, nationalised industries with monopoly powers often use full cost formula arithmetic to justify price increases. A large part of their full cost schedule relates to depreciation and more recently to replacement cost provisions. These provisions introduce a fair amount of flexibility into the pricing formula and enable politically acceptable price rises to be cost justified.

4:2:3 Cost minus pricing This kind of formula pricing calculation is normally linked to a market pricing method. For instance parity pricing or price following markets provide the decision maker with a clear idea of the price that should be set. The required margin is then deducted leaving the target total cost. At this point we will quickly clarify the difference between margins and mark ups. The formulae are:—

$$\text{Mark up} = \frac{(\text{Selling price} - \text{Cost price})}{\text{Cost price}} \%$$

$$\text{Margin} = \frac{(\text{Selling price} - \text{Cost price})}{\text{Selling price}} \%$$

From the formulae it can be seen that the cost plus methods relate to mark-ups and price minus methods to margins.

Example

A company is going to diversify into a market that has established price leaders. The pricing strategy will be to price their product at 10% below the price leader with a first year sales target of 10,000 units. The price leader's product is £10.00. The required profit margin is 20% on variable costs. The balance of variable costs are expected to be 40% direct labour, 30% direct materials and 10% direct expenses. Based on this information the following budget has been constructed:—

	£	£
Sales (10,000 x £9.00)		90,000
less variable costs:—		
Direct labour (60% of 72,000)	43,200	
Direct materials (30% of 72,000)	21,600	
Direct expense (10% of 72,000)	7,200	
		72,000
Contribution towards fixed costs (20% of 90,000)		18,000

4:2:4 Rate of return pricing Most companies have a target rate of return on capital employed. The significance of return on capital employed (ROCE is explained in *Volume 1 Financial accounting for non-accountants.)* The ROCE is a primary performance measure for most businesses and the rate of return pricing method attempts to calculate a percentage mark up that directly relates to the target ROCE. The arithmetic for this method is:

Capital turnover x target ROCE = % mark up

Where; capital turnover represents the capital employed divided by the total costs of one year's normal production.

Example

A company with an average capital employed of £500,000 and an average profit before tax, interest and extraordinary items of £50,000 wishes to increase its ROCE by 20% and has adopted a pricing strategy based on this decision. At normal production levels of 100,000 units a year the total cost function is 300,000 + 3q. With these basic figures the mark up on full cost to achieve the target ROCE is calculated as follows:—

$$\text{Target ROCE} = \frac{50,000}{500,000} \% \times 1.2 = 12\%$$

$$\text{Capital turnover} = \frac{500,000}{300,000 + (100,000 \times 3)} = .83'$$

$$\text{Mark up} = 0.83 \times 0.12 = \underline{0.0996}$$

= 10% on full cost at an output level of 100,000 units.

The mark up percentage calculated on this basis could be used in cost minus pricing calculations (refer to sub section 4:2:3). However some caution is necessary when making ROCE mark up calculations in multi-product firms. This is because some products need far more capital than others and it is often difficult to identify some fixed costs as specifically relating to a single product. The problem of separable fixed costs makes any form of full cost formula pricing difficult for multi-product firms.

4:2:5 Contract pricing For pricing purposes we can broadly divide contracts into: special contracts for the supply of an established product (often under a different brand name or for export markets) or, competitive bidding for a specific contract such as a construction project. Pricing for special contracts of existing products was explained in sub section 2:8:6. The contracts we are concerned with in this sub section are in the latter category of competitive bidding. Large orders for specialised equipment, services and/or construction work are normally priced on a formula basis because a market price cannot be determined. It is common practice for the buyer to publicly invite tenders or privately invite selected companies to submit sealed bids for a contract. At a stated date the buyer will then open the sealed bids and select the lowest price. However, the lowest priced bid will not necessarily win the contract. The supplier has to be convinced that the bidding company has the technical ability, financial resources and adequate productive capacity to meet the contract requirements. In principle, competitive bidding should result in the buyer securing a good contract price, but in practice the following factors may tend to distort the pricing process.

(i) Collusion between suppliers to raise the general price level of bids. The suppliers agree what the price level will be and which company will get the contract.
(ii) Collusion between individuals in the supplying and buying companies to ensure the contract is awarded to a specific company.
(iii) A company that does not want the contract will tend to bid a very high price.
(iv) Companies that want the contract may add a safety factor to the calculations that takes the profit margin above their normal return because of uncertainty in the cost estimates.

If true open market conditions for competitive bidding exist, then a potential supplier needs precise terms of reference for contract costing. There is then a substantial amount of work to be done for this kind of formula pricing. Material specifications and labour time estimates are difficult to compile for complex projects. Input cost inflation clauses, exchange rate clauses and project delay clauses are required. An error with this kind of pricing can cause a company to go into liquidation. Accordingly many businesses include a safety factor in their contract costing formula.

4:3 Optimal pricing In the preceeding explanations of pricing principles and methods no mention has been made of the firm's objectives. Many pricing decisions have an implied assumption of a profit maximisation objective. However, marketing directors may have quite different objectives such as; market penetration, restraining competition and maximising sales, even though they constantly refer to profits. Few marketing directors would willingly support a decision to limit sales so that profits are maximised. Yet, optimal pricing is concerned with a level of output at a specific price that will maximise the firm's profit. In sub sections 4:1 and 4:2 we have tackled the pricing problem with market and cost criteria but did not combine these two broad approaches. Attempts at optimal pricing have to combine market and cost data to derive an optimal price/output position. An important optimal pricing model is the economist's marginal analysis which identifies the optimal price/output position at the point where marginal cost equals marginal revenue. In this sub section we will first look at the principles of marginal analysis and then at possible applications.

Marginality is about the costs and revenues arising from the production and sale of one extra unit, or batch of units. Economists have developed a number of models that prove the optimum output for different markets such as monopoly and perfect competition is where marginal cost equals marginal revenue. (MC = MR). Diagram 89 in sub section 2:9:2 showed an optimum price/output position in a form of break even diagram. If these total cost and total revenue functions are shown as marginal cost and revenue functions then the same optimal point will be where MC = MR. This is shown in diagram 99.

The marginality principle illustrated in diagram 99 does have practical applications for pricing decisions. Before working through a simplified example, let us first define marginal cost and marginal revenue.

DIAGRAM 99 *PRINCIPLES OF OPTIMAL PRICING*

Marginal cost is the increase in total cost arising from an increase in the rate of production by one unit. It is calculated as follows:-

$$\frac{\text{Increase in total costs}}{\text{Increase in quantity}}$$

Marginal revenue is the change in total revenue arising from an increase in the rate of sales for a specific period. It is calculated as follows:-

$$\frac{\text{Increase in total revenue}}{\text{Increase in quantity}}$$

Where the marginal revenue and marginal cost curves intersect in the bottom diagram, is the optimal profit position. This optimal position is also illustrated in the top diagram which is a form of break even model.

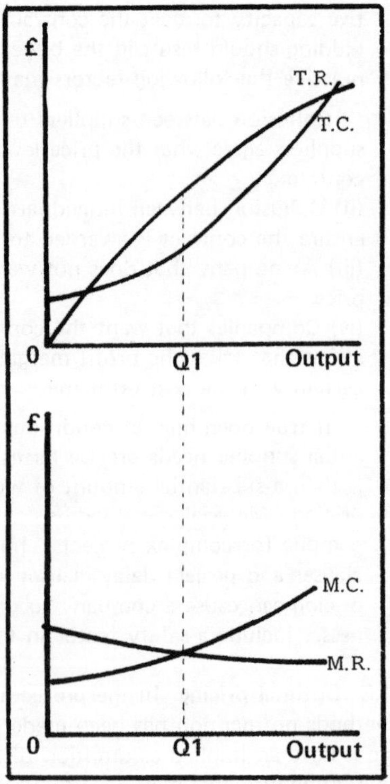

Example

A company is preparing its master budget for the next financial year and is trying to decide the optimum output level for product 'X'. The marketing department has produced the following sales estimates:–

Unit sales	Unit Revenue £	Total Revenue £	Marginal Revenue £
100	1.50	150.00	1.50
500	1.40	700.00	1.375
1,000	1.30	1,300.00	1.20
1,500	1.20	1,800.00	1.00
2,000	1.10	2,200.00	0.80
2,500	1.00	2,500.00	0.60

DIAGRAM 100 CALCULATION OF OPTIMAL PRICE

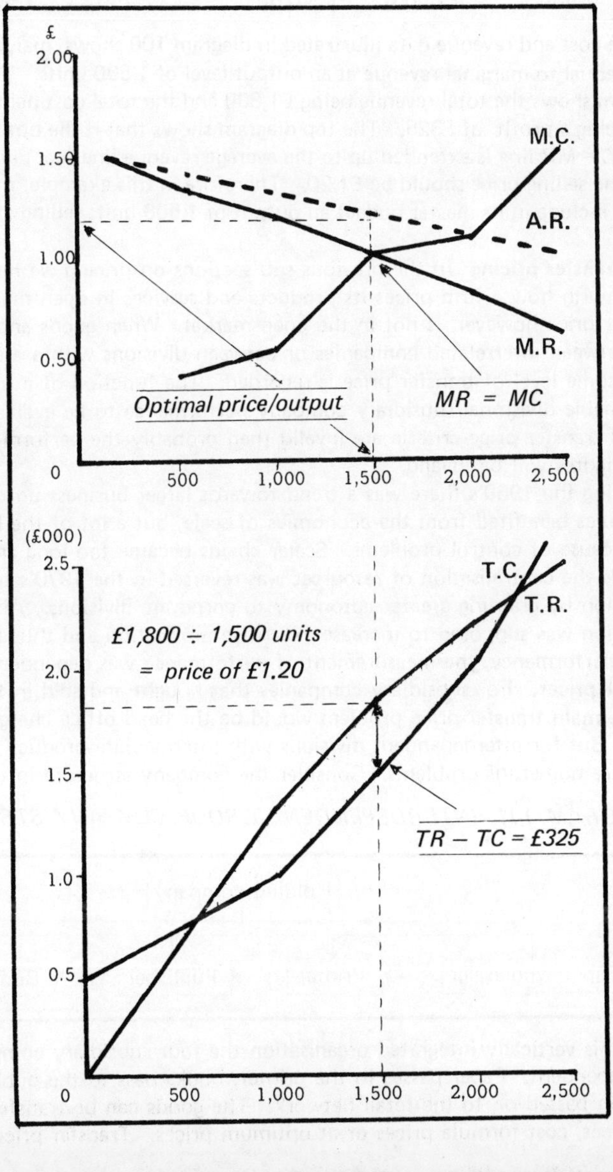

The production department produced cost estimates for batch production of 500 units. The unit variable costs were expected to change because of increased bonus and overtime payments and fixed costs due to the purchase of a machine

Unit production	Fixed costs £	Variable costs per unit £	Total costs £	Marginal costs £
100	500	0.50	550	–
500	500	0.45	725	0.44
1,000	500	0.475	975	0.50
1,500	500	0.65	1,475	1.00
2,000	500	0.75	2,000	1.05
2,500	1,500	0.50	2,750	1.50

The cost and revenue data illustrated in diagram 100 shows marginal cost as being equal to marginal revenue at an output level of 1,500 units. The bottom diagram shows the total revenue being £1,800 and the total cost being £1,475 producing a profit of £325. The top diagram shows that if the optimum output MC = MR line is extended up to the average revenue line (i.e. unit price), then the selling price should be £1.20. Therefore in this example, the company would include in its master budget an output of 1,500 units selling at £1.20 each.

4:4 Transfer pricing In the previous sub sections on pricing we have been concerned with how a firm prices its products and services in open markets. A transfer price however, is not in the open market. When goods and services pass between interrelated companies or between divisions within a single company, some level of transfer price is recorded. The function of a transfer price is to enable divisional/subsidiary company performance to be evaluated. Therefore, if transfer price criteria are invalid then probably the performance assessment figures will be invalid.

During the 1960's there was a trend towards larger business units. Many companies benefited from the economies of scale, but a lot of the benefits were lost because of control problems. Scalar chains became too long and the trend towards the centralisation of resources was reversed in the 1970's back to decentralisation by granting greater autonomy to corporate divisions. Although decentralisation was supposed to increase executive motivation and thus improve divisional performance, the measurement of performance was dependent upon valid transfer prices. For subsidiary companies that bought and sold in the open market the main transfer price problem would be the head office charge for 'services'. But for interdependent divisions with intermediate product transfers there are numerous problems. Consider the company structure in diagram 101.

DIAGRAM 101 INTERDEPENDENT GROUP COMPANY STRUCTURE

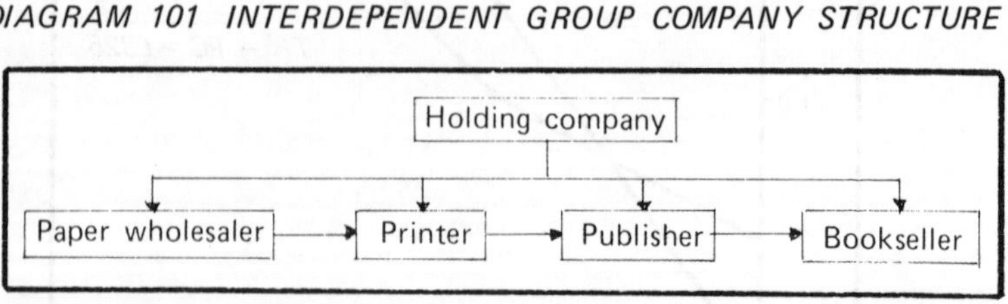

In this vertically integrated organisation the four subsidiary companies are interdependent. Paper passes to the printer, books pass to the publisher, which are then passed on to the retail network. The goods can be transferred at market prices, cost formula prices or at optimum prices. Transfer prices can be imposed by the holding company or negotiated between the transferee and transferor. Head office services such as data processing, personnel, administration and finance are often transferred to subsidiaries at a price that is not negotiable. The holding company can adjust the profit of a subsidiary through transfer prices. For example, assume the printing subsidiary had strong trade unions and high direct labour costs. For local collective bargaining it would be a useful management negotiating tactic to ensure the print subsidiary was always operating at low profits or losses, regardless of labour efficiency. Moreover, profit and/or value added productivity deals could be manipulated through transfer pricing arrangements. Misrepresentation of subsidiary accounts through transfer pricing can also occur internationally. When a holding company wishes to get cash from a foreign wholly (or majority) owned subsidiary that is in a country with politically imposed resource movement restrictions, artificial transactions and transfer prices can be useful. The governments in host countries however, are usually well aware of multinational trade transaction tactics.

It is important to mention that these illustrations of a fraudulent type of transfer pricing would be exceptional cases. Generally, companies make genuine attempts to derive a fair method of transfer pricing, so that divisional profit based performance assessment will be valid and useful. A good transfer pricing system will allow divisional managers to have sufficient autonomy for decision making and at the same time encourage goal congruence (all managers having the same objectives). The system should also enable top management to reliably assess a divisional manager's performance. The following sub sections briefly examine different ways of calculating transfer prices.

4:4:1 Market price This method is really only suitable for products when there is a near perfectly competitive market and the product has a high price elasticity. These market conditions enable a fairly reliable and accurate market price to be obtained. However, many intermediate products are highly specialised and cannot be easily valued on a market price basis because they are price inelastic and their market is imperfect. To use market price as the criteria for transfer pricing the following questions need to be asked?

(a) Are there similar products in the market?
(b) Are the market prices stable?
(c) Would there be significant selling costs if the products were sold in the open market?
(d) Could a buyer obtain discounts on the market price?

If questions like this are asked it should become clear if a market price exists that would be acceptable to the transferor and transferee companies. It is possible that the two companies can negotiate a market price in the same way as open market negotiations. When agreement could not be reached an arbitrator could be appointed by the holding company to make transfer price decisions.

If the products enable a market price based system to be used, then the transfer price criteria of autonomy, goal congruence and performance assessment may be met by this form of transfer pricing system.

4:4:2 Formula price There are two main types of formula transfer prices; full cost plus a mark up and variable cost plus a mark up. The principles are the same as explained in sub sections 4:2:1 and 4:2:2. The cost calculations can be based on actual costs or standard costs. If standards are set and controlled by the holding company, then the problem of transferring inefficiency in the price is resolved. However, if actual costs plus a mark up is used, the greater the inefficiency, the larger the transfer price giving a higher divisional profit to the transferor. When full cost plus a mark up is used the transferor can push up the transfer price and profits by 'adjusting' overhead absorption rates. (Refer to chapter 3 sub-sections 5:1 and 5:3)

Research has shown that full cost plus a percentage is a popular method of transfer pricing because it is precise *(not necessarily valid)* and acceptable to divisional managers. The result of transfer pricing on cost formula criteria can however result in sub optimisation. (The principle of sub-optimality for group company situations is that optimal performance of each subsidiary does not necessarily result in an optimal position for the group.) Moreover, cost formula pricing does not satisfy the three criteria of autonomy, goal congruence and performance assessment. The divisional manager may have autonomy in the short run but to maximise the division's profits requires cost increases not cost reductions. This is certainly not achieving goal congruence. On this basis the holding company cannot assess a subsidiary's performance on an ROCE or other profit based measurement, because of the artificial profit calculation. Accordingly, there appears to be little justification for the purported popularity of cost formula transfer pricing methods.

4:4:3 Optimal price The two previous sub sections have highlighted some of the problems of developing a valid transfer pricing system. The problems are especially difficult for interdependent companies that must accept intermediate products from one another. Often, market pricing cannot be used because there are few comparable products in the market. If cost formula pricing is used, then there is a risk of sub optimal performance and a lack of goal congruence. Let us therefore consider the possibility of an optimal transfer pricing system based on the principles of MC = MR.that were explained in sub section 4:3.

The marginal analysis model is theoretically sound but difficult to apply in practice. However, if marginal cost schedules could be calculated for each division, then a group marginal cost curve could be constructed to be set against a marginal revenue curve for an optimal output/price position. Once an optimal output position was established the transfer prices could be at the marginal costs for specified output levels. The divisional targets would then be to break even. Inefficient divisions would make losses and efficient divisions profits. This possible optimal transfer price application is illustrated in the following simplified example:—

Example

A product passes through three separate, but interdependent processes, before being sold in the open market. Each process is controlled by separate wholly owned subsidiary companies that have a high degree of autonomy. There have been continual disagreements over the transfer prices resulting in excess production and profits in some companies accompanied by high stock levels of intermediate products. The holding company wishes to try a transfer pricing system based on marginal costs and has asked the three companies to submit marginal cost schedules on a value added basis. The three detailed cost schedules have been summarised in the following table:—

Unit Output	500	1,000	1,500	2,000	2,500
MC	£	£	£	£	£
Division A	3.00	3.15	3.30	3.60	3.75
Value added MC					
Division B	1.10	1.20	1.30	1.70	1.80
Division C	2.50	2.75	3.00	3.50	3.75
Group MC	6.60	7.10	7.60	8.80	9.30

DIAGRAM 102 OPTIMAL TRANSFER PRICING MODEL

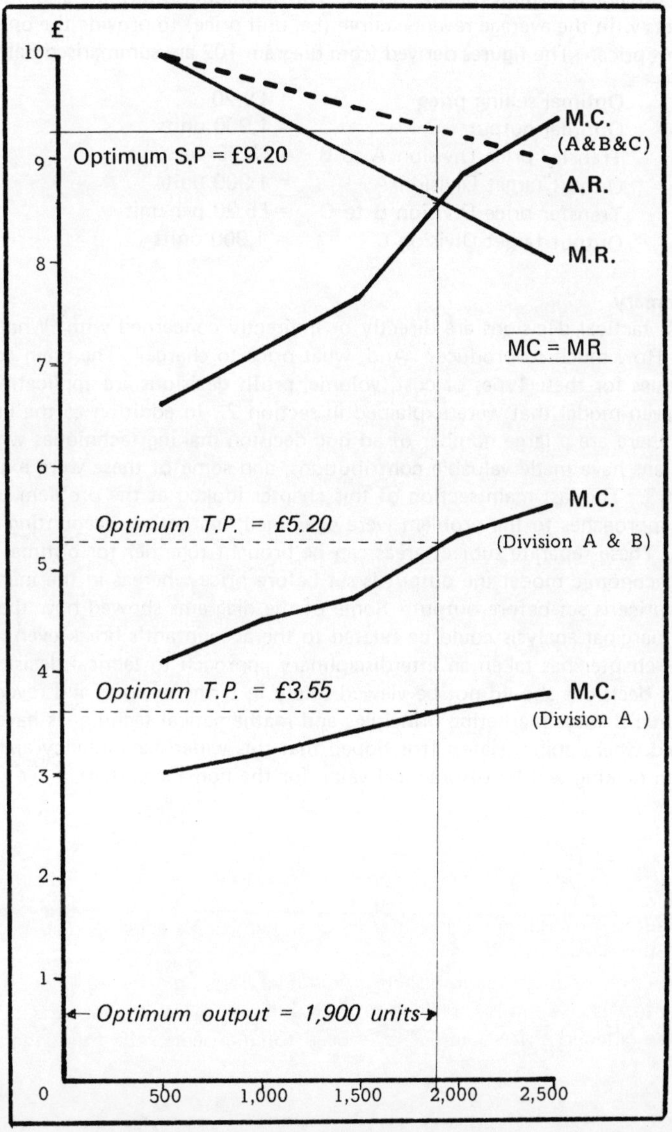

The marketing department in the holding company has estimated that sales would be:-

Unit price	*£10.00*	*£9.75*	*£9.50*	*£9.25*	*£9.00*
Unit sales	500	1,000	1,500	2,000	2,500
giving a:					
Total revenue	£5,000	£9,750	£14,250	£18,500	£22,500
Marginal revenue	£10.00	£9.50	£9.00	£8.50	£8.00

This data is illustrated on diagram 102 that shows the point where MC = MR as being at an output level of 1,900 units. This optimum output level is then intersected with the marginal cost curves of division A and division B to provide optimum transfer prices. The optimum output line also intersects with the average revenue curve (i.e. unit price) to provide the optimal unit price. The figures derived from diagram 102 are summarised below:-

Optimal selling price	= £9.20
Optimal output	= 1,900 units
Transfer price Division A to B	= £3.55 per unit
Output target Division A	= 1,900 units
Transfer price Division B to C	= £5.20 per unit
Output target Division C	= 1,900 units

5 Summary

Most tactical decisions are directly or indirectly concerned with: What to produce? How much to produce? And, what price to charge? The main accounting techniques for these types of cost, volume, profit decisions are applications of the break even model that were explained in section 2. In addition to the break even model there are a large number of ad hoc decision making techniques where mathematicians have made valuable contributions, and some of these were explained in section 3. The last main section of this chapter looked at the problem of pricing. Three approaches to the problem were examined; marketing, accounting and economics. These separate subject areas can be brought together for optimal pricing. In the economic model, the output is set before price, whereas in the marketing model price is set before output. Some of the diagrams showed how the economist's marginal analysis could be related to the accountant's break even model.

This chapter has taken an interdisciplinary approach to tactical decision making because decisions should not be viewed solely in terms of costs and revenues. Economic theory, marketing principles and mathematical techniques have been included where appropriate. It is hoped that this wider accountancy approach to decision making will be of practical value for the non-accountant.

Accountancy Quiz No.6.

1. Explain the function of the break even model and construct a break even graph. *(2, 2:1, 2:2, 2:3).*

2. Explain the following terms:–

Profit graph	*(2:4)*	Operating leverage	*(2:5)*
Margin of safety	*(2:5)*	Profit/volume ratio	*(2:6)*

3. What is meant by 'downside risk' and how can it be minimised? *(2:7, 2:7:1, 2:7:2, 2:7:3).*

4. How do limiting factors affect break even calculations? *(2:8:4, 2:9:5, 3:7).*

5. Does the linearity assumption invalidate break even calculations? *(2:9:2).*

6. Explain the difference between:–

Differential costs	*(3:1)*	Opportunity costs	*(3:3)*
Incremental costs	*(3:2)*	Relevant costs	*(3:4)*

7. What are networks and how do they help the decision maker? *(3:6:1, 3:6:2).*

8. Explain the following terms:-

Parity pricing	*(4:1:1)*	Formula pricing	*(4:2)*
Price follower	*(4:1:2)*	Variable cost pricing	*(4:2:1)*
Promotion pricing	*(4:1:3)*	Full cost pricing	*(4:2:2)*
Psychological pricing	*(4:1:4)*	Cost minus pricing	*(4:2:3)*
Multi product pricing	*(4:1:6)*	Rate of return pricing	*(4:2:4)*

9. Explain the principles of optimal pricing. *(4:3).*

10; Explain the problems of transfer pricing and describe three methods for calculating a transfer price. *(4:4), 4:4:1, 4:4:2, 4:4:3).*

7 Strategic decision making

Objective

To help the decision maker understand the principles, practice and limitations of investment appraisal techniques.

Page No.

Content

An outline of the administration and information requirements for investment appraisal.

An explanation of the investment appraisal techniques that do not take into consideration the time value of money.

A brief explanation of time value principles and the problems of deriving an appropriate discount factor.

Strategic decision making

1 Introduction

In this chapter we will be looking at the principles and problems of strategic decision making and the related decision making techniques. The forecasting and planning elements of this subject were explained in chapter 2. We can therefore now focus our attention on investment appraisal.

Investment is a widely used and abused term. Politicians, economists, trade union representatives, employers' organisations and managers often speak about the need for more investment and then draw upon statistics for support, rather than illumination. It is therefore appropriate that we begin this chapter by taking a closer look at some of the characteristics of investment.

The economist defines investment as the production of capital goods such as build ings, roads, railways and machinery. This man made factor of production is referred to as the stock of capital in a country. The stock of capital will be increased with investment expenditure. But as the capital stock wears out each year, a certain level of investment expenditure is necessary for its replacement. Therefore when looking at investment statistics it is important to be aware of the difference between gross and net investment. (Gross investment refers to total investment and net investment refers to net additions to the stock of capital). Not only are there problems for measuring the stock of capital, but equally important are the difficulties for determing the quality of capital.

Diagram 103 shows the UK industries' gross capital expenditure for the period 1970 to 1980. Supporting data is given in the accompanying table. The diagram reveals two interesting features about UK industry investment. Firstly, the shift of economic emphasis from manufacturing to service industries is quite clear from the investment trends. Secondly, the trends show that investment levels are closely related to the business cycle. The oil price induced recession in 1975 correlates with the fall in total investment. The mini boom that subsequently occurred between 1977 and 1979 correlates with the strong rise in total investment that probably represents the postponement of investment decisions during the recession. As the economy downturned in 1979 into the deep 1980/81 recession, the investment trend in manufacturing industries (except electronics) also downturned. Thus the pattern of UK industry investment expenditure has been a shift away from manufacturing towards the service industries and a positive correlation between the level of investment and the business cycle.

From an accounting viewpoint, expenditure falls into two broad categories; revenue and capital. Revenue expenditure is where the benefit is consumed during one accounting period and capital expenditure where the benefit is consumed over more than one accounting period. ***(Refer to Volume 1 Financial accounting for non-accountants).*** Even with the precision necessary for accounting, there is still an area of discretion between capital and revenue expenditure. For example, the costs of installing machinery are in principle capital expenditure and should be considered as investment. However, it may be more 'convenient' to treat some installation costs such as wages, as revenue expenditure. The strict application of the capital/revenue distinctions would also mean capitalising low cost items that are expected to last several years. As this would create a lot of paperwork, low cost investments are often written off as revenue expenditure. With large businesses the annual revenue write off could be substantial.

UK CAPITAL EXPENDITURE 1970 – 1980 (Source: British Business)

Year	*Manu-facturing industry*	*Distributive and service industries (excluding shipping)*	*Total*
		£ million at 1975 prices	
1970	4,177	3,610	7,787
1971	3,898	3,810	7,708
1972	3,370	3,987	7,356
1973	3,440	4,519	7,959
1974	3,782	4,477	8,259
1975	3,522	3,851	7,373
1976	3,341	3,929	7,270
1977	3,637	4,390	8,027
1978	3,853	4,709	8,562
1979	3,858	5,226	9,084
1980 (estimate)	3,450	5,400	8,850

DIAGRAM 103 UK CAPITAL EXPENDITURE 1970 - 1980

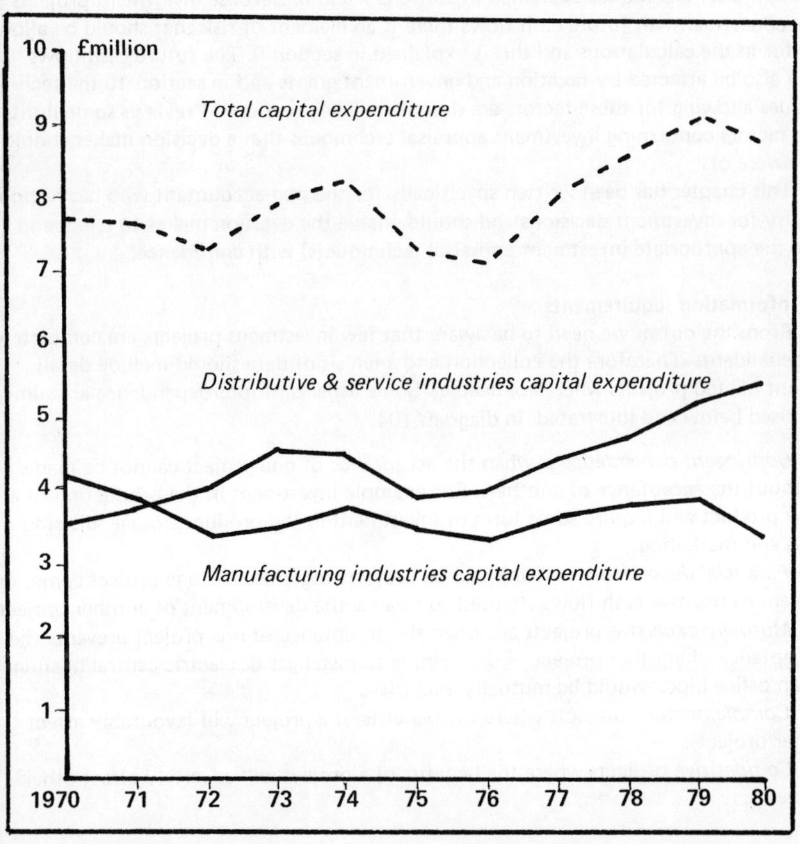

So far we have considered the difficulty of measuring and controlling investment in the economy and the capital/revenue expenditure decisions that are made by accountants. Let us now look at some of the features of an investment decision and how this chapter can help the decision maker.

Features of investment decisions

(a) The decision relates to a future time period exceeding one year.

(b) The decision often requires a commitment of substantial resources for more than one year.

(c) The decision can be difficult and costly to reverse once the resources are committed to the project.

(d) The length of the future time period and the commitment of resources require a detailed investment appraisal to be undertaken.

(e) The decision can be a corporate life risk decision. (Refer to chapter 2.)

From these investment decision features it is clear that the decision maker needs a lot of information before committing business resources. The information requirements and administration for investment decisions are explained in section 2. Once the necessary information is collected it needs to be analysed. Section 3 explains the traditional project analysis techniques. However, the traditional methods do not allow for the time value of money and sections 5 and 6 examine the problems of assessing time based values. The principles of time value are then applied in the project appraisal techniques explained in sections 7 and 8. Because investment projects are concerned with future cash flows there is an element of risk that should be allowed for in the calculations and this is explained in section 9. The future cash flows will also be affected by taxation and government grants and in section 10 the techniques allowing for these factors are described. Then section 11 reviews some limiting factors concerning investment appraisal techniques that a decision maker should be aware of.

This chapter has been written specifically for the non-accountant who has responsibility for investment decisions and should enable the decision maker to select and use the appropriate investment appraisal technique(s) with confidence.

2 Information requirements

From the outset we need to be aware that few investment projects are completely independent. Therefore the collection and analysis of data should include detail about related projects where applicable. Some aspects of interdependence are summarised below and illustrated in diagram 104.

(a) Contingent dependence is when the acceptance of one project cannot be made without the acceptance of another. For example investment in the production of a new product will require some form of investment in the product storage, distribution and marketing.

(b) Financial dependence can link several projects together. As one project comes on stream its positive cash flows are used to finance the development of another project

(c) Mutually exclusive projects are when the acceptance of one project prevents the acceptance of another project. For example to instal gas or electric central heating in an office block would be mutually exclusive.

(d) Complementary projects where the benefits of a project will favourably affect other projects.

(e) Competitive projects where the benefits of a project will adversely affect other projects.

DIAGRAM 104

INTERDEPENDENCE OF PROJECTS

This diagram illustrates different projects and their relationship in a specific accounting period. For instance the production expansion will be partly dependent on existing projects and on related planned projects.

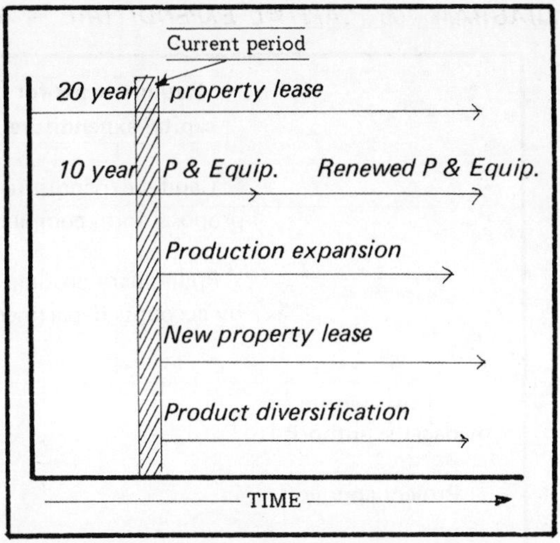

In the following sub sections on information for investment decisions we will be looking at the administrative requirements, terotechnology, estimating project lives, revenues and costs, and how all this data can be collated.

2:1 Capital expenditure administration The administration of capital expenditure comprises of three elements: management procedures, planning and control. The procedures are concerned with capital expenditure authorisation. Planning is concerned with quantifying proposed investment expenditure and control relates to the system of records that advise management of a project's progress. Let us look at each of these three elements in a little more detail.

2:1:1 Authorising capital expenditure The following chapter on budgetary control explains how planned capital and revenue expenditure is co-ordinated in the master budget. Part of the budgetary process requires managers to estimate their future capital expenditure. Based on this information a Capital Expenditure Committee (CEC) will co-ordinate the information and authorise individual/departmental capital expenditure limits. The purpose of this co-ordinated approach is to enable the finance director to estimate the company's financial requirements for the next accounting period. The CEC will normally be a sub-committee of the budget committee and should include senior representatives from finance, production and marketing, who would also be on the budget committee. (Refer to chapter 8). Once budgetary authorisation has been made each project needs to be authorised as it arises. Large capital expenditure projects would be subjected to detailed investment appraisal and then accepted/rejected by the CEC. However, there will always be a lot of small projects such as the purchase of an inexpensive machine, calculator, typewriter or special tools. For this type of capital expenditure individual managers require authorisation limits, i.e.

Individual	*Authorisation limit*	
	Each project	*Annual total*
Production manager – A. Black	1,000	10,000
Office manager – A. White	400	5,000
Marketing manager – A. Green	800	12,000

DIAGRAM 105 CAPITAL EXPENDITURE – ADMINISTRATIVE PROCEDU

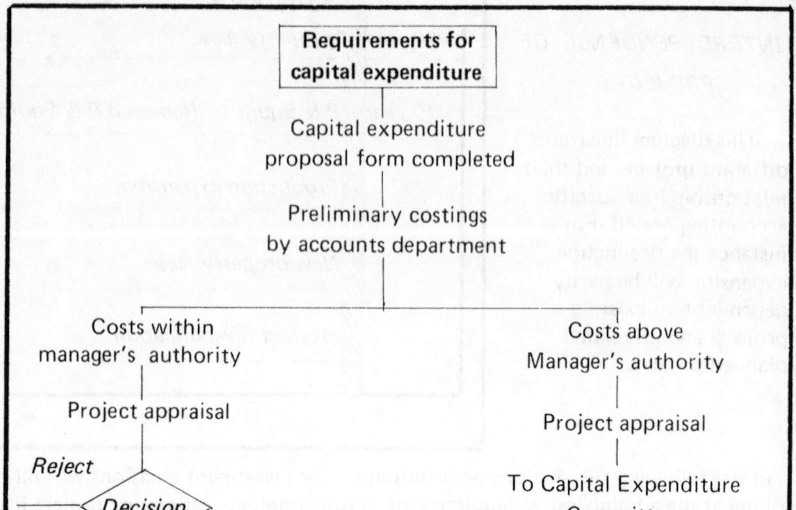

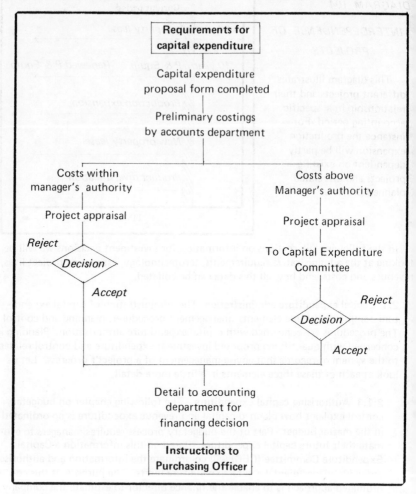

The illustration of an administrative procedure in diagram 105 shows that all specific requests for capital expenditure need to be documented. The proposal then requires a preliminary independent costing by the accounting and purchasing departments. If the total costs of a project fall within a manager's capital expenditure authority then he/she may make the project appraisal and decision. When the project costs exceed a manager's expenditure authority then it would require a full independent investment appraisal and be submitted to the CEC for a decision. Preliminary budgetary approval for a project should not exclude it from a detailed appraisal procedure. If the project is accepted then the paperwork is passed to the accounting department for the financing to be arranged and the final approval to commit resources is passed to the purchasing department. Although this may seem to be an elaborate procedure it is necessary because the authority for capital expenditure needs to be tightly controlled With this kind of control, managers are constantly reminded of the importance of capital expenditure decisions.

2:1:2 Planning capital expenditure The principles of planning and control were explained in chapter 2 and methods of quantifying plans are described in this chapter and chapter 8. The administrative aspects of capital expenditure planning are related to the design of procedures that ensure projects are properly planned. The planning procedure should recognise five aspects of investment appraisal; objectives, interdependence, relevant costs, cash flows and risk.

(i) Objectives Every investment decision should be directly related to corporate objectives. Before attempts are made to quantify and assess a project,management need to be certain that the project will help the business achieve its goals.
(ii) Interdependence. This aspect of investment appraisal was explained in Section 2. The project interdependencies need to be known and attempts made to quantify their effect.
(iii)Relevant costs. When quantifying the project only the relevant costs should be included in the analysis (Refer to chapter 6 sub-section 3:4)
(iv)Cash flows. All relevant costs should be calculated as positive or negative cash flows. This is explained in detail later in this chapter.
(v) Risk. The calculations should make allowance for risk as described in Section 9 of this chapter.

These five aspects of quantifying capital expenditure would not all be considered for relativity small projects that are within the expenditure authority of a manager. But for larger projects, a full investment appraisal covering all five aspects would be required by the C.E.C.

2:1:3 Controlling capital expenditure. Effective control depends upon quantified plans and a recording system that enables actual results to be compared with planned results. It is quite common for overspending to occur with capital expenditure, especially with public expenditure that has been appraised on political rather than economic criteria. For enterprises that cannot rely on an open public purse and require results instead of excuses, tight expenditure control is necessary during the life of the project. An incomplete project that is overspending should be re-submitted through the investment appraisal administrative procedure. Costs that have been incurred are irrelevant for the decision. The relevant costs are a comparison between alternatives such as disinvestment, continue with the project as planned or revise the project. Projects should not be allowed to overspend without a thorough re-appraisal of the investment alternative.

To control projects a reliable system of records is necessary. The administrative procedures should provide for regular, reliable and accurate cost/revenue data, that is related to the plan. Indeed, the control function of a C.E.C. is just as important as their planning function. It is absurd to fully investigate and carefully plan a project without a back-up administrative system that ensures actual project performance and expenditure can be controlled

2:2 Project life patterns One difficulty that arises when comparing projects is their different life patterns. From the outset of the investment appraisal procedure estimates have to be made of the project life and the pattern of cash flows. Consider the following types of project life patterns:-
(a) Purchase of equipment causing an initial outflow of cash followed by net cash inflows over an estimated project life as shown in diagram 106.

DIAGRAM 106 PROJECT LIFE PATTERN — PURCHASE OF EQUIPMENT

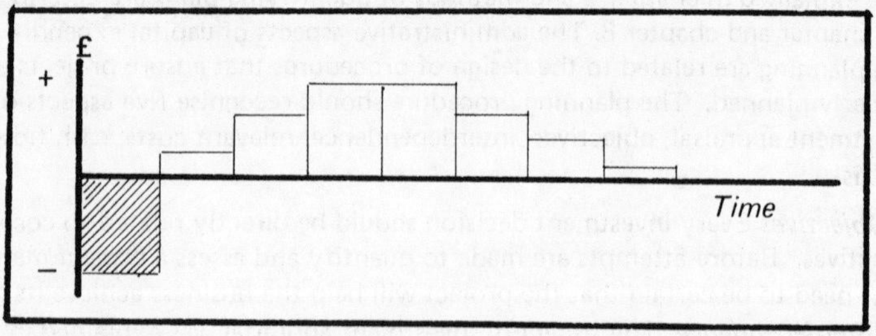

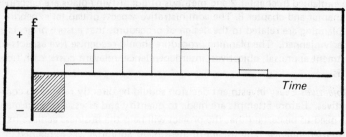

(b) Construction contract causing initian net cash outflows until stage payments are made and then a large terminal net cash inflow as shown in diagram 107.

DIAGRAM 107 PROJECT LIFE PATTERN — CONSTRUCTION CONTRACT

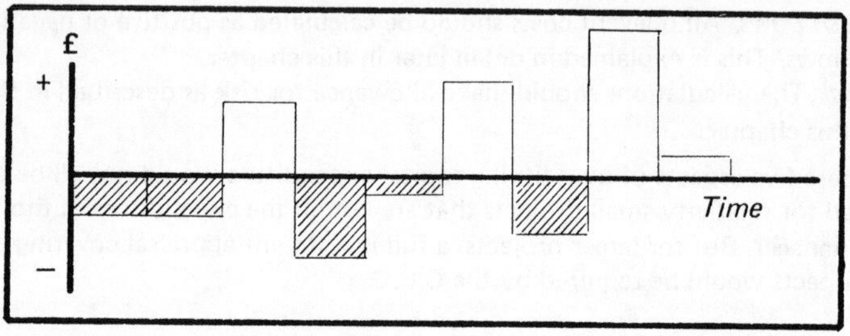

(c) Oil exploration and exploitation (assuming oil found) will have substantial initial net cash outflows over several years and then high net cash inflows over many years after the oil has come on stream, as shown in diagram 108.

DIAGRAM 108 PROJECT LIFE PATTERN — OIL EXPLORATION

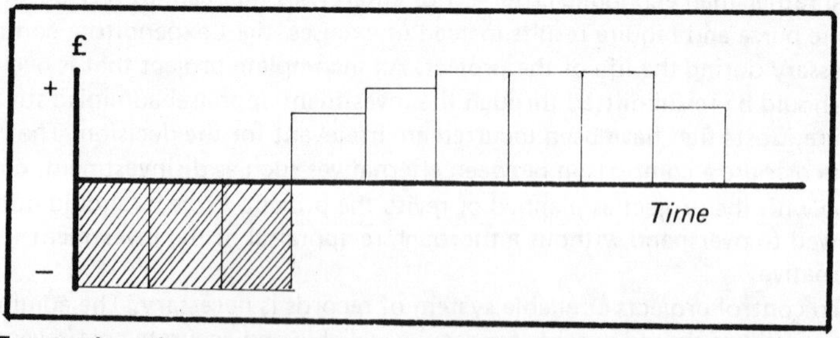

(d) Forestation of open landscape with an estimated 15 year cycle before timber can be cut, giving long net cash outflows followed by large net cash inflows as shown in diagram 109.

DIAGRAM 109 PROJECT LIFE PATTERN — FORESTATION

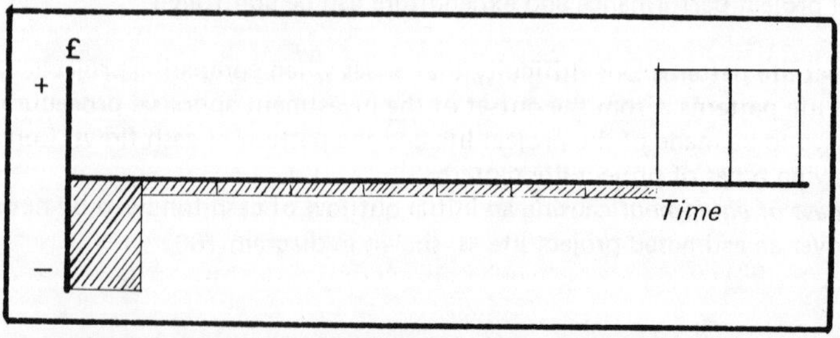

2:2;1 Time horizon How far into the future are you prepared to estimate cash flows? This is a critical question for strategic decision making. The project time horizon (sometimes called planning horizon) can substantially alter the outcome of an investment appraisal. The time horizon is effectively a cash flow cut off point where the decision maker will not allow for subsequent cash flows. Unfortunately this cut off point can be fairly subjective for some projects where there is a strong element of uncertainty. Risk can be built into the calculations as explained in Section 8 but uncertainty will probably be subjectively allowed for by adjusting project life and/or the discount factor. For many projects there is an acceptable level of certainty for estimating project lives. However, when a decision maker is handed an investment appraisal he/she should always question the analyst on the criteria for assessing the time horizon. In the examples in this chapter we will assume a high level of certainty and accurate assessment of project lives.

2:2:2 Product life cycle The product life cycle concept needs to be applied in the appraisal of product based investment projects. For example, if a company was considering diversifying into a new product range requiring capital expenditure on plant and equipment then the cash inflows would be directly related to the sales of the new product. Accordingly, marketing revenue estimates over the life of the project would be required. It is now well established that most products have a life cycle profile as illustrated in diagram 110.

DIAGRAM 110 PRODUCT LIFE CYCLE

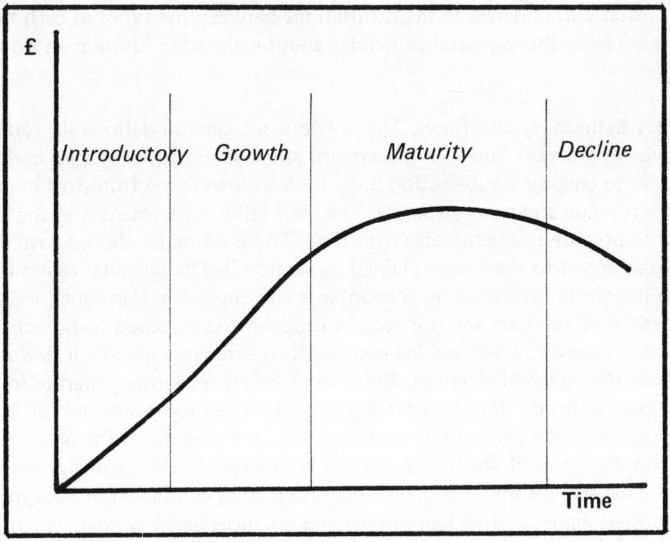

The diagram illustrates how the cash inflows from a new product will pass through four stages. The length of time in each phase would be estimated by the marketing department. Marketing refinements can be built into the estimates. For example, the decline phase can sometimes be postponed by increased advertising and product modifications. This would be a separate investment decision to be made at the appropriate time or built into the initial project appraisal calculations. The main point to note is that cash flows will only tend to be regular during the product maturity phase.

2:3 Project cash flows The accounting analysis in investment appraisal is always made in terms of cash flows and not in terms of profit. The profit calculation is total revenue minus total cost for a specific accounting period. The cost part of the calculation includes non cash items generally referred to as provisions. The provisions may be for expected bad debts, to recover the cost of assets over their expected lives (depreciation) and/or to retain funds in the business for the replace ment of assets. The cash flow approach to investment appraisal is to only include *relevant cash flows over the life of the project.* In this chapter we will be referring to six types of relevant cash flow that are defined below:-

(i) Capital cash flow refers to the initial outflow of cash used to pay for capital equipemnt and any subsequent payments of a capital nature.
(ii)Cash inflow refers to receipts of cash over the life of the project.
(iii)Cash outflow refers to revenue cash payments, i.e. any cash payments that are not capital cash flows.
(iv)Net cash inflows/outflows refers to the difference between cash inflows and cash outflows and is the most frequently used cash flow category. It represents the differential cash flow for each period, such as the sales revenue less relevant costs of production, sales and administration.
(v) Net cash flow refers to the total net cash inflows minus the capital cash inflows
(vi)Discounted cash flow refers to the net cash flows that have been adjusted for the time value of money.

In some sub-sections later in this chapter these cash flows will get a little complicated as they are adjusted for risk and the impact of taxation. It is therefore important that you understand the distinctions between the types of cash flow. Let us now consider these general principles about estimating future cash flows.

2:3:1 Estimating cash flows. The previous sub-section defined six types of cash flow. All the cash flows for investment appraisal must be relevant cash flows. (Refer to chapter 6 sub-section 3:4). Cash inflows come from two main sources: sales revenue and asset disposals. The marketing department is in the best posit ion to provide sales estimates over time. These estimates should have probabilities attached to them as explained in section 9. The terminal values of assets can be jointly estimated by accountants and engineers. Cash outflows should be easier to estimate and not require probabilities attached to expected outcomes However, when making cash outflow estimates specific inflationary trends (Not general inflation. Refer to inflation accounting chapter in *Volume 1 Financial accounting for non-accountants)* need to be allowed for. If some input costs for a project represent a substantial amount of the project costs then some form of sensitivity analysis is necessary. (Refer to sub-section 9:3) For example, assume a project's operating costs comprised of 80% specially imported material, 15% labour cost and 5% miscellaneous cost. The project's net cash inflows would be very sensitive to changes in exchange rates and material cost changes due to economic and/or political reasons. Accordingly when estimating cash outflows, potential project sensitivities need to be identified. The same principle also applies to cash inflows if there is a strong element of demand uncertainty and price inelasticity. The principles of project costing are discussed in the following sub-section on terotechnology and life cycle costing

2:3:2 Terotechnology. This is a cost/engineering concept that was developed in the 1960's, The prefix *tero* is taken from the Greek *terco* meaning *to care for.* This is an application of *life cycle costing* that has been developed in the U.S.A. In the U.K. a government department set up a terotechnology committee in 1970, mainly to improve the attitudes towards design for reduced maintenance costs. Indeed, it was the maintenance aspect of assets where accountants and engineers were supposed to work together at the design stage. The terotechnology principle is therefore highly relevant for investment appraisal because maintenance costs over the life of a project can be very substantial. The cost of lost production from machinery breakdowns can be so high that maintenance costs may not be questioned. Therefore the time for questioning maintenance costs is *before* the asset is acquired. It is at this stage that accountants and engineers can work together in investment appraisal.

The Department of Industry Committee for Terotechnology defines the scope of the subject as:-

> A combination of management, financial, engineering and other practices applied to physical assets in pursuit of economic life-cycle costs. Its practice is concerned with the specification and design for reliability and maintainability of plant, machinery, equipment, buildings and structures, with their installation, commissioning, maintenance and replacement, and with feedback of information on design, performance and costs.

This definition makes terotechnology broader than life cycle costing because it covers all related disciplines and is not simply a costing technique. For the purposes of this chapter the scope is too broad and we will just concentrate on some practical aspects of life cycle costing for estimating cash flows (Further detail about this subject can be obtained from The National Terotechnology Centre. Address and telephone number in appendix 3).

2:3:3 Life cycle costing. The life cycle of any project will of course depend upon its nature and the company's circumstances. The life cycle can however be broken down into the following seven stages:

(i) *Specification stage.* The resources will be drawn up to meet the project's objectives. The specifications do not necessarily have to be precise. Indeed loose specifications enable the designer, engineer, purchasing officer some flexibility in the choice of technology and techniques.

(ii) *Design stage.* This is where the principles of terotechnology should be applied. Accountants and engineers should direct their attention toward 'economic life cycle costs'. The costs of reliability/maintenence are assessed at this stage.

(iii) *Make or buy stage.* At this point the company makes a definite committment of resources. Also at this stage there are related decisions such as how to finance the acquisition or whether to lease or buy?

(iv) *Installation stage.* These costs can sometimes be surprisingly high. For example, the dust-free conditions, anti-static floor and special power arrangements for computer hardware can be very expensive.

(v) *Start up stage.* The time lag between equipment being installed and coming 'on stream' can be long and expensive. With a computer installation for example, there is file loading, staff training and getting the software right. This is often more expensive than the cost of the hardware.

(vi) *Operating stage.* This stage has two main cost elements, production and maintenance. For some projects there may be requirements for additional costs.

(vii) *Terminal costs.* At the end of a project there are costs associated with

equipment disposal and where applicable, redundancy payments. These costs are often netted off against capital revenues arising from the sale of assets.

All of these seven costing stages require costing estimates in terms of releva cash flows for investment appraisal.

2:3:4 Cost minimisation. Many projects do not result in separable identifiable positive cash inflows. For example, new equipment for a small part of a large production process, or capital purchases that are purported to improve the efficiency of administration and/or management. If the decision has been mad to commit resources to capital purchases for reasons other than optimal use o these resources, then an investment appraisal can still be made on cost minimi ation criteria. Often the decision will not need net cash flows to be estimated because the alternatives are limited and the ramifications arising from the deci ion are insignificant. However for investment decisions that are significant the alternatives can be assessed in net cash flow terms and investment appraisal techniques applied to find the least cost alternative. A common problem that can be evaluated on this basis is whether to lease or buy equipment. The important point to note about cost minimisation appraisal is that it does not que tion the decision to commit resources, it simply finds the cheapest alternative.

3. Preliminary investment appraisal techniques.

The administrative system outlined in the previous sub-sections was based on an assumption that all employees would be encouraged to submit ideas, proposals, etc. that may result in investment decisions being taken. With an active ideas system ever proposal should be passed through an appraisal system and be seen to pass through the system. If a system is likely to produce a lot of proposals then some kind of preliminary appraisal is needed as a filter device. The filter needs a series of investment criteria that allow (or reject) a proposal to pass on to the next stage. The advanced stages of investment appraisal would be in depth surveys, risk analysis and calculations for the time value of money. The results of these advanced appraisal techniques would then be considered by a Capital Expenditure Committee for the final decisio to commit resources to a project.

In this section we are going to look at some preliminary investment appraisal tec niques that can act as a filter for investment proposals. In general these techniques should only be used as filtering devices. The final decision on any substantial investment proposal should have taken into consideration risk and the time value of mone The principles and techniques for risk and time value are explained in sections 5, 6 7, 8 and 9.

3:1 Urgency. An early stage of any project appraisal is to determine the level of urgency for the investment. Some kind of urgency ranking can be established by a company as an initial screening for investment proposals. The projects with hig urgency ranking should then be passed through the necessary administrative stage as priority projects. A possible ranking could be:

Urgency ranking	*Description*
1	Absolutely essential investment. Immediate action required. *Example* - Machine broken beyond repair. production halted, replacement machine available ex-stock
2	Essential investment. Urgent action required. *Exampl* Machine continually breaking down and causing production delays.

3 Useful investment. Action required to improve ion efficiency. *Example* - New machine availa will increase output and reduce unit costs. Ex.. machinery ageing but still reliable.

4 Desirable investment. Discussion required on need to purchase asset. *Example* - Purchasing a computer with associated software for administration and finance.

This kind of project appraisal is not concerned with profitability, it is simply an urgency rating to ensure a priority 1 project does not have to stand in an administrative queue.

3:2 Net cash flow (NCF) This is a very basic project calculation that should be made for every investment proposal. It is simply total revenue minus total cost in relevant cash flow terms (Refer to sub section 2:3) When cash flows are being compared on a cost minimisation basis then a differential costing approach (Refer to chapter 6 sub-section 3:1) can be used. Consider the following summary of investment proposals and their cash flows:-

Investment description	*Urgency*	*Cash inflow* £	*Cash outflow* £	*NCF* £
Purchase machine A	2	20,000	17,000	3,000
Purchase machine D	3	70,000	60,000	10,000
Purchase equipment	4	22,000	29,000	(7,000)

The NCF figures are only a preliminary guide for the decision maker and should not be used for project making. Projects with a negative NCF would only be considered under priority conditions of urgency. In the above example the first two projects would require further analysis. But the third project that has a negative rating would be rejected.

Thus the NCF and urgency appraisal techniques can be used for preliminary screening of investment proposals and ensure that time and effort is not wasted on full evaluation of invalid project proposals.

3:3 Payback This is a simple and useful technique that asks one basic question: How quickly do I get my money back? For example if £4,000 spent now would yield £2,000 p.a. for four years the payback period is two years. The formula for calculating the payback period is:-

$$\frac{\text{Net Cash Outlay}}{\text{Average Net Cash Receipts Per Annum}} = \text{Payback period}$$

This formula is satisfactory for regular cash flows such as the above example :-

$$\frac{\text{Net cash outlay}}{\text{Average net cash receipts Per Annum}} \quad \frac{£4{,}000}{£2{,}000} = 2 \text{ year payback}$$

However, for irregular cash flows it is better to just add up the net cash flows per annum until they equal the initial cash outflow i.e.

		£
Initial Cash Outflow		(10,000)
Net Cash Inflows	Year 1	6,000
	Year 2	3,000
	Year 3	1,000 = *Payback in three years*

Year 4	1,000
Year 5	500
Year 6	500

The payback in this example is three years. If the formula method was used it would be :-

$$\frac{10,000}{(12,000 \div 6)} = 5 \text{ year payback}$$

There are two weaknesses of the payback method. One big disadvantage with the payback method is that it ignores cash flows after the payback period. In the following example two projects are compared using the payback method.

	Project 'A' £	Project 'B' £
Initial cash outflow	(10,000)	(10,000)
Net cash inflow Year 1	6,000	2,000
Year 2	3,000	2,000
Year 3	1,000	2,000
Year 4	1,000	2,000
Year 5	1,000	2,000
Year 6	-	2,000
Year 7	-	2,000
Year 8	-	2,000
Year 9	-	2,000
Year 10	-	2,000
Payback	3 years	5 years

Using payback as the decision criteria project 'A' would be selected but on a net cash flow basis project 'B' is better because it has £20,000 compared with £12,000 for project 'A'.

The second weakness is that the method ignores the timing of cash flows. The following example shows how two projects with the same payback of three years have different cash flows

	Project Y £	Project Z £
Cash outflows	(6,000)	(6,000)
Year 1	1,000	3,000
Year 2	2,000	2,000
Year 3	3,000	1,000
Year 4	2,000	2,000
Year 5	2,000	2,000
Net cash flows	4,000	4,000

Using the payback or net cash flow criteria there is no difference between project Y and Z. They both have a three year payback and £4,000 net cash flows. However, project Z would be preferable because of the cash flow timing in the first three years.

Providing a user of the payback technique is aware of the weaknesses of comparing projects using payback criteria it is still a very useful calculation to make for the following reasons:-

a) The longer the project the greater the risk of error in estimating cash flows therefore a cut off payback period is a useful criteria.

b) High technology projects should have a payback limit because of the danger of rapid technological obsolescence.

c) A company with cash flow problem will probably want to have quick payback projects.

d) Businesses operating in markets where consumer preference changes quickly such as ladies' fashions, need a quick payback.

Accordingly, payback can be considered as a useful complementary investment appraisal technique but should not be the sole criteria for evaluating projects. Under no circumstances should project ranking occur solely on the payback method.

3:4 Average rate of return The popularity of this investment appraisal method is probably due to its simplicity and apparent relevance. Most people are aware of rates of return. For example the rate of return on a deposit account or building society account is easily understood. Similarily most managers understand the principles of return on capital employed. Therefore, it is easy for this awareness to be applied to investment projects. Consider diagram 111 and its related table that lists the rates of return for U.K. industry and commerce from 1960 to 1969.

RATES OF RETURN AT CURRENT REPLACEMENT COST FOR INDUSTRIAL COMMERCIAL AND MANUFACTURING COMPANIES

	All industrial and commercial companies		*Industrial and commercial companies excluding North Sea oil*		*Manufacturing companies*	
	%Gross(a)	*%Net(b)*	*%Gross(a)*	*%Net(b)*	*%Gross(a)*	*%Net(b)*
1960	11.2	13.0	11.2	13.0	11.1	13.1
1961	10.1	11.2	10.1	11.2	9.7	10.9
1962	9.5	10.3	9.5	10.3	9.0	9.8
1963	10.3	11.3	10.3	11.3	9.5	10.5
1964	10.7	11.8	10.7	11.8	10.0	11.3
1965	10.3	11.2	10.3	11.2	9.5	10.5
1966	9.4	9.9	9.4	10.0	8.6	9.2
1967	9.4	9.9	9.5	10.0	8.6	9.2
1968	9.5	10.0	9.6	10.1	8.7	9.2
1969	9.4	9.7	9.4	9.8	8.5	9.0
1970	8.6	8.6	8.6	8.6	7.5	7.5
1971	8.7	8.7	8.8	8.8	7.6	7.6
1972	9.0	9.2	9.0	9.2	7.9	8.1
1973	8.7	8.8	8.7	8.9	7.7	8.0
1974	5.9	5.0	6.0	5.1	4.4	3.3
1975	6.1	4.9	6.2	5.3	4.9	3.9
1976	6.4	5.3	6.3	5.4	5.0	4.1
1977	7.5	6.7	6.9	6.2	6.1	5.6
1978	7.6	6.8	7.0	6.3	6.2	5.8
1979	7.2	6.1	5.9	4.7	5.0	4.1

Basis of estimates:

Profits	*Capital employed*
(a) Gross operating surplus on U.K. operations, i.e. gross trading profits less stock appreciation plus rent received.	Gross capital stock of fixed assets (excluding land) at current replacement cost plus book value of stocks, in U.K.
(b) Net operating surplus on U.K. operations, i.e. gross operating surplus less capital consumption at current replacement cost.	Net capital stock of fixed assets (excluding land) at current replacement cost plus book value of stocks in U.K.

(Source: Department of Trade & Industry)

DIAGRAM 111 RATES OF RETURN ON CAPITAL 1960 - 1979

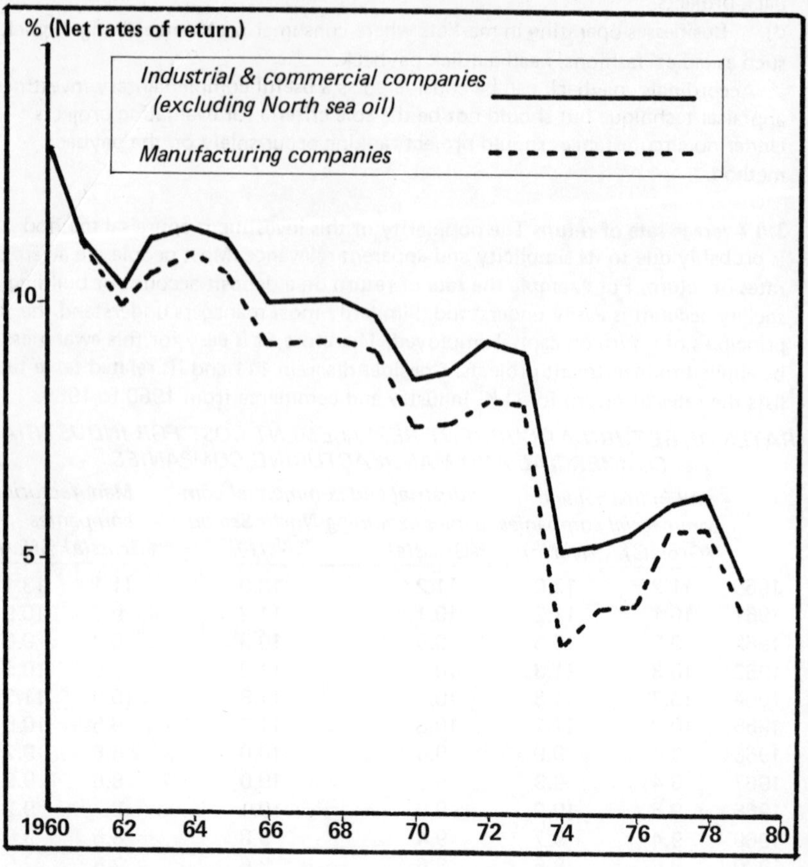

A company director in an industry with an R.O.C.E. of say 10% could apply the knowledge of the industry and/or the company R.O.C.E. as the sole criteria for investment decisions, by requiring all projects to have an annual return greater than say 15%.

There are a number of ways of calculating the annual return on an investment. The easiest is as follows'-

$$\frac{\text{Total cash inflows} - \text{Total cash outflows}}{\text{Total cash outflow x number of years}} \times 100$$

Applying this formula to the two project examples in the payback method section is as follows:-

Project A

$$\frac{(12{,}000 - 10{,}000) \times 100}{10{,}000 \times 5} = \text{4\% Annual Rate of Return}$$

Project B

$$\frac{(20{,}000 - 10{,}000) \times 100}{10{,}000 \times 10} = \text{10\% Annual Rate of Return}$$

Using the accounting rate of return as the decision criteria Project 'B' would be selected whereas using the payback method, Project 'A' would be chosen. Although the accounting rate of return allows for all cash flows its main disadvantage is it does not allow for the time value of money. Consider the following example:-

		Project 'X'	Project 'Y'
Initial cash outflow		(10,000)	(10,000)
Net cash inflows	Year 1	6,000	1,000
	Year 2	3,000	1,000
	Year 3	1,000	1,000
	Year 4	1,000	3,000
	Year 5	1,000	6,000

Calculations $\dfrac{(12{,}000 - 10{,}000)}{10{,}000 \times 5}$ $\dfrac{\text{Accounting rate of Return}}{}$ = $\dfrac{4\%}{}$

Both projects have the same accounting rate of return but Project 'X' is the better project because the high net cash inflows are in the first two years. One further point to note is that the annual rate of return method is based on relevant cash flows not, before tax profits. Accordingly, an annual rate of return cut off point for project acceptance should be above the company's R.O.C.E. to ensure that the project will generate sufficient net cash flows towards paying the general overheads and maintaining the company's R.O.C.E. at the required level.

4 Complementary investment appraisal techniques

There is no single appraisal technique that is suitable for all kinds of investment proposals. Each technique tends to examine a project from a different viewpoint. However, most appraisal techniques are based on the principle that cash inflows should exceed cash outflows over the life of the project. In this section we are going to briefly look at some appraisal techniques that do not readily fit into this broad cash flow comparison category. Some of these complementary appraisal techniques such as decision trees, networks, linear programming and simulation have been explained in the tactical decision making chapter. The following subsections explain: feasibility studies, cost benefit analysis and cost effectiveness analysis.

4:1 Feasibility study This type of appraisal is quite common for projects such as computer installations. Strictly speaking, a feasibility study is undertaken when there is some doubt if the objective of a project can be met within specified financial and time constraints. So called feasibility studies are often limited to the choice of equipment, because the decision to buy has already been made. Accordingly, the starting point of any feasibility study is to seek answers to the following questions:—

(i) Why is this project being proposed?
(ii) What objectives have been set for the investment proposal?
(iii) What are the financial, legal, social, organisational, time and other constraints affecting the project?
(iv) Can the objectives be achieved within the relevant set of constraints?

This type of feasibility study questions the foundations of an investment proposal. For instance, a feasibility study for a computer installation would first examine the need for electronic data processing. If a need was identified, then alternatives such as the use of a computer bureaux or time sharing arrange ments would be considered. The study should not simply be a comparison of hardware and software alternatives. Arising out of the feasibility study for a computer installation would be a specification of the system's requirements. This specification would be part of the 'Statement of Requirements' that need to be drawn up if a computer is to be purchased. Consider the following outlir 'Statement of Requirements' that would be sent to potential suppliers:—

Outline Statement of Requirements

(i) Description of the company and its trading activities.
(ii) Existing equipment.
(iii) Data processing requirements.
(iv) Special management information requirements.
(v) Hardware requirements.
(vi) Software requirements.
(vii) Delivery dates and completion times.

A substantial feasibility study would include the collection of data from po ential suppliers regarding price, performance, delivery and after sales service. The following listing gives an indication of the tremendous amount of detail that a potential supplier of a computer installation should provide:—

The short listed suppliers should be asked to include specifically in their pro osals the following points:—

1. Proposed Configuration

a. The equipment units proposed.
b. The operating characteristics and specification of each unit.
c. Optional units and characteristics.
d. Any alternative configurations.
e. The expansibility of the system (e.g. maximum memory size compared to the size proposed: maximum number of terminals that can be supported co pared to number proposed, etc.)
f. Special requirements as to siting of the machine.

2. Cost of Proposed Configuration

a. Rental/purchase price per unit.
b. Constraints of rental proposed (e.g. single-shift working).
c. Additional costs for operating outside constraints (e.g. two shift working).
d. Maintenance contract for units purchased, (year-by-year over a minimum 5-year period).
e. Rental or purchase price of Operating Software.

3. Software Availability

a. Software proposed, e.g. applications, packages, specially commissioned soft-ware, etc.
b. Languages available for the machine and the version of each.
c. Software history — e.g. how long have the packages been in use: are the language compilers in full operation.
d. Costs of software (rental/purchase, etc.)
e. Maintenance costs of software (over a five-year period).

4. Systems Support

a. How much systems analysis/design is included in the price?

b. What programming is included?
c. What education/training is included?
d. What maintenance is included?
e. What are the extra costs for provision of more of the above services?
f. What maintenance guarantee is given? (e.g. that an engineer will service a hardware fault within x hours of its report).
g. What penalties will be accepted for failure to meet the guarantee?
h. What back-up is available in the event of major hardware failure?
i. What support is provided for the software? (e.g. costs of tailoring packages, amending software, etc.)
j. Are package programs provided in a form which allows user amendment?

5. Terms

a. Does the supplier accept the proposed delivery date or what is their alternative?
b. Payment terms.
c. Penalty clauses accepted.
d. Lease/rental/purchase and other options.
e. Amount of test time provided free of charge.
f. Length of guaranteed maintenance (Some suppliers have come into dispute due to abrogating service agreements within 12 months of selling the system).

6. Systems Performances and Specified Applications

The questions here will be specific to the applications for which proposals were required and to the type of service being sought. These questions assume an installation intending to rely wholly upon pre-written packages. For each application:—

a. Changes in design if different from that specified in requirements.
b. Size of configuration required.
c. Liveware required.
d. Timings — how long does the application take to run under conditions of maximum, minimum and average volumes.
e. Changes in timings (or liveware requirements) if optional equipment were used
f. Costs of running the application - including costs of change-over or implementation
g. How the system will interface with other applications and existing systems
h. List of existing users of the application package

The supplier should also be required to propose a timetable for implementation of the set of applications

7. Çustomer History

a. List of customers already serviced by supplier
b. Experience in applications area/s
c. History of the company (including annual accounts where possible)

The evaluation of all this data falls into two categories:-

a. Evaluation of the supplier company
b. Evaluation of the proposal itself

The installation of a computer system supplied by a particular company places the user very much in the hands of that company. Errors made in the supply and installation of adequate systems can be recovered from, but the time,cost and disruption of doing so can far exceed those associated with the original installation. It is therefore important to be certain of the on-going reliability of a proposed supplier

With regard to the evaluation of the proposal,the data needs to be analysed in a wa that enables suppliers' proposals to be compared. A common approach is to list the important factors and allocate points for each proposal.The supplier with the high rating is then selected.

4:2 Cost benefit analysis (CBA) This technique can be applied to *any* investment proposal, including non-profit making projects such as the provision of say, a work canteen or a social/sports club for employees. A CBA of an investment proposal attempts to place values on all the possible benefits arising from the project and th compare the total value with the total cost. This includes the costs and benefits to third parties. The comparison is sometimes expressed in the form of a cost/benefit ratio :-

$$\frac{\text{Estimated total value of all benefits arising from the project}}{\text{Total costs of the project}}$$

On a simple arithmetic basis, projects with a CB ratio above 1 would be acceptable. However, placing a value on the benefits of some projects is so arbitrary, that the calculation would have little meaning.

The stages of a cost benefit analysis are:-

Stage 1 Assess the life of the project and list all possible benefits (including the ber fits to third parties) for each year.
Stage 2 Estimate values for each benefit and derive a total value of benefits for eac year of the project's life.
Stage 3 Estimate all possible costs that would be avoided (including the costs of th parties) if the project was not undertaken for each year of the project's life.
Stage 4 Deduct costs from benefits for each year
Stage 5 Analyse results on a DCF basis (refer to section 7) and/or as a CB ratio.

A decision maker needs to exercise great caution with CBA to ensure that the computations have been honestly made to evaluate an investment proposal and not to support a vested interest.

4:3 Cost effectiveness analysis (CEA) This appraisal technique was developed in the USA and subsequently used to assess defence projects. The analysis is aimed at:

(a) Finding the cheapest way of achieving a defined objective: and
(b) Getting the best value from a stated level of expenditure.

The main difference between CEA and CBA is that CEA is concerned with effectiv ness and CBA with benefit. A CEA appraisal does not necessarily have to measure effectiveness in terms of value, whereas CBA always converts benefits into values. The stages, in a cost effective analysis would be:-

Stage 1 Define the objective(s) of the project in terms that enable the effectiveness of a proposal to be assessed
Stage 2 List all possible methods of achieving the objective(s)
Stage 3 Calculate the total cost of each method
Stage 4 Remove from the list any method that has a total cost exceeding the stated expenditure limits
Stage 5 Establish an equitable way of measuring the effectiveness of alternative methods in relation to the defined objectives
Stage 6 Grade each method according to effectiveness
Stage 7 Compare costs and effectiveness ratings of each method and select the mos cost effective method.

This type of analysis is suitable for evaluating service and/or social projects. For example corporate objectives such as improving the moral of staff and their loyalty to the company could possibly be measured by labour turnover and labour productivity statistics. Once the objectives and measurement criteria had been determined then the possible methods of achieving the objectives could be listed, such as increasing wages, improving staff facilities and staff welfare arrangements. Attempts could then be made to estimate the costs and assess the effectiveness of each proposal.

5. Time value of money

Supposing you were asked do you prefer to receive £1,000 now or £1,000 in a year's time? Almost certainly you would say £1,000 now, because:-

(a) The money could be invested for one year.

(b) The purchasing power of the money will be less in one year because of inflation.

(c) You have an urgent use for the money.

This is what the time value of money is all about. If people prefer money now to money later then today's cash inflow of say £1,000 is worth more than the same amount next year. How much more depends upon the person or the company and is referred to as a time preference for money. This time preference is expressed as a percentage. There are two main types of percentage calculations relating to the time value of money; compounding and discounting. Compounding is used to calculate the future value of present cash flows. For example, consider the following illustration of £1,000 invested at 10% compound interest.

DIAGRAM 112 TIME VALUE OF MONEY — COMPOUNDING @ 10%

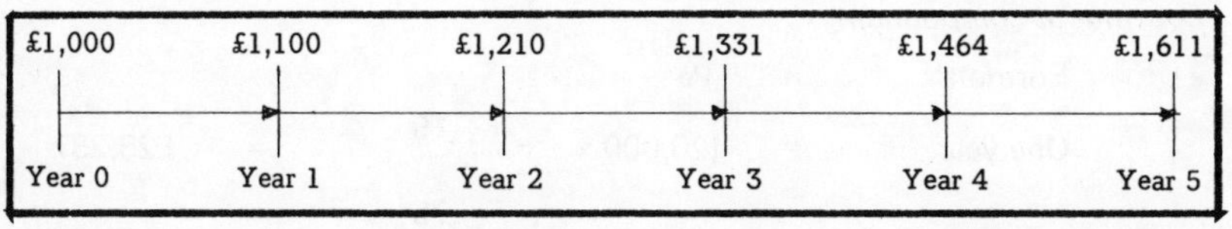

Using the above illustration we could say if a £1,000 was invested at a compound interest rate of 10% it would be worth £1,611 in five years time. Using the discounting calculation we could also say that £1,000 in five year's time is worth £621 in present value terms. Thus the £1,611 in year 5 is worth in present value terms £1,000 (i.e. 1,611 x 0.621). Thus the difference is: compounding calculates the future value of present cash flows and discounting calculates the present value of future cash flows The following sub-sections examine these two techniques in a little more detail.

5:1 Compounding The practice of compounding is usually associated with investments or deposit accounts. Where compound interest is meant to represent the time value of money then there are two factors that have to be considered; the interest rate and the frequency of compounding. Consider the following example of an investment of £20,000 invested at 15% compounded annually, every six months or continuously.

Interest rate Compounded	*£ @ 15% annually*	*£ @ 15% six monthly*	*£ @ 15% continuously*
Today	20,000	20,000	20,000
One year's time	23,000	23,112	23,937
Five year's time	40,227	41,221	42,340
Ten year's time	80,911	84,957	89,634

These figures have been calculated using compound interest formulae with the following notations:

P = the initial sum invested (the principal)
n = the total number of years the principal is invested
r = the rate of interest per annum (the nominal rate)
c = the number of compoundings per annum
i = the interest rate per conversion period (i.e. r/c)
e = the relevant figure from exponential tables

Annual compounding

Formula = $P(1 + r)^n$

One year = $20{,}000\ (1 + 0.15)^1$ = £23,000
Five years = $20{,}000\ (1 + 0.15)^5$ = £40,227
Ten years = $20{,}000\ (1 + 0.15)^{10}$ = £80,911

Six monthly compounding

Formula = $\left(P + \frac{r}{c}\right)^{cn}$

One year = $20{,}000\left(1 + \frac{0.15}{2}\right)^2$ = £23.112

Five years = $20{,}000\left(1 + \frac{0.15}{2}\right)^{10}$ = £41.221

Ten years = $20{,}000\left(1 + \frac{0.15}{2}\right)^{20}$ = £84.957

Continuous compounding

Formula = Pe^{rn}

One year = $(20{,}000 \times e^{*})^{.15}$ = £23,237

Five years = $(20{,}000 \times e^{*})^{.75}$ = £42,740

Ten years = $(20{,}000 \times e^{*})^{1.5}$ = £89,634

* *Figures taken from exponential tables*

For compound interest calculations it is sometimes easier to use the appropriat table. An extract of an annual compound interest table is shown below.

Compound interest table (extract) $P(1 + r)^n$

Year	*2%*	*4%*	*6%*	*8%*	*10%*
1	1.020	1.040	1.060	1.080	1.100
2	1.040	1.082	1.124	1.166	1.210
3	1.061	1.125	1.191	1.260	1.331
4	1.082	1.170	1.262	1.360	1.464
5	1.104	1.217	1.338	1.469	1.611

Assuming a sum of £500 was to be invested at 10% for five years the terminal val calculation would simply be £500 x 1.611 = £805.50

There is one other main type of compound interest calculation generally referred to as an annuity. Annuities are equal payments or receipts at fixed time intervals such as assurance or rent. Annuity calculations can be done with the appropriate table. Compare the annuity table extract below with the above extract from a compound interest table.

Future value of an annuity table (extract) $\frac{(1+r)^n - 1}{r}$

Year	*2%*	*4%*	*6%*	*8%*	*10%*
1	1.000	1.000	1.000	1.000	1.000
2	2,020	2.040	2.060	2.080	2.100
3	3.060	3.122	3.184	3.246	3.310
4	4.122	4.246	4.375	4.506	4.641
5	5.204	5.416	5.637	5.867	6.105

Assume a regular sum of £500 was to be invested every year, for five years at an annual compound rate of 10%. The terminal value of the annuity would be £500 x 6.105 = £3,052.50.

Sometimes a business may want to provide funds for the replacement of an asset by investing regular payments outside the business. Accountants call this a *sinking fund*. Consider the following example:-

Example

A company wishes to replace a machine in five years time and needs to accumulate a fund of £12,200 for this purpose. An external investment providing 10% annual compound interest is available and the directors wish to know how much has to be invested annually. The following calculations have been made:-

Formula $$a = \frac{Ar}{(1+r)^n - 1}$$

Where a = annual payment and A = annuity value

$$a = \frac{12{,}200 \times 0.1}{(1.1)^5 - 1} = \text{£2,000 per annum}$$

From these calculations we can see that the time value of money in future, or terminal value, terms is based upon the rate of interest, the frequency of compounding and the number of years into the future. Investment appraisal is concerned with future cash flows and clearly the time value of money has to be brought into the calculations. However, most investment appraisal techniques discount future values back to the beginning of a project instead of compounding present and future value to the end of a project.

5:2 Discounting The mathematics of discounting are the reciprocal of compounding that were explained in the previous sub section. Thet are used to determine the present value of future cash flows. For instance, a £1,000 payment in one year's time is worth £909 in present value terms at a discount rate of 10%. Or, a £1,000 payment in five years' time is worth £621 in present value terms at a 10% discount rate. The principle is that you should not add future cash flows to present cash flows because they have different values. To bring future cash flows to a common value you apply discount factors that bring all future cash flows to a present value. The principle of discounting is illustrated in diagram 113 overleaf. This should be compared with diagram 112 on page 303.

DIAGRAM 113 TIME VALUE OF MONEY – DISCOUNTING @ 10%

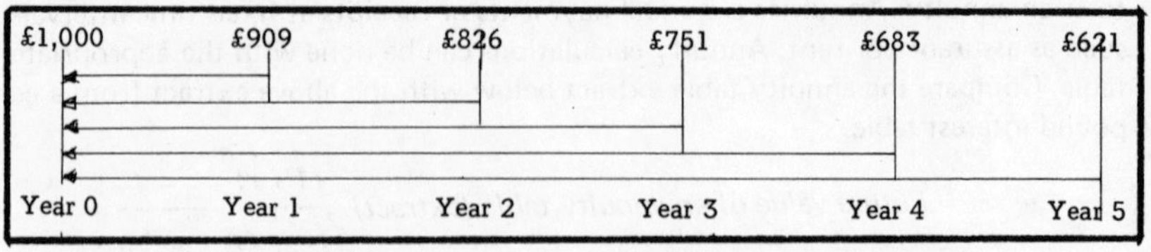

Discounting calculations are generally made on an annual basis when dealing with long future cash flows. However, where large future sums are involved over a relatively short period, the frequency of discounting can be increased. The following table illustrates the difference that arises from altering the frequency of discounting. This table and calculations should be compared with the detail given on compounding frequencies on page 303.

Discount rate	*£0.15% annually*	*£0.15% six monthly*	*£0.15% continuously*
Today	20,000	20,000	20,000
One year's time	17,391	17,307	17,214
Five year's time	9,943	9,703	9,447
Ten year's time	4,944	4,708	4,663

These figures have been calculated using the discounting formulae which are the reciprocals of the compounding formulae given in the previous sub-section. i.e.

Annual discounting

Formula $= P(1 + r)^{-n}$

One year $= 20{,}000\,(1 + 0.15)^{-1} =$ £17.391

Five years $= 20{,}000\,(1 + 0.15)^{-5} =$ £ 9,943

Ten years $= 20{,}000\,(1 + 0.15)^{-10} =$ £ 4,944

Six monthly discounting

Formula $= P\,(1 + {}^{r}/_{c})^{-cn}$

One year $= 20{,}000\left(1 + \frac{0.15}{2}\right)^{-2} =$ £17,307

Five years $= 20{,}000\left(1 + \frac{0.15}{2}\right)^{-10} =$ £9,703

Ten years $= 20{,}000\left(1 + \frac{0.15}{2}\right)^{-20} =$ £4,708

Continuous discounting

Formula $= Pe^{-rn}$

One year $= \left(20{,}000 \times e^{*}\right)^{-.15} =$ £17,214

Five years $= \left(20{,}000 \times e^{*}\right)^{-.75} =$ £9,447

Ten years $= \left(20{,}000 \times e^{*}\right)^{-1.5} =$ £4,663

* *Figures taken from exponential tables*

Present value calculations are often easier if discounted cash flow tables are used. An extract from a DCF table is shown below. Compare this with the compoundin table given in the previous sub-section.

Present value table (extract) $(1 + r)^{-n}$

Year	2%	4%	6%	8%	10%
1	.980	.962	.943	.926	.909
2	.961	.925	.890	.857	.826
3	.942	.889	.840	.794	.751
4	.924	.855	.792	.735	.683
5	.906	.822	.747	.681	.621

Using this table we can see how much future cash flows are worth in present value terms. For instance assume you were to receive £5,000 in five years time and your time preference for money was 10%. The present value of this sum would therefore be £5,000 x 0.621 = £3,105. If the future cash flows are regular then the calculation is for the present value of an annuity. The appropriate table for this type of calculation is the annuity table that was explained earlier. Compare the extract from a present value annuity table shown below, with the annuity table shown earlier.

Present value of an annuity table (extract) $\frac{1 - (1 + r)^{-n}}{r}$

Year	2%	4%	6%	8%	10%
1	0.980	0.962	0.943	0.926	0.909
2	1.942	1.886	1.833	1.783	1.736
3	2.884	2.775	2.673	2.577	2.487
4	3.808	3.630	3.465	3.312	3.170
5	4.713	4.452	4.212	3.993	3.791

This table can only be used for regular cash flows. For example suppose a department store was offering a washing machine for £1,000 cash or five equal annual payments of £250. Assume the prospective buyer's personal time preference for cash is equivalent to 10% then the calculation would be £250 x 3.791 = £947.75 This means it is better to take the instalment plan. If the buyer's cash time prefer ence was 6% then it would be better to pay the £1,000 cash (i.e. £250 x 4.212 = £1,053).

5:3 Timing of cash flow. With time value investment appraisal techniques the foregoing arithmetic for compounding or discounting is applied to a project's cash flows. Most techniques use annual discounting. An underlying assumption of the annual discounting techniques is that the net cash flows generated over one year occur at the end of the year. For most projects where cash flow data is based on estimates, annual compounding or discounting is adequate. With some financial arrangements where fixed interest is charged more than once a year then the appropriate compounding/discounting arithmetic can be applied. However, the continuous compounding/discounting is rarely used except in some economic theoretical models. If cash flows are known to occur regularly during each year of a project's life then a mid year average may be used.

Example
A project lasting four years is expected to produce regular net cash flows of £10,000 per annum. The initial outlay is £30,000 and the company applies a discount factor of 10% for all its projects. As the cash flows for this project occur regularly throughout each year semi-discounting and mid-year averages can be usec providing NPV's of:-

$$30{,}000 - \left[5{,}000 \left(1+\frac{0.1}{2}\right)^{-8} \right] = £2{,}316$$

Using annual discounting the NPV would be :-

$$30{,}000 - \left[10{,}000\ (1 + 0.1)^{-4} \right] = £1.700$$

For most practical purposes annual discounting is adequate for investment appraisal but care is still needed with the timing of cash flows. For instance the timing of cash flows within a single year need to be distinguished-in the first year of a project's life. For example, assume a machine is purchased on the 1st January 1980 for £15,000 and produces annual net cash inflows of £5,000 per annum for 5 years. The initial outflow is usually referred to as year 0 and the 1980 net cash inflow would then be year 1. With a discount factor of 10% the DCF calculations would be as follows:-

	£
Year 0 initial cash outflow	(15,000)
Years 1 to 5 net cash inflows (5,000 x 3.791)	18,955
Net present value	£3,955

Supposing this machine has to be replaced in precisely five years time at a cost of £27,500 producing a further five years net cash inflows of £6,000 per annum. The cash flow timing problem is does the £27,500 outflow on the 1st January 1985 have a 1984 discount factor or 1985 discount factor? The year 0 principle applies again. It would therefore be a 1984 discount factor. The DCF calculations would be as follows:-

	£
Year 0 initial cash outflow	(15,000)
Years 1 to 5 net cash inflows (5,000 x 3.791)	18,955
Year 4 subsequent cash outflow (27,500 x 0.683)	(18,783)
Years 6 to 10 net cash inflows 6,000 (6.145 – 3.791)	14,124
Net present value	£ (704)

If the subsequent cash outflow of £27,500 had been discounted for year 5 the the NPV would be £1,001. Thus the timing of this cash flow makes the difference between rejection and acceptance of the project. Accordingly great care is necessa when calculating the timing of cash flows for investment appraisal.

6. Deriving the discount factor

In the previous section we established money has a time value that can be expressed as a percentage compound interest rate, or discount factor. As most time value basec investment appraisal techniques use discounting, we need to consider how the disco factor is derived. The choice of a discount factor can significantly affect the results of the calculations and hence the investment decision, It is therefore important that the discount factor is derived by using valid criteria. Let us consider some of the criteria that may be taken into consideration when calculating a discount factor.

6:1 Discount factor criteria There have been a number of studies of how companies evaluate projects and the criteria they use for estimating their 'cut off' rate and/or discount factor. Some companies for example used the bank overdraft rate or 'risk free' interest rate. Allowances were also made by some companies for inflation, risk and expected rates of return. From a theoretical viewpoint there is a lot of literature concerning investment opportunity rates and the weighted average cost of capital but these solutions are difficult to apply in practice. Therefore in this subsection we will just review some of the factors that could be taken into consideration when trying to determine the appropriate discount factor.

(i) Cost of finance. This criteria may appear to be relevant to a company that has a lot of debt and will be funding the project with external finance. However, the financing of projects should be separated from the investment decision and the costs of finance excluded from cash flows. (Refer to section 8:4) It is therefore questionable whether finance costs should be used as a basis for deciding on the project cut off rate. Moreover, the costs of finance can be calculated in a number of ways, i.e.

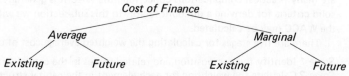

Cost of Finance

- *Average*
  - *Existing*
  - *Future*
- *Marginal*
  - *Existing*
  - *Future*

The bank overdraft rate which is used by some companies, will certainly not be constant during the life of the project. But an assumption of a constant rate has to be made if it is to be used as the sole criteria for the discount factor. Clearly, some caution is needed if the cost of finance is going to be used as a discount factor or cut off rate.

(ii) Investment opportunity rate The return on capital employed represents an average return on all existing projects. Some projects may be yielding high returns and others low returns or losses. A company's ROCE would therefore rarely be the same as its investment opportunity rate. For instance the average ROCE for U.K. carpet manufacturers in the accounting period 78/79 was 6.6%* This is clearly not the industry's investment opportunity rate because a higher return could be achieved from a 'risk free' deposit account. Moreover, the ROCE and the investment opportunity rate will probably change during the life of the project. Therefore if a rate of return criteria is to be used, it should reflect an average required rate of return for the life of the project based on expected investment opportunities.

(iii) Rate of inflation The effect of rising costs and corresponding increases in selling prices should be allowed for in the cash flow estimates. It is the expected specific price increases that are relevant to the project and not the existing average price increase. Although the RPI is often indirectly linked to wage increases and loosely linked to other costs, it represents a very broad averaging process *(Refer to Volume 1 Financial accounting for non-accountants, chapter 10, Inflation accounting).* In most circumstances the use of the RPI percentage as a cut off criteria would be invalid.

(iv) Level of risk A pract approach to this problem of selecting a discount factor is to use a base figure equivalent to a 'risk free' rate of interest such as a bank deposit account. Each project is then given a subjective risk loading rate that is added to the general risk free rate to determine the discount factor. Alternative

**ICC Business Ratios (Refer to Volume 1 Financial accounting for non-accountants).*

methods of allowing for risk are explained in section 9 in this chapter.

(v) Cost of capital This criteria gained a lot of theoretical support as a suitable basis for determining the discount factor. Earlier theories struggled with the problem of calculating a weighted average cost of capital. These were then refined making allowance for inflation interest rate movements and the risk 'profile' of the business. However, in practice it is very difficult to calculate a cost of capital that can be used as a valid cut off rate or discount factor.

6:2 Weighted average cost of capital There is a substantial amount of accounting theory on whether a change in a company's capital structure will affect its total valuation. Probably, there is an optimal financial mix of debt and equity where the weighted average cost of capital (WACC) will be minimised, but in practice it is difficult to calculate. The reason for using the weighted average cost of capital as a criteria for investment decisions is that by financing a project in specified debt/equity proportions and only accepting projects yielding more than the weighted average cost will result in an increase in the total value of the firm. Although there are many practical complications concerning the WAC it is generally accepted as a solid criteria for deriving a discount factor. In this sub-section we will look at how the WACC may be calculated.

There are five stages for calculating the weighted average cost of capital:-

Stage 1 Identify the composition and related values in the capital structure
Stage 2 Calculate the weighting for each element in the capital structure
Stage 3 Determine the nominal costs in terms of interest rates for each element in the capital structure
Stage 4 Adjust all nominal rates to real rates of interest with appropriate calculations such as tax adjustments
Stage 5 Multiply the weights by their related real rates of interest and total the results to derive the WAC.

This can become quite complicated, we will therefore consider each stage separately and then work through a simplified example.

Stage 1 The capital structure of a company is broadly divided into debt and equity Where equity represents ownership rights of control, capital gain and income gain. Whereas debt represents the right to receive payments of interest and the repayment of principal. The composition of equity and debt may consist of:-

Equity	Issued ordinary shares
	Issued preference shares
	Retained earnings
	Provisions
Debt	Long and medium term finance

The retained earnings and some provisions can create a number of theoretical and practical complications that are beyond the scope of this book. On the grounds of expediency, we will avoid these complications by treating these elements at the same cost as the ordinary shares because they belong to the ordinary shareholders.

Stage 2 The weighting of the different elements in the capital structure is best explained by example. In the following simplified illustration, we have taken the market value and the nominal value of the ordinary shares to be the same. i.e. £1.00 each. In the example that follows the illustration, you will note that the market value is £3.00 per £1.00 (nominal) share.

Capital composition	Value £	Weighting
50,000 ordinary shares @ £1.00	50,000	50%
10,000 preference shares @ £1.00	10,000	10%
Retained earnings	20,000	20%
Long term debt	20,000	20%
Total	100,000	100%

Stage 3 The nominal cost of finance is usually the rate of interest that is stated on the legal document. For example a 10% debenture has a nominal rate of 10%. However, if the debenture was issued at a discount and the effect of taxation is taken into consideration the real rate is quite different. For equity, if a £1.00 ordinary share has a market value of say £5.00 the dividend in percentage terms would be five times as high for the nominal value of £1.00 as the market value,i.e. a £0.50 dividend would represent a 10% dividend yield but a 50% nominal rate.

Stage 4 Once the nominal rates have been determined for each element in the capital structure they need to be adjusted for discounts, premiums and taxation to establish the real rates of interest.

Stage 5 The final stage of the calculation is best illustrated by example. Using the data from stage 2 we will include some real rates of interest, i.e.

Capital composition	Weighting	x	Cost	=	Weighted Cost
Ordinary shares	.5		.12		0.06
Preference shares	.1		.06		0.006
Retained earnings	.2		.12		0.024
Long term debt	.2		.08		0.016
			WAC		0.106 *(10.6%)*

Example

A company has the following capital structure:-

(i) 100,000 issued ordinary shares @ £1.00 with a market value of £3.00 each

(ii) Retained earnings and capital reserves of £20,000

(iii) 30,000 10% preference shares @ £1.00 each issued at £0.90 per share

(iv) A £50,000 mortgage debenture 15%, 1990 issued at a 5% discount

The company's dividend policy has been to regularly pay an annual dividend equivalent to 10% of the market price of the shares. The company does not expect their market share price to alter within the foreseeable future and will not alter their dividend policy.

The company is embarking on a substantial investment programme that will be financed by debt and equity in the same proportions as the existing capital structure and has decided to use the WACC as the cut off rate for investment appraisal. The WACC has been calculated as follows:-

Stages 1 & 2

Capital composition	Value £	Weighting %
Ordinary shares	100,000	50
Retained earnings and capital reserves	20,000	10
Preference shares	30,000	15
Long term debt	50,000	25
Total	£200,000	100%

Stages 3 & 4

Capital composition	*Nominal rate x adjustment*			=	*Cost*
Ordinary shares (Note 1)	10%	x	3		30%
Retained earnings and capital reserves (Note 2)	10%	x	3		30%
Preference shares (Note 3)	10%	x	1.1		11%
Debenture (Note 4)	15%	x	(1.05 x 0.5)		7.9%

Notes

(1) It is assumed that no shares have been issued at a premium. Therefore the initial capital of £100,000 is costing £30,000 per annum with no allowance for ta
(2) All profits retained by a business belong to the shareholders. It is therefore assumed that their cost is the same as the ordinary shares. Although it could be argued that a high share value could arise from a high retention policy and therefore the cost of the retained earnings is included in the cost of the ordinary shares
(3) As preference shares were issued at a 10% discount only £27,000 was recei (30,000 x 0.9) and is costing £3,000 per annum which is 11% with no allowance for tax.
(4) The debenture was issued at a 5% discount therefore only £47,500 was received (50,000 x 0.95) and is costing £7,500 gross per annum. Assuming profits are made and corporation tax is 50% then the net cost is £3,750 which is a real rate of 7.9%

Stage 5

Capital composition	*Weighting*	*x*	*Cost*	*= Weighted Cost*
Ordinary shares	0.5		0.3	0.15
Retained earnings and capital reserves	0.1		0.3	0.03
Preference shares	0.15		0.11	0.0165
Debentures	0.25		0.079	0.0197
			WAC	0.21625

In this example the company would use a discount factor of 22% for its investment appraisal

7. Time value investment appraisal techniques

So far we have considered the principles of investment appraisal, some preliminary project appraisal techniques and the time value of money. In this sub-section we will look at the main investment appraisal techniques that make allowance for the time value of money. Before examining each technique in detail there are a few general points that you need to be aware of:-

(a) The techniques are totally dependent on the accuracy of the source data. Ther is little point in applying time value techniques to unreliable data (Refer to section 2
(b) For some of the techniques that use a discount factor its choice must be basec on valid criteria (Refer to sections 5 and 6).
(c) No allowance is made in the following calculations for: uncertainty, risk and project sensitivity. (Refer to section 9.)
(d) No allowance is made in the following calculations for tax and investment incentives (Refer to section 10.)
(e) There are some limitations on the use of time value investment appraisal techniques (Refer to section 11.)

The main time value methods are; net present value (NPV) and percentage yield. The latter may also be called; internal rate of return (IRR), yield, time adjusted rate of return and marginal effeciency of capital. There are other discounting methods such as the present value index (PVI) and compounding methods such as the net terminal value (NTV). These time value investment appraisal techniques are explained in the following sub-sections.

7:1 Net present value method (NPV) The NPV calculation multiplies the net cash inflows for each year of a project's life by a discount factor to derive *Discounted cash flows (DCF)*. The initial capital cash outflow in present value terms is then deducted from the discounted cash flows to derive a *net present value.* To apply this technique the following information is required:-

(a) Length of the project, usually in years.
(b) Timing of the cash flow, usually in years.
(c) Value of the cash flows, usually in years.
(d) Discount factor.

Example

A company is considering purchasing a machine for £10,000 that is expected to last four years with a terminal value of £1,000. The net cash inflows for the project are expected to be £3,000 per annum. The company uses a discount factor of 15% for investment appraisal.

Calculation of NPV using DCF tables

Year	*Detail*	*Cash flow* £	*Discount factor* 15% *	*DCF* £
0	Purchase machine	(10,000)	1.0	(10,000)
1	Net inflow	3,000	0.8696	2,609
2	Net inflow	3,000	0.7561	2,268
3	Net inflow	3,000	0.6575	1,973
4	Net inflow	3,000	0.5717	1,715
4	Sale of machine	1,000	0.5717	572
			Net Present Value	(863)

Because this project has regular cash flows the cumulative DCF tables may be used, i.e.

Detail	*Cash flows* £	£
Capital outflow at beginning of year 1		(10,000)
Net cash inflows years 1 -4		
3,000 x 2.855	8,565	
Sale of machine 1,000 x 0.5717	572	9,137
	Net Present Value	(863)

Calculation of NPV using a calculator

The NPV formula can be stated as reject the project if:-

$$\frac{a_1}{(1+r)^1} + \frac{a_2}{(1+r)^2} + \ldots\ldots\ldots\ldots \frac{a_n}{(1+r)^n} \leqslant C$$

Where:

a = the annual cash flow
r = the rate of interest (discount factor)
C = the initial capital outflow

$$C - \left[\frac{a_1}{(1+r)^1} + \frac{a_2}{(1+r)^2} + \frac{a_3}{(1+r)^3} + \frac{a_4}{(1+r)^4}\right]$$

$$10{,}000 - \left[\frac{3000}{(1{+}0.15)^1} + \frac{3000}{(1{+}0.15)^2} + \frac{3000}{(1{+}0.15)^3} + \frac{4000}{(1.015)^4}\right]$$

$$= 10{,}000 - (2{,}609 + 2{,}268 + 1{,}973 + 2{,}287)$$

Net Present Value = £(863)

Note: The programmable calculators and micro/mini computers usually have DCF programs where only the basic data is needed for input.

Example Summary

The negative NPV in this example would mean that the project should be rejected because it does not meet the company's 15% DCF rate. If the company had chose a 5% DCF rate then the NPV would be a positive £1,491 - (try calculating this) and therefore acceptable.

7:2 Present value index method (PVI) The PVI is a form of cost/benefit ratio in present value terms where the present value of future net cash flows is divided by the initial outlay. The index allows large and small projects to be compared on a cost/profitability basis. Consider the following mutually exclusive projects:-

Projects	*A* £	*B* £	*C* £
Present value of net cash flows	15,000	90,000	165,000
less initial outlay	12,000	72,000	132,000
Net present value	3,000	18,000	33,000

Each of these projects has a PVI of 1.25, therefore on a cost/profitability basis there is no difference between them. For a single project the acceptance criteria is a PVI above 1 and this is the same as accepting a project with a positive NPV. However, when comparing mutually exclusive projects, the PVI should not provide the sole accept/reject criteria. In the following illustration project X has a higher NPV than project Y but the PVI is higher for project Y

Projects	*X* £	*Y* £
Present value of net cash flows	30,000	15,000
less initial outlay	20,000	9,000
Net present value	10,000	6,000
Present value index	*1.5*	*1.67*

The main use for the PVI is for project ranking under single period capital rationing (Refer to sub-section 11:2). The PVI used in this instance is the net PVI explained above. There is also a gross PVI. The difference is:-

$$\text{Net PVI} = \frac{\text{Present value of net cash flows}}{\text{Initial outlay}}$$

$$\text{Gross PVI} = \frac{\text{Present value of cash inflows}}{\text{Present value of cash outflows}}$$

Example

A company is considering two mutually exclusive projects with the following cash flows:-

Year	*Project A*		*Project B*	
	Inflow	*Outflow*	*Inflow*	*Outflow*
	£	*£*	*£*	*£*
0	-	(15,000)	-	(25,000)
1	18,000	12,000	40,000	31,000
2	18,000	12,000	40,000	31,000
3	18,000	12,000	40,000	31,000
4	18,000	12,000	40,000	31,000

Projects	*A*	*B*
	£	*£*
Present value of net cash flows @ 10%	19,020	28,530
less initial outlay	(15,000)	(25,000)
Net present value	4,020	3,530

Net PVI $\frac{19,020}{15,000} = 1.27 \qquad \frac{28,530}{25,000} = 1.14$

Gross PVI $\frac{57,060}{53,040} = 1.08 \qquad \frac{126,800}{123,270} = 1.03$

In most instances the net PVI is the most suitable index because it shows the relationship between the initial cash outflow and subsequent net cash flows. Where as, the gross PVI aggregates all outflows and provides a measure that is no better than other more established investment appraisal methods.

7:3 Percentage yield method This method is easily distinguished from the NPV method because it appraises a project in percentage terms called the internal rate of return (IRR). Using the NPV method a project will have a positive or negative NPV which partly depends on the choice of the discount factor. In the previous example a 15% discount factor gave a negative NPV of £(863) and a 5% discount factor a positive NPV of £1,461. Between these positive and negative NPV's will be a rate of interest that will equate the cash inflow and outflow of the project. Consider the detail in the following table that is illustrated in diagram 114.

Discount factor	*Net Present Value*
%	£
15	(863)
10	193
5	1,461

The table shows that the IRR is somewhere between 10% and 15%. This can be estimated graphically as shown in diagram 114, or calculated by linear interpolation. The method of calculating the IRR, shown overleaf, only provides an approximate figure because the NPV function is not linear.

DIAGRAM 114 INTERNAL RATE OF RETURN

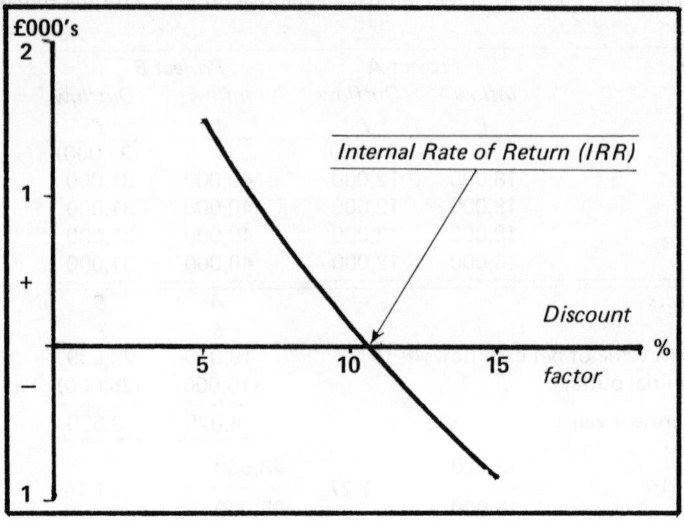

Linear Interpolation calculation

$$10\% \quad + \left(\frac{193}{193 + 863}\right) \quad \times \quad (15\% - 10\%)$$

$$= 0.1 \quad + (0.1828 \times 0.05)$$

$$= 0.109$$

The IRR is therefore approximately 11%.

· The IRR technique does not require the company to calculate a discount facto because every project will be appraised in percentage terms. However, the compan still needs to decide on a 'cut off rate', or 'hurdle rate' which represents the accep ance criteria for projects. The problems of choosing a discount factor, that were explained in section 6, also apply for choosing a cut off rate. Moreover, the use of the IRR for project making will not necessarily produce the optimum project mix. (Refer to sub-section 11:1)

7:4 Net terminal value method (NTV) In section 5 we looked at the mathematics of compounding and discounting. The technique of compounding produces a tern inal value of a series of cash flows whereas its reciprocal discounting, produces a present value. The three time value methods we have looked at in the previous sub sections have all used discounting and are the most widely accepted investment appraisal techniques. However there are instances where compounding can be usec to produce a net terminal value instead of using discounting for a net present valu

Enterprises that are heavily financed by debt capital such as local authorities and public corporations often use NTV annuity type computations for project appraisal. Local government for example tends to identify two costs relating to capital projects: the cost of servicing the debt and the consumption of capital measured by depreciation. The provision for repayment of the principal at the en of a project's life is often made by using a sinking fund (Refer to sub-section 5:1) Thus the net cash inflows after payment of interest, need to be greater than the annuity payments for repayment of the principal. An investment appraisal technique called the *annual capital charge* method is used for this calculation. Consider the following simplified NTV calculation, that for illustration purposes is contrasted with an NPV calculation.

Example

An investment with an initial cash outflow of £10,000 is expected to yield net cash flows of £5,000 per annum for three years.

Calculation of NTV using 10% compounding			£
Net cash flows	£5,000 x 3.31*		16,550
less initial outflow	£10,000 x $(1 + r)^n$		13,310
		NTV	3,240

Calculation of NPV using 10% discounting			£
Net cash flows	£5,000 x 2.487*		12,435
less initial outflow			10,000
		NPV	2,435

Reconciliation — NTV to year 0 3,240 x .751* = 2,433

(** Figures taken from tables in Appendix 4.*)

8. Applications of investment appraisal techniques.

The applications we will consider in this section relate to new and replacement investment decisions for single projects, selecting between mutually exclusive non-productive investment proposals, financing decisions such as to lease or purchase and disinvestment decisions. All the examples will use simplified data. Complications such as risk, sensitivity, taxation and capital rationing are excluded because they are explained in sections 9, 10 and 11.

The most complex investment decision is probably the purchase of an existing business. There are so many variables in this decision that it is difficult to estimate relevant cash flows. If the business is being purchased with intentions of rationalisation and synergy, then the relevant cash flows would be the estimated aggregate net cash flows after taking over the business, less the aggregate net cash flows if the business was not taken over. These differential cash flows can then be discounted normally and set against the expected gross purchase price. In Volume 1 *Financial accounting for non-accountants* five methods of company valuation were explained. The general conclusion was that the valuation techniques provide little more than yardsticks and levers in a bargaining process. Factors such as market conditions, the number of bids, whether payment is in cash and/or shares, the quality of management and any industrial complications can probably alter the opinions of the negotiators far more than any discounted cash flow computation. Accordingly we will not include company acquisitions in this section on applications of investment appraisal techniques.

8:1 New investment This kind of investment decision should take into consideration the following factors:-

(i) How the proposal will affect other aspects of the business (Refer to section 2 - project interdependence)

(ii) The reliability and relevance of the cash flow estimates (Refer to section 9).

(iii) The effect of taxation and government investment incentives (Refer to section 10).

(iv) The financial limitations of the business (Refer to section 11:2)

(v) Non-quantifiable factors such as labour reactions and staff capabilities.

Once the cash flows have been derived the appraisal techniques are quite simple. In the following example we will use the payback, NPV and IRR appraisal method. to help with the investment decision.

Example

A company wishes to diversify by increasing its productive capacity with a new kind of product. Market research has provided the following demand estimates for a four year period:-

Price £	*Year 1* *(units)*	*Year 2* *(units)*	*Year 3* *(units)*	*Year 4* *(units)*
10	50,000	60,000	70,000	70,000
9	100,000	120,000	140,000	120,000

Because of the expected high price elasticity of demand the company has narrowed the choice of production down to two alternatives:-

(a) High volume production with high fixed costs and low unit variable costs. The cost estimates are:-

Initial outlay £400,000
Relevant fixed cash costs of £200,000 p.a. for four years
Variable cash costs £6 per unit for four years
Profit function = 9q – (300,000 + 6q). *Refer to chapter 6*

(b) Low volume production with low fixed costs and high unit variable costs. The cost estimates are:-

Initial outlay £200,000
Relevant fixed cash costs of £50,000 p.a. for four years
Variable cash costs £8 per unit for four years
Profit function 10q – (100,000 + 8q) *Refer to chapter 6*

The following calculations have been made using the company's WACC of 15%.

Year	*Cash inflow £000*	–	*Cash outflow £000*	=	*Net cash flow £000*	x	*Discount factor @ 15%*	=	*D.C.F. £*
Project A									
0	-		400		(400)		1.0		(400,000)
1	900		800		100		0.869		86,900
2	1,080		920		160		0.756		120,960
3	1,260		1,040		220		0.657		144,540
4	1,080		920		160		0.572		91,520
			Project A Net present value						£ 43,920
Project B									
0	-		200		(200)		1.0		(200,000)
1	500		450		50		0.869		43,450
2	600		530		70		0.756		52,920
3	700		610		90		0.657		59,130
4	700		610		90		0.572		51,480
			Project B Net present value						£ 6,980

Safety assumptions of nil terminal values and only a four year project life have been adopted for both projects. In addition to the NPV calculations, IRR, Payback and breakeven calculations have been made to help with the decision process. The results of these appraisal methods are tabulated below:-

Appraisal method	Project A	Project B
Net present value	£43,920	£6,980
Internal rate of return	21%	17%
Payback	2.6 years	2.9 years
Break even (annual unit sales)	100,000	50,000

From this appraisal it seems that the company should opt for high volume low priced output, because project 'A' has a higher NPV, higher IRR and a shorter payback. However, if there are financial constraints and/or the marketing data is considered unreliable then project 'B' may be chosen because of the lower initial outlay and lower break even point.

8:2 Replacement investment There is a point in the life of most assets when it is necessary to consider their replacement. The replacement decision should take into consideration the following factors:-

(i) The future requirements of the business and the need for the asset
(ii) The alternative courses of action such as not replacing the asset, sub-contracting and the replacement options.
(iii) The costs of retaining the existing asset such as maintenance and lost production time (Refer to sub-section 2:3:2)
(iv) The comparative costs and benefits of replacement options
(v) How the replacement will affect other aspects of the business (Refer to section 2)
(vi) The effect of investment incentives (Refer to section 10)

Once the best replacement alternative has been selected, based on similar principles to new investment appraisal, the decision is then narrowed down to replacing or retaining the asset.

Example

A four year old machine producing a specialised product has been breaking down and requiring increasing maintenance. An investigation into the choice of replacement machines has decided on a machine with the following cost detail:-

Initial cost £30,000
Output capacity 100 units per hour
Expected useful life 4 years
Maintenance costs: year 1 - £1,000, year 2 - £2,000, year 3 - £3,000, year 4 - £5,000

In cash flow terms, all other operating costs will be the same as the old machine. The capacity of the old machine is 80 units per hour. For the old machine to run satisfactorily for another four years the following costs would be incurred:-

Complate overhaul £15,000
Maintenance costs: year 1 - £3,000, year 2 - £4,000, year 3 - £6,000, year 4 - £8,000.

Exisitng working practices and labour agreements enable the machine to be used for a maximum of 2,000 hours a year. Demand for the product for the following four years has been estimated as :

	Year 1	Year 2	Year 3	Year 4
Unit demand	150,000	160,000	170,000	180,000

The cash flow contribution will be maintained at a constant £0.10 for the next four years. The following tables show two types of discounting calculations for this problem, both producing the same results.

Year	*Cash inflow*	–	*Cash outflow*	=	*Net cash flow*	x	*Discount factor @15%*	=	*D.C.F.*
Replace machine									
0	-		30,000		(30,000)		1.0		(30,000)
1	15,000		1,000		14,000		0.869		12,166
2	16,000		2,000		14,000		0.756		10,584
3	17,000		3,000		14,000		0.657		9,198
4	18,000		5,000		13,000		0.572		7,436
							NPV		£ 9,384
Retain machine									
0	-		15,000		(15,000)		1.0		(15,000)
1	15,000		3,000		12,000		0.869		10,428
2	16,000		4,000		12,000		0.756		9,072
3	16,000*		6,000		10,000		0.657		6,570
4	16,000*		8,000		8,000		0.572		4,576
							NPV		£15,646

* *Maximum capacity of machine*

Differential Cash Flows	*0* £	*1* £	*2* £	*3* £	*4* £	*NPV* £
Replace (a)	(30,000)	12,166	10,584	9,198	7,436	9,384
Retain (b)	(15,000)	10,428	9,072	6,570	4,576	15,646
(a - b)	(15,000)	1,738	1,512	2,620	2,860	(6,262)

From this analysis it appears that the old machine should be retained for four years unless demand changes and the higher output machine becomes viable.

8:3 Non-productive investment When an investment proposal does not produce positive net cash flows such as expenditure on office furniture or new carpets, then investment appraisal techniques can only be used to identify the least cost alternative. In most instances this will be quite apparent and time value appraisal techniques are unnecessary. However, when the choice of non-productive investment proposals involves cash outflows over time then discounting techniques can be used.

The same principles apply to quasi productive projects where the benefits cannot be converted into positive cash flows. For example the benefits from purchasing a computer and its associated software cannot be quantified with any degree of acceptable accuracy. For computer instalations, attempts are sometimes made to quantify the benefits from improved data handling and purported staff reductions But this kind of analysis is often for support rather than illumination. The investment decision relating to computers is no longer a 'should I buy' type of decision, it is a 'when should I buy' decision. Accordingly, the investment appraisal would concentrate on price and technology trends, competing equipment and the optimum time in the business growth cycle to introduce or expand electronic data processing. The following example illustrates the appraisal of a 'non-productive' type of investment

Example

A company's executive car fleet is due for renewal. The fleet consists of five identical cars that are held on a 'pool basis' where executives can draw a car from the pool for business use only. The average mileage for each car has been a constant 10,000 miles per annum and this is not expected to change. The choice of car and dealers has been narrowed down to the following:-

Dealer A providing 5 type 'Z' cars costing £5,000 each. A trade in allowance of £10,000 has been agreed for the existing fleet. 'Z' cars average 20 miles per gallon and the estimated fleet service costs are: year 1 - £500, year 2 - £1,000, year 3 - £2,000, year 4 - £3,000.

Dealer B providing 5 type 'Y' cars costing £6,000 each. A trade in allowance of £12,000 has been agreed for the existing fleet. 'Y' cars average 25 miles per gallon and the estimated fleet service costs are: year 1 - £500, year 2 - £1,500, year 3 - £1,500, year 4 - £2,000.

The company has estimated that petrol prices per gallon will be: year 1 - £1.30 year 2 - £1.40, year 3 - £1.60, year 4 - £1.80. The following calculations have been made using the company's discount factor of 15%.

Year	*Dealer A*	*D Factor*		*(£)*
0	(5,000 x 5) – 10,000	x 1.0	=	15,000
1	(2,500* x £1.30) + 500	x 0.869	=	3,259
2	(2,500* x £1.40) + 1,000	x 0.756	=	3,402
3	(2,500* x £1.60) + 2,000	x 0.657	=	3,942
4	(2,500* x £1.80) + 3,000	x 0.572	=	4,290
			NPV	£29,893

* *Fuel consumption = 10,000 ÷ 20 x 5*

Year	*Dealer B*	*D Factor*		*(£)*
0	(6,000 x 5) – 12,000	x 1.0	=	18,000
1	(2,000* x £1.30) + 500	x 0.869	=	2,694
2	(2,000* x £1.40) + 1,500	x 0.756	=	3,251
3	(2,000* x £1.60) + 1,500	x 0.657	=	3,088
4	(2,000* x £1.80) + 2,000	x 0.572	=	3,203
			NPV	£30,236

* *Fuel consumption = 10,000 ÷ 25 x 5*

The analysis shows that over a four year period Dealer A is offering a slightly better contract. However the difference of £343 is so small that the decision should not be based on this analysis. In DCF terms there is no significant difference between the two offers and this enables the decision maker to make the choice on other criteria such as car comfort and style.

8:4 Investment financing There is a close relationship between project appraisal and project financing. In principle, if the discounted yield of a project is higher than the costs of financing the initial outlay, then it should be accepted. However, *financing and investment decisions should be separated.* The reasons for this are illustrated in the following example.

Example

A project has an initial outlay of £20,000 and will last for four years with regular net cash inflows of £7,000 per annum. The company's discount factor is 15% and the project can be financed from internally guaranteed funds or from external finance at 10%. The following calculations have been made:-

Financing from internally generated funds	£
Initial outlay	(20,000)
Years 1 - 4 (7,000 x 2.855)	19,985
NPV	(15)

Financing 50% external finance	£	D.Factor		£
Initial outlay	(20,000)			
less financed portion	(10,000)			
	(10,000)	x 1.0	=	(10,000)
Year 1 Net cash inflow	7,000			
Less finance costs*	(500)			
	6,500	x 0.869	=	5,648
Year 2 Net cash inflow	7,000			
Less finance costs*	(500)			
	6,500	x 0.756	=	..4,914
Year 3 Net cash inflow	7,000			
Less finance costs*	(500)			
	6,500	x 0.657	=	4,271
Year 4 Net cash inflow	7,000			
Less finance costs*	(500)			
repayment of principal	(10,000)			
	(3,500)	x 0.572	=	(2,002)
			NPV	£2,831

Finance costs with assumed 50% Corporation Tax are £10,000 x 0.1 x 0.5 = £500 per annum

From these calculations it can be seen that as external finance increases the NPV increases, providing the after tax cost of borrowing is below the company's discount factor. Indeed, the effect of external finance on a project can change a negative NPV to a positive NPV. If the project in the above example was 100% externally financed then the NPV would be:-

		£
Years 1 - 3	(6,000 x 2,283)	13,698
Year 4	(7,000 – 21,000) 0.572	(8,008)
	NPV	5,690

The effect of external finance on this project is shown in diagram 115. It is ther fore clear that the investment decision and the financing decision need to be separated. Accordingly, *the cost of finance should not be included in the cash flows.* Once the investment appraisal process has determined that a project is acceptable under whatever criteria the company is applying (refer to section 6), then a separate appraisal process is necessary to determine the method of financing. The financing options include:-

i) Internally generated funds
ii) Issue of equity
iii) Issue of debenture
iv) Debt/equity mix
v) Bank loan
vi) Hire purchase
vii) Leasing

DIAGRAM 115 EFFECT OF EXTERNAL FINANCE ON NPV APPRAISAL

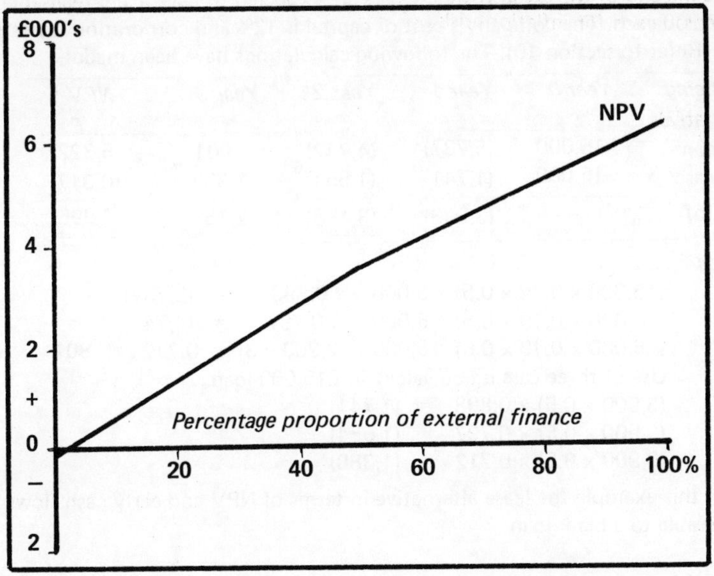

Before we proceed any further it is important to briefly clarify the nature of the financing decision. A decision is a choice between alternatives. The financing choice is to identify the best way of providing funds for a project that has been accepted under investment appraisal criteria. Therefore all we really need to know is 'how much for how long'. Let us now apply this basic principle to the most common type of financing decision - the lease/purchase problem. Firstly we need to distinguish between the two main types of lease:-

Operating leases This is when the lease period is far shorter than the asset life and the lessor bases the lease payments on the assumption that the asset will be re-leased or sold at the end of the lease period.

Finance leases Generally arranged to last for the whole useful life of the asset. The reality of this type of lease is that the lessee has effectively purchased the asset.

Secondly we need to consider the nature of the asset that is being leased. For our purposes the division can be into appreciating and depreciating assets.

Appreciating assets being mainly freehold property, and

Depreciating assets being most kinds of plant, equipment fixtures and fittings and motor vehicles. With appreciating assets, or depreciating assets with high terminal values, the financing decision has to recognise the project's potential terminal cash flows. This point is illustrated in the following example.

Example

A company has decided to acquire three new cars. The make of car and dealer have been chosen and the total price of £15,000 agreed. The main financing options are a bank loan or to lease the cars with an operating lease provided by the dealer. The details are:

i) Bank loan at 19% on the outstanding balance calculated at the end of each year. Repayment of principal to be £5,000 a year for three years.

ii) *Operating lease* of £3,900 per annum for three years. Cars to be returned to dealer at end of the three years.

At the end of the three years the cars are expected to have a net realisable value of £2,200 each. The company's cost of capital is 12% and corporation tax rate 50% (Refer to section 10). The following calculations have been made:-

Financing alternatives	*Year 0* £	*Year 1* £	*Year 2* £	*Year 3* £	*NPV* £
(a) Loan	15,000	(5,737)[1]	(4,742)[2]	801[3]	5,322
(b) Lease	15,000[4]	(1,741)[5]	(1,554)[6]	(1,388)[7]	10,317
(a) - (b)	–	(3,996)	(3,188)	2,189	(4,995)

Notes

1 (15,000 x 0.19 x 0.5) + 5,000 x 0.893 = (5,737)
2 (10,000 x 0.19 x 0.5) + 5,000 x 0.797 = (4,742)
3 (5,000 x 0.19 x 0.5) + 5,000 – 2,200 x 3) x 0.712 = 801
4 Use of three cars is equivalent to £15,000 loan
5 (3,900 x 0.5) x 0.893 = (1,741)
6 (3,900 x 0.5) x 0.797 = (1,554)
7 (3,900 x 0.5) x 0.712 = (1,388)

In this example the lease alternative in terms of NPV and early cash flows is preferable to a bank loan

8:5 Disinvestment Whenever a project reaches a stage where its abandonment value is greater than its discounted future cash flows then some form of disinvestment appraisal is necessary. Later in sub-section 9:5 we will be looking how abandonment value can be built into the initial cash flow appraisal to help determine a *future* project's life. In this sub-section, we are concerned with the abandonment decision for *existing* projects generally referred to as disinvestment.

The disinvestment decision can be broken down into the following stages.

i) Calculate costs of disinvestment such as redundancy payments, re-organisation costs and negative cash flow effects on other projects.
ii) Determine the benefits of disinvestment in terms of reduced net operating cost sale of assets and positive cash flow effects on other projects
iii) A cost/benefit analysis in terms of cash flows from (i) and (ii) (Refer to sub-section 4:2)
iv) Discount cash flows using accepted investment appraisal techniques and compare results with new investment proposals .

A disinvestment problem will often have variables that are not quanitifable such as its effect on the goodwill of suppliers, customers and employees. However, a DCF disinvestment appraisal provides the decision maker with a quantified assessment of many variables and should therefore be a necessary part of the decision process.

Example
The market for a specific product is forecasted to decline rapidly due to a change in technology. A company with a 70% market share for the product has decided to invest in the new technology, but is uncertain what to do about the old product line. The two main alternatives are:-

(a) To gradually disinvest by phasing out the old product, or
(b) To totally disinvest by selling the entire production process

The quantifiable aspects of these alternatives are summarised below;

Year	*Net operating cash flows* £	*Net terminal cash flows* £
0	-	120,000
1	60,000	90,000
2	40,000	80,000
3	30,000	50,000
4	20,000	20,000
5	5,000	10,000

The company has established that its investment opportunity rate for the next five years would be 10% and has decided to use this rate as the criteria for the disinvestment decision.

Year	*Disinvestment calculation*	*NPV* £
0	120,000 x 1.0	120,000
1	(60,000+ 90,000) 0.909	136,350
2	(40,000 + 80,000) 0.826 + 54,540	153,660
3	(30,000 + 50,000) 0.751 + 87,580	147,660
4	(20,000 + 20,000) 0.683 + 110,110	137,430
5	(50,000 + 10,000) 0.621 + 123,770	133,085

The above simplified example shows that disinvestment should take place at the end of year 2. However, this type of disinvestment appraisal is only an aid in the decision decision making process, because there will probably be many unquantifiable factors in this kind of strategic decision.

9. Allowing for risk and uncertainty

Before looking at some of the techniques that attempt to make allowance for risk we must first define three related terms that are frequently used in investment appraisal.

Risk situations are where there is some evidence of the expected outcome of events For example,insurance statistics for car accidents, fire and theft are quantifiable situations where data can be used to assess the risk.
Uncertainty situations are where there is no reliable data to help predict future events. The data is simply based on subjective estimates. For example, a project to launch an entirely new product in an unknown market would have a high degree of uncertainty.
Sensitivity situations relate to critical variables in a project that can significantly affect its profitability if conditions change and/or estimates are wrong (Refer to sub-section 2:3:1)

An investment appraisal technique should attempt to identify and measure risk, uncertainty and/or sensitivity. Inevitably a lot of the data for the techniques will be subjective and it is for the manager to decide whether to opt for a simple technique such as adjusting the discount factor or more complex methods such as risk adjusted cash flows. Managers will have different attitudes to risk ranging from risk seeking to risk averse. But the worst kind of manager is the one who is unaware of risk or ignores it. As most investment decisions relate to uncertain future events it is clear that the user of investment appraisal techniques should recognise that the different risk profiles of projects must be taken into consideration in the decisior process. In the following sub-sections we will be looking at the information requi ments for evaluating risk, some risk and sensitivity analysis techniques and projec failure calculations.

9:1 Information requirements for evaluating risk There are a number of almos risk free or certainty investments which virtually guarantee a fixed percentage return on an investment, such as government stocks or bank deposit accounts. Our concern here however, is with investments that have an element of risk, uncertainty and/or sensitivity.

All investment decisions are made under conditions of economic uncertaint There are many forecasts of economic activity but they all have to be based o assumptions. Similarly, investment decisions are based upon assumptions and i is these assumptions that enable the level of risk, uncertainty and sensitivity tc be assessed. The assumptions have to be organised and quantified in some kinc of assumptions file as illustrated in diagram 116.

DIAGRAM 116 ASSUMPTIONS FILE FOR RISK & UNCERTAINTY

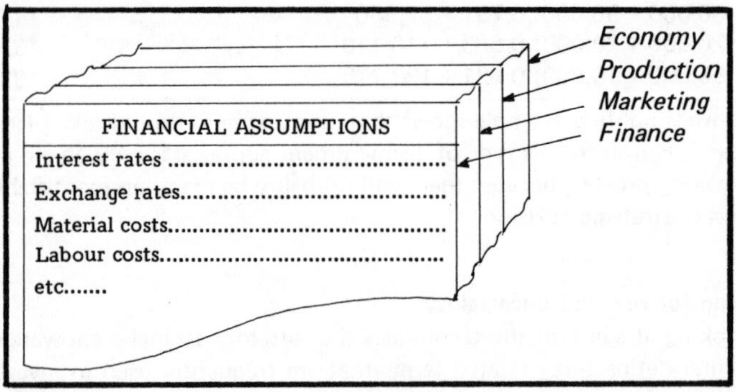

It is the quality of the information provided in the assumptions file that enat valid risk conditions to be made. In the previous chapter we looked at risk in relation to tactical decision making. The same principles apply to strategic de ion making but because the future time period is longer, greater attention to risk is needed. In the following sub-sections we will briefly look at some of t well known methods of analysing data for assessing risk, such as: expected va ues, probability distributions, measures of dispersion and decision trees.

9:1:1 Expected values In the previous chapter the principles of probabilit were explained: There are two basic rules:-

The addition rule - where the probability of a single six from three throws of a six sided dice would be : $^1/_6 + ^1/_6 + ^1/_6 = ^3/_6$ or 50%, and

The multiplication rule - where the probability of a six being thrown three consecutive times would be $^1/_6 \times ^1/_6 \times ^1/_6 = ^1/_{216}$ or 0.46%.

These rules can be applied to cash flows in investment appraisal. Consid the following simplified example.

Example
A company has estimated that there is a 50% probability of a cash flow being £10,000, a 20% probability of it falling to £6,000 and a 30% probability of it increasing to £15,000. The expected monetary value (EMV) of this cash flow would be calculated as follows:

Cash Flow	x	*Probability*	=	*E.M.V.*
10,000		0.5		5.000
6,000		0.2		1,200
15,000		0.3		4,500
				£10,700

This simple EMV calculation is often used in investment appraisal.

9:1:2 Probability distributions If risk is defined as the possibility of variation from the predicted results, then the probability distribution explained in the previous chapter (sub-section 2:7:1) can be used to compare project risk profiles. Consider the following figures for two projects having the same life and initial cash outflow but having different probabilities for their regular cash inflows.

Project 'A'		*Project 'B'*	
Probability	*Cash Flow*	*Probability*	*Cash Flow*
	£		£
0.10	1,000	0.05	5,000
0.25	5,000	0.20	7,500
0.30	10,000	0.50	10,000
0.25	15,000	0.20	12,500
0.10	19,000	0.05	15,000

The probability distributions are illustrated in diagram 117, and show that

DIAGRAM 117 PROJECT RISK PROFILE

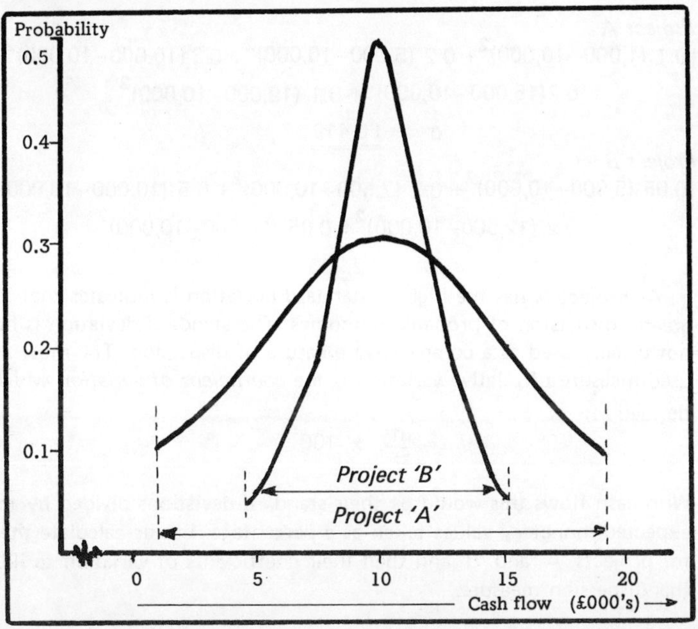

Project 'A' has a higher risk profile because the dispersion of possible outcomes is far wider. Thus the possibility of variation from the predicted result is greater with project 'A' and this should be taken into consideration in the investment appraisal process.

Instead of drawing probability distributions for every project, what is neede is some form of measurement that gives information about the dispersion of the distribution. The most well known measure of dispersion is the standard deviation and this is explained in the next sub-section.

9:1:3 Measures of dispersion Looking at the normal distribution curves in diagram 117 it is clear that the probability of expected outcomes becomes less as one moves away from the centre. The generally accepted method of calculating the expected deviation from the centre (the mean) is called the standard deviation. The standard deviation is expressed by the following formula:-

$$\sigma = \sqrt{\frac{\Sigma\,(x - \bar{x})}{n}}$$

Where

σ = The Greek lower case sigma representing the standard deviation
x = Any single measurement in the series
$\bar{x}$ = The arithmetic mean of the series
Σ = The Greek upper case sigma representing the sum of
n = The number of measurements in the series

Therefore the standard deviation is the square root of; the sum of all the squared deviations divided by the number of measurements in the series. We will not do any extensive standard feviation calculations or proofs because the calculation can easily be made on programmable calculations. Let us jus calculate the standard deviations for the two projects 'A' and 'B' illustrated in diagram 117 in the previous sub-section

Project A

$$\left[0.1\ (1{,}000-10{,}000)^2 + 0.2\ (5{,}000-10{,}000)^2 + 0.3\ (10{,}000-10{,}000)^2 + 0.2(15{,}000-10{,}000)^2 + 0.1\ (19{,}000-10{,}000)^2\right]^{½}$$

$$\sigma = \underline{\underline{£6{,}419}}$$

Project B

$$\left[0.05\ (5{,}000-10{,}000)^2 + 0.2\ (7{,}500-10{,}000)^2 + 0.5\ (10{,}000-10{,}000)^2 + 0.2\ (12{,}500-10{,}000)^2 + 0.05\ (15{,}000-10{,}000)^2\right]$$

$$\sigma = \underline{\underline{£2{,}236}}$$

As project A has the highest standard deviation it indicates that it has a greater dispersion of probable outcomes. The standard deviation is however not usually used as a comparative measure of dispersion. The most widely used measure of relative variation is the *coefficient of variation* which is defined as:-

$$V = \frac{\sigma}{\bar{x}} \times 100$$

With cash flows this would be their standard devistions divided by their expected monetary values taken as a percentage. Let us calculate the EMV's for projects 'A' and 'B' and then their coefficients of variation to illustrate this dispersion measure.

Project A			Project B		
Cash Flow	P	EMV	Cash Flow	P	EMV
1,000	.1	100	5,000	.05	250
5,000	.25	1,250	7,500	.2	1,500
10,000	.3	3,000	10,000	.5	5,000
15,000	.25	3,750	12,500	.2	2,500
19,000	.1	1,900	15,000	.05	750
		10,000			£10,000

$$\text{Project A} \quad V = \frac{6{,}419}{10{,}000} \times 100 = \underline{\underline{64.2\%}}$$

$$\text{Project B} \quad V = \frac{2{,}236}{10{,}000} \times 100 = \underline{\underline{22.4\%}}$$

Project A has the highest coefficient of variation and is therefore the project with the highest risk

Before moving on to another method of analysing risk there is just one further point to be noted about the standard deviation. With a normal distribution 68% of the area under the curve falls within one standard deviation, 95% within two standard deviations and 99% within three standard deviations (Refer to diagram 118). We can therefore re-state projects A and B standard deviation date as follows:

Probability	Project A £			Project B £		
68%	3,581	to	16,419	7,764	to	12,236
95%	(2,838)	to	22,838	5,528	to	14,472
99%	(9,257)	to	29,257	3,292	to	16,708

The methods considered so far have been concerned with single accept/reject decision situations. However many investment decisions are part of a decision sequence and the popular method for identifying and measuring risk in sequential decision situations is explained in the next sub-section.

DIAGRAM 118 NORMAL DISTRIBUTION

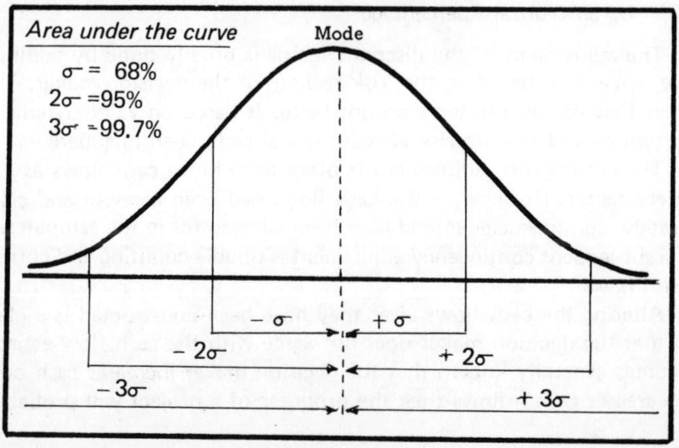

9:1:4 Sequential decisions In section 2 of this chapter it was explained that few investment decisions were completely interdependent and that several forms of interdependency will exist. Our concern in this section is with contingent dependency, where the acceptance of one project cannot be made without the acceptance of another. The main methods used for assessing risk for sequential decision making are decision trees and program evaluation and review techniques (PERT). These techniques were explained in chapter 6 sub sections 3:5 and 3:6 respectively. Both techniques allow probabilities to be applied at different stages of the decision process and their use is applicable to investment decisions.

9:2 Risk evaluation techniques Companies have different risk profiles and any noticeable alteration in the risk complexion of a company will affect its share valuation and possibly its credibility in the market. For example, financial institutions that are dependent on client confidence, opt for low risk profiles, and this is reflected in the risk averse attitude of bank managers. Conversely, the entrepreneur, by definition, tends to be a risk taker. The bank manager type of decision maker would tend to operate in a deterministic framework placing equal emphasis on project failure calculations (usually called security or collateral) as on project success calculations. Any risk evaluation technique would tend to be fairly crude, such as lowering expected cash inflows and raising cash outflows by an arbitary percentage. An entrepreneur however, needs to adopt risk evaluation techniques within a stochastic framework on an assumption of project success.

In the following sub-sections we will be looking at some srude stochastic methods for evaluating risk in investment projects.

9:2:1 Crude methods There is little research to support the contention that complex risk calculations are more valid than simple risk calculation methods For example, the payback criteria explained in sub-section 3:3 can be used as a crude risk evaluation technique. If the decision maker feels uncertain about the future then a short payback could be placed as an investment appraisal hurdle. The main ways of making crude adjustments for risk are to:

(a) Adjust the discount factor
(b) Include contingency cash outflows
(c) Reduce cash inflows and increase cash outflows by an arbitrary percentage

(a) The adjustment of the discount factor is usually done by adding a sub jective percentage based on the 'risk feeling' of the decision maker. This metho assumes that the unadjusted discount factor is based on valid criteria (Refer to section 6) and that no risk element has already been included.
(b) The contingency adjustment is often added into cash flows as a form of safety factor. However, if the cash flows had been assessed and calculated accurately, contingencies should have been allowed for in the estimates. Therefore, a subsequent contingency adjustment is double counting and corrupting the cash flows.
(c) Altering the cash flows after they have been constructed is a clear indication that the decision maker does not agree with the cash flow estimates. If it becomes generally known that the decision maker increases cash outflows and decreases cash inflows then the proposer of a project will probably make

compensating adjustments to their cash estimates before submitting them for a decision.

9:2:2 Certainty equivalent method This is similar to the risk adjusted discount factor method, except that the cash flows are adjusted for risk instead of the discount factor. Each cash flow is adjusted to a certainty equivalent by asking the question:- How certain is the cash flow? For example if a cash flow was expected to be £10,000 but the certainty of £10,000 was say 80% then the certainty equivalent cash flow would be £8,000. The certainty equivalent cash flows are then multiplied by a risk free rate such as the return on government stocks or bank deposit account interest rates.

Example

A company is considering a project using the NPV appraisal method and wishes to make some allowance for risk. The proposer is asked to ascribe the certain probability of the cash flows and the accountant has estimated that a suitable risk fee rate is 10%. The calculations are set out below:-

Year	*Cash flow* £	*Certainty* %	*Certainty flow* £	*Risk free rate (10%)*	*D.C.F.* £
0	(20,000)	100	20,000	1.0	(20,000)
1	9,000	90	8,100	0.909	7,363
2	10,000	70	7,000	0.826	5,782
3	11,000	60	6,600	0.751	4,457
				NPV	(£1,898)

On this basis of assessment the project would be rejected.

The certainty equivalent method is better than the risk adjusted discount rate method because it allows the risk to be varied over the life of the project. Generally speaking, the further into the future the higher the risk and this can be built into the certainty equivalent calculations. However, this method does not take into consideration the full range of probabilities that is allowed for in the EMV method described in the next sub-section.

9:2:3 Expected monetary value method The EMV principles were explained in sub-section 9:1:1. The calculations are similar to the certainty equivalent method except several probabilities are used and the discount factor is not altered to the risk free rate.

Example

The following data has been collected about a project for manufacturing and selling a new kind of product.

Marketing estimates at a constant selling price of £10.00 each.

Year 1		*Year 2*		*Year 3*	
Volume sales	*P*	*Volume sales*	*P*	*Volume sales*	*P*
8,000	.2	10,000	.25	8,000	.3
10,000	.5	12,000	.5	10,000	.4
12,000	.3	14,000	.25	14,000	.3

Production and distribution costs are estimated at a constant cash variable cost per unit of £8.00 and initial cash costs of £50,000. The company's WACC of 15% is used as a discount factor.

The following calculations were made:-

		£	£
Revenue Year 1	(8,000 x 0.2 x £10)	16,000	
	(10,000 x 0.5 x £10)	50,000	
	(12,000 x 0.3 x £10)	36,000	
			102,000
Less variable cash costs	(10,200 x £8)		81,600
	Net cash flow (EMV)		20,400
Revenue Year 2	(10,000 x 0.25 x £10)	25,000	
	(12,000 x 0.5 x £10)	60,000	
	(14,000 x 0.25 x £10)	35,000	
			120,000
Less variable cash costs	(12,000 x £8)		96,000
	Net cash flow (EMV)		24,000
Revenue Year 3	(8,000 x 0.3 x £10)	24,000	
	(10,000 x 0.4 x £10)	40,000	
	(14,000 x 0.3 x £10)	42,000	
			106,000
Less variable cash costs	(10,600 x £8)		84,800
	Net cash flow (EMV)		21,200

Year	*Net cash flow*	*Discount factor*	*D.C.F.*
	£	15%	£
0	(50,000)	1.0	(50,000)
1	20,400	0.870	17,748
2	24,000	0.756	18,144
3	21,200	0.657	13,928
		NPV	(£180)

9:3 Sensitivity analysis The purpose of this type of analysis is to identify the critical variables in a project. Just as some of the network methods (Refer to chapter 6 sub-section 3:6) highlight critical stages in a project, sensitivity analy helps the decision maker identify variables that can significantly alter the cash flows. The analysis seeks to answer the ' What if........?' type of questions such as:-

i) What if market conditions change and prices have to be reduced?
ii) What if interest rates rise?
iii) What if there are large movements in exchange rates?
iv) What if the costs of raw materials and/or labour rise by a significant amount?
v) What if the employees will not accept the new technology?
vi) What if......etc.?

There are many ways the 'what if' problems can be converted into calculati The calculations can be made to show the effect on:-

(a) Net present values
(b) Internal rates of return
(c) Accounting rates of return

or any other appraisal method preferred by the decision maker. There are also a number of ways the information can be presented, but most analy are presented as graphs or tables. i.e.

Example of tabular presentation of a sensitivity analysis

Changes in critical variables	*Net Present Values* *Adjusted*	—	*Expected*	=	*Variance*
	£		£		£
10% reduction in selling price with no change in volume	16,000		20,000		(4,000)
50% increase in oil costs	9,000		20,000		(11,000)
20% increase in labour costs	15,000		20,000		(5,000)
3% increase in interest rates	18,000		20,000		(2,000)
1 year delay in project coming in stream	5,000		20,000		(15,000)

From the table it can be seen that the critical variables are the timing of the project and the cost of oil. Accordingly, PERT would be used to assess the risk of a project delay (Refer to chapter 6 sub-section 3:6) and price trends of oil would be examined more closely.

Example of graphical presentation of a sensitivity analysis

DIAGRAM 119 PROJECT SENSITIVITY FOR A SINGLE VARIABLE

Where:-
(a) = Lowest NPV of £3,000
(b) = NPV range of £10,000
(a + b) = Highest NPV of £13,000
Shaded area = range of possible outcomes.

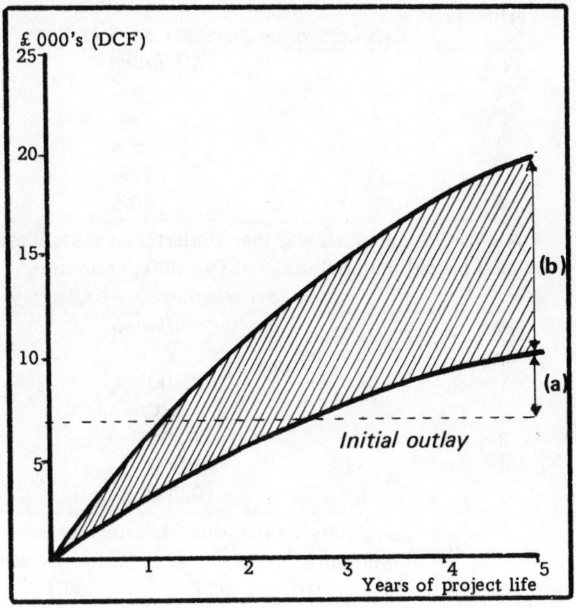

Diagram 119 illustrates a project's sensitivity to a single variable by plotting the range of possible outcomes of high and low expectations. The diagram shows how the payback period can be between one to three years and the NPV between £3,000 and £10,000. A diagram can be useful to illustrate the critical variables that are listed in a sensitivity analysis table.

Example of sensitivity analysis calculations

A managing director of a medium sized engineering company is considering a project that constitutes a corporate life risk decision (Refer to chapter 2). He has been presented with an investment appraisal folio that is summarised below:-

	£
Initial cash outflow	(35,000)
Net cash inflow for five years discounted at 15% (20,000 x 3.352)	67,040
NPV	£32,040

Being a cautious man, he analysed the cost structure which provided the foll owing constant proportions per annum'-

	%
Direct materials	48
Direct labour	20
Miscellaneous	12
Net cash flow	20
Gross cash flow	100%

Because of the high proportion of direct materials a further investigation was undertaken by an engineer to determine the proportions of different materials. The survey revealed that 80% of the direct material costs were for a special kin of aluminium alloy that had to be imported. A separate study was then made on the expected price trends of this metal. The study provided the following estimates:-

Expected price increases on year 0

Year	*Minimum*	*Maximum*
1	5%	10%
2	9%	16%
3	15%	35%
4	25%	60%
5	40%	90%

A sensitivity analysis was then undertaken using these estimates on an expected material usage of £48,000 per annum.

Reduction of Net Cash Flow

Year	*Minimum*	*Maximum*
	£	£
1	2,400	4,800
2	4,320	7,680
3	7,200	16,800
4	12,000	28,800
5	19,200	43,200

Sensitivity to material price increases

	Minimum			*Maximum*		
Year	*NCF*	*DF*	*DCF*	*NCF*	*DF*	*DCF*
	£	*15%*	£	£	*15%*	£
0	(35,000)	1.0	(35,000)	(35,000)	1.0	(35,000)
1	17,600	0.87	15,312	15,200	0.87	13,224
2	15,680	0.76	11,917	12,320	0.76	9,363
3	12,800	0.66	8,448	3,200	0.66	2,112
4	8,000	0.57	4,560	(8,800)	0.57	(5,016)
5	800	0.5	400	(23,200)	0.5	(11,600)
		NPV	£5,637		NPV	(£26,911)

The information from this example is illustrated in diagram 120 which shows that with minimum material price movements the NPV is reduced from £32,400 o £5,637. If the maximum price movements occurred then the project would perate at a loss. Because the project is so sensitive to material price movement nd project failure may mean the end of the company the risk is too great and he project should be rejected.

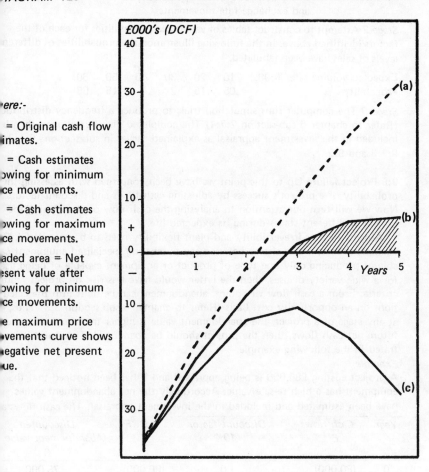

DIAGRAM 120 *PROJECT SENSITIVITY TO MATERIAL COSTS*

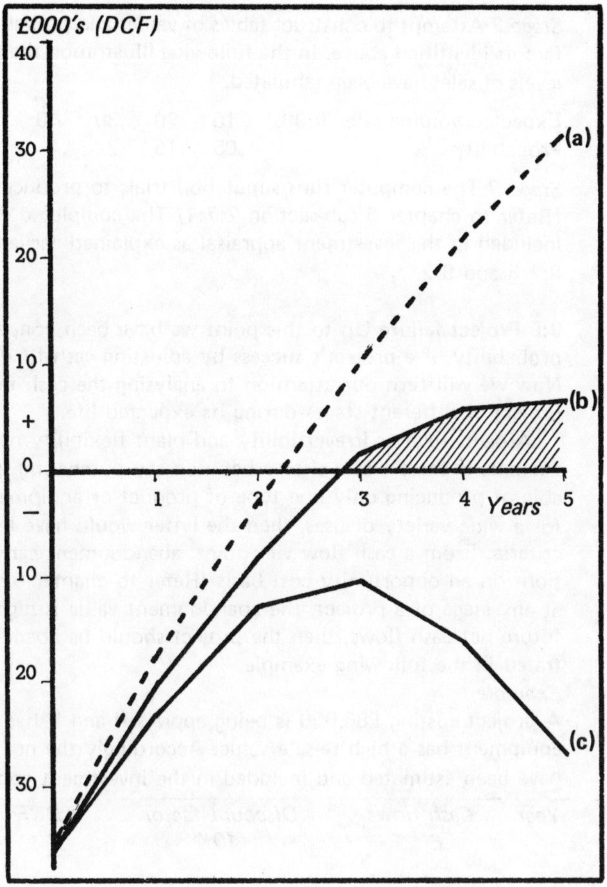

ere:-

= Original cash flow imates.

= Cash estimates owing for minimum ce movements.

= Cash estimates owing for maximum ce movements.

aded area = Net esent value after owing for minimum ce movements.

e maximum price ovements curve shows negative net present ue.

4 Simulation The developments in computer hardware and software packages ve brought financial simulation models within the reach of most businesses. A od computerised financial simulation model is one of the most powerful man ement tools available today, providing the manager knows how to use it. In is sub-section we will be looking at just one simulation model that can be used r risk analysis in investment appraisal. It is called the 'Monte-Carlo' technique. he principles of the technique are based on the study of chance. For example roulette the chance of winning numbers and combinations of numbers can be lculated by simulating a large number of games. These same simulation principles or calculating chance can be applied to investment appraisal. There are three ain stages:-

Stage 1 Identify the factors that are considered to be important in the investment proposal. i.e.

Marketing	-	Nature of the market such as size, growth rate, competition, market shares, selling prices and sales volumes.
Production	-	Cost structures paying special attention to cost elements that are sensitive
Finance	-	Initial cash outflows, expected inflows, interest rate moveme and exchange rate movements.

Stage 2 Attempt to construct tables of values and probabilities for each of the factors identified above. In the following illustration the probabilities of differen levels of sales have been tabulated.

Expected volume sales (000s)	10	20	30	40	50	60
Probability	.05	.15	.2	.4	.15	.05

Stage 3 The computer runs simulation trials to produce a frequency distributic (Refer to chapter 6 sub-section 2:7:1) The completed distribution may then b included in the investment appraisal as explained earlier in sub-sections 9:1:2, 9:1:3 and 9:2.

9:5 Project failure Up to this point we have been concerned with assessing the probability of a project's success by adjusting cash flows and discount factors. Now we will turn our attention to analysing the cash flow of abandoning the project at different stages during its expected life.

Aspects such as irreversibility and plant flexibility need to be considered. F example if there was a choice between say purchasing specialised equipment c able of producing only one type of product or equipment capable of being us for a wide variety of uses, then the latter would have less risk on project failu criteria. From a cash flow viewpoint, abandonment can be built into the calcu tions on an opportunity cost basis (Refer to chapter 6 sub-section 3:3) Thus, at any stage of a project, the abandonment value is higher than its discounted future net cash flows, then the project should be abandoned. This point is illu trated in the following example.

Example

A project costing £80,000 is being appraised and it has been noticed that the equipment has a high re-sale value. Accordingly the net abandonment values have been estimated and included in the investment appraisal. The cash flows a

Year	*Cash flows* £	*Discount factor* 10%	*DCF* £	*Discounted Abandonment value* £
0	(80,000)	1.0	(80,000)	78,000
1	30,000	0.909	27,270	70,000
2	30,000	0.826	24,780	60,000
3	25,000	0.751	18,775	40,000
4	20,000	0.683	13,660	30,000
5	15,000	0.621	9,315	20,000
		NPV	£13,800	

If the project is abandoned at the end of year 4 the NPV is increased to £24,9 Moreover, the high abondonment values reduce the project risk, in cash flow tern For instance if it became evident in the second year that the project was going to fail then the net cash flows up to the abandonment point would only have to be £20,000 to break even.

Therefore if a project appears to have high abandonment values then they should be included in the cash flow calculations.

10. Allowing for taxation and investment incentives

The effect of taxation and investment incentives will make a substantial difference to the cash flows of a project and should be included in the calculations. For example if a project included the purchase of £100,000 plant and equipment which was eligible for a 100% first year tax allowance (tax allowances are explained later in sub-section 10:1) this would reduce the company's corporation tax assessment by £52,000. Providing the company had earned sufficient profits, the following year's cash flow would therefore be increased by £52,000. Clearly, the tax implications should be included in the investment appraisal calculations and the time value appraisal techniques are ideally suited for making time based tax adjustments. If tax allowances are to be taken into consideration then of course tax payments on the project's profits also need to be built into the calculations. The result of all these calculations will be for the decision maker to have *before tax and after tax NPV's and/or IRR's.*

Some forms of investment attract financial assistance from the government. There are two main forms of government financial assistance: revenue based grants and capital based grants. The revenue grants usually relate to some form of employment and/or training subsidy and the capital grants for the acquisition of 'approved' fixed assets. These grants must be included in the cash flow calculations and allowed for in the tax computations where applicable. Government grants and taxation are *explained in greater detail in Volume 3 Finance and taxation for the non-accountant.* In this sub-section we will briefly look at investment appraisal related aspects of tax assessment and the timing of tax payments, then work through some simplified examples.

10:1 Investment incentives The main difference between the calculation of taxable profit and financial profit is in the treatment of depreciation. Normally the depreciation charged in the financial accounts is not an allowable expense for tax purposes. Instead of depreciation the Inland Revenue have a set of rules for *capital allowances.* For example if an investment proposal consisted of a new factory, plant and machinery and some motor vehicles, the tax calculations would take into consideration the following capital allowances:-

Factory building An initial allowance of 50% and a writing down allowance of 4% per annum

Plant and machinery A first year allowance of 100%

Motor vehicles A 25% writing down allowance for cars costing under £8,000

(The rates of capital allowance change quite frequently, refer to Volume 3 Finance and Taxation for the non-accountant)

With the exception of the motor vehicles these capital allowances are greater than the depreciation that would normally be charged when computing the financial profit. The purpose of large capital allowances such as 100% on plant and machinery is to encourage companies to invest. Thus a company making large profits can reduce their tax burden by investing in plant and equipment. This point is illustrated in the following simplified example.

Example

A company had not made any new investment for several years and had constan financial and taxable profits as shown below:-

	£
Financial profit	200,000
add back depreciation and other adjustments	50,000
	250,000
deduct capital allowances and other adjustments	40,000
Taxable profit	210,000
less corporation tax @ 52%	109,200
After tax profit	100,800

A new investment proposal was being considered that included £100,000 to be spent on new plant and equipment. It was estimated that there would be no change in profitability etc for the first two years (For the purpose of illustrating the tax effect all factors will be held constant). The effect on the company's tax assessment has been calculated as follows:-

	£
Taxable profit before investment	210,000
Capital allowances for the investment	100,000
Taxable profit	110,000
less corporation tax @ 52%	57,200
After tax profit	52,800

Reduction of tax payment - 109,200 – 57,200 = £52,000

This reduction of tax from investment expenditure constitutes an investment incentive that needs to be taken into consideration in investment appraisal. Befo moving on to the other main form of investment incentive, the investment grant we need to briefly look at the tax implications that arise when assets are sold.

When assets such as land and buildings are sold above their cost price, capital ga tax of $^{15}/_{26}$ of the profit is chargeable for companies. However most assets are sold below their cost price and a tax calculation called a *balancing allowance* or *balancing charge* is then made. For instance, assume the £100,000 plant and machinery in the previous example was sold three years later for £50,000. This would result in half of the capital allowance that had been claimed being paid back to the Inland Revenue through a balancing charge calculation (i.e. £50,000 @ 52% = £26,000) Thus if a project is likely to have a high terminal value for assets on which capital allowances have been claimed then corresponding balanci charges need to be built into the tax adjusted cash flows.

We will now look at the other main form of investment incentive; the govern ment grant. The grant system is directed at regional development, employment and selected industries as part of government policy. From an investment apprais viewpoint, agreed government grants must be included in the cash flows. This is simply a matter of determining the amount and timing and adding the figures into the calculations. There can be some complications where the grant affects the total capital allowance (not the rate) but once the facts are available the tax adjusted cash flows can be altered *(Refer to Volume 3 Finance and taxation for the non-accountant for more detail about government grants).*

10:2 Tax assessment Our concern in this sub-section is how the tax assessment will affect the cash flows of a project. The main point to note is that a business pays tax on its *total* profits. This means that a single project's profits may not be subject to tax if the business is: making losses, has accumulated losses brought forward and/or has large capital allowances. Thus tax adjusted cash flows for a single project can become very complicated, or an assumption can be made that the project's net cash flows will be classed as taxable profits. There seems little advantage in complicating subjective cash flow estimates with refined tax adjust ments. Accordingly it is suggested that tax adjusted cash flows are based on an assumption that *all* net cash inflows are taxable and net cash outflows allowable

The corporation tax rates (1981) are, 52% with a small companies rate of 40%. A small company is one making profits below £70,000. For profits between £70,000 and £130,000 the rate is 52% less $^{7}/_{50th}$ of the amount by which they are less than £130,000. For unincorporated businesses the rate can be between 30% to 60% (1980/81) depending on the total taxable income after allowances and deductions: i.e.

Total income after deductions and allowances			*Tax Rate*	*Tax Payable*		
£		£	%	£		£
0	to	11,250	30	0	to	3,375
11,250	to	13,250	40	3,375	to	4,175
13,250	to	16,750	45	4,175	to	5,750
16,750	to	22,250	50	5,750	to	8,500
22,250	to	27,750	55	8,500	to	11,525
	above	27,750	60		above	11,525

As individual projects' net cash flows are subject to the *business rate of tax*, this creates a further complication for assessing the after tax cash flows. Not only is there the difficulty of identifying the appropriate rate for the following year, but for subsequent years the rates may change. However, there have only been two substantial changes in business taxation (the introduction of corporation tax in 1965 and the change to the imputation system in 1972) that would significantly affect tax adjusted cash flows in investment appraisal.

10:3 Tax payment For investment appraisal the timing of tax payments and related capital allowances is most important. For businesses subject to corporation tax, there are two tax payments:-

Advance corporation tax (ACT) If a company pays a dividend it is paid gross to the shareholders and tax of $^{3}/_{7ths}$ of the dividend is payable to the Inland Revenue within three months of the dividend being paid to shareholders. ACT is applicable in the appraisal of a project's finance if it is being partly financed by equity and estimated dividends are being included in the cash flows

Mainstream corporation tax (MCT) This is the total tax liability less ACT that should be paid nine months after the end of each 12 month accounting period. Thus for investment appraisal, tax adjustments should allow one year between the assessment period and the cash flow effect.

Consider the following example that illustrates the timing of tax payments.

Example

A large company with a regular corporation tax rate of 52% is considering purchasing £100,000 of equipment on which there is a 100% first year allowance. The project will yield before tax net cash inflows of £30,000 per annum for three years and at the end of the third year the equipment will be sold for £50,000. The company discount factor is 10%.

Before tax NPV calculations		£	£
Initial cash outflow			(100,000)
Net cash inflows	30,000 x 2.49	74,700	
Terminal cash inflow	50,000 x 0.75	37,500	112,200
		NPV	£12,200

After tax NPV calculations		£	*Discount factor*	£
Initial cash inflow				(100,000)
Year 1	Capital allowance (100,000 x 52%)	52,000		
	Net cash flow	30,000		
		82,000	x 0.91 =	74,620
Year 2	Net cash flow	30,000		
	less 52% (Year 1)	(15,600)		
		14,400	x 0.83 =	11,952
Year 3	Net cash flow	30,000		
	less 52% (Year 2)	(15,600)		
	terminal cash flow	50,000		
		64,400	x 0.75 =	48,300
Year 4	52% (Year 3)	(15,600)		
	balancing charge (50,000 x 52%)	(26,000)		
		(41,600)	x 0.68 =	(28,288)
			NPV	£6,584

In this example there was an important difference between the before tax an after NPV's. The difference in the cash flows is illustrated in diagram 121. The main point to note is that the tax effect on cash flows is delayed one ye Thus the three year project in after tax cash flow terms becomes a four year project.

The timing of tax adjusted cash flows for businesses subject to income tax c be a little more complicated because of the basis of assessment. The normal method of assessing the taxable profit of incorporated businesses is on the annu accounts ending in the preceeding tax year. This means that the cash flow gap c be two years instead of the one year for corporation tax.

DIAGRAM 121 TAX ADJUSTED CASH FLOWS

Before tax discounted cash flow

	(100,000)	27,300	24,900	60,000	NPV = £12,200
Year:	*0*	*1*	*2*	*3*	

After tax discounted cash flow

	(100,000)	74,620	11,952	48,300	(28,288)	NPV = £6,584
Year:	*0*	*1*	*2*	*3*	*4*	

10:4 Tax adjustments in cash flows At this stage you will be aware that there are two types of tax adjustments for cash flows. The capital adjustment for capital allowances and balancing charges and a revenue adjustment based on the project's net cash flows.

A single capital adjustment is best dealt with individually as illustrated in the earlier example. However, the revenue adjustment needs to be made to every net cash flow. As it is a constant adjustment it is easier to alter the discount formula. Thus we have two types of discount formulae that are programmable, gross and net, i.e.

Gross $P\,(1+r)^{-n}$

Net at 42% $P.\,(1+r)^{-n} + \left[P_2(1+r)^{-n} - .42\,P\,1\,(1+r)^{-n}\right] + \left[P_3(+r)^{-n} + P_2(1+r)^{-n}\right] + \left[P_4 \ldots\ \text{etc}\right.$

Net at 52% $P_1(1+r)^{-n} + \left[P_2\;(1+r)^{-n} - .52P_1\;(1+r)^{-n}\right] + \left[P_3(1+r)^{-n} - .52P_2(1+r)^{-n}\right] + \left[P_4 \ldots\ \text{etc}\right.$

A number of discounted cash flow tables have been constructed that make allowance for tax and government grants. However they only relate to capital adjustments and their usefulness is questionable when there are usually only a few capital adjustments in a project. It is not possible to create a discount factor table that makes allowance for revenue adjustments. But the formulae can be programed, and as the majority of investment appraisal will soon be done by using packaged software, it is important that the software has a cash flow tax adjustment facility. Let us now work through a simplified example with taxation and investment grant data in the cash flows.

Example

A company is considering starting production of a new product in a development area. The details are as follows:-

(a) Factory rent free for 3 years then fixed rental of £10,000 per annum then thereafter.

(b) Plant and equipment £200,000 Government grant of £75,000 agreed payable at the end of the first year of operation. A 100% first year allowance will be available on the balance of £125,000.

(c) The project is expected to last six years with the following risk adjusted net cash flows:

Year 1	(£20,000)	whilst project is coming 'onstream'
Year 2	£30,000	
Year 3	£60,000	
Year 4	£80,000	
Year 5	£50,000	
Year 6	£10,000	
End ofYear 6	£50,000	from sale of plant and equipment at end of year.

(d) The company's corporation tax rate is 52% and total corporate profits are expected to be substantial during the life of the project.

(e) The company's weighted average cost of capital is expected to remain constant during the life of the project at 15%.

The following calculations show before tax and after tax cash flows and includes the government grant on the assumption that its payment will not be delayed.

Before tax NPV calculations		£	*Discount factor*		£
Initial cash outflow					(200,000)
Year 1	Net cash flow	(20,000)			
add government grant		75,000			
		55,000 x	.869	=	47,795
Year 2	Net cash flow	30,000 x	.756	=	22,680
Year 3	Net cash flow	60,000 x	.657	=	39,420
Year 4	Net cash flow	80,000 x	.572	=	45,760
Year 5	Net cash flow	50,000 x	.497	=	24,850
Year 6	Net cash flow	60,000 x	.432	=	25,920
			NPV		£6,425

After tax NPV calculation		£	*Discount factor*		£
Initial cash outflow					(200,000)
Year 1	Net cash flow	(20,000)			
add government grant		75,000			
		55,000 x	.869	=	47,795
Year 2	Net cash flow	30,000			
	Capital allowance				
	(125,000 x 52%)	65,000			
	52% of year 1 NCF	10,400			
		105,400 x	.756	=	79,682
Year 3	Net cash flow	60,000			
	52% of year 2 NCF	(15,600)			
		44,400 x	.657	=	29,171
Year 4	Net cash flow	80,000			
	52% of year 3 NCF	(31,200)			
		48,800 x	.572	=	27,914
Year 5	Net cash flow	50,000			
	52% of year 4 NCF	(41,600)			
		8,400 x	.497	=	4,175
Year 6	Net cash flow	60,000			
	52% of year 5 NCF	(26,000)			
		34,000 x	.432	=	14,688
Year 7	balancing charge	(26,000)			
	(50,000 x 52%)				
	52% of year 6 NCF	(5,200)			
		(31,200) x	.354	=	(11,045)
			NPV		(£7,620)

In this example the before tax NPV of £6,425 was converted to a *negative* after tax of £7, 620 and illustrates the importance of calculating after tax cash flows in addition to before tax cash flows.

11 Limitations of investment appraisal techniques
So far we have looked at four preliminary, three complementary and four time value investment appraisal techniques. We have also considered how risk, uncertainty, sensitivity, abandonment, taxation and government grants can be included in the cash flows. Unfortunately, all these cash flow refinements and appraisal techniques do not necessarily result in valid information for investment decisions. We can group the problems into the following broad categories:

i) Estimating the cash flows (Refer to sub-section 2:3, 9, 10)
ii) Acceptance criteria in terms of IRR cut off rate or the criteria for the NPV discount factor.
iii) Using the appropriate investment appraisal technique

In this section we will be taking a fairly critical look at the appraisal techniques that have been explained in this chapter and the common problem of project ranking under capital rationing.

The inadequacy of the non-discounting techniques was explained in section 3. It was suggested that some of these techniques such as payback, may be used as preliminary hurdles in a project appraisal process. The problem with using simple appraisal techniques as preliminary hurdles is that a good project may not pass the first hurdle because of an invalid appraisal technique. Moreover, if a company has the software (or access to software) for project appraisal, then once the cash flows have been estimated, the investment appraisal is simply a data processing function. Most investment appraisal software produces NPV and/or IRR output because it is quite easy to program. A few sophisticated packages may be capable of handling risk, sensitivity tax and government grant data. But the output will still probably be NPV and/or IRR. It is therefore appropriate to direct our attention to these two popular investment appraisal methods.

11:1 NPV and IRR From the outset we need to be clear that it is not necessary to choose between these two techniques. The use of NPV does not necessarily exclude the use of IRR and vice versa. It is however, necessary to be aware of their respective limitations. Consider the following example.

Example

A company was considering a choice between two mutually exclusive projects with the following cash flows:-

	Risk adjusted, before tax, net cash flow	
Year	*Project A* £	*Project B* £
0	(25,000)	(25,000)
1	14,000	0
2	10,000	5,000
3	7,000	10,000
4	6,000	25,000
	12,000	15,000

The company's discount factor was 5%. A local computer bureaux ran the cash flow data and provided the following output:-

	Project A	*Project B*
NPV @ 5%	£8,384	£8,749
IRR	21.4%	14.5%

The directors were confused, beacuse under the NPV method project B was preferable but using the IRR method project A should have been chosen. They then asked a management consultant for advice. He produced a graph (refer to diagram 122 and the following explanation:-

DIAGRAM 122 CONFLICT OF NPV & IRR

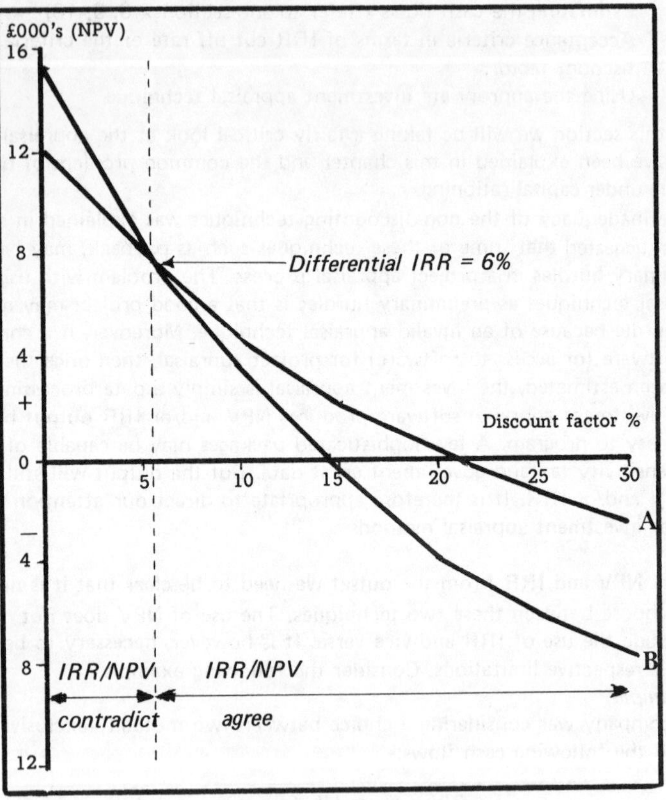

	Net Present Values	
D. Factor %	Project A £	Project B £
5	5,384	8,749
10	5,345	3,718
15	2,758	(345)
20	551	(3,693)
25	(1,356)	(6,430)
30	(3,032)	(8,738)

'The reason the two methods sometimes provide contradictory results is becaus of the difference in the implicit compounding of the interest rates *(Refer to section 6)* The NPV method for both projects had a compounding assumption of 5%. Whereas the IRR method had compounding assumptions of 21.4% for project A and 14.5% for project B. The effect of these different compounding assumptions are shown in the graph. It can be seen that at any discount factor below 6% NPV and IRR results for these two projects will be in conflict. When the discount factor is above 6% the two methods will be in agreement on the choice of project A'. As the company has a discount factor of 5% it is probable that the cut off rate is below the IRR's for projects A and B. Accordingly, to choose between A and B on an IRR basis the differential cash flows can be discounted as follows:-

Differential cash flow calculations

Year	*0* £	*1* £	*2* £	*3* £	*4* £	*NPV @ 5%*
Project A	(25,000)	14,000	10,000	7,000	6,000	-
Project B	(25,000)	0	5,000	10,000	25,000	-
A – B	0	14,000	5,000	(3,000)	(19,000)	(366)
B – A	0	(14,000)	(5,000)	3,000	19,000	366

The differential IRR of 6% is the same for A – B and B – A as shown in diagram 122. However, the differential NPV is greater for B – A. Therefore with a discount factor of 5%, project B should be chosen, even though its IRR is lower than project A.

From this example we can draw a few useful conclusions:-

i) For mutually exclusive projects it is possible for NPV and IRR to be in conflict

ii) The conflict arises when the discount factor is below the differential IRR

iii) Under these circumstances the decision should be based on the NPV

One point that needs to be mentioned at this stage relates to the compounding calculations that give rise to the NPV/IRR conflict. This compounding is often referred to as the *re-investment assumption*, on the basis that funds from a project are re-invested at the project's rate of return over its useful life. In practice, this is highly improbable, but the mathematics of compounding and discounting are made on a re-investment basis. This tends to support the argument that the appropriate discount factor for a project should be a rate applicable to the enterprise and not specific projects, because re-investment in the enterprise is a reasonable assumption. Accordingly, the IRR calculation that is based on specific project re-investment assumptions is not as sound as an NPV calculation based on an enterprise re-investment assumption.

There is one other criticism that is often levelled at the IRR method concerning multiple rates of return. When a project has more than one large negative cash flow over its life, it is possible for there to be more than one IRR. The NPV curves shown in previous diagrams have all been downward sloping but with the following type of cash flow it is possible for the curve to rise and fall as shown in diagram 123.

If a project is likely to have multiple IRR's none of the rates will be of use to the decision maker, because one IRR will not measure the project over its full life. Under these circumstances the NPV method is more appropriate.

As a general rule, when there is a conflict between NPV and IRR the NPV should be used.

DIAGRAM 123 MULTIPLE INTERNAL RATES OF RETURN

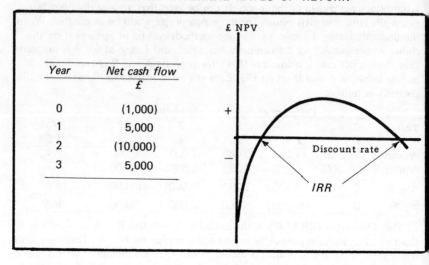

Year	*Net cash flow* £
0	(1,000)
1	5,000
2	(10,000)
3	5,000

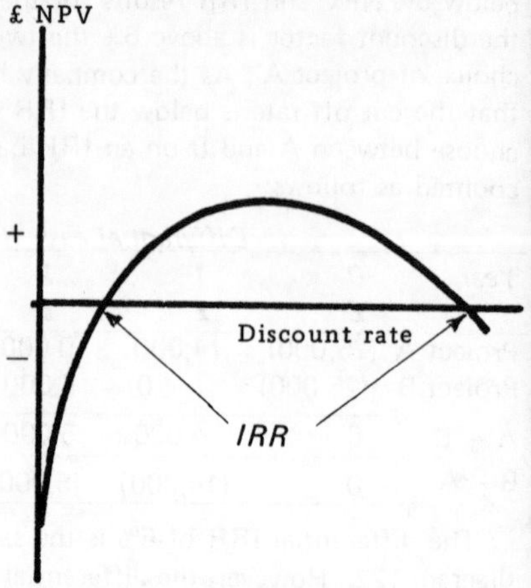

11:2 Capital rationing This term is used to describe investment conditions that are subject to financial constraint such as availability of funds. It is often said that finance will always be available for profitable projects. However, a company may impose its own capital expenditure limits based on internally generated funds Or, a subsidiary company will usually have a capital expenditure budget set by the holding company. The problem that arises with capital rationing is that a company may have many good investment proposals that have high positive NPV and IRR's above the cut off rate. But because of a financial constraint on the business not all the projects can be accepted.

The capital rationing problem can be broadly divided into two categories:-

(a) *Single-period rationing* where the financial constraint is limited to just one period; and

(b) *Multi-period rationing* where the financial constraint is set over several periods.

The objective for either of these categories is to select the projects that will optimise the use of available funds. As all the projects will have satisfied the NPV and/or the IRR criteria some form of project ranking is needed. Under single period rationing the present value index (PVI) method can be used. The PVI method was explained in sub-section 7:2.

Example

A company has a self-imposed financial constraint in its next accounting period of £80,000 based on internally generated funds for projects with positive NPV's The company's weighted average cost of capital is 12% and it can borrow at 15%. The project details are summarised below:-

Project A	$\frac{\text{Net Present Value}}{\text{Initial outlay}}$	$\frac{38,000}{20,000}$	PVI	=	1.9
Project B	$\frac{\text{Net Present Value}}{\text{Initial outlay}}$	$\frac{72,000}{53,000}$	PVI	=	1.36
Project C	$\frac{\text{Net Present Value}}{\text{Initial outlay}}$	$\frac{27,000}{18,000}$	PVI	=	1.5

Project D	$\frac{\text{Net Present Value}}{\text{Initial outlay}}$	$\frac{25{,}000}{14{,}000}$	PVI =	1.78
Project E	$\frac{\text{Net Present Value}}{\text{Initial outlay}}$	$\frac{75{,}000}{40{,}000}$	PVI =	1.87
Project F	$\frac{\text{Net Present Value}}{\text{Initial outlay}}$	$\frac{39{,}000}{25{,}000}$	PVI =	1.56

Project ranking	*PVI*	*Initial outlay* £	*Finance required* £
A	1.9	20,000	20,000
E	1.87	40,000	60,000
D	1.78	14,000	74,000
F	1.56	25,000	99,000
C	1.5	18,000	117,000
B	1.36	53,000	170,000

Although all the projects have favourable NPV's the financial constraint of £80,000 will allow only projects A, E and D to be accepted. If project F, C or B was divisible (i.e. the initial outlay could be divided and produce a proportionately reduced series of cash flows), then the remaining £6,000 could be allocated to a divisible project. The opportunity foregone from not financing projects F, C and B is illustrated in diagram 124.

DIAGRAM 124

INVESTMENT OPPORTUNITIES FOREGONE FROM CAPITAL RATIONING

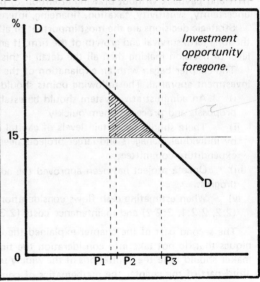

D = The demand curve for finance for all investments having positive NPV's at varying rates of return.

OP_1 = Projects accepted totalling £74,000.

OP_2 = Capital rationing limit of £80,000.

OP_3 = Projects with a rate of return above the marginal cost of finance totalling £120,000.

$OP_3 - OP_1$ = The investment opportunities foregone.

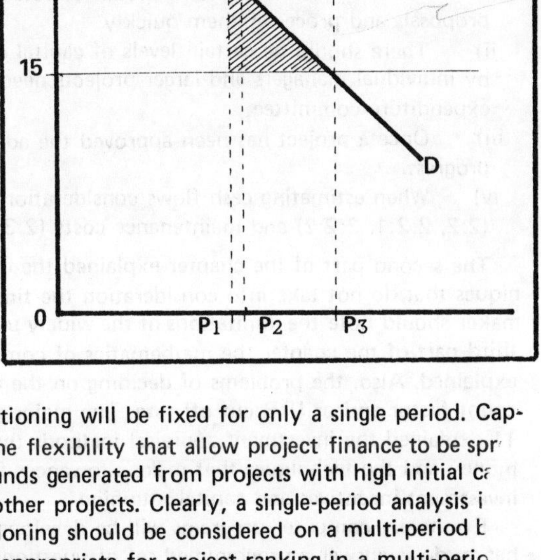

It is unlikely that capital rationing will be fixed for only a single period. Capital budgets normally have some flexibility that allow project finance to be spr over several years. Also, the funds generated from projects with high initial ca flows can be used to finance other projects. Clearly, a single-period analysis i too rigid, therefore capital rationing should be considered on a multi-period b The PVI method is not really appropriate for project ranking in a multi-perio capital rationing analysis. For instance lets assume a company expected its investment finance to be limited over a three year period to say £100,000 per annum and that it had many high yield investment proposals available. If severa of these proposals had high 'early' net cash inflows then these could be used to help finance projects in years two and three. Thus the opportunity value of thes early net cash inflows under capital rationing are related to subsequent investment proposals. The terms used to denote the opportunity value of these additiional funds are *'shadow prices'* or *'dual prices'.*

The ranking of projects in a multi-period analysis should take into considerat ion these shadow prices and the PVI method cannot do this. However mathematical models have been developed based on linear programming and integral programming that can cope with multi-period capital rationing. Eventually these advanced techniques will be incorporated into standard investment appraisal sof ware packages. All the decision maker will have to do is answer the questions required for input data and within seconds an optimal project ranking will appe on a visual display unit.

11. Summary

The author is aware that the substantial coverage of investment appraisal technique in this chapter may perplex the non-accountant. It is however very important that decision makers appreciate there is no single appraisal technique that will always provide the right accept/reject signals. Every technique has its limitations and it would be irresponsible to just explain the well established methods such as NPV, IRR and payback without drawing attention to practical problems such as risk, uncertainty, sensitivity, taxation, financing, interdependence and capital rationing.

Strategic decisions are the most important of all decisions because they determine the long term survival and growth of the firm. If an executive is responsible for this level of decision making then all the detail is this chapter is essential reading.

The chapter began with an explanation of the information requirements for investment appraisal. The following points should be noted:-

i) An administrative system should be established that encourages investment proposals and processes them quickly.

ii) There should be certain levels of capital expenditure that can be authorise by individual managers and larger projects need to be approved by a capital expenditure committee

iii) Once a project has been approved the administration should monitor its progress.

iv) When estimating cash flows consideration must be given to project life (2:2, 2:2:1, 2:2:2) and maintenance costs (2:3:2, 2;3;3)

The second part of the chapter explained the different investment appraisal tech niques that do not take into consideration the time value of money. The decision maker should note the limitations of the widely used payback method (3:3). In the third part of the chapter the mathematics of compounding and discounting were explained. Also, the problems of deciding on the appropriate criteria for the discount factor and/or IRR cut off rate. The major part of the chapter, sections 7 to 11 explained the investment appraisal methods that allow for the time value of money and the techniques that make allowances for risk, sensitivity, taxation, investment incentives and capital rationing.

Eventually computer programs will be developed where all the decision maker has to do is answer a programmed set of questions. The computer will then make all the appropriate calculations that have been explained in this chapter and provid a full investment appraisal. Currently (1980) most investment appraisal programs provide little more than a simple NPV and IRR analysis. This is inadequate for strategic decision making.

Accountancy Quiz No.7

1. Explain how you would organise the administration of investment appraisal in a medium sized company. *(2, 2:1, 2:1:1, 2:1:2, 2:1:3, 2:3, 2:3:1)*

2. What is terotechnology and its relationship to investment appraisal? *(2:3:2, 2:3:3)*

3. Explain how the following investment appraisal techniques are used:-

   Payback *(3:3)*
   Average rate of return *(3:4)*
   Cost benefit analysis *(4:2)*
   Cost effectiveness analysis *(4:3)*

4. What criteria would you apply when deriving a discount factor for investment appraisal? *(6, 6:1, 6:2)*

5. Explain how and why you would use, or not use, the following appraisal techniques:-

   Net present value method *(7:1, 11:1)*
   Present value index method *(7:2, 11:2)*
   Discounted yield method *(7:3, 11:1)*

6. Why should the financing decision for a project be separated from the investment decision? *(8:4)*

7. Explain three methods of making allowance for risk and uncertainty in investment appraisal and state which you would use and why. *(9:1, 9:1:1, 9:1:2, 9:1:3, 9:1:4, 9:2, 9:2:1, 9:2:2, 9:2:3)*

8. What is sensitivity analysis and how can it be applied to an investment proposal ? *(9:3)*

9. Explain how cash flows can be adjusted for:-

   Taxation *(10:2, 10:3, 10:4)*
   Investment incentives *(10:1)*
   Abandonment of a project *(8:5, 9:5)*

10. State some of the limitations of the NPV and IRR techniques and explain what investment appraisal methods you would use under conditions of capital rationing *(11, 11:1, 11:2)*

Budgeting Systems

Objective

To explain, for the non accountant, the principles, practices and problems of budgetary planning and control systems.

Content

Page No.

An explanation of the budgetary planning process, including descriptions of different individual budgets.

An explanation of the budgetary control process, including budget administration and the investigation of variances.

Budgeting Systems

1. Introduction

Any budgeting system can be divided into two inter-related components:-

(a) Budgetary planning; and
(b) Budgetary control.

The principles of planning and control were explained in chapter 2. In this chapter we are going to look at specific planning and control techniques. There are many kinds of planning and control techniques, but almost all of them work on the same control principle of comparing actual results with planned results. This principle is fundamental to the most widely established planning and control technique generally referred to as 'budgeting'.

Before going into the detail of budgetary planning and control it is worthwhile attempting to define a budget and to consider some of the objectives for establishir a budgeting system.

Definition of a budget

A budget is a quantitive statement relating to a future period of time of a policy to be pursued during that period towards stated objectives. A budget can therefore be viewed as an expected level of future performance against which actual performance is measured to determine whether actual results are proceeding in accordance with planned results. There are key words in this lengthy definition that require further explanation:-

Quantitive statement	The statements will cover costs, revenues and output and may be divided according to function, i.e. sales production etc. and/or relate to the organisation structure.
Future periods	The budget period is always in the future and the time perioc must be clearly defined.
Objectives	Objectives may relate to the long, medium or short term strategy of the firm. Policies are formed from the objectives and budgets should reflect these policies and objectives.
Expected/actual performance	The comparison of actual performance with expected performance is the main feature of the budgeting process as a control technique.

Objectives of a Budgetary System

The primary objective of a budgetary system is the provision of information to management that will assist in the control and direction of business activities for maximum efficiency. There are also a number of subsidiary objectives:

i) To improve co-ordination between departments and ensure departmental objectives fit into the corporate objectives.
ii) To improve functional co-ordination - for example between sales and product ion. If the demand was for product X and production insisted producing product Y then stock and cash flow problems would quickly develop.
iii) To provide a quantitative total plan for a future period of time.
iv) As a performance measure.
v) To assist the management delegation function where an individual can be given a budget responsibility.
vi) To increase motivation by involving people in the planning and control proces Also by linking a reward/penalty system to budget responsibilities.

vii) To increase awareness of cost control.

viii) To assist management to manage by the principle of management by exception. If actual performance is proceeding according to plan in one area management may then direct attention to another area where there is a significant variation between actual and planned results.

Now we have some idea of what budgets are and why budgeting systems are so widely used in industry, commerce and government, we can look at the budgeting process.

In most enterprises the budgeting process begins with budget planning. The planning horizon is usually one year, although some planning horizons are longer, such as capital budgeting (Refer to chapter 7). But in this chapter we will be directing our attention to budget periods of 1 year or less. Once the plans have been agreed, detailed budgets can be constructed that act as performance yardsticks during the budget period.

The following sections examine the main budgetary planning techniques, the administration of budgetary control, how budgets affect people and some different types of budgeting systems.

2. Budgetary planning

A large number of accounting techniques are concerned with recording, analysing and reporting on *past activities.* Although a lot of this work is legally necessary, it is of little use to managers, employees and owners who are concerned with *future activities* of a business. Accordingly, budgetary planning is a very important accounting technique. This first stage in the budgeting process provides managers with an opportunity to take a fresh look at the next accounting period. They can set new objectives and discuss ways of achieving them within the constraints that are expected to apply during the period under review. Indeed, the value of an enterprise is often more dependent on future plans than on past performance. Naturally, past results are often taken as an ability indicator of future performance. But the strength of an enterprise depends on management's capability of developing plans and converting them into results. It is therefore surprising that senior executives sometimes ignore the opportunity of proper budgetary planning and take the easy option of simply 'adjusting' the previous year's figures. We have already examined the principles of planning and control in chapter 2. Thus in the following sub sections we can look at budgetary planning in a little more detail.

2:1 Sales forecasting Let us begin by distinguishing between a forecast and a budget. Forecasts are *predicted outcomes* based upon a stated set of assumptions Whereas budgets represent *planned outcomes* that are part of the corporate strategy. Forecasting the level of business activity will normally depend upon sales expectations and therefore the sales forecast would be the starting point of the budgetary process. Sales forecasting involves two main activities:

General forecasting of economic conditions such as the trade cycle and terms of trade: and,
Specific forecasting relating to the industry, competition and the markets.

The general forecast can be obtained by analysing published details of well established macro-economic models such as the Treasury model. Also a lot of useful macro-economic information and general forecasting is published in bank reviews and economic journals. However, for most businesses, this aspect of forecasting is just to provide a general picture of expected economic activity over several years. It is particularly important for capital budgeting and the state of the economy can have a significant effect on specific sales forecasts.

Specific forecasting would be seeking the answers to questions such as:-

i) How large is the total market for a specific product or service is likely to be
ii) Is the market growing, static or declining?
iii) What is the company's existing market share?
iv) Will the company's market share increase, remain constant or decline?
v) Who are the major competitors and what are their market shares?
vi) What actions are the major competitors likely to take over the next year(s) that will affect the company's sales?

To answer this type of question the company would need to undertake market research. This can be very expensive. Diagram 125 shows how market research data can be presented. The important point for the decision maker is to know how the forecasts were derived. Market researchers generally use mathematical forecasting techniques. Most of the techniques identify data as belonging to specific time intervals and are referred to as *time series*. When analysing time series there are four movements that need to be identified:-

Secular trends	The smooth and regular movement over a long period of time
Seasonal trends	Short term movement such as the increase in food retailing receipts on Saturdays
Cyclical trends	Medium term movements after smoothing out seasonal trends
Irregular movements	Unpredictable variations that are unrelated to any trends

DIAGRAM 125 *SALES FORECASTING*

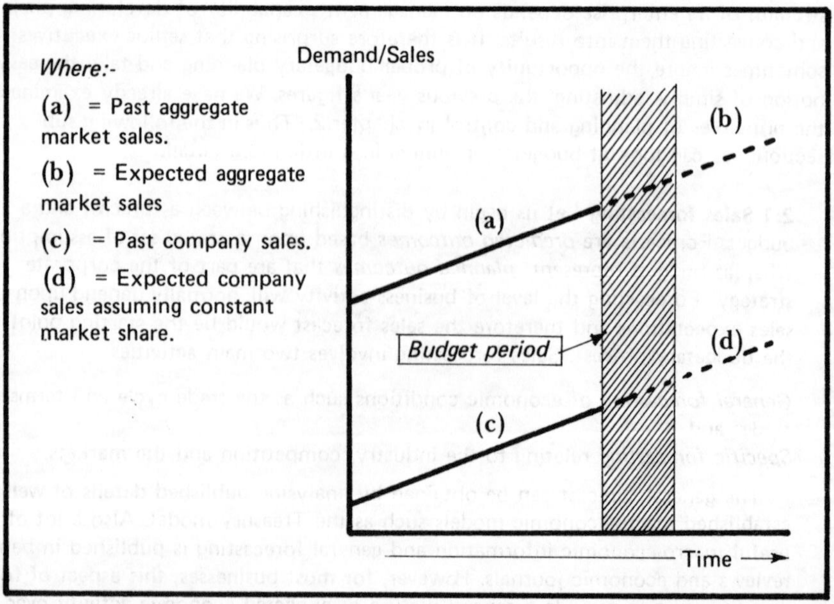

There are a number of techniques that can be used for smoothing out fluctuations and extrapolating the trend. Computer programs for this kind of forecasting tend to be based on mathematical models such as: polynominal models (i.e. linear and quadratic), logarithmic and exponential models. The point to note about these types of program is that generally they only extrapolate past data. A similar result can be achieved with simple techniques such as moving averages or just drawing an approximate smoothing line through a graph of historical data. Past events are not necessarily the best indicator of the future. Therefore, any forecasting program that only uses past data, regardless of the elegance of the mathematics and systems design, will produce an inadequate and possibly misleading forecast.

A forecasting program should be capable of allowing for: relationships between variables such as; the forward order book, salesmens' expectations, general economic forecasts, possible actions by competitors, as well as past sales data. The program should allow key variables to be adjusted on a 'what if.....?' basis. (Refer to chapter 7 sub-section 9:3). For the smaller business that does not have access to sophisticated software, sales forecasting will tend to be intuitive. An intuitive sales forecast can be an acceptable base for budget planning if it is constructed on objective criteria and all relevant data has been considered

2:2 Estimating capacity It is most unlikely that the sales forecast will exactly equal the productive capacity of a company. The sales forecast will be either above or below the capacity of one or more of the productive departments. Let us consider each of these conditions separately.

2:2:1 Sales forecast greater than productive capacity. Under these conditions, the firm would normally attempt to try and meet the expected demand whilst maintaining production flexability. The company would, therefore, consider the following alternatives to arrive at an output capability figure:

i) Overtime and other production incentives
ii) Shift working
iii) Hire, lease or purchase machinery
iv) Sub contract output requirement that cannot be met internally

Each of these alternatives have financial implications that need to be calculated For instance if more plant and machinery was needed to increase caoacity to meet the sales forecast, then capital budgeting would be needed (Refer to chapter 7). Even if additional fixed assets were not needed, the planned inccreased level of activity would require more working capital. Thus financing calculations would be undertaken. There would also need to be profit/volume calculations based on the planned figures to ensure that the proposals were profitable (Refer to chapter 6).

2:2:2 Sales forecast less than productive capacity. The main problems of operating below capacity are overhead recovery and laying off labour or short-time working. Consequently every effort would be made to maintain output. The company could consider the following possible course of action:

i) Try to increase sales by:
   (a) Increased advertising
   (b) Increased sales effort

(c) Price reduction and discounts
(d) Investigate export potential

ii) If the sales are expected to increase the following year then consider building up stocks

iii) Try to utilise the idle capacity by:
(a) Sub contract work
(b) New product

iv) Disinvestment decision if sales not expected to increase and above methods not possible. Sell excess equipment and lay off excess labour - (Refer to chapter 7 sub-section 8:5).

There are many problems associated with a planned total capacity reduction such as managerial motivation and industrial relations difficulties. Accordingly if the sales forecast is below productive capacity it may not be truly reflected in the budgets. There would probably be a tightening of cost control which may include a 'trimming of output' in selected areas. But the decision to significantly reduce capacity by laying off labour and possibly disinvestment is often delayed until it is forced upon management by increasingly adverse cash flows.

2:3 Co-ordinating sales, production and finance In the previous two sub-sections we have briefly looked at the problem of coordinating the sales forecast and a company's productive capacity. The linkage between production and sales is finance. Capacity can usually be increased providing:-

(a) The increased capacity will result in increased profits, and
(b) There are sufficient funds available to finance the expansion.

Conversely the problem of potential excess capacity requires financial calculations to determine the differential cost between disinvestment/capacity reduction and stock piling.

It is therefore clear that budgetary planning first requires the sales and production plans to be evaluated by the finance department to determine an optimum output/sales plan. The iterative process is illustrated in diagram 126. The reason why these separate activities need to be co-ordinated is because there will always be one or more factors that tend to limit all business activities. For example the sales forecast may not be converted into actual sales because of say: a shortage of skilled labour to produce the product. In this instance the limiting factor is skilled labour and thus becomes the *principal budget factor.*

DIAGRAM 126 CO–ORDINATING SALES, PRODUCTION & FINANCE

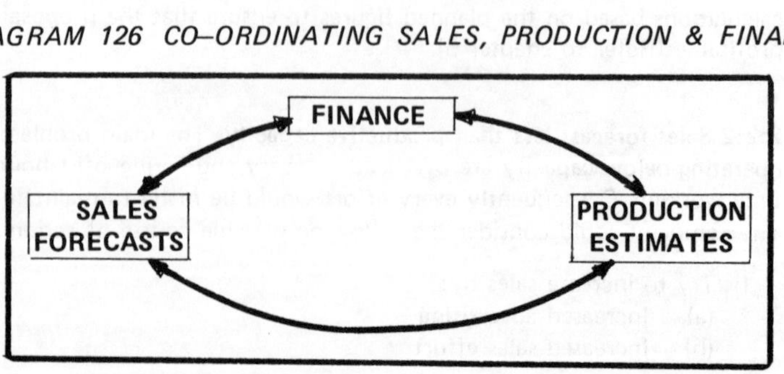

2:3:1 Principal budget factor (PBF) an essential part of the budget co-ordination process is to identify the principal budget factor. For example, assume a skilled labour PBF was ignored and investment in machinery and marketing was undertaken to increase capacity and market share. A crisis would soon develop because the PBF would prevent production targets being met then delivery promises would be broken and consequently orders would be cancelled To prevent this kind of crisis the budgetary planning process would seek to find the optimal output/sales plan based on maximising the principal budget factor. The principles and calculations for maximising the contribution in relation to limiting factors were explained in chapter 6 sub-sections 2:8:4 and 3:7.

2:4 Preparing the budgets Once the sales, production and finance budgets have been co-ordinated and the planned level of business activity agreed, the detailed functional budgets can be constructed. The inter-relationship of all these budgets is illustrated in diagram 127 and details about each type of budget are given in the following sub-sections.

DIAGRAM 127 INTER–RELATIONSHIPS OF BUDGETS

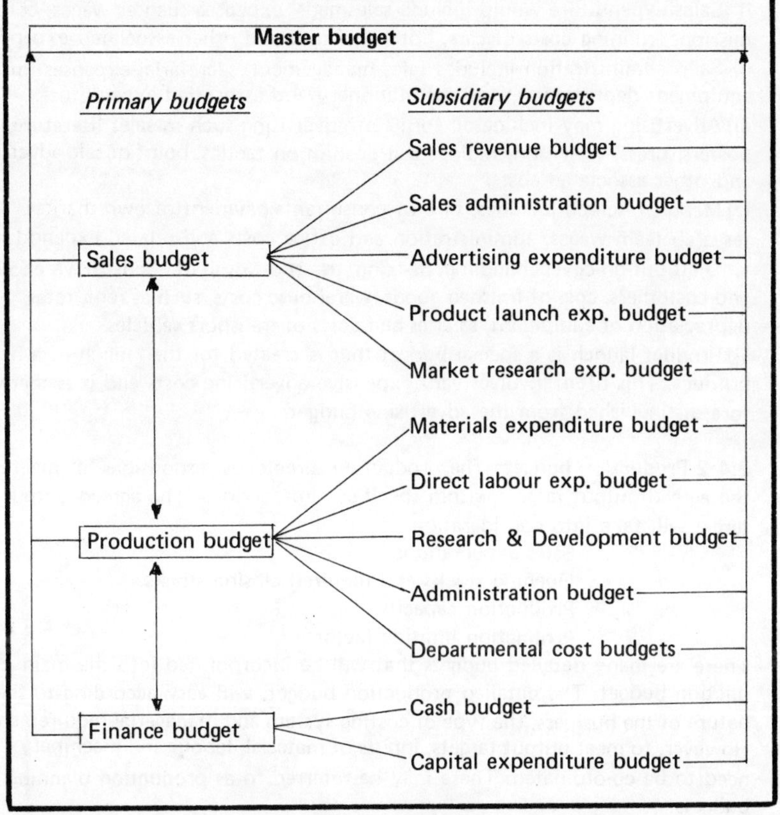

2:4:1 Sales budgets There are many kinds of detailed sales budgets. As a general classification they can be divided into sales revenue, budgets and sales cost budgets.

Sales revenue budgets are sales targets expressed in quantity and/or value terms They may be analysed in three ways:-

i) Area analysis, where sales targets are set on a geographical basis
ii) Product analysis where sales targets are set by product or groups of products
iii) Responsibility analysis where sales targets are set for individual salesmen and sub managers.

Often all three types of budgets (sales targets) are operated in one system and integrated into a total sales budget. For instance, an area may be allocated a sales target by product. The area manager would then allocate sales targets by product, or in total, to each salesman.

Sales cost budgets represent expenditure limits that are usually controlled according to function. These functions may include:

i) Sales expenditure
ii) Sales Administration
iii) Advertising
iv) Market research
v) Product launch

i) Sales expenditure would include salesmens' expenses such as wages, commissions, running costs of cars, hotel expenses and other associated expenditure.
ii) Sales administration includes sales management, secretarial expenses, office equipment depreciation, postage, stationery and associated expenditure.
iii) Advertising may include all forms of advertising such as sales literature, posters, press, television, radio, local promotion tactics, point of sale advertising and other associated costs.
iv) Market research includes, hire of consultants,payment of own market research team wages, administration and office costs and related expenditure.
v. Distribution covers handling, packing, transportation of goods to warehouse and customers, cost of finished goods, warehouse costs, such as rent, rates, depreciation of equipment, salaries and costs of transport vehicles.
vi) Product launch is a special budget that is created for the launch of a new product. This often involves very expensive advertising costs and it is therefore distinguished from the advertising budget.

2:4:2 Production budgets The production director is responsible for meeting the agreed output targets within specified time periods. The agreed output target will take into consideration:

Sales expectations
Opening stocks and required closing stocks
Production capacity
Production limiting factors

There are many detailed budgets that will be incorporated into the main production budget. The detailed production budgets will vary according to the nature of the business, the type of costing system and managerial requirements. However, to meet output targets, inputs of material, labour and machinery need to be co-ordinated. These may be referred to as production planning budgets.

Production Planning Budgets Production planning is the co-ordination and control of inputs to ensure that output targets are achieved in the correct quantity and quality at the required time. The production inputs that require co-ordination and control may be grouped under the following broad headings:

i) Materials
ii) Direct labour
iii) Overheads

(i) *Materials* The responsibility for providing the right quantity and quality of materials at the right time without excessive stock holding rests on the purchasing department. Sometimes the function of calculating all production input requirements is undertaken by a department called production planning or progress. Whatever the department title, the functions are , in principle, the same, i.e:-

(a) Calculating material requirements in relation to expected production levels and stock level requirements.

(b) Ordering materials from reliable suppliers at competitive prices so that delivery dates fit the production requirements.

(c) Making decisions on quantities ordered, taking into consideration: quantity discounts, expected price rises, costs of late deliveries and balancing them against the costs of holding stock and the company's cash flow.

The purchasing department budget will therefore be divided into two main parts: the costs of the purchasing department and the costs and quantities of the materials to be purchased. The costs of the purchasing department would include: wages and salaries, telephone, postage and a proportion of overheads. The most important part however, is the materials budget. This is usually drawn up by the production planning department and is a vital part of budget co-ordination in the budgeting planning process. An outline materials budget is illustrated in diagram 128. The quantity totals would be multiplied by expected prices to determine the total cost.

DIAGRAM 128 OUTLINE MATERIALS BUDGET

Ref: No.	*Description*	*Unit of Measure*	*Opening Stock & on order*	*Production Requirement*	*Required Closing Stock*	*Purchase Requirements*
AV989	1mm Nuts	Each	8,000	90,000	5,000	87,000
AK128	1mm Bolts	Each	11,000	90,000	5,000	84,000
2.391	3mmSteel Tube	Metres	200	1,000	300	1,100
728	Oil	Litres	600	4,000	1,000	4,400

(ii)Direct Labour The first stage of the direct labour budget is to calculate the manpower requirements for each department. The direct labour hours requirements at basic rate and overtime rate would then be written in to a direct labour cost budget. Indirect labour costs would be included in overhead cost budgets. An example of a manpower budget is shown in diagram 129. Manpower planning is explained in greater detail in chapter 4 section 4

DIAGRAM 129 *MANPOWER PLANNING BUDGET*

Manpower Budget Department 'C'

	Hours
Direct labour calculations: Total direct labour hours per employee after making allowance for holidays and annual leave	
48 weeks x 40 hours per week	1,920
Add normal overtime of 10 hours per week	480
	2,400
Deduct estimates from non productive time due to sickness, tea breaks, etc. 10%	240
	2,160
Total productive hours per employee x number of employees	10
Total productive direct labour hours available	21,600
Deduct production hours requirement 10,000 units taking 3 hours per unit	30,000
Additional direct labour hours required	8,400
Suggested plan: Three extra employees	7,200
Additional overtime	1,200
	8,400

(iii) *Overheads* Overhead budgets include machine utilisation and indirect expenses. Machine utilisation budget calculations are similar in principle to the direct labour calculations shown in diagram 129. The departmental indirect expe diture budgets will list all the indirect costs of each production department. The costs will be based upon the previous budget period figures adjusted according to circumstances. An illustration of an overhead planning budget is given in diagram 130.

DIAGRAM 130 *MACHINE UTILISATION BUDGET*

Machine Utilisation Budget Department 'A'

	Machine Hours
Normal machine usage including overtime (Similar calculations as in manpower budget)	3,000
Less downtime for repairs and maintenance 10%	300
	2,700
x number of machines	10
	27,000
Less output requirement in machine hours 10,000 units using 3 machine hours per unit	30,000
Additional machine hours required	3,000

Suggested plan - Purchase new machine
Alternatives: - (a) Overtime
(b) Shift working
(c) Sub contract

2:4:3 Research and development budgets. The basic purpose of a research budget is to limit expenditure. The problems associated with research expenditure are how much to allocate and whether the company is getting value for money The amount of money spent will depend upon the following factors:

(a) The nature of the industry
(b) Size of the organisation
(c) Actions of competitors
(d) Expected cash flows
(e) Existing commitment to research
(f) Success or failure of research to date
(g) Management attitude to research

Whether the company is getting value for money is very difficult to measure. In the long run, it will become evident if funds have been well utilised, but the very nature of research means it is risk expenditure.

2:4:4 Finance budgets At any point in time the company accountant should have a clear idea of expected cash inflows/outflows over the budget period. If a business unexpectedly runs out of cash, it is a clear indicator of bad financial planning and control. Within budgeting systems there exist many types of finance budget. But the main classifications are: cash budgets for short and medium term cash flows, capital budgets for medium and long term cash flows and final accounts' budgets that provide an estimate of future profit/loss and the expected asset/liability structure. In this sub section we will be briefly reviewing these main types of finance budget. (Additional detail is given in *Volume 3 - Finance & Taxation for the non accountant.*)

Cash Budgets For most high growth businesses the critical factor is cash. Consequently the cash budget is a vital budget in the planning and control process. To construct a cash budget all future estimates must be converted into:

(a) Specific costs and revenues; and
(b) Timing of each cost and revenue item

Once all the cash flows have been listed, a columnar budget is constructed that lists cash inflows and cash outflows against time. This is best illustrated by example.

Cash Budget Example

White Limited is to be formed with an ordinary share capital of 20,000 £1 shares to be paid on the 1st January. The company will purchase small 'X' type machines for re-sale at £100 each. Sales are expected to be as follows:

	Units		*Units*
January	50	April	100
February	70	May	100
March	100	June	100

Sales are on two months credit.

Deliveries will be	January	300 units
	April	300 units

Cost per unit £60. Payments due one month after each delivery.

Wages and other expenditure: £2,000 per month, payable in the same month
Initial equipment purchases £3,000 payable in January
Rent and rates payable £1,000 January, £1,000 June.
Using this basic detail a cash budget can be prepared to determine the finance requirements.

Detail	*January*	*February*	*March*	*April*	*May*	*June*
Cash Inflows						
Ordinary shares	20,000					
Sales	-	-	5,000	7,000	10,000	10,000
Total Inflows(a)	20,000	-	5,000	7,000	10,000	10,000
Cash Outflows:						
Purchases		18,000			18,000	
Salaries	2,000	2,000	2,000	2,000	2,000	2,000
Equipment	3,000					
Rent & Rates	1,000					1,000
Total outflows(b)	6,000	20,000	2,000	2,000	20,000	3,000
(a–b)	14,000	(20,000)	3,000	5,000	(10,000)	7,000
Balance B/F (c)	nil	14,000	(6,000)	(3,000)	2,000	8,000
Balance C/F						
(a – b) + c	14,000	(6,000)	(3,000)	2,000	(8,000)	(1,000)

This example illustrates how cost and revenue detail can be converted into a cash budget that will show the timing and value of finance requirements. In the example the business would have tried for overdraft facilities of £8,000. If a loan of £8,000 was arranged the money would not be fully utilised. It is important that the distinction between cash flow and profit is appreciated. White Ltd's budgeted profit statement would be:-

Budgeted Profit Statement for the Six Months ended 30th June

	£	£
Sales (520 @ £100)		52,000
Purchases (600 @ £60)	36,000	
less closing stock (80 @ £60)	4,800	
		31,200
Budgeted Gross Profit		£20,800
less:		
Wages and administration (6 x £2,000)	12,000	
Rent and Rates	2,000	
Depreciation estimated (10% of 3000 x .5)	150	
		14,150
Budgeted Net Profit		£6,650

Although White Limited has an estimated net profit of £6,650 there is a negative cash flow limit of £8,000 that is due to:

(a) The timing of the cash flows, and

(b) The inclusion of capital expenditure in the cash flow budget whereas in the profit calculation only the depreciation of capital expenditure is included.

Consequently a budgeted profit statement does not inform the business if there will be sufficient cash to meet future requirements. The cash budget is an essential part of the budget co-ordination process because unless finance is available to meet future operational requirements, then budget targets cannot be achieved.

Capital expenditure budgets. The main characteristics of capital expenditure budgets are:-

(a) The time period is usually longer than the operational budget period, and

(b) Large initial cash outflows are generally required.

An illustration of a capital budget expenditure budget is given in diagram 131 and capital budgeting is explained in detail in chapter 7.

DIAGRAM 131 OUTLINE CAPITAL EXPENDITURE BUDGET

Capital Expenditure Budget for the Five Years Ending 19- -								
Project Author-isation Number	*Brief Descrip tion*	*Cash Outflows (not discounted)*					*Total Re-placement Investment*	*Total Additional Investment*
		1977	*1978*	*1979*	*1980*	*1981*		
839	Grinding Machine	–	–	10,000	–	–	10,000	
840	Lathe	15,000	–	–	–	–	3,000	12,000
841	Delivery Vans		–	3,000	–	3,500	3,000	3,500
etc.								

2:4:5 Administration and miscellaneous services budgets. Departmental budgets for administration and miscellaneous services are constructed for expenditure control. Each budget will list all cost items related to relevant departments. Normally the head of a department will be responsible for cost control within the limits laid down in his department's budget. The arrangement and content of departmental cost budgets will vary according to the organisation's requirements. An example of a departmental cost budget is given in diagram 132

Service department managers sometimes need to be placed under strict cost controls, because the size and expenditure of a service department is often viewed as reflecting the organisational seniority of its manager. Thus a manager can enhance his/her status by increasing their department's staff and spending more money. Accordingly, budgetary planning should require *all* service departments' expenditure to be fully justified on a cost benefit basis. (Refer to chapter 7 sub section 4:2) can help to eliminate this bad management practice. This topic is discussed in more detail in a later sub-section on zero base budgeting.

DIAGRAM 132 OUTLINE ADMINISTRATION BUDGET

Administration Department Budget for Period Ending				
Last Year			*This Year*	
Budget	*Actual*	*Description*	*Budget*	*Actual*
		Salaries		
		Telephone		
		Postage		
		Stationery		
		etc.		

2:4:6 The Master budget. Master budgets are generally constructed in the form of a budgeted profit and loss account and a budgeted balance sheet. These budgeted statements will normally be far more detailed than the published accounts *(Refer to Volume 1 Financial accounting for non-accountants)*, but the total figures should be comparable with previous years. A budgeted profit and loss account is illustrated in diagram 133 and a budgeted balance sheet in diagram 134

DIAGRAM 133 *BUDGETED INCOME STATEMENT*

Budgeted Profit and Loss Account for the period ending	£	£
Sales revenue (from sales budgets)		x
Other revenue (from financial budgets)		x
		x
less cost of sales:-		
Direct materials (from materials budget)	x	
Direct labour (from production budget)	x	
Factory overhead (from production budget)	x	
Adjustment for opening /closing stocks	x	
Gross profit		x
less expenses:-		
Marketing costs (from sales cost budgets)	x	
Administration costs (from administration budgets)	x	
Other costs (from miscellaneous budgets)	x	x
Net profit before tax		x
Estimated tax		x
Net profit after tax		x
Estimated dividends		x
Retained profit for the year		x

DIAGRAM 134 *BUDGETED BALANCE SHEET*

Budgeted Balance Sheet as at	£	£
Fixed Assets (Existing plus capital expenditure budget)	x	
less depreciation	x	x
Current Assets		
Stock (from production budgets)	x	
Debtors (from sales budgets)	x	
Cash (from cash budget)	x	
Less current liabilities		
Trade creditors (from materials budget)	x	
Bank overdraft (from cash budget)	x	
Net Current Assets		x
Net Assets		x
Financed by:-		
Ordinary share capital	x	
Retained profits and reserves	x	
Retained profits and reserves		x
Equity interests		
Long term debt		x
Capital employed		x

The diagrams show how the budgeted final accounts derive their data from all the subsidiary budgets. These master budgets can then be compared with previous years' accounts by the board of directors. Once the master budgets are approved by the board of directors the budgetary emphasis moves from planning to control.

3. Budgetary Control

The previous sub-sections have been concerned with the planning part of a budgetary system. We will now turn our attention to the control aspects of budgeting. From the outset we need to be aware that good budgetary planning does not necessarily imply good budgetary control. Although plans provide useful yardsticks for control the real difficulties tend to arise during the implementation phase. Successful implementation of plans depends upon the effectiveness of management.(Refer to chapter 1) The ineffective manager will usually be able to provide a number of reasons why targets are not being achieved, but excuses rarely produce positive cash flows. However,if managers have not participated in the planning process and receive budget performance levels that are not achievable, then the budgetary system will simply produce adverse variances and may lose creditability as a control technique. In the following sub-sections we will be looking at the administration of budgets, flexible budgeting and the relationship between budgeting and standard costing.

3:1 Administration of budgets. The method of administering a budgetary system will vary according to the nature and needs of each organisation. However, in any organisation there are two key elements of budget administration that need to be identified:

(a) The allocation of responsibility for the budgetary system; and,

(b) The recording, analysing and communicating of budget information.

3:1:1 Allocation of budget responsibilities. The ultimate responsibility for a budgetary control programme rests with the chief executive. The function will be delegated to a person titled a *Budget Controller* or *Budget Officer.* The responsibility for budgets is shared by a *Budget Committee.* The Committee should have representatives from all major departments of the organisation to assist in the co-ordination stage of the budgeting process. The Budget Officer is often the Chairman of the Budget Committee. It is important that the Budget Officer has executive authority because he is responsible for preparing a *Budget Time Table* that requires many people to prepare budgets within time constraints If some departments are late in preparing their budgets, this can delay budget co-ordination and may result in budgets being issued during the budget period. When departments are under work pressure budget preparation may not be seen as priority work unless the chief executive gives the Budget Officer his full support. Therefore, the burden of responsibility should not be placed on an individual unless he is also given authority.

Budget responsibilities can also be divided on an organisational basis where budget cost allowances and their related actual costs are assigned to department and/or individuals. These are called *'budget centres'*. Example of budget centres are given in sub-section 5:3 - Responsibility accounting.

3:1:2 Communicating budgetary information. The 'people problems' associated with communication are discussed in section 4. What we are concerned with here are the principles and techniques of collecting, analysing and presenting budgeta information. Budgetary control is based on comparing actual results with planned results. The results are for specific time periods. The budget period does not necessarily have to be the company financial year. For example, the fashion industry is geared to the season of the year, therefore the budget period is most suited to a particular season. Alternatively, the budget period may be longer tha a year Nationalised industry capital expenditure plans may be as long as twenty years. However, for many organisations the use of the accounting year as a budget basic time period is the most suitable choice. The basic time period of one year is often divided into shorter control periods; quarterly, monthly, weekly or daily. A popular time period breakdown is thirteen four week periods.

Once the budget periods have been clearly defined, care is needed to ensure that the actual data collected over the time period is related to its comparable planned data. This requires precise cost and revenue definitions in the planning stage and a good costing system that is capable of collecting and analysing comparable data. Assuming the collection and analysis of data is satisfactory then attention can be given to effective communication. A common method of communicating budgetary information as a means of control is a four column analys illustrated in diagram 135. Although form design is an important aspect of budg communication a more important issue is *follow up.*

DIAGRAM 135 BUDGETARY CONTROL — FOUR COLUMN FORMAT

Department XYZ			*Budget Period* 3	
Detail	*Budget* £	*Actual* £	*Variance* £	*Variance to date* £
Materials	40,000	41,000	(1,000)	(3,000)
Wages	30,000	32,000	(2,000)	(8,000)
etc.				

Budgetary control needs to be linked to some kind of reward/penalty system If the actual results of a department are significantly different from the planned results and no follow up action occurs then the budgetary system loses its effectiveness. The fountain of control is the chief executive. If a manager over or unde performs in relation to the budget then he/she should be made aware that the performance has been noticed by a senior executive. This can create 'people problems', (refer to section 4) but without some form of reward/penalty linkage to budgetary control the system can become just a paper exercise. Under a 'paper exercise' budgetary system budgets are created, agreed, filed and forgotte until next year when the exercise is repeated again.

3:2 Budgetary control and standard costing These two accounting techniques both apply the same control principle of comparing actual and expected cost and revenu data. The main difference is that budgeting is a total concept aimed at co-ordinatin and planning business activity. These plans are then subsequently used as a means of control. Whereas standard costing is a unit concept, specifically directed at cost control, Standard costing tends to be far more detailed, where every cost item, is given a standard cost. These standard costs can be set as objectives and may not be achievable, whereas budgeted costs should represent expected costs. The two syste are not mutually exclusive. Indeed, many budgetary control systems are linked to standard costing. The principles and techniques of standard costing are explained in chapter 9.

3:2 Flexible budgeting. Budgetary planning produces fixed output, cost and revenue data in what are generally described as fixed budgets. When this fixed data is applied to budgetary control it is usually necessary to adjust some of the figures in relation to output. This is called flexing the budget. For example, assume the 'plan' was to produce/sell 1,000 units a month and the actual production/sales were 1,200 units a month. The production department may have been very efficient, but some cost budgets will show adverse variances indicating inefficiency. To overcome this problem the control part of budgeting will adjust the budget figures at the end of an accounting period to allow for changes in output. Fixed and flexible budgets are defined below

Fixed budgets are constructed during budgetary planning for future periods. The budgeted figures are fixed regardless of the level of actual activity.
Flexible budgets are constructed at the end of an accounting period as part of budgetary control. The budgeted figures are flexed to make allowance for the level of actual activity.

To flex a budget, the costs are divided into two categories, costs that vary with output and costs that remain fixed regardless of output. When the actual output level is known a *Budget Cost Allowance (BCA)* is calculated. Thus in flexible budgeting actual costs are compared with their related budget cost allowances. There are two methods of calculating the budget cost allowance:-

Formula method where costs are divided into variable costs per unit of activity and fixed costs. The following formula is applied when actual activity is known:-

BCA = Fixed costs + (Unit variable costs x actual units of activity)

Multi-activity method where budgets are prepared for different levels of activity and the budget cost allowance is calculated by interpolating between the relevant activity levels.

One of the problems with the formula method is that variable costs are generally not linear throughout the activity levels. Also the formula makes no allowance for stepped fixed costs that can occur at various activity levels (Refer to chapter 6, sub-section 2:9:2) Accordingly it is suggested that the multi-activity method should be applied whenever non linearity and stepped fixed costs are likely to occur.

An application of the multi-activity method for flexible budgeting is to plot the expected total costs of various levels of activity on a graph and draw in a line of best fit as shown in diagram 136. The line is usually curved and is therefore often referred to as *'curve expenses'*.

Example
A company has a 100% productive capacity of 100,000 units of output over a four week budget period. From past experience and future cost estimates the following cost data has been compiled:-

Level of activity	*20%*	*40%*	*60%*	*80%*	*100%*
Cost detail	*£000*	*£000*	*£000*	*£000*	*£000*
Fixed costs	10	10	10	10	12
Variable costs	10	15	22	24	26
Total costs	20	25	32	34	38

DIAGRAM 136 CURVE EXPENSES

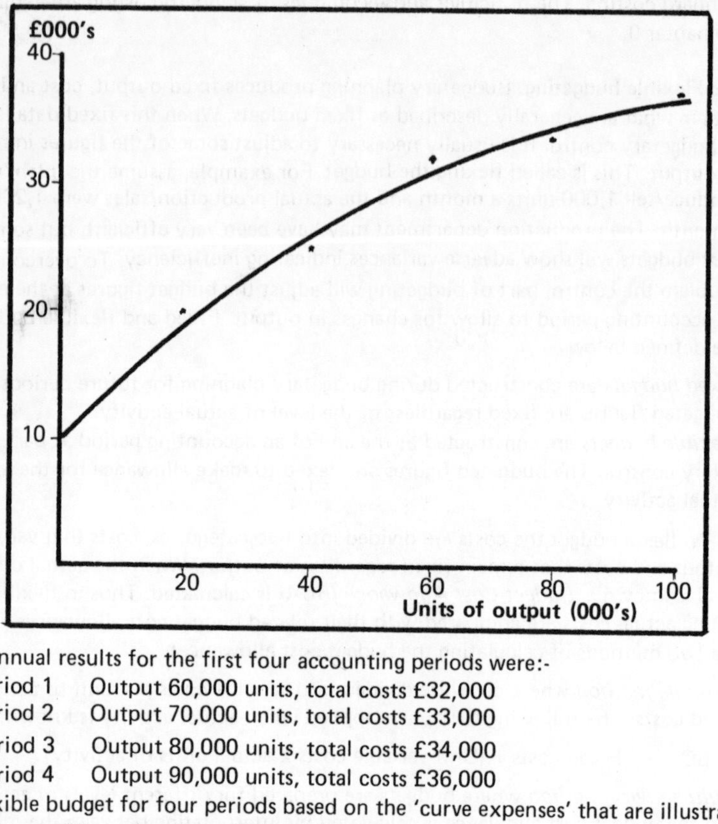

The annual results for the first four accounting periods were:-

Period 1 Output 60,000 units, total costs £32,000
Period 2 Output 70,000 units, total costs £33,000
Period 3 Output 80,000 units, total costs £34,000
Period 4 Output 90,000 units, total costs £36,000

A flexible budget for four periods based on the 'curve expenses' that are illustrated in diagram 136 produced the following results:-

Summary budget for the period ending
Production Department 'X'

Period	*Activity*	*Budget*	*Actual*	*Variance*	*Variance to date*
	%	*£*	*£*	*£*	*£*
1	60	32,000	33,000	(1,000)	(1,000)
2	70	33,000	34,000	(1,000)	(2,000)
3	80	34,000	35,000	(1,000)	(3,000)
4	90	36,000	36,000	nil	(3,000)

3:4 Allowing for inflation Rising prices during the budget period are almost certain to affect every budget. For a budgetary system to be an effective planning and control technique, allowance must be made for inflation. Before looking at ways of allowing for inflation it is necessary to distinguish between general and specific inflation. General inflation is measured by the Retail Price Index which represents an averaging of price movements for the average U.K. household. *(Refer to Volume 1 Financial accounting for non-accountants, chapter 10)* This basket 'index' is of little use for budgetary planning and control. It provides a general indication of potential wage claims but it is too broad an average for detailed cost estimates. Our interest is in specific inflation that relates to rising prices for specific categories of goods and services.

For example details about rising costs of energy in the form of gas, electricity, coal or oil are available from government statistical publications. Many price increases are known in advance, such as electricity, gas, coal, telephone and postage Specific price indices for raw material can be be maintained and extrapolated and estimates made of expected increases in wages, rents and rates. The following table illustrates the kind of calculations that need to be made:-

Description	*Previous year's cost* £	*Expected price increases* £	*Current cost* £
Rents	20,000	10%	22,000
Wages and salaries	50,000	15%	57,500
Rates	4,000	50%	6,000
Telephone	1,000	20%	1,200
Postage	1,500	25%	1,875
Electricity	900	30%	1,170
Materials	40,000	8%	43,200
	117,400		132,945

(Note: These are price adjustments to derive current costs. Subsequent activity (adjustments should then be made on the current costs, not on historic costs)

There are a variety of ways that inflation adjustments can be made to budgets. Clearly they need to be distinguished from activity adjustments that were explained in the previous sub-section. If inflation adjustments are not included in budgetary planning and control calculations then the system will simply produce adverse variances and may lose credibility.

3:5 Budget variances A budget variance is the difference between budgeted and actual cost/revenue data. Budget cost variances are sometimes referred to as 'overspend' or 'underspend'. Whatever the terminology, the principle is still the same, comparison of actual results with planned results. The analysis of variances is explained in some detail in the following chapter about standard costing. In this sub-section we will consider the use of budget variances as a control technique. There are three aspects of budget variances that need to be examined, significance, trend and controllability. The investigation of budget variances regarding these three aspects is illustrated in diagram 137 and explained in the following notes.

3:5:1 Significance of variances. Budgets are *estimates* of future output, costs and revenue and therefore represent *approximate* measures. Accordingly, variances will always arise. Managers therefore have to decide if each variance is significant and thus require investigation. Statistically, a variance is significant if it could not have arisen by chance. The principle of statistical significance is illustrated in diagram 138. (Refer to chapter 6 sub-section 2:7:1, 2:7:2 and chapter 7 sub-section 9:1:2). Clearly the budgetary control system should highlight statistically significant variances to ensure they receive management attention. An advanced budgetary control system would have a program that made probability calculations for variances and produced a budget range as illustrated in diagram 139.

DIAGRAM 137 FLOWCHART FOR INVESTIGATING BUDGET VARIANCES

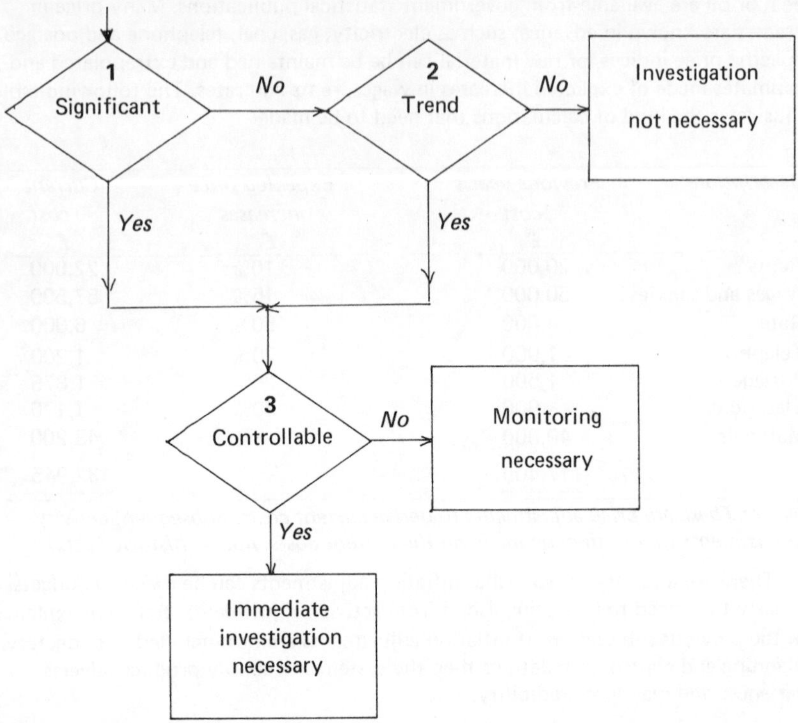

The significance, trend and controllability aspects of variance accounting are illustrated in this flow chart. The chart shows that the first point to establish about a variance is, if it is significant. If it is not significant, is there an adverse trend? If there is no significance or adverse trend then no investigation is needed. However, if there is an adverse trend and/or a significant variance then its controllability has to be considered. If it is not controllable within the accounting period then the costs are closely monitored until corrective action can be taken. If the variance is controllable, then an immediate investigation is needed and subsequent appropriate corrective action taken.

1.*Significance* A decision is needed for the action level for a variance. In some instances a 5% difference between actual and standard may be considered significan whilst in other instances the significance of a variance may not be until there is a 25% difference. Probability calculations can be used to determine significance leve

2.*Trend* The trend of variances is equally important as their significance. Ideally the trend indicators should enable minor corrective action to be taken to prevent a variance going above the significance level.

3.*Controllable* The controllability of variances is usually related to time. In the long run all costs can be controlled. But within an accountancy control period, some costs may not be controllable, therefore no immediate action is possible.

DIAGRAM 138 STATISTICAL SIGNIFICANCE AT BUDGET VARIANCES

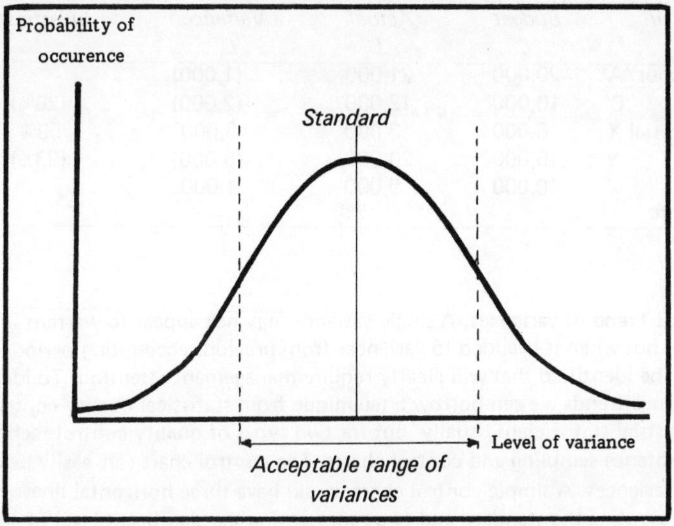

DIAGRAM 139 KEY FACTOR BUDGET VARIANCE CONTROL CHART

These two diagrams illustrate the principles of the significance levels for variances. The same principles apply for standard costing and budgeting. The normal distribution above, shows that there should be an acceptable range for a variance based on its probability of occurence. Whilst the control chart approach shows that a variance trend can be established. A good accountancy control software package should provide upper and lower significance levels for variances based on their probability of occurence. The package should also provide a control chart display, on request, for any variance. This would show the trend of a variance over time and thus help with cost control and standard setting.

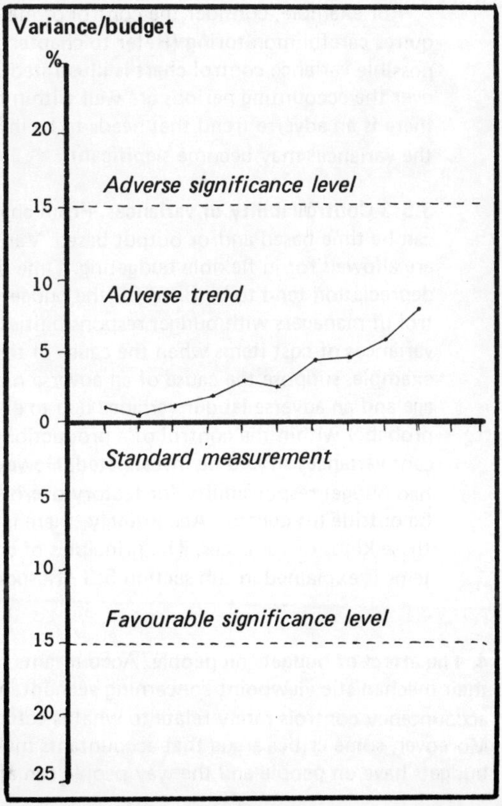

A simpler method would be a percentage calculation of variance divided by th budget. In the following illustration the investigation level has been set at 15%

Detail	*Budget*	*Actual*	*Variance*	*Investigate*
	£	*£*	*£*	*%*
Labour 'A'	20,000	21,000	(1,000)	-
'B'	10,000	12,000	(2,000)	(20%)
Material X	6,000	3,000	3,000	50%
Y	15,000	20,000	(5,000)	(33%)
Z	10,000	9,000	1,000	-
etc				

3:5:2 Trend of variances. A single variance may not appear to warrant investig tion, but when it is added to variances from previous accounting periods a tren may be identified that will clearly require management attention. To identify variance trends we can borrow a technique from statistical quality control. Industrial statisticians usually opt for two types of quality control techniques, acceptance sampling and control charts. The control chart can easily be adapte for variances. A simple control chart would have three horizontal lines: one representing the standard and two representing the significant level of adverse and favourable variances. The significance levels can be determined by probabi ity calculations or simple percentages.

For example, consider the control of maintenance costs for an area that requires careful monitoring (Refer to chapter 7 sub-section 2:3:2 terminology) A possible variance control chart is illustrated in diagram 139. It shows the varia over the accounting periods are well within the 15% significance limits. Howev there is an adverse trend that needs to be investigated and corrected, otherwise the variances may become significant.

3:5:3 Controllability of variances. From chapter 2 you will be aware that costs can be time based and/or output based. Variations in costs due to output chan are allowed for in flexible budgeting. Time based costs such as rent, rates and depreciation tend to be fixed for the budget period and are not within the con trol of managers with budget responsibilities. There is little point in investigati variances of cost items when the cause of the variance is not controllable. For example, suppose the cause of an adverse materials variance was excessive wast age and an adverse labour variance due to excessive overtime. These costs are probably within the control of a production manager and therefore the significant variances should be investigated. However if the production manager also had budget responsibility for factory overhead costs such as rates, they would be outside his control. Accordingly, there is no valid reason for investigating these kinds of variances. The principles of cost controllibility in budgeting systems is explained in sub-section 5:3 - Responsibility accounting.

4. The effect of budgets on people. Accountants have been frequently criticised for their mechanistic viewpoint concerning accountancy control systems. It is claimed th accountancy controls rarely relate to what is actually happening in an organisation. Moreover, some critics argue that accountants make no attempt to determine the ef budgets have on people and the way people can affect budgets. To a certain extent these criticisms are valid and there is some useful accounting research being undertaken on the behavioural implications of accounting systems.

For some while, the behavioural schools in management theory have been influencing managers to such an extent that an accepted definition of management is now'getting things done with and through people'. These developments in participative management styles have resulted in practical changes of accountancy control systems. The changes can be just involving managers at the planning stage and then democratic discussions about results. Or more advanced motivation systems such as management by objectives. (This technique is explained later in sub-section 5:4) The point to note here is that *managers decide on the nature of their control systems, not accountants.* If a company's management style is autocratic then the control system will be designed accordingly. Only when managers are prepared to change their style can accountancy planning and control systems begin to make allowances for the effect of budgets on people. In the following sub-sections we will be looking at some of the 'people problems' associated with budgetary control. Many of these problems are the subject of continued debate in the accountancy profession and frequently appear in accounting journals.

4:1 Motivation. There is a substantial amount of theory on motivating employees with a view to increasing output. The prime motivators seem to be money, leadership, supervision, personal recognition, work groups and individual attitudes. Budgets can in one way or another affect all of these motivators, because budgets set goals and measure performance. Empirical studies of employees and managers in their place of work have revealed that budgets are often viewed by employees as pressure devices to improve efficiency. Some studies have attempted to draw general conclusions on how employees react to budgetary pressure[1]. One such conclusion is that individuals join groups for emotional support, security within a group and relief from pressure. These cohesive groups then develop tactics to combat management and budgetary pressure. If management pressure is subsequently reduced this will not cause the groups to break up. Thus a possible 'people effect' from the use of budgets as pressure devices, is to create employee pressure groups working against the budgets.

Supervisors are often placed under budgetary pressure. Researchers interviewing supervisors, have reported that they did not usually pass the pressure-on to the shop floor, because it may cause trouble. The problem therefore was to learn how supervisors relieved themselves from budgetary pressure. There appeared to be three forms of pressure relief:-

(a) Blaming other departments or supervisors for errors
(b) Blaming accountants for irrelevant budgets and/or wrong actual data
(c) Internalizing the pressure

In the long run this kind of pressure is bad for the individual and consequently counter productive for the firm. Although these research findings are not applicable to all work situations the general message is applicable. *Great care is necessary if budgets are to be used as a pressure device.*

When middle and higher level management are subjected to budgetary pressure the biggest risk is the effect of failure. If a manager feels he/she has failed then this can have serious adverse effects on work performance and personal relationships. Some research experiments on success and failure at work produced the following list of tendencies for people who had experienced failure:-[2]

---

1) Chris Argyris in Harvard Business Review Vol.31, No.1
2) Ronald Lippet and Leland Bradford in Personnel Administration 4 December 1945

i) Lose interest in their work
ii) Lose confidence in themselves
iii) Lower their standards of achievement
iv) Give up quickly
v) Fear and resistance to change
vi) Expect failure
vii) Escape from failure by daydreaming
viii) Become difficult to work with
ix) Become overcritical of other people

The consequences of widespread managerial apathy could damage a company. Thus if budgetary pressure is to be applied to managers as a motivational device care is needed to ensure that managers do not experience *constant* failure.

One of the prime motivators in a company is the reward/penalty systems. A good system would encourage managers to act like entrepreneurs by rewarding them for successful risk taking and applying penalties for failure. Indeed, one of the reasons for decentralisation of power in large businesses was that by granting managers more autonomy, it created higher motivation and improved business performance. Budgets tend to concentrate more on penalties than on reward. The entrepreneurial manager is not encouraged to take risks under a budgetary control system. Indeed a budgeting system tends to favour the inward looking 'play it safe, organisation man'. The dynamic entrepreneur will rarely fit into a budgetary control system.

The problems of linking rewards into a budgetary system can be divided into two parts; monetary and non-monetary rewards. Monetary reward motivation systems such as productivity deals and profit sharing were explained in chapter 4. Labour management. In this sub-section we will briefly consider the non-monetary rewards. The appropriate starting point is to summarise Maslow's hierarchy of needs theory[(3)] The theory is based on man being a wanting animal and subject to the following principles:-

(a) Man always wants, and wants more
(b) Needs and wants are arranged in a hierarchy of importance (See diagram 140)
(c) Satisfied needs do not motivate behaviour

Diagram 140 shows the hierarchy of needs as a five level pyramid with the basic drives such as food and shelter at the bottom working up to the ultimate personal needs that are probably never fulfilled.

In some political/economic systems motivation is based on the bottom two levels of the pyramid. But in civilised societies, no individual should be entirely work motivated by physiological or safety needs. A caring society will provide a social safety net of safeguards to ensure no person is denied the right to survive.

The importance of this theory for reward/penalty systems and budgeting is that it is directed at the top two levels of the pyramid. This is especially true for managers whose behaviour is goal-directed. If the goal setting part of a budgeting system can help create high corporate aspiration levels within employees, then this can be a powerful kind of non-monetary motivation. We will return to this part in a later sub-section on participation in the budgetary planning process.

4:2 Budgetary bias. The budgetary principles and practice explained in this chapter are based on the assumption that managers are rational economic decision makers. A substantial amount of economic theory is also based on the same assumption. However, managers are not rational decision makers. Boundaries upon rational

(3)A.H. Maslow in Motivation and Personality (Harper & Brothers 1954)

DIAGRAM 140 HIERARCHY OF NEEDS

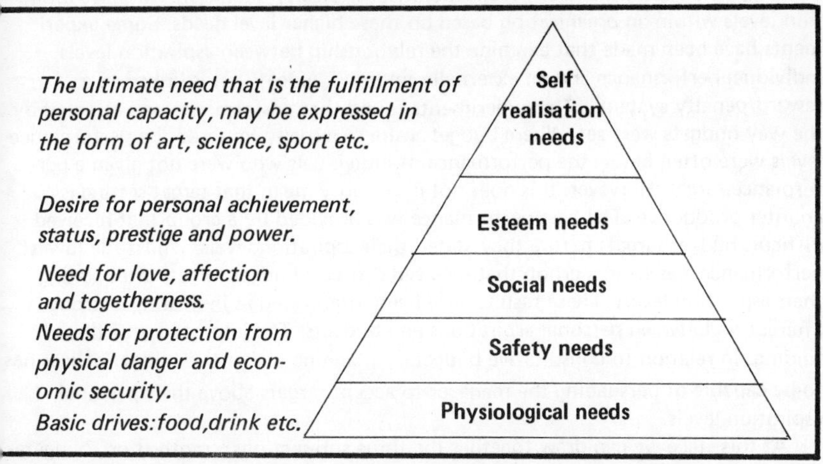
The ultimate need that is the fulfillment of personal capacity, may be expressed in the form of art, science, sport etc.
Self realisation needs
Desire for personal achievement, status, prestige and power.
Esteem needs
Need for love, affection and togetherness.
Social needs
Needs for protection from physical danger and economic security.
Safety needs
Basic drives: food, drink etc.
Physiological needs

decision making are created by attitudes, motivations and lack of knowledge. This bounded rationality can emerge in the budgetary planning process. Managers may attempt to bias the budgets by understating revenue estimates and overstating cost estimates so that the budgets are more easily attainable. Budgetary bias can occur at any level in the planning process and thus create *budgetary slack.* For instance a cautious production manager may state that full capacity at peak efficiency is say 100,000 units when in reality the figure could possibly be 120,000 units. The budgetary slack in this instance would therefore be a positive 20,000 units.

Budgetary slack will not necessarily always be positive. Negative and positive slack has been identified by researchers. Sales managers appear to be prone to negative slack by making optimistic sales forecasts to impress their chief executive. Although optimism is a necessary quality in salesmen, realism is even more neeessary for budgetary planning. Accordingly, the budget officer should ideally be objective independent and capable of identifying bias in management estimates. Even with the ideal budget officer it would still be very difficult to remove budgetary slack, especially if the budgeting system was linked to a reward/penalty system.

4:3 Participation. The problem we are concerned with in this sub-section is: should managers participate in the budgetary planning process? To develop a participative budgetary planning system is an important policy decision that reflects the managerial style of the company. Chief executives often refer to *participative planning* when what they are really describing is *consultative planning.* There is a very important difference. With consultative planning, senior executives retain the right of decision. Whereas with participative planning, decision making is shared. The behavioural schools in management theory have considerably weakened the resolve of traditional authoritarian managers. Even so, there must surely be few chief executives that will freely and genuinely hand over their power to junior executives. Thus we can assume that most discussions on participation in budgetary planning are really referring to consultation. Whatever the title, there is a trend in budgetary planning away from the remote externally imposed budget system and towards increased managerial involvement in setting target performance levels.

The problem of motivating managers has attracted many researchers. Earlier we referred to Maslow's hierarchy of needs, that indicates managerial motivation tends to be based on esteem and self-realisation needs. Clearly, managers will have aspiration levels within an organisation based on these higher level needs. Some experiments have been made that examine the relationship between aspiration levels, individual performance and an externally imposed budget that is linked to a reward/penalty system[4]. The experiments found that performance was affected by the way budgets were set. Where budgets were externally imposed the performance levels were often below the performance of individuals who were not given a performance target. However, this does not necessarily mean that target setting is counter productive. The best performance was provided by a group that received difficult budget targets before they stated their aspiration levels. Whilst the lowest performance was from a group that received difficult budget targets after stating their aspiration levels. These results have been interpreted as indicating a strong interaction between personal aspirations and budgets. The importance of these findings in relation to consultative budgetary planning is that the budget officer has to be capable of persuading the manager to accept targets above their personal aspiration levels.

At this stage we can draw together the three sub-sections: motivation, budgetary bias and participation, and attempt to draw some conclusions. It is clear that there is a 'People effect' on budgets. We have identified just two areas where this can adversely affect performance.

(a) Reduced employee motivation; and
(b) Sub optimal target setting

The use of budgets as pressure devices for increased performance carries a risk of increasing internal conflict between employee pressure groups and management. There is also a risk that high target setting linked to a reward/penalty system may produce failure tendencies in managers. Fears of high target setting and budgetary pressure can cause budgetary bias in the planning process, resulting in budgets not representing the real position and thus losing credibility.

Planning, control and motivation are management functions and it is for the chief executive to decide on the appropriate budgetary system. This really depends on the managerial style. But even the most autocratic chief executive will surely recognise that managers have aspirations and attempt to reconcile these needs with in the corporate plan. To allow managers at *all levels* to participate in planning does not necessarily mean an erosion of executive power. The process could just be consultative and still be a valid method of resolving some of the 'people problems'. The point to note here is that accountants and systems analysts produce budgetary systems to meet management requirements. If the system is faulty due to the 'people effect', it is the responsibility of the chief executive to alter the organisation and managerial style. When executives are prepared to widen their planning franchise then the budgetary system can be altered. It is therefore inappropriate to direct the blame on accountancy planning and control systems when the chief executive has the responsibility for an appropriate budgetary system and the power to direct change.

5. Types of budgeting systems

A feature of any budgeting system is that it should be tailor made to meet the needs of the organisation and suit the management style. Accordingly, no two budgeting

---

(4) A.C. Stedry Budgeting and Employee Behaviour in the Journal of Business (1964)

systems will be identical, except in subsidiary companies having to comply with a uniform costing system (Refer to chapter 3 sub-section 5:5). There are however broad categories of budgeting applications that have gained popularity during the last two decades. Generally speaking these applications fall into two broad areas:

i) Systems developments; and
ii) Behavioural developments

In the first two sub-sections we will look at two types of systems developments: zero budgeting and planning, programming and budgeting systems (PPBS). Both of these systems applications have been developed in the public sector, but they do have some private sector relevance. In the last two sub-sections we will look at budgetary applications that make allowance for the 'people effect' explained in section 4. Responsibility accounting being based on the principle of identifying budgetary responsibilities for people and management by objectives based on the principle of full participation in objective setting.

There are of course many other applications of budgeting but they tend to be based on principles of one or more of the systems explained in this chapter. For instance, *Response Budgeting* identifies key areas for control and provides two levels of figures to provide an incentive for managers to strive for a higher level of efficiency. There are many similar kinds of 'tag on' motivational devices attached to productivity deals or profit sharing incentives for managers. Whatever the budgetary system, they will all follow the same basic rules of setting performance targets that are subsequently used as yardsticks against which actual performance is measured.

5:1 Zero budgeting. This type of budgeting system may be referred to as *Zero Base Review, Zero base budgeting or Program Analysis and Review (PAR).* Although technically, PAR really describes a form of control on a budgeting system that is usually part of a *Planning Programming Budgeting System (PPBS).* This is explained in the next sub-section. Whatever the choice of title, a zero budgeting system will be based on the concept of having to justify all existing activities in the same way as new proposals. Thus,established activities will have to be compared with alternative uses for available resources during the budgetary planning phase.

As we have noted in earlier sections in this chapter, planning and control procedures can easily drift into an *'incremental budgeting'* process. When incremental budgeting takes over the main justification for future expenditure is the level of past expenditure. For instance, established service departments are not required to justify their planned expenditure and right to claim resources in the same way as resource claims for a new proposal. All that is required is to justify the *increase* in planned expenditure over past expenditure. This incremental approach to budgetary planning tends to allow overmanning and inefficiency to continue unchallenged. New projects however,are always subjected to the rigors of justifying resource allocation (Refer to chapter 7)

A zero budgeting system takes away the implied right of existing activities for continued allocation of resources by asking some fundamental questions such as:-

(a) What are the objectives of the activity?
(b) Are the objectives satisfied?
(c) Is the activity really necessary?
(d) Are there alternative ways of meeting the objectives?
(e) Are any of the alternatives more cost effective?
(f) What would be the consequences and cost savings if the activity was stopped?

Clearly this places a tremendous burden on the budgetary planning process because it requires:-

(i) The organisation to be divided into spheres of activity that can be costed and then appraised under the same criteria as new proposals.

(ii) The costing and appraisal process is then undertaken for every activity from a *zero base*. i.e. No activity has an established right for resources. (Refer to chapter 6 sub-section 3:3 - Opportunity costs)

However, once a zero budgeting system has been established, the burden of appraising each activity every year during the budgetary planning process can be eased by incorporating a simple review procedure. The purpose of a review procedure would be to ensure that all activities are subject to annual cost/effective review. (Refer to chapter 7 sub-section 4:3) This would tend to break the incremental budgeting process. In addition to the annual review every activity would be required to face a full zero base review at intervals of say every three or five years. The system would also allow for immediate zero base reviews if trading circumstances changed and an activity was considered unnecessary.

Zero budgeting systems are not well established in the U.K. The practice gained some status in the U.S.A. after former President Carter had introduced the system into the Georgia State budgets. Indeed the zero base principle is particularly applicable for central and local government budgets where *'budgetary creep'* (the continued unquestioned increase in expenditure) may conceal continued unnecessary functions.

5:2 Planning, programming budgeting system (PPBS) This is a wide ranging management technique that encompasses many other techniques. Such a system may be referred to as: *Program Analysis and Review, Performance budgeting, Function costing, Programme budgeting* or *Output budgeting.* The term 'output budgeting' is also used to describe a quantitative statement of future production. The PPBS principle is illustrated in diagram 141. The diagram shows that PPBS is a total system concept for planning and control. In the planning stage the principles of cost/benefit analysis are applied (Refer to chapter 7 sub-section 4:2) to determine the best course(s) of action to achieve the organisation's objectives. Once the best use of resources has been determined the programming stage mainly comprises deriving a total programme structure. When the programme structure has been agreed then the normal budgetary planning and control systems can be applied. (Refer to sections 2 and 3).

Programme budgeting made a significant impact on American defence expenditure programmes during the 1960's. Before it was used, defence budgets were drawn up individually for numerous defence projects in terms of input categories such as staffing, construction, purchasing and research for each of the different services. The PPBS examined defence objectives from a total viewpoint and each of the services were assessed in output terms towards achieving these objectives. A smaller example of a PPBS application was the Greater London Council's (GLC) attempts during the 1970's to rationalise its services. The GLC examined the totality of all its services and divided them into the main programme groups; strategic planning, housing, transportation, health & safety, arts & recreation and general serices. They then built up a programme structure upon which the budgeting systems were to be based. There are other PPBS examples in the UK but they are mostly connected with the public sector. The private sector does not seem to have widely adopted PPBS. This is probably because the totality principle is already being applied within existing corporate budgeting systems.

DIAGRAM 141

PRINCIPLES OF PLANNING, PROGRAMMING BUDGETING SYSTEM

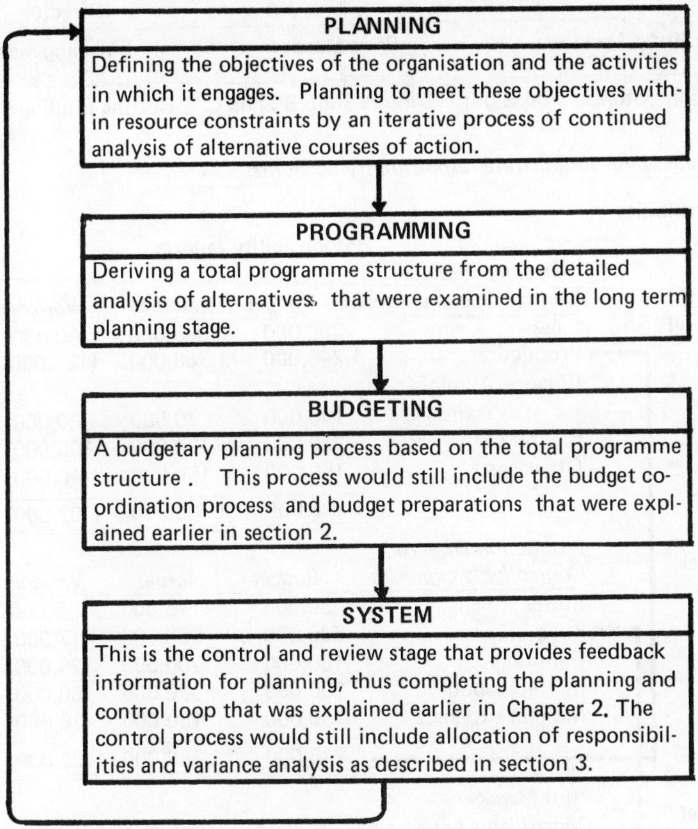
PLANNING
Defining the objectives of the organisation and the activities in which it engages. Planning to meet these objectives within resource constraints by an iterative process of continued analysis of alternative courses of action.
PROGRAMMING
Deriving a total programme structure from the detailed analysis of alternatives, that were examined in the long term planning stage.
BUDGETING
A budgetary planning process based on the total programme structure . This process would still include the budget co-ordination process and budget preparations that were explained earlier in section 2.
SYSTEM
This is the control and review stage that provides feedback information for planning, thus completing the planning and control loop that was explained earlier in Chapter 2. The control process would still include allocation of responsibilities and variance analysis as described in section 3.

5:3 Responsibility accounting This type of budgetary system is based on the principle that a manager's performance should be assessed only on the variables that are within his/her span of control. Responsibility accounting systems tend to have the following characteristics:-

(i) The system operates within a clearly defined organisation structure where managers are aware of their responsibilities and authority.

(ii) The budgets are targeted at individual managers' areas of responsibility.

(iii) The costing system has cost classifications of controllable and non-controllable costs (Refer to chapter 2 sub-section 3:5)

iv) Each manager's budget only contains costs (and revenues where applicab that are within his/her span of control.

The technique of responsibility accounting is illustrated in the following example

Example

A printing and publishing company with a clearly defined organisation structure has recently introduced a responsibility accounting system. The organisation struc ure and responsibility budgets are shown overleaf.

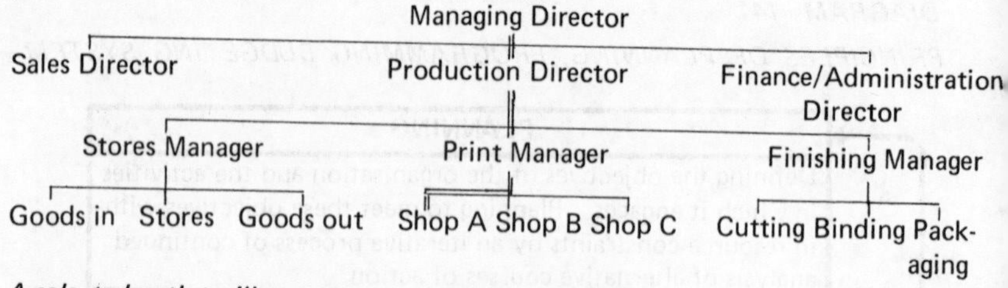

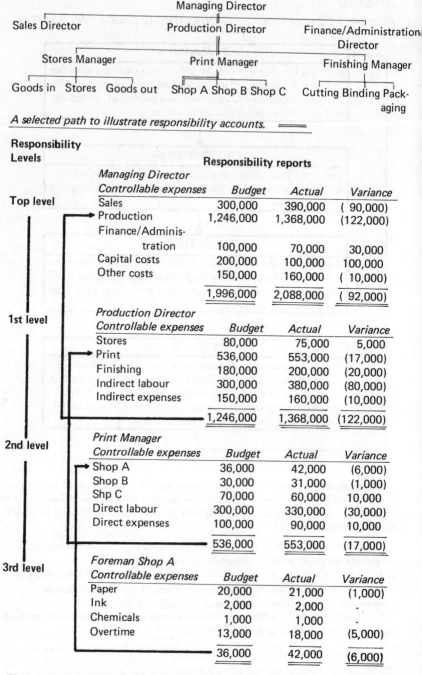

A selected path to illustrate responsibility accounts.

Responsibility Levels — **Responsibility reports**

Top level

Managing Director *Controllable expenses*	*Budget*	*Actual*	*Variance*
Sales	300,000	390,000	(90,000)
Production	1,246,000	1,368,000	(122,000)
Finance/Administration	100,000	70,000	30,000
Capital costs	200,000	100,000	100,000
Other costs	150,000	160,000	(10,000)
	1,996,000	2,088,000	(92,000)

1st level

Production Director *Controllable expenses*	*Budget*	*Actual*	*Variance*
Stores	80,000	75,000	5,000
Print	536,000	553,000	(17,000)
Finishing	180,000	200,000	(20,000)
Indirect labour	300,000	380,000	(80,000)
Indirect expenses	150,000	160,000	(10,000)
	1,246,000	1,368,000	(122,000)

2nd level

Print Manager *Controllable expenses*	*Budget*	*Actual*	*Variance*
Shop A	36,000	42,000	(6,000)
Shop B	30,000	31,000	(1,000)
Shp C	70,000	60,000	10,000
Direct labour	300,000	330,000	(30,000)
Direct expenses	100,000	90,000	10,000
	536,000	553,000	(17,000)

3rd level

Foreman Shop A *Controllable expenses*	*Budget*	*Actual*	*Variance*
Paper	20,000	21,000	(1,000)
Ink	2,000	2,000	-
Chemicals	1,000	1,000	-
Overtime	13,000	18,000	(5,000)
	36,000	42,000	(6,000)

The example shows a single scalar chain from the managing director down to the foreman of.workshop A. The four levels of management each have increasing areas of responsibility that are illustrated in the responsibility budget structure. The foreman, for example, only has control over costs such as overtime and printing ink usage. Whereas at the next level, the print manager is responsible for each of the foremen, direct labour and direct expenses. Thus the controllable expenses at one level are included in the next management level until it reaches the chief executive who has overall responsibility for all costs. The managing director's budget with an adverse variance of £92,000 shows that both sales and production directors have far exeeeded their budgets. Working down the selected scalar chain, the production director would investigate the indirect labour variance and the print manager would investigate the labour variance.

The purported advantages of this system are that it increases motivation and improves goal congruence. However there are many practical difficulties in the allocation of controllable costs to individual managers. Firstly, the level of management authority has to be clearly defined. Some management functions have clear authority parameters such as a workshop foreman. But there are managers whose area of responsibility can cut across many departments. Also, with interdependent departments, the efficiency of one manager could affect the costs that are the responsibility of another manager. Secondly, it is difficult to divide and allocate *all* costs to individual managers on controllable criteria. A controllable cost is one that can be influenced by a manager within a given time span. The time span is usually the budgetary control period. The decision making cost classification of fixed and variable (Refer to chapter 3 section 3:3) may be converted into controllable and non-controllable for the lower levels of management. But even then, the variable cost of direct labour may be decided by higher management when they determine staffing levels. Higher management are capable of converting fixed costs to variable costs through sub-contracting or hiring assets instead of purchasing them (Refer to chapter 6 sub-section 2:7:3). Or, converting variable costs to fixed costs by reducing direct labour through labour saving capital equipment purchases.

Although there are some practical difficulties for implementing and running a responsibility accounting system the principle is sound. A budgeting system is operated by managers and for these individuals to feel responsible for their budgets they need to be able to control their costs. Thus the system is not only tailored for the organisation, each budget is tailored for an individual.

5:4 Management by objectives (MBO). Throughout this chapter it has been emphasised that the nature of a budgetary system will depend upon the management style. Some enterprises may have an autocratic chief executive who is prepared to allocate responsibilities but not delegate the necessary authority. At the other end of the scale is the truly democratic enterprise with a genuine participative management style. In section 4 we noted that some of the 'people problems' relating to budgetary systems could be removed if:-

(a) Budgets were not used as pressure devices by autocratic managers.
(b) Individual aspiration levels were recognised and where possible incorporated into the budgetary planning process.
(c) Goal setting was not at an unrealistic level and was acceptable to each manager with budget responsibilities

An MBO system will provide a framework for participative management in the setting and achieving of objectives. The principles of an MBO system are illustrated in diagram 142 which follows the planning and control feedback loop that was explained in chapter 2. The main stages in an MBO system are summarised overleaf

DIAGRAM 142 PRINCIPLES OF MANAGEMENT BY OBJECTIVES

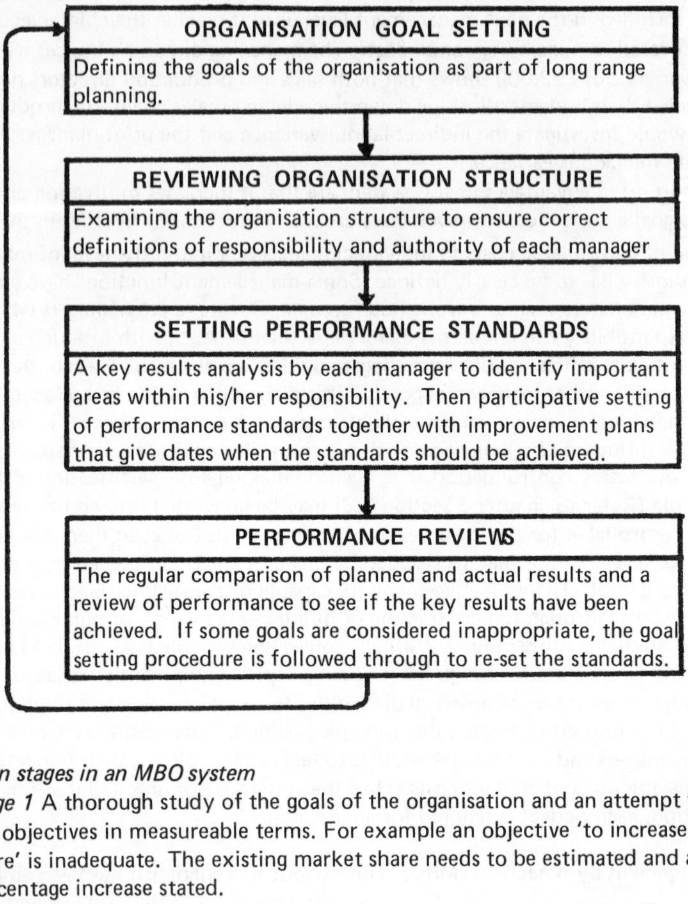

ORGANISATION GOAL SETTING
Defining the goals of the organisation as part of long range planning.
REVIEWING ORGANISATION STRUCTURE
Examining the organisation structure to ensure correct definitions of responsibility and authority of each manager
SETTING PERFORMANCE STANDARDS
A key results analysis by each manager to identify important areas within his/her responsibility. Then participative setting of performance standards together with improvement plans that give dates when the standards should be achieved.
PERFORMANCE REVIEWS
The regular comparison of planned and actual results and a review of performance to see if the key results have been achieved. If some goals are considered inappropriate, the goal setting procedure is followed through to re-set the standards.

Main stages in an MBO system

Stage 1 A thorough study of the goals of the organisation and an attempt to define the objectives in measureable terms. For example an objective 'to increase market share' is inadequate. The existing market share needs to be estimated and a specific percentage increase stated.

Stage 2 A review of the formal organisation structure to ensure clear lines of delegation for: authority, responsibility, functions and any interdependence between managers.

Stage 3. A key result analysis where each manager discusses with his/her supervison and a 'controller' the key areas of personal responsibility. The outcome of this discussion is the setting of minimum standards of performance agreed by all parties.

Stage 4. Regular performance reviews where actual results are compared with planned results. Every manager is encouraged to assess their own performance and their role in the organisation and the support they have given other managers. This review provides feedback into the organisational goal setting system for future budget periods.

Glossary of MBO terminology.

Long range plan	Defining the objectives of the organisation
Unit plans	Outline of steps required to achieve the objective
Key results analysis	Each manager analyses his job in order to identify the most important areas

Performance standard	Express key result areas in terms of the results one expects to achieve
Job improvement plan	The plan giving dates when the performance standard should be achieved
Management guide	A step by step analysis of the above
Control information	The information flow to a manager so that he can determine whether he is achieving results
Performance review	At periodic intervals time is set aside for discussion of the progress made. The discussion should lead to drawing up a new plan for the next period.
Personal goals	The stated objectives of individuals
Divisional goals	The objectives of a department or division as agreed by senior management
Organisation goals	The objectives that determine the long term strategy of the enterprise
Goal congruence	The harmonization of the above goals
Hierarchy of objectives	The ranking of the above goals into a hierarchy with the primary objectives being the organisation goals

It is clear that for an MBO system to exist and perform a valid function, managers at all levels must be willing to participate in the planning process and set their own performance standards. Without the co-operation of managers and the full support of the chief executive the system will just become a paper exercise and a complete waste of resources. Accordingly, before an MBO system is set up a full feasibility study is necessary including a pilot run in a suitable area of the enterprise.

6. Summary

Budgeting is a very important accounting technique that is widely used by industry and commerce in the private and public sectors. Most budgetary planning periods are one year. Therefore every organisation should conduct an annual planning exercise. The principles and techniques for this annual event were explained in section 2. Special note should be made of the budget co-ordination process and principal budget factors Section 3 then looked at the control part of a budgeting system which compáres actual results with planned results. The control process does pose some problems such as variations in output, inflation, allocation of budget responsibilities, communicating budget information and interpreting the variances. These were all discussed in section 3

Section 4 about the effect of budgets on people is probably the most important topic in the chapter. This is because many budgeting systems in operation that have evolved over many years, may not have adapted to the changing nature of the workplace. Management styles have become more participative and the educational aspiration levels of many employees have risen considerably. Thus the externally imposed budgetary process being used as a pressure device may be counter productive in the long run. Section 4 briefly examined some of the ' people effects' on budgets and the effects that budgets have on people and then attempted to draw some general conclusions. There is a lot more work needed in this area and it is hoped that this sub-section will alert the non-accountant to some of the 'people problems' relating to budgetary systems.

The final section looked at some applications of budgetary systems such as zero budgeting, PPBS, responsibility accounting and MBO.

Accountancy Quiz No.8.

1. Define a budget and stste the objectives of a budgetary system *(1)*

2. What is meant by budget co-ordination process and how is it affected by the principal budget factor? *(2:2, 2:2:1, 2:2:2, 2:3, 2:3:1)*

3. What is flexible budgeting and why is it necessary? *(3:3)*

4. How would you decide what budget variances require investigation? *(3:5, 3:5:1, 3:5:2, 3:5:3)*

5. What do you think are the possible consequences of using budgets as pressure devices for increased efficiency? *(4:1)*

6. What is budgetary slack and how can it be avoided? *(4:2)*

7. Do you think managers should participate in the budgetary planning process? Justify your opinion. *(4:3)*

8. What is zero budgeting? *(5:1)*

9. Explain the principles of a Planning Programming, Budgeting System. *(5:2)*

10. Explain the principles of Responsibility Accounting and Management by Objectives. *(5:3, 5:4)*

9
Standard Costing

Objective
To help the non-accountant understand the principles and techniques of standard costing and how to interpret variances.

Page No.

Contents

Standard Costing

1. Introduction

The principle of standard costing is quite simple. A standard is set for each item of cost or revenue against which the actual cost or revenue is compared. Th difference is called a variance. The variances are then used mainly as a control technique by managers. There are however a number of complications that the non-accountant should be aware of. This chapter will explain the basic principles of standard costing and variance analysis and illustrate by example the different types of variances. The explanation of each type of variance with its calculation is mainly for reference purposes and ***the reader is advised not to attempt to under stand all variances in one reading.*** The main point to grasp is the usefulness of va iance analysis for cost control. Variances can simplify the control of large volume of cost data. The manager will not need to study detailed cost sheets because var iance analysis will have done this work. The variances provide pointers to cost areas where management attention should be focused. Once a manager understands variances then he/she will find them an invaluable management tool for cos control.

2. Principles of standard costing

Standard costing may be defined as a system that establishes a detailed listing of expected costs against which actual costs are compared. The resultant figures called variances are then analysed to draw management's attention to areas that are not operating according to expectations. From this definition we can extract several points that require further explanation:—

(a) Expected costs are called standard costs. The system is dependent on relevant standard costs, therefore the criteria for setting standards is very important and is explained in sub section 2:4.

(b) Management's attention needs to be drawn to the variances on the principle of management by exception. However, this assumes managers can understand variance analysis. This aspect is discussed in sub sections 2:1 and 2:5.

Standard costing is an established and proven control technique for managers but like any other tool the manager needs to understand how to use it.

2:1 Management by Exception *(MBE)* The principle of MBE is that managers should arrange their business affairs so that only exceptional cases are brought to their attention. All other cases that are proceeding according to plan are dealt with by sets of instructions and delegation of responsibility and authority In other words 'if things are going alright, leave them alone'. Standard costing is a perfect example of MBE. For example assume a purchasing officer is responsible for purchasing several thousand different items every month. How ca he exercise cost control over this wide range of detailed purchases? With standard costing an expected cost would be given for each item and when it is purchased the actual cost would be compared against the standard, thus producing a variance. The manager no longer needs to look down a long list of costs, he just has to look for significant variances. Indeed with electronic data processing the significant variances can be produced on a separate tabulation. The dat sorting can be programmed to produce a tabulation of all variances that are say $\pm$20% of the standard cost. The manager's attention is therefore focussed on areas that need to be investigated.

2:2 Relationship to other costing bases and methods The costing methods explained in chapter 3 were based on historic costs. The significant difference with standard costing is that it is based on expected costs. Thus the standard costing basis of expected costs can be applied to any of the costing methods based on actual costs. For example a process costing system, a contract costing system or a unit costing system can all be standard costing systems. The costing method is not altered, only the data base is widened to include expected costs as well as actual costs. Similarly, the basis of marginal or absorption costing can become standard marginal costing or standard absorption costing. With regard to budgetary control systems there is a lot of similarity between standard costing and budgetary control. Budgets also use expected cost and revenue data. However the difference tends to be in the level of detail. Standard costing is usually far more detailed than budgetary control. Standard costing is a unit concept whereby all costs elements are given predetermined costs. Budgeting is a total concept that is used for setting plans and co-ordinating the activities of the business. Both control techniques compare actual performance with expected performance. The two systems are often linked in a budgetary control standard costing system where the budgets are constructed using standard cost data. A total variance analysis will use budget figures.

2:3 Advantages and disadvantages of standard costing The following brief notes summarise the advantages and disadvantages of standard costing. The widespread use of standard costing indicates that the advantages tend to outweigh the disadvantages.

2:3:1 Advantages The major advantage is improved control.

(a) Cost control — Most costing systems are based on historic costs therefore management are not aware of all the costs until after they have been incurred. Standard costs are pre-determined costs and enable management to construct a detailed cost plan in advance of operations. Actual costs are then compared with the detailed cost plan as a basis of control.

(b) Management by Exception — Providing costs are behaving in accordance with the plan management attention may be directed into areas where there is a deviation from plan and management action may be needed. Variance analysis directs management attention to the deviations from plan and helps to identify the cause of the deviation.

(c) Pricing decisions — When management has available detailed pre-determined costs then they can price the "one off" operation with greater confidence of full cost recovery.

(d) Control information — Historic costs will not readily provide a manufacturer with the following control information that can be obtained from a standard costing system:

(i) Materials — efficiency of purchasing department, efficiency of production department in the level of scrap and the optimum mix of materials

(ii) Direct labour — efficiency of labour and information on wage rates paid that differ from planned rates.

(iii) Indirect costs — efficient use of indirect materials and efficient utilisation of indirect labour.

(iv) Fixed overhead — efficient use of productive capacity.

2:3:2 Disadvantages The main disadvantages are costs, reliability and management understanding.

(a) Setting accurate standards — It is very difficult to determine an accurate standard. The setting of standards is explained later in this chapter.

(b) Maintaining standards — It is necessary to constantly check standards to ensure they are valid. This is especially true during inflationary times when prices and wage rates are unsettled.

(c) Cost/benefit — The costs of setting up, maintaining and operating a standard costing system must be less than the benefits derived from the system. In some instances an expensive cost control system may not be cost justified.

(d) Management understanding — Standard costing is a control tool. Like any other tool, its effectiveness depends on the user. Standard costing and variance analysis is complicated and it is quite possible that management may not be able to use this tool effectively.

2:4 Setting standards Standard costing is based on the principle of comparing actual with expected results. To make this comparison expectations have to be quantified and regularly updated. Indeed it is not overstating the issue to say that the validity of any standard costing system is dependent on the relevance and reliability of the standard setting process. Let us first consider the principles of standard setting, then the practice.

2:4:1 Principles for setting standards The basic decision is whether the standards are to represent objectives, optimal performance or expected performance. This is especially relevant when setting standard hours of production. If an unattainable objective is set, there will always be adverse efficiency variances and this may vitiate the system's credibility. If the standards were to be set at an optimal performance level then the system may have a motivational effect especially if there was some participation in the standard setting process. To set standards at an expected level may lead to complications if they are used by trade unions in collective bargaining. These three broad alternatives can be summarised as follows:—

Objective standards would be based on corporate objectives and would probably assume perfect machine and material utilisation with maximum possible labour efficiency.

Optimal standards would be achievable but are based on continued peak labour efficiency and best use of machines and material.

Expected standards would be set to allow for normal wastage, machine breakdowns, idle time and expected level of labour efficiency.

The setting of efficiency standards is particularly difficult because direct labour will probably not provide peak performance times if they are aware that standard hours are being set. Moreover, there is a risk that the standard setting process could be drawn into collective bargaining and thus become *'compromise standards'*.

Once standards have been set they need to be regularly revised because of the effects of inflation on costs. Also, the effect of capital and/or the learning curve on efficiency. For example, if the standard hours were measured for a particular product when it was first introduced into production within a short while the learning curve effect would be causing increasing favourable efficiency variances. If participative standard setting is used for revising the standards then there is a risk of *'compromise standards'*.

2:4:2 Practical aspects of standard setting The most practical method of standard setting is to use past costs as a guide and build in an expected inflation factor that will revise the standards at regular intervals. This revision process can be fairly easily programmed for standard costing systems that are computerised. The following notes briefly explain some practical aspects of setting standards for materials, labour and overheads.

Material standard setting requires decisions to be made concerning the material price, expected usage including wastage and the material specifications. The design department will be able to produce standard specifications, the production department should be able to provide expected wastage figures and the buying department the expected prices.

Labour standard setting requires decisions on wage rates, labour grades in relation to job specifications and standard hour calculations. The personnel department can provide the wage rate detail, the production department the labour grade detail and work study and/or production records can provide the detail for standard hour calculations.

Overhead standard setting requires decisions on fixed and variable overhead absorption rates and standard hours of production. Financial accounts and budgets will contain a lot of the necessary overhead cost detail upon which estimates can be made and the standard hour calculations will use labour standard hours as explained above.

From these two sub sections you will appreciate that there are many problems relating to standard setting. Once a valid basis for setting standards has been agreed there are still immense practical difficulties to overcome before the standard costing system becomes operational.

2:5 Variances The output of a standard costing system will be variance reports These reports are sometimes difficult to understand because the accountant has made no concessions for the recipient's lack of specialised knowledge. This chapter provides explanations, formulae and simplified worked examples for 29 different variances. Do not attempt to work through all this detail. Use sections 3, 4, 5 and 6 for reference purposes only. For instance, if you are, say, a purchasing officer in a company that uses a standard costing system, then you should have some knowledge about material variances, because they will influence management opinion about your efficiency. It is important that you only learn about variances you need to know. There are too many variances and they are too complicated for you to learn all of them. However, there are some general points about variances that may be of some use. Firstly, almost all variances are derived by deducting standard costs from actual costs. If actual costs are greater than standard costs this will create an adverse variance denoted with a letter (A). Sometimes this is called an unfavourable variance and denoted with a letter (U). When standard costs are below actual costs this creates a favourable variance denoted with a letter (F). The second point to note is that there is a logical structure for variance analysis. The main divisions are into material, labour, overheads and sales that are explained in sections 3, 4, 5 and 6 respectively. Each of these main divisions are broadly sub divided on the principle of price and quantity, i.e.

Material variances are divided into price and usage.
Labour variances are divided into wage rate and labour efficiency.
Overhead variances are divided into expenditure and output.
Sales margin variances are divided into price and quantity.

To interpret variances and understand variance reports requires an understanding of why variances are structured this way. It is therefore appropriate for you to read the beginning and end of sections 3, 4, 5 and 6 that explain the principles of specific variances and their interpretation. The sub sections on variance formulae and calculations can then be used on a reference basis. Once again it is necessary to advise you not to get involved in variance calculations that are a machine function. If you can understand and interpret variances then standard costing will become a useful part of your 'management toolkit'.

3. Material variances

A materials variance is the difference between the *actual* cost of direct materials used and the *standard* cost of direct materials used for the same level of output. The total cost for materials is calculated by:—

Material usage x material price

Therefore any difference between actual and standard costs will be due to either, or both, quantity used or unit price. This is illustrated in the following example:

	USAGE	*PRICE*	£
Actual cost	11 items of A @	£1.05 each	11.55
Standard cost	10 items of A @	£1.00 each	10.00
		Materials variance	1.55 (A)

The adverse materials variance is due to usage having increased by 10% and unit price by 5%. Therefore the total material variance may be divided into price and usage. This is shown in diagram 143 below.

DIAGRAM 143 MATERIAL PRICE & USAGE VARIANCES

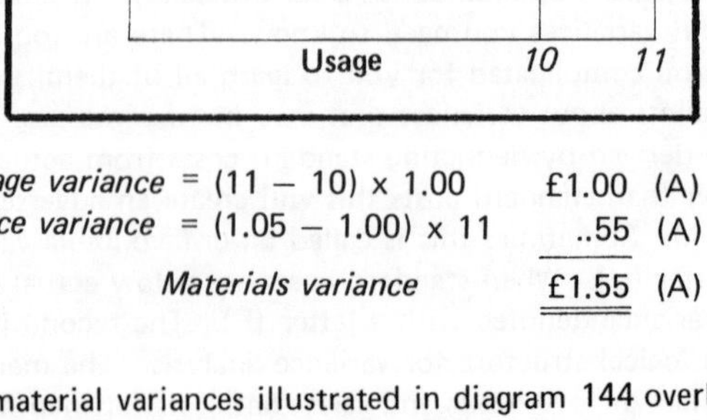

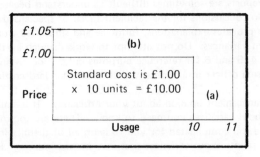

(a) Usage variance	= (11 – 10) x 1.00	£1.00	(A)
(b) Price variance	= (1.05 – 1.00) x 11	..55	(A)
	Materials variance	£1.55	(A)

The hierarchy of material variances illustrated in diagram 144 overleaf, shows the main division of variances into price and usage. The usage variance in standard process costing is then divided into a mixture and a yield variance

DIAGRAM 144 STRUCTURE OF MATERIAL VARIANCES

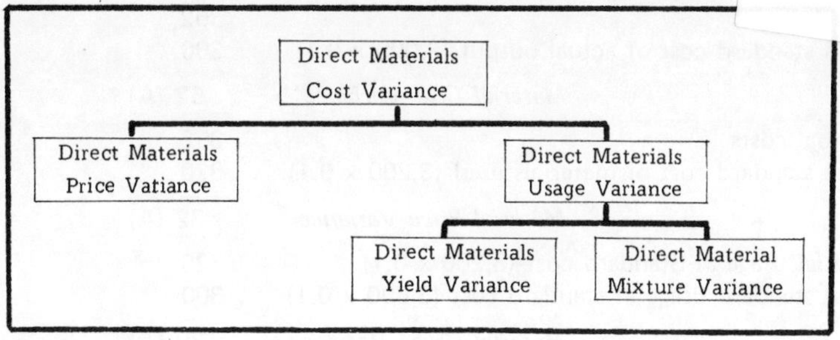

3:1 Formulae

Direct Materials Cost Variance

(Actual cost of direct materials) – (Standard cost of direct materials)

Direct Materials Price Variance

(Actual cost of direct materials per unit) – (Standard cost of direct materials per unit) x Actual quantity used in production

Direct Materials Usage Variance

(Actual quantity of material used) – (Standard usage of material for actual production) x Standard price

Direct Materials Yield Variance

Actual yield – (Standard yield for the actual input) x Standard cost per unit of output

where: Standard cost per unit of output is calculated by

$$\frac{\text{Standard cost per unit of input}}{\text{Yield}}$$

Direct Materials Mix Variance

(Standard cost of actual output using actual mixture quantities) – (Standard cost of actual output using standard mixture quantities)

3:2 Calculations The main calculation for material variances is to find out if the excess (or low) actual material cost is due to usage, price or both. In the following example the excess material expenditure was £2,100.

	Price	*Usage*	*Cost*
	£		£
Actual	1.00	10,000	10,000
Standard cost	1.10	11,000	12,100
Differences	0.10	1,000	2,100

This was due to:

	£
Usage variance = 1,000 x £1.00	1,000 (A)
Price variance = 11,000 x £0.10	1,100 (A)
Cost variance = (10,000 x £1.00) – (11,000 x £1.10)	2,100 (A)

Consider the following example of material costs in a production process where the standard material costs for a unit of output are one kilo of raw material costing £0.10 per kilo. Actual production for the accounting period was

3,000 units using 3,200 kilos of material costing £352. Material cost, price and usage variances would be calculated as follows:–

	£	
Actual costs	352	
Less standard cost of actual output (3,000 x 0.1)	300	
Material Cost Variance	52	(A)
Actual costs	352	
Less standard cost of materials used (3,200 x 0.1)	320	
Material Price Variance	32	(A)
Actual usage at Standard cost (3,200 x 0.1)	320	
Less standard usage at standard cost (3,000 x 0.1)	300	
Material Usage Variance	20	(A)

From the hierarchy of material variances illustrated in diagram 144 you may have noticed that the material usage variance can be divided into mixture and yield variances. The yield variance arises when the actual loss in a production process is different from the expected (standard) loss. This is illustrated in diagram 145 below.

DIAGRAM 145 *YIELD VARIANCE*

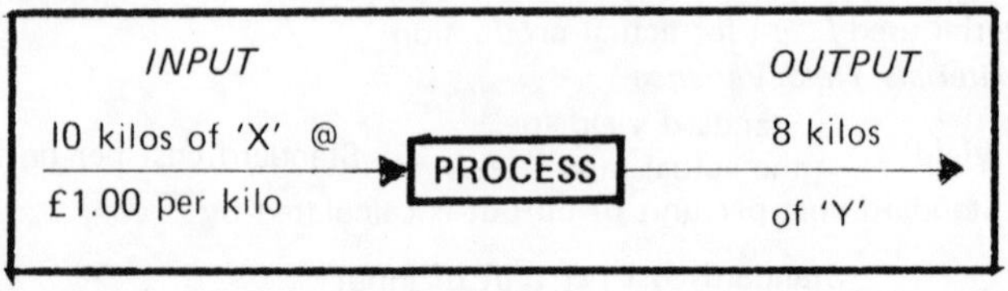

The expected loss in this process is 2 kilos for every 10 kilos of input, therefore the process standard yield is 80%.

$$\text{Standard yield} = \frac{\text{Standard output}}{\text{Standard input}}\ \% \quad \frac{8}{10} = 80\%$$

The standard cost per kilo of Y (output) is 1¼ times the cost per kilo of X

$$\text{Standard cost per unit of output} = \frac{\text{Standard cost per unit of input}}{\text{Standard Yield}}$$

$$\frac{£1.00}{0.8} = £1.25 \text{ per kilo}$$

In the following example of a material yield variance a production process uses 9 litres of X to produce 4 litres of Y. The standard cost of X is £1.00 per litre. Actual production during the accounting period used 1,000 litres of X to produce 450 litres of Y. The yield variance is calculated as follows:–

$$\text{Standard yield} \quad {}^{4}/_{8} = 50\%$$

$$\text{Standard cost per litre of Y} = \frac{£1.00}{0.5} = £2.00$$

	£	
Actual yield x standard cost per litre of Y (450 x 2)	900	
Less Standard yield x standard cost per litre of Y (1,000 x 0.5 x 2)	1,000	
Yield Variance	100	(A)

The mixture variance also arises in production processes but only when there is more than one kind of input. In diagram 146 the production process has an input mixture of products A and B. The mixture variances refers to the difference in costs that arises because of the different proportions of inputs used in a production process

DIAGRAM 146 *MIXTURE VARIANCE*

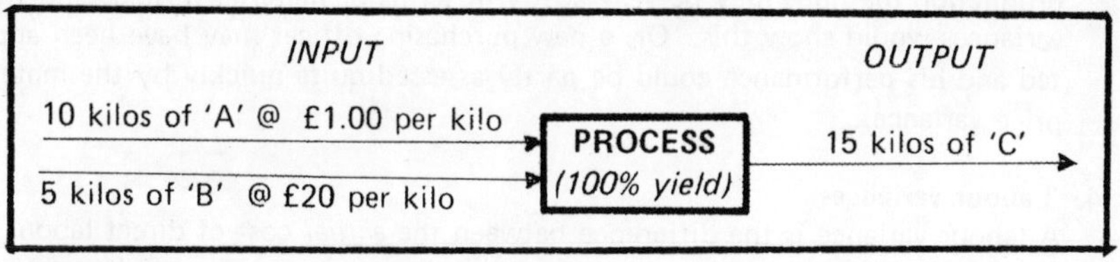

If 150 kilos of "C" were produced then the standard inputs would be:

100 kilos of A at standard price of £1.00 per kilo	100
50 kilos of B at standard price of £20.00 per kilo	1,000
Standard cost of actual output using standard mixture	£1,100

However, if the actual inputs for producing 150 kilos of C were 90 kilos of A and 60 kilos of B, the actual cost would be:

90 kilos of A at a standard price of £1.00 per kilo	90
60 kilos of B at a standard price of £20.00 per kilo	1,200
Standard cost of actual output using actual mixture	1,290
Less standard cost of actual output using standard mixture	1,100
Adverse mixture variance	190

The following example is from a production process that has two types of material input and a 100% yield, therefore no yield variance calculations are needed. The production process uses a standard mixture of 80 kilos of material X costing £20 per kilo and 20 kilos of material Y costing £50 per kilo to produce 100 kilos of product Z. Actual production of Z during the accounting period was 2,000 kilos using 1,500 kilos of material X and 500 kilos of material Y. The material mixture variance is calculated as follows:—

Actual costs for 2,000 kilos of Z

Material X 1,500 x £20	30,000	
Material Y 500 x £50	25,000	55,000

Standard costs for 2,000 kilos of Z

Material X $2{,}000 \times \frac{80}{100} \times £20 =$	32,000	
Material Y $2{,}000 \times \frac{20}{100} \times £50 -$	20,000	52,000
Material mixture variance		3,000 (A)

3:3 Interpretation Variances arising due to price and usage of materials may be caused by any of the following reasons:—

Material price variance The price paid for materials may be different due to; changes in purchase price by the supplier or change in supplier, changes in delivery costs or a change in the specification of material purchased.

Material usage variance The usage of materials may change due to; changes in production methods, poor/good workmanship causing a change in wastage rate pilferage or deterioration because of bad storage or a change in the material specification altering the usage.

In most instances the manager will be aware of faults in production, storag and purchasing. The variances will give an indication how costly these faults are and possibly help him/her to improve the position, for example a change i production methods may be very costly in terms of material wastage and the variances would show this. Or, a new purchasing officer may have been appoi ted and his performance could be partly assessed quite quickly by the materia price variances.

4. Labour variances

A labour variance is the difference between the *actual* cost of direct labour ar the *standard* cost of direct labour for an equivalent output. The total cost for la our is calculated by:—

Direct labour hours x Direct labour rate

When setting the standard for labour hours it is necessary to set a level of effi iency. Therefore the difference between the actual cost and the standard cost m be due to either/both the efficiency of labour and the labour rate. This is illust ted in the following example:—
Production of cost unit X has the following labour cost detail:—

DIAGRAM 147

LABOUR RATE & EFFICIENCY VARIANCES

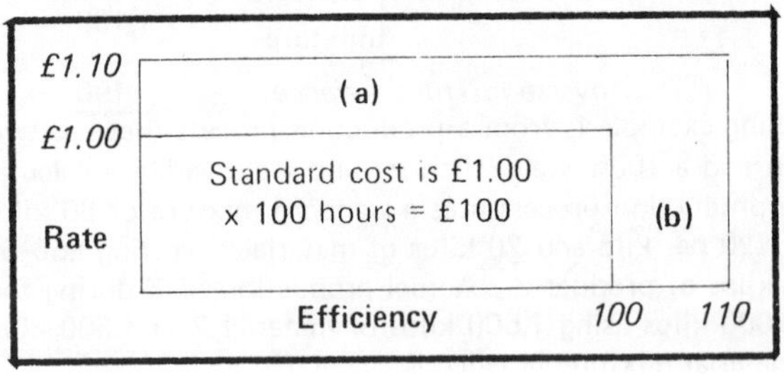

Output	*Rate per hour*		*Total Hours*	*£*
Actual output 100 units	£1.10	x	110	121
Less Standard output for 100 units	£1.00	x	100	100
	Direct Wages Variance			21 (A)

Variances:	*Total hours*
(a) Rate (£1.10 – £1.00) x 110	£11.00 (A)
(b) Efficiency (110 – 100) x £1.00	£10.00 (A)
Wage rate variance (£1.10 x 110) – (£1.00 x 100)	£21.00 (A)

The breakdown of direct labour costs into rate and efficiency is similar in pr ciple to the material cost breakdown into usage and price. However the labour rate will be affected by the amount of overtime and the amount of labour subs tion. This term 'substitution' refers to work conditions where direct labour wil work at a level above or below their grade. For example if a skilled man was t do unskilled work this would result in an adverse substitution variance. The eff iency variance will be affected by the number of hours worked and the amount of abnormal idle time. These aspects of direct labour costs are shown as a hierarchy of labour variances in diagram 148.

DIAGRAM 148 STRUCTURE OF LABOUR VARIANCES

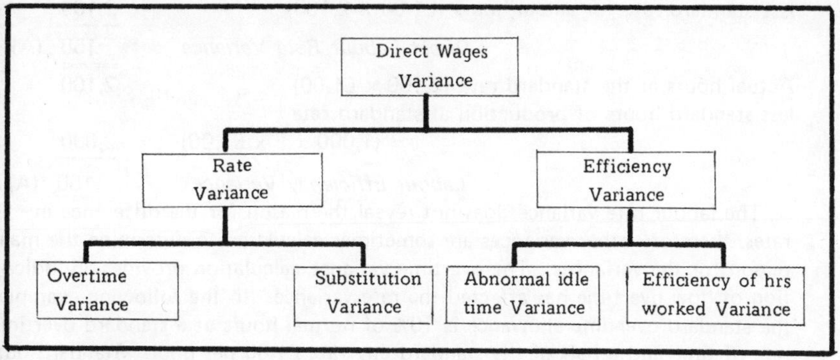

4:1 Formulae

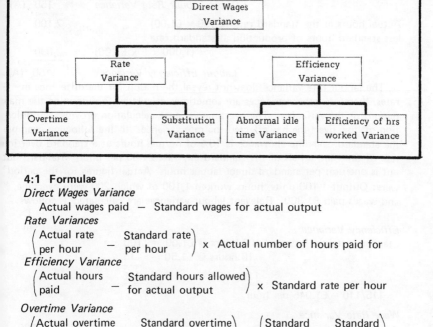

Direct Wages Variance

Actual wages paid − Standard wages for actual output

Rate Variances

(Actual rate per hour − Standard rate per hour) x Actual number of hours paid for

Efficiency Variance

(Actual hours paid − Standard hours allowed for actual output) x Standard rate per hour

Overtime Variance

(Actual overtime hours − Standard overtime hours allowed for actual output) x (Standard overtime rate − Standard rate)

Substitution Variance

(Standard rate for actual labour grade used − Standard rate for standard labour grade) x (Actual hours worked by substituted grade of labour)

Abnormal Idle Time Variance

(Actual hours paid for − Actual hours worked) x Standard rate per hour

(Actual hours worked − Standard hours allowed for actual output) x Standard rate per hour

4:2 Calculations What we are trying to find out with labour variances is if the direct labour has been efficient and if the wage rates were according to expectations (standards). In this first example only the rate and efficiency variances are calculated. From the production records we learn that to produce one unit of X takes 2 Standard Hours of Production (SHP) at a standard rate of £1.00 per hour. The actual output for the accounting period was 1,000 units and the labour records showed 2,100 hours were taken costing £2,250. Direct wages, rate and efficiency variances are calculated as follows:—

	£
Actual direct wages	2,250
less standard cost of actual output (1,000 x 2 x £1.00)	2,000
Direct Wages Variance	250 (A)

Actual direct wages	2,250
less standard rate for actual hours (£1.00 x 2,100)	2,100
Direct Labour Rate Variance	150 (A)

Actual hours at the standard rate (2,100 x £1.00)	2,100
less standard hours of production at standard rate (1,000 x 2 x £1.00)	2,000
Labour Efficiency Variance	100 (A)

The labour rate variance does not reveal the reason for the difference in rates, therefore other variances are sometimes calculated to determine the main reason for the variances. The overtime variance calculation provides an indication of how overtime has affected the rate variance. In the following example the standard overtime allowance is 10% of normal hours at a standard overtime rate of time and a half of the standard pay rate £1.00 per hour. Standard output is one unit per standard direct labour hour. Actual figures for the period were: Output 1,100 units, hours worked 1,100 of which 200 were overtime, and wages paid £1,300. Relevant labour variances are calculated as follows:–

		£	£
Efficiency Variance			Nil
Standard rate per hour =	100 hours @ £1.00 =	100	
	10 hours @ £1.50 =	15	
	110	115	

115/110 = £1.045 per hour

Wage Rate Variance

Actual wages paid	1,300
less standard hours of actual output at standard rate (1,100x£1,045)	1,150
Wage Rate Variance	150 (A

Overtime Variance

Actual overtime hours at overtime premium 200 x (1.50 – 1.00)	100
less standard overtime hours at overtime premium 100 x (150–1.00)	50
Overtime Variance	50 (A

Therefore only £50 of the adverse rate variance was due to excessive overtime.

The substitution variance also helps to identify a possible cause for a rate variance. If, for example, a skilled grade of labour was being used for work allocated to lower paid unskilled labour, then an adverse substitution variance would arise. Assume a company employs two grades of direct labour at the following rates:

Skilled	Grade A	£1.50 per hour
Unskilled	Grade B	£1.00 per hour

Each unit of output "X" required 2 standard grade "B" hours.
During the period 100 units of "X" were produced using 20 hours of grade "A and 180 hours of grade "B". Wages paid £740.00. There was no efficiency variance. First we will calculate the wage rate variance then the substitution variance.

Wage Rate Variance	£
Actual wages paid	240
less standard wages for actual output (100 x 2 x £1.00)	200
Wage Rate Variance	40 (A)

Substitution Variance

(Standard rate for actual labour grade used − Standard rate for standard labour) x Actual hours worked by substituted labour

Substitution Variance = £1.50 – £1.00 x 20 = £10 (A)

Therefore £10.00 of the adverse wage rate variance is due to the use of skilled labour in unskilled work.

The labour efficiency variance does not show the cost of idle production time. Idle time can arise through: machine breakdown, delay in raw materials or parts, labour disputes, fires and a variety of other reasons. For example, if one unit of output took one direct labour hour and 100 hours had been lost through a machine breakdown then output would be less than expected. If 500 units had been produced taking 600 hours, then the variances would be:—

	£	£
Idle time hours lost through machine breakdown (100 x £1.00)		100 (A)
Efficiency of hours worked		
Actual hours worked (500 x £1.00)	500	
less standard hours for actual output (500 x £1.00)	500	Nil
Efficiency variance (600 – 500) x £1.00		100 (A)

The direct labour have not been inefficient, yet there is an adverse efficiency variance. It is, therefore, important to calculate efficiency in terms of hours work ed and separate this from idle time. Consider the following example where one standard hour of production (SHP) at a standard rate of £1.20 per hour produces 80 units of product Y. The actual output was 18,000 units taking 800 hours which were paid at the standard rate of £1.20 per hour. However, 150 direct labour hours were lost because of fire. The efficiency variance for hours worked and idle time variance are calculated below:—

	£
Actual hours at the standard rate (800 x £1.20)	960
less standard hours of production at standard rate (18,000/30 x £1.20)	720
Direct Labour Efficiency Variance	240 (A)
Actual hours worked at the standard rate (800 –150) x £1.20	780
less standard hours of production at standard rate (18,000/30 x £1.20)	720
Direct Labour Efficiency Variance for hours worked	60 (A)
Actual hours paid at the standard rate (800 x £1.20)	960
less Actual hours worked at the standard rate (800 – 150) x £1.20)	780
Idle Time Variance	180 (A)

If this calculation had not been made all of the adverse efficiency variances would probably have been attributed to the fire. The figures show that regardless of the fire the direct labour was still operating below expectations.

Before moving to the next section let us just work through another direct labour variances example. The detail is that one standard hour of production (SHP) at a standard rate of £0.90 per hour produces 20 units of product Z. The actual output was 850 units and 40 hours were paid for, costing £37. There was 4 hours of idle time due to a machine breakdown.

Direct wages, rate, efficiency, hours worked and idle time variances are calculated below:—

	£
Actual direct wages	37
less standard cost of actual output (850/20 x £0.90)	38.25
Direct Wages Variance	1.25 (F)
Actual direct wages	37
less standard rate for actual hours (40 x £0.90)	36
Direct labour rate variances	1 (A)
Actual hours at the standard rate (40 x £0.90)	36
less standard hours of production at the standard rate (850/20x£0.90)	38.25
Direct labour efficiency variance	2.25 (F)
Actual hours worked at the standard rate (36 x £0.90)	32.4
less standard hours of production at the standard rate (850/20x£0.90)	38.25
Direct Labour Efficiency for Hours Worked	5.85 (F)
Actual hours paid at the standard rate (40 x 0.90)	36
less actual hours worked at the standard rate (36 x £0.90)	32.4
Idle Time Variance	3.6 (A)

4:3 Interpretation Wage rate and efficiency variances may be caused by any of the following reasons:—

Direct wages rate A continuing adverse rate variance could probably be due to an increase in wage rates that had not been included in the standard rate. This would possibly occur for individuals who were given a special kind of rate that was not allowed for in the standard. If the standard rate was calculated making an allowance for authorised overtime, then overtime exceeding the authorised level would cause an adverse rate variance. The wage rate could also be altered by using non standard labour as shown in the substitution variance.

Direct labour efficiency Changes in efficiency can be due to two main causes:—

(a) Working conditions such as machine breakdowns, supply of materials irregular, wrong grade of materials, delay in stores issues, or

(b) Employees performance due to poor supervision, lack of motivation, bad training, ability and attitudes.

Interdependence Some care is needed when interpreting variances because of their interdependence. For example an adverse labour efficiency variance may have been caused because poor quality materials were purchased. If faulty raw material had been purchased then this could create high wastage and extra machine 'downtime'. The variances may look as follows:—

	£
Direct materials price	5,000 (F)
Direct materials usage	3,500 (A)
Direct materials variance	1,500 (F)
Direct wage rate	NIL
Direct labour efficiency	3,000 (A)
Direct labour variance	3,000 (A)

At first sight it looks as though the purchasing officer has been very efficient. But the large favourable price variance may be due to the purchase of inferior materials causing an adverse direct materials usage variance and an adverse direct labour efficiency variance. The point to note here is that variances are only a warning light that something is wrong. They sometimes can point to the cause but great care is needed when interpreting the results of a variance report.

5. Overhead Variances

These variances can be a little more complicated than direct materials and direct labour variances. You will recall that total cost is the result of price x quantity. Thus materials and labour variances basically comprised of:–

Direct material variance = Price x Usage

Direct labour variance = Wage Rate x Standard Hours of Production

The same principle applies to overhead variances except the rate is called an overhead absorption rate which may refer to fixed overheads or variable overheads i.e.

Fixed Overhead Absorption Rate FOAR

Variable Overhead Absorption Rate VOAR

Most absorption costing systems collect and analyse costs in cost centres. The overheads collected in the cost centre are then charged to the cost units passing through the cost centre by applying an overhead absorption rate. (Details on absorption costing are given in chapter 3 section 5:1). The overhead absorption rate is calculated using the following formula:-

$$\text{Overhead absorption rate} = \frac{\text{Total overheads from the cost centre}}{\text{Total number of units of selected base}}$$

The selected base may be; units of output, direct labour hours, machine hours or any other measure considered relevant. For standard costing, the selected base is normally the standard hours of production.

The usage part of the overhead cost equation uses standard hours of production (SHP) as a measure of output. A standard hour is a measure of productive activity. The measure is most needed when a business produces more than one type of output. The SHP principle is best illustrated by example.

Assume a factory has a standard output of 10,000 cups, 10,000 saucers and 1,000 plates. To have a number of different products and output figures like this makes it difficult to measure productive activity. For instance if the actual output was 5,000 cups, 12,000 saucers and 2,000 plates, it is difficult to see if production has increased or decreased. Therefore it becomes necessary to reduce the figures to standard hours. The following table multiplies the standard time by the number of units produced to derive the standard hours of production 3,150. These standard hours of production are a measure of output.

Products	Standard time to produce one unit	Number of Units produced	Standard Hours of production
	(Hours)	(Units)	(Standard Hours)
Cup	0.2	10,000	2,000
Saucer	0.1	10,000	1,000
Plate	0.15	1,000	150

The following simplified example illustrates the principles of overhead variances with the use of diagrams. The basic detail is that a cost centre has a budgeted output of 2,000 units. The standard output is one unit of output per two standard hours of production. The budgeted overheads for the period are fixed overhead £10.00, variable overhead £6.00. We will first calculate the fixed overhead variances divided into expenditure and volume variances. These variances are shown on diagram 149. The second part of the calculation will be to derive the variable overhead variances and these are shown on diagram 150.

			£
Budget Fixed Overheads / SHP for budgeted output	£10,000 / (2 x 2,000)	=	2.50
Budgeted Variable Overhead / SHP for budgeted output	£6,000 / (2 x 2,000)	=	1.50
Total Overhead Absorption Rate			£4.00

Using the budgeted figures from the cup, saucer and plate example, assume the actual results for the period were:

SHP	=	3,500 (Actual hours worked 3,500)
Fixed Overheads	=	£10,500
Variable Overheads	=	£6,000

The fixed overheads variances would be:—

DIAGRAM 149 *FIXED OVERHEAD & VOLUME VARIANCES*

Where:-

(a)=FOAR of £2.50 per SHP.

(b)=Budget expenditure level £10,000.

(c)=Actual expenditure level £10,500.

(d)=Acual activity level 3,500 SHP

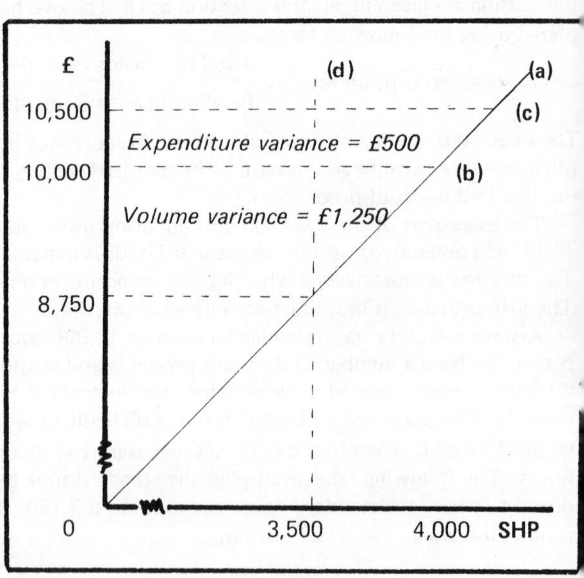

Variances		£
Standard = (SHP x FOAR) — 3,500 x £2.50		8,750
When the actual overheads were		10,500
Leaving a fixed overhead variance of:		£1,750 (A)
This can be divided into	Expenditure	500
and	Volume	1,250
	Total	£1,750 (A)

The variable overhead variances will be:

DIAGRAM 150 *VARIABLE OVERHEAD EXPENDITURE VARIANCE*

Where:-

(a)=VOAR of £1.50 per hour

(b)=Budget expenditure level £6,000

(c)=Actual activity level 3,500 SHP.

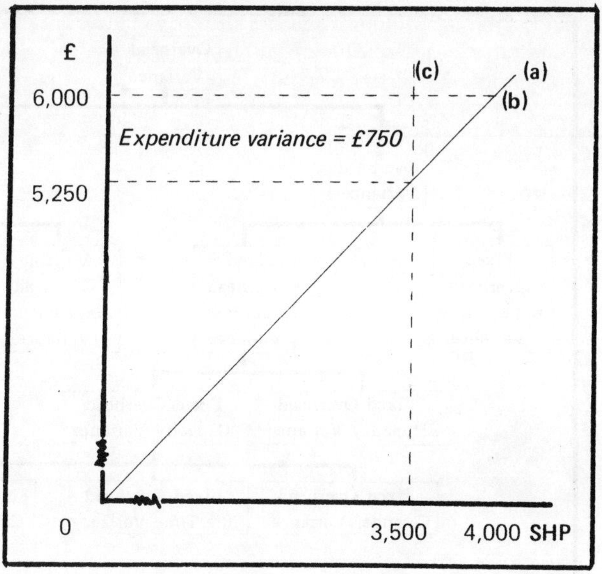

For an activity level of 3,500 SHP the expected variable overhead expenditure would be 3,500 x £1,50 = £5,250. The actual expenditure was the same as the budget, £6,000.

Variances	£
Expenditure = 6,000 – (3,500 x £1,50)	750
Efficiency = (3,500 – 3,500) x £2.50	nil
i.e. (Actual Hours – SHP) x VOAR	
Variable Overhead Variance	750 (A)

The full range of overhead variances are shown in diagram 151. The main division of overheads is into fixed and variable, especially where flexible budgeting systems are in use. The fixed overhead variance is divided into expenditure and volume. The expenditure variance is the difference between the actual fixed costs and the budgeted fixed costs. The volume variance is the difference between normal/budget capacity output and actual output multiplied by the overhead absorption rate. Therefore, if the output was below budget, then overheads would be under-absorbed and the volume variance unfavourable. The variable overheads are divided into expenditure and efficiency. The variable expenditure variance calculation is not the same as the fixed expenditure variance because the variable overheads are expected to "flex" in relation to output. In both the variable expenditure and efficiency variances actual hours are used in relation to standard hours. The fixed overhead volume variance can be divided into efficiency and capacity variances. The capacity variance can be further analysed into calender, idle time and usage variances.

DIAGRAM 151 STRUCTURE OF OVERHEAD VARIANCES

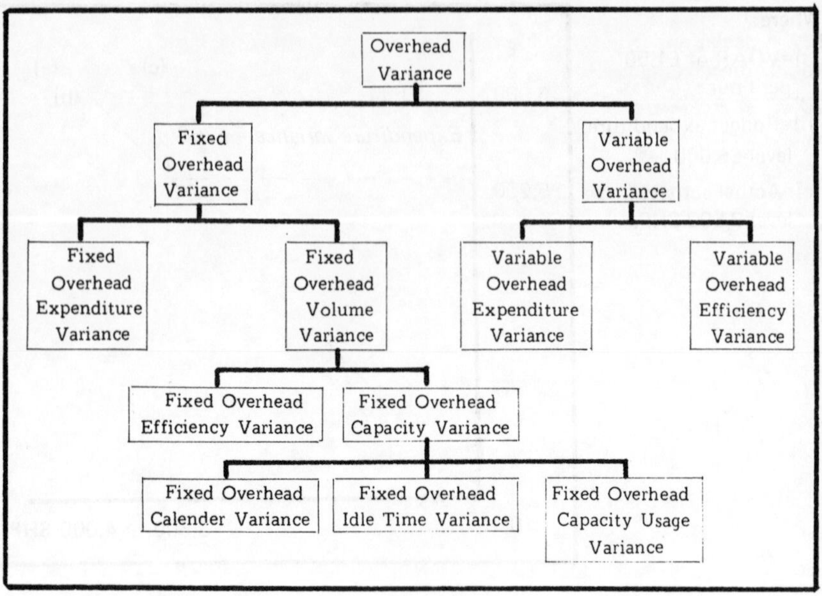

5:1 Formulae

Abbreviations:– SHP = Standard Hours of Production
VOAR = Variable Overhead Absorption Rate
FOAR = Fixed Overhead Absorption Rate

Overhead Variance
Actual overhead – SHP x (VOAR + FOAR)

Fixed Overhead Variance
Actual fixed overheads – (SHP x FOAR)

Variable Overhead Variance
Actual variable overheads – (SHP x VOAR)

Fixed Overhead Expenditure Variance
Actual fixed overhead – Budgeted fixed overhead

Fixed Overhead Volume Variance
(Actual SHP – Budgeted SHP) x FOAR

Variable Overhead Expenditure Variance
Actual variable overhead – (Actual hours worked x VOAR)

Variable Overhead Efficiency Variance
(Actual hours worked – SHP) x VOAR

Fixed Overhead Efficiency Variance
(Actual Hours Worked – SHP) x FOAR

Fixed Overhead Capacity Variance
(Actual hours paid for – Budgeted hours) x FOAR

Fixed Overhead Calender Variance
Standard Working Hours per day x (Actual working days in period – Normal Budget working days in period) x FOAR

Fixed Overhead Idle Time Variance
(Actual hours worked – Actual hours paid for) x FOAR

Fixed Overhead Capacity Usage Variance
(Actual hours worked — Budgeted Hours) x FOAR

5:2 Calculations The following simplified examples show the basic calculations for overhead variances:—

EXAMPLE Fixed and variable overhead variances

A cost centre's budget is as follows:—

FOAR £0.50 per SHP
VOAR £0.25 per SHP
Output 400 units, 4 units = 1 SHP

The actual results were:

Output 400 units = 100 SHP
Fixed Overheads £60, Variable Overheads £50

Total overhead, fixed overhead and variable overhead variances are:—

		£
Fixed overhead variance	60 — (100 x £0.5)	10 (A)
Variable overhead variance	30 — (100 x £0.25)	25 (F)
Total overhead variance	(60 + 30) — (100 x 0.75)	15 (F)

EXAMPLE Fixed overhead expenditure and volume variances

A cost centre fixed cost budget was £2,000
Budgeted output 1,000 units with 1 SHP = 1 unit
Actual production was 1,100 units with actual fixed costs £2,100

Fixed overhead expenditure and volume variances are:—

		£
Expenditure variance	2,100 — 2,000	100 (A)
Volume variance	(2,200 — 2,000) x £1.00	200 (F)
Fixed Overhead Variance	2,100 — (2,200 x £1.00)	100 (F)

EXAMPLE Overhead expenditure and efficiency variances

Budget = 950 SHP with a VOAR £0.50
Actual = 1,000 hours worked. Variable overheads £475
Variable overhead, expenditure and efficiency variances are:—

		£
Expenditure variance	475 — (1,000 x 0.5)	25 (F)
Efficiency variance	(1,000 — 950) x 0.5	25 (A)
Variable Overhead Variance	475 — (950 x 0.5)	nil

EXAMPLE Fixed overhead efficiency and capacity variances

A cost centre has the following budget figures:

Output 2,000 SHP Fixed Overheads £2,000

Actual results for the period were:

Fixed overheads £4,200, output 2,100 SHP and the payroll showed that 2,400 hours were paid for.

Fixed overhead, volume and efficiency variances are:—

Calculation of FOAR $\frac{£4{,}000}{2{,}000 \text{ SHP}}$ = £2.00 per SHP

		£
Efficiency variance	(2,400 — 2,100) x £2.00	600 (A)
Capacity	(2,400 — 2,00) x £2.00	800 (F)
Fixed Overhead Volume	(2,100 — 2,000) x £2.00	200 (F)

EXAMPLE Fixed overhead capacity, idle time and capacity usage variance

A cost centre has the following budget figures:

Output 5,000 SHP where one labour hour = 1 SHP
Fixed cost £10,000

Relevant results for the period were:

Hours worked according to the clock cards	6,000
Hours paid for according to the payroll	6,500

Fixed overhead capacity, idle time and capacity usage variances are:—

$$\text{Calculation of FOAR} = \frac{£10{,}000}{5{,}000 \text{ SHP}} = £2.000 \text{ per SHP}$$

		£
Idle time variance	(6,000 – 6,500) x £2.00	1,000 (A)
Capacity usage variance	(6,000 – 5,000) x £2.00	2,000 (A)
Fixed Overhead Capacity	(6,500 – 5,000) x £2.00	3,000 (A)

5:3 Interpretation To interpret overhead variances the user must be aware of th relationship of overheads to output especially for the capacity variances. Basical if a capacity variance changes it is because output has altered from the standard and that can be due to a variety of reasons such as labour disputes, late deliveries machine breakdowns or just poor labour efficiency. All of these will cause an ad verse capacity variance. The same principles apply to overhead efficiency variances. The expenditure variances will alter if the actual costs of the overheads alter

6 Sales Variances

There are two main approaches to sales variances, sales value variances and sales margin variances. During the early development of standard costing and budgetary control, sales variance analysis was based on the amount of sales. For example, if th budget sales were 10,000 units @ £10.00 each and the actual sales were 1,000 units £9.00 each, then the variance analysis would be:

		£
Sales Quantity Variance	(11,000 – 10,000) x £10.00	10.000 (F)
Sales Price Variance	(£9.00 – £10.00) x 11,000	11,000 (A)
Sales Variance	(11,000 x £9.00) – (10,000x £10.00)	£1,000 (A)

Although this is a useful analysis the concern is on sales profitability rather than sales value. The profitability referred to is standard profit being the difference between the unit selling price and the standard total costs per unit. Thus in the above example, if the standard cost per unit was £8.00 the sales margin variances would b

		£
Sales Margin Quantity Variances	(11,000 – 10,000) x £2.00	2,000 (F)
Sales Margin Price Variance	(£1.00 – £2.00) x 11,000	11.000 (A)
Sales Margin Variance	(99,000 – 88,000) – 20,000	£9,000 (A)

From these figures it can be appreciated that the sales margin variance provides more essential information. A £1,000 adverse sales variance does not seem so bad a drop in profit of £9,000. It is for this reason that sales margin variances are more widely used. Although there is nothing to prevent both types of sales variances bei used by a company. The following chart and notes only refer to sales margin varia

DIAGRAM 152 STRUCTURE OF SALES MARGIN VARIANCES

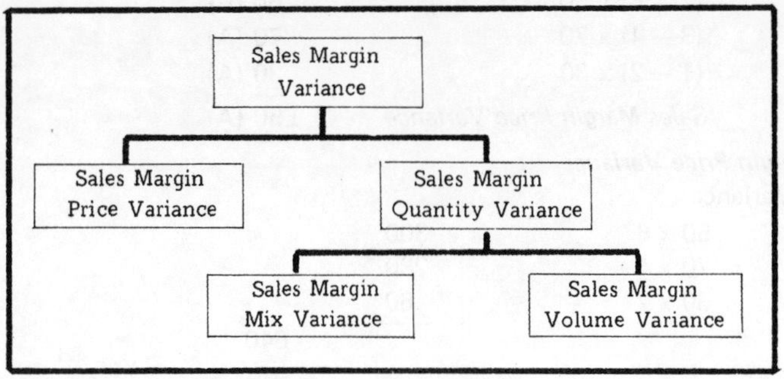

6:1 Formulae

Sales Margin Variance

Actual sales – Standard cost of actual sales – Budgeted margin for budgeted sales

Sales Margin Price Variance

(Actual unit selling price standard unit cost – Budget unit selling price standard unit cost) x Actual units sold

i.e. Actual Margin — i.e. Standard Margin

Sales Margin Quantity Variance (Sometimes referred to as Volume Variance)

Sales Margin Mix Variance

(Actual quantities in actual proportions x Standard Margins) – (Actual quantity in standard proportion x Standard Margin)

Sales Margin Volume Variance

(Actual quantity in standard proportions x Standard Margin) – (Budgeted units x Standard Margin)

6:2 Calculations We will use just one simplified example to illustrate the sales margin price, quantity, volume and mix variances. The basic detail is as follows:–

Product	*Standard Margin £*	*Standard Selling Price £*	*Budgeted Sales Units*
A	6	12	60
B	4	10	20
C	2	8	20

Actual results:

Product	*Actual Selling Price £*	*Actual Sales Units*
A	13	50
B	9	70
C	7	30

The sales margin variance calculations are shown below:-

Sales Margin Variance		£
A	(60 x 6) – (50 x 7)	10 (A)
B	(20 x 4) – (70 x 3)	130 (B)
C	(20 x 2) – (30 x 1)	10 (A)
	Sales Margin Variance	£110 (F)

Price Variance

A	(7 – 6) x 50		50 (F)
B	(3 – 4) x 70		70 (A)
C	(1 – 2) x 30		30 (A)
	Sales Margin Price Variance		£50 (A)

Sales Margin Price Variance

Mix Variance

A	50 x 6	300	
B	70 x 4	280	
C	30 x 2	60	
			640
less			
A	(150 x 0.6) = 90 x 6	540	
B	(150 x 0.2) = 30 x 4	120	
C	(150 x 0.2) = 30 x 2	60	
			720
	Sales Margin Mix Variance		£80 (A)

Sales Margin Volume Variance

Reconciliation of Variances

Mix		80 (A)	
Volume		240 (F)	
	Quantity		160 (F)
	Price		50 (A)
	Sales Margin Variance		110 (F)

6:3 Interpretation The same principles for cost variances apply to sales margin variances. There are sales margin quantity and sales margin price variances. If variances arise in the quantity variances it is because different quantities have been sold than expected. If variances arise in the price variances this is due to change in price or discounts. None of the variances arise due to changes in costs because only standard costs are used in the calculations.

7 Production ratios

From your reading of this chapter you will be aware that standard costing and variance analysis can help management control production. An additional feature of some standard costing systems is to produce control ratios that provide an overview of production efficiency, capacity and activity. The ratios are calculated from standard costing data and are summarised in diagram 153 and the following notes.

DIAGRAM 153 STRUCTURE OF PRODUCTION RATIOS

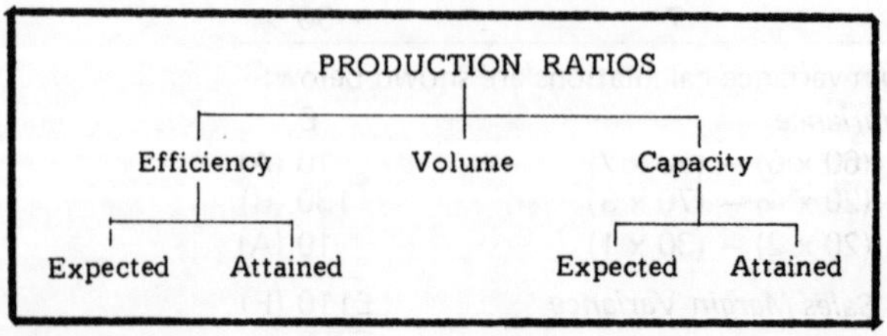

7:1 Formulae

Efficiency expected $\dfrac{\text{Budgeted output in standard hours}}{\text{Budgeted clock hours}}$ %

Efficiency attained $\dfrac{\text{Actual standard hours of production}}{\text{Actual clock hours}}$ %

Volume $\dfrac{\text{Standard hours of production}}{\text{Budgeted standard hours of production}}$ %

Capacity expected $\dfrac{\text{Budgeted hours for the period}}{\text{Maximum hours for the period}}$ %

Capacity attained $\dfrac{\text{Actual clock hours for the period}}{\text{Budgeted hours for the period}}$ %

7:2 Calculations We will use a simplified example to illustrate the calculation of production ratios. Assume a company's production budget for an accounting period was an output of 260 standard hours of production using 300 direct labour hours. The maximum possible direct labour hours for the period was 340. The actual output was 240 hours and direct labour clock records totalled 280 hours. This data can be converted into production ratios as follows:—

Efficiency expected $\dfrac{260}{300} \times 100 = 86.7\%$

Efficiency attained $\dfrac{240}{280} \times 100 = 85.7\%$

Volume $\dfrac{240}{260} \times 100 = 92.3\%$

Capacity expected $\dfrac{300}{340} \times 100 = 88.2\%$

Capacity attained $\dfrac{280}{300} \times 100 = 93.3\%$

7:3 Interpretation The efficiency ratios are concerned with the relationship between actual hours and standard hours of production. The *level of efficiency* is not so important as the *trend of efficiency* because the level is mainly determined by the standard setting criteria. (Refer to section 2:4). However in the short run a comparison between the expected and attained efficiency is adequate.

The volume ratio is sometimes called the 'activity ratio' and is concerned with ensuring sufficient volume to recover the fixed overheads. The budgeted standard hours provide the yardstick for a level of output that is acceptable to managements. Accordingly if the percentage of actual standard hours to budgeted standard hours is low then output is insufficient.

The capacity ratio is concerned with the relationship between actual hours and budgeted hours. The budgeted hours indicate the expected level of production capacity during the period assuming sufficient labour is available and the machines are working. Machine breakdowns, material shortages, labour shortages or labour disputes will tend to lower the actual hours and cause the company to be operating below capacity.

8 Summary

The falling hardware costs for electronic data processing make it possible for many more businesses to include standard costing in their management information system. (Refer to chapter 10). Already there are a number of software packages available for standard costing and variance analysis which will enable many more businesses to use this powerful management tool. Even though the data pro cessing side of standard costing can be purchased as a package, management still need to exercise caution in the following areas:

(a) Cost collection system. The existing costing system must be capable of provic ing all the detail necessary for actual data to be compared frequently with standard data.

(b) Setting standards. Before starting on the detail of setting all the cost, output and efficiency standards management must be absolutely clear on the criteria for standard setting and have ensured that the standards will be regularly revised.

(c) Understanding variances. The output of the system will be variance based reports. If managers do not understand variances then the entire operation is serving no valid function.

The principles of costing and cost collection explained in chapter 3 are applicable to standard costing. In this chapter we have covered the problems of setting standards, how variances are calculated and how to interpret the results.

Accountancy Quiz No.9.

1. What is standard costing and how does it help managers? *(1, 2, 2:1, 2:2, 2:3).*

2. Assume you are setting up a standard costing system and trying to decide on the criteria for standard setting. You have narrowed your choice down to the following alternatives:–

Alternatives	*Materials*	*Labour*	*Overheads*
Average of past	costs and usage	rates and efficiency	costs
Expected	costs and usage	rates and efficiency	costs
Best possible	costs and usage	rates and efficiency	costs

State which alternative you would choose and give your reasons. *(2:4).*

3. Discuss the statement that variance reports attach too much importance to figures and no importance to reasons. *(2:5, 8).*

4. Assume you are trying to convince a managing director of the need for a standard costing system in his/her company. What would you say? *(2:1, 2:3:1, 8).*

5. Explain how material variances are divided into two main parts and how this division helps managers. *(3, 3:2, 3:3).*

6. Explain how labour variances are divided into two main parts and how this division helps managers. *(4, 4:2, 4:3).*

7. What is meant by interdependence of variances and why is it important to look for interdependence when interpreting variance reports? *(4:3).*

8. What is a standard hour of production? *(5).*

9. What is the relationship between overhead variances and production ratios? *(5, 5:3, 7, 7:3).*

10. Explain how sales variances are structured and how they can help managers. *(6, 6:2, 6:3).*

10 Management Information Systems

Objective
To provide the reader with a general understanding of management information systems and computers, and to integrate the contents of this book into an MIS structure.

Page No.

Content
An explanation of the principles, applications, terminology and likely developments of computers.

An explanation of the principles and problems of management information systems.

A review of techniques explained in this book that have practical applications in management information systems

Management Information Systems

1. Introduction
The purpose of a management information system is to provide relevant, reliable and timely information, within cost constraints, that will help managers plan and control business activity for the optimal use of scarce resources. The methods of achieving this broad objective will of course vary between different organisations. But one common feature of many information systems is the use of the computer. Although in principle an MIS is not dependent upon the use of a computer, in practice new information systems and the computer are almost always linked. Because the rate of technological change in electronic data processing is so fast a large knowledge gap has developed. It is therefore appropriate to begin this chapter with an explanation of how computers work and how recent developments are likely to affect information systems. The explanation of computers in section 2 covers a very wide area. It is intended to provide the reader with an understanding of how computers work, some computer terminology and most important an appreciation of how recent technological developments are going to change established work methods.

Section 3 explains the general principles and problems of management information systems in three stages. The first stage outlines some systems theory as an introduction to the subject. The second stage some characteristics and problems related to information systems. And the last stage looks at management information systems and how they can meet the needs of individual managers and the organisation. As section 3 takes a fairly broad approach to management information systems it was necessary to review some practical aspects of an MIS.

In section 4 the practical aspects of an MIS are first divided into the three broad categories of planning, control and communication. Some of the sub sections in these categories adopt a critical viewpoint about oversold software applications packages. Other practical issues discussed in this section cover areas such as: common data base, MIS security and communication networks.

2. General principles of electronic data processing
The rapid development and application of computers has probably created a knowledge gap for many managers, between what they should know and what they actually know, about electronic data processing. It is hoped that the following detail will help to fill that gap.

This section is divided into three main parts. The first part explains some principles and applications of computers. The second part looks at recent developments and the final part provides a quick reference glossary of computer terminology.

2:1 What is a computer? A computer is a machine which will perform logical operations on input data according to a set of instructions. These logical operations include mathematical functions such as: adding, subtracting, multiplying, dividing, powers, roots, logarithms, etc. and operations such as counting, ranking, listing, comparing and choosing between alternatives. Many of the computer's operations such as memory, adjusting for changing circumstances and making logical decisions appear to give the machine human attributes. However a computer will blindly follow a set of instructions with no ability whatsoever for critical analysis (unless programmed) and creative thinking. The computer's only advantage over the human brain is its capacity to process vast amounts of data precisely in accordance with instructions.

There are two basic kinds of computer: digital and analog. Digital computers operate by counting discrete data. Early mechanical digital computers such as the Pascal mechanical calculator in 1642 used the decimal system where each wheel had ten teeth numbered from 0 to 9. But the modern electronic digital computers use the binary system of 0 and 1 because the electronic components used have only two stable states - on and off. The analog computer operates by setting up an analogy of a problem. A variety of measuring devices used by engineers are based on analogue principles, where fluids, levers, cogs or cables provide some form of scale measurement. For instance the mechanical speedometer in a car is a form of analogue computer. The combination of gears and a rotating flexible inner cable move a pointer on a scale to indicate speed and miles travelled. The slide rule is a common example of an analog computer. Although low cost electronic calculators have virtually replaced the slide rule. Analog computers tend to be used for very specific measuring applications by engineers and scientists. As most computers used in a wide variety of applications are digital, all of this section will be concerned with this category of machine.

The operating principles of an electronic digital computer are illustrated in diagram 154.

DIAGRAM 154 PRINCIPLES OF AN ELECTRONIC DIGITAL COMPUTER

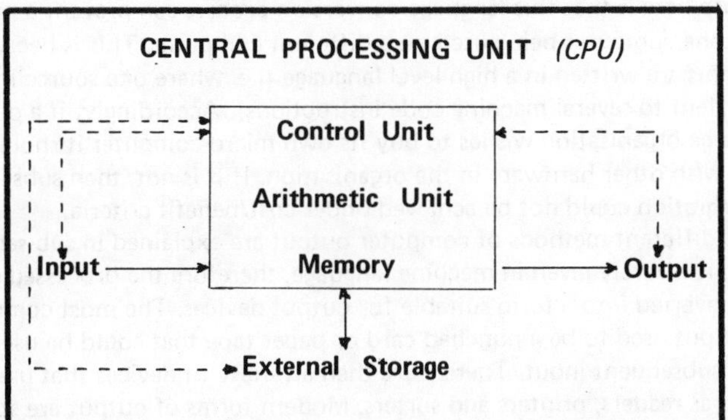

The CPU has three parts; memory, arithmetic unit and the control unit. The external devices for input, output and backing storage all feed into and out of the memory and are switched on/off (controlled) by the control unit.

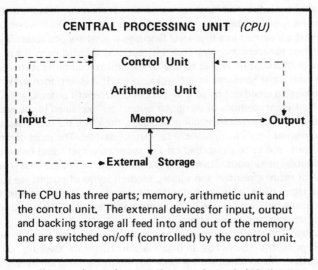

The above diagram shows the central processing unit (CPU) as being the 'brain' of the computer. The main part of this brain is the memory. Processing cannot begin until the program instructions and data input are in the memory and the output from the computer also passes through the memory. The control unit that directs the step by step operations of the system also takes its instructions from the memory. These three functions of the CPU; storage,processing and control are described in the following notes:-

Memory This is the part of the computer where instructions and data are stored. The instructions are called a program. Before any problem can be solved the program and the data has to be in the memory. The larger the program the less room there is for data and vice versa. It therefore follows that the capacity of the memory is a very important factor to consider when purchasing a computer.

Arithmetic unit This part is similar to an electronic calculator. It receives data and instructions from the memory and processes the data in accordance with the instructions. The results of processing are then fed back into the memory where the program instructs how they are to be fed to an output device. Sometimes the results can be fed direct to an output device from the arithmetic unit.
Control unit This unit directs operations by extracting the program instructions one by one from the memory. It controls all movements of data throughout the system from input through the CPU to output so that the computer becomes a fully integrated system.

Diagram 154 shows the computer's brain being serviced by three other parts input, output and external storage. These are briefly explained in the following notes:-

Input There are a number of ways that data may be put into a computer. Many of these input methods are explained in sub-section 2:1:1. The point to note at this stage is, that whatever input method is used the data has to be converted into machine language (i.e. binary) before it can be stored and processed. This conversion process is done by a *compiler* that is supplied by the computer manufacturers (Some computers have *assemblers.* The difference is that a compiler program generates more than one machine code instruction for each source statement whereas an assembler program converts on a one to one basis). The important point to grasp here is that this language conversion process can prevent a program written for one computer being used on a different computer. This is because most programs are written in a high level language (i.e. where one source instruction is equivalent to several machine code instructions). Accordingly, if a department in a large organisation wishes to buy its own micro-computer it should be compatible with other hardware in the organisation. If it is not, then subsequent systems integration could not be achieved under cost/benefit criteria.
Output The different methods of computer output are explained in sub-section 2:1:4. Output is rarely given in machine language, therefore the processed data has to be converted into a form suitable for output devices. The most common forms of output used to be a punched card or paper tape that could be used for storage and subsequent input. There were then a variety of devices that used cards or tape such as readers, printers and sorters. Modern forms of output are stored on magnetic tapes, disks or drums and output for users appears on printed tabulations and/or visual display units (VDU's). Output also occurs as electronic pulses to control machinery and forms of oral output.
External storage The size of a computer's memory is usually too small to hold all the data and programs required by an organisation. Therefore 'backing ' or 'file' storage is needed. The external storage generally holds the program library and separate files of data. The methods of storing programs and data vary and are explained in sub-section 2:1:2.

We have now covered the operating principles of an electronic digital computer as illustrated in diagram 154. From this explanation it can be appreciated that there is an important distinction between hardware and software. Basically, hardware represents all the tangible components relating to input, storage, processing and output. Whilst software relates to the sets of instructions (programs) that tells the hardware what to do. We will be examining different kinds of software in sub-section 2:1:3.

To summarise, we have established that a computer performs four basic operations - input, storage, processing and output. For communication to occur between humans and the computer language translation is necessary. During the input phase,the programing language is converted into machine language for storage and processing. Then during the output phase the machine language is converted into a form that is acceptable to the user. These four basic operations of input. storage, processing and output are explained in greater detail in the following subsections.

2:1:1 Input So far we have established that there are two main categories of input; programs (lists of instructions) and data which is to be processed. The most common form of input used to be punched cards and/or punched paper tape. Punching data can take a long time because it is usually a three stage process of punching, verification and input reading. With these earlier forms of input a system known as batch processing was developed. Data was prepared in batches with control totals. The punch operators then punched the data and part of the verification process was checking manual batch totals with punched batch totals. To shorten the input time,visual display units connected to typewriter style keyboards were developed. The typed input is displayed on a screen for the operator to check. Once the input is checked a 'send' button is pressed which transfers the data into the CPU. Some computers have input validation programs that make checks for obvious errors such as numbers in data that should be alphabetic. When such errors are identified the input is returned to the VDU screen with instructions for correction. The input VDU may be 'on-line' where it is connected directly to the CPU of the main computer as well as being an output device. Alternatively the input VDU may be 'off-line' with its own validation, storage and processing. The data input on this type of VDU is stored on a 'floppy disk' or cassette tape which is then used as direct input into the main computer. This is similar to the batch input of punched data.

Faster ways of getting input into the CPU are oonstantly being developed. Optical Character Recognition (OCR) machines that can read source documents such as cheques, typed forms (i.e. invoices) and even handwriting are now being used by large organisations. But the real breakthrough in input devices will be voice recognition. This is discussed in sub-section 2:2:3.

2:1:2 Storage An electronic digital computer stores data in the machine language of binary digits. Examples of binary notation are given below:

Number	*Binary Notation*
0	0
1	1
2	10
3	11
4	100
5	101
6	110
7	111
8	1000
9	1001

The abbreviation for a binary digit is 'bit' or 'character'. Thus storage space for say a number 9 would require 4 bits. We established earlier that programs and data for processing are stored in machine language in the memory. It therefore follows that one measure of a computer's power is the storage size of its memory. This is usually expressed in characters (bits), bytes or words.

Characters	A binary digit or bit
Byte	A set of bits that are usually a sub-division of a word. The byte size may vary according to the storage method.
Kilobyte (k)	1,024 bytes
Megabyte (m)	1,000,000 bytes
Word	The computer word can be either a data word or instruction word. Both types of word normally have a space allowance of 34 bits.

Let us apply some of this storage jargon to a simple problem. Say a business wanted to use a 32k byte micro-computer for control of a 1,000 customers' accounts. To store the names, addresses and account details of 1,000 customers would probably require between 100,000 and 200,000 bits. Storage space would also be needed for the programs. Clearly the 32k machine would not be able to hold all the data and programs in memory. Therefore external storage would be required. The important point to note about memory and external storage, is the difference in access time. The time to read from, or write to ory is so fast that fine time measurements are used i.e.

1,000	*milliseconds*	equal one second
1,000,000	*microseconds*	equal one second
1,000,000,000	*nanoseconds*	equal one second

Whereas access to external storage is generally dependent upon an electro-mechanical operation and is therefore far slower. As a general guide, in the time it takes to access one item in external storage, about 100,000 items could be accessed from memory. Indeed access to data is sometimes more important than processing of data. With the larger computers, punched tape and punched cards are used in older systems, or for specialised functions. In newer systems magnetic drums and disk packs are used. The characteristics of different storage methods are given in the following notes and table.

Characteristics of Storage Methods

Type of Storage		*Average capacity* *(bytes)*	*Average access time* *
Memory	- Micro	4k - 64K	5 microsecs
	- Mini	64k - 1,024K	5 microsecs
	- Mainframe	1m - 1000m	5 microsecs
		(characters)	
Disks	- Fixed	5m - 80m	10 millisecs
	- Exchangeable	5m - 100m	50 millisecs
	- Floppy	125k - 1m	50 - 500 millisecs
Tapes	- Cassette	50k - 250k	Can range from
	- Cartridge	500k - 10m	millisecs to minutes
	- Open reel	1m - 20m	depending on position tape
Drum		1m - 50m	10 millisecs

*(*Note: The averages are crude approximations intended as guidelines for the non-specialist. The range will be very wide due to the number of manufacturers and technological developments)*

(a) *Memory* This term is generally used to describe the *internal* storage of the CPU (Refer to diagram 154, sub section 2:1). External storage such as disks and cassettes are sometimes referred to as memory units. Therefore when determining the size of a computer's memory be sure that figures relate to internal storage. We have established that the relevant data and programs must be in the memory before processing can be undertaken. Also,that processed data usually returns to memory before going to an output device. Thus the size of the memory is a major factor for determining the power of a computer. A computer memory will normally have two modes:

Read Only Memory *ROM*
Random Access Memory *RAM*

The ROM is a fixed memory for control and program languages. Whereas the RAM is the working memory that can be used for programs and data that will be changed. However, machines vary in the way programs and data are stored. For instance a 32k RAM may have 30k of usable memory. Some memories are *volatile*, which means they do not retain the data and programs when the power is switched off. These can be contrasted with *non-volatile* memories that are a feature of some modern micro/mini computers. Because of these complications concerning memory definition and memory size, potential buyers need to carefully examine the written specifications of different machines and obtain written classification from the manufacturers where necessary.

Memory size can be increased by adding on memory units and by skillful programming. It was suggested earlier, that external storage was an economic and practical solution to limited internal memory. One aspect of this limitation, is that large programs cannot themselves, be retained in memory in their entirety. A solution is to reduce the work a single program does, thus reducing its size but increasing the number of programs required. With small systems this lowering of efficiency may not be significant but an alternative which uses disk backing store is available on some machines. Here a too large program is divided into logical segments or sets and each set is called up from the disk store when, and only when, it is required. The technique is particularly useful because the lengthy call-up process can be going on whilst another section of the program in main memory is doing its work and there is thus no delay. The concept of *virtual memory* whereby fixed fast access backing storage is permanently allocated as an immediate feeder to main memory effectively expands the latter at a much lower cost then buying the extra memory modules otherwise required.

(b) *Magnetic disks* There are three main types of magnetic disk arrangement: fixed, exchangeable and floppy. They all work on the same principle, except the heads touch the surface of floppy disks, whereas with the others they float close to the surface. The heads are similar to the record/playback head of a tape recorder in that they can transfer signals to and from the surface of the disk. Floppy systems wear more because the heads are in contact with the disk. The mechanism for rotating the disk is referred to as the disk drive and the heads more fully described as 'read/write heads'. The drive also houses the electronic circuitry needed to operate the disk by the control unit in the CPU.

Fixed disks are permanently mounted on the drive. Their use for mass storage has now largely been superseded by more flexible arrangements. Typically the surfaces are divided into several concentric sectors, each of which is provided with a moving read/write head. Normally there are a number of disks mounted concentrically on the drive with a set of heads for each surface.

Exchangeable disks are also permanently mounted in a cartridge or 'pack' in use but these packs can be exchanged on the drive. Therefore a number of packs can be used to store all the data required by an organisation and mounted on the drive in turn when required. A single read/write head is provided for each surface and the set of heads move between the disks in unison. (The exact nature of the mechanism varies with the manufacturer).

Floppy disks were introduced in the early 1970's and have been very successful. Their name derives from their physical flexibility, in contrast to the rigidity of other disks. The standard version is 8 inch in diameter but there are several variations. The capacity of a single 'floppy' is low compared with most other disk storage but in quantity they can provide a very effective backing storage for small computers. They have a particular advantage in some applications in that their lightness, flexibility and comparative robustness enables them to be easily stored and transported.

(c) *Magnetic tapes* The principal feature which differentiates tape from disk, is that on tape,data is stored consecutively and once the tape is running, the data follows in the order in which it was stored in the first place. On disk it is possible (though not always required) to access a given record or group of records directly regardless of physical location on the disk. With tape it is not possible to know the position of a record except as relative to its preceding or succeeding record. Getting information from a reel of tape, therefore, can be quite fast if it is near its start or very slow (perhaps 15-20 minutes) if it is near its end. Accordingly, if a computer must have access to a program which is stored in some form of external store and needs to access different parts of that medium at different times, a magnetic tape would rarely be appropriate.

However, tape storage has a role to play with both main frame and mini-computers. It can be appropriate to store programs on tape when they are not segmented for virtual memory operation. Tape is a very cheap medium and provides a secure and convenient way of holding the program library. Many applications specifically require the reading of consecutive records right through the file, such as payroll, therefore tape could be used.

There are two main types of magnetic tape systems; open reel and cassette. They are similar in appearance to open reel and cassette tape recorders. Open reel systems generally use ½ inch wide tape of varying reel lengths. Cassette tapes are mainly used with micro computers because they have a small storage capacity. Although large cassettes, called 'cartridges' have a storage capacity equivalent to small reel systems. A common application for cassettes is the preparation of input data at sites remote from the computer. The cassette is robust enough to use in the post. A typical example of their use might be to store a day's trading transactions for a small business. They have also been found ideal for storing programs.

(d) *Drum* An alternative form of fixed storage is a smaller disk or drum. For each track of the drum, there is a single fixed read/write head. Because there is no mechanical movement of the heads, access to the recorded data is very fast. Costs of the equipment are high however, and the capacity of the unit is comparatively small. Their use is principally for storing programs (or parts of programs) or data to which very fast access is essential.

2:1:3 Processing For data processing to occur the computer has to have a set of understandable instructions. The process for getting the computer to understand instructions is shown in diagram 155. For example, if a user wanted the computer to print out a list of customer accounts ranked in terms of value, the

DIAGRAM 155 COMPUTER LANGUAGE CONVERSION PROCESS

Normal Language →	**Flowchart Language** →	**Procedural Language** →	**Machine Language**
User requirements for systems designs are usually collected by systems analysts	*Work usually done by systems analysts See example in chapter 2 sub-section 2:3:6*	*Sequence of instructions in procedural language such as BASIC, COBOL or FORTRAN is usually done by programmers*	*Conversion into machine language is usually done by a compiler in the computer*

instructions would have to go through the three stage conversion process before the computer could process the data. Computer manufacturers now build into their hardware,programs called compilers,that convert a procedural language into the machine language. For micro computers the compiler generally uses the procedural language of BASIC. Whereas the compilers in small business systems may use the procedural language of COBOL, that is an acronym for Common Business Orientated Language. The manufacturers also provide utility programs with their equipment. These programs perform many processing tasks such as: file creation, labelling, transfers, editing, copying and updating.

Although the fixed stage of the conversion process into machine language is done automatically, the task of converting normal language into the appropriate procedural language can be complex and very expensive. This is why software can sometimes cost far more than the hardware. Moreover, software needs to be maintained, because application programs often have to be altered to meet changing circumstances. We will not get involved in the detail of flowcharting and procedural languages because it is outside the scope of this introduction. However it is worthwhile just summarising what is involved in making the computer understand what we want it to do.

GETTING A COMPUTER TO WORK

Problem definition ↓	-	The problem must be precisely defined and where possible in a mathematical form.
Analysis ↓	-	The defined problem to be analysed from all view points including effect of solution on existing and future procedures and systems. A system is proposed by systems analysts.
Procedure ↓	-	Programmers examine proposed system to see if it is within the computer's capabilities and if it can be written in a procedural format.
Machine conversion	-	Agreed system written in procedural format (the program) is tested on the computer and *de-bugged*. (i.e. errors are removed).

In addition to instructions that tell the computer what to do with data, we also need to tell the computer when to switch on/off input/output devices and when to pass data etc. from the memory into the arithmetic unit (Refer to diagram 154, sub section 2:1) This set of instructions is generally referred to as an *operating system* and is often provided by the manufacturers with the equipment. With small machines a fairly simple *executive or supervisory program* is used that just ensures only one process at a time is carried out by the computer. But with larger machines using many terminals,different activities are run simultaneously and tailor made operating systems have to be designed. The design and maintenance of these types of systems can be very expensive.

In this sub-section we have established that there are three main categories of software required for a computer to process data: compilers and utility programs, operating systems and application programs. With the smaller machines the first two categories are usually provided by the manufacturer with the hardware. For application programs there are basically two options:

(a) To use packaged software that can be adapted to meet requirements. Or alter requirements to suit the software.
(b) To have software written specifically to meet requirements using in-house analysts and programmers, or using the services of a bureau.

If the user has the time and inclination then 'simple' programs can be written. But prospective buyers should not underestimate just how much time, patience and skill is required to get a computer to understand what you want it to do.

2:1:4 Output The output from the CPU is in machine language and has to be decoded and presented in a form acceptable to the user. The most common forms are printed on paper or displayed on a screen. There are specialised applications such as computer controlled machines that have specialised output devices. But in this sub-section we will only be reviewing print and visual display output devices. Let us first consider the different types of printer. The characteristics we are looking for are:-

(a) Speed of printing mechanism
(b) Price
(c) Quality of print
(d) Reliability
(e) Ability to produce multiple copies on one print run

(i) Dot matrix printer These tend to be used with small computers, are quite cheap and have low print speeds of about 30 to 300 characters per second.
(ii) Character printer These generally use typewriter mechanisms , are cheaper and slower then matrix printers. Average print speed is about 30-45 characters per second. Mainly used by small computers.
(iii) Line printer As the name implies these machines print a line at a time instead of a single character. A line can be up to 132 characters and print speeds average 16 - 32 lines per second. They are generally used for large print runs.
(iv) Electrostatic printers These are based in electrostatic photocopying machine principles and can produce up to 48 lines per second.
(v) Thermal printers These use special thermal photocopying type paper and can produce about 30 to 300 characters per second.
(vi) Ink jet printers These produce high quality print at high speed.
(vii) Laser printers These also produce high quality print at high speeds.

There is a wide range of printers available, but for small computers, dot matrix and character printers tend to be chosen because they are cheap, have some flexibility in print style and high print speeds are not needed. Some printers can produce line diagrams in multiple colours. One other form of printed output that needs to be mentioned is COM. This is an acronyn for Computer Output to Microfilm. As microfilm and microfiche gains wider acceptance as a data storage method COM systems will become increasingly popular. A COM system would often be far cheaper in the long run than a paper based hard copy output system.

The other main form of output is the Visual Display Unit (VDU). These are normally a cathode ray tube similar to a television set. Indeed, in some micro computer systems a domestic television set is used for display of input and out put. A typical VDU will display about 25 lines, each holding up to 80 characters. The VDU will be connected to a keyboard for input/output instructions and probably some form of printer that enables selected displayed information to be printed. Thus the VDU is really an important communication device between humans and computers.

2:2 Recent developments From reading the foregoing sub-sections you should have acquired some knowledge of how a computer works, what it can do and understand some of the jargon. It is useful to have this knowledge before reading the following sub-sections. Computing really is an exciting field of activity because there are some remarkable technological developments happening that are drawing industry and commerce into a new era. It is outside the scope of this book to discuss in detail these important developments, but it is hoped that the following review will provide the reader with an awareness of what is happening. In the first sub-section an attempt is made to summarise the current state of affairs of mini/micro computers. The trends identified are that machines are generally getting smaller, more powerful and cheaper. The following sub-section deals with the related topic of word processing that will become an important application for small computers. The third sub-section on semi conductor technology (chips and microprocessors) is most important because chips are the driving force in this technological revolution. Developments such as speech input and speech output chips, and super size memory chips will give equipment manufacturers the opportunity to make products that will completely alter the nature of work. One area of work that will certainly be affected is the office and the final sub-section reviews some aspects of office automation that will be part of the office of the future.

2:2:1 Micro/mini computers Any discussion about micro, mini or mainframe computers creates a problem of definition. A decade ago it was quite easy to distinguish a mainframe computer by characteristics such as a CPU, backing storage, input and output devices. Now all these characteristics can exist in a micro computer that costs just a few hundred pounds. Thus the distinction between small, medium and big computers that is now being drawn is their processing/storage access capability. But even this distinction is becoming blurred at the edges, because a modern mini computer can have a larger processing storage access capability than a ten year old mainframe. Even calculators are taking on the characteristics of computers. Therefore before we start talking about 'super minis' and 'micromainframes' let us first try and establish a starting point. The following summary lists the hardware components of different categories of 'computers'.

PROGRAMMABLE CALCULATOR
Processor
Single line visual display
Keyboard
2k bytes memory
Cassette interface for programs
Interface for printer

MICROCOMPUTER BASIC
Processor
Television screen
Keyboard
Cassette Deck
4 to 8k bytes memory

MICROCOMPUTER - FOR COMMERCIAL USE
As above plus
Twin Floppy Disk
Thermal printer
32k bytes memory

DESK TOP COMPUTER
Processor
V.D.U. Display
Keyboard
Twin Floppy Disk
64k bytes memory
Character or Dot Matrix Printer

SMALL BUSINESS SYSTEM
Processor
V.D.U. Display
Keyboard
Four Floppy Disks
64k bytes memory
Character or Dot Matrix Printer

VISIBLE RECORD COMPUTER WITH DISK
Processor
Keyboard
Dot-matrix printer
Twin Floppy Disk
64k bytes memory
Magnetic ledger card feed

MINICOMPUTER - SMALL
Processor
64k bytes memory
2 V.D.U. displays
Disk system e.g. 5m bytes fixed
+ 5m bytes interchangeable
Matrix printer

MINICOMPUTER - MEDIUM
Processor (enhanced)
128k bytes memory
Two 14m bytes exchangeable disks
Printing terminal
Real-time operating system

MINICOMPUTER - LARGE
Processor
512k bytes memory
Virtual memory
1024m bytes (4 exchangeable units) disk
Line printer (300 lines/minute)
Mag. Tape Unit
Console typewriter
32 V.D.U. displays

Having identified some computer categories we can now discuss possible trends. The discernible trend is that computers are getting smaller in size and cheaper in terms of processing/storage power. The once popular visible record computers (VRC's) used for accounting applications are probably being replaced with minis or micros. Also some mainframe installations will probably be replaced by more robust minis that do not need special computer room conditions. And low cost micros are now bringing computers to a very wide cross section of society that a decade ago related the term 'hardware' with a shop that sold pots and pans. A good indicator of what is going to happen with small computers is the history of the calculator.

In the 1950's a lot of mechanical equipment began appearing in offices such as addlisting machines, mechanical calculators and book-keeping machines. This equipment was often large, noisy and unreliable. It was not until the early 1970's that quieter, more reliable electronic machines started to replace the electro-mechanical devices. The early electronic calculators using printed circuit boards and large display tubes were then costing several hundred pounds. The equipment suppliers were developing a back up service using the same organisation method as used for the servicing of mechanical machines. Within ten years electronic calculators were costing about one per cent of the original price (i.e. 1971 cost circa £300 and 1981 £10) in constant purchasing power terms. The back up service had completely disappeared, because calculators are sold on a single replacement basis. This dramatic change was brought about mainly by the microprocessor which we will be discussing in the section on semi-conductors.

Now let us apply the experience of the calculator market to small computers. During 1976 a mini computer costing say £15,000 would have less processing power and storage capacity than a 1981 micro costing around £2,000. And micros are getting cheaper and more powerful. Moreover the lucrative home computer market is driving prices down to a level where a micro can be purchased (in 1981) for under £75. The hardware is becoming smaller, cheaper and better, in the same way as the calculator experience. In the following subsections we will be considering related developments.

2:2:2 Word processing The term 'word processing' was introduced by IBM in the late 1960's to summarise office activities such as: dictating, transcribing, typing, editing, communicating and filing that could be undertaken by a computer. Since then, hardware and software has been specifically designed for the following word processing functions:-

(1) *Repetitive letters* where just the address, name and a few personal details are different. The main letter is held in memory and relevant alterations, additions are made via a VDU and keyboard. The letter is then typed automatically at high speed to any width setting.
(2) *Long documents* such as legal statements, budgets, reports of meetings, tenders, etc. that may require 'adjustments' after they have been typed. The original is held in memory, the adjustments are entered via the V.D.U. keyboard and the document is then retyped automatically at high speed.
(3) *Filing and retrieval* of correspondence and other documents can be undertaken by the machine without the need for nard copies. The filing system could also include an analysis function.

Thus a word processing machine can reduce the amount of typing, photocopying and filing undertaken in an office. There are basically four categories of word processing systems:

1) Add on system which is a software package that enables a computer user to have some word processing capability without having to buy a separate word processing machine.
2) Stand alone system where the machine is completely self contained with its own keyboard, memory. storage, printer and in most instances a V.D.U.
3) Cluster system where several machines share one or more facilities such as memory, storage and/or printing.
4) Shared logic system which is specifically designed as an integrated system where most of the facilities are shared between the users.

The developments in word processing seem to be towards systems that combine data processing and word processing. Some word processing machines are providing limited data processing facilities and data processing machines are providing limited word processing facilities. Indeed the convergence of data and word processing is a necessary step towards the office of the future.

2:2:3 Semi-conductor technology The dictionary definition of a semiconductor is a solid substance that is non conductive at low temperature but has a conductivity between insulators and most metals at higher temperatures. This does not seem like a substance that will radically alter the nature of industry and commerce until one appreciates that semiconductor technology was responsible for early developments such as the transitor and is currently producing an astonishing range of microchips. The chip is a miniturised solid state electronic circuit constructed on a wafer of silicon. The first high value output of chips provided the computational circuits for electronic calculators. These calculators also had memory chips (Refer to earlier description of ROM's and R.A.M's) By the mid 1960's, memory and computational chips were being built as a single chip often referred to as a microprocessor. It is these microprocessors that are the brain of all modern computers. Let us now briefly look at some of the recent developments in chips and microprocessors. We will use the four classifications of: input, storage, processing and output that were used in section 2.
Input In sub-section 2:2:1 the main forms of input were identified as punched cards, punched paper tape, keyboard via a visual display unit and sensing devices such as an optical character recognition machine. The revolution for input devices will be when a chip is manufactured that will convert speech into

digital input. In section 2:1 the difference between digital and analog computers was explained. You may recall that many measurements such as temperature, pressure, time, light, speed and *sound* are anologue. But the most efficient form of electronic data processing is digital. Therefore an important stage is for analog input signals to be converted into digital data. There are many analog-to-digital converter chips in use in scientific and industrial measurement devices. It is only a matter of time before speech amplification is digitised and available in mass produced chips. This is a particularly important development for the Japanese, because their complex language creates input difficulties. Once cheap and reliable speech input chips are available, it will dramatically change communications in industry and commerce. For instance, language schools would be virtually wiped out when hand held translating machines become available. With speech chips, the user could input one language and have speech output in a choice of languages. Speech chips in word processing machines would also drastically reduce the need for secretaries because oral input could be displayed on a VDU, corrected orally and then typed according to oral instructions. Probably input speech chips will be mass produced within the next decade and it does not require much foresight to appreciate the impact this tiny semiconductor device will have on commercial activity.

Storage In section 2:1:2 we identified two main types of storage: internal and external. Internal storage being the memory part of the CPU that holds programs and data awaiting processing. Whilst the external storage in magnetic disks, cassettes or drums being necessary because the memory was not large enough for all the data and programs. Semiconductor memories store information in cells made up of tiny transistors. With read only memories (R.O.M's), the transistors are fixed in the on and off position in the manufacturing process. These chips are now being programmed in high level languages instead of machine language (Refer to sub-section 2:1:3) With read/write memory chips (R.A.M's), the tiny transistors are turned on/off instead of being fixed. The storage capacity of these R.A.M.'s is getting larger with 64k R.A.M. chips becoming widely available. With these larger capacity chips micro-computers are becoming far more powerful.

The really exciting storage development is the bubble memory. It is quite different from semi conductor memories. A bubble memory stores data in magnetic domains (bubbles) moving under a track on the surface of a 'chip' External magnetic fields around the chip keep the bubbles moving. A circuit then tells a bubble generator whether or not to place a bubble in a specific location on a particular track. Because the bubbles are very small, up to one million can be stored on a single chip. Not only does the bubble memory have a tremendous storage capacity, it can be non volatile if it is packaged with a permanent magnet. Whereas semi conductor R.A.M's are volatile. This means that bubble memories will be able to replace storage whilst using a fraction of the space and far less hardware.

Processing Diagram 155 in sub section 2:1:3 showed how difficult it can be to tell the computer what to do. This unfriendliness on the part of the computer, has created many difficulties and provided high paid employment for systems analysts and programmers. However, with the lucrative personal and small business computer markets offering virgin ground for hardware manufacturers, there are tremendous pressures to make computers more 'user friendly'. It is evident that the hardware can easily cope with most user's processing requirements. The demand/supply gap is for software that provides a sufficient range of processing applications at the right price. As a result manufacturers are providing far more built in software in R.O.M.'s and 'friendly' software packages covering a wide variety of applications.

Output The output devices explained in sub-section 2:1:4 were mainly printers and visual display units. Recent developments with printers have concentrated on making them faster, more reliable and in some instances cheaper. There are however, a large number of specific output devices designed to control some kind of production process, or display a form of measurement. Many of these devices use digital to analog converters. A wider general use of digital to analog converters will be speech chips. National Semi-conductors Corporation for ex-example, produce a speech chip called 'Digitalker'. This chip set consists of a speech processor and a read only memory that stores the words. When connect ed to an external filter and amplifier, the synthesizer produces life-like speech, a duplicate of the original recorded voice whether male,female, adult or child. Digitalker works on a speech compression principle. A human voice is used to record a message; this is converted (by an analog-to-digital converter) into digital data that is fed to a computer. This computer compresses the data which is then put into a memory. During playback, the speech data is taken from the memory and fed to the Digitalker processor chip where it is decompressed and reconverted to an analog signal. This is then filtered and amplified and sent to a loudspeaker.

The real benefits of speech input devices will come when speech input is fully developed and users can converse with a computer. This is not science fiction, it is a reality. Semiconductor technology is rapidly getting nearer to the point of convergence when the developments in speech input, super size memories and speech output chips will combine to produce some truly remarkable machines

2:2:4 Office automation A substantial amount of management accounting techniques are related to production cost control and efficiency. One result of this emphasis on lower unit costs has been the introduction of more capital equipment per worker to a point where some production processes are almost entirely automated. The office worker however has had few fears about being replaced by a machine. Loss of employment in offices has tended to be governed more by personalities than by performance. Some research in the U.S.A. noted that the average office worker was supported by about $3,000 of capital equipment compared with $ 35,000 for a factory worker and $50,000 for a farm worker. Although these are fairly crude statistics they do indicate that there is substantial scope for office automation. In this sub-section we will just briefly review recent developments in office automation to provide some indication of what the office of the future will look like.

(i) *Data processing* Businesses generate a vast amount of internal data relating to matters such as production, storage, costs and revenue. Office automation has tended to focus on the processing of this data but still produced hard copy reports for circulation. The office of the future will tend to move away from hard copy output of processed data and provide wide access to on-line terminals and V.D.U's. Once management and employees have access to information through terminals then the need for hard copy records is reduced.

(ii) *Word processing* Previous sub-sections have explained how word processing reduces the need for hard copy records of letters, reports and internal communications. Hard copy communications would only be needed for people, or

businesses that did not have access to a compatible electronic system. Thus the office of the future would need less typewriters, filing cabinets, photocopying machines, office space and fewer office staff. However, the conversion to a paperless office would probably be unacceptable to many people. Therefore electronic word and data processing systems will tend to be duplicated by unnecessary print outs and print out filing systems.

(iii) Teleconferencing Management meetings can be expensive and time consuming when executives have to travel for group discussions. With rising costs and increasing inconvenience related to travelling, the benefits of teleconferencing are becoming cost justified. A decade ago only television studios could justify the high costs associated with recording studios and powerful transmitters. But modern video equipment and telecommunications have substantially reduced the cost of transmitting live pictures on closed circuits. The Post Office operates a confravision service and multinational corporations are seeing definite cost benefits in running meetings on a teleconference basis. Thus the television screen for closed circuit conference facilities will become a feature of the office of the future.

(iv) External data bases The television screen will also be used in the office of the future as a communication device with external data bases. In the U.K. the major data base owned by the Post Office is called Prestel. The system uses the GPO telephone lines and modified television sets and provides users with a wide range of information. In Europe there are about 400 commercial data bases available on line to the customer's premises. However, most of these data bases originate from the USA and mainly contain data relating to American corporations. However the trend indicates that the office of the future will have access to several external data bases.

(v) Networks The breakthrough in office automation will be when the different internal and external information systems can be linked together. The main problems are systems' compatability and complexity. With regard to compatability, few items of hardware are 'plug compatible'. The smaller manufacturers attempt to make their peripheral equipment compatible with larger manufacturers' equipment. Whilst the larger manufacturers often attempt to 'lock in' their customers by making it extremely expensive to change their hardware. Thus systems integration is difficult to cost justify. Even with compatible hardware, the complexity of integrating information systems can be a long and expensive process. However some large companies are moving towards integrated networks using private automatic branch exchanges (PABX) for centralised communication. These PABX systems are using cable, microwave antennas and even satelites. Thus the office of the future in large corporations will have an astonishing communication network. Executives will have private teleconferencing facilities, instant access to large internal and external data bases with visual displays and private facsimile transmission of hard copy documents over large and small distances.

Office automation is well advanced in many large companies where the benefits of improved communication for planning and control are cost justified. For the medium sized and small businesses, office automation is happening with word and data processing machines, but systems integration is currently too expensive. The paperless office, with visual display units, television sets and speech input/output devices is technically possible but is unlikely to become a commercial reality in the near future.

2:3 Glossary of computer terminology All trades and professions tend to develop their own specialised words and phases. Computer specialists certainly have quite a large esoteric vocabulary. Many of these specialised terms are in common usage and need to be understood by the layman if he/she is working with computers. The purpose of this glossary is to provide brief explanations of common computer words and phrases as a reference for the non-specialist. The explanations are brief, and will not necessarily correspond to specific interpretations,because hardware and software suppliers sometimes apply different interpretations for the same word. However, it is hoped that the reader finds this glossary useful.

GLOSSARY OF COMPUTER TERMINOLOGY

Algol A high level programming language intended mainly for mathematical and scientific applications.

Algorithm A prescribed process for the solution of a given problem in a finite number of defined steps.

Alphanumeric Containing alphabetic and numeric and/or special characters

Applications program A program for a specific application which is written with the intention of processing transaction data provided by a user department.

Applications package A set of general programs usually designed to carry out the processing of a specific application for a number of users with differing requirements (e.g. Payroll for weekly and/or monthly wages)

Arithemetic unit The section of the central processor in which arithematic and logical operations are performed. (Refer to diagram 154)

Audit trail A means of tracing output back to source data and vice versa used by auditors.

Backing Store Storage devices such as magnetic disks, tapes, and drums which are attached to, but not always in use by the computer.

Backup A set of precautions to restore programs or data if the originals are destroyed or a provision to run an application on an alternative machine, or by manual procedures in the event of a machine break down.

Batch processing Data collected over a period of time for submission to the computer in batches.

Bit or Binary digit The smallest unit of data which can be stored in a computer as I or O

Block A convenient size unit of information for processing or the area of storage in which a block of information is recorded.

Bug An error in a program

Byte Adjacent bits which are used as a unit and represent either a character or one or two digits. This unit is fixed by the manufacturer and is the basic unit used for determining the memory size of the CPU. However, some mini/micro compute manufacturers use 'word' rather than 'byte' as a unit of storage.

Card punch A manually operated keyboard machine used to prepare punched cards from source documents for input into a data processing system, or an output device on-line to the computer which punches patterns of holes into cards to store data.

Card reader A machine that reads the data recorded as punched holes in cards, and passes it to the CPU for processing,

Cathode ray tube An electronic vacuum tube for displaying data (See also Visual Display Unit).

Central processing unit (CPU) The central electronic part of a computer which contains the internal storage, control unit and arithmetic unit (Refer to diagram 154).

Character recognition The process of sensing characters by machine and passing them to the CPU. The characters may be printed in magnetic ink and read by 'MICR' (magnetic ink character recognition) equipment or they may be printed in normal ink and read by equipment which recognises the light/shade patterns (OCR).

Check digit An additional digit included in a reference number which checks for clerical or punching errors.

Cobol Common Bussiness Orientated Language. A high level programming language intended mainly for commercial applications. Now available on minicomputers.

Coding The writing of program instructions in a programming language.

Com The transfer of computer data to microfilm without an intermediate printing stage.

Compiler A computer program which converts a 'high level language' program into a 'machine language' program for use by the computer. The original program is called the 'source program' and the compiled version the 'object program'

Configuration The equipment making up a computer system, i.e. the size of core storage and number and types of peripheral units. Except, with the smallest computers there is a great deal of flexibility in how a particular installation is configured

Console typewriter An automatic typewriter electronically attached to the CPU through which the operator can communicate with the computer and vice versa.

Control unit The portion of the CPU which directs the sequence of operating, interprets the coded instructions and issues the commands to the computer circuit to execute the instructions.

Debug To correct the mistakes in a program

Decision table A table which lists the conditions which may be encountered within a problem and the actions to be taken for all possible combinations of the conditions.

Disk A magnetic storage device in which data is stored on concentric tracks on a rotating disk. Disks can now be divided into 'floppy' and 'rigid' varieties. The former are especially prevalent with small computers. Both provide Direct Access capabilities.

Disk pack A portable set of rigid magnetic disks that can be removed from the disk drive, allowing another set of disks to be placed on the drive and accessible by the computer.

Down time The time during which a computer is not available for use, which may be due to a breakdown, or for maintenance.

Executive program A permanent program in the computer to control the operation of the various peripherals in use (See operating system).

File A collection of related records in either serial, sequential or random order, held on a storage device.

File maintenance Updating of file records covering a specific period.

Flowchart A diagram showing the sequence of operations in a clerical or computer system. There are standard conventions adopted in drawing such diagrams.

Fortran FORmula TRANslation. A high level programming language for scientific applications, although at least one minicomputer has extended FORTRAN into a viable commercial language.

Hard copy Printed computer output, such as reports, listings and other documents.

Hardware Electronic and/or mechanical equipment which is attached to or fed by a computer. The term is often applied more generally to any equipment associated with the computer installation.

High level language A programming language which approximates to English or mathematical notation, e.g. BASIC, COBOL, FORTRAN.

Input A general term used to describe the process of feeding data into the computer.

Interface A boundary between two systems or devices (e.g. the central processor and a peripheral device). The term is also used in relation to boundaries between manual parts and computerised parts of a system).

K 1K = 1024 units of storage capacity

Key Characters used to identify a record. In any set of records the key characters will all be in the same position relative to the start of the record.

Key processing A mechanism whereby data instead of being punched into cards is transferred directly to a magnetic medium (usually disk - floppy or rigid, or tape, including cassettes).

Line printer An output device which prints one line at a time.

Liveware The people involved in running a computer systeme.g. programmers, analysts, operators, etc.

Low level language A computer language in which programs can be written but which is usually specific to a machine or family of machines. It is close to the machine code of the computer.

Magnetic tape (Mag-tape) Coated tape on which data is magnetically recorded.

Magnetic tape deck or Magnetic tape unit. A device which is used for reading from and writing on to, magnetic tape (also known as tape drive or tape transport).

Multi-programming The processing of two or more independent programs by one central processor, apparently simultaneously. Each program in the computer is given a priority, the computer processes the program with the highest priority most readily, and when this program goes into a wait condition, due to some slow input/output operation, the executive program utilises the wait time to process the program of the next high priority. Only one instruction can be processed at a time, therefore multi-programming is not, in fact executed simultaneously.

Off-line Devices or operations which although part of the data processing system are not directly controlled by the CPU.

On-line Peripheral equipment connected to, and operated by the CPU. The term is also used to refer to systems where the user is in interactive connection with the computer (See Real-time)

Operating system A manufacturer's program in the computer which allows the work of the computer to be organised and carried out with a minimal human interruption.

Output The information which is given out by a computer by means of an output device (e.g. lines printed on a printer, cards punched on a punch). Such information does not need to be human readable form and output can be to magnetic disk or tape.

Package A set of subroutines that may be incorporated into a program to perform certain processes, usually with the object of easing the task of writing the program - or a program designed to carry out some specific task - or a suite of programs to carry out all the processing for a given application.

Paging A method whereby a programmer may write programs which require more memory than available in the computer (see virtual memory). Program segments (pages) are stored on a very fast direct access device, each segment being called into core as it is required overlaying part of the program already there.

Paper tape Strips of paper tape, usually one and a half inches wide, in which data is recorded by a pattern of holes punched sequentially. This medium is common as an input medium to mainframe computers and is often a by-product from an accounting machine or transmission unit.

Parallel running A method of systems testing in which the suite of programs and associated manual procedures run concurrently with the existing method (usually manual) of performing the procedures. The two sets of results are compared to ascertain if the system is producing the correct results.

Peripheral equipment Devices which are connected to, and controlled by, the CPU.

Pilot running A method of systems testing in which the suite of programs and associated manual procedures are run for a section of the system only (e.g. one product group of the Stock File). The results are evaluated for accuracy/acceptability before a further section of the new system is taken on.

Printer A device which prints lines of information which a program requires to be printed. Depending upon the type of printer,it may produce the line,character by character or all characters effectively simultaneously.

Program A sequence of instructions written in an appropriate language that tell the computer what to do and how to do it.

Programmer A person who writes instructions in a programming language.

Punched card A card on which data is represented by a pattern of holes.

Real time A system in which data is processed virtually simultaneously with the activity generating the data.

Remote batch processing Entering batches of data from remote terminals into a time shared computer system.

Serial access A method of storing data on a magnetic medium whereby records are processed serially, the next record to be processed must be the one which follows that currently being processed.

Serial processing The processing of data in the order they occur.

Software Computer programs of all kinds such as operating systems, compilers, applications packages and applications programs.

Systems analysis The detailed investigation of an application area where problems of organisation or method are suspected (what is done at present, what is required to be produced by the system, what improvements can be introduced). Following analysis of the requirements a solution will be devised (with or without the use of a computer) and then implemented.

Terminal An input/output device, usually remote from the computer, but with facilities to provide the computer with information, interrogate files and activate processing within the computer. Terminals can include visual display units interrogating typewriters and other features such as their own data processing and storage facilities (See visual display unit).

Time sharing The simultaneous use of computers by two or more peripheral devices, such as providing computing services to numerous users through the use of remote on-line terminals.

Update To revise a master file with current data.

Verifier A device for checking the accuracy of data punched into cards or paper tape, whereby the same data is keyed by a second operator, the machine compares the two results; if an individual character does not agree, the verifier operator will be warned, the machine is locked and some exceptional action has to be taken by the operator to ensure the correct character is punched.

Vetting Checking the validity of input data. Usually applied by a program which determines whether the data conforms to certain criteria, and rejecting or making assumption about incorrectly prepared data. Also called validity checking.

Virtual memory A concept whereby the programmer can write programs which are larger than the main storage available in the computer with which he is working (see Paging)

Visual display unit (VDU) A terminal which incorporates a cathode ray screen similar to a television set. Data which is keyed into the terminal is displayed on the screen before transmission to the central processor, information being transmitted back from the computer for checking or further processing. Sophisticated versions are themselves mini computers and can be programmed to do much of the vetting before data is sent to the main computer.

Word The basic unit of information for certain types of computer, consisting of a fixed number of bits in which a fixed number of characters can exist. Small computers usually feature words of 8 or 16 bits although 32 bit words are being introduced on some machines.

Working store Part of the memory which is available for holding application programs and data.

3. General principles of a management information system

The term management information system has been defined, described and discussed from many viewpoints and the subject is still not free from controversy. The approach taken in this chapter is to positively link the MIS with computers with a view to total systems integration. Of course an MIS can exist without electronic data processing but the capacity of any manual system to store and process data in hard copy form has physical limitations. Whereas the capacity of computers enables vast amounts of data to be stored and processed at high speed.

To describe the principles of an MIS this section is divided into three parts. The first part examines some systems theory to answer the question - What is a system? (The systems approach to problem solving was explained in chapter 2, sub-section 2 2:3:5) The second part of this section then moves on to describe the principles of information systems paying special attention to defining an information system's boundaries, the data base and converting data into information. The data base aspect is particularly important and is frequently referred to throughout this chapter. Indeed, an MIS is frequently called a data base system. The third part builds upon the systems and information systems sub-sections to answer the question - What is a management information system? The MIS discussion has three elements; how the system can meet the needs of individual managers, how it meets the needs of the organisation and the characteristics of the system.

3:1 What is a system? A system may be defined as any group of interrelated components which work together to achieve an objective. Thus a system can be described by identifying its parts and the way they are related. For example, planets revolving around the sun are referred to as a solar system, the development of life on a planet is often called an 'eco' (ecological) system and the way man organises activity can be called an economic system. It therefore follows that the word 'system' can be applied to any set of elements that are interrelated in some way. Also, the word 'system' rarely stands alone, because it needs to be described. Some of the general descriptions relating to systems are summarised in the following sub-section

3:1:1 Classification of systems There are many types of systems that have very specific titles such as an invoicing system or production control system. Our concern here is with the division of systems based upon their *general* characteristics. These broad classifications are summarised below:-

Closed system	-	Where the components of the system are in no way dependent upon the environment or other systems (Refer to diagram 157)
Open system	-	Where there is a flow of energy or materials across the system's boundaries. This is the most common type of system and one of the difficulties is defining the boundaries. (Refer to diagram 158)
Natural systems	-	A system made by nature such as human beings

Manmade systems	-	There are numerous examples ranging from mechanical and electrical systems to economic and political systems
Simple systems	-	Where there are only a few components with a simple interrelationship
Complex systems	-	Where there are many components with complicated interrelationships
Tangible systems	-	These are physical systems that can be seen and touched such as a mechanical object
Intangible systems	-	These are conceptual systems that represent ideas or intangible relationships
Deterministic systems	-	A mechanistic type of system where it is possible to predict the output with certainty
Probabalistic systems	-	Where the output can be predicted on the basis of statistical probability
Cybernetic system	-	These are self organising systems that automatically adapt to a changing environment. Most natural systems are cybemetic

The important point to note about these broad classifications is that they describe the characteristics of a system. For example, a production system would be: *open, manmade, complex, tangible and probabalistic.* Having established some broad systems' classifications we can now move on to consider how a system works.

3:1:2 How a system works Every system has some form of input and output passing through a process. The form and variety of the inputs and outputs will naturally depend upon the kind of system. Generally, when describing a system only the'important' inputs and outputs need to be established as illustrated in diagram 156. In some information systems however, attempts are sometimes made to collect all the data. This point will be examined later in this chapter when we consider the cost/benefit of information.

DIAGRAM 156 IDENTIFYING IMPORTANT INPUTS & OUTPUTS

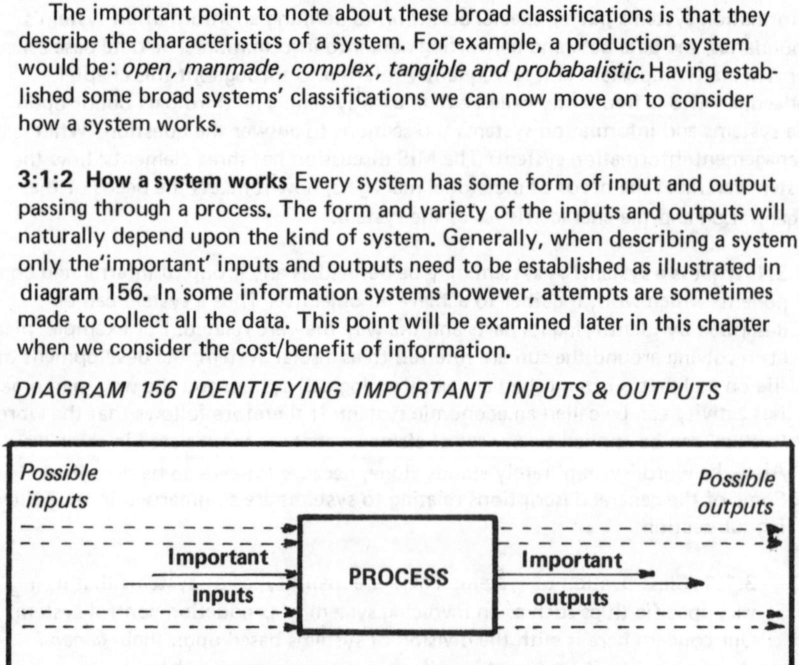

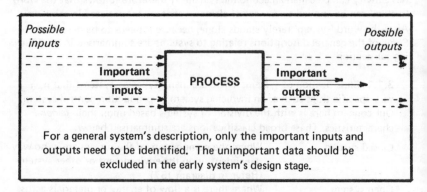

For a general system's description, only the important inputs and outputs need to be identified. The unimportant data should be excluded in the early system's design stage.

By measuring the inputs and outputs of a system the performance of the process can be assessed. But to do this, a feedback loop is needed. If the input and/or system's process are to be adjusted, then a control function is required. A system with a feedback loop and control is illustrated in diagram 157.

DIAGRAM 157 SYSTEM WITH FEEDBACK LOOP

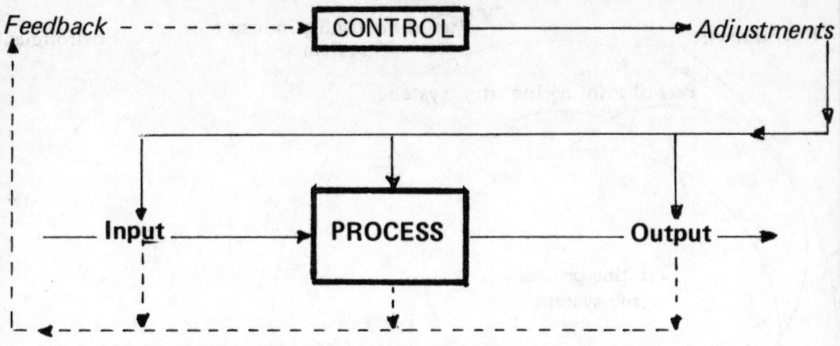

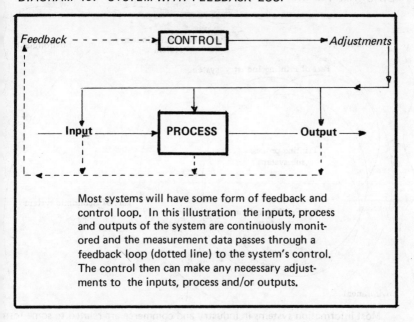

Most systems will have some form of feedback and control loop. In this illustration the inputs, process and outputs of the system are continuously monitored and the measurement data passes through a feedback loop (dotted line) to the system's control. The control then can make any necessary adjustments to the inputs, process and/or outputs.

So far we have established the main parts of a system being input, process, output, feedback and control. We now need to consider the interrelationship of one system with another and with the environment. As an example we will consider how a printing process sub system interrelates with other sub-systems and the environment. The principle is illustrated in diagram 158, that shows the printing process sub system interrelation with other sub systems in the publishing company. The publishing company is itself a sub system of other systems such as the publishing industry and economic system which are all part of the environment. Thus the inputs of one system are the outputs of other systems and this can make it very difficult to define the boundaries of any system. This point is particularly important for information systems. These are explained in the next sub-section.

3:2 What is an information system? An example of a good information system that all readers will be familiar with, is the newspaper. It is quite remarkable how the mass of data entering an editorial office is sifted, sorted., analysed, investigated, reported, edited and structured within such tight time constraints. Just imagine if all the data collected by the editorial staff was presented in data form with no headlines or editing. Few people would bother reading it. This is basically what an information system is all about - sorting data and presenting it as information. The nature of the sorting and presentation process will depend upon the purpose of the information system. The objectives of a newspaper are usually to inform, educate and entertain their readers. Although, some newspapers place a greater emphasis on entertainment than on information, they still serve a valid function, because they give their readers what they want. The newspaper criteria of providing the right kind of information at the right time and at the right price applies to any information system.

DIAGRAM 158 INTER–RELATIONSHIP OF SYSTEMS

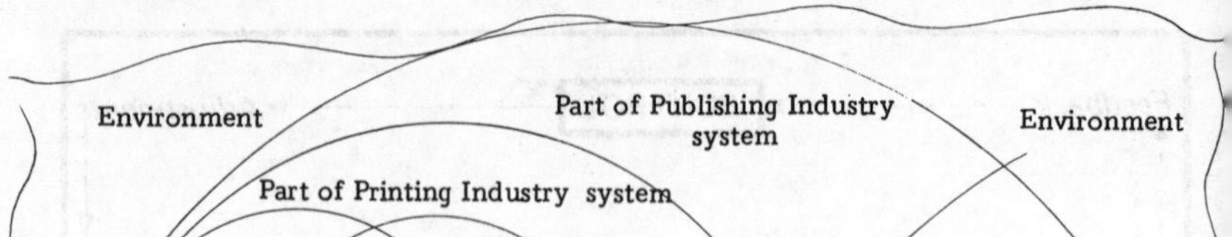

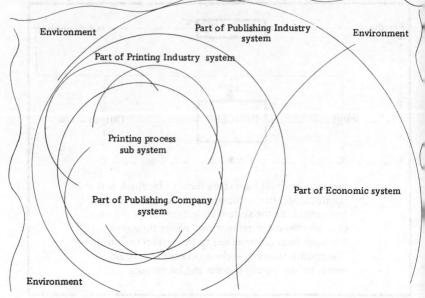

Most information systems in industry and commerce are related to some forn of control function as illustrated earlier in diagram 157. For instance, a quality trol systems needs two sets of data:

(a) The *desired* level of quality in terms of weight, size and/or performance, and

(b) The *actual* level of quality

The comparison of these two sets of data provides quality, control information. There are many examples of this kind of control information system. Indeed, th previous two chapters in this book explain the important management control information systems of standard costing and budgeting.

In addition to control information systems, businesses also have advisory information systems such as a house journal. briefing meetings and notice board: Thus information systems can range from a simple notice board to a complex standard costing and budgeting system. Whatever the size and complexity of the system there are still certain principles that need to be considered. In the follow- ing sub-sections we will be looking at; the boundaries of a system, collecting dat and constructing a data base, then converting the data into useful information.

3:2:1 Establishing a system's boundaries Earlier we distinguished between a closed and open system (sub-section 2:1:1) by stating that a closed system w in no way dependent upon the environment or other systems. Information sy tems tend to be open systems that are dependent upon several systems and th environment. Accordingly, some care is needed when defining the boundaries of an information system. Even when an information system's boundaries hav been defined, they still need to be constantly reviewed to keep up to date wit the changing nature of business activity and changes in data processing techno logy. The appropriate starting point for establishing the boundaries of an information system is to define the system's objectives. There will be the usual objectives of relevance, timeliness and easy to understand. But the objective we are going to focus our attention on here, is the level of systems integration.

All activities within a business are, in some way, interrelated. It can therefore, be argued that an information system should be integrated to allow for this interrelationship of business activity. Indeed, some definitions of a management information system imply a totally integrated system that draws data from all activities within a business and related data from the business environment. The degree of integration will be somewhere along the following scale:-

Single information system relating to a limited area of user requirements	————————	Fully integrated information system capable of satisfying a wide range of users' needs

With the development of relatively low cost electronic data processing and the tendency towards larger business units, attempts have been made to achieve economies of scale with information systems. Although the hardware is often capable of handling the data load, the software can be so complex that system interface problems become insurmountable. Even the most skilled systems analysts may be incapable of producing integrated software within a reasonable time period. Thus the attention of a fully integrated information system with wide boundaries needs to be assessed on a cost/benefit basis. Diagram 159 illustrates the principle of a cost/benefit assessment for an information system. The marginal cost of information is assumed to be lowest for the simple single information system and rises fairly steadily until the system becomes complex when marginal costs rise steeply. The marginal benefit of information is assumed to be very high initially and then fall steeply. The cost/benefit intersection is meant to represent a practical level of integration that will help define the information system's boundaries. The point to grasp, is that the criteria for determining an information system's boundaries are its costs and benefits in relation to the system's objectives.

DIAGRAM 159

COST/BENEFIT OF INFORMATION

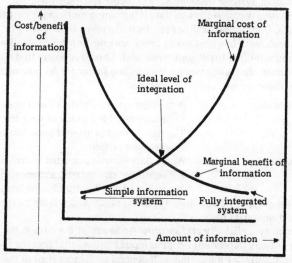

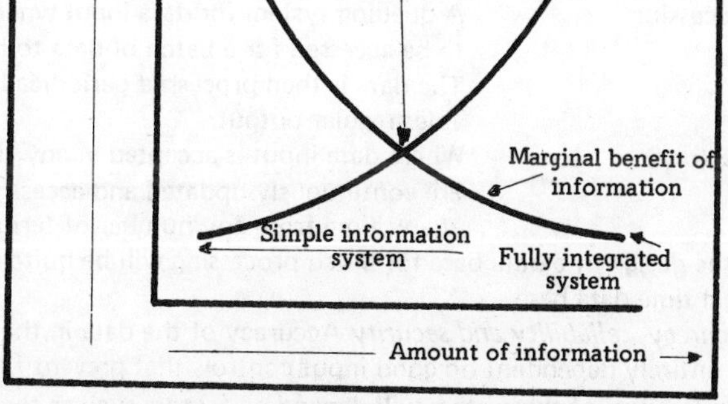

3:2:2 The data base Once an information system's boundaries have been defined the data base may be planned. Traditional data bases operated by individual departments, tended to be simple alpha/numeric systems stored in filing cabinets. But these information system data bases had restricted boundaries and provided few facilities for data analysis. With the trend towards the electronic office and reduction of hard copy storage, the information system data base needs far more careful planning. Ideally each information data base should be part of an overall systems strategy. The strategy would include an objective of providing information for decision making and control. Thus where possible, cost/benefit terms, information data bases should be capable of integration. Even a simple information system data base can be planned to allow for subsequent integration into a larger system. The data base plan needs to take into consideration the following factors:-

(i) User requirements Probably not all the user requirements will be satisfied within the system's cost constraints. However a full listing of user information requirements is still needed. Once the listing is complete and then rationalised, the data base content can be determined.

(ii) Data content There are several points to be considered under this heading. What to include, exclude? The level of data aggregation. To use existing files or start afresh. File loading time scale, including parralel running. Preventing corrupt data entering the files and any interface problems where linked access to other data bases is required. An estimate has to be made of the maximum data content to ensure that the proposed data base has sufficient storage capacity.

(iii) File design So far we have considered: what is required of the data base and what is to be stored. Now it is necessary to consider how the data is to be stored? Ideally the data should be stored in common files that are independent of any application program. The coding and structure of the common files should enable multiple use to be made of the data by a variety of application programs. Where possible, the coding and structure of the files should be capable of integration with other information data bases. When a data base is structured for a single application program then it lacks flexibility and integration with other systems becomes very difficult and expensive.

(iv) Data base access Access to data is becoming more important than computing data. Computing facilities can be undertaken by any mini or micro computer. Indeed, with low cost micro processors many terminals will have computing capability (i.e. Intelligent terminals). Thus it is access to data, not processing of data, that will often be the limiting factor for an information system. Basically, there are two types of operation:-

Batch processing	-	A queuing system for data input where a file has to be accessed for a batch of data to be loaded. The data is then processed periodically and provides regular output.
Real time (or on line)	-	Where data input is accepted at any time, files are continuously updated and access is available at any time from any number of terminals.

Clearly, the design of a data base for batch processing will be quite different from a real time data base.

(v) Accuracy, reliability and security Accuracy of the data in the data base is almost entirely dependent on good input controls that prevent file corruption. The reliability of the system will depend on factors such as the programm-

ing, staff training and maintenance of hardware and software. Safety factors such as father and grandfather files would be part of the system so that any 'lost' file could be recreated. Security aspects for a data base would be to identify confidential files and have restricted access to them via special coding or some form of identity device at the terminal.

From the foregoing review of factors to consider when planning an information system data base, it should be evident that this can be a very detailed and complex task. Later in this chapter we will be reviewing some of the practical complications for establishing a *Common Data Base.*

3:2:3 Converting data into information A distinction that is often drawn between data and information is that data is processed to produce information. This is illustrated in diagram 160, which shows data being collected, analysed and transmitted as information. The conversion of data into information is a

DIAGRAM 160

CONVERTING DATA INTO INFORMATION

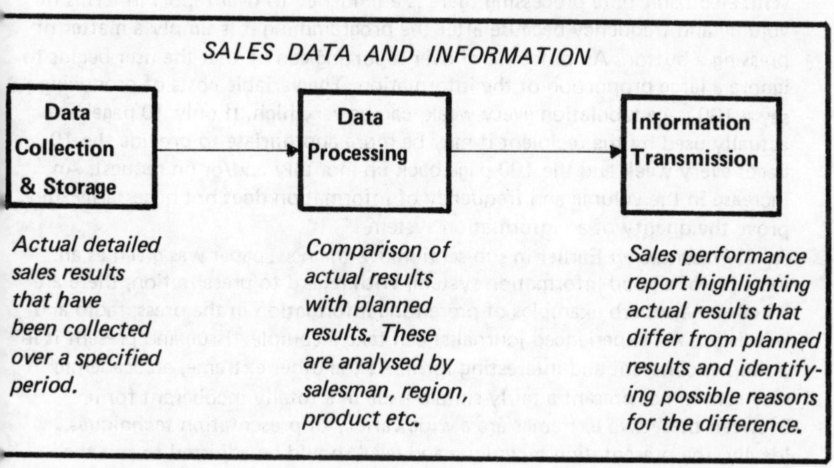
SALES DATA AND INFORMATION
Data Collection & Storage
Data Processing
Information Transmission
Actual detailed sales results that have been collected over a specified period.
Comparison of actual results with planned results. These are analysed by salesman, region, product etc.
Sales performance report highlighting actual results that differ from planned results and identifying possible reasons for the difference.

characteristic of all information systems. But this conversion process can create a number of problems. Some of these problems are summarised below:-

(i) *Volume* Data is often identified by its volume and lack of structure and analysis. To reduce the volume of data into meaningful information requires aggregation and selection. The conversion process that reduces the data volume, can produce misleading results. On the other hand, if the data volume is not substantially reduced and a decision maker is simply handed an enormous computer print out, then essential information will be concealed in a mass of data. A single page of good information is generally worth far more than 100 pages of data. For routine reporting the volume decision requires a careful analysis of the system user's needs and the application of established analytical techniques for the reduction of data volume.

(ii) *Importance* When analysing the information needs of the system's users,

some form of ranking is needed to distinguish the relative importance of different aspects of information. For example, if the information system was to meet the needs of say a credit controller, then key information would include a debtors age analysis, large debtors requiring close attention and details of debtors that have recently placed substantial orders so as to determine their credit worthiness.

(iii) *Accuracy* It is important to determine the level of accuracy required from an information system. Generally speaking, the higher the level of management, the lower the need for precise information. At the supervisory management level, say in production, accuracy is essential in matters such as production quantities, stock levels and product inspection. But at the strategic management level, the information is mainly to provide indications of trends and does not have to be so precise. However, with electronic data processing a high level of accuracy is possible providing there are sufficient input controls and the application programs are correct.

(iv) *Frequency* Decisions need to be made regarding the frequency of reporting from an information system. The options are: routine reporting on a daily weekly, monthly, etc. basis, reporting on request or a combination of both. With electronic data processing there is a tendency to over report in terms of volume and frequency because after the programming it is simply a matter of pressing a button. An outcome of over reporting can be that the user begins to ignore a large proportion of the information. The variable costs of producing say a 100 page tabulation every week, can be very high. If only 10 pages are actually used by the recipient it may be more appropriate to provide the 10 pages every week and the 100 page back up monthly and/or on request. An increase in the volume and frequency of information does not necessarily improve the quality of an information system

(v) *Presentation* Earlier in sub-section 3:2 the newspaper was given as an example of a good information system. With regard to presentation, there are often some superb examples of presenting information in the press, radio and television. An experienced journalist can take a complex issue and present it in a simple, coherent and interesting form. At the other extreme, an academic may sometimes present a fairly simple issue in a totally incoherent form. Between these two extremes are a wide variety of presentation techniques. Ideally, the presentation technique and level should be adjusted to suit the ability of the recipient. For example, an information system processing accounting data would have different types of presentation for accountants and non-accountants.

We have briefly considered a number of problems that can arise when an information system converts data into information. From the author's experience with computer based information systems there is a tendency to produce too much information too frequently. In one instance, this was evidenced by computer print outs being stacked in corridors because there was insufficient room left in the offices. What was actually happening was the print outs were providing data and reports were then constructed manually to provide information. The conversion of data into information by administrative staff then produced a whole new set of problems, such as lack of understanding of complex print outs, work overload, human error and personal bias. When all these factors were combined the final output of the computer/manual information system was not very reliable.

3:3 What is a management information system? The preceeding sub-sections have provided the foundations for an understanding of management information systems. The sub-section on systems theory explained how a system has an input, process and output with feedback and controls. The systems principle were then developed in the sub-sections on information systems that covered issues such as establishing a system's boundaries, the size of data base, level and costs of systems integration and the problems of converting data into information. With this general background we can now move to the more specific area of management information systems.

The appropriate starting point is to establish some MIS objectives. As a general objective we can say that the purpose of an MIS is to provide relevant, reliable an and timely information, within cost constraints, that will help managers plan and control business activity for the optimal use of scarce resources. Under this general objective a hierarchy of specific objectives could be constructed such as:

An MIS should be capable of meeting the needs of individual users.
An MIS should fit into the organisation structure and become part of the organisation
An MIS should have the level of systems integration that is appropriate for the organisation and individual users

In the above objectives we have established three MIS aspects relating to the individual, the organisation and the characteristics of the system. These three aspects are discussed in the following sub-sections.

3:3:1 Meeting the needs of individual managers There are two main areas for consideration regarding information for individual managers, functional information requirements and the characteristics of the individual. With manual information systems these two areas tend to merge. Thus when a manager is replaced, the new manager often changes the system to suit his/her personal requirements. Such changes are generally called 'improvements' but as the functional information requirements are still the same, most of the changes are probably just to suit individual preference. With a computerised MIS however, a manager does not have this opportunity to tailor the system for his/her personal needs. Minor programming changes may eventually be made, but the manager loses that personal control over information. Therefore an inbalance can arise between information wanted and information provided. There are two possible outcomes from this inbalance

(a) The manager accepts the system and uses it as an excuse for sub-optimal performance or,
(b) The manager sets up a separate departmental information system that is under his/her personal control.

Both outcomes are unsatisfactory. With the former the system is not providing the right kind of motivation and with the latter; ad hoc information system tems make systems integration increasingly difficult and are probably a waste of corporate resources. From the author's experience there seems to be a tendency for managers to set up their own information systems. In some instances the output of these personal systems was then used as an organisational climbing device, because *information is power.* This aspect of information will be discussed in the next sub-section on the MIS meeting the needs of the organisation.

Meeting individual functional information requirements is really just a shopping list of information content and frequency that is needed to do a particular job. But meeting the needs of individuals is quite a different matter. Here we are entering the field of psychology in areas such as perception, attitudes and motivation. Two managers with identical functional responsibilities and authority could easily attach totally different values to the same information. The problem of satisfying the information requirements of all individual managers in an organisation can be partially resolved by:-

(a) MIS discussion groups where managers meet to discuss their information needs.
(b) The MIS could provide a choice of information models instead of a routine pre-structered report on a take it or leave it basis
(c) If possible within cost constraints the MIS would have direct access to the data base with data storage (limited) and processing capability at the terminal. This would enable a manager to call up data, then store and process to meet his/her personal requirements.
(d) Management training to ensure managers know how to make the best use of their MIS

Probably an on line system with terminal storage and processing facilities would be too expensive for many organisations. However, batch systems with routine reporting can become more user friendly if systems analysts are guided by MIS discussion groups and managers are given the opportunity to learn about information systems and their applications.

3:3:2 Meeting the needs of the organisation Organisations vary in size, nature and management styles. It therefore follows that an MIS needs to be tailored to meet the existing and future needs of an organisation. This can be a very expensive exercise and great care is needed at the planning stage to ensure that MIS objectives are not set too high. For example, the attractions of a totally integrated common data base are far beyond the hardware, software or brainware' capabilities of most organisations. Even with the falling costs of hardware, multiple online access to a large common data base may still not be feasible on a cost benefit basis (Refer to diagram 159 in sub section 3:2:1). Thus the first point to consider regarding the MIS needs of an organisation, is the relevant level of investment. The appropriate investment level is usually established through a feasibility study as explained in chapter 7 sub-section 4:1.

Manual information systems for managers have traditionally been organised on a departmental basis where the manager had personal control over input, storage, processing and output. The linking of these information systems was achieved through informal grouping which established organisational power relationships and formally through internal memoranda and management meetings. But with the enormous data storage and processing capability of computers, the potential for integrating these separate systems increased. The concept of single recording in common files for multiple access held the promise of tremendous cost savings that would greatly reduce the need for administrative staff and hard copy filing space. Thus the application of the common data base concept could fundamentally change the nature of an organisation. Let us briefly consider how fundamental this change could be.

An integrated MIS allows, in principle, decision making to be more centralised and enables routine decision making such as ordering and production scheduling to be programmed. As a result the organisation could operate with a reduction in the number of management levels. Moreover, systems integration reduces the need for information exchange between departments through internal memoranda and meetings. Whilst the common data base substantially reduces the need for departmental filing systems. Therefore great savings would be possible due to reduced administrative staff and office space requirements. Alongside these purported benefits are some disadvantages such as the flow of information tends to become more rigid and incapable of quickly adjusting to changing circumstances. Thus the organisation may be required to adapt to the MIS instead of the other way round. The centralisation of data and alteration of information flows may erode the power and prestige of some individual managers. Conversely the power and prestige of the new departments directly related to the MIS will increase.

It is therefore evident that an integrated MIS can change an organisation. This is not necessarily an undesirable outcome, providing the MIS is improving the organisation's ability to meet its objectives. Earlier however, we established that total systems integration would rarely be cost justified. Thus we need to consider how different levels of systems integration will meet the needs of the organisation. There are basically three ways a computerised MIS can be introduced into an organisation :-

(a) Through packaged software for specific management information needs.
(b) Computerizing existing procedures.
(c) An attempt to develop an integrated MIS with relevant adjustments to the organisation.

Cost constraints and managerial attitudes usually cause MIS development to begin in categories (a) and/or (b) so that it does not require substantial changes to the organisation. This piecemeal approach can be a starting point for an integrated system providing there is a total systems strategy that ensures the separate systems developments are all compatible. Then gradually the systems can be integrated and the organisation altered to suit the new working methods.

3:3:3 MIS characteristics The characteristics of an MIS are determined by the nature of the organisation and the information needs of its managers. The list of characteristics does not necessarily have to include computers. For instance double entry book keeping information systems have been providing management information long before the computer was invented. However, as electronic data processing will eventually be the method used for most information systems, we will assume that a computer is to be used for storing and processing MIS data.

The structure of any MIS is a combination of many variables that are brought together in a balanced mixture. Attempts to identify just a few critical variables will tend to produce misleading results because most of the variables are capable of causing an MIS to fail. In the preceeding sub-sections we have identified variables such as: the level of systems integration, system boundaries and interface with other systems, individual user needs, organisational needs, cost/benefit of information, training of users, user involvement in the system's development, security, frequency, recency and accuracy of information, the data base design, mode of system (batch or on line) input, processing. output and converting data into information. In this sub-section we will just consider some variables that would contribute towards an *ideal* MIS.

(i) Mode of operation This would be an on-line real-time system with multiple access through user terminals that would have storage and processing capability.

(ii) *Data base* This would be a common data base where data was only handled once so that good input controls could be established. The data base would be constructed with common files that are independent of any application program and capable of interrogation by a user.

(iii) *Security* Access to restricted files in the data base would be controlled by terminal personal identity devices and coding.

(iv) *Regular reports* The system would produce regular reports to meet user needs and be sufficiently flexible to quickly alter the output to meet changing circumstances.

(v) *Integration* The MIS should aim to integrate all systems and external data with a view to developing financial, production, inventory and marketing models to aid the managerial planning function by answering the 'what if' type of questions.

(vi) *Cybemetic control* The MIS would be able to provide some elementary cybemetic controls (Refer to chapter 2 sub-section 5:1:1) in areas such as inventory management and production scheduling.

By the year 2000 many businesses will have integrated management information systems that can draw data from a wide variety of sources. Indeed with the convergence of developments in telecommunications, robotics and computer hardware and software, automation with cybemetic control systems will become commonplace. The MIS will be the central system in this kind of development and will become increasingly important with each technological stride. Almost all the management and accounting techniques explained in this book will probably be available in packaged MIS software.

4. Practical aspects of management information systems
So far in this chapter we have looked at the dymanic world of computing and considered the principles and problems of management information systems. We can now move on to some practical aspects of this subject and the importance of appropriate software. The practical considerations relating to hardware are mainly capacity problems and have been discussed in section 2. On the software side an MIS can be viewed under three broad categories. Software for planning, control and communication. Under the planning category the most powerful decicision making aid is the simulation model and these are reviewed in sub sections 4:1:1 to 4:1:4. The control category is covered in sub sections 4:2:1 to 4:2:5. And the communication category in sub section 4:3. The remainder of this section considers three other practical issues: the common data base, MIS security and communication networks. There are of course many other practical considerations, but a full discussion would be outside the scope of this chapter.

4:1 Simulation models The principles of model building are explained in chapter 2 sub-section 2:3:4. Basically, a decision model establishes the relationship between variables. For example total revenue is a function of unit sales and unit price. If these variables are altered, then total revenue is altered. Most decision models have a far more complex set of variables and relationships. But once all the main variables have been defined and their relationships established then simulation exercises can be undertaken to answer the: what if ......? type of questio. The computer is an ideal machine for model building because decision problems such as - what if I increase the price of unit X by 10%? - can be run as a simulation exercise. There are of course many practical complications, but for plannin decision making, a simulation model is a very powerful management tool. In the following sub-sections we will be reviewing some important areas for simulation models.

4:1:1 Price/output decisions The principles, problems and techniques relating to price/output decisions are explained in chapter 6. A simple decision model could be programmed based on break even analysis. The only variables in such a simple model would be price, quantity, variable cost and fixed cost. However you will recall from chapter 6 that the break even model is a fairly crude decision technique that is well suited for 'back of an envelope' calculations. The model makes no allowance for risk, limiting factors and where different products are produced, it will not give an optimal mix. There exist a number of software packages that claim to be decision models when all they actually do is some fairly simple break even calculations. This kind of oversold software can produce misleading results. (Refer to chapter 6 sub-section 2:9). Accordingly, if an MIS is to have a price/output decision model it should have facilities for risk adjustments and optimal product mix decisions using established techniques such as linear programming. (Refer to chapter 6 sub-section 2:7).

In the early stages of the system's development the relevant data would probably have to be entered by the user. But the objective would be for the system to be able to draw the necessary data direct from s common data base. Ideally, all the user would have to do is call up the program, follow the instructions and input the relevant data.

4:1:2 Investment decisions The techniques for investment appraisal are explained in chapter 7. After reading chapter 7 you will be aware that a good simulation model would need to take into consideration the following factors'-

(a) Cash flow estimates. (Ch. 7 sub-section 2:3)
(b) The time value of money, (Ch. 7 sections 5, 7 and 8)
(c) Allowances for risk (Ch. 7 sub-section, sub sections 9:1 and 9:2)
(d) Allowances for sensitivity (Ch. 7 sub-section, sub section 9:3)
(e) Allowances for tax and investment incentives (Ch. 7 section 10)
(f) Allowance for capital rationing (Ch. 7 sub-section 11:2)

There exist a number of software packages that claim to 'solve the problems of investment appraisal'. On close examination one finds that all the package really does is apply simple discounting formulae to the input (cash flow) and produce a range of NPV's and an IRR. This kind of software is not really very useful. Discounting calculations as described in chapter 7 are more suitable for programable calculators. If investment appraisal software is to be purchased it must do far more than a few simple DCF calculations.

A good software package for investment appraisal would enable cash flows to be adjusted for risk, uncertainty and sensitivity. The program should also be capable of answering what if questions such as:-

What if the cost of material X increases by 20%?
What if exchange rates alter by......?
What if the cost of finance increases by 5%?
What are the levels of sales per annum where cash flows break even?

In addition to answering these types of questions the output would also give before tax and after tax results. Moreover, the system should be capable of handling the common problem of multi-period capital rationing and simply provide the decision maker with project rankings for given sets of circumstances and assumptions. To make all these calculations the computer would ask the user for specific information and provide guidance in the interpretation of the results.

4:1:3 Inventory decisions The administration, valuation, planning and control of inventories is explained in chapter 5. Most of the problems relating to inventories end up in the two basic decisions of: how much to order and when to order. With the how much to order question: calculations are required on the costs of carrying stock and the penalty costs of not carrying enough stock. The outcome of these calculations produce an economic order quantity (EOQ) for each stock item. The related question of when to order requires calculations that will produce re-order stock levels and safety stock levels. All these calculations were explained in chapter 5 section 6.

Stock control simulation models have been developed by mathematicians for a wide range of applications. These simulation models are particularly important for large retail organisations where the costs of carrying stock are a substantial part of the company's total cost. Thus, some stock control software packages have been developed to a high level of sophistication. Demand estimates based on probability calculations are related to stock data such as existing stock levels, outstanding orders, average delivery times, unit costs and quantity discounts to determine re-order levels, safety stocks and EOQ's. Ideally, these simulation programs would draw data direct from a common data base and at the 'press of a button' automatically produce the necessary inventory purchase orders. Some truly remarkable inventory control systems have been developed by major retailing chains. Some systems can now record at each part of sale, through magnetic ink character recognition, the sale of each individual stock item. These advanced cash registers are on-line to a data base that will provide management with instant stock level information. Then through inventory simulation models, the expected sales of each item can be estimated and EOQ's etc. adjusted accordingly.

In previous sub sections so called decision making software has been criticised as often being inadequate and misleading. But in the area of inventory control, it seems as though a lot of effort has been directed into producing some very useful software packages.

4:1:4 Financial decisions Most business decisions can be described as financial decisions because money is involved. Therefore simulation models with business applications are often referred to as financial models. For our purposes we will be using a fairly narrow definition. A financial model is one that produces a profit (or loss) figure and return on capital figure from a given set of data. Most of the data would be from the financial accounting double entry data base. Such a data base should be capable of producing a 'press button' balance sheet and income statement. *(Refer to Volume 1 Financial accounting for non-accountants).*

With this data processing facility for instant final accounts, a simulation model would enable the decision maker to determine what would happen to profit and ROCE if specified events occurred. For example, if a 10% fall in demand was expected accompanied by a rise in interest rates and an increase in the value of the pound, the simulation model would show what effect these events would have on profit and ROCE over a given period.

There is certainly a lot of work being done by accountants and systems analysts on financial modelling. As a result, a number of software packages are being sold. Unfortunately some extravagant claims are being made about the capability of these packages. For a financial simulation model to be useful, it would have to include a wide range of variables that can significantly affect profit. As many of these variables are interdependent and their relationships not easily defined, the prediction of profit or loss becomes a very complex matter. Accordingly, some caution is needed when dealing with a model that purports to predict profit from an input of just a few variables.

4:2 Control information The principles of control were explained in chapter 2 section 5 and various control techniques have been explained throughout this book. Control information systems of some kind would almost certainly exist in all organisations. The control information could be just a simple production estimate/target that is compared with actual production. Or, a full standard costing budgetary control system. Each manager may have his/her own system of control that requires specific data collection and analysis. It is therefore clear that a vital function of any management information system is to provide managers with relevant and timely information for control.

The following sub-sections review areas where separate control information systems can exist. Ideally these separate systems should be integrated into a management information system. Therefore, when separate systems are being designed /updated, constant attention needs to be given to the objective of subsequent integration with other systems.

4:2:1 Financial controls The financial accounts record revenues and costs to determine profit or loss and the value of assets and liabilities. (The principles and practice of financial accounting are fully explained in *Volume 1 Financial accounting for the non-accountant).* Earlier in sub-section 4:1:4 it was explained how an MIS can contain a simulation model that produces forecasts of profit or loss and return on capital employed. The control function of a financial accounting system can produce information for areas such as credit control, cash control, wages control and capital expenditure control.

Software packages are readily available for many aspects of financial control such as credit control and payroll. However, these separate systems are often self contained with their own input, storage, process and output, and are not easily integrated into an MIS. Indeed, it is not uncommon for financial accountants to have their own hardware and software completely independent of other data processing systems. If this situation is allowed to develop then a fully integrated MIS becomes impossible. Ideally, the financial accounting records should be part of a common data base and any software development for financial control would have a common data base interface.

4:2:2 Cost controls Basic costing principles and techniques are explained in chapter 3 and the major cost control techniques of budgeting and standard costing are fully explained in chapters 8 and 9. Most of the control techniques explained in this book can be part of an MIS. For instance, let us briefly consider the most commonly used planning and control technique - budgeting. After reading chapter 8 you will appreciate that a budgeting system contains two main categories of data: *planned* revenues and costs and *actual* revenues and costs. Generally, control cannot exist without planning, because there must be some yardstick against which actual results are compared. Thus the starting point for a cost control system is to input planned results. Ideally these planned results would be derived by using MIS simulation models that were explained earlier. Using simulation models drawing upon a common data base a plan could be constantly updated to meet changing circumstances and cost control yardsticks improved. With regard to actual costs and revenues; an ideal situat-ion would then be when a common data base was constantly updated by on line activity terminals where costs and revenues were recorded as they occurred. The cost control system would then draw actual cost data from the common data base.

4:2:3 Labour controls A large proportion of management time is devoted to controlling labour. This difficult task has been discussed in chapters 2 and 4 and section 4 in chapter 8. Labour data is rarely centralised. Personnel departments keep extensive employee personal details, the accounts department keeps pay-roll details and many departments maintain some form of personal performance assessment for each employee. Clearly an MIS has an important role to play in integrating these different data systems into a common data base. An integrated labour information system would assist in labour control at two levels. At the labour planning level (Refer to chapter 4 section 4) management would be pro-vided with aggregate information to help with forecasting labour requirements and producing a labour plan. At the individual level on matters such as perform-ance, salary and promotion the system could display all the relevant data at the touch of a button. Naturally this part of an MIS would require strict access and update safeguards and all employees should have the right to inspect their own personal file.

4:2:4 Inventory controls The administration and control of inventories is fully explained in chapter 5. Earlier in this chapter, sub section 4:1:3, we briefly considered inventory simulation models for determining how much to order and when to order. It was noted that some simulation models can become part of an integrated inventory control system. In such a control system an MIS can become partly cybernetic. It is important to note the difference between a cybernetic system and an information system. An information system such as an MIS, provides information to help managers make decisions. Whereas a cybe-netic system is designed to take decisions without reference to a manager. Stock control is just one of the many areas of routine decision making where an MIS can become partly cybernetic and thus reduce the demands made on middle and lower level managers. Some of the very advanced inventory control systems run by large retail chains have gone even further and linked a partly cybernetic system to automated storage. The vital input for these advanced systems is through MICR (magnetic ink characters recognition) on product packaging. Thus control of different types of stock can be exercised from the warehouse right through to the point of sale terminal in the retail outlet. In time, this kind of advanced inventory control software should become avail-able at a 'packaged price' suitable for a wide range of applications. However, the cost of integrating this kind of advanced software package into existing systems would probably prevent an MICR cybernetic inventory system be-coming an integral part of an MIS.

4:2:5 Production controls The traditional tasks of production line manage-ment were mainly related to controlling people and machines in an attempt to achieve target output quantities and quality. For this task, many separate in-formation systems would exist often containing a vast amount of detail. To just control the production of even a simple component through several pro-duction processes could require a large amount of line management time.

This was because so much of the integration of control information was undertaken by individual managers. Although there are probably many line managers capable of controlling production processes in this way it does represent an inherent organisational weakness. An MIS can reduce this kind of organisational dependence on individual managers by integrating the separate production information systems. Moreover, an integrated system could become partly cybemetric, thus relieving line managers from routine decisions that are based on arithmetic rather than knowledge and experience. With semi automated and fully automated production processes many routine controls have already become a programming function. Just as automation can replace craft skills so a cybemetric MIS can replace a large part of the middle management function.

4:3 Communication So far we have considered some planning and control uses of an MIS. Although improved planning and control is the main justification for developing management information systems, it is still appropriate to review MIS communication applications. A suitable starting point is to identify possible company information flows. Diagram 161 identifies six possible information flows that need to be co-ordinated in a disclosure policy (Refer to *Volume 1 Financial Accounting for non accountants).*

DIAGRAM 161

POSSIBLE COMPANY COMMUNICATION CHANNELS

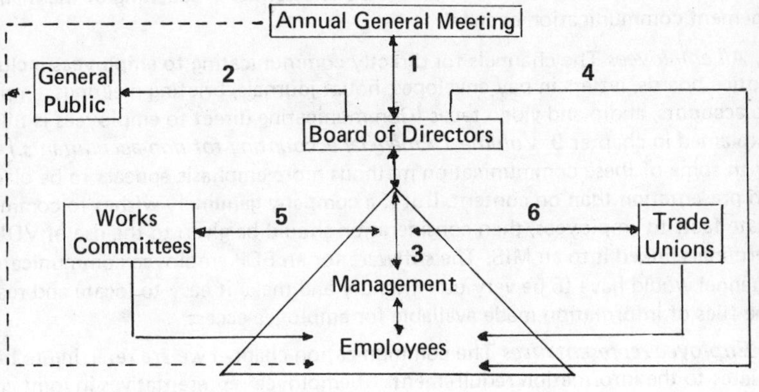

Communication channels:-

1. To shareholders in accordance with company law requirements.
2. To the general public.
3. To management for planning and control.
4. To all employees.
5. To employee representatives for joint consultation.
6. To trade unions for collective bargaining.

The existence of an integrated MIS could affect some areas of a disclosure policy. It is therefore worthwhile briefly considering the effect that an MIS could have on the different formal communication channels shown in diagram 161

1. Shareholders It is unlikely that the existence of an advanced MIS would alter the well established communication method of the printed annual report and accounts. However, there is no reason why a majority shareholder should not demand access to an MIS.

2. General public Under this heading, interest groups such as creditors, customers potential investors and 'local communities' are included. With the exception of powerful creditors such as large financial institutions, the existing communication channels will probably be affected by an MIS. It is unlikely that a journalist would be allowed access to an MIS terminal. Thus the established methods of carefully worded press releases and out of date historical cost accounts will continue to be the main information link between a business and the general public.

3. Management This is the communication channel that will be the most affected by an MIS. In earlier sub sections we have discussed how an MIS can improve planning and control. But in addition to specific control information about the company a lot of general information flows through informal communication channels. Although informal communication networks are important there is a tendency for information to become distorted and sometimes misleading. Accordingly, an MIS has an important support communication role to play where managers can access the data base to determine the facts that relate to rumours. There are of course, a few truly confidential file classifications in a common data base, such as personnel files, that require restricted access. But if managers are given a wide data base access,then this represents a substantial broadening of the management communication channel.

4. All employees The channels for directly communicating to employees include: notice boards, letters in pay envelopes, house journals, briefing meetings, employee accounts, audio and video tapes (Communicating direct to employees is fully explained in chapter 9 *Volume 1 Financial accounting for non-accountants.)* With some of these communication methods more emphasis appears to be placed on presentation than on content. But if a company genuinely wishes to communicate facts to employees, then consideration should be given to the use of VDU terminals linked into an MIS. The software for an EDP employee communication channel would have to be very user friendly and make it easy to locate and read the files of information made available for employee access.

5. Employee representatives The communication channel we are referring to here relates to the information requirements of employee representatives in joint consultative committees. (Refer to chapter 2 sub-section 4:2:1 and chapter 4 subsection 4:1:3) If the consultative process in a company was genuine and not just a rubber stamping procedure, then employee representatives should have access to the MIS so that all the committee are using the same information. However, giving rights for MIS access would probably represent a substantial change in a disclosure policy. This is because information has traditionally been under the complete control of management. In the consultative process,management generally retain control over information and the right of decision. Thus to hand over access to an MIS would constitute a move towards participation. Indeed, an open MIS is an ideal information system for participation(Refer to chapter 2, sub sections 4:2:3 and 4:2:4)

6. Trade unions Aspects of trade unions and staff associations have been discussed in chapter 2 sub-section 4:2:2 and chapter 4 sub-sections 4:1:1 and 4:3. The communication channel to trade unions for collective bargaining is normally a negotiated issue. Recognised trade unions have a legal right to demand information for collective bargaining (Refer to chapter 4 sub-section 4:3:1). These demands have generally been related to specific areas such as investment plans and salary details. However, if a company was operating a fully integrated MIS, a trade union claim could be made for full access to the data base. If such a claim was upheld by the CAC, then it would cause many companies to reconsider their MIS integration policy.

4:4 Common data base A common data base is a file of records which is not designed to meet a specific application but is used as a data source for a variety of recording, analysis and reporting functions. Throughout this chapter we have frequently referred to the importance of systems compatability with a view to integrating all files into a common data base. From a practical viewpoint, file control software can be extremely expensive and at present is only cost justified when large amounts of data are constantly accessed by many different people. For example, an airline ticket booking system handles a vast amount of rapidly changing data that needs to be accessed by many ticket selling agencies. The software for an on line data base in this instance is cost justified, because there are fewer double bookings and better utilisation of the aircraft. The same principles of large amounts of data requiring multiple access also apply to certain files in most organisations. Stock detail for example often needs to be known by numerous departments such as purchasing, goods in, accounts, sales, administration and production. Many of these departments will be holding aspects of stock detail in their own filing systems and a large amount of duplicated effort occurs in maintaining separate filing systems. Under these circumstances, an on-line data base stock file could probably be cost justified.

Earlier in sub-section 2:2 it was explained how recent developments in hardware, made on line systems well within the financial reach of small users. However common data base software is expensive and can be very complex. Moreover, if some files are to be centralised into a common data base, then there must be very tight controls on the system Any system design changes need to be carefully planned and tested before use and good input controls are needed to avoid file corruption. Thus the costs of buying and maintaining common data base software will be a practical limitation on the development of integrated management information systems. Small and medium size computer users tend to opt for single application software packages such as payroll, bought ledger, sales ledger, inventory control and fairly simple decision making packages that provide DCF and break even types of calculations. Once a business is committed to separate application packages the cost benefits of a change to an integrated MIS using a large common data base will almost certainly be negative.

4:5 MIS security The trend of replacing hard copy records with electronic digital storage is taking place in many organisations. With large organisations vast amounts of data are stored on magnetic disks, drums and tapes. The centralisation of data storage that is generally associated with an MIS means that security precautions are needed against the following types of risk:-

(a) Accidental damage through loss of power supply, fire or natural disaster
(b) Deliberate damage by individuals or groups

(c) Unauthorised access to confidential files
(d) Corruption of files
(e) Fraud
(f) Shutdown during an industrial dispute by trade union action

These kinds of risks also exist with hard copy records, but with electronic systems the damage can be far greater. It is therefore necessary to consider what security would be needed for an MIS.

(a) Accidental damage through loss of power is usually safeguarded by having back up generators and special fire precautions. Also, data and programs on backing storage are duplicated or even triplicated and copies held in separate locations.

(b) Deliberate damage is generally safeguarded by restricted access to the computer and computer files.

(c) Unathorised access to confidential files is achieved by data coding and user identity codes, discs or keys controlled at the terminal. The very confidential files not requiring constant access may be physically separated in secure containers, with restrictions on key holders.

(d) File corruption through faulty input or bad programming should be prevented by systems analysts and programmers that monitor the systems in operation and control all systems changes.

(e) Fraud mainly occurs with payroll and bought ledger systems where payments to employees or suppliers, real or fictious, are adjusted. Safeguards include programmed confidential analysis figures, manual checks on detail and confidential checks on individuals that are in a position to perpetrate fraud.

(f) System shutdown during an industrial dispute as a trade union bargaining lever, is becoming increasingly common as information systems become more centralised. Indeed, with data centralisation a small group of employees can exercise considerable 'industrial muscle'. Accordingly, for companies that have poor industrial relations, the costs and likely occurence of information systems being shutdown in industrial disputes need to be taken into consideration when deciding on the level of systems integration.

4:6 Communication networks In section 3:2:1 we considered the problems of defining the boundaries of an information system. The boundaries of an MIS are generally determined by practical considerations such as costs, benefits and availability. Thus MIS boundaries were usually within a company's internal information flows. However, rapid technological change and massive investment in external data bases are making it possible to expand MIS boundaries to include external data bases. The key to this expansion is a suitable communication network that can link data bases. Large organisations have developed their own networks with private telecommunications systems. But the real breakthrough in the U.K. will be when British Telecom have System X fully operational. This electronic digital network using optical fibres for data transmission will enable data bases to be connected through the telephone system. Thus a company could cost justify access to numerous external data bases as part of its own MIS. Communication networks are clearly going to expand MIS boundaries. An example of how external data bases will be 'plugged into' corporate information systems, are the plans for automated banking. The big five clearing banks will be working through the Prestel network to provide full banking services via customer terminals. The probable long term outcome of this network will be direct linking of different company accounting systems' bought and sales ledgers via the banking system.

This would dramatically reduce the volume of invoices, cheques and associated hard copy documentation that is part of existing accounting systems. It would also broaden the information system by making it partly cybernetic.

5. Summary

It is appropriate that a book on management accounting should have management information systems as the final chapter. After all, management accounting has been providing information for managers long before the MIS gained popularity. Indeed it can be argued that in practice, there is not a lot of difference between a full management accounting system and a management information system. In principle an MIS would cover a wider area than management accounting, but in the foreseeable future a fully integrated MIS is most unlikely, because the software would not be cost justified.

In this final chapter, attempts have been made to link different aspects of an MIS to various chapters in the book. For example, simulation models were linked to chapters 6 and 7 and control information to chapters 3, 4, 5, 8 and 9. Many of these chapters are complicated because they cover large areas in great detail, but the non-accountant using an MIS would not have to get immersed in the detail. This is the best part about well designed information systems; the detail is looked after by the software. All the user has to do is ask the right questions.

It is sincerely hoped that this book will help the non-accountant to know what questions to ask and how to interpret the answers.

Accountancy Quiz No.10.

1. Explain in detail the four main parts of an electronic data processing system. *(2:1, 2:1:1, 2:1:2, 2:1:3, 2:1:4)*

2. Explain the following terms:-

Closed system	Open system
Deterministic system	Probabilistic system
Complex system	Cybernetic system

(3:1:1)

3. What factors would you take into consideration when designing an information system? *(3:2:1, 3:2:2, 3:2:3)*

4. What is a management information system? *(3:3, 3:3:3)*

5. How would the needs of individual managers and the organisation be taken into consideration when designing an MIS? *(3:3:1, 3:3:2)*

6. How can an MIS help with decision making? *(4:1, 4:1:1, 4:1:2, 4:1:3, 4:1:4)*

7. How can an MIS help with controlling business activity? *(4:2, 4:2:1, 4:2:2, 4:2:3, 4:2:4, 4:2:5)*

8. How can an MIS help with corporate communication? *(4:3)*

9. What is a common data base? *(3:2:2, 4:4)*

10. How do you see the future for corporate management information systems? *(2:2, 2:2:1, 2:2:2, 2:2:3, 2:2:4, 4:6)*

Appendix 1 Glossary

This glossary is intended as a reading aid for non-accountants and provides brief explanations of over 100 'specialised' words and phrases used in this book. Additional glossaries on management techniques and computer terminology are contained in chapters 1 & 10.

Absorption costing. A costing technique that charges all costs incurred in bringing a product to its current condition and location to operations, products or processes. *Chapter 3 section 5:1*
Activity sampling. A work measurement technique to produce standard work times for planning, pricing and incentive payment schemes. *Chapter 4 section 3:3:4*
Algorithm. A structured series of procedural steps necessary for solving a problem. A list of instructions is a form of algorithm. A flowchart is a diagramatic representation of an algorithm. *Chapter 2 section 2:3:6*
Allocation of costs. The charging of all the cost elements to a cost centre or cost unit. Distinguish from cost apportionment. *Chapter 3 section 3:1:3*
Analytical estimating. A work measurement technique for planning, pricing and incentive schemes where a job is broken down into parts and times given for each part. *Chapter 4 section 3:3:4*
Apportionment of costs. The equitable division of a cost elements between cost centres or cost units. Distinguish from cost allocation. *Chapter 3 section 3:1:2*
Average cost. Total cost divided by related output. *Chapter 3 section 5:2:1*
Average rate of return. An investment appraisal method that calculates the annual return on an investment without allowing for the time value of money. *Chapter 7 section 3:4*

Batch costing. A costing system suitable for an enterprise that produces identical cost units, i.e. nuts, bolts, etc. The cost units are then costed in batches by totalling all the related costs and dividing by the batch quantity. *Chapter 3 section 5:12*
Binomial distribution. A calculation that measures the likelihood of events taking place where the probability is measured between: O = the event will certainly not occur and 1 - the event is absolutely certain. *Chapter 6 section 2:7:1, chapter 7 sections 9:1:2 and 9:1;3*
Break even graph. A graph that plots the total revenue and total cost functions for a specific product. *Chapter 6 section 2:2*
Break even model. A decision making technique that determines the effect on profit if cost, price or output is altered. *Chapter 6 section 2:1*
Break even point. The level of output/sales where total cost equals total revenue. *Chapter 6 section 2:2*
Budget. A quantitative plan relating to a future period of time of a policy to be pursued during that period towards stated objectives. *Chapter 8 section 1*
Budgetary bias. The attempt by managers to bias budgets during the planning phase by understating revenues and overstating costs so that the targets are more easily achievable. *Chapter 8 section 4:2*
Budgetary control. The detailed comparison of planned activity with actual activity to ensure the business is meeting its objectives. *Chapter 8 section 3*

B.C.

Budget cost allowance (BCA). A set of cost control figures that are calculated when the actual level of output is known in a flexible budgeting system. In a fixed budgeting system the BCA figures are determined during the planning phase. *Chapter 8 section 3:2*

Budgetary planning. A goal directed quantitative planning technique that integrates the sales forecast with the production and financial capacity of the business, to determine the future (usually one year) level of business activity. *Chapter 8 section 2*

Budgetary slack. Created by budgetary bias and represents the difference between the budgeted cost/revenue estimates and the achievable cost/revenue estimates. Usually the slack is positive, i.e. understated revenues and overstated costs. But there can also be negative slack. *Chapter 8 section 4:2*

Budget variance. The difference between the planned and actual cost or revenue figures. *Chapter 8 section 3:5*

By-product costing. A costing system for relatively low value output from a production process, i.e. scrap metal. *Chapter 3 section 5:7:2*

Capital allowances. A set of rules used by the Inland Revenue for calculating tax allowances for capital expenditure. *Chapter 7 section 10:1*

Capital expenditure. Where the benefit arising from the expenditure is consumed over more than one accounting period, i.e. purchase of a machine or motor vehicle. *Chapter 7 section 1*

Capital expenditure committee. A committee appointed to co-ordinate, supervise and approve/reject capital expenditure proposals. *Chapter 7 section 2:1:1*

Capital rationing. Investment conditions that are subject to financial constraint. Single period rationing is where the constraint is set for one accounting period and multi-period rationing where the constraint covers several periods. *Chapter 7 section 11:2*

Certainty equivalent. A method that makes allowance for risk in projects by adjusting the cash flow to a 100% certainty then using a risk free rate as a discount factor. *Chapter 7 section 9:2:2*

Controllable costs. Cost elements that a manager is capable of influencing within specified time periods. Refer to responsibility accounting. *Chapter 3 section 3:5*

Conversion costs. The cost of converting raw materials into finished goods. *Chapter 3 section 3:2*

Compounding. A calculation used to estimate the future value of present cash flows. *Chapter 7 section 5:1*

Computer data base (CDB). A file of records held in the computer which is not designed to meet a specific application but is used as a data source for a variety of analysis and recording requirements. *Chapter 3 section 4:1:2*

Contract costing. A costing system where all relevant costs are specifically identified with a single contract. *Chapter 3 section 5:11*

Contribution. An important figure derived in marginal costing systems by deducting the variable costs from related sales. *Chapter 3 section 5:2:2*

Contribution graph. A graph that plots the total cost, total revenue and variable costs for a specific product, thus highlighting a product's contribution. *Chapter 6 section 2:4*

C.D.E.

Cost benefit analysis. An appraisal technique that attempts to place values on all benefits arising from a project and then compares the total value with the project's total cost. *Chapter 7 section 4:2*

Cost centre. This is a department, person or item of equipment which is charged with costs that relate to location and sphere of operations. *Chapter 3 section 2:3*

Cost effectiveness analysis. An appraisal technique aimed at finding the cheapest way of achieving a defined objective and of getting the best value from a specified expenditure level. *Chapter 7 section 4:3*

Cost element. The primary division of expenditure into materials, labour and expense, where expense represents any expenditure that is not for materials and labour. Distinguish from cost classifications and methods. *Chapter 3 section 2:1*

Cost unit. A unit of product or service for which a cost is ascertained. *Chapter 3 sections 2:2 and 5:6*

Critical path analysis (CPA). A networking technique that breaks a project down into separate tasks and places them in sequence in an arrow chart. *Chapter 6 section 3:6:1*

Curve expenses. A term often used to describe a curvilinear total cost function. The curved total cost line can be drawn on a graph to determine a budget cost allowance for different levels of activity. *Chapter 8 section 3:2*

Decision tree. A decision making technique that shows a branching off of events arising from different courses of action. The probability of the events occurring can be included in the decision branches. *Chapter 6 section 3:5*

Differential costing. A decision making technique where only the relevant costs that are likely to differ between alternative courses of action are used. *Chapter 6 section 3:1*

Direct costs. A cost that belongs exclusively to a cost centre or cost unit. *Chapter 3 section 3:4*

Disinvestment appraisal. A project appraisal method that takes into consideration abandonment values. When the project's abandonment value is greater than its discounted future net cash flows then disinvestment appraisal is necessary. *Chapter 7 sections 8:5 and 9:5*

Discounted cash flow. The net cash flows of a project that have been adjusted to allow for the time value of money. *Chapter 7 sections 2:3, 5:2 and 7*

Discounting. A calculation used to estimate the present value of future cash flows. *Chapter 7 section 5:2*

Discount factor. A percentage figure representing a firm's or individual's time preference for money that is used in investment appraisal calculations. *Chapter 7 section 6*

Downside risk. A term that refers to the side of the business activity probability distribution that will result in the business trading at a loss. *Chapter 6 section 2:7:2*

Economic order quantity. A calculation that equates the cost of holding stock and the costs of not carrying enough stock to determine the quantity of specific items to be ordered. *Chapter 5 section 6:1:3*

E.F.H.I.J.K.

Expected monetary value (EMV). A cash flow value that has been adjusted for risk. *Chapter 7 sections 9:1:1 and 9:2:3*

Factor comparison. A job evaluation method where each job is ranked in a job hierarchy and a payment hierarchy, to derive a ranking of all jobs and wage rates. *Chapter 4 section 3:1:2*

Feasibility study. A study, not necessarily quantitive, to determine if an investment proposal can meet corporate objectives. *Chapter 7 section 4:1*

First in first out. A stock valuation system where goods are priced and issued to work in progress on the assumption that the first stock received is issued first. *Chapter 5 section 5:3:1*

Fixed budgets. These are constructed during the budgetary planning phase and have fixed levels of business activity. During the budgetary control phase the fixed budgets may be flexed to allow for different levels of activity. *Chapter 8 section 3:2*

Fixed costs. Costs that are fixed regardless of the level of output within a specified range. *Chapter 3 section 3:3*

Fixed overhead absorption rate (FOAR). A calculation that divides the total fixed overheads of a cost centre by a measure of output such as units, volume, labour hours or machine hours. *Chapter 3 section 5:1 and chapter 9 section 5*

Flexible budgets. A budgetary control technique applied at the end of an accounting period that makes allowance for differences between the budgeted and actual levels of activity. *Chapter 8 section 3:2*

Formula pricing. A pricing method based on a cost calculation plus a percentage for profit. Or conversely, a price less a specified margin to determine a target cost figure. *Chapter 6 section 4:2*

Human resource accounting. Attempts by accountants to place a value on human assets in an enterprise. Also called 'Human-asset' accounting. *Chapter 4 section 5:1:3*

Incremental costing. A decision making technique used to calculate the change in total costs and revenues arising from a change in the level of activity. *Chapter 6 section 3:2*

Indirect costs. A cost that is not directly related to the cost centre or unit being costed. *Chapter 3 section 3:4*

Internal rate of return. The percentage discount factor that equates a project's discounted cash inflows and outflows. It is the discount rate where the net present value will be zero. *Chapter 7 sections 7:3 and 11:1*

Job costing. A costing system for 'one off jobs' where costs are totalled on an absorption costing base for each job. *Chapter 3 section 5:10*

Job grading. A job evaluation scheme based on an organisation's hierarchy of job grading. *Chapter 4 section 3:1:2*

Job ranking. A job evaluation scheme based on job descriptions. *Chapter 4 section 3:1:2*

Joint costing. A costing system used for production processes that automatically produce more than one product. (Distinguish from by-product costing). *Chapter 3 section 5:7:1*

Key factor. Refer to limiting factor. *Chapter 6 section 2:8:4*

L.M.N.

Labour variance. The difference between the actual cost and standard cost of labour that may be due to a difference in labour efficiency or wage rate. *Chapter 9 section 4*

Last in first out. A stock valuation system where goods are priced when issued to work in progress on the assumption that the last stock received is issued first. *Chapter 5 section 5:3:2*

Life cycle costing. The division of a project's life cycle into seven costing stages: specification, design, make or buy, installation, start up, operating and terminal stage. *Chapter 7 section 2:3:3*

Limiting factor. A factor that restricts the growth of a business. The limiting factor may be sales, finance, skilled labour or materials (Also called key factor) *Chapter 6 section 2:8:4*

Marginal costing. A costing system that divides costs into fixed and variable. Only the variable costs are used in product costs and stock values. The system has gained wide acceptance for price/output decision making. *Chapter 3 section 5:2 and 5:3 and chapter 6 section 2*

Margin of safety. The difference between the break even point and the budgeted level of output for a specific product. *Chapter 6 section 2:5*

Market pricing. The determination of a product's price based on market conditions and marketing criteria. *Chapter 6 section 4:1*

Master budget. A budgeted profit and loss account and balance sheet based upon all the detail in the primary and subsidiary budgets. *Chapter 8 sections 2:4 and 2:4:6*

Materials variance. The difference between the actual cost and standard cost of materials that may be due to a difference in price or usage. *Chapter 9 section 3*

Measured daywork. A group incentive payment scheme where a fixed sum is paid above the basic rate if agreed performance targets are achieved. *Chapter 4 section 3:5*

Merit rating. A method of evaluating personnel usually linked to an incentive payment scheme. Points are awarded against a list of 'desirable' personal characteristics to derive an individual's rating. *Chapter 4 section 3:3:3*

Monte-Carlo technique. A simulation model that can be used to make allowance for risk in a project's cash flows. The principle is based on the study of chance using combinations of numbers. Tables are constructed for different factors and probabilities and simulation trials are run to produce a frequency distribution. *Chapter 7 section 9:4*

Net cash flow. The total net cash inflows of a project minus the capital cash outflow. *Chapter 7 sections 2:3 and 3:2*

Net present value (NPV). An investment appraisal calculation that multiplies the annual net cash flows of a project by a discount factor to derive discounted cash flows. The initial cash outflow is then deducted from the discounted cash flows to derive a net present value for the project. *Chapter 7 sections 7:1 and 11:1*

Net terminal value (NTV). An investment appraisal technique that uses compounding calculations to determine a future value of present cash flows. *Chapter 7 section 7:4*

Network. A diagramatic illustration of complex problems involving interrelated activities. Refer to Critical Path Analysis (CPA) and Program evaluation and Review Techniques (PERT). *Chapter 6 section 3:6*

N.O.P.R.

Non-controllable costs. Cost elements that are outside the control of a manager over a specified time period. Refer to responsibility accounting. *Chapter 3 section 3:5*

Operating leverage. Refers to the total cost structure that determines the contribution per unit. Generally, capital intensive cost structures have a large operating leverage. *Chapter 6 sections 2:5 and 2:7:2*
Operational gearing. The same principle as operating leverage. *Chapter 6 sections 2:5 and 2:7:2*
Opportunity costs. An economic concept that represents the benefit foregone or opportunity lost by not using a resource in its best alternative use. *Chapter 6 section 3:3*
Optimal pricing. A calculation that relates output to price to determine a price and output level that will maximise profit. *Chapter 6 section 4:3*
Overhead. A cost that is not usually charged direct to a cost unit and tends to be fixed in relation to putput. *Chapter 3 section 3:1:3*
Overhead variance. The difference between the actual cost and standard cost of overheads that arise, due to differences in planned and actual expenditure and/or the level of activity. *Chapter 9 section 5*

Payment by results. A range of incentive payment schemes that are directly linked to levels of output. *Chapter 4 section 3:3*
Performance review. A personnel evaluation method usually linked to a salary review procedure. The employee's performance is assessed against predetermined tasks and objectives. *Chapter 4 section 3:1:3*
Piecework. A remuneration system where the wage level is directly related to output levels. *Chapter 4 section 3:2:1*
Points rating. A job evaluation scheme where the 'value' of a job is assessed by totalling points that have been allocated to selected job functions. *Chapter 4 section 3:1:2*
Present value index (PVI). A form of cost/benefit ratio in present value terms where the present value of future net cash flows is divided by the initial outlay. The PVI enables projects to be compared and ranked under single period capital rationing. *Chapter 7 section 7:2*
Prime costs. A cost category in a manufacturing account mainly comprised of direct material and direct labour. *Chapter 3 section 3:2*
Primary budgets. The general term used to describe the sales production and finance budgets. All other budgets (except the master budget) are then referred to as subsidiary budgets. *Chapter 8 section 2:4*
Production ratios. A set of production related ratios that are calculated from standard costing data. The ratios measure production efficiency, capacity and volume. *Chapter 9 section 7*
Profit sharing. A group incentive payment scheme that is supposed to improve employee goodwill towards the enterprise. *Chapter 4 section 3:6*
Profit volume graph. A graph that plots the profit function (i.e. total revenue - total costs) for a specific product and enables the profit or loss to be read direct from the graph at any level of output. *Chapter 6 section 2:4*
Profit volume ratio. The relationship that exists between contribution and sales is expressed as a fraction, percentage or decimal. (P/V ratio = contribution ÷ sales). *Chapter 6 section 2:6*

Relevant costs. A cost element that is relevant to a specific decision and tends to have two characteristics: it is a future cost and will be different for the decision alternatives. *Chapter 6 section 3:4*

R.S.T.U.V.

Relevant range. A range of output/sales where unit costs and revenue are expected to be linear. *Chapter 6 section 2:9:2*
Risk. Conditions where the expected outcome of events is quantifiable. Distinguish from uncertainty. *Chapter 7 section 9*
Rucker plan. A cost reduction incentive payment scheme based on a labour cost/added value ratio. *Chapter 4 section 3:4:2*

Safety stock. A stock holding level of specific items below which stock will not fall during normal trading conditions. Sometimes physically separated and called *'base stock'. Chapter 5 section 6:2:2*
Sales variance. There are two types: sales value variances and sales margin variances. Sales value variances represent the difference between the budgeted and actual sales. Sales margin variances represent the difference between the actual and standard selling price multiplied by the actual quantity sold. *Chapter 9 section 6*
Scanlon plan. A cost reduction incentive payment scheme based on a single labour cost/sales ratio. *Chapter 4 section 5:4:1*
Sensitivity analysis. A method that identifies critical variables that can significantly affect a project's profitability if conditions change or estimates are wrong. The analysis attempts to measure the effect that a change in the variables will have on a project's cash flow. *Chapter 7 section 9:3*
Standard hour of production (SHP). A measure of productive activity based on an agreed level of labour efficiency. Often used to measure total output of different products for a specified time period. *Chapter 9 section 5*
Stepped fixed costs. The increase in fixed costs that occurs at specific levels of output. *Chapter 6 section 2:9:2*

Time horizon. (Also called planning horizon) Refers to the length of time for which cash flows will be estimated. It is a cash flow cut off point where the decision maker will not allow for any subsequent cash flows. *Chapter 7 section 2:2:1*
Time value of money. The allowance in cash calculations for the time preference for money. *Chapter 7 section 5*
Transfer price. The price to be charged for goods and services that are transferred between inter-related companies or between divisions within a company. *Chapter 6 section 4:4*

Uncertainty. Conditions where there is no reliable data to help predict future events. Distinguish from risks. *Chapter 7 section 9*
Unit costing. A costing technique where the total cost is divided by the related unit output to derive an average cost per unit. *Chapter 3 section 5:6*

Variable costs. Costs that vary directly in relation to output such as direct materials in a production process. *Chapter 3 section 3:3*
Variable overhead absorption rate (VOAR). A calculation that divides the total variable overheads of a cost centre by a measure of output such as units, volume, labour hours or machine hours. *Chapter 3 sections 5:1 and chapter 9 section 5*

W.Z.

Weighted average cost of capital (WAC). A calculation that attempts to measure the cost of a company's capital to determine an optimal debt/equity mix. The WAC is often used as a discount factor in investment appraisal calculations. *Chapter 7 section 6:2*
Work in progress. The value given to partly finished goods in the production process. *Chapter 5 section 2*
Working capital cycle. The time it takes for cash to flow through stock, debtors and creditors. *Chapter 5 section 1*

Zero base review. Refer to zero budgeting. *Chapter 8 section 5:1*
Zero budgeting A budgeting system where all existing activities are assessed and cost justified in the same way as new proposals. The system removes the implied right of existing activities for the continued allocation of resources. *Chapter 8 section 5:1.*

Appendix 2 Abbreviations

(A)	Adverse variance
AC	Absorption costing
AC	Average cost
ACAS	Advisory Conciliation and Arbitration Service
ACT	Advance corporation tax
ADT	Automatic data processing
ALGOL	Algorithmic language
BCA	Budget cost allowance
B/E	Break even
BEP	Break even point
CBA	Cost benefit analysis
CBI	Confederation of British Industry
CCA	Current cost accounting
CDB	Common data base
CEA	Cost effective analysis
CEC	Capital expenditure committee
CLR	Corporate life risk
COBOL	Common business orientated language
COM	Computer on to microfilm
CPU	Central processing unit
DBMS	Data base management system
DCF	Discounted cash flow
DDP	Distributed data processing
DF	Discount factor
DL	Direct labour
DM	Direct materials
EDP	Electronic data processing
EMV	Expected monetary value
EOQ	Economic order quantity
EPA	Employment Protection Act
(F)	Favourable variance
FC	Fixed costs
FG	Finished goods
FIFO	First in first out
FOAR	Fixed overhead absorption rate
FOH	Fixed overhead
FORTRAN	Formula translation
FWH	Flexible working hours
IFC	Inter-firm comparison
IRA	Industrial Relations Act
IRR	Internal rate of return
ISX	Information switching exchange
JIC	Joint industrial council
JPC	Joint production committee
LIFO	Last in first out
LRP	Long range planning

MBE	Management by exception
MBO	Management by objectives
MC	Marginal cost
MCT	Mainstream corporation tax
MDW	Measured day work
MICR	Magnetic ink character recognition
MOS	Margin of safety
MTM	Methods time measurement
NBPI	National Board for Prices and Incomes
NCF	Net cash flow
NIFO	Next in first out
NPV	Net present value
NRV	Net realiseable value
NTV	Net terminal value
OCR	Optical character recohnition
O/H	Overhead
P	Probability
PABX	Private automatic branch exchange
PAR	Program analysis and review
PBF	Principal budget factor
PBR	Payment by results
PBX	Private branch exchange
PEAT	Programme evaluation and review technique
PMTS	Predetermined motion time system
PP	Profit planning
PPBS	Programming planning budgeting system
RAM	Random access memory
RC	Replacement cost
RM	Raw materials
ROCE	Return on capital employed
ROM	Read only memory
SHP	Standard hour of production
SSAP	Statement of standard accounting practice
SWOT	Strengths, weaknesses, opportunities and threats
TC	Total cost
TR	Total revenue
TUC	Trades Union Congress
Var	Variance
V+A	Valuable and attractive
VC	Variable cost
VDU	Visual display unit
VO/H	Variable overhead
VOAR	Variable overhead absorption rate
WACC	Weighted average cost of capital
WIP	Work in progress
ZBR	Zero base review

Appendix 3 Useful addresses

Association of British Chambers of Commerce
6 - 14 Dean Farrar Street,
London SW1H ODX
Telephone: 01 222 0201

Confederation of British Industry
21, Tothill Street,
London SW1H 9LP
Telephone: 01 930 6711

Trade Union Congress
Great Russell Street,
London WC1
Telephone: 01 636 4030

British Institute of Management
Management House,
Parker Street,
London WC2B 5PT
Telephone: 01 405 3456

Institute of Cost and Management Accountants *
63, Portland Place,
London W1N 4AB
Telephone: 01 637 2311

Institute of Management Consultants Consultants
23 - 24 Cromwell Place,
London SW7 2LG
Telephone: 01 584 7285

Association of Business Executives
10, Dryden Chambers,
119, Oxford Street,
London W1R 1PA
Telephone: 01 437 3063

Association of Chambers of Commerce of Ireland
7, Clare Street,
Dublin 2
Telephone: Dublin 764291

Institute of Directors
10, Belgrave Square,
London SW1X 8PW
Telephone: 01 235 3601

Institute for Workers Control
Betrand Russell House,
Gamble Street,
Nottingham N67 4ET
Telephone: 0602 74504

Institute of Chartered Secretaries and Administrators
16, Park Crescent,
London W1H 4AH
Telephone: 01 580 4741

British Computer Society
13, Mansfield Street,
London W1M OBP
Telephone: 01 637 0471

Institute of Management Specialists
2, Hamilton Terrace,
Royal Lemington Spa,
Warwickshire
Telephone: 0926 55498

Institute of Supervisory Management
22, Bore Street,
Lichfield,
Staffordshire WS13 6LP
Telephone: 054 32 51346

(A full list of UK accountancy bodies is given in Volume 1 Financial Accounting for non - accountants.)*

Management Consultants
Association
23 - 24 Cromwell Place,
London SW7 2LG
Telephone: 01 584 7283

Institute of Adminstrative
Management
205, High Street,
Beckenham,
Kent BR3 1BA
Telephone: 01 658 0171

Institute of Public Relations
1, Great James Street,
London W1RN 3DA
Telephone: 01 405 5505

Public Relations Consultants
Association
44, Belgrave Square,
London Sw1X 8QS
Telephone: 01 235 6225

Institute of Commerce
1, Lincoln's Inn Fields,
London WC2A 3AD
Telephone: 01 242 3669

Institute of Internal Auditors
(UK Chapter)
1, Ashurst Road,
Tadworth, Surrey.
Telephone: Tadworth 2732

Institute of Purchasing and
Supply
York House,
Westminster Bridge,
London SE1 7UT
Telephone: 01 928 1851

Institute of Marketing
Moor Hall,
Cookham,
Berkshire SL6 9QH
Telephone: 062 85 24922

Institute for Operational
Research
56 - 60 Hallam Street,
London W1M 5LH
Telephone: 01 580 2196

Institute of Production Control
46, Ruther Street,
Stratford upon Avon,
Warwichshire CV37 6LT
Telephone: 0789 5266

Institute of Personnel
Management
Central House,
Upper Woburn Place,
London WC1M OHX
Telephone: 01 387 2844

Institute of Practioners in
Work Study
9 - 10 River Front,
Enfield,
Middlesex EN1 3TE
Telephone: 01 363 7452

The National Terotechnology
Centre
Cleeve Road,
Leatherhead,
Surrey KT22 7SA
Telephone: Leatherhead 78242

The Centre for Interfirm
Comparison
25, Bloomsbury Square,
London WC1A 2PJ
Telephone: 01 637 8406

Appendix 4
Discounting & Compounding Tables

WHAT THE TABLES REPRESENT

Table A *(Pages 468 - 477)* The present value of 1 from 1 to 50 years at rates of 1% - 50%. For example, the present value of £1.00 received/paid in year 10 using a 10% discount rate would be £0.385. Refer to 10% column on page 468.

Table B *(Pages 478 - 487)* The present value of 1 per annum for 1 to 50 years at rates of 1% to 50%. For example, the present value of £1.00 received/paid every year for 10 years at a discount rate of 10% would be £6.14. Refer to 10% column on page 478.

Table C *(Pages 488 - 497)* The future value of 1 per annum for 1 to 50 years at rates of 1% to 50%. For example, the value in year 10 of £1.00 received/paid every year for 10 years at a compound rate of 10% would be £15.94. Refer to 10% column on page 488.

HOW TO USE THE TABLES

Example of NPV and NTV calculation An investment with an initial cash outlay of £20,000 will yield £4,000 per annum for eight years and give a terminal cash flow of £1,000. The investment will be appraised using a 10% factor.

NPV calculation		£
Regular cash inflows £4,000 x 5.33493 *(Table on page 478)*		21,340
Terminal cash flow £1,000 x 0.466507 *(Table on page 468)*		467
Initial cash outflow £20,000 x 1.0		(20,000)
	NPV	£1,807

NTV calculation		£
Regular cash inflows £4,000 x 11.4359 *(Tables on page 488)*		45,744
Terminal cash inflow £1,000 x1.0		1,000
Initial cash outflow £20,000 x $(1 + r)^n$ *		(42,880)
	NTV	£3,864

Reconciliation of NPV & NTV (Allowing for rounding)
Present value of NTV = 3,864 x 0.467 = £1,804
Terminal value of NPV = 1,807 x 2.144 * = £3,874

(The compound interest calculation was explained in chapter 7 section 5:1)*

Acknowledgements – These tables originally appeared in The Finance and Analysis of Capital Projects by A.J. Merrett and Allen Sykes. Longman ISBN 0 582 45038 1

TABLE A *The present value of 1* $v_{n|r} = (1 + r)^{-n}$

YEAR	PERCENTAGE 1	2	3	4	5	6	7	8	9	10
1	0·990099	0·980392	0·970874	0·961538	0·952381	0·943396	0·934579	0·925926	0·917431	0·909091
2	0·980296	0·961169	0·942596	0·924556	0·907029	0·889996	0·873439	0·857339	0·841680	0·826446
3	0·970590	0·942322	0·915142	0·888996	0·863838	0·839619	0·816298	0·793832	0·772183	0·751315
4	0·960980	0·923845	0·888487	0·854804	0·822702	0·792094	0·762895	0·735030	0·708425	0·683013
5	0·951466	0·905731	0·862609	0·821927	0·783526	0·747258	0·712986	0·680583	0·649931	0·620921
6	0·942045	0·887971	0·837484	0·790315	0·746215	0·704961	0·666342	0·630170	0·596267	0·564474
7	0·932718	0·870560	0·813092	0·759918	0·710681	0·665057	0·622750	0·583490	0·547034	0·513158
8	0·923483	0·853490	0·789409	0·730690	0·676839	0·627412	0·582009	0·540269	0·501866	0·466507
9	0·914340	0·836755	0·766417	0·702587	0·644609	0·591898	0·543934	0·500249	0·460428	0·424098
10	0·905287	0·820348	0·744094	0·675564	0·613913	0·558395	0·508349	0·463193	0·422411	0·385543
11	0·896324	0·804263	0·722421	0·649581	0·584679	0·526788	0·475093	0·428883	0·387533	0·350494
12	0·887449	0·788493	0·701380	0·624597	0·556837	0·496969	0·444012	0·397114	0·355535	0·318631
13	0·878663	0·773033	0·680951	0·600574	0·530321	0·468839	0·414964	0·367698	0·326179	0·289664
14	0·869963	0·757875	0·661118	0·577475	0·505068	0·442301	0·387817	0·340461	0·299246	0·263331
15	0·861349	0·743015	0·641862	0·555265	0·481017	0·417265	0·362446	0·315242	0·274538	0·239392
16	0·852821	0·728446	0·623167	0·533908	0·458112	0·393646	0·338735	0·291890	0·251870	0·217629
17	0·844377	0·174163	0·605016	0·513373	0·436297	0·371364	0·316574	0·270269	0·231073	0·197845
18	0·836017	0·700159	0·587395	0·493628	0·415521	0·350344	0·295864	0·250249	0·211994	0·179859
19	0·827740	0·686431	0·570286	0·474642	0·395734	0·330513	0·276508	0·231712	0·194490	0·163508
20	0·819544	0·672971	0·553676	0·456387	0·376889	0·311805	0·258419	0·214548	0·178431	0·148644
21	0·811430	0·659776	0·537549	0·438834	0·358942	0·294155	0·241513	0·198656	0·163698	0·135131
22	0·803396	0·646839	0·521893	0·421955	0·341850	0·277505	0·225713	0·183941	0·150182	0·122846
23	0·795442	0·634156	0·506692	0·405726	0·325571	0·261797	0·210947	0·170315	0·137781	0·111678

24	0·787566	0·621721	0·491934	0·390121	0·310068	0·246979	0·197147	0·157699	0·126405	0·101526
25	0·779768	0·609531	0·477606	0·375117	0·295303	0·232999	0·184249	0·146018	0·115968	0·092296
26	0·772048	0·597579	0·463695	0·360689	0·281241	0·219810	0·172195	0·135202	0·106393	0·083905
27	0·764404	0·585862	0·450189	0·346817	0·267848	0·207368	0·160930	0·125187	0·097608	0·076278
28	0·756836	0·574375	0·437077	0·333477	0·255094	0·195630	0·150402	0·115914	0·089548	0·069343
29	0·749342	0·563112	0·424346	0·320651	0·242946	0·184557	0·140563	0·107328	0·082155	0·063039
30	0·741923	0·552071	0·411987	0·308319	0·231377	0·174110	0·131367	0·099377	0·075371	0·057309
31	0·734577	0·541246	0·399987	0·296460	0·220359	0·164255	0·122773	0·092016	0·069148	0·052099
32	0·727304	0·530633	0·388337	0·285058	0·209866	0·154957	0·114741	0·085200	0·063438	0·047362
33	0·720103	0·520229	0·377026	0·274094	0·199873	0·146186	0·107235	0·078889	0·058200	0·043057
34	0·712973	0·510028	0·366045	0·263552	0·190355	0·137912	0·100219	0·073045	0·053395	0·039143
35	0·705914	0·500028	0·355383	0·253415	0·181290	0·130105	0·093663	0·067635	0·048986	0·035584
36	0·698925	0·490223	0·345032	0·243669	0·172657	0·122741	0·087535	0·062625	0·044941	0·032349
37	0·692005	0·480611	0·334983	0·234297	0·164436	0·115793	0·081809	0·057986	0·041231	0·029408
38	0·685153	0·471187	0·325226	0·225285	0·156605	0·109239	0·076457	0·053690	0·037826	0·026735
39	0·678370	0·461948	0·315754	0·216621	0·149148	0·103056	0·071455	0·049713	0·034703	0·024304
40	0·671653	0·452890	0·306557	0·208289	0·142046	0·097222	0·066780	0·046031	0·031838	0·022095
41	0·665003	0·444010	0·297628	0·200278	0·135282	0·091719	0·062412	0·042621	0·029209	0·020086
42	0·658419	0·435304	0·288959	0·192575	0·128840	0·086527	0·058329	0·039464	0·026797	0·018260
43	0·651900	0·426769	0·280543	0·185168	0·122704	0·081630	0·054513	0·036541	0·024584	0·016600
44	0·645445	0·418401	0·272372	0·178046	0·116861	0·077009	0·050946	0·033834	0·022555	0·015091
45	0·639055	0·410197	0·264439	0·171198	0·111297	0·072650	0·047613	0·031328	0·020692	0·013719
46	0·632728	0·402154	0·256737	0·164614	0·105997	0·068538	0·044499	0·029007	0·018984	0·012472
47	0·626463	0·394268	0·249259	0·158283	0·100949	0·064658	0·041587	0·026859	0·017416	0·011338
48	0·620260	0·386538	0·241999	0·152195	0·096142	0·060998	0·038867	0·024869	0·015978	0·010307
49	0·614119	0·378958	0·234950	0·146341	0·091564	0·057546	0·036324	0·023027	0·014659	0·009370
50	0·608039	0·371528	0·228107	0·140713	0·087204	0·054288	0·033948	0·021321	0·013449	0·008519

TABLE A *The present value of 1 (continued)* $v_{n|r} = (1 + r)^{-n}$

YEAR	PERCENTAGE 11	12	13	14	15	16	17	18	19	20
1	0·900901	0·892857	0·884956	0·877193	0·869565	0·862069	0·854701	0·847458	0·840336	0·833333
2	0·811622	0·797194	0·783147	0·769468	0·756144	0·743163	0·730514	0·718184	0·706165	0·694444
3	0·731191	0·711780	0·693050	0·674972	0·657516	0·640658	0·624371	0·608631	0·593416	0·578704
4	0·658731	0·635518	0·613319	0·592080	0·571753	0·552291	0·533650	0·515789	0·498669	0·482253
5	0·593451	0·567427	0·542760	0·519369	0·497177	0·476113	0·456111	0·437109	0·419049	0·401878
6	0·534641	0·506631	0·480319	0·455587	0·432328	0·410442	0·389839	0·370432	0·352142	0·334898
7	0·481658	0·452349	0·425061	0·399637	0·375937	0·353830	0·333195	0·313925	0·295918	0·279082
8	0·433926	0·403883	0·376160	0·350559	0·326902	0·305025	0·284782	0·266038	0·248671	0·232568
9	0·390925	0·360610	0·332885	0·307508	0·284262	0·262953	0·243404	0·225456	0·208967	0·193807
10	0·352184	0·321973	0·294588	0·269744	0·247185	0·226684	0·208037	0·191064	0·175602	0·161506
11	0·317283	0·287476	0·260698	0·236617	0·214943	0·195417	0·177810	0·161919	0·147565	0·134588
12	0·285841	0·256675	0·230706	0·207559	0·186907	0·168463	0·151974	0·137220	0·124004	0·112157
13	0·257514	0·229174	0·204165	0·182069	0·162528	0·145227	0·129892	0·116288	0·104205	0·093464
14	0·231995	0·204620	0·180677	0·159710	0·141329	0·125195	0·111019	0·098549	0·087567	0·077887
15	0·209004	0·182696	0·159891	0·140096	0·122894	0·107927	0·094888	0·083516	0·073586	0·064905
16	0·188292	0·163122	0·141496	0·122892	0·106865	0·093041	0·081101	0·070776	0·061837	0·054083
17	0·169633	0·145644	0·125218	0·107800	0·092926	0·080207	0·069317	0·059980	0·051964	0·045073
18	0·152822	0·130040	0·110812	0·094561	0·080805	0·069144	0·059245	0·050830	0·043667	0·037561
19	0·137678	0·116107	0·098064	0·082948	0·070265	0·059607	0·050637	0·043077	0·036695	0·031301
20	0·124034	0·103667	0·086782	0·072762	0·061100	0·051385	0·043280	0·036506	0·030836	0·026084
21	0·111742	0·092560	0·076798	0·063826	0·053131	0·044298	0·036991	0·030937	0·025913	0·021737
22	0·100669	0·082643	0·067963	0·055988	0·046201	0·038188	0·031616	0·026218	0·021775	0·018114

23	0·090693	0·073788	0·060144	0·049112	0·040174	0·032920	0·027022	0·022218	0·018299	0·015095
24	0·081705	0·065882	0·053225	0·043081	0·034934	0·028380	0·023096	0·018829	0·015377	0·012579
25	0·073608	0·058823	0·047102	0·037790	0·030378	0·024465	0·019740	0·015957	0·012922	0·010483
26	0·066314	0·052521	0·041683	0·033149	0·026415	0·021091	0·016872	0·013523	0·010859	0·008735
27	0·059742	0·046894	0·036888	0·029078	0·022970	0·018182	0·014421	0·011460	0·009125	0·007280
28	0·053822	0·041869	0·032644	0·025507	0·019974	0·015674	0·012325	0·009712	0·007668	0·006066
29	0·048488	0·037383	0·028889	0·022375	0·017369	0·013512	0·010534	0·008230	0·006444	0·005055
30	0·043683	0·033378	0·025565	0·019627	0·015103	0·011648	0·009004	0·006975	0·005415	0·004213
31	0·039354	0·029802	0·022624	0·017217	0·013133	0·010042	0·007696	0·005911	0·004550	0·003511
32	0·035454	0·026609	0·020021	0·015102	0·011420	0·008657	0·006577	0·005009	0·003824	0·002926
33	0·031940	0·023758	0·017718	0·013248	0·009931	0·007463	0·005622	0·004245	0·003213	0·002438
34	0·028775	0·021212	0·015680	0·011621	0·008635	0·006433	0·004805	0·003598	0·002700	0·002032
35	0·025924	0·018940	0·013876	0·010194	0·007509	0·005546	0·004107	0·003049	0·002269	0·001693
36	0·023355	0·016910	0·012279	0·008942	0·006529	0·004781	0·003510	0·002584	0·001907	0·001411
37	0·021040	0·015098	0·010867	0·007844	0·005678	0·004121	0·003000	0·002190	0·001602	0·001176
38	0·018955	0·013481	0·009617	0·006880	0·004937	0·003553	0·002564	0·001856	0·001347	0·000980
39	0·017077	0·012036	0·008510	0·006035	0·004293	0·003063	0·002192	0·001573	0·001132	0·000816
40	0·015384	0·010747	0·007531	0·005294	0·003733	0·002640	0·001873	0·001333	0·000951	0·000680
41	0·013860	0·009595	0·006665	0·004644	0·003246	0·002276	0·001601	0·001129	0·000799	0·000576
42	0·012486	0·008567	0·005898	0·004074	0·002823	0·001962	0·001368	0·000957	0·000671	0·000472
43	0·011249	0·007649	0·005219	0·003573	0·002455	0·001692	0·001170	0·000811	0·000564	0·000394
44	0·010134	0·006830	0·004619	0·003135	0·002134	0·001458	0·001000	0·000687	0·000474	0·000328
45	0·009130	0·006098	0·004088	0·002750	0·001856	0·001257	0·000854	0·000583	0·000398	0·000273
46	0·008225	0·005445	0·003617	0·002412	0·001614	0·001084	0·001730	0·000494	0·000335	0·000228
47	0·007410	0·004861	0·003201	0·002116	0·001403	0·000934	0·000624	0·000418	0·000281	0·000190
48	0·006676	0·004340	0·002833	0·001856	0·001220	0·000805	0·000533	0·000355	0·000236	0·000158
49	0·006014	0·003875	0·002507	0·001628	0·001061	0·000694	0·000456	0·000300	0·000199	0·000132
50	0·005418	0·003460	0·002219	0·001428	0·000923	0·000599	0·000390	0·000255	0·000167	0·000110

TABLE A *The present value of 1 (continued)* $v_{n|r} = (1 + r)^{-n}$

	PERCENTAGE									
YEAR	21	22	23	24	25	26	27	28	29	30
1	0·826446	0·819672	0·813008	0·806452	0·800000	0·793651	0·787402	0·781250	0·775194	0·769231
2	0·683013	0·671862	0·660982	0·650364	0·640000	0·629882	0·620001	0·610352	0·600925	0·591716
3	0·564474	0·550707	0·537384	0·524487	0·512000	0·499906	0·488190	0·476837	0·465834	0·455166
4	0·466507	0·451399	0·436897	0·422974	0·409600	0·396751	0·384402	0·372529	0·361111	0·350128
5	0·385543	0·369999	0·355201	0·341108	0·327680	0·314882	0·302678	0·291038	0·279931	0·269329
6	0·318631	0·303278	0·288781	0·275087	0·262144	0·249906	0·238329	0·227374	0·217001	0·207176
7	0·263331	0·248589	0·234782	0·221844	0·209715	0·198338	0·187661	0·177636	0·168218	0·159366
8	0·217629	0·203761	0·190879	0·178907	0·167772	0·157411	0·147765	0·138778	0·130401	0·122589
9	0·179859	0·167017	0·155187	0·144280	0·134218	0·124930	0·116350	0·108420	0·101086	0·094300
10	0·148644	0·136899	0·126168	0·116354	0·107374	0·099150	0·091614	0·084703	0·078362	0·072538
11	0·122846	0·112213	0·102576	0·093834	0·085899	0·078691	0·072137	0·066174	0·060745	0·055799
12	0·101526	0·091978	0·083395	0·075673	0·068719	0·062453	0·056801	0·051699	0·047089	0·042922
13	0·083905	0·075391	0·067801	0·061026	0·054976	0·049566	0·044725	0·040390	0·036503	0·033017
14	0·069343	0·061796	0·055122	0·049215	0·043980	0·039338	0·035217	0·031554	0·028297	0·025398
15	0·057309	0·050653	0·044815	0·039689	0·035184	0·031221	0·027730	0·024652	0·021936	0·019537
16	0·047362	0·041519	0·036435	0·032008	0·028147	0·024778	0·021834	0·019259	0·017005	0·015028
17	0·039143	0·034032	0·029622	0·025813	0·022518	0·019665	0·017192	0·015046	0·013182	0·011560
18	0·032349	0·027895	0·024083	0·020817	0·018014	0·015607	0·013537	0·011755	0·010218	0·008892
19	0·026735	0·022865	0·019580	0·016788	0·014412	0·012387	0·010659	0·009184	0·007921	0·006840
20	0·022095	0·018741	0·015918	0·013538	0·011529	0·009831	0·008393	0·007175	0·006141	0·005262
21	0·018260	0·015362	0·012942	0·010918	0·009223	0·007802	0·006609	0·005605	0·004760	0·004048
22	0·015091	0·012592	0·010522	0·008805	0·007379	0·006192	0·005204	0·004379	0·003690	0·003113
23	0·012472	0·010321	0·008554	0·007101	0·005903	0·004914	0·004097	0·003421	0·002860	0·002395

24	0·010 307	0·008 460	0·006 955	0·005 726	0·004 722	0·003 900	0·003 226	0·002 673	0·002 217	0·001 842
25	0·008 519	0·006 934	0·005 654	0·004 618	0·003 778	0·003 096	0·002 540	0·002 088	0·001 719	0·001 417
26	0·007 040	0·005 684	0·004 597	0·003 724	0·003 022	0·002 457	0·002 000	0·001 631	0·001 333	0·001 090
27	0·005 818	0·004 659	0·003 737	0·003 003	0·002 418	0·001 950	0·001 575	0·001 274	0·001 033	0·000 839
28	0·004 809	0·003 819	0·003 038	0·002 422	0·001 934	0·001 547	0·001 240	0·000 996	0·000 801	0·000 645
29	0·003 974	0·003 130	0·002 470	0·001 953	0·001 547	0·001 228	0·000 977	0·000 778	0·000 621	0·000 496
30	0·003 284	0·002 566	0·002 008	0·001 575	0·001 238	0·000 975	0·000 769	0·000 608	0·000 481	0·000 382
31	0·002 714	0·002 103	0·001 633	0·001 270	0·000 990	0·000 774	0·000 605	0·000 475	0·000 373	0·000 294
32	0·002 243	0·001 724	0·001 328	0·001 024	0·000 792	0·000 614	0·000 477	0·000 371	0·000 289	0·000 226
33	0·001 854	0·001 413	0·001 079	0·000 826	0·000 634	0·000 487	0·000 375	0·000 290	0·000 224	0·000 174
34	0·001 532	0·001 158	0·000 877	0·000 666	0·000 507	0·000 387	0·000 296	0·000 226	0·000 174	0·000 134
35	0·001 266	0·000 949	0·000 713	0·000 537	0·000 406	0·000 307	0·000 233	0·000 177	0·000 135	0·000 103
36	0·001 046	0·000 778	0·000 580	0·000 433	0·000 325	0·000 244	0·000 183	0·000 138	0·000 104	0·791 4*
37	0·000 865	0·000 638	0·000 472	0·000 349	0·000 260	0·000 193	0·000 144	0·000 108	0·809 4*	0·608 4
38	0·000 715	0·000 523	0·000 383	0·000 282	0·000 208	0·000 153	0·000 114	0·843 4*	0·627 4	0·468 4
39	0·000 591	0·000 429	0·000 312	0·000 227	0·000 166	0·000 122	0·895 4*	0·659 4	0·486 4	0·360 4
40	0·000 488	0·000 351	0·000 253	0·000 183	0·000 133	0·966 4*	0·704 4	0·515 4	0·377 4	0·277 4
41	0·000 403	0·000 288	0·000 206	0·000 148	0·000 106	0·767 4	0·555 4	0·402 4	0·292 4	0·213 4
42	0·000 333	0·000 236	0·000 167	0·000 119	0·851 4*	0·609 4	0·437 4	0·314 4	0·227 4	0·164 4
43	0·000 276	0·000 193	0·000 136	0·961 4*	0·681 4	0·483 4	0·344 4	0·245 4	0·176 4	0·126 4
44	0·000 228	0·000 159	0·000 111	0·775 4	0·544 4	0·383 4	0·271 4	0·192 4	0·136 4	0·969 5
45	0·000 188	0·000 130	0·900 4*	0·625 4	0·436 4	0·304 4	0·213 4	0·150 4	0·106 4	0·746 5
46	0·000 156	0·000 107	0·732 4	0·504 4	0·348 4	0·242 4	0·168 4	0·117 4	0·818 5	0·574 5
47	0·000 129	0·873 4*	0·595 4	0·407 4	0·279 4	0·192 4	0·132 4	0·914 5	0·634 5	0·441 5
48	0·000 106	0·716 4	0·484 4	0·328 4	0·223 4	0·152 4	0·104 4	0·714 5	0·492 5	0·339 5
49	0·878 4*	0·587 4	0·393 4	0·264 4	0·178 4	0·121 4	0·820 5	0·558 5	0·381 5	0·261 5
50	0·726 4	0·481 4	0·320 4	0·213 4	0·143 4	0·958 5	0·645 5	0·436 5	0·295 5	0·201 5

* The final digit is the power of 10 by which the given tabular value has to be divided.

TABLE A *The present value of 1 (continued)* $v_{n|r} = (1 + r)^{-n}$

YEAR	PERCENTAGE 31	32	33	34	35	36	37	38	39	40
1	0·763359	0·757576	0·751880	0·746269	0·740741	0·735294	0·729927	0·724638	0·719424	0·714286
2	0·582717	0·573921	0·565323	0·556917	0·548697	0·540657	0·532793	0·525100	0·517572	0·510204
3	0·444822	0·434789	0·425055	0·415610	0·406442	0·397542	0·388900	0·380507	0·372354	0·364431
4	0·339559	0·329385	0·319590	0·310156	0·301068	0·292310	0·283869	0·275730	0·267880	0·260308
5	0·259205	0·249534	0·240293	0·231460	0·223014	0·214934	0·207204	0·199804	0·192720	0·185934
6	0·197866	0·189041	0·180672	0·172731	0·165195	0·158040	0·151243	0·144786	0·138647	0·132810
7	0·151043	0·143213	0·135843	0·128904	0·122367	0·116206	0·110397	0·104917	0·099746	0·094865
8	0·115300	0·108495	0·102138	0·096197	0·090642	0·085445	0·080582	0·076027	0·071760	0·067760
9	0·088015	0·082193	0·076795	0·071789	0·067142	0·062828	0·058819	0·055092	0·051626	0·048400
10	0·067187	0·062267	0·057741	0·053574	0·049735	0·046197	0·042933	0·039922	0·037141	0·034572
11	0·051288	0·047172	0·043414	0·039980	0·036841	0·033968	0·031338	0·028929	0·026720	0·024694
12	0·039151	0·035737	0·032642	0·029836	0·027289	0·024977	0·022875	0·020963	0·019223	0·017639
13	0·029886	0·027073	0·024543	0·022266	0·020214	0·018365	0·016697	0·015190	0·013830	0·012599
14	0·022814	0·020510	0·018453	0·016616	0·014974	0·013504	0·012187	0·011008	0·009949	0·008999
15	0·017415	0·015538	0·013875	0·012400	0·011092	0·009929	0·008896	0·007977	0·007158	0·006428
16	0·013294	0·011771	0·010432	0·009254	0·008216	0·007301	0·006493	0·005780	0·005149	0·004591
17	0·010148	0·008918	0·007844	0·006906	0·006086	0·005368	0·004740	0·004188	0·003705	0·003280
18	0·007747	0·006756	0·005898	0·005154	0·004508	0·003947	0·003460	0·003035	0·002665	0·002343
19	0·005914	0·005118	0·004434	0·003846	0·003339	0·002902	0·002525	0·002199	0·001917	0·001673
20	0·004514	0·003877	0·003334	0·002870	0·002474	0·002134	0·001843	0·001594	0·001379	0·001195
21	0·003446	0·002937	0·002507	0·002142	0·001832	0·001569	0·001345	0·001155	0·000992	0·000854
22	0·002630	0·002225	0·001885	0·001598	0·001357	0·001154	0·000982	0·000837	0·000714	0·000610
23	0·002008	0·001686	0·001417	0·001193	0·001005	0·000848	0·000717	0·000606	0·000514	0·000436

24	0·001533	0·001277	0·001066	0·000890	0·000745	0·000624	0·000523	0·000439	0·000370	0·000311
25	0·001170	0·000968	0·000801	0·000664	0·000552	0·000459	0·000382	0·000318	0·000266	0·000222
26	0·000893	0·000733	0·000602	0·000496	0·000409	0·000337	0·000279	0·000231	0·000191	0·000159
27	0·000682	0·000555	0·000453	0·000370	0·000303	0·000248	0·000203	0·000167	0·000138	0·000113
28	0·000520	0·000421	0·000341	0·000276	0·000224	0·000182	0·000149	0·000121	0·990 4*	0·810 4*
29	0·000397	0·000319	0·000256	0·000206	0·000166	0·000134	0·000108	0·878 4*	0·712 4	0·578 4
30	0·000303	0·000241	0·000193	0·000154	0·000123	0·986 4*	0·791 4*	0·636 4	0·512 4	0·413 4
31	0·000232	0·000183	0·000145	0·000115	0·911 4*	0·725 4	0·578 4	0·461 4	0·369 4	0·295 4
32	0·000177	0·000139	0·000109	0·856 4*	0·675 4	0·533 4	0·422 4	0·334 4	0·265 4	0·211 4
33	0·000135	0·000105	0·818 4*	0·639 4*	0·500 4	0·392 4	0·308 4	0·242 4	0·191 4	0·151 4
34	0·000103	0·795 4*	0·615 4	0·477 4	0·370 4	0·288 4	0·225 4	0·175 4	0·137 4	0·108 4
35	0·786 4*	0·602 4	0·463 4	0·356 4	0·274 4	0·212 4	0·164 4	0·127 4	0·987 5	0·768 5
36	0·600 4	0·456 4	0·348 4	0·266 4	0·203 4	0·156 4	0·120 4	0·921 5	0·710 5	0·549 5
37	0·458 4	0·346 4	0·262 4	0·198 4	0·151 4	0·115 4	0·874 5	0·668 5	0·511 5	0·392 5
38	0·350 4	0·262 4	0·197 4	0·148 4	0·112 4	0·842 5	0·638 5	0·484 5	0·368 5	0·280 5
39	0·267 4	0·198 4	0·148 4	0·110 4	0·826 5	0·619 5	0·465 5	0·351 5	0·264 5	0·200 5
40	0·204 4	0·150 4	0·111 4	0·824 5	0·612 5	0·455 5	0·340 5	0·254 5	0·190 5	0·143 5
41	0·156 4	0·114 4	0·836 5	0·615 5	0·453 5	0·355 5	0·248 5	0·184 5	0·137 5	0·102 5
42	0·119 4	0·863 5	0·628 5	0·459 5	0·336 5	0·246 5	0·181 5	0·133 5	0·985 6	0·729 6
43	0·906 5	0·654 5	0·472 5	0·342 5	0·249 5	0·181 5	0·132 5	0·966 6	0·709 6	0·521 6
44	0·692 5	0·495 5	0·355 5	0·255 5	0·184 5	0·133 5	0·964 6	0·700 6	0·510 6	0·372 6
45	0·528 5	0·375 5	0·267 5	0·191 5	0·136 5	0·979 6	0·704 6	0·508 6	0·367 6	0·266 6
46	0·403 5	0·284 5	0·201 5	0·142 5	0·101 5	0·720 6	0·514 6	0·368 6	0·264 6	0·190 6
47	0·308 5	0·215 5	0·151 5	0·106 5	0·749 6	0·529 6	0·375 6	0·266 6	0·190 6	0·136 6
48	0·235 5	0·163 5	0·114 5	0·792 6	0·555 6	0·389 6	0·274 6	0·193 6	0·137 6	0·968 7
49	0·179 5	0·124 5	0·854 6	0·591 6	0·411 6	0·286 6	0·200 6	0·140 6	0·982 7	0·691 7
50	0·137 5	0·936 6	0·642 6	0·441 6	0·304 6	0·210 6	0·146 6	0·101 6	0·707 7	0·494 7

* The final digit is the power of 10 by which the given tabular value has to be divided.

TABLE A *The present value of 1 (continued)* $v_{n|r} = (1 + r)^{-n}$

	PERCENTAGE									
YEAR	*41*	*42*	*43*	*44*	*45*	*46*	*47*	*48*	*49*	*50*
1	0·709220	0·704225	0·699301	0·694444	0·689655	0·684932	0·680272	0·675676	0·671141	0·666667
2	0·502993	0·495933	0·489021	0·482253	0·475624	0·469131	0·462770	0·456538	0·450430	0·444444
3	0·356732	0·349249	0·341973	0·334898	0·328017	0·321323	0·314810	0·308471	0·302302	0·296296
4	0·253002	0·245950	0·239142	0·232568	0·226218	0·220084	0·214156	0·208427	0·202887	0·197531
5	0·179434	0·173204	0·167232	0·161506	0·156013	0·150743	0·145684	0·140829	0·136166	0·131687
6	0·127258	0·121975	0·116946	0·112157	0·107595	0·103248	0·099105	0·095155	0·091387	0·087791
7	0·090254	0·085898	0·081780	0·077887	0·074203	0·070718	0·067418	0·064294	0·061333	0·058528
8	0·064010	0·060491	0·057189	0·054088	0·051175	0·048437	0·045863	0·043442	0·041163	0·039018
9	0·045397	0·042600	0·039992	0·037561	0·035293	0·033176	0·031199	0·029352	0·027626	0·026012
10	0·032197	0·030000	0·027967	0·026084	0·024340	0·022723	0·021224	0·019833	0·018541	0·017342
11	0·022834	0·021127	0·019557	0·018114	0·016786	0·015564	0·014438	0·013401	0·012444	0·011561
12	0·016195	0·014878	0·013676	0·012579	0·011577	0·010660	0·009822	0·009054	0·008352	0·007707
13	0·011486	0·010477	0·009564	0·008735	0·007984	0·007302	0·006682	0·006118	0·005605	0·005138
14	0·008146	0·007378	0·006688	0·006066	0·005506	0·005001	0·004545	0·004134	0·003762	0·003425
15	0·005777	0·005196	0·004677	0·004213	0·003797	0·003425	0·003092	0·002793	0·002525	0·002284
16	0·004097	0·003659	0·003271	0·002926	0·002619	0·002346	0·002103	0·001887	0·001694	0·001522
17	0·002906	0·002577	0·002287	0·002032	0·001806	0·001607	0·001431	0·001275	0·001137	0·001015
18	0·002061	0·001815	0·001599	0·001411	0·001246	0·001101	0·000973	0·000862	0·000763	0·000677
19	0·001462	0·001278	0·001118	0·000980	0·000859	0·000754	0·000662	0·000582	0·000512	0·000451
20	0·001037	0·000900	0·000782	0·000680	0·000592	0·000516	0·000450	0·000393	0·000344	0·000301
21	0·000735	0·000634	0·000547	0·000472	0·000409	0·000354	0·000306	0·000266	0·000231	0·000200
22	0·000521	0·000446	0·000382	0·000328	0·000282	0·000242	0·000208	0·000180	0·000155	0·000134
23	0·000370	0·000314	0·000267	0·000228	0·000194	0·000166	0·000142	0·000121	0·000104	0·891 4*

24	0·000262		0·000221		0·000187		0·000158		0·000134		0·000114		0·965	4*	0·820	4*	0·697	4*	0·594	4
25	0·000186		0·000156		0·000131		0·000110		0·924	4*	0·778	4*	0·656	4	0·554	4	0·468	4	0·396	4
26	0·000132		0·000110		0·915	4*	0·763	4*	0·637	4	0·533	4	0·446	4	0·374	4	0·314	4	0·264	4
27	0·936	4*	0·773	4*	0·640	4	0·530	4	0·440	4	0·365	4	0·304	4	0·253	4	0·211	4	0·176	4
28	0·664	4	0·544	4	0·447	4	0·368	4	0·303	4	0·250	4	0·207	4	0·171	4	0·142	4	0·117	4
29	0·471	4	0·383	4	0·313	4	0·256	4	0·209	4	0·171	4	0·141	4	0·115	4	0·950	5	0·782	5
30	0·334	4	0·270	4	0·219	4	0·177	4	0·144	4	0·117	4	0·956	5	0·780	5	0·637	5	0·522	5
31	0·237	4	0·190	4	0·153	4	0·123	4	0·994	5	0·804	5	0·650	5	0·527	5	0·428	5	0·348	5
32	0·168	4	0·134	4	0·107	4	0·856	5	0·686	5	0·550	5	0·442	5	0·356	5	0·287	5	0·232	5
33	0·119	4	0·943	5	0·748	5	0·594	5	0·473	5	0·377	5	0·301	5	0·241	5	0·193	5	0·155	5
34	0·844	5	0·664	5	0·523	5	0·413	5	0·326	5	0·258	5	0·205	5	0·163	5	0·129	5	0·103	5
35	0·599	5	0·468	5	0·366	5	0·287	5	0·225	5	0·177	5	0·139	5	0·110	5	0·868	6	0·687	6
36	0·425	5	0·329	5	0·256	5	0·199	5	0·155	5	0·121	5	0·947	6	0·742	6	0·582	6	0·458	6
37	0·301	5	0·232	5	0·179	5	0·138	5	0·107	5	0·830	6	0·645	6	0·502	6	0·391	6	0·305	6
38	0·214	5	0·163	5	0·125	5	0·960	6	0·738	6	0·568	6	0·438	6	0·339	6	0·262	6	0·203	6
39	0·152	5	0·115	5	0·875	6	0·667	6	0·509	6	0·389	6	0·298	6	0·229	6	0·176	6	0·136	6
40	0·107	5	0·810	6	0·612	6	0·463	6	0·351	6	0·267	6	0·203	6	0·155	6	0·118	6	0·904	7
41	0·762	6	0·570	6	0·428	6	0·321	6	0·242	6	0·183	6	0·138	6	0·105	6	0·793	7	0·603	7
42	0·541	6	0·402	6	0·299	6	0·223	6	0·167	6	0·125	6	0·939	7	0·706	7	0·532	7	0·402	7
43	0·383	6	0·283	6	0·209	6	0·155	6	0·115	6	0·857	7	0·639	7	0·477	7	0·357	7	0·268	7
44	0·272	6	0·199	6	0·146	6	0·108	6	0·794	7	0·587	7	0·435	7	0·322	7	0·240	7	0·179	7
45	0·193	6	0·140	6	0·102	6	0·748	7	0·548	7	0·402	7	0·296	7	0·218	7	0·161	7	0·119	7
46	0·137	6	0·988	7	0·715	7	0·519	7	0·378	7	0·275	7	0·201	7	0·147	7	0·108	7	0·794	8
47	0·970	7	0·696	7	0·500	7	0·361	7	0·260	7	0·189	7	0·137	7	0·995	8	0·725	8	0·529	8
48	0·688	7	0·490	7	0·350	7	0·250	7	0·180	7	0·129	7	0·931	8	0·672	8	0·486	8	0·353	8
49	0·488	7	0·345	7	0·245	7	0·174	7	0·124	7	0·885	8	0·633	8	0·454	8	0·326	8	0·235	8
50	0·346	7	0·243	7	0·171	7	0·121	7	0·854	8	0·606	8	0·431	8	0·307	8	0·219	8	0·157	8

* The final digit is the power of 10 by which the given tabular value has to be divided.

TABLE B *The present value of 1 per annum*

$$a_{n|r} = \frac{1 - (1 + r)^{-n}}{r}$$

	PERCENTAGE									
YEAR	*1*	*2*	*3*	*4*	*5*	*6*	*7*	*8*	*9*	*10*
1	0·990099	0·980392	0·970874	0·961538	0·952381	0·943396	0·934579	0·925926	0·917431	0·909091
2	1·97040	1·94156	1·91347	1·88609	1·85941	1·83339	1·80802	1·78326	1·75911	1·73554
3	2·94099	2·88388	2·82861	2·77509	2·72325	2·67301	2·62432	2·57710	2·53129	2·48685
4	3·90197	3·80773	3·71710	3·62990	3·54595	3·46511	3·38721	3·31213	3·23972	3·16987
5	4·85343	4·71346	4·57971	4·45182	4·32948	4·21236	4·10020	3·99271	3·88965	3·79079
6	5·79548	5·60143	5·41719	5·24214	5·07569	4·91732	4·76654	4·62288	4·48592	4·35526
7	6·72819	6·47199	6·23028	6·00205	5·78637	5·58238	5·38929	5·20637	5·03295	4·86842
8	7·65168	7·32548	7·01969	6·73274	6·46321	6·20979	5·97130	5·74664	5·53482	5·33493
9	8·56602	8·16224	7·78611	7·43533	7·10782	6·80169	6·51523	6·24689	5·99525	5·75902
10	9·47130	8·98259	8·53020	8·11090	7·72173	7·36009	7·02358	6·71008	6·41766	6·14457
11	10·3676	9·78685	9·25262	8·76048	8·30641	7·88687	7·49867	7·13896	6·80519	6·49506
12	11·2551	10·5753	9·95400	9·38507	8·86325	8·38384	7·94269	7·53608	7·16073	6·81369
13	12·1337	11·3484	10·6350	9·98565	9·39357	8·85268	8·35765	7·90378	7·48690	7·10336
14	13·0037	12·1062	11·2961	10·5631	9·89864	9·29498	8·74547	8·24424	7·78615	7·36669
15	13·8651	12·8493	11·9379	11·1184	10·3797	9·71225	9·10791	8·55948	8·06069	7·60608
16	14·7179	13·5777	12·5611	11·6523	10·8378	10·1059	9·44665	8·85137	8·31256	7·82371
17	15·5623	14·2919	13·1661	12·1657	11·2741	10·4773	9·76322	9·12164	8·54363	8·02155
18	16·3983	14·9920	13·7535	12·6593	11·6896	10·8276	19·0591	9·37189	8·75563	8·20141
19	17·2260	15·6785	14·3238	13·1339	12·0853	11·1581	10·3356	9·60360	8·95011	8·36492
20	18·0456	16·3514	14·8775	13·5903	12·4622	11·4699	10·5940	9·81815	9·12855	8·51356
21	18·8570	17·0112	15·4150	14·0292	12·8212	11·7641	10·8355	10·0168	9·29224	8·64869
22	19·6604	17·6580	15·9369	14·4511	13·1630	12·0416	11·0612	10·2007	9·44243	8·77154

23	20·4558	18·2922	16·4436	14·8568	13·4886	12·3034	11·2722	10·3711	9·58021	8·88322
24	21·2434	18·9139	16·9355	15·2470	13·7986	12·5504	11·4693	10·5288	9·70661	8·98474
25	22·0232	19·5235	17·4131	15·6221	14·0939	12·7834	11·6536	10·6748	9·82258	9·07704
26	22·7952	20·1210	17·8768	15·9828	14·3752	13·0032	11·8258	10·8100	9·92897	9·16095
27	23·5596	20·7069	18·3270	16·3296	14·6430	13·2105	11·9867	10·9352	10·0266	9·23722
28	24·3164	21·2813	18·7641	16·6631	14·8981	13·4062	12·1371	11·0511	10·1161	9·30657
29	25·0658	21·8444	19·1885	16·9837	15·1411	13·5907	12·2777	11·1584	10·1983	9·36961
30	25·8077	22·3965	19·6004	17·2920	15·3725	13·7648	12·4090	11·2578	10·2737	9·42691
31	26·5423	22·9377	20·0004	17·5885	15·5928	13·9291	12·5318	11·3498	10·3428	9·47901
32	27·2696	23·4683	20·3888	17·8736	15·8027	14·0840	12·6466	11·4350	10·4062	9·52638
33	27·9897	23·9886	20·7658	18·1476	16·0025	14·2302	12·7538	11·5139	10·4644	9·56943
34	28·7027	24·4986	21·1318	18·4112	16·1929	14·3681	12·8540	11·5869	10·5178	9·60857
35	29·4086	24·9986	21·4872	18·6646	16·3742	14·4982	12·9477	11·6546	10·5668	9·64416
36	30·1075	25·4888	21·8323	18·9083	16·5469	14·6210	13·0352	11·7172	10·6118	9·67651
37	30·7995	25·9695	22·1672	19·1426	16·7113	14·7368	13·1170	11·7752	10·6530	9·70592
38	31·4847	26·4406	22·4925	19·3679	16·8679	14·8460	13·1935	11·8289	10·6908	9·73265
39	32·1630	26·9026	22·8082	19·5845	17·0170	14·9491	13·2649	11·8786	10·7255	9·75696
40	32·8347	27·3555	23·1148	19·7928	17·1591	15·0463	13·3317	11·9246	10·7574	9·77905
41	33·4997	27·7995	23·4124	19·9931	17·2944	15·1380	13·3941	11·9672	10·7866	9·79914
42	34·1581	28·2348	23·7014	20·1856	17·4232	15·2245	13·4524	12·0067	10·8134	9·81740
43	34·8100	28·6616	23·9819	20·3708	17·5459	15·3062	13·5070	12·0432	10·8380	9·83400
44	35·4555	29·0800	24·2543	20·5488	17·6628	15·3832	13·5579	12·0771	10·8605	9·84909
45	36·0945	29·4902	24·5187	20·7200	17·7741	15·4558	13·6055	12·1084	10·8812	9·86281
46	36·7272	29·8923	24·7754	20·8847	17·8801	15·5244	13·6500	12·1374	10·9002	9·87528
47	37·3537	30·2866	25·0247	21·0429	17·9810	15·5890	13·6916	12·1643	10·9176	9·88662
48	37·9740	30·6731	25·2667	21·1951	18·0772	15·6500	13·7305	12·1891	10·9336	9·89693
49	38·5881	31·0521	25·5017	21·3415	18·1687	15·7076	13·7668	12·2122	10·9482	9·90630
50	39·1961	31·4236	25·7298	21·4822	18·2559	15·7619	13·8007	12·2335	10·9617	9·91481

TABLE B *The present value of 1 per annum (continued)*

$$a_{n|r} = \frac{1 - (1 + r)^{-n}}{r}$$

	PERCENTAGE									
YEAR	*11*	*12*	*13*	*14*	*15*	*16*	*17*	*18*	*19*	*20*
1	0·900901	0·892857	0·884956	0·877193	0·869565	0·862069	0·854701	0·847458	0·840336	0·833333
2	1·71252	1·69005	1·66810	1·64666	1·62571	1·60523	1·58521	1·56564	1·54650	1·52778
3	2·44371	2·40183	2·36115	2·32163	2·28323	2·24589	2·20958	2·17427	2·13992	2·10648
4	3·10245	3·03735	2·97447	2·91371	2·85498	2·79818	2·74324	2·69006	2·63859	2·58873
5	3·69590	3·60478	3·51723	3·43308	3·35216	3·27429	3·19935	3·12717	3·05763	2·99061
6	4·23054	4·11141	3·99755	3·88867	3·78448	3·68474	3·58918	3·49760	3·40978	3·32551
7	4·71220	4·56376	4·42261	4·28830	4·16042	4·03857	3·92238	3·81153	3·70570	3·60459
8	5·14612	4·96764	4·79877	4·63886	4·48732	4·34359	4·20716	4·07757	3·95437	3·83716
9	5·53705	5·32825	5·13166	4·94637	4·77158	4·60654	4·45057	4·30302	4·16333	4·03097
10	5·88923	5·65022	5·42624	5·21612	5·01877	4·83323	4·65860	4·49409	4·33893	4·19247
11	6·20652	5·93770	5·68694	5·45273	5·23371	5·02864	4·83641	4·65601	4·48650	4·32706
12	6·49236	6·19437	5·91765	5·66029	5·42062	5·19711	4·98839	4·79322	4·61050	4·43922
13	6·74987	6·42355	6·12181	5·84236	5·58315	5·34233	5·11828	4·90951	4·71471	4·53268
14	6·98187	6·62817	6·30249	6·00207	5·72448	5·46753	5·22930	5·00806	4·80228	4·61057
15	7·19087	6·81086	6·46238	6·14217	5·84737	5·57546	5·32419	5·09158	4·87586	4·67547
16	7·37916	6·97399	6·60388	6·26506	5·95423	5·66850	5·40529	5·16235	4·93770	4·72956
17	7·54879	7·11963	6·72909	6·37286	6·04716	5·74870	5·47461	5·22233	4·98966	4·77463
18	7·70162	7·24967	6·83991	6·46742	6·12797	5·81785	5·53385	5·27316	5·03333	4·81219
19	7·83929	7·36578	6·93797	6·55037	6·19823	5·87746	5·58449	5·31624	5·07003	4·84350
20	7·96333	7·46944	7·02475	6·62313	6·25933	5·92884	5·62777	5·35275	5·10086	4·86958
21	8·07507	7·56200	7·10155	6·68696	6·31246	5·97314	5·66476	5·38368	5·12677	4·89132
22	8·17574	7·64465	7·16951	6·74294	6·35866	6·01133	5·69637	5·40990	5·14855	4·90943

23	8·26643	7·71843	7·22966	6·79206	6·39884	6·04425	5·72340	5·43212	5·16685	4·92453
24	8·34814	7·78432	7·28288	6·83514	6·43377	6·07263	5·74649	5·45095	5·18223	4·93710
25	8·42174	7·84314	7·32998	6·87293	6·46415	6·09709	5·76623	5·46691	5·19515	4·94759
26	8·48806	7·89566	7·37167	6·90608	6·49056	6·11818	5·78311	5·48043	5·20601	4·95632
27	8·54780	7·94255	7·40856	6·93515	6·51353	6·13636	5·79753	5·49189	5·21513	4·96360
28	8·60162	7·98442	7·44120	6·96066	6·53351	6·15204	5·80985	5·50160	5·22280	4·96967
29	8·65011	8·02181	7·47009	6·98304	6·55088	6·16555	5·82039	5·50983	5·22924	4·97472
30	8·69379	8·05518	7·49565	7·00266	6·56598	6·17720	5·82939	5·51681	5·23466	4·97894
31	8·73315	8·08499	7·51828	7·01988	6·57911	6·18724	5·83709	5·52272	5·23921	4·98245
32	8·76860	8·11159	7·53830	7·03498	6·59053	6·19590	5·84366	5·52773	5·24303	4·98537
33	8·80054	8·13535	7·55602	7·04823	6·60046	6·20336	5·84928	5·53197	5·24625	4·98781
34	8·82932	8·15656	7·57170	7·05985	6·60910	6·20979	5·85409	5·53557	5·24895	4·98984
35	8·85524	8·17550	7·58557	7·07005	6·61661	6·21534	5·85820	5·53862	5·25122	4·99154
36	8·87859	8·19241	7·59785	7·07899	6·62314	6·22012	5·86171	5·54120	5·25312	4·99295
37	8·89963	8·20751	7·60872	7·08683	6·62881	6·22424	5·86471	5·54339	5·25472	4·99412
38	8·91859	8·22099	7·61833	7·09371	6·63375	6·22779	5·86727	5·54525	5·25607	4·99510
39	8·93567	8·23303	7·62684	7·09975	6·63805	6·23086	5·86946	5·54682	5·25720	4·99592
40	8·95105	8·24378	7·63438	7·10504	6·64178	6·23350	5·87133	5·54815	5·25815	4·99660
41	8·96491	8·25337	7·64104	7·10969	6·64502	6·23577	5·87294	5·54928	5·25895	4·99717
42	8·97740	8·26194	7·64694	7·11376	6·64785	6·23774	5·87430	5·55024	5·25962	4·99764
43	8·98865	8·26959	7·65216	7·11733	6·65030	6·23943	5·87547	5·55105	5·26019	4·99803
44	8·99878	8·27642	7·65678	7·12047	6·65244	6·24089	5·87647	5·55174	5·26066	4·99836
45	9·00791	8·28252	7·66086	7·12322	6·65429	6·24214	5·87733	5·55232	5·26106	4·99863
46	9·01614	8·28796	7·66448	7·12563	6·65591	6·24323	5·87806	5·55281	5·26140	4·99886
47	9·02355	8·29282	7·66768	7·12774	6·65731	6·24416	5·87868	5·55323	5·26168	4·99905
48	9·03022	8·29716	7·67052	7·12960	6·65853	6·24497	5·87922	5·55359	5·26191	4·99921
49	9·03624	8·30104	7·67302	7·13123	6·65959	6·24566	5·87967	5·55389	5·26211	4·99934
50	9·04165	8·30450	7·67524	7·13266	6·66051	6·24626	5·88006	5·55414	5·26228	4·99945

TABLE B *The present value of 1 per annum (continued)*

$$a_{n|r} = \frac{1 - (1 + r)^{-n}}{r}$$

YEAR	PERCENTAGE 21	22	23	24	25	26	27	28	29	30
1	0·826466	0·819672	0·813008	0·806452	0·800000	0·793651	0·787402	0·781250	0·775194	0·769231
2	1·50946	1·49153	1·47399	1·45682	1·44000	1·42353	1·40740	1·39160	1·37612	1·36095
3	2·07393	2·04224	2·01137	1·98130	1·95200	1·92344	1·89559	1·86844	1·84195	1·81611
4	2·54044	2·49364	2·44827	2·40428	2·36160	2·32019	2·27999	2·24097	2·20306	2·16624
5	2·92598	2·86364	2·80347	2·74538	2·68928	2·63507	2·58267	2·53201	2·48300	2·43557
6	3·24462	3·16692	3·09225	3·02047	2·95142	2·88498	2·82100	2·75938	2·70000	2·64275
7	3·50795	3·41551	3·32704	3·24232	3·16114	3·08331	3·00866	2·93702	2·86821	2·80211
8	3·72558	3·61927	3·51792	3·42122	3·32891	3·24073	3·15643	3·07579	2·99862	2·92470
9	3·90543	3·78628	3·67310	3·56550	3·46313	3·36566	3·27278	3·18421	3·09970	3·01900
10	4·05408	3·92318	3·79927	3·68186	3·57050	3·46481	3·36439	3·26892	3·17806	3·09154
11	4·17692	4·03540	3·90185	3·77569	3·65640	3·54350	3·43653	3·33509	3·23881	3·14734
12	4·27845	4·12737	3·98524	3·85136	3·72512	3·60595	3·49333	3·38679	3·28590	3·19026
13	4·36235	4·20277	4·05304	3·91239	3·78010	3·65552	3·53806	3·42718	3·32240	3·22328
14	4·43170	4·26456	4·10816	3·96160	3·82408	3·69485	3·57327	3·45873	3·35070	3·24867
15	4·48901	4·31522	4·15298	4·00129	3·85926	3·72607	3·60100	3·48339	3·37264	3·26821
16	4·53637	4·35673	4·18941	4·03330	3·88741	3·75085	3·62284	3·50265	3·38964	3·28324
17	4·57551	4·39077	4·21904	4·05911	3·90993	3·77052	3·64003	3·51769	3·40282	3·29480
18	4·60786	4·41866	4·24312	4·07993	3·92794	3·78613	3·65357	3·52945	3·41304	3·30369
19	4·63460	4·44152	4·26270	4·09672	3·94235	3·79851	3·66422	3·53863	3·42096	3·31053
20	4·65669	4·46027	4·27862	4·11026	3·95388	3·80834	3·67262	3·54580	3·42710	3·31579
21	4·67495	4·47563	4·29156	4·12117	3·96311	3·81615	3·67923	3·55141	3·43186	3·31984
22	4·69004	4·48822	4·30208	4·12998	3·97049	3·82234	3·68443	3·55579	3·43555	3·32296

23	4·70251	4·49854	4·31063	4·13708	3·97639	3·82725	3·68853	3·55921	3·43841	3·32535
24	4·71282	4·50700	4·31759	4·14281	3·98111	3·83115	3·69175	3·56188	3·44063	3·32719
25	4·72134	4·51393	4·32324	4·14742	3·98489	3·83425	3·69429	3·56397	3·44235	3·32861
26	4·72838	4·51962	4·32784	4·15115	3·98791	3·83670	3·69630	3·56560	3·44368	3·32970
27	4·73420	4·52428	4·33158	4·15415	3·99033	3·83865	3·69787	3·56688	3·44471	3·33054
28	4·73901	4·52810	4·33462	4·15657	3·99226	3·84020	3·69911	3·56787	3·44551	3·33118
29	4·74298	4·53123	4·33709	4·15853	3·99381	3·84143	3·70009	3·56865	3·44614	3·33168
30	4·74627	4·53379	4·33909	4·16010	3·99505	3·84240	3·70086	3·56926	3·44662	3·33206
31	4·74898	4·53590	4·34073	4·16137	3·99604	3·84318	3·70146	3·56973	3·44699	3·33235
32	4·75122	4·53762	4·34205	4·16240	3·99683	3·84379	3·70194	3·57010	3·44728	3·33258
33	4·75308	4·53903	4·34313	4·16322	3·99746	3·84428	3·70231	3·57039	3·44750	3·33275
34	4·75461	4·54019	4·34401	4·16389	3·99797	3·84467	3·70261	3·57062	3·44768	3·33289
35	4·75588	4·54114	4·34472	4·16443	3·99838	3·84497	3·70284	3·57080	3·44781	3·33299
36	4·75692	4·54192	4·34530	4·16486	3·99870	3·84522	3·70302	3·57094	3·44792	3·33307
37	4·75779	4·54256	4·34578	4·16521	3·99896	3·84541	3·70317	3·57104	3·44800	3·33313
38	4·75850	5·54308	4·34616	4·16549	3·99917	3·84556	3·70328	3·57113	3·44806	3·33318
39	4·75909	4·54351	4·34647	4·16572	3·99934	3·84569	3·70337	3·57119	3·44811	3·33321
40	4·75958	4·54386	4·34672	4·16590	3·99947	3·84578	3·70344	3·57124	3·44815	3·33324
41	4·75998	4·54415	4·34693	4·16605	3·99957	3·84586	3·70350	3·57128	3·44818	3·33326
42	4·76032	4·54438	4·34710	4·16617	3·99966	3·94592	3·70354	3·57132	3·44820	3·33328
43	4·76059	4·54458	4·34723	4·16627	3·99973	3·84597	3·70358	3·57134	3·44822	3·33329
44	4·76082	4·54473	4·34734	4·16634	3·99978	3·84601	3·70360	3·57136	3·44823	3·33330
45	4·76101	4·54486	4·34743	4·16641	3·99983	3·84604	3·70362	3·57138	3·44824	3·33331
46	4·76116	4·54497	4·34751	4·16646	3·99986	3·84606	3·70364	3·57139	3·44825	3·33331
47	4·76129	5·54506	4·34757	4·16650	3·99989	3·84608	3·70365	3·57140	3·44825	3·33332
48	4·76140	4·54513	4·34762	4·16653	3·99991	3·84610	3·70367	3·57140	3·44826	3·33332
49	4·76149	4·54519	4·34766	4·16656	3·99993	3·84611	3·70367	3·57141	3·44826	3·33332
50	4·76156	4·54524	4·34769	4·16658	3·99994	3·84612	3·70368	3·57141	3·44827	3·33333

TABLE B *The present value of 1 per annum (continued)*

$$a_{n|r} = \frac{1 - (1 + r)^{-n}}{r}$$

	PERCENTAGE									
YEAR	*31*	*32*	*33*	*34*	*35*	*36*	*37*	*38*	*39*	*40*
1	0·763359	0·757576	0·751880	0·746269	0·740741	0·735294	0·729927	0·724638	0·719424	0·714286
2	1·34608	1·33150	1·31720	1·30319	1·28944	1·27595	1·26272	1·24974	1·23700	1·22449
3	1·79090	1·76629	1·74226	1·71880	1·69588	1·67349	1·65162	1·63024	1·60935	1·58892
4	2·13046	2·09567	2·06185	2·02895	1·99695	1·96580	1·93549	1·90597	1·87723	1·84923
5	2·38966	2·34521	2·30214	2·26041	2·21996	2·18074	2·14269	2·10578	2·06995	2·03516
6	2·58753	2·53425	2·48281	2·43314	2·38516	2·33878	2·29394	2·25056	2·20860	2·16797
7	2·73857	2·67746	2·61866	2·56205	2·50752	2·45498	2·40433	2·35548	2·30834	2·26284
8	2·85387	2·78595	2·72079	2·65824	2·59817	2·54043	2·48491	2·43151	2·38010	2·33060
9	2·94189	2·86815	2·79759	2·73003	2·66531	2·60326	2·54373	2·48660	2·43173	2·37900
10	3·00907	2·93041	2·85533	2·78361	2·71504	2·64945	2·58667	2·52652	2·46887	2·41357
11	3·06036	2·97759	2·89874	2·82359	2·75188	2·68342	2·61800	2·55545	2·49559	2·43826
12	3·09951	2·01332	2·93139	2·85342	2·77917	2·70840	2·64088	2·57641	2·51481	2·45590
13	3·12940	3·04040	2·95593	2·87569	2·79939	2·72676	2·65758	2·59160	2·52864	2·46850
14	3·15221	3·06091	2·97438	2·89231	2·81436	2·74027	2·66976	2·60261	2·53859	2·47750
15	3·16963	3·07644	2·98826	2·90471	2·82545	2·75020	2·67866	2·61059	2·54575	2·48393
16	3·18292	3·08822	2·99869	2·91396	2·83367	2·75750	2·68515	2·61637	2·55090	2·48852
17	3·19307	3·09713	3·00653	2·92087	2·83975	2·76287	2·68989	2·62056	2·55460	2·49180
18	3·20082	3·10389	3·01243	2·92602	2·84426	2·76681	2·69335	2·62359	2·55727	2·49414
19	3·20673	3·10901	3·01687	2·92986	2·84760	2·76972	2·69588	2·62579	2·55919	2·49582
20	3·21124	3·11288	3·02020	2·93273	2·85008	2·77185	2·69772	2·62738	2·56057	2·49701
21	3·21469	3·11582	3·02271	2·93488	2·85191	2·77342	2·69907	2·62854	2·56156	2·49787
22	3·21732	3·11805	3·02459	2·93648	2·85327	2·77457	2·70005	2·62938	2·56227	2·49848

23	3·21933	3·11973	3·02601	2·93767	2·85427	2·77542	2·70077	2·62998	2·56279	2·49891
24	3·22086	3·12101	3·02707	2·93856	2·85502	2·77604	2·70129	2·63042	2·56316	2·49922
25	3·22203	3·12198	3·02788	2·93922	2·85557	2·77650	2·70167	2·63074	2·56342	2·49944
26	3·22293	3·12271	3·02848	2·93972	2·85598	2·77684	2·70195	2·63097	2·56361	2·49960
27	3·22361	3·12326	3·02893	2·94009	2·85628	2·77709	2·70215	2·63114	2·56375	2·49972
28	3·22413	3·12369	3·02927	2·94036	2·85650	2·77727	2·70230	2·63126	2·56385	2·49980
29	3·22452	3·12400	3·02953	2·94057	2·85667	2·77741	2·70241	2·63135	2·56392	2·49986
30	3·22483	3·12425	3·02972	2·94072	2·85679	2·77750	2·70249	2·63141	2·56397	2·49990
31	3·22506	3·12443	3·02986	2·94084	2·85688	2·77758	2·70255	2·63146	2·56401	2·49993
32	3·22524	3·12457	3·02997	2·94092	2·85695	2·77763	2·70259	2·63149	2·56403	2·49995
33	3·22537	3·12467	3·03006	2·94099	2·85700	2·77767	2·70262	2·63152	2·56405	2·49996
34	3·22547	3·12475	3·03012	2·94104	2·85704	2·77770	2·70264	2·63153	2·56407	2·49997
35	3·22555	3·12481	3·03016	2·94107	2·85706	2·77772	2·70266	2·63155	2·56408	2·49998
36	3·22561	3·12486	3·03020	2·94110	2·85708	2·77773	2·70267	2·63155	2·56408	2·49999
37	3·22566	3·12489	3·03022	2·94112	2·85710	2·77775	2·70268	2·63156	2·56409	2·49999
38	3·22569	3·12492	3·03024	2·94113	2·85711	2·77775	2·70269	2·63157	2·56409	2·49999
39	3·22572	3·12494	3·03026	2·94114	2·85712	2·77776	2·70269	2·63157	2·56410	2·50000
40	3·22574	3·12495	3·03027	2·94115	2·85713	2·77777	2·70269	2·63157	2·56410	2·50000
41	3·22576	3·12496	3·03028	2·94116	2·85713	2·77777	2·70270	2·63157	2·56410	2·50000
42	3·22577	3·12497	3·03028	2·94116	2·85713	2·77777	2·70270	2·63158	2·56410	2·50000
43	3·22578	3·12498	3·03029	2·94117	2·85714	2·77777	2·70270	2·63158	2·56410	2·50000
44	3·22578	3·12498	3·03029	2·94117	2·85714	2·77777	2·70270	2·63158	2·56410	2·50000
45	3·22579	3·12499	3·03029	2·94117	2·85714	2·77778	2·70270	2·63158	2·56410	2·50000
46	3·22579	3·12499	3·03030	2·94117	2·85714	2·77778	2·70270	2·63158	2·56410	2·50000
47	3·22580	3·12499	3·03030	2·94117	2·85714	2·77778	2·70270	2·63158	2·56410	2·50000
48	3·22580	3·12499	3·03030	2·94117	2·85714	2·77778	2·70270	2·63158	2·56410	2·50000
49	3·22580	3·12500	3·03030	2·94117	2·85714	2·77778	2·70270	2·63158	2·56410	2·50000
50	3·22580	3·12500	3·03030	2·94118	2·85714	2·77778	2·70270	2·63158	2·56410	2·50000

TABLE B *The present value of 1 per annum (continued)* $a_{n|r} = \frac{1 - (1 + r)^{-n}}{r}$

	PERCENTAGE									
YEAR	*41*	*42*	*43*	*44*	*45*	*46*	*47*	*48*	*49*	*50*
1	0·709220	0·704225	0·699301	0·694444	0·689655	0·684932	0·680272	0·675676	0·671141	0·666667
2	1·21221	1·20016	1·18832	1·17670	1·16528	1·15406	1·14304	1·13221	1·12157	1·11111
3	1·56895	1·54941	1·53030	1·51160	1·49330	1·47539	1·45785	1·44068	1·42387	1·40741
4	1·82195	1·79536	1·76944	1·74416	1·71951	1·69547	1·67201	1·64911	1·62676	1·60494
5	2·00138	1·96856	1·93667	1·90567	1·87553	1·84621	1·81769	1·78994	1·76293	1·73663
6	2·12864	2·09054	2·05361	2·01783	1·98312	1·94946	1·91680	1·88509	1·85431	1·82442
7	2·21889	2·17643	2·13540	2·09571	2·05733	2·02018	1·98422	1·94939	1·91565	1·88294
8	2·28290	2·23693	2·19258	2·14980	2·10850	2·06862	2·03008	1·99283	1·95681	1·92196
9	2·32830	2·27952	2·23258	2·18736	2·14379	2·10179	2·06128	2·02218	1·98444	1·94798
10	2·36050	2·30952	2·26054	2·21345	2·16813	2·12451	2·08250	2·04202	2·00298	1·96532
11	2·38333	2·33065	2·28010	2·23156	2·18492	2·14008	2·09694	2·05542	2·01542	1·97688
12	2·39953	2·34553	2·29378	2·24414	2·19650	1·15074	2·10676	2·06447	2·02377	1·98459
13	2·41101	2·34601	2·30334	2·25287	2·20448	2·15804	2·11344	2·07059	2·02938	1·98972
14	2·41916	2·36338	2·31003	2·25894	2·20999	2·16304	1·11799	2·07472	2·03314	1·99315
15	2·42493	2·36858	2·31470	2·26315	2·21378	2·16647	2·12108	2·07751	2·03566	1·99543
16	2·42903	2·37224	2·31798	2·26608	2·21640	2·16881	2·12318	2·07940	2·03736	1·99696
17	2·43194	2·37482	2·32026	2·26811	2·21821	2·17042	2·12462	2·08068	2·03850	1·99797
18	2·43400	2·37663	2·32186	2·26952	2·21945	2·17152	2·12559	2·08154	2·03926	1·99865
19	2·43546	2·37791	2·32298	2·27050	2·22031	2·17227	2·12625	2·08212	2·03977	1·99910
20	2·43650	2·37881	2·32376	2·27118	2·22091	2·17279	2·12670	2·08251	2·04011	1·99940
21	2·43723	2·37944	2·32431	2·27165	2·22131	2·17314	2·12701	2·08278	2·04035	1·99960
22	2·43775	2·37989	2·32469	2·27198	2·22160	2·17339	2·12722	2·08296	2·04050	1·99973

23	2·43812	2·38020	2·32496	2·27221	2·22179	2·17355	2·12736	2·08308	2·04060	1·99982
24	2·43838	2·38043	2·32515	2·27237	2·22192	2·17367	2·12745	2·08316	2·04067	1·99988
25	2·43857	2·38058	2·32528	2·27248	2·22202	2·17374	2·12752	2·08322	2·04072	1·99992
26	2·43870	2·38069	2·32537	2·27255	2·22208	2·17380	2·12756	2·08326	2·04075	1·99995
27	2·43880	2·38077	2·32543	2·27261	2·22212	2·17383	2·12759	2·08328	2·04077	1·99996
28	2·43886	2·38082	2·32548	2·27264	2·22215	2·17386	2·12762	2·08330	2·04079	1·99998
29	2·43891	2·38086	2·32551	2·27267	2·22218	2·17388	2·12763	2·08331	2·04080	1·99998
30	2·43894	2·38089	2·32553	2·27269	2·22219	2·17389	2·12764	2·08332	2·04080	1·99999
31	2·43897	2·38091	2·32555	2·27270	2·22220	2·17390	2·12765	2·08332	2·04081	1·99999
32	2·43898	2·38092	2·32556	2·27271	2·22221	2·17390	2·12765	2·08333	2·04081	2·00000
33	2·43900	2·38093	2·32556	2·27271	2·22221	2·17390	2·12765	2·08333	2·04081	2·00000
34	2·43900	2·38094	2·32557	2·27272	2·22221	2·17391	2·12766	2·08333	2·04081	2·00000
35	2·43901	2·38094	2·32557	2·27272	2·22222	2·17391	2·12766	2·08333	2·04081	2·00000
36	2·43901	2·38094	2·32558	2·27272	2·22222	2·17391	2·12766	2·08333	2·04082	2·00000
37	2·43902	2·38095	2·32558	2·27272	2·22222	2·17391	2·12766	2·08333	2·04082	2·00000
38	2·43902	2·38095	2·32558	2·27273	2·22222	2·17391	2·12766	2·08333	2·04082	2·00000
39	2·43902	2·38095	2·32558	2·27273	2·22222	2·17391	2·12766	2·08333	2·04082	2·00000
40	2·43902	2·38095	2·32558	2·27273	2·22222	2·17391	2·12766	2·09333	2·04082	2·00000
41	2·43902	2·38095	2·32558	2·27273	2·22222	2·17391	2·12766	2·08333	2·04082	2·00000
42	2·43902	2·38095	2·32558	2·27273	2·22222	2·17391	2·12766	2·08333	2·04082	2·00000
43	2·43902	2·38095	2·32558	2·27273	2·22222	2·17391	2·12766	2·08333	2·04082	2·00000
44	2·43902	2·38095	2·32558	2·27273	2·22222	2·17391	2·12766	2·08333	2·04082	2·00000
45	2·43902	2·38095	2·32558	2·27273	2·22222	2·17391	2·12766	2·08333	2·04082	2·00000
46	2·43902	2·38095	2·32558	2·27273	2·22222	2·17391	2·12766	2·08333	2·04082	2·00000
47	2·43902	2·38095	2·32558	2·27273	2·22222	2·17391	2·12766	2·07333	2·04082	2·00000
48	2·43902	2·38095	2·32558	2·27273	2·22222	2·17391	2·12766	2·08333	2·04082	2·00000
49	2·43902	2·38095	2·32558	2·27273	2·22222	2·17391	2·12766	2·08333	2·04082	2·00000
50	2·43902	2·38095	2·32558	2·27273	2·22222	2·17391	2·12766	2·08333	2·04082	2·00000

TABLE C *The amount of 1 per annum*

$$s_{n|r} = \frac{(1 + r)^n - 1}{r}$$

YEAR	PERCENTAGE 1	2	3	4	5	6	7	8	9	10
1	1·00000	1·00000	1·00000	1·00000	1·00000	1·00000	1·00000	1·00000	1·00000	1·00000
2	2·01000	2·02000	2·03000	2·04000	2·05000	2·06000	2·07000	2·08000	2·09000	2·10000
3	3·03010	3·06040	3·09090	3·12160	3·15250	3·18360	3·21490	3·24640	3·27810	3·31000
4	4·06040	4·12161	4·18363	4·24646	4·31012	4·37462	4·43994	4·50611	4·57313	4·64100
5	5·10101	5·20404	5·30914	5·41632	5·52563	5·63709	5·75074	5·86660	5·98471	6·10510
6	6·15202	6·30812	6·46841	6·63298	6·80191	6·97532	7·15329	7·33593	7·52333	7·71561
7	7·21354	7·43428	7·66246	7·89829	8·14201	8·39384	8·65402	8·92280	9·20043	9·48717
8	8·28567	8·58297	8·89234	9·21423	9·54911	9·89747	10·2598	10·6366	11·0285	11·4359
9	9·36853	9·75463	10·1591	10·5828	11·0266	11·4913	11·9780	12·4876	13·0210	13·5795
10	10·4622	10·9497	11·4639	12·0061	12·5779	13·1808	13·8164	14·4866	15·1929	15·9374
11	11·5668	12·1687	12·8078	13·4864	14·2068	14·9716	15·7836	16·6455	17·5603	18·5312
12	12·6825	13·4121	14·1920	15·0258	15·9171	16·8699	17·8885	18·9771	20·1407	21·3843
13	13·8093	14·6803	15·6178	16·6268	17·7130	18·8821	20·1406	21·4953	22·9534	24·5227
14	14·9474	15·9739	17·0863	18·2919	19·5986	21·0151	22·5505	24·2149	26·0192	27·9750
15	16·0969	17·2934	18·5989	20·0236	21·5786	23·2760	25·1290	27·1521	29·3609	31·7725
16	17·2579	18·6393	20·1569	21·8245	23·6575	25·6725	27·8881	30·3243	33·0034	35·9497
17	18·4304	20·0121	21·7616	23·6975	25·8404	28·2129	30·8402	33·7502	36·9737	40·5447
18	19·6147	21·4123	23·4144	25·6454	28·1324	30·9057	33·9990	37·4502	41·3013	45·5992
19	20·8109	22·8406	25·1169	27·6712	30·5390	33·7600	37·3790	41·4463	46·0185	51·1591
20	22·0190	24·2974	26·8704	29·7781	33·0660	36·7856	40·9955	45·7620	51·1601	57·2750
21	23·2392	25·7833	28·6765	31·9692	35·7193	39·9927	44·8652	50·4229	56·7645	64·0025
22	24·4716	27·2990	30·5368	34·2480	38·5052	43·3923	49·0057	55·4568	62·8733	71·4027

23	25·7163	28·8450	32·4529	36·6179	41·4305	46·9958	53·4361	60·8933	69·5319	79·5430
24	26·9735	30·4219	34·4265	39·0826	44·5020	50·8156	58·1767	66·7648	76·7898	88·4973
25	28·2432	32·0303	36·4593	41·6459	47·7271	54·8645	63·2490	73·1059	84·7009	98·3471
26	29·5256	33·6709	38·5530	44·3117	51·1135	59·1564	68·6765	79·9544	93·3240	109·182
27	30·8209	35·3443	40·7096	47·0842	54·6691	63·7058	74·4838	87·3508	102·723	121·100
28	32·1291	37·0512	42·9309	49·9676	58·4026	68·5281	80·6877	95·3388	112·968	134·210
29	33·4504	38·7922	45·2189	52·9663	62·3227	73·6398	87·3465	103·966	124·135	148·631
30	34·7849	40·5681	47·5754	56·0849	66·4388	79·0582	94·4608	113·283	136·308	164·494
31	36·1327	42·3794	50·0027	59·3283	70·7608	84·8017	102·073	123·346	149·575	181·943
32	37·4941	44·2270	52·5028	62·7015	75·2988	90·8898	110·218	134·214	164·037	201·138
33	38·8690	46·1116	55·0778	66·2095	80·0638	97·3432	118·933	145·951	179·800	222·252
34	40·2577	48·0338	57·7302	69·8579	85·0670	104·184	128·259	158·627	196·982	245·477
35	41·6603	49·9945	60·4621	73·6522	90·3203	111·435	138·237	172·317	215·711	271·024
36	43·0769	51·9944	63·2759	77·5983	95·8363	119·121	148·913	187·102	236·125	299·127
37	44·5076	54·0343	66·1742	81·7022	101·628	127·268	160·337	203·070	258·376	330·039
38	45·9527	56·1149	69·1594	85·9703	107·710	135·904	172·561	220·316	282·630	364·043
39	47·4123	58·2372	72·2342	90·4091	114·095	145·058	185·640	238·941	309·066	401·448
40	48·8864	60·4020	75·4013	95·0255	120·800	154·762	199·635	259·057	337·882	442·593
41	50·3752	62·6100	78·6633	99·8265	127·840	165·048	214·610	280·781	369·292	487·852
42	51·8790	64·8622	82·0232	104·820	135·232	175·951	230·632	304·244	403·528	537·637
43	53·3978	67·1595	85·4839	110·012	142·993	187·508	247·776	329·583	440·846	592·401
44	54·9318	69·5027	89·0484	115·413	151·143	199·758	266·121	356·950	481·522	652·641
45	56·4811	71·8927	92·7199	121·029	159·700	212·744	285·749	386·506	525·859	718·905
46	58·0459	74·3306	96·5015	126·871	168·685	226·508	306·752	418·426	574·186	791·795
47	59·6263	76·8172	100·397	132·945	178·119	241·099	329·224	452·900	626·863	871·975
48	61·2226	79·3535	104·408	139·263	188·025	256·565	353·270	490·132	684·280	960·172
49	62·8348	81·9406	108·541	145·834	198·427	272·958	378·999	530·343	746·866	1057·19
50	64·4632	84·5794	112·797	152·667	209·348	290·336	406·529	573·770	815·084	1163·91

TABLE C *The amount of 1 per annum (continued)*

$$s_{n|r} = \frac{(1+r)^n - 1}{r}$$

	PERCENTAGE									
YEAR	*11*	*12*	*13*	*14*	*15*	*16*	*17*	*18*	*19*	*20*
1	1·00000	1·00000	1·00000	1·00000	1·00000	1·00000	1·00000	1·00000	1·00000	1·00000
2	2·11000	2·12000	2·13000	2·14000	2·15000	2·16000	2·17000	2·18000	2·19000	2·20000
3	3·34210	3·37440	3·40690	3·43960	3·47250	3·50560	3·53890	3·57240	3·60610	3·64000
4	4·70973	4·77933	4·84980	4·92114	4·99337	5·06650	5·14051	5·21543	5·29126	5·36800
5	6·22780	6·35285	6·48027	6·61010	6·74238	6·87714	7·01440	7·15421	7·29660	7·44160
6	7·91286	8·11519	8·32271	8·53552	8·75374	8·97748	9·20685	9·44197	9·68295	9·92992
7	9·78327	10·0890	10·4047	10·7305	11·0668	11·4139	11·7720	12·1415	12·5227	12·9159
8	11·8594	12·2997	12·7573	13·2328	13·7268	14·2401	14·7733	15·3270	15·9020	16·4991
9	14·1640	14·7757	15·4157	16·0853	16·7858	17·5185	18·2847	19·0859	19·9234	20·7989
10	16·7220	17·5487	18·4197	19·3373	20·3037	21·3215	22·3931	23·5213	24·7089	25·9587
11	19·5614	20·6546	21·8143	23·0445	24·3493	25·7329	27·1999	28·7551	30·4035	32·1504
12	22·7132	23·1331	25·6502	27·2707	29·0017	30·8502	32·8239	34·3911	37·1802	39·5805
13	26·2116	28·0291	29·9847	32·0887	34·3519	36·7862	39·4040	42·2187	45·2445	48·4966
14	30·0949	32·3926	34·8827	37·5811	40·5047	43·6720	47·1027	50·8180	54·8409	59·1959
15	34·4054	37·2797	40·4175	43·8424	47·5804	51·6595	56·1101	60·9653	66·2607	72·0351
16	39·1899	42·7533	46·6717	50·9804	55·7175	60·9250	66·6488	72·9390	79·8502	87·4421
17	44·5008	48·8837	53·7391	59·1176	65·0751	71·6730	78·9792	87·0680	96·0218	105·931
18	50·3959	55·7497	61·7251	68·3941	75·8364	84·1407	93·4056	103·740	115·266	128·117
19	56·9395	63·4397	70·7494	78·9692	88·2118	98·6032	110·285	123·414	138·166	154·740
20	64·2028	72·0524	80·9468	91·0249	102·444	115·380	130·033	146·628	165·418	186·688
21	72·2651	81·6987	92·4699	104·768	118·810	134·841	153·139	174·021	197·847	225·026
22	81·2143	92·5026	105·491	120·436	137·632	157·415	180·172	206·345	236·438	271·031

23	91·1479	104·603	120·205	138·297	159·276	183·601	211·801	244·487	282·362	326·237
24	102·174	118·155	136·831	158·659	184·168	213·978	248·808	289·494	337·010	392·484
25	114·413	133·334	155·620	181·871	212·793	249·214	292·105	342·603	402·042	471·981
26	127·999	150·334	176·850	208·333	245·712	290·088	342·763	405·272	479·431	567·377
27	143·079	169·374	200·841	238·499	283·569	337·502	402·032	479·221	571·522	681·853
28	159·817	190·699	227·950	272·889	327·104	392·503	471·378	566·481	681·112	819·223
29	178·397	214·583	258·583	312·094	377·170	456·303	552·512	669·447	811·523	984·068
30	199·021	241·333	293·199	356·787	434·745	530·312	647·439	790·948	966·712	1181·88
31	221·913	271·293	332·315	407·737	500·957	616·162	758·504	934·319	1151·39	1419·26
32	247·324	304·848	376·516	465·820	577·100	715·747	888·449	1103·50	1371·15	1704·11
33	275·529	342·429	426·463	532·035	664·666	831·267	1040·49	1303·13	1632·67	2045·93
34	306·837	384·521	482·903	607·520	765·365	965·270	1218·37	1538·69	1943·88	2456·12
35	341·590	431·663	546·681	693·573	881·170	1120·71	1426·49	1816·65	2314·21	2948·34
36	380·164	484·463	618·749	791·673	1014·35	1301·03	1669·99	2144·65	2754·91	3539·01
37	422·982	543·599	700·187	903·507	1167·50	1510·19	1954·89	2531·69	3279·35	4247·81
38	470·511	609·831	792·211	1031·00	1343·62	1752·82	2288·23	2988·39	3903·42	5098·37
39	523·267	684·010	896·198	1176·34	1546·17	2034·27	2678·22	3527·30	4646·07	6119·05
40	581·826	767·091	1013·70	1342·03	1779·09	2360·76	3134·52	4163·21	5529·83	7343·86
41	646·827	860·142	1146·49	1530·91	2046·95	2739·48	3668·39	4913·59	6581·50	8813·63
42	718·978	964·359	1296·53	1746·24	2355·00	3178·79	4293·02	5799·04	7832·98	10577·4
43	799·065	1081·08	1466·08	1991·71	2709·25	3688·40	5023·83	6843·86	9322·25	12693·8
44	887·963	1211·81	1657·67	2271·55	3116·63	4279·55	5878·88	8076·76	11094·5	15233·6
45	986·639	1358·23	1874·16	2590·56	3585·13	4965·27	6879·29	9531·58	13203·4	18281·3
46	1096·17	1522·22	2118·81	2954·24	4123·90	5760·72	8049·77	11248·3	15713·1	21938·6
47	1217·75	1705·88	2395·25	3368·84	4743·48	6683·43	9419·23	13273·9	18699·6	26327·3
48	1352·70	1911·59	2707·63	3841·48	5456·00	7753·78	11021·5	15664·3	22253·5	31593·7
49	1502·50	2141·98	3060·63	4380·28	6275·41	8995·39	12896·2	18484·8	26482·6	37913·5
50	1668·77	2400·02	3459·51	4994·52	7217·12	10435·6	15089·5	21813·1	31515·3	45497·2

TABLE C *The amount of 1 per annum (continued)*

$$s_{n|r} = \frac{(1 + r)^n - 1}{r}$$

YEAR	PERCENTAGE 21	22	23	24	25	26	27	28	29	30
1	1·00000	1·00000	1·00000	1·00000	1·00000	1·00000	1·00000	1·00000	1·00000	1·00000
2	2·21000	2·22000	2·23000	2·24000	2·25000	2·26000	2·27000	2·28000	2·29000	2·30000
3	3·67410	3·70840	3·74290	3·77760	3·81250	3·84760	3·88290	3·91840	3·95410	3·99000
4	5·44566	5·52425	5·60377	5·68422	5·76562	5·84798	5·93128	6·01555	6·10079	6·18700
5	7·58925	7·73958	7·89263	8·04844	8·20703	8·36845	8·53273	8·69991	8·87002	9·04310
6	10·1830	10·4423	10·7079	10·9801	11·2588	11·5442	11·8366	12·1359	12·4423	12·7560
7	13·3214	13·7396	14·1708	14·6153	15·0735	15·5458	16·0324	16·5339	17·0506	17·5828
8	17·1189	17·7623	18·4300	19·1229	19·8419	20·5876	21·3612	22·1634	22·9953	23·8577
9	21·7139	22·6700	23·6690	24·7125	25·8023	26·9404	28·1287	29·3692	30·6639	32·0150
10	27·2738	28·6574	30·1128	31·6434	33·2529	34·9449	36·7235	38·5926	40·5564	42·6195
11	34·0013	35·9620	38·0388	40·2379	42·5661	45·0306	47·6388	50·3985	53·3178	56·4053
12	12·1416	44·8737	47·7877	50·8950	54·2077	57·7386	61·5013	65·5100	69·7800	74·3270
13	51·9913	55·7459	59·7788	64·1097	68·7596	73·7506	79·1066	84·8529	91·0161	97·6250
14	63·9095	69·0100	74·5280	80·4961	86·9495	93·9258	101·465	109·612	118·411	127·913
15	78·3305	85·1922	92·6694	100·815	109·687	119·347	129·861	141·303	153·750	167·286
16	95·7799	104·935	114·983	126·011	138·109	151·377	165·924	181·868	199·337	218.472
17	116·894	129·020	142·430	157·253	173·636	191·735	211·723	233·791	258·145	285·014
18	142·441	158·405	176·188	195·994	218·045	242·585	269·888	300·252	334·007	371·518
19	173·354	194·254	217·712	244·033	273·556	306·658	343·758	385·323	431·870	483·973
20	210·758	237·989	268·785	303·601	342·945	387·389	437·573	494·213	558·112	630·165
21	256·018	291·347	331·606	377·465	429·681	489·110	556·717	633·593	720·964	820·215
22	310·781	356·443	408·875	469·056	538·101	617·278	708·031	811·999	931·044	1067·28

23	377·045	435·861	503·917	582·630	673·626	778·771	900·199	1040·36	1202·05	1388·46
24	457·225	532·750	620·817	723·461	843·033	982·251	1144·25	1332·66	1551·64	1806·00
25	554·242	650·955	764·605	898·092	1054·79	1238·64	1454·20	1706·80	2002·62	2348·80
26	671·633	795·165	941·465	1114·63	1319·49	1561·68	1847·84	2185·71	2584·37	3054·44
27	813·676	971·102	1159·00	1383·15	1650·36	1968·72	2347·75	2798·71	3334·84	3971·78
28	985·548	1185·74	1426·57	1716·10	2063·95	2481·59	2982·64	3583·34	4302·95	5164·31
29	1193·51	1447·61	1755·68	2128·96	2580·94	3127·80	3788·96	4587·68	5551·80	6714·60
30	1445·15	1767·08	2160·49	2640·92	3227·17	3942·03	4812·98	5873·23	7162·82	8729·99
31	1749·63	2156·84	2658·40	3275·74	4034·97	4967·95	6113·48	7519·74	9241·04	11350·0
32	2118·06	2632·34	3270·84	4062·91	5044·71	6260·62	7765·12	9624·98	11921·9	14756·0
33	2563·85	3212·46	4024·13	5039·01	6306·89	7889·38	9862·70	12321·0	15380·3	19183·8
34	3103·25	3920·20	4950·68	6249·38	7884·61	9941·62	12526·6	15771·8	19841·6	24939·9
35	3755·94	4783·64	6090·33	7750·23	9856·76	12527·4	15909·8	20189·0	25596·7	32422·9
36	4545·68	5837·05	7492·11	9611·28	12322·0	15785·6	20206·5	25842·9	33020·7	42150·7
37	5501·28	7122·20	9216·30	11919·0	15403·4	19890·8	25663·2	33079·9	42597·7	54796·9
38	6657·55	8690·08	11337·0	14780·5	19255·3	25063·4	32593·3	42343·2	54952·0	71237·0
39	8056·63	10602·9	13945·6	18328·9	24070·1	31580·9	41394·5	54200·4	70889·1	92609·1
40	9749·52	12936·5	17154·0	22728·8	30088·7	39793·0	52572·0	69377·5	91448·0	120393·0
41	11797·9	15783·6	21100·5	28184·7	37611·8	50140·2	66767·4	88804·1	117969·0	156512·0
42	14276·5	19257·0	25954·6	34950·0	47015·8	63177·6	84795·6	113670·0	152181·0	203466·0
43	17275·6	23494·5	31925·1	43339·1	58770·7	79604·8	107691·0	145499·0	196314·0	264507·0
44	20904·4	28664·3	39268·9	53741·4	73464·4	100303·0	136769·0	186240·0	253246·0	343860·0
45	25295·3	34971·4	48301·8	66640·4	91831·5	126383·0	173698·0	238388·0	326689·0	447019·0
46	30608·4	42666·1	59412·2	82635·1	114790·0	159243·0	220597·0	305137·0	421430·0	581126·0
47	37037·1	52053·7	73078·0	102468·0	143489·0	200648·0	280160·0	390577·0	543645·0	755465·0
48	44815·9	63506·5	89886·9	127062·0	179362·0	252817·0	355804·0	499939·0	701303·0	982106·0
49	54228·3	77478·9	110562·0	157558·0	224204·0	318550·0	451872·0	639923·0	904682·0	1276740·0
50	65617·2	94525·3	135992·0	195373·0	280256·0	401374·0	573878·0	819103·0	1167040·0	1659760·0

TABLE C *The amount of 1 per annum (continued)*

$$s_{n|r} = \frac{(1+r)^n - 1}{r}$$

	PERCENTAGE									
YEAR	*31*	*32*	*33*	*34*	*35*	*36*	*37*	*38*	*39*	*40*
1	1·00000	1·00000	1·00000	1·00000	1·00000	1·00000	1·00000	1·00000	1·00000	1·00000
2	2·31000	2·32000	2·33000	2·34000	2·35000	2·36000	2·37000	2·38000	2·39000	2·40000
3	4·02610	4·06240	4·09890	4·13560	4·17250	4·20960	4·24690	4·28440	4·32210	4·36000
4	6·27419	6·36237	6·45154	6·54170	6·63288	6·72506	6·81825	6·91247	7·00772	7·10400
5	9·21919	9·39833	9·58054	9·76588	9·95438	10·1461	10·3410	10·5392	10·7407	10·9456
6	13·0771	13·4058	13·7421	14·0863	14·4384	14·7987	15·1672	15·5441	15·9296	16·3238
7	18·1311	18·6956	19·2770	19·8756	20·4919	21·1262	21·7790	22·4509	23·1422	23·8534
8	24·7517	25·6782	26·6384	27·6333	28·6640	29·7316	30·8373	31·9822	33·1676	34·3947
9	33·4247	34·8953	36·4291	38·0287	39·6964	41·4350	43·2471	45·1354	47·1030	49·1526
10	44·7864	47·0618	49·4507	51·9584	54·5902	57·3516	60·2485	63·2869	66·4731	69·8137
11	59·6701	63·1215	66·7695	70·6243	74·6967	78·9982	83·5404	88·3359	93·3977	98·7391
12	79·1679	84·3204	89·8034	95·6365	101·841	108·437	115·450	122·904	130·823	139·235
13	104·710	112·303	120·439	129·153	138·485	148·475	159·167	170·607	182·844	195·929
14	138·170	149·240	161·183	174·065	187·954	202·926	219·059	236·438	255·153	275·300
15	182·003	197·997	215·374	234·247	254·738	276·979	301·111	327·284	355·662	386·420
16	239·423	262·356	287·447	314·891	344·897	377·692	413·522	452·652	495·370	541·988
17	314·645	347·309	383·305	422·954	466·611	514·661	567·524	625·659	689·565	759·784
18	413·185	459·449	510·795	567·758	630·925	700·939	778·509	864·410	959·495	1064·70
19	542·272	607·472	680·358	761·796	852·748	954·277	1067·56	1193·89	1334·70	1491·58
20	711·376	802·863	905·876	1021·81	1152·21	1298·82	1463·55	1648·56	1856·23	2089·21
21	932·903	1060·78	1205·81	1370·22	1556·48	1767·39	2006·07	2276·02	2581·16	2925·89
22	1223·10	1401·23	1604·73	1837·10	2102·25	2404·65	2749·31	3141·90	3588·81	4097·24

23	1603·26	1850·62	2135·30	2462·71	2839·04	3271·33	3767·56	4336·83	4989·45	5737·14
24	2101·28	2443·82	2840·94	3301·03	3833·71	4450·00	5162·55	5985·82	6936·34	8033·00
25	2753·67	3226·84	3779·45	4424·38	5176·50	6053·00	7073·70	8261·43	9642·51	11247·2
26	3608·31	4260·43	5027·67	5929·67	6989·28	8233·09	9691·97	11401·8	13404·1	15747·1
27	4727·89	5624·77	6687·81	7946·76	9436·53	11198·0	13279·0	15735·4	18632·7	22046·9
28	6194·53	7425·70	8895·78	10649·7	12740·3	15230·3	18193·2	21715·9	25900·4	30866·7
29	8115·84	9802·92	11832·4	14271·5	17200·4	20714·2	24925·7	29969·0	36002·6	43214·3
30	10632·7	12940·9	15738·1	19124·9	23221·6	28172·3	34149·2	41358·2	50044·6	60501·1
31	13929·9	17082·9	20932·6	25628·3	31350·1	38315·3	46785·4	57075·3	69563·0	84702·5
32	18249·2	22550·5	27841·4	34342·9	42323·7	52109·8	64097·1	78764·9	96693·5	118585·0
33	23907·4	29767·6	37030·1	46020·5	57137·9	70870·3	87814·0	108697·0	134405·0	166019·0
34	31319·7	39294·3	49251·0	61668·5	77137·2	96384·6	120306·0	150002·0	186824·0	232428·0
35	41029·8	51869·4	65504·8	82636·8	104136·0	131084·0	164820·0	207004·0	259686·0	325400·0
36	53750·1	68468·6	87122·4	110734·0	140585·0	178275·0	225805·0	285667·0	360965·0	455561·0
37	70413·6	90379·6	115874·0	148385·0	189791·0	242456·0	309354·0	394221·0	501742·0	637787·0
38	92242·8	119302·0	154113·0	198837·0	256218·0	329741·0	423816·0	544026·0	697423·0	892903·0
39	120839·0	157480·0	204972·0	266442·0	345896·0	448448·0	580629·0	750757·0	969419·0	1250060·0
40	158300·0	207874·0	272613·0	357034·0	466960·0	609890·0	795462·0	1036050·0	1347490·0	1750090·0
41	207374·0	274395·0	362577·0	478426·0	630398·0	829452·0	1089780·0	1429740·0	1873020·0	2450130·0
42	271661·0	362202·0	482228·0	641092·0	851038·0	1128060·0	1493010·0	1973050·0	2603490·0	3430180·0
43	355877·0	478108·0	641364·0	859065·0	1148900·0	1534160·0	2045420·0	2722810·0	3618860·0	4802260·0
44	466200·0	631104·0	853015·0	1151150·0	1551020·0	2086450·0	2802220·0	3757470·0	5030210·0	6723160·0
45	610723·0	833058·0	1134510·0	1542540·0	2093880·0	2837580·0	3839050·0	5185310·0	6992000·0	9412420·0
46	800048·0	1099640·0	1508900·0	2067000·0	2826730·0	3859110·0	5259500·0	7155730·0	9718880·0	13177400·0
47	1048060·0	1451520·0	2006840·0	2769790·0	3816090·0	5248390·0	7205510·0	9874910·0	13509200·0	18448400·0
48	1372970·0	1916010·0	2669100·0	3711510·0	5151720·0	7137810·0	9871550·0	13627400·0	18777800·0	25827700·0
49	1798590·0	2529140·0	3549900·0	4973430·0	6954830·0	9707420·0	13524000·0	18805800·0	26101200·0	36158800·0
50	2356150·0	3338460·0	4721370·0	6664400·0	9389020·0	13202100·0	18527900·0	25952000·0	36280700·0	50622300·0

TABLE C *The amount of 1 per annum (continued)* $s_{n|r} = \frac{(1+r)^n - 1}{r}$

	PERCENTAGE									
YEAR	*41*	*42*	*43*	*44*	*45*	*46*	*47*	*48*	*49*	*50*
1	1·00000	1·00000	1·00000	1·00000	1·00000	1·00000	1·00000	1·00000	1·00000	1·00000
2	2·41000	2·42000	2·43000	2·44000	2·45000	2·46000	2·47000	2·48000	2·49000	2·50000
3	4·39810	4·43640	4·47490	4·51360	4·55250	4·59160	4·63090	4·67040	4·71010	4·75000
4	7·20132	7·29969	7·39911	7·49958	7·60113	7·70374	7·80742	7·91219	8·01805	8·12500
5	11·1539	11·3656	11·5807	11·7994	12·0216	12·2475	12·4769	12·7100	12·9469	13·1875
6	16·7269	17·1391	17·5604	17·9911	18·4314	18·8813	19·3411	19·8109	20·2909	20·7812
7	24·5850	25·3375	26·1114	26·9072	27·7255	28·5667	29·4314	30·3201	31·2334	32·1719
8	35·6648	36·9793	38·3393	39·7464	41·2019	42·7073	44·2641	45·8737	47·5378	49·2578
9	51·2874	53·5106	55·8252	58·2348	60·7428	63·3527	66·0682	68·8931	71·8313	74·8867
10	73·3153	76·9850	80·8301	84·8582	89·0771	93·4950	98·1203	102·962	108·029	113·330
11	104·375	110·319	116·587	123·196	130·162	137·503	145·237	153·383	161·963	170·995
12	148·168	157·653	167·719	178·402	189·735	201·754	214·498	228·008	242·324	257·493
13	209·917	224·867	240·839	257·899	276·115	295·561	316·312	338·451	362·063	387·239
14	296·983	320·311	345·400	372·374	401·367	432·519	465·979	501·908	540·474	581·859
15	419·746	455·841	494·921	537·219	582·982	632·477	685·989	743·823	806·306	873·788
16	592·842	648·294	708·738	774·595	846·324	924·417	1009·40	1101·86	1202·40	1311·68
17	836·907	921·578	1014·49	1116·42	1228·17	1350·65	1484·82	1631·75	1792·57	1968·52
18	1181·04	1309·64	1451·73	1608·64	1781·85	1972·95	2183·69	2415·99	2671·93	2953·78
19	1666·26	1860·69	2076·97	2317·44	2584·68	2881·50	3211·03	3576·67	3982·18	4431·68
20	2350·43	2643·18	2971·07	3338·12	3748·78	4207·99	4721·21	5294·47	5934·44	6648·51
21	3315·11	3754·31	4249·63	4807·89	5436·73	6144·67	6941·18	7836·81	8843·32	9973·77
22	4675·31	5332·13	6077·97	6924·36	7884·26	8972·22	10204·5	11599·5	13177·5	14961·7

23	6593·18	7572·62	8692·49	9972·08	11433·2	13100·4	15001·7	17168·2	19635·5	22443·5
24	9297·39	10754·1	12431·3	14360·8	16579·1	19127·6	22053·4	25410·0	29258·0	33666·2
25	13110·3	15271·8	17777·7	20680·5	24040·7	27927·4	32419·6	37607·8	43595·4	50500·3
26	18486·5	21687·0	25423·1	29781·0	34860·0	40774·9	47657·7	55660·5	64958·1	75751·5
27	26067·0	30796·6	36356·1	42885·6	50548·1	59532·4	70057·9	82378·5	96788·6	113628·0
28	36755·5	43732·1	51990·2	61756·3	73295·7	86918·3	102986·0	121921·0	144216·0	170443·0
29	51826·3	62100·6	74346·9	88930·0	106280·0	126902·0	151391·0	180444·0	214883·0	255666·0
30	73076·0	88183·9	106317·0	128060·0	154107·0	185278·0	222545·0	267059·0	320176·0	383500·0
31	103038·0	125222·0	152034·0	184408·0	223456·0	270506·0	327142·0	395248·0	477064·0	475251·0
32	145285·0	177816·0	217410·0	265548·0	324012·0	394940·0	480900·0	584968·0	710826·0	862878·0
33	204853·0	252500·0	310898·0	382390·0	469818·0	576613·0	706924·0	865754·0	1059130·0	1294320·0
34	288843·0	358551·0	444585·0	550643·0	681237·0	841857·0	1039180·0	1281320·0	1578110·0	1941480·0
35	407270·0	509144·0	635757·0	792927·0	987794·0	1229110·0	1527600·0	1896350·0	2351380·0	2912220·0
36	574252·0	722986·0	909134·0	1141820·0	1432300·0	1794500·0	2245570·0	2806600·0	3503560·0	4368330·0
37	809696·0	1026640·0	1300060·0	1644220·0	2076840·0	2619980·0	3300980·0	4153770·0	5220300·0	6552490·0
38	1141670·0	1457830·0	1859090·0	2367670·0	3011420·0	3825170·0	4852450·0	6147570·0	7778250·0	9828740·0
39	1609760·0	2070120·0	2658500·0	3409450·0	4366560·0	5584750·0	7133100·0	9098410·0	11589600·0	14743100·0
40	2269760·0	2939570·0	3801660·0	4909610·0	6331510·0	8153730·0	10485700·0	13465700·0	17268500·0	22114700·0
41	3200360·0	4174190·0	5436370·0	7069840·0	9180690·0	11904400·0	14413900·0	19929200·0	25730100·0	33172000·0
42	4512510·0	5927360·0	7774010·0	10180600·0	13312000·0	17380500·0	22658400·0	29495200·0	38337800·0	49758000·0
43	6362650·0	8416850·0	11116800·0	14660000·0	19302400·0	25375500·0	33307900·0	43652800·0	57123300·0	74637000·0
44	8971330·0	11951900·0	15897100·0	21110400·0	27988500·0	37048300·0	48962600·0	64606200·0	85113700·0	111955000·0
45	12649600·0	16971700·0	22732800·0	30399000·0	40583300·0	54090500·0	71975100·0	95617200·0	126819000·0	167933000·0
46	17835900·0	24099900·0	32507900·0	43774600·0	58845800·0	78972100·0	105803000·0	141513000·0	188961000·0	251900000·0
47	25148600·0	34221800·0	46486300·0	63035400·0	85326400·0	115299000·0	155531000·0	209440000·0	281552000·0	377850000·0
48	35459600·0	48595000·0	66475500·0	90771000·0	123723000·0	168337000·0	228631000·0	309971000·0	419512000·0	566775000·0
49	49998000·0	69004800·0	95059900·0	130710000·0	179399000·0	245772000·0	336087000·0	458757000·0	625073000·0	850162000·0
50	70497200·0	97986900·0	135936000·0	188223000·0	260128000·0	358827000·0	494048000·0	678961000·0	931359000·0	1275240000·0

Index